John G. Morris

Fifty years in the Lutheran ministry

John G. Morris

Fifty years in the Lutheran ministry

ISBN/EAN: 9783742897664

Manufactured in Europe, USA, Canada, Australia, Japa

Cover: Foto ©ninafisch / pixelio.de

Manufactured and distributed by brebook publishing software (www.brebook.com)

John G. Morris

Fifty years in the Lutheran ministry

IN THE

LUTHERAN MINISTRY.

BY

JOHN G. MORRIS.

BALTIMORE:
PRINTED FOR THE AUTHOR BY JAMES YOUNG,
112 West Baltimore Street.
1878.

NOTICE.

To my deep regret I was compelled to omit many good things which were properly comprehended within the scope of my book, but I found its size growing so fast upon me, that I was reluctantly obliged to retrench. The subjects of Home Missions, the Book Company, Histories of Synods, numerous private reminiscences of persons, a large number of piquant and original anecdotes and other interesting matters will probably appear in another volume under consideration. I direct the reader's attention to the following

ERRATA.

Page 121, 10th line from bottom, for *reorganized* read *surprised*.
Page 126, top line, for *on* read *no*.
Page 267, 17th line from bottom, for *salvation* read *salutation*.
Page 340, last line, for *two* read *three*.
Page 417, 10th line from top, for *legatees* read *testators*.
Page 465, 5th line from top, for *Olshausen* read *Hengstenberg*.

Index.

INDEX.

Almanacs	526
Anecdotes	545
Ansgari College	510
Anti-Rebellion Resolutions	269
"Arrivals"	384
Augsburg Confession	8
Augustana College	540
Bachman, Dr., Sketch of	76
Baker, Dr., Sketch of	146
" " Anecdotes of	152
Baptism, Romish	295
Baugher, President	191
Baum, Dr., on Dr. Stork	202
" " " C. A. Morris	247
Beates, Dr., Sketch	49
Beneficiary Education	520
Bernheim, German Settlements	43
Bittle, D. F.	221
Bolzius	6
Bread in Communion	358
Brobst, S. K.	226
Brown, J. A., Letter of	19
" " on Definite Platform	339
" A. J.	45
Burial of Non-Members	362
Cake and Wine at Funerals	425
Carthage College	515
Centennial Celebration	293
Christlieb, Prof.	467
Church Literature	506
" Music	531
" History, Books on	516
" Trials in Civil Courts	109
Coal Furnaces	355

Colleges, Lutheran	498
Colloquium	457
Concordia College	518
Conrad, F. W., on S. S. Schmucker	131
Council, General	299
Crape at Funerals	367
Cult	349
D. D's. in Lutheran Church	438
Definite Platform	337
Demme, Dr	119
"Departures"	383
Dewitt, W. R., Letter of	30
Diehl, Dr. D., Letter of	46
" " Maryland Synod Question	485
Diet, The	457
Donation Parties	366
Dorner, Prof	465
Ebenezer	6
Education Society	520
Education, Theological	522
Eichelberger, Dr. L	180
Endress, Dr. C	33
Episcopal Church	259
Evangelical Review on Definite Platform	342–46
Evangelisches Magazin	22
Fabricius	5
Feltz, Rev. Dr. P., Letter of	244
Finckel, Dr. S	235
Flowers in Churches	354
Forms of Worship	8
Franckean Synod	273, 281, 413
Funerals	424
Gas in Churches	355
Geissenhainer, Dr. F. W	34, 36
General Council	299
General Synod	257
" " South	297
German Reformed	262
Glenn, Rev., Murder of	404
Goering, Rev	12, 24
Government, Form of	7
Gown, use of	351
Gronau, Rev	6
Gunn, Rev. W	180
Gustavus Adolphus	5
Hay, Dr. C. A., Letters of	20, 181
" " Arrest of	401
Hazelius, Dr. E. L	66

Henkel, Rev. Paul	43
" Andrew, Letter of	45
Heyer, Rev. F.	211, 216
Hutter, Dr. E. W.	194
Hymn Books	492
Ignorance Concerning our Church	482
Insurance League	391
Jacobs, D.	229
Jacobs, Prof. M.	228
" H. E	239
Jubilee in 1868	293, 426
" Publications	428, 430
Keller, B.	155
" E.	182
Kneeling at Communion	356
Kraft, Prof.	467
Krauth, Dr. C. P., Sketch of	101
" " " Letter of	27
Kurtz, Dr. J. D.	21
" Dr. B.	137, 140-6
Leading Men in 1826	10
Lectureship and Prizes	433
Legacies	405
Lehmanowsky	228
Lintner, Rev. G. A., Letter of	59
" Sketch of	206
Literature of Lutheran Church	261, 306, 428
Liturgy	349
Lochman, Rev. G.	29
" Rev. A., Letter	32
Luther, Books on	445, 47
Luther College	515
Lutheran Church, History of	5
" " Books in	316
" Colleges	498
" Writers on Science	411
" Ministers, College Professors	436
" Laymen Writers	441
" Pastors' Fund	390
" Members of Learned Societies	441
" Commentators	444
" Members of Foreign Societies	441
" Settlements	5
Maine, Lutheran Settlement in	6
Martin, Rev. J.	233
Maryland Synod Question	485
Matthews, Rev. J. M., Letter	38
Mayer, Rev. Dr. P. F.	90

INDEX.

Miller, Rev. G. B., Letter 68
" " " Sketch 89
" Rev. J. 92
Ministers from Germany, early 7
" Number in 1826 9
" Visitors to this Country 462
" Who have left 382
" Who have joined us 382
" Summer Vacations 469
" Fees 365
" Presents to 365
Professors in other Colleges 436
Missions, Foreign 474
Missionary Institute 537
Morris, C. A. 247
" J. G., Letters 13, 72
Muhlenberg, Rev. H. Melchior 6, 7
" " H. A. 48
" H. H., Letter 93
" College 513
Naming Churches 362
New Measures 386
Noel, Counsellor 466
North Carolina College 543
Ockershausen, A. 250
Oxenstiern 5
Pacific Overture 341
Pastors' Fund 390
Paxton, Rev. Dr., Letter 186
Pennsylvania College 498
Pennsylvania Synod and General Synod..258, 260, 266, 276, 277, 279, 283-92
Pictures in Churches 355
Plitt, Rev. J., Letter 159
Pohlman, Rev. H. N., Letters 70, 87
" " " Sketch 217
Political Office 408
Prayer Meetings 352
Preaching, Method of 352
Presbyterian Delegate 267
Prizes 433
Quitman, Rev. Dr. 56
Reck, Rev. A. 162, 163-75
Reformation Day 293, 435
" Literature of 428
Relief Fund 389
Revivalism 386
Richards, Rev. J. W. 176
Rizer, Rev. P., Letter of 239

INDEX.

Roanoke College 511
Roedelsheimer's Legacy... 417
Romish Baptism... 295
Rosenmiller, Rev. D. P., Letter................................... 40
Ruthrauff, Rev. J. F.. 46
    "   " F... 176
Sacred Music.. 353
Saltzburgers.. 6
Schaeffer, Rev. C. F., Letter..................................... 25
    " F. D.. 23
    " F. C.. 86
    " D. F.. 96, 100
Schmidt, Rev. Dr. H. J., Letter................................... 67
Schmucker, Rev. Dr. J. G.. 11
    "   " S. S.. 15, 121, 341
Schoharie... 5
Semi-Centennial Jubilee... 426
Senderling, Rev. J. Z... 244
Settlements of Lutherans.. 5
Sheeleigh, Rev. M., Library....................................... 520
Shober, Rev. G.. 39
South Carolina College.. 509
Spaeth, Rev. Dr. A.. 299
Sprague's Annals... 11, 24, 45
Sprecher, Rev. Dr. S.. 184
Stained Glass... 354
State of the Country..................................... 269, 271, 282
State of Theology... 392
Statistics.. 424
Stephan... 322
Stoever, Prof.. 49, 64, 104, 182, 252
Stork, Rev. Dr. T... 202
Streit's Legacy... 417
Strobel, Rev. Dr.. 217
Suicides, Burial of... 362
Summer Vacations.. 469
Sunday School Hymn Books.. 496
Swedes.. 5
Synod General... 257
Synods in 1826.. 9
Synodical Visits to Presidents.................................... 468
Theological Education... 522
    " Seminary... 527
    "   " of South Carolina............................... 535
Theology, State of.. 392
Thiel College... 516
Titus, Rev. T. T.. 198
Uhlhorn, Rev. J... 95

Union Army, Ministers and Students in.................... 397
Wackerhagen, Rev. Dr................................ ....57, 63
Wafers in Sacrament..356–58
Wartburg Seminary...514
Weiser, Rev. R., Letter..249
Why We Lose Members..368
Why so few Germans join English Churches.........................374
Witchcraft, belief in... 37
Wittenberg College..505
Women Praying in Meeting..352
Worship, Mode of..349
Wyneken, Rev...264, 360

Historical Introduction.*

The origin of the Lutheran Church in America was in an emigration from Holland, which dates back nearly to the first settlement of the Dutch in New Amsterdam, in 1621. So long as the territory belonged to Holland, the Lutherans were obliged to hold their religious services in private; but from 1664, when British rule commenced, they were permitted to conduct their worship publicly—a privilege which was continued to them under all the successive Governors. Their first minister was Jacob Fabricius, who arrived in this country in 1669 but after having served them for eight years, withdrew and took charge of the Swedish Church at Wicaco, now Southwark, Philadelphia. Here, after having labored fourteen years, during nine of which he was blind, he died in 1692.

The next Lutheran settlement was that of the Swedes on the Delaware, in 1636. This Colony was first contemplated during the reign of Gustavus Adolphus, and with his hearty concurrence; but, being delayed by the Thirty Years' War, the plan subsequently took effect under the auspices of his illustrious Prime Minister, Oxenstiern. The Colony prospered for some time, but, not receiving any accessions from the parent country, it came gradually to languish until the Swedish language was entirely abandoned, and the congregations, three or four in number, became incorporated with the Episcopal Church.

The third settlement of Lutherans was that of the Germans, which, beginning in Pennsylvania, extended to Maryland, Virginia, the interior of New York and the Western States. In 1710 about three thousand Germans, chiefly Lutherans, came to New York, by way of England, having been driven from their native land by Romish persecution, and settled on the Hudson River. In 1713 one hundred and fifty families of these settled in Schoharie, and in 1717, and again in 1727, large numbers more planted themselves in different parts of Pennsylvania. This Colony was for a long time without a regular ministry, but, as many of them possessed the truly Christian spirit, they kept up public worship, sustaining their services

---

* Various publications of Dr. Schmucker.— Early History of the Lutheran Church in America, by C. W. Schaeffer, D. D.— Brief sketch of the American Lutheran Church, by Professor Stoever; also his Discourse before the Historical Society of the Lutheran Church, &c. Lutheran Almanac for various years.

sometimes by reading devotional books, which they had brought with them from Germany, and sometimes by putting their school-masters forward to perform the office of Preachers of the Gospel. During the twelve years immediately preceding the arrival of Dr Henry Melchior Muhlenberg, in 1742, the Germans were often favored with the gratuitous labors of the Swedish Ministers.

The fourth settlement of Lutherans in this country was that of the Saltzburgers, who established themselves in Georgia in the year 1733, and, in testimony of their gratitude for the Divine protection, called the place of their residence *Ebenezer*. These emigrants came hither to escape Romish persecution, and to find a place in these Western wilds where they could freely worship God—pecuniary aid being afforded them by the British Society for the Promotion of Christianity. Their first Pastors were Messrs. Bolzius and Gronau. In 1738 these Colonists, by the powerful aid of George Whitefield, erected the far-famed Orphan House at Ebenezer. Many of the descendants of these people are still connected with the Lutheran Church in the South.

Not long after the settlement of the Saltzburgers, numerous Germans from Pennsylvania and other Provinces migrated to North Carolina, where they formed a Lutheran community that has been extending with the lapse of years. In 1735 a settlement of Lutherans was formed in Virginia, supposed to be the church in Madison County, but there were some circumstances attending it which proved unfavorable as well to its numerical as its spiritual growth. In 1739 a few Germans made their way to Waldoborough, Maine, who were subsequently joined by several hundred more; but, the title to their land proving unsound, many of them, after a while, withdrew, and the Colony never prospered.

The most important of these several Colonies was that which planted itself originally in Pennsylvania, and gradually worked its way into several of the neighboring States. In 1742 this body of Lutherans, and, indeed, the cause of Lutheranism throughout the country, was greatly strengthened by the arrival of the Rev. Henry Melchior Muhlenberg from Germany, a man of extraordinary powers and high culture, and intense devotion to his work, whose labors were probably more influential in moulding the destinies of the Lutheran Church than those of any other individual have ever been. Educated, as he had been, in the school of Francke, and possessing a large measure of the spirit of that illustrious man, he became, by common consent, the leader of his denomination, laboring in season and out of season to sustain the interests of evangelical religion for almost half a century.

Muhlenberg was soon joined by other men of kindred spirit and excellent education, most of whom were, like himself, emigrants from Germany. Among them were Brunnholtz and Lemke, in 1745; Handschuh, Weygandt and Hartwig, the founder of the Seminary that bears his name, in 1748; Heintzelman and Schultz, in 1751; Gerock, Hausil, Wortman, Wagner, Schartlin, Shrenk and Rauss, in 1753; Bager, in 1758; Voight and Krug, in 1764; Helmuth and Schmidt, in 1769; and Kunze, in 1770.

When the first Lutheran Synod was held, in 1748, there were only eleven regular ministers in this country; but three years afterwards there were reckoned about forty congregations.

The most of these men were eminently devoted ministers, but they were compelled to prosecute their labors amidst manifold discouragements, growing out of the unsettled state of the country, the dissolute habits of not a small part of the population, and constant exposure to the barbarity of the Indians. During the War of the Revolution the Lutheran Church, in common with other denominations, was temporarily retarded in its growth, though it subsequently shared in the happy results which that grand enterprise was destined to work out.

In 1786 the number of Lutheran Ministers in the Middle States was twenty-four. From that time till 1820, when the General Synod was formed, there was a very considerable increase of the number both of congregations and of ministers, though the standard of theological education, owing to the want of a suitable institution for the purpose, was far from being elevated, and there was a proportional depression in the tone of piety in most of the churches. Previous to the formation of the General Synod, in 1820, the Church had gradually become divided into five or six different, distant and unconnected Synods. There were serious difficulties to be encountered in bringing these several bodies together as an harmonious whole, but the result has proved most auspicious to the interests of Lutheranism throughout the country.

The *Form of Government* adopted from the beginning by the Lutheran Churches in this country recognizes "the parity of Ministers, the co-operation of the Laity in Church Government, and the free, voluntary convention of Synods." Such was the character of the first Synod, held in Philadelphia in 1748. It was composed of a due proportion of lay delegates, who shared equally with the Clergy in the transaction of business. In the discipline of the Church, Muhlenberg adopted substantially the Congregational mode, which has always been adhered to till the present time.

The *Creed* of the Lutheran Church, as it exists in this country, is embodied in the Augsburg Confession.

As to *Forms of Worship and Church Order*, the Lutheran Church retains and observes the festivals of Christmas, Good Friday, Easter, the Ascension and Whitsunday. She also maintains the institution of Infant Church-membership and Baptism, and, in connection with it, the rite of Confirmation. Cathechetical instruction is considered as an important part of pastoral duty. At least once a year the Minister is expected to hold a series of meetings with those who are applicants for admission to the Sacrament of the Lord's Supper, or to the rite of Confirmation, and with all who feel a special concern for their salvation. At the close of these meetings, which are generally continued once or twice a week, through a period of from six to twelve weeks, the catechumens are examined in respect to their qualifications for Communion.

The following is the statistical view of the condition of the Lutheran Church in the United States in 1877-78:

56 Synods; 2935 Ministers; 5004 Churches; 650,000 Communicants; 22 English Periodicals, 31 German, 8 Norwegian, 3 Danish, 7 Swedish—total 71; 16 Theological Seminaries; 18 Colleges; 22 Orphan Houses, Infirmaries and Hospitals.

Fifty Years in the Lutheran Ministry.

CHAPTER I.

The Leading Men of Fifty Years Ago.

In 1826, to which period these reminiscences extend, there were fewer than two hundred Lutheran ministers in the United States, and these were limited to the States of New York, Pennsylvania, Maryland, Virginia, North Carolina, South Carolina, Georgia, Tennessee and Ohio. They had divided themselves into eight small Synods, but, for the most part, they were united in sentiment. They had an immense field to cultivate, and much ignorance, prejudice and religious apathy to encounter. Our people, though as a class thrifty, honest and quiet, were to a great extent behind other communities in intelligence, enterprize and education. Not a few of our ministers also were men of superficial training, and the wonder is not that we have not made further progress in the course of years, but that with the formidable and peculiar obstructions in our way, the prejudice of foreigners, the ignorance of natives, the parsimony of both, the spiritual deadness, the formality of worship, the incompetence of not a few of the clergy, the insane opposition to the introduction of the English language into the services of the sanctuary, the indifference to the support of religious literature, the lack of sympathy with the religious activity of some other denominations which prevailed to a great extent—I say, that with all these, and still other difficulties, constantly encountered by the working ministers of those early days and for years subsequently, the wonder is that our men have accomplished so much. No intelligent man will deny that this was the condition of things to a great extent fifty years ago, and no honest historian will conceal it.

Even a superficial glance at the state of the church now, in contrast with what it was then, will satisfy any candid observer that the true men of those days deserve unspeakable credit for preparing the way for the improved and encouraging condition of things which we happily see at the present time. They struggled against mighty odds, but they persevered, and their descendants now enjoy the results of their self-denial and devotedness.

Fifty years ago, the LEADING OLDER ministers in the church were, John George Schmucker, of York, Pa.; Frederick David Schaeffer, of Philadelphia; John Daniel Kurtz, of Baltimore; George Lochman, of Harrisburg, Pa.; Christian Endress, of Lancaster, Pa.; Frederick William Geissenhainer, of New York; Gottleib Shober, of North Carolina; Paul Henkle, of Virginia; John Frederick Ruthrauff, of Franklin county, Pa.; Henry Augustus Muhlenberg, of Reading, Pa.; and William Baetes.

I call them *leading* men, not because they were all the most learned or the only efficient of our clergy of that day, but because most of them, from their geographical proximity and influential position, took a more or less active part in shaping the church of that day into something like symmetrical harmony and evangelical activity, and I mention these only because it was my privilege as an ecclesiastical neophyte to see them all and to know several of them very intimately in subsequent years. It is my purpose to record only that which I have seen or heard during my "Fifty Years." I may occasionally deviate, but not often.

There were not a few *younger* men of that generation, who were following their noble predecessors in the path of usefulness and devotedness to the interests of the church, whose names and services shall be commemorated in a subsequent chapter, but they cannot be reckoned among the "fathers" of fifty years ago. They were the rising and promising *sons*, who zealously carried on their work side by side with the venerated "ancients" whose names are recorded above.

I shall proceed to give mere outline sketches of these men, not biographies, for I have not room for that, but the chief characteristics of these servants of the Lord, so that the Lutherans of modern times may learn what sort of men our fathers were. In these and subsequent sketches of distinguished laborers in our apostolic church, the propriety of confining myself to those who are deceased will be apparent.

For many of the facts concerning these men, whom I did not know intimately, I am indebted to "*Sprague's Annals of the Lutheran Pulpit*," which are authentic, because furnished to that distinguished annalist by our own ministers, and because many of our ministers and people have never seen Dr. Sprague's impartial and invaluable book. For sketches of more modern men, which will appear subsequently, besides my own personal reminiscences, I am indebted to the liberality of some of my clerical brethren, and to those masterly pen and ink portraits of many of our deceased ministers drawn by the lamented Professor Stoever, in the Evangelical Review, whom I designated some years ago as the Plutarch of the Lutheran Church of America.

DR. JOHN GEORGE SCHMUCKER

was my pastor when I was a boy, and, as he lived until 1854, I was intimately associated with him in various enterprizes of the church.

He was a model of christian courtesy, and a finished gentleman. His temper was amiable, and his entire deportment discreet and dignified. He never censured any one severely, and was most tender towards the faults of others. He was kind to young preachers, and indulgent in his criticism. I never heard him utter an objectionable word, and he never related a story that was not perfectly pure.

As a student all his life through, he was diligent, and as a reader he was discriminating and untiring; as a theologian, he belonged to the old Lutheran school, although he never introduced that subject for the sake of controversy. It was from him that I first learned the scriptural doctrine of the Lord's supper as maintained by the church. I distinctly remember the day on which his rich elucidation of the truth was made to me. It was in my student years, and one vacation day, when, in his study, he began and unfolded to me in language never forgotten, the sublime doctrine taught by Luther, and which with more or less power has influenced my theological *tendency* ever since. Sometimes, owing to adverse associations, my faith was shaken, but when I got free from the influence of living teachers, and began independent investigation, my old pastor's interpretation of the scripture argument would come back with redoubled force.

He was born in the Duchy of Darmstadt, Germany, in 1771, and came to this country with his parents in 1785, who, after having lived in Northampton and Lancaster counties for two years, moved to Shenandoah county, Virginia; he began his studies for the ministry under Rev. Paul Henkle, but, in 1790, he repaired to Philadelphia, and became the student of Rev. Drs. Helmuth and Schmidt, where he remained two years. In 1792 he took pastoral charge of several congregations in York county. During his residence here he continued the study of the Hebrew language, and of theology, with the aid of the Rev. Mr. Goering, who was then the pastor at York, and who was regarded as among the learned ministers of his time.

In 1792 he accepted a call to Hagerstown, Md., in his twenty-second year; so youthful was his appearance, and so pale and emaciated his face, that he was sportively designated the *boy preacher*.

At the death of Dr. Kunze, in 1807, he was called to succeed him in the city of New York, which he declined.

In 1809 he became the successor of Mr. Goering, in the borough of York, where he remained until 1852, when he removed to Williamsburg, Pa., where several of his children resided, and where he died in October, 1854, in the eighty-fourth year of his age, and was buried in York.

In 1825 he received the degree of D. D. from the University of Pennsylvania.

Dr. Schmucker occupied many important places, and rendered much valuable service in connection with the public interests of the church. He was one of the founders and most zealous advocates of the General Lutheran Synod. He was President of the Foreign Missionary Society from its formation till a short time before his death, when he declined a re-election. He was also the early and active supporter of the Theological Seminary of the General Synod, and, for many years, served as President of its Board of Directors. He had an important agency in the establishment of Pennsylvania College, and, for more than twenty years acted as a Trustee. At the time of his death he was the Senior Vice President of the American Tract Society. Various other benevolent institutions found in him an efficient auxiliary.

I will here insert a letter furnished by me for "*Sprague's Annals*," which will be followed by several others:

BALTIMORE, April 11, 1861.

DEAR SIR: My earliest recollections are associated with Dr. Schmucker, of York. As a boy I was conducted to his church every Sunday, where, with other boys, I sat on the foot-board of the circular railing that enclosed the communion table. Though not understanding a word of his sermons at that time, which were German, yet there I sat every Sunday, a silent and sometimes sleeping, if not a profited, hearer. This was more years ago than I care about telling; and I mention it only in connection with the lasting impression which his personal appearance of that period made upon my juvenile mind. He was of a compact frame, firm and elastic step, hair dark as a raven, and eye black and glistening like anthracite coal. His voice was strong, though not loud, and of touching tenderness. Even many years later it did not lose this admirable quality, and it was "as good as a sermon" to hear him lead the singing of one of those good old German hymns in the prayer-meetings. There was a peculiar softness and impressive tremulousness in its tones which ring in my ears even to this day.

As I grew up and became his companion during my student life, I could appreciate the fine qualities of his character more distinctly. I never spent an hour with him without learning something useful. He poured forth his stores of practical wisdom, theological learning, rich personal experience and instructive anecdote, without effort or display.

His disinterestedness was remarkable, and his fear of giving offence was sometimes, as I think, carried to extremes. On one occasion that occurs to me, he sacrificed his better judgment to his apprehension of blame, in deciding the location of an institution of learning by his vote. He feared he would be charged with acting from interested motives if he voted differently. And yet, when deep principle was involved, he was unflinchingly firm. In the early days of the Temperance movement he braved the fierce opposition and even threats of his warmest personal friends and most liberal supporters.

Though not superstitious, he was not entirely free from belief in supernatural influences. If his mind had not been well balanced, he was just the man to be wrought on by the presumed revelations of modern Spiritualism. I believe this infirmity was fostered by his high admiration of, and thorough acquaintance with, some of the mystic theologians of the last century, especially Jung Stilling.

Quite unintentionally, and to his great annoyance, he once acquired the reputation of being a semi-miraculous healer of wens, warts, and similar ugly excrescences. On one occasion a plain countryman came into his study and complained of a wen on his head. "Let me see it," said the Doctor. He examined it, as a matter of curiosity, and touched it. The man declared that, from that moment, it began to diminish until it disappeared altogether. His neighbors heard of it, and, for miles around, all who were affected with similar unnatural protuberances, hastened to the "Pastor" to be healed by the magic touch; and it required some effort to convince the simple people that he possessed no supernatural powers, and he dismissed them to their deep chagrin.

I remember the first English sermon he preached. It was quite an event in the church. I do not mean the sermon, but the fact. Every body knew he was fully competent to the task; but the introduction of a new language into the church was an epoch in its history. The spacious house was crowded. The members of other churches left their own to hear Dr. Schmucker preach English. They and his own people were anxious to hear whether those church walls would echo English sounds. It was a success —the sermon was an admirable defence of the Inspiration of the Bible, and an eminent lawyer of the place was so deeply interested in it that he sent for it the next day for his private perusal and study. The Doctor, after this, continued to preach English several times a month, until he secured an assistant. The English service was designated to the town people by a peculiar ringing of the bells, so that the sexton would always go to the Doctor's house of a Sunday evening and ask whether he was to "ring English or German."

If the Doctor had, in early life, cultivated his talent for poetry, he would have excelled in that department.

He was one of the most unaffectedly polite men I ever knew. There was no superfluous bowing and scraping and fulsome complimenting, but he was so regardful for the feelings of others, so careful to avoid wounding them, so forbearing towards their faults, so condescending to inferiors, and so patient with gainsayers, as to compel their admiration and respect.

As a preacher no man was more methodical, logical and impressive. His extreme observance of system in his sermons often verged on stiffness. Every thing seemed to be laid down by rule and compass, and his hearers were so accustomed to his regular divisions as to length and place, that, at the conclusion of each, there was a general shifting of position and other demonstrations of relief from protracted and absorbed attention. At the announcement of the next head or division, the whole congregation would *subside* into the most fixed and silent listening to his well-set argument and tender appeal.

His extremely defective vision prevented him from reading his proof texts from the Pulpit Bible, and hence, for that purpose, he always used a small copy, which he was obliged to hold close up to his eyes.

As a Pastor, he was faithful, affectionate and tender; as a member of Synod and other Church Bodies, he was judicious, attentive and influential; as a friend, firm, candid and instructive; and, as a promoter of benevolent and literary enterprises, active, liberal and successful. Very truly yours,

JOHN G. MORRIS.

FROM THE REV. SAMUEL S. SCHMUCKER, D. D.

THEOLOGICAL SEMINARY, GETTYSBURG, December 24, 1857.

In person, my father was of about the medium stature, rather thick set, though not corpulent; his eyes were deep seated, and, like his hair, jet black. His complexion was dark; his constitution vigorous; and, even in old age, his person was very erect, and his bodily movements, whilst they were deliberate and dignified, were also prompt and firm. His countenance was expressive of great amiability, benevolence and dignity, whilst his keen black eye and well developed head indicated the excellence of his intellectual powers. His character was unusually symmetrical and well balanced, and his temper so uniformly placid that I have scarcely ever seen it ruffled by the most trying annoyances of life. He had a quick sensibility for the sufferings of humanity. Nor did his sympathy evaporate in mere mental emotion—he was also a generous and active friend of the poor, the afflicted and the oppressed, in our own and foreign lands. Of the expansiveness of his benevolence I will state a single example. When the Orphan House at Halle, in Germany, was almost destroyed during the Bonapartean Wars, so strong was his sympathy for that suffering institution, whose alumni were the chief founders of our Church in this country, that his response to the appeal of its Directors to our churches in this Western world for pecuniary aid was the most liberal of all our ministers. He was possessed of strong common sense, great discernment of character and singular soundness of judgment. Though modest and unassuming, he was distinguished for conscientiousness and moral courage, was unwavering in his defence of truth and righteousness, and an unfaltering friend of the great moral reforms of the day. Of this his noble defence of the Temperance cause in its infancy, when not only the populace generally, but the majority of professing Christians, and even some of the neighboring ministers of the Gospel, were yet opposed to it, affords a striking example. So violent was this opposition amongst the German community at large (they regarding it as an attempt to infringe upon their civil rights), that some even menaced personal violence; and so extensive amongst his own church members that their contributions to his salary fell off one-half during that year. He, however, faltered not; gradually the truth gained the victory, and, in a few years, he, who had previously enjoyed the public confidence in an unusual degree, found it again reposed in himself in a higher measure than before.

He was warmly attached to the great National Societies of our land, in which different Christian denominations co-operate, such as the American Bible and Tract Societies. He was especially interested in the operations of the American Tract Society, and regarded that mass of truth taught in its publications, and held by the Evangelical denominations in common, as the grand instrumentality for the conversion of the world. Yet, he was warmly attached to the Evangelical Lutheran Church, as organized under the Biblical constitution of our General Synod. He was an attentive student of the Prophetic Scriptures, as well as a careful observer of the signs of the times, and wrote with acknowledged ability on both topics.

As a Preacher he was eloquent, instructive and impressive, generally fixing the attention of the audience to his subject and holding it there to the close of his discourse. He was especially a good textuary. He enriched his discourses with copious citations of Scripture proof and illustration, not unfrequently naming the chapter and verse. Few men employed the power of the pulpit more faithfully in reproving current vices. Soon after his removal to York, he learned that some ten or more of the most respectable and influential citizens of the town, who were also professedly members of his church, were in the habit of meeting frequently for the purpose of playing cards as an innocent diversion. This he deemed highly criminal, not only as a waste of time, which Christians should apply to better use, but as an example calculated to sanction and encourage the gambling habits of the young and profligate. After repeated but fruitless private admonition, he determined on another and more hazardous measure to break up the practice, which was generally known to the community. On the ensuing Sabbath he introduced the subject into the pulpit, and exposed the evils of the practice in so fearless a manner, and with such distinct allusion to the parties concerned, that I well remember seeing members turning round in the church and looking at the offenders, whilst a sensation of surprise and concern filled many minds, all expecting disturbance in the church, and offence to the families concerned, as the result of the discourse. The effect, however, was favorable. The practice was abandoned; and, although the parties felt individually aggrieved at the exposure, they made no public demonstration against the Preacher, and eventually admitted the justice and propriety of his course.

Sacred Music and Poetry found a deep response in his heart. He also occasionally committed some Hymns and other poetical effusions to the press, which, if they do not prove him a special favorite of the Muses, are distinguished for ease and smoothness of versification, as well as the deep-toned piety which they breathe.

As a Pastor, he was most laborious and faithful. Such was his punctuality in attending the Judicatories of the Church that his presence was calculated on by all as a matter of course; and such were his administrative talents that he was repeatedly elected to the highest offices of the Church. He was an ardent friend of the General Synod—was one of its original founders, and, ever after among its ablest defenders. In short, for about thirty years he was one of the leading minds in our American Lutheran Church, was actively engaged in all her important measures, and was ever known as the firm champion of piety and of revivals of religion, as well as of all such enterprises as tend to advance the spiritual triumphs of the Redeemer in the Church universal. His own ministry was blest not only by numerous conversions occurring every year, but by five or six special outpourings of the Holy Spirit, each resulting in the conversion of multitudes of souls. In one of these revivals, the number of converts was so large that they divided themselves into three classes, and each conducted a separate weekly prayer-meeting in a different part of the congregation.

A striking trait in my father's character was the depth of his religious experience, and his unusually advanced progress in the Divine life. The following remarks, which I find written by his own hand in his pocket Greek Testament, will throw some light on his internal religious history:

"1. From the time of my conversion in my eighteenth year, my life was, though in different degrees, a continual prayer, a longing and sighing after God. 2. It was a continual repentance, on account of my sins and the depravity of my heart. 3. It was a continual longing after the holiness and grace to live according to the will of God. 4. A continual longing for union and communion with God. 5. Through life I had a continued desire for the conversion of souls, which influenced every sermon I preached, though it was often defiled by the intermixture of selfish aims. 6. I had a constant desire for the society of the pious. 7. At the same time, I had many infirmities and sins, and all my virtues were defective. In 1840 I enjoyed a special manifestation of the Divine love shed abroad in my heart, which was exceedingly refreshing to me. And, soon after, I had also a special view of the Divine majesty and goodness. In 1841 I had an extraordinary view of Christ, and beheld his image, as it were, in the chamber of my soul."

For several months before his death, he was much abstracted from the world, and engaged in almost constant communion with God. During this time, he, on one occasion, was lying on his bed in the night-watches, and called to my mother, who was at his side—"Oh, if you could see what I have seen beyond the Jordan of death, how happy you would be!" Such was the holy frame of mind in which he awaited the call of his Redeemer, and such the foretaste vouchsafed to him of his future inheritance until he calmly yielded his life into his Redeemer's hands.

Very fraternally yours,

S. S. SCHMUCKER.

FROM REV. J. ALLEN BROWN, D. D.

PROFESSOR IN THE THEOLOGICAL SEMINARY, GETTYSBURG, PA.

GETTYSBURG THEOLOGICAL SEMINARY, March

My DEAR SIR: In complying with the request to furnish something touching the late venerable Dr. J. G. Schmucker, I will confine myself strictly to my own personal recollections; and, as these extend only over a small part of his life, you will not be troubled with a very lengthy account. It affords me, however, great pleasure to be able, even in this humble way, to record my high regard for him while living, and the delight with which I recall the intercourse with him which I was privileged to enjoy.

Our first meeting, which I cannot call acquaintance, since I was then but a youth, was in the year 1840, when he was on a visit to his son-in-law, Dr. Sprecher, at Middletown, Pa. He had already retired from the active duties of the Ministry. As I was then a student, not yet entered college, I have little recollection beyond his venerable, dignified appearance, his apparent interest in study, and his friendly condescension to a mere youth. Some remarks about theological opinions, and concern about Buttmann's Greek Grammar, leave the impression that, even at that period, he maintained habits of careful investigation.

My acquaintance proper began early in the year 1848, when I settled in York, Pa., where a large part of his life had been spent, and where it was my lot to officiate in the church of which he had been so long Pastor, and in which he was then a regular worshipper. During a period of some two years I was a frequent visitor at his house, sharing not only his friendship, but enjoying his friendly counsels. A few items, the freshest in my memory, of this venerable father, I will now give.

No one who ever saw him could forget his personal appearance and manner. Of about medium stature, and singularly erect in old age, with a fine countenance, and full supply of hair in perfect order, he presented an appearance of dignity that was truly commanding; whilst his manner, combining gravity and softness, was attractive and pleasing. In his intercourse he exemplified the precept—"Be courteous," and was a model of Christian politeness. Nature and grace had both contributed to the formation of his character, and the result was one of much beauty and excellence.

His manner towards young preachers was very kind and encouraging. Usually at the close of the service he had some kind word to cheer. After my first sermon in his presence, he said, as I came from the pulpit—"I think the Lord was with you to-day." There were no flippant criticisms, no eulogies to gender or nourish pride, but judicious words of counsel and encouragement. On another occasion, after I had preached on Matt. xxviii, 19, 20, he expressed gratification, but said there was too much in the text for a single discourse. It was very evident that he had made preaching a study, and knew how to divide the Word of truth. His criticisms of some men, though never harsh, were discerning, and showed that he had detected the weak points. He loved to speak of the great preachers in our own and other churches, and especially to tell of their spiritual power.

He was interested in the study of the Word. Olshausen, at this time, was a favorite commentator with him. He expressed a decided preference for Olshausen over Tholuck, as more spiritual and giving more of the mind of the inspired writer. Tholuck he regarded as too profuse in his exhibition of learned authorities, and less instructive than Olshausen. My first acquaintance with Olshausen was made with a borrowed volume from his library.

The prosperity of Zion and the welfare of the country both seemed to be near his heart. He loved to hear of what God was doing. The cause of Christ at home and abroad had his sympathies and his prayers. He believed that the coming of the Messiah to reign over the earth was drawing nigh. The revolutions among nations he regarded as preparatory to the establishment of the Kingdom which shall not pass away. He was cheerful, hopeful, and looking forward with confidence in God.

But he has gone to join the band of Prophets, Apostles, Confessors and Ministers of Jesus. His name is fragrant on the earth, his record was on high, and he has entered on his reward.

Truly yours,
J. A. Brown.

EXTRACT OF A PRIVATE LETTER TO J. G. M.

December, 1876.

I used to like to listen to old Dr. Schmucker, as he told of his early experiences in the West when he was travelling in Ohio and Kentucky, as a candidate. You know the Synod used to send the licentiates as a sort of circuit riders, or rather as exploring missionaries, to hunt up the scattered settlers, baptize their children, hold communion services with them, and, when possible, organize them into churches. Once Rev. Schmucker came suddenly upon a smouldering camp fire that had just been deserted by a bivouacking party of a hostile tribe of Indians. He was discovered by them just as he turned to flee in the direction from which he came, and they gave chase. I do not remember how many miles he led them, but it was a long and breakneck race, his faithful steed bringing him back into the settlement just as his pursuers were about closing upon him.

DR. JOHN DANIEL KURTZ,

who, for fifty years, continued to be pastor of the same church in Baltimore, became a worshipper with my congregation after he resigned his position as pastor. Owing to a slight defect in his hearing after he had become an old man, he usually took his seat beside me in the pulpit, that he might hear more distinctly, and, he was one of the most attentive hearers I had. He was too polite to express any disapprobation of what was said, or rather of the manner which, doubtless, he often felt, but he would frequently signify his assent by an undertone *hem* with a falling inflection, as much as to say, " All right young man! go on."

He was the most blameless man I ever knew. He lived in Baltimore nearly sixty years, and had encountered some troublesome spirits in his church, but in all that time not the slightest whisper of wrong doing on his part was ever heard, and he went down to his grave with a name untarnished as the whitest snow. His piety was profound, but he seldom spoke of his religious experience. His extreme modesty forbade him to speak of himself on any occasion, and yet he once told me when speaking of the nature of conversion, that " He did not remember the time when he did not love God."

He was not, what we now call, a learned man, but still well read in the old Lutheran theology, and perhaps more in the practical than the dogmatical. He was a diligent reader of the old orthodox devotional books, and always had one of these precious volumes near at hand.

In early life he paid some attention to natural history, but the want of time and of books prevented any extended research. but, still in our country visits, he would let no butterfly or beetle escape which he could capture, not for the purpose of keeping it for his cabinet, but to explain its beauties to me, and it is principally to him that I am indebted for my taste in that same direction and my subsequent operations in that enticing field of study.

During one of these visits to an old country friend, Dr. Kurtz returned from a walk among the bushes and brambles of a neglected garden, and as he approached the house he was amazed at the violent exclamations of the people, while they pointed to his feet. He looked down and saw that a snake had wound itself around his leg, and of which he was perfectly unconscious. He quickly shook it off and allowed it to escape, remarking that it was a harmless creature, and nobody need be frightened at it.

He contributed several excellent articles on Justification to the old Evangelisches Magazin, published in Philadelphia by Dr. Helmuth. Some years after, a minister of our church from the country and I were paying him a visit, when the stranger incidentally remarked that he had lately been looking at the old "Magazin," and was delighted with several articles on Justification. The modest old doctor said not a word, nor changed countenance, but I, who always sought to honor him and give him his due, said, "And you are speaking to the author of those articles." The visitor expressed his pleasure in knowing it, and was proceeding to compliment him still further, but the doctor instantly changed the subject.

He had some troubles in his church during his long pastorate, but he bore them all like a christian martyr, glad to know that his worst opponent could never charge him with neglect of duty or violation of moral principle. Upon his retirement from the pulpit, the congregation voted him an annuity of one thousand dollars and the use of the parsonage during his life.

Although I have seen him exposed to severe trials of patience, yet I never saw him excited to any degree, excepting once. It was at a meeting of our Synod, when a number of us prevented the election of an objectionable candidate for the Presidency by withholding a majority. Five or six elections were held, and with the same result. The old gentleman arose and most severely rebuked us for our obstinacy, and for occasioning the loss of so much time. We yielded, and bore the infliction of an incompetent man in the presidential chair for one year. He died in 1856, in the ninety-third year of his age.

He was the first man I ever heard preach from a text in the Apocrypha, but it was a very unusual practice with him.

He never preached English, but was a vigorous, systematic and earnest German preacher. He adhered all his life time to the old pietistic school both in sentiment and arrangement, and could hold an audience in silence and perfect attention for an hour. I heard his nephew, the modern Dr. Kurtz, say, that his uncle once preached for him in Chambersburg, when he began his sermon thus: "For over fifty-five years have I preached the same unchangeable gospel of salvation by faith in Jesus Christ, and I have nothing else to present to you to-day." He then proceeded to tell them what this gospel was, and my narrator added, that this simple declaration, associated as it was with his earnest manner and voice trembling with emotion, his venerable appearance and yet unabated vigor had an overwhelming effect upon the aged hearers present.

I was almost daily at his bedside during his final illness, and I often told him that I had come to learn patience and resignation, and not to teach or support him. And yet he would listen to the simplest truths of christianity with an intentness as though he did not understand them better than I did, and would sometimes supplement my remarks with observations, exhibiting the profoundest insight into the plan of salvation, and the richest christian experience.

He was fond of repeating some of those grand old German hymns, which he would do until perfectly exhausted. He was a good man, and full of the Holy Ghost.*

DR. FREDERICK DAVID SCHAEFFER OF PHILADELPHIA.

I never had much intercourse with this worthy and venerated father. I dined with him once when I was quite a young man, in company with the sainted Dr. Krauth, and was pleased with his condescending attention. A few years later he called on me

---

*See an interesting autobiography in Lutheran Observer, beginning in number for July, 1856; also, Evangelical Review, 1857, page 519.

in Baltimore, soon after the death of his son, Rev. F. C. Schaeffer, of New York, of whom he spoke with the most tender paternal affection. I remember, particularly, how gratefully he spoke of some gentleman in New York, who offered the bereaved father a place in his vault in the cemetery for the remains of the son, and closed by saying with deep emotion, "We deposited his body there to await the resurrection of the Just."

I met him subsequently at the house of his son, David F., in Frederick, but old age had crept upon him, and other circumstances had combined to sadden the evening of his days.

From his conversation, which was always grave when I was in his company, I soon learned that he was of the Arndt and Spener school in theology and feeling. Indeed, a majority of these fathers had the same *Richtung*.

Although Dr. Schaeffer never, to a great extent, indulged in authorship, he was a more learned man than many whose books are more numerous.

He was born in Germany and came to this country in 1775 or '76. He was cherished by Rev. Mr. Goering, of York, under whom young Schaeffer studied for the ministry. He had previously taught school in York county for several years. He was licensed in 1786, and took charge of the churches in and around Carlisle. In 1790 he became pastor of the Germantown district, and in 1812 he removed to Philadelphia and became the colleague of Rev. Dr. Helmuth, in St. Michel's and Zion Churches. In 1814 he was honored with the title of D. D. by the University of Pennsylvania. In 1834 he retired from the active duties of the ministry and removed to Frederick, Md., where his son David Frederick was pastor, and where he died in 1836, aged 76 years.

Four of his sons became ministers; David F., who died in Frederick, Md, in 1837; Frederick Christian, who died in New York in 1832; Frederick Solomon, who died in Hagerstown in 1815, aged 25, who was the father of Rev. Dr. C. W. Schaeffer, of Germantown; and Charles Frederick, one of the most learned of our clergy, still surviving (1878) and professor in the Theological Seminary, Philadelphia.

The following letters from Sprague's Annals, pp. 82-4, represent his character truly:

FROM THE REV. CHARLES F. SCHAEFFER, D. D.

EASTON, PA., November 16, 1854.

Those who were best acquainted with my father in private life esteemed him, I believe, as a devout and holy man. He devoted himself especially to those duties of the pastoral office which, least of all, attract public attention. A large portion of his time was given to the visitation of the sick and poor. The former he loved to visit, and his great experience, combined with his own clear views of Divine truth and the wants of the heart, account for the deep impressions which the afflicted received when he prayed with them or conversed on religious subjects. For the latter he almost systematically collected alms by applying to benevolent Christian friends, who gladly availed themselves of his services as their almoner. Many instances occurred in which he sought out the needy, and afforded relief under circumstances which would have admitted of aid from no other source.

His deep interest in the spiritual welfare of the young, and his warm attachment to them, were also among his characteristic features. He seemed to regard those as his happiest hours in which he regularly gave religious instruction to the young on the evening of the Lord's Day. When he paid pastoral visits it was usual to bring the children of the family to him, as he devoted as much attention to these, in his own gentle and pleasant mode, as to adults. He described the Saviour to the little children, who loved to gather around him, attracted their attention by familiar descriptions of Christ's miracles and parables, and taught them to pray to their Divine Redeemer.

He was eminently a man of prayer, and devoted much time daily to his private devotions. His children who survive gratefully remember his mode of conducting family worship, his explanations of the portion of Scripture which he or one of them read, and the hymns which he taught the family to sing as a delightful part of the daily worship.

His mild and forgiving spirit was often tested. At one period of his life, during his residence in Philadelphia, unusual difficulties arose in the German congregation of which he was pastor, connected with the question of introducing the English language into the public worship. He never permitted a word expressive of anger to escape his lips, but exhorted his friends to be forbearing and submissive. He embraced every opportunity to soothe the excited minds of those who seemed to be unfriendly, and his consistent and kind course disarmed many, removed their prejudices, and converted them into sincere and admiring friends.

He never accumulated money. Several small amounts, obtained by the practice of strict economy during many years, and entrusted to those whom he considered as his friends, were all lost. Though he had hoped to preserve the money for his family, and of course regretted the loss of it, he fully retained his equanimity, and always said "The Lord will provide."

He was of average height, rather thin in person, but favored with an uncommonly good constitution. Even in his advanced years he retained much of that manly beauty of features by which he had once been distinguished. His very dark hair and eyes, his healthy color, and his unusually powerful voice, which was also well toned, arrested attention and predisposed persons to a kindly estimate of him. There was, besides, a gentleness of expression in his countenance, which did not fail to add to the effect produced by his addresses.

It is probable that his feelings were very excitable in early life. Even in later years traces of sensitiveness occasionally appeared, indicating that if Divine grace had not renewed his heart, he might have often displayed even great warmth of temper. Remarks which he occasionly made on this subject led his family to understand that he deemed it especially necessary to watch over himself, and, by Divine aid, control his feelings. His prayers were evidently heard; for even when circumstances occurred adapted to arouse the angry passions, he was enabled to overcome the temptation, and was never known to yield. His family never saw him gay or excessively lively, but neither did they ever witness anything that resembled melancholy or gloom. He was rather characterized by a uniform gravity, tempered by a calm cheerfulness. Among the favorite texts which he often quoted in the family circle were two which had evidently exercised a predominating influence over his own character, namely, "Our conversation is in Heaven," and "Set your affections on things above, not on things on the earth."

In place of adding any further remarks of my own, I will conclude by appending a brief extract from a sketch of my father's character, which Professor Stoever, of Pennsylvania College, prepared, and which I regard as a very faithful view of some of his leading characteristics.*

"Dr. Schaeffer was a man of solid abilities and of studious habits. He was a close student, and carefully read the Hebrew Bible and the Septuagint. No day passed without the deliberate perusal of the sacred original. His intellect had been invigorated and enriched by earnest effort and constant diligence. It was single in its aims, and more effective than many minds of greater brilliancy. * * * * He was peculiarly interested in geographical studies, and had accumulated a large collection of maps. After his professional studies, this seems to have been his favorite pursuit. He was also enthusiastic in his love of music, and from this source frequently sought recreation. It was his usual practice every night before retiring to play on the piano and sing a few choice stanzas. He had likewise a poetic talent, which, in earlier life, he was disposed to cultivate. He composed quite a number of hymns. In later years he does not seem to have exercised this gift. * * * * * * * *

"As a preacher Dr. Schaeffer was plain and unostentatious, but instructive and experimental. His views on all subjects of Christian faith were evangelical. The teachings of Divine Revelation he implicitly received. After the Sacred Scriptures he revered the volume of our Symbolic Books, a Latin copy of which he always read. These, in his judgment, contained a summary of Christian Doctrine, the truths of God's Word. He never, however, exalted them above the Bible. He was tolerant in his views, liberal in his spirit, and conciliatory in his intercourse. His sermons were eminently practical, designed to reach the heart and affect the conduct. His partialities were all in favor of the Arndt and Spener School. These predilections which he acquired in his youth he retained through life."

With great regard, I am very sincerely yours,
CHARLES F. SCHAEFFER.

FROM THE REV. C. P. KRAUTH, D. D.,
PROFESSOR IN THE THEOLOGICAL SEMINARY, GETTYSBURG.

GETTYSBURG, April 5, 1855.

MY DEAR SIR: My first introduction to Dr. Schaeffer was in the year 1819, in the city of Baltimore, at a meeting of the Evangelical Lutheran Synod of Pennsylvania and the adjacent States.

* Evang. Rev. VI, 275.

then in my youth, and applying to that venerable body for authority to preach the Gospel, Dr. Schaeffer was a member of the committee appointed by Synod to examine the applicants. I retain a very distinct recollection of the appearance and bearing of the doctor during that (to me) trying process. Grave, dignified, earnest, kind, he executed his task with a faithful and gentle spirit. He manifested a special interest in the examination of a young gentleman, who had made in Germany considerable proficiency in Hebrew, an attainment now so common, but then rare in all our churches. Amongst the divines of his day he held a very high rank in respect to Oriental learning, and particularly the Hebrew; and I believe he continued to cherish his fondness for it till the close of life. To what extent he had pursued the dialects cognate with the Hebrew I do not know, but have reason to believe that he had studied them to some extent.

It was eight years after this when, from a change of residence, Philadelphia became my home, that I was brought into closer relations and more intimate communion with him. He was then advanced in life, and had long and faithfully served his Master in preaching the Gospel and performing the arduous duties of a pastor. I found him hospitable, accessible to his younger brethren, and uniformly urbane. In conversation he was remarkably unpretending and modest; indeed no trait in him was more strongly developed than freedom from ostentation. He was unjust to himself in this respect—if any reference were made to his attainments he would, with perfect sincerity, disclaim all pretensions to any superior knowledge. Consulted in casuistical cases, he was always ready to counsel his younger brethren in the ministry, and his oracles were given forth with no uncertain sound. Moving much amongst his people, diligent in his visits from house to house, attentive to the sick and afflicted, he was a model minister of Jesus Christ. I have seen him when he was cast upon a bed of sickness, and when his recovery seemed at least very doubtful, and he was calm, resigned, ready to depart and be with Christ. I have marked the deep reverence and solemnity with which he partook in the devotional exercises which he solicited, and had evidence not to be resisted that he was a man of large experience in the Divine life, a devoted soldier of the Cross. His mind was solid rather than brilliant, and his discourses were adapted to instruct and profit rather than merely to please. Evangelical in his views, setting forth the doctrine of Justification by Faith, as held by our church, aiming to win souls by true conversion, enforcing all his lessons by a holy example, he finished the work which had been given him, and I doubt not entered into the joy of his Lord.

Faithfully yours,
C. P. KRAUTH.

DR. GEORGE LOCHMAN

I never was acquainted with, though I distinctly remember his appearance, having seen him in the pulpit when I was a boy, in York. He did nothing more on that occasion than announce the opening of the Synod the next day, and yet, juvenile as I was, to this day his mild, amiable, handsome countenance is present to my view, and the sweet mellifluous tones of his voice still sound in my ears. He and Dr. Schmucker, Sr., were intimate as brothers, and I have often heard the latter speak of him as he would of a favorite younger brother. I remember him telling me how deeply Dr. Lochman was wounded at the severe criticism of one of his publications by Dr. Ely, of Philadelphia. He, who could never utter or write a word that would hurt the feelings of any man living, thought it hard that other men should indulge in sharp language and unsparing criticism of others. I have been told that he was equally the favorite of all men of sensibility who knew him.

He was born in Philadelphia in 1773, graduated in the University of Pennsylvania in 1789, licensed in 1794, elected pastor at Lebanon, where he remained twenty-one years. In 1815 he was elected to Harrisburg, where he remained till his death, in 1826, aged fifty-three. For a list of his writings, see my Bibliotheca Lutherana.

One of his pupils thus describes him:

The doctor took great pains and pleasure in imparting to us such instruction as we needed. He was a father to us, always pleasant and communicative. He was easily approached, ever ready to solve our difficulties, and unravel the many hard questions which made us halt. He would spend his time cheerfully for our good. He was the kind father, the patient and condescending instructor, and affable and social christian, the light of whose handsome and benevolent countenance illuminated the circle which his benevolent heart attracted around him. He delighted, between the recitation hours, to gather his students around him and explain the points of difference between other creeds and the Lutheran. He prided in the distinctive characteristic liberality of Lutheranism; of not having an endless creed run out into the minor distinctions of theological disputants, but set up the Bible as the only rule of faith. He ascribed the union and harmony of the Lutheran church to the liberty her ministers enjoyed in non-essentials, and union in the fundamentals of our holy religion.

EXTRACTS OF A LETTER IN SPRAGUE'S ANNALS.
FROM THE REVEREND WILLIAM R. DEWITT, D. D.

HARRISBURG, January 16, 1852.

MY DEAR SIR: When I came to Harrisburg, in 1818, to take charge of the church to which I now minister, Dr. Lochman was the Pastor of the Evangelical Lutheran Church of this place. Dr. Lochman preached a portion of his time in the English language. When the Presbyterian and Methodist Churches were not supplied, his church was the resort of all the English inhabitants of Harrisburg who were accustomed to attend public worship. He was also frequently called on for the performance of funeral services and the visitation of the sick in the English families. He was prominent in all the educational interests of the Borough; was, from its organization to his death, the President of the Harrisburg Bible Society, and gave his countenance and support to every measure that promised to advance the public welfare. He thus became intimately associated with the citizens of Harrisburg, and, to this day, his name is held in affectionate remembrance by our older inhabitants of all denominations.

This was the prominent feature in Dr. Lochman's character—a childlike simplicity, combined with unmeasured kindness of heart, which nothing could disturb, except indeed some invasion of what he esteemed the rights and prerogatives of the good old Lutheran Church, for which he entertained an affection next in strength and devotedness to that he felt for his Divine Master. I do not mean to intimate that Dr. Lochman was a bigot—nothing could be farther from his nature. He could not be otherwise than genial and kind to all of every denomination. But the Lutheran Church, the *Great Lutheran Church*, lay very near his heart.

His preaching, his prayers, all his public as well as private ministrations, bore the impress of his pastoral character. He was esteemed among the most learned of the Lutheran Divines in this country. He always had a greater or less number of students of Divinity residing with him in his family, to whom he gave instruction by way of preparing them for the sacred office. But in the pulpit he invariably laid aside the doctor, and was the kind and affectionate pastor. As a pastor he was indefatigable. During his ministry here he had, for a time, the charge of several small country congregations in addition to the one in town, which rendered his pastoral labors very severe. But he was ever prompt to the call of duty when his health would permit. Storm or sunshine, cold or heat, day or night, he was ever ready to go and administer the consolations of the Gospel to the sick and dying, to the afflicted and distressed. Often, in my early ministry, have I come from my study with my head throbbing in my efforts to get out something that might be useful to my people, and have met the Doctor, with cane in hand, walking the streets, with his fresh ruddy countenance lighted up with an expression of benignity, either coming from or going to visit some afflicted family, some child of want, or some members of his congregation, at whose houses he was welcome, and I dare not say I never envied the leisure he enjoyed from his studies for pastoral visitation. Methinks I see him now walking the streets, with his golden-headed cane, a pattern of neatness in his dress, a perfect gentleman of the old school in his manners, bowing politely and complacently to all he met, and smiling benignantly on the little children, who rejoiced to be recognized by the good Doctor, and thought they had much to tell their parents at home when they could say that they had met Dr. Lochman in the street and that he had spoken to them and laid his hands on their heads and blessed them. In those days Whitsuntide was a great day in Harrisburg. It was a high day. On that day all the youth of a certain age of the Lutheran families marched in procession through our streets, dressed in white, with a plain white cap on their heads, to the Lutheran Church, where they were confirmed and received the benediction of their Pastor. As I recall in my musings the scenes of other days, I seem to meet again in our streets the good Lutheran Pastor, to see the benignant smile on his countenance, and to hear from his lips the "How do you do, my dear friend?" in that peculiar tone of kindness which it is impossible to imitate. But he is gone. Notwithstanding four or five other excellent Pastors have occupied his place since his death, the memory of Dr. Lochman still seems almost as fresh and fragrant as ever.

Yours most respectfully,

W. R. DEWITT.

EXTRACT OF A LETTER FROM THE REV. A. H. LOCHMAN, D. D.

YORK, PA., January 19, 1863.

I think I may safely say that his most prominent characteristics as a man and a christian were a childlike simplicity and an ardent affection. These qualities tempered and modeled the whole man. His piety was more of the type of that of John than of Peter. Though ardently attached to the Church of his fathers and of his choice, yet no one ever accused him of a bigoted or sectarian spirit. His hand was ever cordially extended, and his heart open to welcome all who loved the Lord Jesus Christ, and who received what he regarded as the cardinal truths of our holy religion.

Neither in his intercourse with others, nor in his discussions at Synodical meetings, nor on any other public occasions, was there anything that approached to ostentatious display. You always knew where to find him. He spoke directly to the point without any formality or any concealment. To his students of Divinity, of whom he had at different times upwards of twenty, he always said "Be plain and simple; speak so that the common people will be able to understand you, and you are sure that the learned will."

He scarcely ever passed a person, not even a child, for whom he had not a smile and a kind word.

The love of God in the redemption of the world through the atonement of Christ was the theme upon which, above all others, he loved to dwell. This seemed to set his soul on fire, and he discoursed upon it with an eloquence and a pathos which often proved quite irresistible.

In his judgment of others he always leaned to the side of mercy. His family government, though firm and decisive, was a constant exhibition of love. He scarcely ever administered a severe reproof; and I never knew him correct any of his children but once or twice, and then I was myself the unfortunate subject, and I richly deserved it. Something may be inferred concerning the influence that he exerted upon his children from the fact that all of them who came to years of maturity (seven) became consistent members of the church. In his dying moments he said to a minister of another denomination, who visited him, "Brother, what would I do now if I had not an Almighty Saviour to rest upon?"

ANECDOTE OF DR. LOCHMAN.

When George was a boy his father determined that he should learn his business and thus help to support the family. By the depreciation of the continental currency he had lost the little means he had possessed. The importunities of the son, however, made an impression upon him, and he consented to allow him to acquire a knowledge of the languages. On a certain occasion a new book was to be purchased. The previous week he had bought a dictionary and other books which he required. He was afraid to mention it to his father, lest he might refuse to furnish him with the money. In this difficulty he resorted to prayer. As he was returning from school he simply stated his case to his Heavenly Father and asked his assistance. "After I had prayed," he said, "my mind became easy, and taking a feather which was lying in my path, I blew it in the air and ran after it. As it was descending I blew it up again, when a slight breeze caught it and bore it away before me. I followed it. It fell down into the street and lighted upon a silver dollar, the price of the book I wanted to buy. I took it up, praising God, brought it home, told my father all the circumstances." The old man was much affected, and as he brushed away the tears from his eyes and said "George, this dollar may not be ours, but take it. God has sent it. We will make enquiry, and if the owner is found I will give him another."

DR. CHRISTIAN ENDRESS, OF LANCASTER,

was one of the most intellectual of our ministers of that day. He died in 1827, too early for any intimate acquaintance with him. I never saw him but once, when he was on a visit to Dr. Schmucker, whom he came to consult about the publication of a new translation of Paul's Epistle to the Romans. It never was put to press, though advertisements were issued.

He was the author of those exhaustive articles in the Lutheran Intelligencer, entitled, "Was Luther an absolute predestinarian?"

In his youth he was a tutor in the University of Pennsylvania, and is said by those who knew him to have been a first rate classical scholar.

Any person who ever saw

DR. FREDERICK WILLIAM GEISSENHAINER

but once, as I did years ago, must have been struck with the intense brilliancy of his eye, and of course with his profoundly penetrating look. I met him only once, and that was in his own house in New York. He was slight in person and had a deeply pockmarked face, if I remember correctly. His movements were quick, his conversation animated, and his thoughts betokened the man of reflection and experience. Without any pretence he soon impressed you that he was a man of learning, if there were any occasion to draw him out. I confess that my previous associations had led me to entertain a prejudice against him, but an hour's interview dispelled such unfavorable feelings, and he proved himself to be a polite christian gentleman.

When I was with him a German woman came in with a boy, whom she represented as incorrigibly bad, and requested the doctor to give him a good lecture. He did it in proper style, and held the menace over him that if he did not reform he would not confirm him! This seemed to have a better effect than any thing else, at least so it appeared, but the way in which the poor frightened lad replied over a dozen times to the doctor's remonstrance, "Ya, Herr Pfarrer!" was very amusing.

When he first arrived in this country, in 1793, he was of slender stature, delicate constitution, and timid disposition. He fell among thieves at the public house in Philadelphia at which he stopped, and the savage landlord still further tried to alarm the young and inexperienced foreigner by telling him that it was a common thing in the rural districts of this country for the people to chastise their preachers if their sermons reproved the sins of the hearers, or otherwise did not satisfy them. The credulous young missionary was so dreadfully alarmed by this report and other ill treatment that he resolved to return to Europe by the first opportunity. Through the persuasion of Dr. Helmuth, he consented to delay his voyage a short time, and to preach at Barren Hill for Rev. Dr. Schaeffer. He rode out on horseback, but all the time was much depressed in spirit, and when he reached the place he tied his horse to a tree and stood for a considerable time at some distance from the church, as if afraid to venture in. The congregation waited for a whole hour, but at length growing impatient, one of the elders approached the stranger, who was not recognized as a clergyman, perhaps from his youth and his unclerical light colored overcoat. On the elder making enquiry whether he knew of any minister who was coming on that morning to preach for them, Mr. G. summoned up courage to say that he had come for that purpose. He then entered the pulpit and preached, but as soon as the sermon was ended he hurried off as fast as he could, in dread of the chastisement which he feared would be inflicted. Being a good rider, he quickened his pace, but how great was his alarm when, suddenly looking back, he saw some one riding after him at a most rapid rate! And now the race began. The man called upon him to stop, but the louder he called the faster the preacher urged on his steed. The pursuer at last overtook him, but the preacher's fears of a castigation were soon dispelled by the gentle and kind words of the elder, who invited him home to dinner. He said that he wished to converse with him on a matter of conscience, as he was convinced from his sermon that he could give him the best advice. But regarding this as only a cunning device to get him into his power, he declined and hastened to Philadelphia. On relating to Doctor Helmuth the circumstances, the doctor told him he should, by all means, have gone with the elder, and tried to deliver his young friend from the false and painful misrepresentations under which his mind was laboring. He finally succeeded so far that Mr. Geissenhainer decided he would accept the call to the congregations tendered him in Montgomery county, about forty miles from Philadelphia, and for a season, at least, make trial of the ministry in this country. An incident, however, occurred at the very beginning of his experience that almost made him regret the step he had taken, and served to confirm him in the opinion he had conceived with regard to the rudeness of the country people. On his arrival at Goschenhoppen he put up at an inn, and on the following Sabbath preached his first sermon. After the services the vestry met and decided that as it was improper for the pastor to remain at a public house, one of their own number must take him into his own family. But so profound a reverence for the youthful preacher was entertained that all made objection to his reception. Finally, two who lived on fine farms and possessed ample accommodations were selected, one of whom, it was said, must consent to the arrangement. Both still expressing very great aversion to the proposition, they resolved to cast lots for the purpose of ascertaining upon whom the necessity should be laid. Mr. Geissenhainer had been all the time a silent spectator to the discussion, but now he could no longer restrain his feelings and keep silence. He told them that he did not wish to obtrude upon any man's hospitalities, that under the circumstances he could not remain, and that he would at once return to Philadelphia. His host of the inn, a christian-minded man who was present, now interfered, and asserted that there was not a member of the Board who would not most cheerfully receive him into his family, and consider himself highly honored to have the minister dwell under his roof, but they all feared that the accommodations they could furnish would not be good enough for such a man as he was. This explanation presented the case in quite a different aspect, and the preacher assuring them that on that point there need be no difficulty, Mr. Michael Reiter offered to give him a home in his family. Ev. Rev. viii, 503.

A POPULAR MINISTER.

This same Mr. G ....., who was one of our old time ministers, became so renowned in his vicinity, that persons, from a feeling of curiosity, would come from remote points to visit him. On a certain occasion an elderly gentleman from a great distance called and enquired for *old* Mr. G ....., supposing that a man so distinguished for wisdom and possessing so much influence must necessarily be advanced in life. When the young minister presented himself, appearing even more youthful than he really was, the stranger surveyed him from head to foot and said, "I wish to see your father!" "My father," he replied, "died many years ago in Europe!" "Then," said the gentleman, "I have been misdirected. Is there any other clergyman in these parts by the name of G .....? for I have come a considerable distance to see that renowned old pastor, and to converse with him on the subject of religion." The preacher said, "They call me old pastor G......, inasmuch as I have a younger brother in the ministry." The stranger still seemed incredulous. He thought that this could scarcely be the man he sought, but he remarked, "As I have come so far, I may as well communicate my difficulties and freely unbosom to you my mind." After talking with him for some hours, apparently much delighted and fully satisfied, he took his leave, remarking, "I now believe, sir, that you are old Mr. G.....' Ev. Rev. viii, 507.

He had great difficulty in overcoming the general belief in witchcraft in his churches. Observing the deleterious effects of the delusion, he felt that it was his duty to direct his energies, in the pulpit and out of it, to the removal of these superstitious errors. He, however, found a most strenuous opponent to his efforts in a notorious impostor, who feigned that he possessed the power of exorcism. As he derived no small gain from his craft, he regarded Mr. G..... with little favor, and put forth the most active exertions to counteract his influence. Fortunately, a most trifling circumstance exposed the ridiculous pretensions of the fellow, turned the current of sentiment against him, and arrested the evil, accomplishing that which argument had failed to secure.

It happened that one Sabbath evening Mr. G....., in passing from one church to another, was obliged to go through a thick dismal woods for a distance of three miles. It was already quite dark, and, as he was not able to see the road, he let his faithful white horse pick out the way as well as he could. Content to ride leisurely along, he lighted his German Meerschaum, and thus in his gloomy solitude, resolved to indulge in his wonted luxury. When he had reached the middle of the thicket, he heard a human sound which saluted him with "Good evening!" Not being able to discern any one, he felt that he was not recognized, yet he at once detected the voice of the magician, who had been the terror of the whole neighborhood. The idea immediately occurred to him that he would ascertain whether the breast of the man who had made others his victims was himself entirely free from the influence of superstition. He, therefore, determined to keep perfectly silent; and, when the salutation was uttered the second time, he blew the sparks of his tobacco pipe through the holes of the lid. This so alarmed the pretended enchanter that he at once took to his heels and ran as if for his life a mile and a half to the first house, which he reached pale and trembling. At first he was unable to speak, but, after a little, recovering from his fright, and being asked the cause, he answered that he had just encountered, in the centre of the dreaded woods, a most frightful ghost—a white horse without a head, and upon it a spirit with a head of fire. Soon after the man had departed, the young clergyman leisurely approached the house. It was the house of one of his deacons, who expressed his surprise that he would venture out alone on so dark a night, and along so dreary a road. The clergyman asked why he should be afraid. "Because," said the deacon, "the wood is haunted. The exorcist, this very evening, escaped from a most formidable apparition, and came hither a few minutes ago almost frightened to death." "What is it?" inquired the clergyman. The deacon answered, "It was a white horse without a head, and a spirit rider with a fiery head!" "Why, sir, that apparition was I and my Whitey," said Mr. G......, and he told how he had purposely frightened the impostor. The family enjoyed the joke, and, on relating the ludicrous story to others, it soon spread through the community, so that the poor fellow's gain was now at an end, and feeling very much mortified with what had occurred, he went to other parts, and after this there was little more heard of witchcraft. Ev. Rev. Vol. viii, 508.

Mr. G.... was on intimate terms with those who differed from him in sentiment. Although he had no sympathy with what are called Calvinistic doctrines, yet he cherished so high a regard for many distinguished divines of the Calvinistic faith that the walls of his study were adorned with their likenesses. On a certain occasion, when some Lutheran ministers were partaking of his hospitality, some reference was made to these portraits, and one of them remarked, "Ah, sir, you must be a *crypto* (secret) Calvinist!" "So *crypto*," he replied, "that I have never yet made the discovery myself." Ib. 517.

FROM THE REV. JAMES M. MATHEWS, D. D.*

NEW YORK, March 3, 1852.

MY DEAR SIR: I cannot claim to have been a very intimate friend of the Rev. Dr. Geissenhainer, concerning whom you enquire, and yet I had considerable knowledge of him during the latter years of his residence in this city. I first became acquainted

*Sprague, 106.

with him in consequence of his calling upon me on business, about the year 1815 or '16, and the impression which that first interview made upon my mind led me to feel a strong desire to cultivate an acquaintance with him, as I might have opportunity. I frequently met him in subsequent years, and always with great pleasure, and the more I knew of him the greater was my respect for his character and attainments.

In stature Dr. Geissenhainer was rather small, but he had an uncommonly expressive countenance. His eye was remarkably clear, and, when lighted up, as it usually was in conversation, it beamed with intelligence. Indeed, when he was earnestly engaged, he seemed to talk to you not merely with his lips but with every part of his face. He impressed you at once with the idea that he had a vigorous, discriminating and well furnished mind. He had the reputation, and I have no doubt justly, of being a man of very extensive learning. His acquirements were not merely professional but extended to various other departments of knowledge, in some of which he was allowed to be eminent. He was strong in his moral nature as in his intellectual. He spoke and acted out of the abundance of his heart.

Dr. Geissenhainer generally preached in German, so that I am not able to express an intelligent opinion concerning him in this respect. I know, however, that he was in excellent repute as a preacher among the German population, and I have often heard that in his religious opinions he was a faithful follower of Martin Luther. He always seemed to me to evince great honesty of purpose and great simplicity of religious feeling. He was highly respected while he lived, and his memory is still fragrant in the various circles in which he moved. Very truly yours,

J. M. MATHEWS.

GOTTLIEB SHOBER.

At a meeting of the General Synod held in Frederick in 1825, before I was licensed, I met for the only time in my life that bluff, honest, homespun, good old man, GOTTLIEB SHOBER, of North Carolina. In dress, appearance and manners, he was a regular backwoodsman, and his disregard of some of the more refined conventionalities of polite society offended the taste of some of his more precise brethren, whilst they were amused with his drollery and wit. He had a broad, open, German face, though a native of this country; an expanded chest and a large head. He was fifty years old before he entered the ministry, having been a lawyer as well as a tradesman. He never attained to theological eminence, but he was a warm-hearted, laborious worker in the struggling church in North Carolina, and had a commanding influence upon her destiny.

At that meeting of the General Synod he was elected President.

I remember that at the dinner table, after a profitable morning session, some one remarked that the session just closed was the most pleasant and best they had as yet had. "No," he replied, "this is the most agreeable, for here there is no dispute, no difference of opinion, no long and tedious speeches, and I, as your president, am not compelled to call you to order!"

He was one of the founders of the General Synod, but, owing to his distant residence, as it was then considered, he did not often attend the meetings.

He bequeathed a large tract of land to the Theological Seminary, but very little advantage was ever realized from it.

FROM THE REV. D. P. ROSENMILLER.

LANCASTER, PA., March 20, 1862.

DEAR SIR: My first personal knowledge of the Rev. G. Shober dates back to the year 1825, when I attended a meeting of our General Synod in Frederick, Md., at which he was present. From 1829 to 1832, while I was a resident of Lexington, N. C., I was often in his company at his own house, and he assisted me on several sacramental occasions in the country churches in Stokes county, which he had previously served as pastor, and in which I became his successor.

In person Mr. Shober was broadly built, about five feet ten inches in height, and had usually enjoyed excellent health. He had a cheerful expression of countenance which encouraged the familiar advances of strangers on their first introduction to him. In his conversation he was free and easy, and his unbounded flow of good humor sometimes manifested itself in witty sayings and droll anecdotes, which were sure to draw loud bursts of laughter from his auditors. At such times I have seen his broad merry face illumined as if by a sudden flash of electricity, while his proportionally broad chest would be convulsed with muscular agitation, and the very spectacles on his patriarchal nose would seem to share in the fun. So expanded was his chest that in its projection there was a corresponding depression across his back of sufficient depth to allow an ordinary sized infant to be laid in it. Picture to yourself a gray-haired patriarch with a ruddy full-moon face all glowing with good humor, and you will have a good idea of the personal appearance of Mr. Shober.

His general character was well illustrated in his history, for he was emphatically a self-made man. Commencing as a tinner, he married the daughter of a Moravian and soon made himself at home in the pleasant town of Salem. Whilst working at his trade he undertook to study law and accomplished his purpose. In due time he commenced practice, and was somewhat extensively employed in the neighboring counties of Stokes, Davidson, Rowan and Surry, being the only member of the bar acquainted with the German language and able to transact business with the large number of Germans then living in that region. Combining a book and stationery store with his tin shop, which he contrived to have carried on, he also became proprietor of a paper mill, kept the post-office, which he caused to be made a distributing office, and was the owner of a farm with numerous slaves, and thousands of acres of low-priced lands in the western part of the State.

Mr. Shober was eminently a cheerful and genial Christian, his religious character taking its hue in no small degree from his natural temperament. He had a firm faith in the great truths of the Gospel, and evinced a most benevolent spirit in all his intercourse with his fellow-men. After he had passed the meridian of life he expressed a wish to become a minister of the Gospel, and was eventually received as a member of the Evangelical Lutheran Ministerium of North Carolina, and served his churches gratuitously until near the time of his death. But there were not wanting those who looked suspiciously upon his professions, and were disposed to find unworthy motives for even his best actions. Such persons gave him little credit for preaching gratuitously, because, they said, he continued to make money as fast as ever by means of his tin shop, book store, paper mill, farm and post-office. Whilst he was frequently treading on the toes of the Methodists and

Baptists, he in turn encountered their serious opposition; and to weaken his influence the former would pray publicly for his conversion, and the circuit riders, being strangers to him, would ask him if he had any religion.

What Mr. Shober lacked as an orator he supplied by the use of drollery and tact. It cannot be denied that he sometimes, in obedience to an impulse that seemed quite irresistible, approached very near to the former in the pulpit, while he resorted to the latter abundantly in his legal practice. When he determined to become a minister of the Gospel it was his wish to take orders in the Moravian Church, but he found that he could not be admitted there without going through a regular course of theological training, which at his advanced age seemed impossible. He also knew that he could not continue to reside in the town of Salem if he became connected with another denomination. He, therefore, made it clear to the Corporate Fathers that a certain alteration in their rigid and exclusive borough laws was called for. This being adopted and duly confirmed by legislative act, the way was open for him to carry out his already meditated plan. He then applied to the Rev. Charles Stork, of Cabarras, who prescribed for him a course of reading; and he also accompanied that faithful man in his catechetical lectures, carefully observing and taking notes. In due time he applied for admission to the Synod and was received. When the indignant Moravians called a meeting to compel him to leave their town, he calmly adduced their recent enactment as proof that they were acting without a warrant.

Mr. Shober once told me that a clergyman from Germany had settled in Lexington, and a report was started so highly injurious to the purity of his character that he was compelled to prosecute for slander, and he employed him (Mr. S.) as his counsel. "When I had examined the case," said he, "I found it was rotten and wholly indefensible. On the day of the trial I employed several persons to mingle with the witnesses of the defence and report their conversation to me. They did so. When those witnesses were called up I objected to their testimony on the ground of a conspiracy. I could prove that one agreed to say so, and another so, and did prove it. Their testimony was set aside and full damage given to my client. I then said to him, 'I have helped you out of this scrape and I want you now to follow my advice. Sell what property you have, return to Germany, and never show your face in this country again.' He did so, and the country was well rid of a bad man."

Mr. Shober was a warm friend and zealous supporter of Sunday Schools. He supplied them liberally with books, and by this means, in a country exceedingly destitute of the means of grace, undoubtedly accomplished much good.

For many years he was Treasurer of the North Carolina Synod and kept his accounts satisfactorily. But at length some of his brethren thought that he should not have a life-estate in the honors (emoluments there were none) of that dignified position. I was present when the movement was made for a change. But he frowned it down as an outrageous rebellion against authority, which the lapse of many years had sanctioned. "I kept the money," said he, "when there was none to keep, and will continue to do so now whilst there is any thing in the treasury." The election resulted in his favor. In taking his usual time-honored seat his radiant face showed that a gratifying result had been realized. "Brethren," said he, "I am obliged to you for my re-election. If I did not say so I would be a hypocrite."

His family continued regular members of the Moravian Church.* His only son, *Emanuel*, is a lawyer of respectability.

Very truly yours,
D. P. ROSENMILLER.

THE REV. PAUL HENKEL

was, in early life and for many years, a laborious missionary among the scattered Anglo-German population in the South. He may indeed be considered as one of the pioneers of the church in that region, which was in those days truly desolate. His narrative, which was printed, has all the interest of romance, and if he

---

* "'Mr. Shober was no Lutheran.' He was a member of the Moravian Church and never disconnected himself from communion with the same. He lived and died as a member of that church. This information the writer received from his own daughter, the widow of Bishop Herrman. He merely served the Lutheran Church in the capacity of one of its ministers, being the pastor of several neglected Lutheran congregations in the vicinity of his place of residence, Salem, N. C." — *Bernheim, German Settlement of Lutheran Churches*, p. 441.

had performed the same self-denying labors in the service of any other church he would have received a greater earthly reward.

I remember seeing him in New Market, Va., in 1825, and soon afterward attended his funeral at the same place. He was at that day already superannuated. He was tall in stature, emaciated and feeble and tottering in his gait. I once saw him in a Methodist church, seated "in the altar," as they called it. The old gentleman was exceedingly nervous, and the preacher bellowed as if addressing a camp meeting. It had a singular effect upon Mr. Henkel. He writhed and every feature of his face was distorted with pain. His whole nervous system was racked by the obstreperous bawlings of the man in the pulpit. Young as I was, I really pitied old Mr. Henkel, and it was a relief to him and to those of us who observed his agony when the noisy preacher stopped.

Five of his sons became ministers in our church, of whom David was the best educated and the most energetic. It was he who by his writings and preaching became the leader of what was for years popularly and reproachfully called "Henkelism," but which distinguished itself only by a more rigid adherence to the old Lutheran theology, and by a want of sympathy and co-operation with what was called the "evangelical" section of the church. David Henkel was a strong man among the men with whom he was associated, and exercised an unlimited control over their ideas and actions. The other brothers, while firm in their maintenance of the original faith, were less inclined to controversy, and mingled more freely with ministers of other Synods. There are to this day five ministers of that name in our church, probably all of whom are sons of the five sons of Paul.

The Henkel family deserve credit for their activity in publishing catechisms, hymn books and other useful books. They began this as early as 1809, and have continued it to this day. They translated and published on their own account the first English edition of the Book of Concord ever issued, as well as of Luther on the Sacraments, Luther's House Postil, and other religious works.*

The early and arduous missionary labors of Paul Henkel deserve a more extended notice than I have room to give. The materials are at hand in his own journal, in which are recorded many stirring events. He was in many respects a remarkable man, and

---

* For a list of Paul Henkel's writings, see Bibliotheca Lutherana.

no one ever doubted his sincerity and christian zeal. He was a man of strong prejudices, undoubtedly, and of contracted views on the wants of the church and the proper mode of supplying those wants, but he never or very seldom went out of the limited sphere of his own operations, and had no opportunity of expanding his views by intercourse with other leading men or other sections of the church.

He and his sons were violent and uncompromising enemies of the General Synod and all its institutions, and did much to influence their friends against most other Lutheran ministers and measures. For a while they even opposed Sunday schools, missionary and education societies, and other religious and benevolent enterprises. Their descendants, however, do not cherish these ideas, but are enlightened supporters of the true interests of the church. The writings of Rev. A. J. Brown, now of the Holston Synod, contributed much to create a wholesome change in the minds and church activity of some of those men, all of whom now are ranged on the side of evangelical measures.

Andrew Henkel thus speaks of his father in Sprague's Annals:

My father was a large man, within half an inch of six feet in height, with physical organs well developed, with a keen black eye, as erect as an Indian, somewhat inclined to corpulency, and yet athletic and rapid in his movements. Though his health was not always good, yet he was almost constantly employed either in reading, writing, preaching or travelling, and, when necessary, he did not hesitate to labor with his hands. He had no desire for this world's goods beyond what was wanting for daily use. Whatever savored of ostentation was foreign to his nature. His manner of living was frugal and his dress plain, and yet in performing the services of the sanctuary he uniformly wore a gown of rich black silk. He had great equanimity and serenity of temper, and his friendships were sincere and constant, and his friends numerous. In the social circle he always rendered himself agreeable, and often communicated important instruction by means of some pertinent and sometimes humorous anecdote.

As a preacher he possessed much more than ordinary power. In the commencement of his discourse he was slow and somewhat blundering, but as his subject opened before him he would become animated and eloquent, with a full flow of appropriate thought and glowing language. His illustrations were lucid and forcible, simple and natural. He assisted in training a goodly number of young men for the ministry, some of whom have occupied responsible stations with great fidelity and usefulness.

After faithfully serving his generation for a long course of years, it pleased the Great Master to call him from his labors to his reward. A stroke of palsy rendered him almost helpless for a time before his departure. He died on the 17th of November, 1825, when he had nearly completed his seventy-first year. His remains are deposited in front of the Lutheran church in the town of New Market.*

REV. JOHN F. RUTHRAUFF,

of Greencastle, Pa., was a modest, retiring man, and did not hold a prominent position among our ministers of "fifty years ago." He did his plain, pastoral work, removed from the broad society of men, and hence his name does not stand out conspicuously in the list. He gave two excellent sons to our ministry, Frederick and Jonathan, and one grandson. He died in 1837, aged 74.

Dr. Diehl characterizes him fairly in the following letter in Sprague's Annals:

DEAR SIR: My recollections of the Rev. John F. Ruthrauff date back chiefly to my very early life. During his last years I saw very little of him, being myself away from the neighborhood, prosecuting my studies at college. The image of the man, however, with his tall and muscular frame, his benevolent countenance and gray hairs, his stately walk, his courteous bow, his easy conversation with the elders of his church, and his kind remarks to children, are deeply impressed upon my memory. He was capable of severe and unintermitted labor. His parish was very large, extending some twenty-five miles from mountain to mountain, across the whole of the Cumberland Valley, in the northern part of Franklin county. His life was eminently an active one.

Nature must have endowed him with strong mental qualities—quickness of perception, clearness of insight, and tenacity of memory. He enjoyed few early advantages for intellectual culture, and could never be said to be a man of studious habits. His

---

* For a fuller account of what was once called Henkelism, see a subsequent chapter under that head.

reading scarcely extended beyond the Bible, a good Commentary, and a few practical works. But his native vigor of mind enabled him to produce, with but little effort, discourses, each of which would have cost most other men days of intellectual labor. His temper was quick and sensitive. In early life he must have been somewhat impetuous; and even in old age he would sometimes utter burning words to those whom he regarded as wilfully perverse.

Few men were gifted with a keener sagacity, or possessed a more thorough knowledge of men and things, than Mr. Ruthrauff. He was as little likely to be imposed on in a bargain as any other man. His deportment was always grave and dignified. In his intercourse with his parishioners he was ordinarily bland, but his personal reproofs were sometimes very caustic, and not unfrequently, for the time being at least, procured for him enemies. He had great moral courage—no man's presence ever intimidated or embarrassed him in the performance of any duty to which he believed himself called.

As a preacher, he was fluent, animated and instructive, and his appeals were often exceedingly earnest and pathetic. While he expounded his text in a luminous and satisfactory manner, his sermons were generally rather practical than doctrinal. He frequently selected, as the basis of his discourse, the Gospel or the Epistle of the day. He delivered himself with great ease, and while he always spoke to edification, he left you with the impression that he was giving utterance to the thoughts which first occurred to him. His voice was pleasant and of considerable compass, though he seldom spoke louder than was necessary to fill his audience room. He was particularly happy in the instruction of the youth of his charge. His catechumens, on the day of Confirmation, were often deeply moved, and sometimes bathed in tears, while his own voice became tremulous and his venerable frame shook with emotion.

Mr. Ruthrauff, though not indeed without infirmities (for these cling even to the best), was a man of substantial Christian excellence, and labored earnestly for the conversion of souls and the extension of the Redeemer's Kingdom. And his labors were not without their reward; for many were the seals to his ministry. Some who were brought to a knowledge of the truth, through his instrumentality, are yet to be found in the district over which his labors extended. His memory is still reverently and gratefully cherished by his surviving parishioners.

Very respectfully, yours,
GEORGE DIEHL.

REV. HENRY A. MUHLENBURG

was for some years pastor in Reading, Pa., and was a prominent representative of that time-honored and influential family. His nephew, Rev. Prof. Muhlenburg, of the University of Pennsylvania, is at present the only one of that well known name in our ministry. There are others who are adorning other callings, but the professor is the only one who has donned the clerical toga.

Henry A. wielded an immense influence upon the church and community in which he lived. He was a man of commanding talent and energy of character. So popular was he in that section of Pennsylvania that the people insisted (about 1829) upon his being a candidate for Congress, to which he was elected for four successive terms (1838), when he resigned his seat.

It was at Washington where I first met him, the only time in my life. I had some interest in the Revolutionary Pension Bill which he had in charge as chairman of the committee, and I called upon him for some information. He was coldly polite; and after I had received what I went for, I introduced the subject of the church, but he showed no disposition to converse upon that subject, probably because engaged on other business, and I bowed myself out.

During his membership, some pedantic orator of the House frequently indulged in Latin quotations. Muhlenburg, in a speech one day, said he would also quote a foreign language, and exclaimed what was appropriate to the occasion: "*Fürchte Gott und scheue niemand.*" (Fear God, and be not afraid of any man.)

In 1835 he was nominated as the candidate of the Democratic party for Governor of Pennsylvania, but was defeated by Governor Wolf. In 1837 President Van Buren tendered him a position in the Cabinet, as Secretary of the Navy, and also the mission to Russia, both of which he declined; but in 1838 he accepted the mission to Austria, and was unanimously confirmed by the Senate. After an absence of nearly three years, he was recalled at his own request, and returned in December, 1840. In 1844 he was again nominated by the Democratic party as candidate for Governor, and would undoubtedly have been chosen had not his death occurred previous to the election. He died on the 12th of August, 1844, at the age of 62, leaving behind him the well-earned reputation of an accomplished and useful minister of the Gospel and an upright and able statesman. Whilst he was abroad, he visited all the more interesting parts of Italy, Germany and Switzerland, in doing which he found much to gratify his fine classical tastes.

[The following article is an abridgement of a sketch by Prof. Stœver in the Evangelical Review, Vol. . . . , p. 405]:

REV. WM. BEATES

was born in Philadelphia, June 14, 1777, whilst the city was in possession of the British. In after life he often spoke with deep interest of the thrilling scenes which transpired during the days of his childhood, of the alienation and bitterness among neighbors, and of the zeal and earnestness with which even the boys would respectively espouse the interest of the two parties. Long after peace was declared, England still had her warm advocates in this " land of the free and the home of the brave." He vividly remembered how a Tory, in the vicinity of his father's residence, would take him by the hair, and, as he attempted to escape his firm grasp, would pull out large bunches, because the patriotic lad, in the buoyancy of his spirits and in bold defiance, would lustily cry: " Hurrah for General Washington !" " Hurrah for the Continental Congress!" He had very distinct recollections of the appearance of Washington, whose residence in Philadelphia was, for a season, on Market street, above Fifth, just opposite the house of his father. He frequently saw him as he daily rode out on his gray war-horse with bright hoofs, polished with shoe blacking, as was the fashion in those days.

He was a youth of steady, industrious habits, free from vicious tendencies, although indifferent and careless on the subject of religion.

He was reared under Christian influences, and regularly attended the services of the sanctuary in the German churches, then under the pastoral care of Drs. Helmuth and Schmidt. In his sixteenth year his attention to the truth was arrested and a concern for the salvation of his soul awakened, under circumstances very peculiar. He was returning from Zion's Church, where Dr. Helmuth had delivered a most solemn discourse on the miraculous restoration of the paralytic. He had listened with earnest attention, as was his custom, to the eloquent preacher; yet the sermon seemed to have made no deeper impression than on previous occasions. But, as he was in the act of crossing Arch street homeward, he imagined that he heard a voice, in the most emphatic tones, saying to him: "You shall never enter that church again as you now are." The words continued to ring in his ears—he could not divest his mind of the impression. It was in the year 1793, when the yellow fever was so fearfully raging in Philadelphia, and thousands were the daily victims of its ruthless ravages. No one left home without carrying with him camphor, ammonia, or some disinfectant, as a safeguard from the dreaded pestilence. He had with him, on this occasion, a sponge saturated with lavender, which he immediately applied to his nostrils, and with great trepidation were his steps accelerated. As he reached the Market House he sought shelter beneath its roof; but, just as his home was in sight, he encountered a hearse. A cold shudder passed over his frame; the whole atmosphere seemed impregnated with death. Breathless, he rushed into the house, and soon the little family, unconscious of what was agitating his youthful breast, were gathered around the table, where was spread the simple but substantial meal. It had not for him, however, on this occasion, the usual zest: his appetite had gone. He longed for solitude; but whither could he flee? "Hell," he says, "seemed to be getting fast hold of me, and I was filled with indescribable misery." He retired to the shop—it was Sunday—that he might be alone. In his mental distress, he thought he again heard the voice, which had previously addressed him, saying: "Look within!" "The wages of sin is death!" "These you are now reaping!" His eyes are partially opened. He is awakened to a sense of his danger and his guilt. He now realizes, as he never before had, his true spiritual condition. He begins to feel how odious a thing sin is, and how ruinous are its consequences. The scriptural injunction, "Seek the Lord," appeared to sound in his ears, as if uttered by a human voice. The prompt inquiry was: "How?" The reply came: "By prayer." "I immediately fell upon my knees," he says, "and commenced with the only prayer I knew, 'Our Father;' but ere I had finished, my tongue seemed loosened, my lips were unsealed, and, for full an hour, I continued in earnest supplication at the mercy-seat, pleading with God for the forgiveness of my sins." His supplications were not long unanswered. He thought he heard the same voice saying: "Thy sins are forgiven thee!" He now enjoyed peace of mind — that peace which passeth knowledge. He hastened in the afternoon to God's house, with devout gratitude, "no longer a child of hell," to use his own language, "but an heir of heaven." His spiritual enjoyment, however, was not unalloyed. Sorrow was sometimes mingled with his cup of happiness. He had his difficulties, his trials, and his fears.

Dr. Helmuth, some time after, on becoming acquainted with the change that had taken place in the young man's religious views, urged him to unite in the exercises of the "Mosheim Society," an association connected with the church, designed to promote the mental and spiritual improvement of its members. The theological students connected with the seminary belonged to this Society. The exercises consisted of singing and prayer, the reading and exposition of the Scriptures, and the discussion of questions on religious topics. Committees were appointed at these meetings to assist in the Sunday Schools of the church, in the city and vicinity. He was also a teacher in the church Sunday School, and frequently opened and closed the services with prayer. On one of these occasions his pastor, being present, for the first time suggested to him the subject of the Christian ministry. "William," said he, "you must preach the Gospel." "I? No! If the Lord needs workmen, He has many more worthy to do His work. I cannot." "You do not know," answered Dr. Helmuth; "the Lord chooses His workmen, and He knows best." "True," says the young man; "but how could I preach? In one half hour I could tell all I know, and what then?" "William," replied the venerable doctor, "your head is now like an apothecary shop, upside down; all that is required to be done is to set the materials in order."

A noted infidel happened to visit his father, and, turning to the young man, very much to the surprise of the family, said: "William, you must preach the Gospel." Personal friends were earnestly directing his attention to the subject; but, modest in reference to his own abilities, his timid spirit shrank from the responsibilities of the office. Whilst his mind was thus deeply exercised as to duty, and earnestly engaged in meditation and prayer, he took up Bogatsky, and as he opened the book the first word that met his eye was *Predige* (Preach). He closed the book. "I then felt," said he, "'Woe is unto me, if I preach not the Gospel.' Prostrate upon my knees, I prayed: 'Take away *my* spirit, O God, rather than I should enter upon the work without *Thy* spirit'" He was slow to believe that the Lord wanted him to labor, as a minister, in His vineyard. He dreamed that he was accosted by his pastor in the following language: "William, why do you not call to see me? Is it because you fear I will urge you to study for the ministry? Are you afraid to suffer for Christ's sake?" "I am not afraid to suffer," was the reply; "but I have no time to come, except on Saturday." "Well, then," said the good man, "come at that time." He met the pastor in the course of a few days, and what struck him as most remarkable was, that this identical conversation occurred.

On the morning of May 12th, 1807, in the thirtieth year of his age, as a theological student Mr. Beates entered the study of Dr. Helmuth. Under his instructions and those of his colleague, Dr. Schmidt, he continued his studies for three years.

He was licensed by the Synod of Pennsylvania, and on the 8th of July, 1810, preached his introductory discourse in the Warwick Pastorate. His labors were arduous during these twenty-six years, but his success was very great. As his health, however, suffered from constant exposure to all kinds of weather, for his congregations were distant and his members scattered, he felt the importance and necessity of rest. He accordingly resigned his position and removed to Lancaster, preaching occasionally, and performing other religious services when an opportunity offered. At a subsequent period he was prevailed upon to take charge of Zion's (German Lutheran) Church in Lancaster, which was in a distracted and languishing condition. With his accustomed zeal and energy he took hold of the enterprise, refusing all compensation for his services, yet stipulating with the congregation that they regularly raise the promised amount of salary and appropriate it to the liquidation of the church debt. He was their pastor for fifteen years, but in 1853 the increasing infirmities of age constrained him to retire from the active duties of the ministry, to resign to other hands the work in which he had been so long engaged. His visitations to the sick and the infirm he continued so long as he was able until within a few months of his death. He frequently spoke of his approaching change with satisfaction and delight, and referred to the eternal world as a place of activity. "Heaven I look upon," he said, "as a High School. The schools on earth are only primary. In that very thing in which we most excel here below will we advance with the greatest rapidity in the world above."

He embraced every opportunity which occurred to preach the truths of the Gospel to his children and to all who approached him. "In view of death," he remarked, "I have three things to say to my family: Serve the Lord, be liberal to the Church, be kind to the poor." His son Henry observed: "Father, you have been serving the Lord all your life, at least for seventy-five years, do you feel that you merit any thing for all these years of service?" "No!" was his emphatic reply, "I have nothing in the way of merit; I depend entirely upon the merits of Christ." He added: "Here I am, aged and helpless, and though I had untold wealth it would avail nothing in the hour of eternity. What a miserable creature I would be now were it not for religion, true religion."

"I never saw him," says Dr. Muhlenberg, "without being more and more deeply impressed with the thought that he was a good man, an Israelite, indeed, in whom there was no guile."

His sermons were also eminently scriptural, and the truth was always presented with great originality and force. His fidelity no one could doubt. On a certain occasion, as he descended from the pulpit, he was accosted by one of the church officers who was apprehensive that the discourse just preached was entirely too pointed and would give offence. "Did I utter anything," said the preacher, "not contained in the Bible?" "No, I cannot say that you did," was the reply. "When I came hither I found that Bible," said Mr. Beates, pointing to it in the pulpit, "and I presumed that you wanted me to preach from it. According to your own admission I confined myself to its teachings. Then why find fault with me?" This response, if it did not entirely satisfy, completely silenced the fault-finder. In the pulpit his manner was exceedingly natural.

On a certain occasion an individual came to him, apparently in the deepest distress, perplexed in reference to some mystery in the Bible. He at first supposed that he was concerned with regard to the salvation of his soul, and he rejoiced in the opportunity of directing an awakened sinner to the Saviour. But how great his disappointment on learning that the man's solicitude was occasioned by the difficult question, "Where did Cain obtain his wife?" "Sir," said the reverend father, without being in the least ruffled by the inquiry, "Sir, go home and sleep a night, return to me to-morrow morning, and bring with you some proof that it will be of any benefit to you to have the question answered and I will answer it for you." The next day the man returned, when Mr. Beates exhorted him to repent of his sins and believe on the Lord Jesus Christ and be converted. He engaged with him in earnest and importunate prayer, and soon found him rejoicing in Christ.

Referring one day to his pastoral labors, he said, "I discriminate between the rich and the poor, but it is always in favor of the latter." Ministerial brethren often sought his counsel and direction. To a young man in the tide of his popularity, caressed and admired, who had just been called to one of our most prominent churches, he said, "To-day it is 'Hosanna,' to-morrow it will be 'Crucify him'."

We heard him once speak, among other trials connected with his ministry, of a suit brought against him, when seventy-eight years of age, to recover, in accordance with a legislative act of 1729–30, the penalty of £50 for marrying a minor without the consent of the parents. Although it was clearly shown in the trial that there was no intention on his part to violate the law or do the plaintiff any injury, that the defendant had taken every means in his power to ascertain the age of the parties and was assured that all was right; also that there was a trap laid, a preconcerted arrangement between the father and the son to induce the minister to perform the ceremony, so that the £50, just the sum of money required by the father for the completion of a dwelling then in process of erection, might be secured, the Court imposed the fine, alleging that the publication of the bans was necessary, a law regarded as obsolete, of which Mr. Beates had never heard during a ministry of nearly half a century. There was no redress and he had to submit. In speaking of the injustice done him in this case, said he, "The figure of Justice which surmounts the steeple of the Court House has a pair of scales in her hand to show justice is to be administered in the court-room below, while there is a rod (lightning-rod) behind." "This," he continued, "should be reversed. The rod should be placed in the hand and the scales in the rear."

He had an aversion for controversy, and carefully avoided all discussions conducted in a spirit of recrimination and unfriendly criticism. "I hold," said he, "to neither party in the Church. I am no party man. I will not share in the family quarrel. My time is nearly out. My mind is fixed. I am waiting to go where we shall know all these things. Some things I know, others I do not know. The Lord's Supper is a mystery. Why the bread and wine are called the body and blood of Christ I do not know. But I believe, else I make Christ a liar. Yet I do not believe that I eat his carnal body, the body that hung upon the tree." On another occasion he said, "That Christ is present in the Sacrament I have no doubt. My God has said so and that is sufficient. *How* belongs to Him. To receive Him belongs to me. I have enough to do with *my hows*. *How* I live, *how* I love, *how* I fight, *how* I partake of the Supper, and if I am not careful my *how* (*sic*) will at last be turned into *woe*. The Saviour is present at my Communion, He is with me in the Supper, the *manner* belongs to Him." He added: "Many a so-called doctor disputes and disputes and reaps no comfort from the Sacrament, whilst the honest trusting tradesman, who labors from Monday morning till Saturday night, reads, believes, partakes and is blessed. No one who attempts to go behind the simple words of Christ can give any satisfactory explanation."

A prominent trait in his character was the exemplification of the apostolic command, "Follow peace with all men." "If individuals," he said, "would only turn their ire against Satan and the old Adam they might fight as much as they pleased." Some of his parishioners were very anxious to know what his political sentiments were. One of them approached him one day and inquired "What his politics *might be*, as he subscribed for the newspapers of both parties?" "Oh," he replied, "I am a Lutheran." They never could tell whether he was Whig or Democrat.

He possessed a fund of rich quaint humor which would spring forth in spontaneous expressions. He loved a little pleasantry and often made a playful or witty remark. Even during his last days this natural vein of humor would manifest itself. Speaking of his death, he looked up at those who were present, with that twinkle of the eye which was peculiar to him, and said, "After I have gone it will be asked of what did he die?" To which it may be truly answered, "He died of hardness of heart," alluding to the disease, ossification of the heart, from which he was suffering. Some years ago, when a general interest prevailed in almost every community on the temperance question, and individuals were disposed to sign the pledge of total abstinence, his neighbor, Bishop Bowman, called to see him, and inquired, "If he, too, had joined the society?" "Oh, yes," he replied, "many years ago. When I was a youth I was confirmed, and then I promised to renounce the Devil and all his works." His friend was amused with the novelty of his reply, but agreed with him that he was a member of the temperance society. Some one connected with his congregation once sent him a verbal message, expressing his dissatisfaction and displeasure with something he had presented in one of his discourses. "Give him my compliments," said Mr. Beates, "and tell him I am not at all satisfied with myself, and, therefore, I cannot censure him for being dissatisfied with me."

REV. DR. FREDERICK HENRY QUITMAN

never attended any of the General Meetings of the Church, nor any Synod but the one to which he belonged, and hence was personally known to but few of our ministers south of New York.

He was born in Westphalia in 1760, and after his admission to the ministry he became pastor on the Dutch island of Curacoa, West Indies, where he remained fourteen years. In 1795 he came to the State of New York, and served the Church in various places until 1828. He died in 1832, aged 72. For a list of his published writings, see Bibliotheca Americana. The following extracts from Sprague's Annals are interesting:

FROM THE REV. AUGUSTUS WACKERHAGEN, D. D.

The opportunities which I enjoyed for becoming acquainted with the late Dr. Quitman were various and ample, both of us being fellow-laborers in the same portion of our Lord's vineyard, members of the same Ministerium, fellow officers to the same body, and still more closely connected by my marriage with the only daughter of his second wife.

Dr. Quitman's personal appearance was very imposing. His well-proportioned and ever erect frame stood full six feet high and was of great bulk, weighing generally about, and sometimes above, three hundred pounds. When, as a youth of nineteen years, he entered the University of Halle, one of the professors, surveying his frame, burst out into the exclamation, "*Quanta ossa! Quantum robur!* Young man, you have in you the stamina for a life of a hundred years." His bodily powers were very great. His small grey eyes cast a quick piercing glance, and in the corners of his small mouth a benign smile was almost constantly lurking, so that even young children, to whom he was a great friend, looked at him with confidence. His mind being equal in power to his body, imparted to him a high degree of both moral and physical courage, which manifested itself whenever there was occasion for it.

Dr. Quitman's character in society was conspicuous and of high standing. On account of his various learning, his refined manners and his great conversational powers, he was sought and admired by all. Having, after the termination of his University studies, been for several years private tutor to the children of the Prince of Waldeck, he was accustomed to move in the society of the higher ranks, and when settled as pastor of the Lutheran Church in Rhinebeck was not only received but sought by the distinguished families of the vicinity, as previous to his removal to the United States had been the case on the Island of Curacoa. By his congregation he was deeply reverenced.

As to the religious and theological character of Dr. Quitman, it was of the liberal cast, he having been a disciple of the highly distinguished Professor Semler.

In preaching he was brief, biblical, practical and impressive, inculcating with great energy the Christian ethics—his commanding appearance and deep-toned voice in the pulpit contributing much to the effect of his discourses. Sometimes, when treating particular subjects or preaching on particular occasions, he would elaborate his sermons with great care. When at home he never failed to make a complete skeleton of his discourse, but when away from home he was "semper paratus," and often preached seven or eight times in one week, either in the German, Low Dutch or English language. He never used a manuscript in the pulpit.

Dr. Quitman was a man of great independence of character, and was always ready for any emergency. He had a retentive memory, considerable imagination and quick comprehension of characters and things. Flashes of wit, some pleasing, some scathing, would, on proper occasions, dart forth from his prolific and well furnished mind. He was, in the years of his vigor, fond of horses, so that generally in his frequent travels he handled whip and line himself. When a student at the University he delighted in driving coach and four. His various talents and great acquirements in sciences and languages never left him without one or more students, as well in theology as in the classics, and the business of teaching always had for him peculiar attractions. He had a charitable and generous spirit, and his parsonage was the seat of a cordial hospitality.

To furnish you with anecdotes relating to my friend might be somewhat invidious. I will, however, mention two or three in proof of his courage, determination and ever ready wit. When he was engaged to the lady who became his second wife and who lived on the west side of the river, he came one day to the city of Hudson, intending to pay her a visit with a view to the final settlement of all matters relating to their mutual concerns. But as a most violent wind was raging at the time on the water, and tossing up high waves, no ferryman could be induced, for love or money, to carry the doctor over. Unwilling to be disappointed, he walked and looked about until he met with two rough-looking tars, whom, showing them a hard silver dollar, he asked whether they had sufficient courage, for such a reward, to set him over. Readily consenting, they caried their charge, safe as Cæsar was once carried, through storm and waves, and received their well-earned reward.

An aged female member of his congregation, looking up to his face, asked him, "Dominie, have you had the small pox?" "No, mother, it has had me," was his reply. That disease had left its deep marks over his whole face.

Walking once in company with his step-son, the late Rev. Frederick G. Mayer, in the streets in the city of Albany, they were met by an uncommonly large man, apparently from the country. The man seeing the doctor stopped short, and scanning his frame from foot to head, exclaimed, "I wonder who's the biggest, you or I?" "I know," was the quick reply of the doctor as he walked on, "who is the biggest fool of the two."

The doctor being, at a certain time, sent by the Ministerium to allay some difference between a congregation and their pastor, spoke on the occasion, as was his wont, as a man of authority. An elderly man, being displeased with his authoritative bearing, turned to the reverend pacificator and said, with a taunting air, "And what are ministers then?" "We are grindstones to grind rough people smooth," was the answer. Ibid 118.

One Lord's day, arriving at rather an early hour near the church of a distant congregation, he was informed that a certain man by the name of Finger, living near the church although not a member of it, had slandered him in the congregation. The services of the sanctuary being closed, the doctor alluded to the affair, the guilty man being present, and closed with the following observation: "But I see that the Devil has had a *finger* in this business, and, therefore, no one will believe a word of it."

FROM THE REV. G. A. LINTNER, D. D.

I met Dr. Quitman frequently in our Synodical Conventions, heard him preach some very excellent sermons, and always regarded him as one of our ablest divines and most accomplished pulpit orators. He was President of our New York Ministerium when I was received as a licentiate by that body, in Albany, in the year 1818. I recollect that, during that session of the Ministerium, a complaint was brought by one of the churches against its Pastor for some misconduct; and, while the Ministerium was engaged in investigating the charges against the Pastor, a lawyer from the congregation, who had brought the complaint, delivered himself of a pretty long speech. The Doctor, who was in the chair, listened to it until he became wearied by its length and seeming irrelevancy, when he turned to one of the commissioners from the congregation,—an old acquaintance, in whose honesty and good sense he had the fullest confidence,—and said,—" Mr. ..... is a lawyer—I don't care about law points and law arguments in the case—I want to know the plain truth—tell me, my friend—how is it? Has your minister done wrong? Have you lost your confidence in him, and have matters gone so far that he can no longer be useful among you, and do you really want him to leave you? Tell me, upon your honor, as a Christian, here, in the presence of God and this Ministerium, what you think ought to be done in the case." The appeal was immediately answered in the same frank and candid manner in which it had been made. The aged member of the congregation, whom the Doctor had known for many years, arose and replied,—" I must say, that I think it is best, in view of all circumstances, that we and our minister should part. I am sorry it is so, but I cannot resist the evidence of it." This settled the matter. The Ministerium agreed to dissolve the connection, under certain conditions satisfactory to both parties.

Dr. Quitman was present and presided at my Ordination, as Pastor of the Evangelical Lutheran Church of Schoharie, in June, 1819. He preached the Ordination Sermon, and I preached my Introductory in the afternoon of the same day. After service he came to me in the parsonage and said,—" My dear young brother, this has been to me a solemn day—your sermon awakened within me deep emotion—I feel that the connection this day established between you and this church will be a lasting and happy one, and will result in the salvation of souls." The words seemed to me prophetic. The connection lasted thirty years; and, during that time, we were blessed with several gracious visitations of the Divine Spirit, which resulted in the hopeful conversion of many souls.

It was only a few years after the close of the Revolutionary War that the Doctor took charge of the Church at Schoharie; and, as the people had been deprived, in a great measure, of the means of grace, during the War, they had not much regard for religion, and still less for its ministers and institutions. I recall several anecdotes, illustrative of the then existing state of things, which he related to me. One day, as he was standing at the door of the parsonage, one of his parishioners, who, for some trifling offence, absented himself from the church, came along, and the

Doctor stepped out, and asked,—"Mr. . ..., what is the reason you do not come to church any more?" "Ah," replied he, "I am afraid you are one of those shepherds who care more for the fleece than for the sheep." The Doctor, answering him, said: "You are no longer a sheep—you are a goat." This reply to the insulting language of a refractory member had the desired effect. It brought him to reflection, and he afterwards came to church and acknowledged that he had done wrong.

The Doctor was invited to preach on the occasion of a Masonic celebration. A member of his church heard of it, and came to his house, deeply exercised in respect to the matter, and said to him,—"My dear Pastor, I have understood that you are to preach before that Society which is in league with the Devil; and I could not rest till I had come and told you my feelings on the subject." "I am sorry," said the Doctor, "that you feel so, and to satisfy you that I intend to do no evil, I will read you the sermon which I have written for the occasion." So he produced the sermon; and, as he read the text, the simple-hearted man exclaimed,— "My dear Sir, are you going to preach to these Masons from the Bible? Then I have no objections—it is all right, and I'll come and hear you." So he did, and was much pleased and edified by the sermon.

At one of our Synodical meetings a protest was presented, censuring Dr. Quitman for exercising his authority as President of the Synod, in changing the place of meeting from a locality where a dangerous and fatal disease was prevailing. The protest met the approval of the Synod, thereby implying a censure on the President. He felt himself called upon to repel the charge; and, I well remember the terms in which he did it. "I own," said he, "that I exercised an authority not expressly granted in the Constitution; but I meant it for your good. My object was to save you from imminent danger. Suppose I had suffered you to run into the danger, and you had perished, would that have been right? I tell you nay—I never could have forgiven myself for sacrificing such a fine looking and worthy band of ministers to the *folly* of carrying out their views of constitutional authority."

Dr. Quitman was one of those men who never fail to make an impression, by their fine personal appearance, wherever they are seen. He had a cheerful disposition, was remarkable for his conversational powers, and could readily accommodate himself to any class of society into which he was thrown, always sustaining the honor and dignity of the clerical character. In the pulpit he was highly animated, entering into the spirit of his subject, and generally carrying his hearers with him by his eloquent and forcible appeals. In his theological views he doubtless sympathized with those who have a general dislike for creeds, and hold to free interpretations of Scripture, without much regard to their dogmatic sense and ecclesiastical construction. In his intercourse with his people he was, in a high degree, edifying. There are still some in our churches who have sat under his ministry, and who recollect many of his sayings, and speak of him with respect and veneration.

These were the *leading* older men of "Fifty Years Ago," all of whom I have seen, except Dr. Quitman, and a few of whom I have known intimately. There were a few others of that generation whose names and persons were not so familiar, or who were seldom or never seen in the Church Conventions, however influential they may have been in their immediate circle. These shall be commemorated in another book, Providence permitting.

SECTION II.

There was another but *younger* class of men on the stage of action in those days, whom I designate as the men of the *Transition Period*. Most of them overlap with the *older* men of "Fifty Years Ago," but they properly belong to more modern times.

AUGUSTUS WACKERHAGEN.

I never had the pleasure of meeting Dr. Wackerhagen but once, and that was at the General Synod in Chambersburg in 1859. He was born in Hanover, Germany, May 22, 1774. He was educated at Goettingen, and after the completion of his studies was for a time employed as a teacher in a seminary for young ladies, and also as private tutor in a nobleman's family. He came to this country in 1801, and upon his arrival he became tutor to the only son of Mr. Bohlen, a wealthy merchant of Philadelphia, in whose family he remained three years. Whilst here he received a call from the churches of Schoharie and Coblekill, but did not accept because he had made arrangements to visit Europe. On his return voyage he was shipwrecked and lost every thing he had. Finding Schoharie still vacant, he accepted the call. This was in 1805. He remained there ten years, where he was active in the cause of the Bible society, three years before the American Bible Society was formed.

In 1816 he became pastor of various churches in Columbia county, New York, and for a season taught a class of young ladies at his house. He also, at different times, taught young men the ancient languages, &c., and for several years he had charge of the academy at Clermont, where he died November 1, 1865, in his ninety-first year.

For many years he was a diligent student of the Bible. The Hebrew, Syriac, Greek, German and French versions were daily consulted by him. The degree of D. D. was conferred on him by Union College in 1825. Except a sermon in the Lutheran Pulpit, I, 242, the only work he published was a German volume on "Faith and Morals," Philadelphia, 1804.

He was a faithful pastor, and sometimes would ride fourteen or sixteen miles to see an invalid member of his church.

Dr. Wackerhagen never associated much with our men outside of his own Synod. He was at the General Synod in Chambersburg in 18 9 but he did not seem to sympathize with the men or the policy of that body. I thought that both he and his colleague, Dr. Miller, felt out of place. He took little part in the proceedings, but when he did speak it was to some purpose.

Some subject relating to the Franckean Synod was discussed, during which Dr. Lintner quoted Schmucker's Popular Theology as Lutheran authority, and among other things charged the Franckeans with believing that the Divine nature of Christ suffered upon the cross as well as the human. Dr. W .... , though not favorable to the Franckeans, rather severely rebuked Lintner for quoting as authority a book that had never been officially recognized as such. "And as for the other point," he said, "what you call heresy in those men is taught in your own hymn book," and then quoted the lines:

> "When God, the mighty maker, died,
> For man, the creature's sin."

Lintner yielded the first point and could not deny the second.

Prof. Stoever thus speaks of him: His funeral services were invariably prepared with the greatest care, and much valuable truth communicated, because, as he was want to say, on such occasions many persons were present who, at any other time, seldom or never entered the sanctuary. He always specially addressed the mourners, the bearers and the congregation. In the earlier years of his ministry, the irrepressible instincts of his humanity and his great kindness of heart, led him to dwell on the best qualities of those who had just departed. It was his practice to say nothing but good concerning the dead. *De mortuis nil nisi bonum.* But in after years he modified his course, the result of additional experience, and of having incidentally overheard a conversation between two fishermen, engaged in their regular vocation on the Hudson. They "had toiled all the night and had taken nothing;" drenched with rain and exhausted with labor, disappointed and tired, they were not in a very good humor, which, in the one, showed itself in very profane utterances, the repetition of the most terrific imprecations. This greatly shocked his companion who severely rebuked him, and inquired, "What would become of him when he died, if he used such language?" To which he replied: "Oh! I shall be safe enough; for my friends will get Dr. Wackerhagen to preach my funeral sermon, and he will be sure to send me to heaven."

The unvarying kindness of his manners and heart, his genial hospitality and constant courtesy, were among his prominent characteristics. He was, in the full sense of the word, a Christian gentleman. He was most careful not to wound the feelings, or injure the reputation of another. He was determined in the maintenance of his own rights, but he was equally considerate of the rights of others. He was a man of great humility, always "esteeming others better than himself." The purity of his character was sullied by no stain, by no gross or unworthy acts. His life was beyond reproach or suspicion. He was a Christian from conviction, not from impulse; from love, not from fear, and he endeavored continually to exemplify the sincerity of his principles in his conduct. His faith was simple and child-like in its exercises, his life laborious and useful. You could ever notice the sincere desire, the habitual, honest effort to obey God's word, to bring his life in harmony with its teachings, the struggle of an earnest human soul towards what is good and best. And it was this that gave unity, efficiency and consistency to his character and permeated his entire actions. So calm and self-composed was he at all times, that scarcely a ripple disturbed the tranquility of his life. The impress of his character he left unto those who came under his influence. His ministrations were practical. His great aim was not so much, that his people might profess Christ, as that they might walk in Christ's way—that they might be "neither barren nor unfruitful in the knowledge of our Lord Jesus Christ," but faithful and exemplary Christians, "always abounding in the work of the Lord." He labored with unwearied perseverance, with an unselfish devotion for the good of those committed to his charge. To them he devoted his best energies; to their highest welfare all his labors, his untiring efforts were steadily and uniformly directed.

He was emphatically a man of peace, scrupulously avoiding those measures which so often lead to the separation of friends, and most assiduously "endeavoring to keep the unity of the Spirit in the bond of peace." He had no sympathy with the controversial spirit of the day. He had no taste for the personal polemics and the ecclesiastical strife which so often disturb the Church. He was wont to say that these exhibitions were destructive to holiness of heart and the prosperity of Zion. When differences existed among the brethren, he always tried to assuage asperities, to pour oil upon the troubled waters.

In his sermon on his death, Dr. Pohlman speaks of him as "the faithful, zealous and consistent herald of the cross," and adds that "his character was no ordinary exemplification of the faith and the hope of the gospel," that "his whole life and teachings were in perfect harmony with the gospel of Jesus Christ;" that "piety and prudence, patience and perseverance were associated in lovely combination, and, as heavenly graces, presided over his spirit, formed the habitual temper of his mind, and made him what he was—a perfect gentleman and the exemplary Christian divine." He was certainly a beautiful example of unceasing and honest labor, of Christian serenity, dignity and self-respect, uniting kind, affable and attractive manners with a happy, cheerful disposition, and a cultivated intellect, which rendered his society acceptable to the most intelligent and refined circles. Although his modest and unassuming character was impressed upon everything he said or did, in public and private, yet his influence in the Church was very great, particularly in the ecclesiastical body with which he was connected. He was beloved, honored and trusted. Capacity and integrity gave him authority and won for him the highest confidence. For twelve years he presided over the *New York Ministerium*. He was also an original trustee of Hartwick Seminary, and in this capacity served for thirty years.

THE REV. DR. ERNST L. HAZELIUS

was one of the most popular men of the church—I mean, that everybody was his friend. His blameless life, transparent candor, and sincerity of heart, endeared him to all who knew him. His perfect honesty and simplicity of character closed our eyes to his imperfections of temperament, and we saw nothing but the lineaments of the kind and loving old gentleman.

He was well known in the church for many years as Professor

in Hartwick Seminary; then Professor in the Seminary at Gettysburg, and subsequently in the theological school of the South at Lexington, where he died in 1853, aged 76.

The following letters from those who knew him well, portray his character well in Sprague's Annals:

EXTRACTS FROM THE REV. HENRY I. SCHMIDT, D. D., PROFESSOR IN
COLUMBIA COLLEGE.

NEW YORK, March 27th, 1861.

MY DEAR SIR: You have asked whether I could give you any reminiscences of the late Dr. Hazelius—any incidents of his life not yet made public. He and my father were school-mates in Germany, at the Pedagogium in Barby, and appear, at that time, already to have been much attached to each other. When the Doctor left the Pedagogium for the Theological Seminary, my father went to the University as a student of Medicine. Some time after this—I do not remember how long*—the Doctor came to this country, to become Professor of Theology in the Moravian Seminary at Nazareth. Here he led rather a lonely life for a few years, until my father arrived at the same place, when the two friends were reunited, and for some time occupied rooms in the same building.

I have wonderfully distinct recollections of my earliest childhood, and one or two of them are connected with the subject of this gossiping letter. He was my godfather, and held me at the font, and thus sustained to me a relation which, in those good old-fashioned times, was esteemed second only to that of a parent. The fidelity with which he discharged the duties thus assumed, the many acts of kindness which I received at his hands, especially at the time when I entered the ministry, and when his paternal counsels and guidance were invaluable, will never fade from my memory. My father had then been for years reposing under the sod. As I said, my recollection of him goes back to my earliest childhood; but the incidents which are so distinctly retained by memory, were of too trifling a nature to be recounted in a letter. I may, however, mention one incident which my father used to relate with great glee. Small parties used, in those days, to spend a day, occasionally, in a pleasure excursion from Nazareth to the Blue Mountains, where an old

*A. D. 1800.—J. G. M.

Revolutionary soldier, named Burroughs, had a cottage, not far from the Gap. These parties carried their provision with them, which they enjoyed in the old pensioner's cottage, where the remains of the meal were quite an acceptable donation. On one such occasion, my parents, Dr. Hazelius and another friend named Felgentreff, made up the party, the last named person having contributed, among other delicacies, a roasted goose to the entertainment. When he undertook to carve this *piece de resistance*, it slipped away from under his knife, and fell under the table. He seems not to have had the presence of mind displayed by another noted character in a similar position—at any rate he failed to quickly clap his foot on the lapsed goose. This was a chance not to be neglected by a half-famishing dog, that had been greedily looking out for scraps—he seized the Capitoline fowl, and rushed out of the door. The cottage was near the road where the declivity of the mountain was steep. Out flew poor Felgentreff after the canine robber, calling loudly upon him to relinquish his ill-gotten prey. Vain was the summons. Felgentreff gave chase, but the more he ran and shouted, the more furious became the speed of the dog, that knew the topography of the mountain better than his pursuer, and was soon beyond the reach of the vengeance which so laboriously strove to overtake him. Of course the company assembled in the cottage enjoyed the scene immensely; and it was long ere Felgentreff heard the last of his bootless chase after the stolen goose, from which he returned quite out of breath; for, unable soon to check the rapidly accelerated speed of his career down the mountain, he did not fail to learn that, while the *facilis descensus* is not over disagreeable, the *revocare gradum* is, especially when *minus* a goose, a tedious *opus*, and a hard labor. Regretting that I have nothing of more importance to communicate, I remain, most truly, yours,

H. J. SCHMIDT.

FROM THE REV. GEORGE B. MILLER, D. D., PROFESSOR IN THE HARTWICK SEMINARY.

HARTWICK SEMINARY, September 28, 1854.

DEAR SIR: I had the happiness of a long and intimate acquaintance with Dr. Hazelius, and was called upon to preach on the occasion of his death. I shall barely hint at a few of the more prominent traits of his character.

In his private character Dr. Hazelius was devout, humble, simple-minded, upright,—faithful in the discharge of his onerous duties even to scrupulousness. In his family he was kind, affectionate and loving. In promiscuous company he made himself very agreeable, being at once very sociable and fond of conversing upon useful subjects. He had a peculiar affection for children, though never blessed with any of his own. If he had some prejudices, and was at times somewhat hasty, this, with all who enjoyed the happiness of his acquaintance, served as a mere foil to his noble qualities of heart and mind. As a Public Teacher, whether in the Pulpit or the Theological Chair, or the Classical School, his gifts were rather solid than showy. He was well acquainted with Latin, Greek and Hebrew, as well as with a number of Modern Languages, and was uncommonly familiar with History, both General and Ecclesiastical. He was a learned Theologian, and a good interpreter of Scripture. A respectable Preacher, his sermons were sensible, well digested, evangelical and practical.

That he was an excellent instructor is abundantly testified to by many of his pupils, still living,—some of them occupying important stations in the ministry, and others in civil and political life. He always took the warmest interest in the welfare of his former pupils, doing every thing he could to benefit them; while many of them, in turn, cherish his memory with an affection truly filial.

It would be unjust to his memory not to allude, in this connection, to some of his extra-official labors. He prepared several books, partly translations from the German, partly original, some of which have been published, while others are yet lying in manuscript. His mind, never at rest, was always devising or prosecuting some useful enterprise. As another proof of his active turn, I would mention that, while he was at Hartwick, he frequently employed his summer and fall vacations in visiting destitute congregations in various parts of the State, acting as a sort of volunteer Home Missionary, at his own cost; and I have no doubt that some of our congregations were actually preserved from extinction by his faithful labors. By this means, too, he knew the condition of our churches and could direct young men, when they were licensed, to the places where their services were most needed, and to which they were best adapted.

He also carried on an extensive correspondence till the decay of his strength rendered the exertion too laborious.

If now it is asked what has been the fruit of his more than fifty years' active and laborious exertion, especially of the last thirty-seven, in which he was engaged in preparing young men for the ministry, the answer is, his faithful services have introduced into the ministry a large number of active and useful young men, and thus conduced to the increase and extension of the Church. And whereas, during the period of his labors, as Theological Professor, our Church, by the blessing of the Most-High, has increased tenfold, he has been honored by our Heavenly Master, to contribute a very material share to this increase; and I presume there are few in our connection, whose praise is in all the churches, especially in the Northern and Southern extremities of our land, as is that of Dr. Hazelius. I am, dear sir,

Yours in the bonds of the Gospel,
GEORGE B. MILLER.

FROM THE REV. HENRY N. POHLMAN, D. D.

ALBANY, January 8, 1852.

MY DEAR SIR: When I went to Hartwick, as a theological student, in 1816, I not only became acquainted with Dr. Hazelius, but came under his immediate care and instruction. The relations thus born gave place, in due time, to other relations of a more general character; and there existed between us, to the close of his life, an intimate, not to say confidential, friendship. My memory is full of incidents, some of them touching enough, and some of them laughable enough, that might aptly illustrate his different characteristics.

The personal appearance of Dr. Hazelius was striking, and would make him pretty likely to be noticed in a crowd. He was of about the middle size, and, whether his body was at rest or in motion, there was always an inclination of the head so considerable as to suggest the idea of a natural deformity. He had a fine, round, intellectual face, that gave you the assurance, before he opened his lips, that he was much more than an ordinary man. His movements were rapid; but there was a slight degree of awkwardness about them, growing out of the fact that he was extremely near sighted. I remember, on one occasion, as I was riding to Cooperstown with him, in the winter, he suddenly took off his hat and made a very graceful bow. "Whom are you bowing to, Doctor?" said I. "To that gentleman," said he, "that we just passed." "That gentleman," said I, "was a stump." Of course he enjoyed the joke as much as I did. His manners were those of a well-bred gentleman of the old school. He had great kindliness of spirit, but along with it, as often happens, a full share of irascibility. Of this latter quality, one or two striking instances now occur to me. I was, at one time, an assistant to the Doctor in his school; and, as my boarding place was some two miles distant, I used to take my dinner along with me and eat in my room. He was just returning from *his* dinner, when some of the boys were amusing themselves by rolling a cannon ball through the lower hall of the building, and it actually came near hitting the Doctor as he was entering the door. As I had, at that moment, opened my own door to find out what was going forward, my face was the first that presented itself to Dr. H., and his first thought was that I was the offender, and he instantly drew himself back, and lifted his cane as if to level a terrible blow at me. I exclaimed,—"Why, Dr. Hazelius!" And by that time he discovered his mistake. One of his boys from Albany, rather an unlucky fellow, addressed him in the school in a somewhat impudent manner, and the indignant preceptor, by a tremendous blow, knocked him down. The boy made a great ado, and affected a much more serious injury than he had really experienced, so that the Doctor was prodigiously frightened. He came rushing into my room in great consternation, and said, "I believe I have killed Russell." I immediately went into his room, and there, sure enough, was Russell lying on the floor, apparently writhing in agony, and evidently willing to have it believed that it was the agony of death. I was satisfied, in a moment, that it was all affectation, and that the fellow had really received no serious injury. It was agreed that I should take him to his boarding house, where he might have the requisite attention paid to him. The Doctor was so deeply exercised about him that he could not feel contented to stay away from him; and, accordingly, he had the bell rung for evening prayers at three o'clock in the afternoon, and then hastened away to ascertain the condition of his victim; when, behold, I had the pleasure of telling him that he had gone off skating!

Not only was his knowledge of the classics most thorough, but he had great facility of imparting it to his pupils. His preaching was eminently instructive, and the most cultivated hearer would never find in it any lack of material for his mind to work upon. His voice was mellow and pleasant, and sufficiently flexible, without being very loud. His gesture, though not abundant, was simple and natural. Instead of looking his audience in the face, his eyes seemed to be watching the flies upon the ceiling; and this, of course, detracted somewhat from the force of his manner. He wrote and spoke the English language not only fluently, but with great correctness; insomuch that it would hardly have occurred to you that it was not his mother tongue. Indeed, it became much easier for him to preach in English than in German. I remember once accompanying him some twenty miles below Hartwick, where he went to preach a Funeral Sermon for some old German, and though he began in the German language, he found it so difficult to proceed in it, that long before the sermon was finished he was making free use of the English.

Dr. Hazelius never seemed to take much interest in Deliberative Bodies, and, I think, that neither his taste or talents pointed very decidedly in that direction. He was, however, once President of the General Synod. I remain, as ever, yours sincerely,

HENRY N. POHLMAN.

FROM THE REV. JOHN G. MORRIS, D. D.

BALTIMORE, November 1, 1862.

DEAR DR. SPRAGUE: The first time I ever met Dr. Hazelius was in this city, in 1830, when he was on his way to Gettysburg, where he had been called as Professor of Theology. He was staying at the house of a venerable minister of our Church; and, instead of sending his card to announce his presence, as some fastidious gentlemen do, he called at once, and, with a sort of semi-apologetic mien, observed,—"I owe you this visit and pay it out of gratitude." I replied that I was not conscious of having put him under any obligation to me. "Not you," he continued, "but your parents. In 1800 I landed in this city from Bremen, a stranger; and, on my way to Bethlehem, I passed through York, where your father kindly entertained me for some days, and I shall ever remember his generous hospitality." Very frequently, in our subsequent intimate intercourse, did he allude to that event, and always with evident pleasure. This may be one of the reasons of our confidential relations as long as he lived.

He remained in Baltimore over the following Sunday, and I of course invited him to preach. On our way to church he inquired whether I read my sermons, and to my negative answer he made no reply. I did not then know his mode of preaching or I should have modified my answer. He did not read. I wish he had, for without his manuscript the good Doctor was not a good preacher. He was not fluent in extemporaneous speech nor systematic in arrangement. He was too old to commit his sermons to memory, and had habituated himself entirely to his notes. With his pen he was strong and clear, with his tongue weak and confused. As I gently chided him afterwards for abandoning his habitual track, he remarked that he always tried to conform to the custom of the pulpit in which he preached, even at the risk of blundering. A few years afterwards a similar event occurred. He and I had been invited to speak at the meeting of the Frederick County Bible Society, which was to be held during the meeting of our Synod, at that place. It happened to be on the 31st of October, the anniversary of the Reformation, which affords a glorious theme for a Bible Society speech. The Doctor had elaborated a regular discourse on that subject, expecting to read it from the pulpit, but we were not in the pulpit, and he was too far removed from the light to see distinctly (for he was very near-sighted), and what could he do? He could not recite his written speech, and he was not ready for an off-hand effort. It was a failure.

During his several years residence in Gettysburg, though thirty years his junior, I was his confidential friend. He undertook no important work without consulting me, and minutely related to me all his grievances and sorrows. I could even have taken liberties with him which it was not safe for others to do. For instance, whilst examining his students in the presence of the Board he would forget that he was examining and go on lecturing, and thus exhaust the time allotted before half of the young men had been questioned. I would gently remind him of the nature of the exercise, when he would spasmodically exclaim, "Yes, yes, you are right," and then proceed, "Well, Mr. S...., tell us what you know about the Manicheans—their rise, doctrines, influence, etc." The young fellow would begin, and probably soon come to the end of his line, when off would go the Professor in a regular lecture on the Manicheans, when he was kindly reminded again that the impatient Board had come to hear what the students and not what the Professor knew. The old gentleman would, with a smile, beg pardon, and in less than ten minutes would be off again in another long explanation. He was surprised, and I presume a little mortified, to hear the announcement from the President of the Board, "Your hour is out—let another subject be introduced."

I have met with but very few professors who understood the *art* of examining. They always seem to think they must explain every blunder a pupil makes and correct every error he commits. This belongs to the lecture room and not to the examination.

I should suppose that no professor was ever more loved by his pupils than was Dr. Hazelius. Having no children of his own, he seemed to cherish a paternal feeling towards *all* under his care, and I believe it may be asserted with truth that not one of them was ever heard to utter a disrespectful word of him. They reverenced him for the purity of his character, the artlessness of his conduct, and loved him for the deep interest he always showed in their affairs.

He was painfully afflicted at any of their derelictions, and so perfectly innocent himself that the slightest departure from the strictest propriety would affect him to the very soul. The night previous to a College Examination, some mischievous students had raised a pole with a flag bearing this inscription,—" Menagerie of living animals to be exhibited to-day." Now this, to most of them, was a good joke, though lacking wit and ingenuity; but to the tender-hearted and delicately nerved Hazelius it was a heinous offence, and whilst the rest of them laughed, he sat down and absolutely wept.

I was long aware that his position in Gettysburg was not pleasant, and we often spoke of a change as desirable to him. A letter was received by me, from a leading man in the Synod of South Carolina, inquiring into the qualifications of a minister for the post of Professor in their Seminary. Instead of answering as requested, I proposed the name of Dr. Hazelius, which was received with the most gratifying surprise, never dreaming that reputedly one of the best scholars and best men of the Church would leave her chief Seminary, to go down to the backwoods of South Carolina; but he did go, and was glad to go.

Before he left Gettysburg the students raised a subscription for his portrait, and he came to Baltimore to sit for it. He would insist on my accompanying him every day to the artist, to keep him awake and cheerful. I put forth all my powers to enliven him, for the artist was a dull fellow, and had nothing to say, but all was in vain. After half an hour's constant sitting, the old gentleman would nod: I would rouse him by some piquant story or interesting question in Church History; occasionally I would get up some difficulty in Hebrew Grammar or Exegesis, which would rouse him for a moment, but he would soon collapse. Then I would eulogize some man whom I knew he did not like, or pretend to be a Democrat; and, when all else failed, I brought up the Manicheans; but, before the hour was out, he was again asleep. A man asleep is not the man to be painted, and we would adjourn for that day, with leave to sit again. The picture was finished after much trouble, and is now suspended in the Seminary Chapel, but it is a very imperfect counterfeit of the noble original. The best likeness of him is that in mezzotint by Sartain; but that represents him without spectacles. When a man wears spectacles all his life, and is never seen without them, they are a part of his likeness, and no true artist will leave them off.

The literary labors of Dr. Hazelius have never had much reputation beyond our own Church. His publishers were not of that class who *make* a book sell, and he himself knew absolutely nothing of the ways of trade. Though his books were carefully elaborated (he wrote several of them three times over), yet they have never found many readers beyond his own circle. His translation of the life of Stilling seemed to be his favorite, and yet it is the least meritorious of them all—a lame or sickly child is often the pet of the family. He would read this book in manuscript to the members of his household by the hour, and was deeply mortified that it created no excitement on its subsequent publication.

When the Doctor moved to South Carolina he, like many other northern men who go there, became a slaveholder from necessity, as he used to say. As far as I know he had but one slave, and he a little boy. It is said his discipline was most paternal, and the exercise of it gave him greater pain than the little culprit felt. He would lecture the offending darkey, reason with him as though he had been a man, preach to him, *cry over* him really, whilst the scamp was slyly laughing at "ole massa" all the time. It was a most amusing scene altogether. I have heard frequent recitals of it, with all the moving protestations of the Doctor and the cunning, half jocose apologies of the servant. The Doctor's earnest sincerity and deep emotion were in strong contrast with the boy's giggling countenance and evident and ill concealed enjoyment of the fun.

As a Theologian, Dr. Hazelius was profound; as a Linguist, learned; as a Christian, devout; as a Teacher, successful; as a Man, complete as far as our fallen nature can be.

REV. JOHN BACHMAN,

of Charleston, had been for some years a leading man in the Southern Church before he became personally known to the same class of men in the Central Church. His first appearance among them was as a member of the General Synod in York in 1835, when he endeared himself to them all by his courteous manners, his high social qualities, his varied learning and his churchly activity. He was gay without frivolity, learned without pedantry, and pious without asceticism. He had already at that time acquired great reputation as a naturalist, but he never alluded to science without being asked a question.

On this occasion, at York, a number of us accompanied him on a botanical excursion up the Codorus Creek, when we were compelled not only to admire his familiarity with the Flora of the region, and his facility in discovering the names of the few plants unknown to him, but also to admire, and, at the same time, to deplore his extreme agility, for he outwalked some much younger men than himself, and left the older lagging far behind.

He attended one or two meetings of the General Synod subsequently, and at one of them was elected President.

The same body convened in his church in 1850. It was the first time we had ever met South, and it was a happy meeting.

Among many other acts of kindness shown, Dr. Bachman presented every clerical member of the Synod with a copy of his celebrated book "On the Unity of the Human Race."

It was on this occasion that I became the possessor of a treasure which I prized very highly, and which is now before me on a row of shelves in my study. The Doctor had a large collection of dried plants, kept as Herbariums usually are, in folio volumes. I think he told me it once belonged to Elliott, the botanist, and the author of a book on Southern botany. Without any further words as to how and why, the collection became mine, by gift. Mrs. B..... was glad to get rid of the pile, for she wanted the room for other purposes, and I was so glad to disencumber the house of the annoyance that I immediately engaged a man to pack them in two immense boxes and to cart them to a ship bound for Baltimore. I made two or three good collections out of it, and supplied several friends in Europe with specimens of Southern plants. Many of them have Elliott's and Bachman's original labels. The Doctor sometimes made observations on them, of which I will quote only one example. On the label of a poisonous plant, he writes: "In the summer of 1831 this plant poisoned me and laid me up for several weeks, and nearly put a stop to my botanizing for the rest of my life."

(From the Charleston News and Courier.)

THE STORY OF HIS LIFE AND LABORS.

The venerable John Bachman died at his residence in this city yesterday, in the eighty-fifth year of his age.

HIS LIFE AND PASTORATE.

He was descended from an old German family, although his first American ancestor came from Switzerland to this country as the private secretary of William Penn. During his childhood he knew nothing of the German language, but in after life he spoke and wrote German with great fluency. Dr. Bachman first acquired his knowledge of German at college, and afterward made himself master of that and other modern languages during his visit to Europe. His father, like other farmers around him in those days, was a slaveholder, and to the last years of his long life Dr. Bachman took occasion, from time to time, as opportunity offered, to make inquiry concerning the fate of the negroes who were the companions of his tender years. He has often been heard to speak of those former bondmen, and lament the fate that had befallen them.

Dr. Bachman received a liberal education, and at the early age of twenty-three was licensed by the Lutheran Synod of New

York, having been previously elected pastor of three congregations in the vicinity of his own neighborhood in Rensselaer county, New York, where it was then his expectation to spend the remainder of his days among the friends and relatives of his boyhood and early youth. A hemorrhage of the lungs, however, with which he had been attacked while in college, was making a fearful inroad in his health, and he was advised by his physicians to seek relief in a more southern climate. About this time a call was sent from the Lutheran church in this city to the president of the Synod of New York, Dr. Quitman, with a request that he should recommend some clergyman who might be adapted to this field of labor. Dr. Quitman and Dr. Mayer, of Philadelphia, therefore proposed Mr. Bachman's name to the congregation in Charleston. A call was immediately sent, inviting him to become their pastor. After consultation with his family and congregation, he obtained a leave of absence for nine months, the hope being expressed that during that time his health would become sufficiently restored to enable him to return and resume his ministerial labors at the north. The Lutheran church had then scarcely an existence in the Southern States, and as there was no Lutheran Synod here, an extra meeting of the Synod of New York was convened in December, 1814, at Rhinebeck, for the purpose of ordaining him. The ordination services were performed by Dr. Quitman and the other officers of the Synod in the Lutheran church at Rhinebeck, and, without returning home, the young clergyman proceeded on his way to this city, where he arrived on the tenth of January, 1815. A meeting of the vestry of the church took place on the twelfth, two days afterward, and the charge of the congregation was in due form committed to his trust. On January 10th, the day of his arrival, he attended the first funeral, and on the sixteenth performed the first baptismal service of his ministry in Charleston.

The state of the country at the time of Dr. Bachman's advent in Charleston was graphically described by him in a sermon on the forty-third anniversary of his arrival here, as follows:

"We were in the midst of a three years' war with the most powerful of foreign nations. Fearful battles had occurred on our northern frontiers, on the ocean and on the lakes. The traces of devastation and death were visible in the half-covered graves along the highway between Baltimore and Washington. The blackened walls of the capitol at Washington, and the waste and destruction in every part of the city, presented an awful picture of the horrors of war. On my arrival here I found our citizens working on the lines of defense thrown around the land side of our city—even ladies went there with hoes and spades to cheer the citizen soldiers by their presence, their countenance and example, and I, too, joined, at least in form; for it was our common country that was to be defended. In the meantime the battle of New Orleans had been fought on the 8th of January, and a treaty of peace had been signed at Ghent; but these important events were not known until some time afterward. The war had fallen heavily on our southern people. The principal staple of our commerce—cotton—had for several years during the embargo and war been sold at a mere nominal value, and was stored away in various depositories in King street. Our city was then only a village compared with its present growth, and the grass was growing in our most public streets. Men had the necessaries of life, and these were cheap; but all the means of enterprise, and all the avenues to wealth were closed up. Fortunately, men were driven to the necessity of manufacturing their necessary articles, and they were compelled to deny themselves luxuries; they studied economy, and hence there was not much suffering among our people from any want of the necessaries of life. But the constant dread of invasion, the sufferings and dangers to which our friends, who were in the army and at sea, were constantly exposed, kept the minds of our citizens in an unsettled and feverish state. The means of traveling were very different from what they are now, in the days of steamers and railroads. The roads were almost impassable; as an evidence of this I would state that with the exception of a Sabbath on which I preached for Dr. Mayer, of Philadelphia, I came in the regular stage line, which traveled day and night, and arrived in Charleston on the morning of the twenty-ninth day after leaving Dutchess county, which is one hundred miles north of the city of New York. In the meantime our vehicles were either broken or overturned eight times on the journey."

The congregation then worshiped in a small wooden building situated in the rear of the site of the present church. It was an antiquated building of peculiar construction, resembling some of the old churches in the rural districts of Germany, and had been erected previous to the Revolutionary war. The congregation was composed of Germans, who, during the stormy season of the Revolution, had been the strenuous advocates and defenders of the rights of their adopted country. Its pastors, from 1771 to 1815, when Dr. Bachman was called to the charge of the congregation, were Rev. F. Daser, Rev. Mr. Martin (who was driven from the church by the British officials in consequence of his refusal to pray for the king), Rev. John C. Faber, Rev. Charles Faber and Rev. Mr. Streit. Dr. Bachman entered upon the pastoral duties of his new charge amid gloomy and discouraging surroundings in the temporal condition of the congregation, but brought to the work a fervent spirit of Christian zeal and the robust energy of mental character, which always characterized him; and he had the pleasure, during his long pastorate, of seeing his church rapidly built up in numbers and efficiency, two sister churches of the same denomination established in the community, and a Lutheran Synod, a Theological Seminary, and a flourishing Lutheran College established in the State. He stood amid the revolutions of the changing years, and saw the brethren who welcomed him upon his arrival here, and were his companions in the early history of the Lutheran Church in Charleston, falling by death on every side, until at the close of his eventful life he was the one connecting link between the past and present, surrounded only by the children of his former friends, down to the fourth generation, whom he had come to look upon as the children of his heart as well as the members of his spiritual flock.

In 1835, Dr. Bachman, then in his forty-fifth year, received the degree of doctor of divinity. In the autumn of 1837, the devoted pastor's health again broke down under the arduous labors which devolved upon him, and which included the preaching of three sermons every Sunday, sometimes in English and sometimes in German; and his congregation feeling a profound interest in the preservation of his life and the restoration of his enfeebled health, unanimously requested him to take a respite from his labors. He accordingly left his home and people in 1838, believing, as he said, that he had looked upon the land of his nativity for the last time, and that he was destined to breathe his last among strangers in a foreign land. He was absent eight months, during which time he traversed nearly the whole of Europe, and received on all hands such cordial welcome, appreciation and hospitality, such manifestations of respect, admiration and fraternal regard as his eminent scholastic and scientific attainments, his sturdy piety, and his pure and blameless life, commanded. He returned in January, 1839, his health considerably improved, but still feeble, for which reason an assistant minister was employed by the congregation, who relieved the pastor of a large portion of his work until his health was announced once more restored.

To Dr. Bachman is due much of the credit of reorganizing and re-establishing the Evangelical Lutheran Churches in Georgia. In the winter of 1823-24 he went to Savannah, where he was instrumental in infusing new life into the Lutherans of that city. There were at that time the remnants of two Lutheran congregations in the entire State of Georgia. The church at Savannah had been burnt down in 1797; the congregation at Charleston had contributed $500 toward rebuilding it, but nothing was done toward keeping up the congregation. It had no pastor and gradually became disorganized. The small building which had been erected was occupied as a Sunday school by another denomination. Dr. Bachman's visit was not a moment too soon; a few more years of neglect, says Dr. Bernheim in his history of the Lutheran Church, would have extinguished the name of Lutheranism in Savannah. By means of his well directed and energetic labors, a congregation was at once organized, and in about a month's time was turned over to the pastoral care of the Rev. S. A. Mealy, who had been raised up in the Lutheran Church, at Charleston, and whose theological training had been received from Dr. Bachman. From that time the Lutheran Church in Savannah continued to prosper, under the efficient labors of a succession of devoted pastors. Having completed his good work in Savannah, he now turned his attention to the church at Ebenezer, the aged pastor of which was fast sinking into the grave. By his judicious labors, a son of Dr. Bergmann, who had taken a license to preach the gospel under the auspices of the Presbyterian Church, was induced to rejoin the Lutheran Church, and being subsequently ordained at the newly organized Synod of South Carolina, which met in Lexington district, on the 18th of November, 1824, returned to Ebenezer, and became the esteemed pastor of the Church in which his aged father, now dead, had labored so zealously and so faithfully.

Dr. Bachman was married January, 23, 1816, to Miss Harriet Martin, who died in 1838. In 1848 he married Miss Maria Martin, a sister of his first wife, who died in 1863. He has had fourteen children, of whom five died young, four died grown, and five are now alive. His two eldest daughters married the two only sons of Audubon, the naturalist. They died; one without issue, the other (Mrs. John Audubon) left two daughters, of whom one is now living in West Chester county, New York (Mrs. Delancy Williams), with three children. The other, Harriet Audubon, is now living with her aged grandmother (wife of the naturalist), in Louisville, Kentucky.

Dr. Bachman took no part in politics. He abhorred from his very soul that hybrid in professional life, "a political parson." But he was an ardent lover of his country, and at no time indifferent to her welfare. He took the most anxious interest in the political events which preceded the late war. A friend happened to be with Dr. Bachman on the fast day appointed by Gov. Gist, soon after the election of President Lincoln in 1860. The conversation was about Dr. Darwin's "Origin of Species," then but recently published. Dr. Bachman mentioned that thirty years before he had met the young Charles Darwin in England, just after his return from a cruise on H. M. Ship "Beagle," and there Darwin had told him that he had foresworn science, and thenceforth was going to give himself to the service of the church, and that he would not rest satisfied until he should be made a bishop. While giving these reminiscences, the venerable doctor brightened up with the reflection of the glow of youth that illumined his mind as he was retracing the incidents of earlier years. All at once he broke off abruptly, and with countenance overcast with gloom, said: "My mind is not upon these things. I have this day done the saddest act of life; I have preached a sermon against the Union, and upholding the secession movement of our people. My father fought in the Revolutionary war. I was taught from my earliest childhood to venerate my country's flag." Then walking to the window, and pointing to the United States flag on the Arsenal building, he said: "Many and many a time have I looked upon that flag with pride. It grieves me that I can do so no more. I love the Union, but I must go with my people." Tears were in the old man's eyes when he said this. And faithfully and nobly did he redeem his promise of going with his people. Soon after the commencement of war he organized a society for the relief of wounded soldiers, and until near the close of the war he was unwearied in his efforts to collect funds, provisions, clothing, etc., for this purpose. Although seventy-five years old then, he spared not himself nor his waning strength, but made many fatiguing journeys to Virginia to carry comfort and succor to those who needed his ministrations. It is needless to say that his efforts were crowned with the greatest success.

After the evacuation of Charleston, and the abandonment of the sea coast of South Carolina became certain, Dr. Bachman accepted the invitation of a friend in the northern part of the state, and sought shelter under the hospitable roof of General Cash, near Cheraw. But the hope of safety proved fallacious. Chesterfield county, as is well known, was visited by Sherman's host. Dr. Bachman, doubtless mistaken for the owner of the house, was beaten by the brutal soldiery, because he would not reveal where "the treasure was hid." It is the opinion of many that this beating was the cause of the disease which soon after befell him.

The close of the war found him a mere wreck of his former self. In common with nearly all his fellow-citizens he lost the greater part of his property; his library, a large collection of valuable works on natural science, theology and general literature, the laborious accumulation of over three score years, fell a prey to the flames when Columbia was burned. He was prostrated with paralysis several years ago, and his life despaired of by his friends; but thanks to an iron constitution, he rallied again and again. He preached but rarely, but continued more or less to attend to his duties until about January, 1869, when the Rev. W. W. H...... assistant pastor, was engaged. From this date, with but one or two exceptions, he ceased from the church ministrations. Mr. Honour officiated until February, 1872, when the Rev. Mr. Dosh took charge of the church. Dr. Bachman, however, generally participated in any important public occasion, as for instance in the laying of the corner-stone of the German church in King street, and again at the consecration of the church five years afterward.

HIS SCIENTIFIC AND LITERARY LABORS.

Dr. Bachman was first of all, and above all things, a pious, devoted Christian pastor, and it was this field of labor which commanded the most earnest efforts of his active mind and occupied the first place in his great heart. But he was also eminent as a savant and an author, and in these capacities his name will live as long as the literature of the English language retains a history. He was an ardent devotee of nature, never more at home than when out of doors. He loved nature in all her forms, and was fond of field sports, fishing, boating, and indeed of all healthful and manly exercises. Gardening was one of his favorite recreations, and he took a pride in its pursuit. It was this love of nature, doubtless, which early gave a bent to his studies, and to become a naturalist soon came to be his great ambition. It is not necessary to state that he never allowed his scientific tastes or pursuits to interfere in any manner with the duties of his sacred calling, but all his leisure, and that time which others give to the social amenities, was devoted by him to the study of nature. In forming an estimate of his acquirements and the vast labor achieved by him, it must be borne in mind that in him was exhibited one of the finest specimens of German industry. Of a strong frame, habitually in robust health, at least during the former half of his life, and possessed of a rare buoyancy of spirit, he could work with great rapidity, while his well-trained mind, sound judgment and retentive memory still further facilitated his self-imposed tasks. Nor was he an amateur in science. He was thorough in all he undertook, and shunned no labor to make himself master of his subject. With this view, he studied anatomy carefully, dissecting every animal he studied or described. Comparative anatomy was his favorite subject, and in this he achieved great results. Botany, mineralogy and geology at different times claimed more or less of his attention, but the study of animal nature was his preference, and zoology came to be his specialty. Not to mention innumerable monograms touching upon questions in his branch, he published jointly with Audubon, "The Quadrupeds of North America," to this day the finest work upon the subject that has appeared in this country. Mr. Audubon furnished the designs and Dr. Bachman the text. He also gave Audubon great assistance in his celebrated work on "The Birds of North America." These labors introduced him to the entire world of science, and he everywhere found most gratifying recognition. Honors came pouring in thick and fast. He received the degree of doctor of philosophy from Berlin in 1838, and that of doctor of laws from the South Carolina College at Columbia about the same time. He was elected to membership in almost every scientific association on the habitable globe. The magnates of science in England, France, Germany, Holland, Switzerland, Sweden and Denmark, testified their appreciation of his services by their letters, and with many he maintained a correspondence to his latest years. The great Alexander Von Humboldt was one of his warmest friends, and when, in 1850, he published his treatise on the "Unity of the Human Race," he dedicated it to his friend, the greatest of German physicists. The work just named was among the last of his strictly scientific publications. He had passed his three-score years, disclaimed any further ambition in the republic of letters, and expressed a determination to devote the remainder of his life to his pastoral duties. But the question of the unity or plurality of origin of the human race having become one of the controversies of the day, and from its nature, inferentially at least, partaking somewhat of a theological character, Dr. Bachman was drawn into the arena, and once in, he bent all the energies of his well-stored mind to the demonstration of the truth of his side of the controversy—the unity of origin.

Although a great devotee of science, this study was, as we have stated, secondary with Dr. Bachman, and whenever modern science seemed to clash with revelation, as has happened very frequently in the controversies during the present century, as new discoveries have been made, from time to time, in geology, chronology or ethnology, Dr. Bachman arrayed himself on the side of religious orthodoxy, and in every conflict proved a tower of strength.

Besides these works, most of which are far more scientific than theological, and altogether polemical or combative, Dr. Bachman furnished from time to time a great number of essays, reviews, sermons, editorials, and articles in the various periodicals of the day. From 1835 to 1840, he wrote a great deal for the editorial columns of the *Southern Agricultural Journal*. At another time he delivered and published a sermon against duelling; and besides all these works which have seen the light, he had several scientific works, which were nearly ready for publication, destroyed at the burning of Columbia in February, 1865.

HIS PERSONAL CHARACTER.

There was something simple and childlike in the character of Dr. Bachman which inspired confidence almost instantaneously. He was always at home with children, and for children, and cheerfully gave his time and labor to instruct and entertain the little ones. About 1850 the *Sunday-School Visitor* was established in Charleston, by the M. E. Church, South, edited by the Rev. Thomas O. Summers, D. D. He asked his friend Dr. Bachman to contribute articles on zoology for this journal. The venerable divine thought it not beneath himself, but furnished an article on some bird or animal for each number of the *Visitor* for several years. These sketches, off-hand, though they were, showed the master-hand. It was science popularized, not as is too much the fashion now-a-days by hack-writers who "read up" for the occasion, but as Herschel popularized astronomy. He could make everything clear and intelligible, because he had a perfect comprehension of it himself. Whatever he touched he adorned; for the keen, ripe intellect was always guided by a spirit of justice, and tempered by a loving heart.

For a list of his writings see *Bibliotheca Lutherana*.

FREDERICK CHRISTIAN SCHAEFFER,

of New York, was known by but few men south of New York. He did not take an active part in general church affairs, and never attended the General Synod, to which he was not well disposed. He died as early as 1832, and that was about the transition period, or at least when a class of younger men was displaying increased activity in the church.

Mr. S. had some reputation as a literary man, and also paid some attention to natural science. It was at a time when science had but few votaries in this country, and when opportunities of acquiring knowledge in Natural History were meagre. He made some exchanges of minerals with a professor of Science in Europe, who expressed to me his extreme dissatisfaction with what he had received from Mr. S. in exchange for a box previously sent him. I made every apology for him, but the learned German was inexorable.

A writer in Sprague's Annals (p. 147) mentions a noteworthy fact "that the King of Prussia presented him with a large gold medal as an acknowledgement for his services in extending among his subjects the knowledge of the Natural History of this country."

I never saw Mr. S. but once. One hot Sunday night I observed a stranger in my church, who struck me as a remarkably handsome man, bearing a strong resemblance to his brother, David F., in Frederick. I was not mistaken, and after service I introduced myself, and remarked, "Sir, you are a Schaeffer." I accompanied him to his lodging place, and had an hour's pleasant conversation with him. He was then in bad health, and had already abandoned preaching. He died soon after.

He was a graceful writer, and had a decided talent for composing parables after the Krummacher school, a volume of which was published. He also published a Sermon on the Reformation, and a singular fact was connected with it, showing that as far back as 1817, the Episcopal Church was more tolerant of ministers of other churches than at present. This sermon was preached in St. Paul's Episcopal Church of New York! of course, with the sanction of the high authorities.

A German Reformed minister once told me that Mr. S. preached for him upon the text "I am the rose of Sharon," in which he drew a beautiful analogy between the flower and Christ. As early as 1830, when he was 38 years of age, he was honored with the degree of D. D. by Columbia College.

He had some difficulties with a colleague arising out of that fruitful source of strife in many of our churches of that period, and more recently also, and that is the introduction of English preaching. The result of this quarrel was that Dr. S. and his congregation left the house of worship in which they had assembled for some time and which was sold to the Germans. He and his people removed to the edifice known as St. James' Church, presented to the congregation by Mr. Lorillard, who desired to be, and for a long time was, unknown as the generous donor. Here he continued to labor until the close of his life, in March, 1832, aged 40.

Dr. Schaeffer published The German Correspondent, one volume; Sermon at the Centennial Jubilee of the Reformation, 1817; Parables and Parabolic Sayings, one volume.

FROM THE REV. HENRY N. POHLMAN, D. D.

ALBANY, December 9, 1861.

MY DEAR SIR: In 1820, while I was yet connected with the Hartwick Seminary, I received a letter from the Rev. F. C. Schaeffer, requesting me to come and take charge of a mission in the

State of New Jersey; and thus commenced an acquaintance between us, which grew into a close intimacy that was terminated only by his death.

Dr. Schaeffer was altogether one of the finest looking men whom I have ever met with—if I were to say that there was not a nobler, more beautiful specimen of physical humanity than he in the city of New York, during the period of his residence there, I am confident that I should not be chargeable with exaggeration. His face was of rather the Jewish type—his eyes were black and piercing, his complexion dark, his nose Roman, his whole face beaming with intelligence, and capable of expressing every variety of emotion. Had it not been that there was a slight degree of heaviness in his movements, it would have been difficult to have suggested any improvement in his outer man. And his mind was scarcely less extraordinary than the face which it animated and illumined—it was inventive, brilliant, logical and graceful. He had an uncommonly genial spirit, and was one of the most generous and loving of friends, while those whom he did not like were in no danger of mistaking his feelings towards them. He was a highly educated man, and failed not to make his mark in literary society. For several years he was the German correspondent of the New York Spectator; and he was also a member of a club which used to hold meetings for purposes of intellectual culture and enjoyment, with which Dr. Samuel L. Mitchell was prominently connected. He was a great lover of Natural History. He exchanged many specimens of birds, insects and minerals with several men of science in Prussia; and the King of Prussia presented him with a large gold medal as an acknowledgment for his services in extending among his subjects the knowledge of the Natural History of this country. He was a splendid musician, and played skillfully on a variety of instruments. He had remarkably fine powers of conversation, and not only spoke out of a richly endowed and highly cultivated mind, but had the faculty of communicating what he knew with a most graceful facility. At the same time, he was a devout Christian, and never forgot that his main business was in dealing with men in respect to their higher and immortal interests. While he was faithful to his immediate charge, in the performance of pastoral duty, he took a deep interest in the general advancement of Christ's Kingdom, and was always ready to contribute his time, or lend the influence of his talents, to help forward any truly Christian enterprise.

As a preacher, he was undoubtedly one of the most popular and effective of his day. His voice was of great compass and melody, and his utterance perfectly distinct, and his whole manner graceful, earnest and attractive. He had nothing more than the outline of his sermon before him in the pulpit, but it was evident that his train of thought at least was thoroughly premeditated, and that it was beaten oil that he had brought into the sanctuary. He preached in English and German with equal ease. It was a mark of extraordinary respect for both his talents and virtues that, in 1817, he was allowed to preach in St. Paul's (Episcopal) Church, New York, a Sermon commemorative of the beginning of the great Reformation.

It may safely be said that Dr. Schaeffer, young as he was, was one of the prominent ministers of his denomination; and when he died, the universal feeling was that a great light had been extinguished. As ever, yours sincerely,

HENRY N. POHLMAN.

DR. GEORGE B. MILLER,

of Hartwick Seminary, never appeared among us in the central section of the Church, except at the meeting of the General Synod at Chambersburg, in 1839. I never tried harder to become acquainted with any man, but he seemed unapproachable, and I thought repulsively cold. His friends and pupils, however, told me that this was not his disposition, but that he was eminently unobtrusive and indeed bashful.

He took no part in the discussions, and like Dr. Wackerhagen, his colleague, he seemed little concerned in the affairs of the General Synod. His pupils, who were many, say that he was a thorough scholar and a most successful teacher. He had no oratorical grace as a speaker, but his sermons are sound and thoroughly elaborated. One of his sermons was reviewed by "S. S. S." in Vol. 1 of Lutheran Observer, and I happen to know that a copy of the review was sent to him before publication by the writer of it, to ascertain whether it contained any thing that he might wish to alter. He was for many years instructor in Hartwick Seminary.

"We have no hesitation in asserting," writes Dr. H. I. Schmidt, who knew him well, "that he had not his equal in our church. * * * He possessed the most absolute and ultimate familiarity with the various exact sciences. He had the most perfect command of our own vernacular. He spoke and wrote both French and German with great facility He was a profound Hebraist, and his knowledge of the classical languages was accurate, critical and complete. * * * * * * He seemed to get into the inermost heart of a language, to master its idioms, * * * * and to comprehend its genius with a sort of intuition. His knowledge of the scriptures was absolutely ubiquitous."

It is said that he was so familiar with the sacred volume that he never had occasion to use a concordance, but, with almost unfailing success, could turn to the passage which he required. He was a very able theologian. "His reading," says Dr. Schmidt, "was peculiar. He appropriated what others had to give with extraordinary rapidity, and when most men would have labored painfully through page after page, he got at the pith and marrow of any new book by a marvellously expeditious process, a sort of intellectual affinity, which, aided by a most retentive memory, made him master of his author's meaning in an incredibly short space of time."*

Every person who ever knew

DR. PHILIP F. MAYER,

of Philadelphia, must have admired the courteous gentleman and the agreeable, intelligent conversationalist. Properly, perhaps, he should have his place among the older men of the church, for he was licensed as early as 1802, but he outlived most of them, having died in 1857.

He was the only minister in the church who, in those early days, served an exclusively English congregation, and to this one he preached for fifty years.

Though residing in Philadelphia, yet he retained his connection with the Synod of New York, and seldom attended any other as a delegate and never as a mere visitor. He did not go where he

* For a fuller biographical sketch by Professor Stoever, see Ev. Rev. XXI, 24.

had no business, and he was too jealous of his time to waste it upon Synodical idling.

He was all his life through an opponent of the General Synod, although he was present at its formation at Hagerstown in 1820. He was distrustful of the men into whose hands the control of it afterwards fell, and he always kept aloof from it.

He carefully prepared and fully wrote out every sermon he preached, and being particularly exact and even severe towards himself, he thought he had a right to be so towards others, and hence usually asked to see the sermons which young men, whom he invited to his pulpit, intended to preach. One young man whom the Doctor had invited to preach, and who had heard of this habit of his, when asked what and how he was going to preach, saucily replied, "Sir, if I am to preach for you, your people must be content to hear what my people do, and I am not going to change my manner to accommodate you!" The Doctor said nothing, but was evidently displeased. On another occasion the same young man was in Philadelphia and the Doctor again invited him. It happened to be Ascension Day, and the stranger had no sermon with him adapted to the occasion, and he thought it too late to prepare one. This Dr. Mayer did not like, but consented to the arrangement. After the young man had returned to his boarding house, the Doctor came and, in the politest way possible, said that he could not possibly allow the Festival day to pass without an appropriate discourse, and released the stranger from the engagement. He was right, but the young man did not see it in that light at that time.

He persistently refused to have an assistant though frequently urged upon him. He declared that when he was no longer able to discharge all the duties of the ministry, he would resign, but not until then.

In his younger days, about the year 1806, when he settled in Philadelphia, he was a very popular preacher, and crowds of people went to hear him.

Like many others of our ministers who uphold the English interests in the church, Dr. M. met with violent opposition from the German ministers, and even refused all intercourse with him. He assumed and maintained a resolute stand, and deserves everlasting credit for the perseverance with which he carried out his measures in this regard.

He rendered good service in the cause of education, and was all his life long an active friend of various benevolent societies.

No one ever charged Dr. M. with insincerity or duplicity. He was not a man of policy, and he abhorred petty intrigue and low cunning. He had no respect for men who were not frank, open-hearted and honest. I have heard him severely denounce men whom he suspected of double dealing.

Whilst he was polite, refined and courteous, yet he was rather distant, and maintained a dignity which I have thought excessive. Perhaps with others he may have been more sociable, but I doubt whether he ever admitted any of his brethren to familiar intimacy.

No man was ever more highly respected by his colleagues, for they had confidence in his integrity, sound judgment and unaffected piety.

I regret that my limited space will not permit me to dwell longer upon the admirable character of Dr. Mayer, but I refer my readers to the Ev. Rev. X, 190, and Prof. Stoever's Eulogy, Phila., 1859, for full information.

DR. JACOB MILLER,

of Reading, (though he never accepted the title given him by the University of Pennsylvania), will be remembered by many of us, as a man of large frame, of commanding presence, of dark features and with a head as Websterian as you will meet in a year. He had firmness approximating to obstinacy, depicted on every lineament of his expressive face. To strangers, he was reserved and apparently stern, but his intimate friends said that in society he was frank and genial. I never met him but once, when I thought he was cold, although I was a very young man and had no right to look for courtesies. I soon ascertained that in the Synod he wielded an immense influence and yet he did not always carry his points. He was the most uncompromising opponent of the General Synod, and he had few courtesies to show to those outside of his Synod who were differently disposed. He went so far as to maintain that the General Synod aimed at political influence as well as religious bondage, and conceived violent prejudices against the leaders of that enterprise. He never attended the meetings of any other Synod than his own, and though he had many admirers of his preaching and of his upright life, he had few warm friends.

It was a long time and after a severe struggle that he yielded to the necessity of introducing the English language into his pulpit. He was intensely Pennsylvania German, but was compelled to give way to the overwhelming current. The submission was complete,—he himself recommended a worthy young man as his English assistant, who was elected, and with whom he labored in harmony as long as the young preacher lived. Dr. Miller died in 1850, in the 62 year of his age.

The following letter from Sprague's Annals is a faithful portrait:

FROM H. H. MUHLENBERG, M. D.

READING, January 18, 1862.

DEAR SIR: On the resignation of my father as Pastor of Trinity Church in this place, Mr. Miller was chosen his successor. I had then just concluded my college course, and I commenced my acquaintance with him by finding him my Pastor on my return. I was one of his first class of catechumens, and well remember the interest with which I listened to his explanations of the Catechism, and of the Principles of Natural and Revealed Religion. Although, after a college course, I found myself rusty in the German language, I managed to take down imperfectly his lectures, and write them out at home, from time to time, for my own benefit and the convenience of my friends in the class, some of whom were growing up with an imperfect knowledge of the German. His lectures and explanations were altogether in that language; and, if my recollection serves me, but one of the class, of perhaps sixty or seventy, used the English Catechism and recited in the English language. His lectures were adapted to the humblest capacity, and were at once easily comprehended and easily remembered. His arguments, and in some instances his very words, are vividly in my memory to this day. If any doubt remained in any mind in respect to any thing in his public lectures, there was no hesitation felt in asking him for an explanation; and it was always given so promptly and kindly and satisfactorily, that it became really a pleasure to ask him questions.

He soon acquired the confidence and affection of both the old and the young, and we felt that in our Pastor we had also a faithful and devoted friend. He made it a practice to visit all the members of his church, both high and low, at least once a year; and he was deeply impressed with the idea that it was essential to a minister's highest usefulness that he should have a personal acquaintance with those who constitute his pastoral charge. By his social disposition and winning candour, he made personal friends of all who had the opportunity of becoming well acquainted with him. Although there was a great disparity of years between him and myself (he being in the prime of life, and I a mere youth), I soon learned to look upon him as a friend, and one of my greatest pleasures was to spend as much time as I could in chatting with him in his study. He always seemed disengaged, and just as ready to converse with me on religion, politics or the occurrences of the day, according to the mood we happened to be in, as if I had been, in all respects, his equal.

By years of intercourse of this kind, I learned that his opinions were fixed and positive, but he was always willing to explain his own views, and to listen patiently to the arguments that were brought against them. One of his strong prejudices was in favor of the German language, as excelling the English in copiousness, clearness and facility for expressing ideas. He acknowledged the English as the language of the land, but nothing more, and thought that every person of liberal education, especially every one of German descent, should learn and use the German language. He would never hear it sneered at or decried without an instant word in its defence, and, as he was a man of very decided talents, it required some degree of courage to attack his opinions on any subject, for there was more than an equal chance that the assailant would not come off victorious.

Another strong prejudice that he cherished was that his own Church was vastly superior to any other in respect to both faith and government. Not that he thought other churches were out of the pale of salvation, or denied that they had their good points, and were instrumental of promoting the Redeemer's cause in the salvation of souls, but he thought them exceedingly imperfect as compared with our own. Ours he maintained was the real trunk, while others were mere branches, and the Catholic a decayed stem.

Still another of his strong prejudices was to be seen in his opposition to the General Synod, which he looked upon as a mere scheme for religious and even political influence. Whether this view originated in personal distrust of the men who were at the head of the enterprise, or in general views of human weakness, or both, I am not able to say. He was always in favor of the amplest individual and congregational liberty of religious opinion and connection, consistent with his views of Scriptural truth. I have repeatedly argued this point with him, and could never even get him to agree to the expediency of the General Synod, as a bond of closer union to our churches. Nothing, in his judgment, but similarity of religious faith and principle could be permanent. In this connection I may state that, although he received the degree of Doctor of Divinity from the University of Pennsylvania, he never recognized it, or called himself any thing else than *Jacob Miller*, Lutheran clergyman. Any other title than this was decidedly distasteful to him.

Notwithstanding the fixedness of his opinions, when he became convinced that the young people of his charge in Reading were growing up without such an acquaintance with the German language as to render it a suitable medium for conveying to them religious knowledge, he yielded his strong prepossession in its favor, and consented to the introduction of the English into his congregation; and when, during a protracted illness, which turned out to be his last, he sent in his resignation, the congregation seemed to feel as if his place could never be more than partially filled. Hence the difficulty of finding a successor, for, in the affectionate hearts of his flock, every one who was compared with him was found wanting, and he will never be forgotten, never cease to be loved, by those who sat under his preaching or enjoyed his friendship. See Ev. Rev. XIII, 561.

REV. J. UHLHORN.

Among the many men of versatile talent and high mental culture which our church has furnished, and who, in other spheres, would have far outranked many celebrities of other denominations, none deserves a more exalted position than Rev. Uhlhorn, formerly of Zion's German Church in Baltimore. He came to this country in 1824 or 25, a young, highly accomplished, and rather fashionable ecclesiastic. He wore rings in his ears, and his outer man betrayed other evidences of more expensive and scrupulous attention than is common among clergymen, but gradually he gracefully accommodated himself to our more simple American customs.

He was endowed with an extraordinary retentive memory. I have heard him repeat odes of Anacreon and other Greek poets with perfect correctness. He could recite chapters of the Bible and of other books without scarcely missing a word. But these were not the most striking proofs of the strength of his faculty. Old Dr. D. Kurtz has told me that Uhlhorn could repeat a long German hymn *backwards*, after reading it several times over.

His powers of impromptu versification were wonderful. I have heard him recite long series of good verses upon any subject that may have come up, and on short extempore couplets he was unsurpassed.

His manner in the pulpit would be considered as rather overstrained, at the present day, but, in his more moderate mood, he was grand and impressive.

I remember reading a published lecture *On Action* in Elocution, by some New England writer, which he illustrated by an example which he had witnessed in Baltimore. One Sunday, he remarked, happening to be in that city, he strayed into a church, attracted by the music. He soon discovered it was a German church, and he did not understand one word of the language. He concluded, however, to remain. He then describes the manner of the preacher, and afterwards inquired whether the subject of the sermon had not been The Prodigal Son, which was the fact. He says, from the manner and *acting* of the preacher, he could see the inconsiderate young man leaving home, and the preacher *acted* out his whole subsequent career, even to his return home, so naturally, impressively, speakingly, that the scene could have been no other than that of "The Prodigal Son." I remember showing this article to Uhlhorn, but he had too much good sense to betray any feeling of gratified vanity.

DR. DAVID F. SCHAEFFER, OF FREDERICK.

Those of us who have had the pleasure of stopping at Dr. Schaeffer's parsonage in Frederick, "long, long ago," will never forget his kindness and generous hospitality. No sojourner at his house could look for his company during the day, for he was ever on foot or in the saddle visiting his people or attending to other clerical duties. He was the most indefatigable and faithful pastor for many years that was ever known in all that section. In allusion to his constant habit of visiting his parishioners, when suffering from the slightest indisposition, some persons used to say, "If Parson Schaeffer's people have only the toothache they send for him to pray with them."

He was particularly attentive to the young, and kept up the good old system of cathechization every Sunday morning all the year through. With good old Lutheran doctrine, he inculcated profound veneration for Martin Luther, as a man and a reformer. I have heard him tell some amusing stories concerning answers of some of his pupils to his questions on the difference between Lutheranism and Calvinism, which showed that sometimes their ideas were much confused on the distinctive points of theology.

He was so profoundly venerated even by the children of his church, that a prominent member of our communion told me that when he was a boy, in Frederick, he, with six or eight other boys, would every day, on returning from school, go a square out of their way to pass Parson Schaeffer's house, that they might have the privilege and pleasure of being kindly spoken to and his hand laid upon their heads, and they were much disappointed if they did not see him.

He was by nature a courteous gentleman. In walking the streets of Frederick with him, he would politely salute every man, woman and child of every complexion, and stop and exchange a few words with half of them. I would impatiently hurry him on, when he would say, "Young man! the most of these people are members of my flock—they are worthy of my respectful regard; by these cheap attentions I gain their confidence, and they open their hearts to my preaching." He was right, and I felt the force of the rebuke. He not only verbally saluted every one by name, for he knew everybody, but he had a habit of lifting his hat to every one. One of his pupils says, "It was sometimes said, by way of pleasantry, that he always wore out his hat first at the front brim." Before the establishment of the Theological Seminary at Gettysburg, Mr. Schaeffer always had some young candidates for the ministry under his instruction.

Mr. S. preached exclusively German for many years, and had

great difficulty, as well as many other men, in introducing English preaching, but he managed it in time and succeeded. In this measure he was opposed by some who spoke English as well as German, and whose children did not understand it all, and yet this insane obstinacy and stupidity many of our ministers have encountered.

Mr. S., in his early ministry, received his small salary in small proportions. One day a country deacon came to his house and told him he had some money for him, but did not pay it and leave, but he sat an hour or two until dinner time, when, of course, he was invited to remain; and the hungry countryman, who had probably never sat down to as nice and plentiful a table, ate enormously. He literally gorged his inner man with the good things of the table. After dinner, he remarked, "Well, parson, I don't want to keep you longer out of your money," and deliberately handed over thirty-seven cents!

One day when I was a guest at his house, a shabbily dressed fellow came for alms; the man was ragged and unwashed, and evidently had been reduced to that condition by intemperance. I will never forget the manner in which the "parson" treated him. He rebuked him in terms and tones so tender, and seemed to sympathize with him so deeply, that the man was completely subdued, and went away, I think, a better man. Thus he treated everybody, though I have heard him speak severely of men who he thought had done him wrong, especially in his clerical character and activity.

One of his successors tells a good story of him in demonstration of his patriotism and public spirit. During the war of 1812, when Mr. S. was just 25 years of age, on receiving news of the disgraceful battle at Bladensburg, he mounted his horse and rode with Captain B. up and down the streets of Frederick, calling on the young men to organize a company and fight for their country. In the course of a few hours the company was full. He then rode with them three miles, and delivered an address and offered a prayer while all the soldiers were kneeling. They then marched to meet the enemy." Towards the end of his life Mr. S. got into painful difficulties with our Maryland Synod, and I never performed a more reluctant duty than to inform him personally of the action of the Synod, which was incumbent upon me as President. I persuaded Dr. Kurtz, Sr., to accompany me, and prevailed upon him, a life long friend of Mr. S., to make the communication, which he did with fatherly tenderness and discretion. Mr. S. died a few months after, in May, 1837, in the fiftieth year of his age, and the thirtieth of his ministry. He never was pastor of any other congregation.

For many years he had controlling influence in our Synod, and was seldom out of office.

The degree of D. D. was conferred upon him by St. Johns College, Annapolis. I have reason to know that he keenly felt the apparent neglect of our own college to bestow upon him the same honor.

He was very jealous of any depreciation of the religious character of his church. Some years ago a German Reformed revivalist created considerable commotion among the congregations in Frederick, and, in reporting his operations to a Philadelphia paper, inveighed severely against the coldness and religious apathy of the people, and designated them as a "field of dry bones." This roused the pious wrath of Dr. Schaeffer, and in "The Intelligencer," which he then edited, he entered upon a labored vindication of his church, and showed that his people were faithful attendants upon public worship, that his Sunday school was in good condition, that the prayer meeting was not neglected, and that things in general were not bad. Though he was evidently excited, yet the vindication was made in good temper. He sometimes carried this disposition to apologize for his people a little too far, though I believe it was entirely owing to his paternal regard for them. No person likes to hear his own children blamed. When, at the meetings of the Maryland Synod in his church, some of our zealous young men, in their exhortations, would urge the people to greater activity *in general*, and *seem* to indicate that they were not all doing their duty, Dr. Schaeffer would invariably follow with a recital of their good deeds, as much as to say that such exhortations were not applicable to his congregation, and yet he himself did not spare his people, but he would not allow any body else to rebuke them.

Dr. Diehl, at present pastor of Frederick, has stated some interesting historical facts concerning this old church in his discourse upon that subject.

He edited the Lutheran Intelligencer for five years. He was proud of this position, and, although he was not a forcible writer, yet he well enough met the wants of the Church in that day of small beginnings.

NUMBER OF THE COMMANDMENTS.

Dr. Schaeffer once asked a boy in his catechetical class, "How many commandments are there?" The reply was "Seven?" "No!" "Nine?" "No!" "Twelve?" "Not right yet!" "Fifteen?" "Worse and worse!" "Twenty?" "Charley," said the minister, "leave the class, go home, and do not return until you can bring me the correct answer." On his way home he met another boy who was going to "Catechism," and he asked him the number of commandments. "Why, ten, you goose!" was the reply. "Well," said the inquirer, "you had better not give that answer to Parson S ....., for I said there were twenty, and, that not being enough, he drove me home; so look out!"

SECTION III.

There was still another class of men who, fifty years ago, had stepped into the arena, some of whom subsequently distinguished themselves, and their memory is still precious. A few of them yet survive, but it is of those who have departed that I will now specially speak.

CHARLES P. KRAUTH

was a model man in every relation of life. He adorned every position he ever occupied. He was freer from the usual faults of men than any man I ever knew. I never saw him excited to anger but once, and then the provocation was intense. He was charged with duplicity, and he met the unfounded accusation with a most withering reply, that silenced as well as confounded his opponent. As soon as he had uttered his words of honest indignation, and sent the accuser, as it were, reeling to his seat, he became calm again as usual as though nothing had occurred to provoke him.

I became acquainted with him when I was a student, and from that time to his death, more than thirty years afterwards, we were as brothers, although he was some years my senior. On a visit to him in my student years, at Martinsburg, where he was then pastor, he insisted upon my going to a wedding with him, and to my surprise and gratification the parents of the bride had emigrated from my native place, where they had known our family and gratefully spoke of my father's medical services to their parents years before. During that same visit I accompanied him to one of his country churches, where he had a class of catechumens. I remained reading in a house until he had finished his work. He was a widower then, and his son, who has since become so distinguished, was a small boy, living with his grandfather at Staunton.

Mr. K. was educated as a physician, and attended medical lectures in Baltimore, but he never practiced his profession. He turned his attention to the ministry, of which he was a brilliant ornament. He was a most industrious reader from the beginning, but his reading was miscellaneous. He had at that time no large library of his own, and Martinsburg did not furnish him with a choice of theological books, and hence he read every thing he could lay his hands on. He has told me that he read and remembered as many as fifty volumes in a year, and his reading was thorough. It was only after he had removed to Philadelphia, where he had access to great libraries, that he confined his researches more particularly to theology and languages. His intimate association with Dr. Demmé, who was of similar tastes and pursuits, and his senior in years, aided and encouraged him in his studies. The result was that he became a first class linguist and theologian. These severe studies were continued all his life long, during which he acquired an extensive and valuable library.

In his early ministry he was associate editor with Dr. D. F. Schaeffer of the Lutheran Intelligencer, but in the course of a year or so he withdrew from that position. He became weary of going from Martinsburg to Frederick every month, to aid in making up the paper, a service which he conceived to be necessary under the circumstances.

He contributed considerably to the literature of our Church, as will be seen from the Bibliotheca Lutherana, but he was not particularly elegant as a writer, and he did not study the graces of style. He had too much to say to care about saying it in fine phraseology.

He was exceedingly simple in his habits, and not very particular about his dress during his life as a widower. Every body observed the change after he married the second time. I remember we were once admiring a splendid mansion in Staunton, when he remarked, "It's all very fine, but I would rather live in my plain house in Martinsburg than in that splendid edifice."

He had a singular habit of raising his hat when saluting any person, not in front, as other men do, but from behind. It was there his hat was first worn out, as we have already heard that David Schaeffer's was first worn out before. I often gently rebuked him for this singular departure from universal custom, but he never changed it.

As a preacher he was very instructive, but his voice was so weak that he could scarcely fill an ordinary sized church with its volume.

I never knew him to engage in any game such as backgammon, chess or chequers, in which so many ministers find pleasant recreation; nor did he ever go on excursions of pleasure, and I doubt whether he knew the use of the fishing rod or the gun, at least practically. His recreation was books and nothing else.

He was one of the founders of the Theological Seminary, but he little thought at that time that he ever would be a professor in it.

His whole manner was remarkably mild and tender; his voice, when not strained, was melodious; and he had that personal magnetism which attracts friends and keeps them.

As a teacher, judging from the little I saw of his method, I think he was too indulgent towards his class; he told them what they should have told him—if a student hesitated for a moment in his reply, the professor would at once relieve him of his embarrassment by answering the question himself. Hence, he was popular as a Synodical examiner—the applicants knew that he would let them off easily, of which I can speak from experience, for he examined me at Winchester in 1826, just fifty years ago.

As a theologian he always inclined to the old Lutheran system, though not very demonstratively. He was not a controversialist, and he abhorred strife. He gave offence to some Lutherans of a lower school by his sermon preached at the General Synod in Charleston, in which he assumed higher ground than was usually maintained, and which, if fully carried out, would logically lead to old Lutheranism. He once said, "I find the Lutheran doctrine of the Sacraments hard to accept in view of my puritanic training, but I find the Scripture passages quoted in favor of them still harder to get over and explain away," and this I apprehend is the feeling of many who see the truth, but are slow to make a decided and public demonstration of it.

Dr. Krauth witnessed the first day's conflict of the Union and Rebel armies at Gettysburg. He lived in the Professor's house, north of the Seminary; and when our men were driven from Seminary Hill and the rebels took possession, Dr. Krauth and family came up out of the cellar, whither they had fled, and started for the town. "Stop," said the rebel officer, "I will allow you to leave the house in any direction except towards town." They wandered from farm to farm, finding houses and barns full of wounded rebels, and they finally found shelter at a house two miles away. They remained there from Wednesday until Saturday afternoon, when the enemy had retreated. On returning they found their house crowded with wounded men, the bed clothing torn up for bandages, the plate carried off, books scattered, fences torn down, and all around a scene of ruin.

[The following glowing tribute to the memory of Dr. Krauth is from the classic pen of Prof. Stoever, and no excuse will be necessary for dwelling at such unusual length on this universal favorite in the church and pre-eminently beloved man:]

A character so near perfection, a life so almost blameless as was that of Charles P. Krauth is seldom found. He was one of the purest and best men that ever lived. One more faithful and affectionate, more devoted to high and noble purposes, better in the entire combination of his gifts and graces, has never been given to the Church. He was born in Montgomery county, Pennsylvania, May 7th, 1797. His father was a native of Germany, and came to this country, as a young man, in the capacity of a school teacher and a church organist. His mother was a Pennsylvanian. They lived in York, Pennsylvania, and in Baltimore, Maryland; also, for many years, in Virginia, highly respected and enjoying the confidence of their neighbors. Of his early life comparatively little is known, in consequence of his singular and habitual reticence with regard to himself. He was, however, considered by the children, cotemporary with him at school, as very precocious, quick in his apprehensions and successful in study. "We thought him," writes Charles A. Morris, of York, who knew him when he was about seven or eight years of age, "very far advanced in his arithmetic, but we boys were disposed to ascribe his success to the fact of his having a father who was a teacher." He seems to have been, from a youth, of an inquiring turn of mind and fond of books. His natural love of knowledge led him to improve his opportunities to good purpose, so that, without the advantages of a collegiate education, he attained to a very respectable measure of intellectual culture. He early evinced a decided taste for linguistic studies, and, in the prosecution of the Latin, Greek and French, won for himself high credit. Having selected medicine as his profession, he commenced its study when about eighteen years of age, under the direction of Dr. Selden, of Norfolk, Virginia, and subsequently attended a course of lectures in the University of Maryland. But, his funds having become exhausted, he visited Frederick, Maryland, with the view of procuring pecuniary aid from an uncle, the organist of the Lutheran Church, or of negotiating a loan for the completion of his theological studies.

During a visit to Rev. D. F. Schaeffer, of Frederick, his mind was led to the conclusion that the ministry was the work to which God had called him. He very soon commenced his theological studies under the instructions of Rev. Dr. Schaeffer, and, at every step of his progress, was the more strongly convinced that he was acting in accordance with the divine will.

Whilst he was engaged at Frederick, in the prosecution of his studies, in the year 1818, Rev. Abraham Reck, of Winchester, Virginia, who was in feeble health, wrote to Dr. Schaeffer, inquiring if he could not send him a theological student to aid him in the discharge of his laborious duties. In compliance with his request, Dr. Schaeffer sent young Mr. Krauth, who continued his studies under the direction of Pastor Reck, and assisted him in preaching the gospel and performing other pastoral labor. He studied under Mr. Reck one year, and the testimony of his preceptor is that, "He showed great comprehension of mind, and was a most successful student." "I gather," writes Rev. T. W. Dosh, "that, at this time, he frequently preached in the Lutheran Church, and was very popular with the people. He was highly respected for his uniform piety and zeal."

Mr. Krauth was licensed to preach the gospel by the Synod of Pennsylvania, at its meeting in Baltimore, in 1819. His first pastoral charge embraced the united churches of Martinsburg and Shepherdstown, Virginia, where he labored for several years most efficiently and successfully. It was at a District Conference, held in the church at Martinsburg, whilst Mr. Krauth was pastor, that the enterprise of a Theological Seminary, in connection with the General Synod, originated, and the first funds towards the object contributed. He was, in 1826, elected a member of its first Board of Directors. Dr. Morris, who, after his licensure, spent some days with him at his own residence in Martinsburg, thus speaks of him, at this interesting period of his life: "That week's intercourse was to me of great importance, as a young man of one and twenty. His conversation was so instructive, his counsels were so wise, his manners so gentle, his spirits so buoyant, that I learned more practical wisdom than in any other week of my life, and the visit begat in me the most ardent affection for him, who was afterwards my theological counsellor, my life-long associate in many a good work, and to his dying day my most cherished friend." "From that day," he adds, "our fraternal alliance was consummated, and amid all the ecclesiastical changes of the last thirty-five years, the sharp theological controversies, the personal estrangements, the doctrinal developments, the varying phases of thought, our intimate relations have not been interrupted for a single hour." In 1827 he received and accepted a call to St. Matthew's congregation, recently organized in Philadelphia.

The removal of Mr. Krauth to Philadelphia, in 1827, marks a new epoch, not only in the history of our English Lutheran interests in that city, but of his own life. Brought into new associations, surrounded by active, earnest, living men, with large libraries at his command, the best books on all subjects accessible, new powers seemed to be awakened within him, new energies were developed. As a scholar, a theologian and a preacher, he rapidly advanced, and made a deep impression upon the community. At first he encountered some opposition from the German Churches in the prejudices which existed, even at that day, against the introduction of the English language into the services of the sanctuary, but this all vanished when his character and object were better understood. With the German ministers, Drs. Schaeffer and Demme, he was on the most cordial and confidential terms. His relations with Dr. Demme were of the most intimate character, and continued years after Dr. Krauth left the city. "Their temperaments," says Dr. Morris, "were wholly diverse, but they harmonized delightfully in literary pursuits, in church polity and theological doctrine. Demme had the highest respect for our friend's talents and æsthetic taste, and he held, in profound esteem, Demme's genius and attainments. Many an evening it was my privilege to spend in their company, when wit and anecdote, and the most refined glee blended harmoniously with profound philosophic discussion, and the spontaneous outflow of the richest learning on their part. Demme knew all German philosophy, and Krauth, all literature." Dr. Demme's influence, at this time, on his character and studies, was most favorable, and always acknowledged. He ever referred to him with veneration and affection, and in that remarkable production delivered by him, at the request of the Directors of the Theological Seminary, on the Advantages of a Knowledge of the German Language, he expresses the most ardent gratitude to his benefactor, who had excited and aided him in his acquisitions in the direction of German literature. Dr. Krauth remained in Philadelphia six years, and during the whole period, enjoyed the highest reputation as a pastor and a preacher, gathering around him a large and devoted congregation, and accomplishing an amount of good that can scarcely be estimated.

In the year 1833, when Dr. Hazelius resigned his professorship in the Theological Seminary at Gettysburg, the attention of the Board of Directors was at once turned to Mr. Krauth as the man best qualified for the position. As a Hebraist he had not at the time, in the Church, his superior, the result of his own earnest, indefatigable application. He was unanimously chosen Professor of Biblical and Oriental Literature. The appointment was popular, and was regarded by the Church generally as most judicious. "His character and talents," said the *Lutheran Observer*, at the time edited by Dr. Kurtz, "have long been admired by his numerous friends. He is well known as a gentleman of science, of literature and of piety. He possesses great facility for the acquisition of languages, and has, for several years, paid particular attention to their study." But it was agreed that part of his time should be devoted to instruction in Pennsylvania College, with the understanding that so soon as the proper arrangements could be made his duties should be entirely confined to the Theological Seminary.

Professor Krauth was unanimously elected President of Pennsylvania College in the spring of 1834. The *United States Gazette*, edited by the Hon. J. R. Chandler, in noticing the appointment, said, "Mr. Krauth is known as a sound scholar, who ornaments piety with attainments in science and the arts. Under his supervision, which is never given by halves, we augur well for the new college."

The duties of this office he faithfully performed for nearly seventeen years, during most of the time also giving instruction in the Theological Seminary. With what untiring industry he labored, and how patiently and cheerfully he toiled, year after year, for the temporal and spiritual welfare of the young men committed to his care, only a few, those who were most intimately associated with him in his efforts, know. In all his relations, as president of the college, in his intercourse with the students, with his colleagues and the public, he was a model of Christian propriety and prudence, of humility and conscientiousness, of purity and honor, whom all could approach, whom none could reproach, always ready to listen and advise, considerate and kind, yet independent in his conclusions, and always firm and uncompromising when a question of principle was involved. A more judicious man in his official position, more delicate in his feelings and discreet in his conduct, could nowhere have been found. He brought to the consideration of every practical question, not only the rare qualities of his intellect, but also the impartial and just feelings of his heart. The history of the College, during his connection with it, furnishes an unerring proof of his fidelity and success as a presiding officer. The College graduated, during his presidency, one hundred and sixty-four young men, and of these one hundred and eight devoted themselves to the ministry of reconciliation. During this period, either directly or indirectly, there were brought under the influence of his instructions about one thousand individuals, many of whom here consecrated themselves to the Saviour and commenced their Christian life. Influences, during these seventeen years, were put in motion, imparting an influence to the Church which is, at the present day, moving millions of hearts to God.

On the resignation of Dr. Krauth as President of the College, in order that he might devote his exclusive time to duties in the Theological Seminary, which was the original design of his removal to Gettysburg, the Board of Trustees, in a unanimous vote, expressed "their high estimation of the fidelity with which he had discharged his duties during his long connection with the Institution," and their gratification, "that, by his continued residence in the place, he could still aid the College in promoting its success, by his council and co-operation."

In the autumn of 1850, yet in the vigor of manhood, he relinquished, with great satisfaction, the anxious, toilsome, and often ungrateful work of the College Presidency, for the more quiet, congenial and pleasant duties of theological instruction. Here he was in his element. Here he enjoyed repose. Devoted to his books, and fond of research, loved and revered by his pupils, he was happy and useful, an ornament to the position and a blessing to the Church. For five years, during his connection with the Seminary, he, also, served with great acceptance as pastor of the congregation, with which the Institutions are united. He continued his duties in the Theological Seminary until the close of life, delivering his last lecture to the Senior Class within ten days of his death, the subject, by a singular and interesting coincidence, being the Resurrection. He died May 30th, 1867, in the 71st year of his age, and the 49th of his ministry.

Although only a fortnight before he passed away, just after the anniversary of his birth day, he remarked to us that he had now reached his "three-score years and ten," the time spoken of by the Psalmist, and that his earthly career would probably soon terminate. His death was, nevertheless, unexpected. When summoned to his dying chamber, although so fragile in body, we found his mind remarkably clear and calm; he was scarcely able to speak, yet he was fully conscious, sustained by the promises of God's word and cheered by the faith he had so long and steadily professed. When we remarked that God was good to him, in that his mind was so composed and tranquil. "I am," he said, "very composed." Observing how patient he was in his occasional suffering, we added, "God will not impose upon you more than you can bear—He will not forsake you in this hour of trial,"—the prompt reply was, "His promises are, Yea and Amen!" His heart was full of Christian love towards all who approached him. It was a great privilege to behold his calm serenity, his unfaltering confidence in the Saviour, his trustfulness and humility, his perfect peace in prospect of the speedy change that awaited him. No one could witness the occasion without having his faith strengthened, his hopes confirmed, his affections elevated. The whole scene was indeed a benediction. To Dr. Brown, who inquired on taking leave of him, if he had a message for his colleagues and the students, he replied: "Tell them to be faithful, be faithful!" Dr. Muhlenberg having made an allusion to the sting of death and the victory of the grave being taken away, he said, after some interval: "Thanks be to God, who giveth us the victory through our Lord Jesus Christ!" A short time before his departure, whilst devoted friends were by his side watching his last pulsations, he was asked by the Pastor of the church, "Whether he was aware that his earthly troubles were nearly ended." Answering with a motion of the head in the affirmative, Dr. Hay inquired, "And how do you now feel in view of your approaching end?" "Calm!" "Calm!" he distinctly repeated. "Is Jesus still precious to you?" His glazed eye resumed its lustre and with a strong effort he exclaimed, "O yes!" When reference was made to the fact that this was the hallowed day on which many pious Christians were commemorating the Ascension of our Lord, and that he too was about to rise and meet his glorified Redeemer, and as several familiar and precious passages were repeated, his eye kindled with an expression of intense interest and grateful satisfaction. Although he had lost the power of utterance, his reason remained unclouded till the last. He was calm to the close. The spark of life very soon, however, ceased glowing—the good man had gone to his rest.

As the intelligence of his death spread, the deepest gloom pervaded the community. In every circle, among all classes and denominations, his name was mentioned with reverence, with the most tender affection. Never before in Gettysburg was there so great a public interest felt in any man's departure; never was there a death so universally regretted, so sincerely mourned. All felt that one of the excellent of the earth had been taken away. "Gladly would I exchange places with him," said a young man in the bloom of life, just commencing a successful business career, so high an estimate did he place upon the Christian character of this man of God. "If there be one place nearer the throne than another, he will be sure to occupy it," was the remark of a careful observer, who had long enjoyed his confidence, and been brought into constant contact with him. His funeral was numerously attended. Places of business were closed, ordinary work was suspended, and the whole population came out to testify their profound sorrow, to manifest their high appreciation of his services, and to pay their last tribute of respect to the lamented dead. The church in which for upwards of thirty years he had been a regular and devout worshipper, was heavily draped in mourning, and as the lifeless form of the partiarch lay in front of the pulpit, from which he had so often delivered God's message to attentive audiences, all seemed to realize the solemnity of the occasion. The services conducted by various ministers were most touching and impressive and calculated to inculcate the importance of holy living, as the only means of attaining a calm and peaceful death. The music chants were exquisitely sweet and sad, yet most tender and comforting to the soul. His associates in the Church tenderly carried his body to the grave.

The death of such a man as Dr. Krauth is no subject of common sorrow. Its tidings circulated, in a note of sadness, all over the Church. "*Multis ille bonis flebilis occidit.*" A great and good man," says the *Evangelical Lutheran*, "has been taken from our midst, and though we bow in submission to the will of Him who has called him away from the scene of his earthly labors, we cannot but feel that his death, to the Church, is more than an ordinary affliction." "He has left a memory," says the *Lutheran and Missionary*, "which will be precious forever." It is the memory of one who combined the highest intellectual powers with the most childlike piety, in whom profound learning was united with the deepest humility, who, in the pulpit and with the pen, in the chair of the theologian and in domestic life, never forgot the work to which he had been sanctified, and, untiring to the end, fulfilled the highest vocation given to man." "Honorable in his bearing," says the *Lutheran Observer*, "upright in all his intercourse with men, frank in the expression of his opinions, firm in adhering to what he deemed to be right, he commanded the respect and confidence of all who knew him." The testimony that reaches us from different sections of the Church, from men of all shades of opinion, from those who, for years, were associated with him in labor, is all of the same interesting character. Dr. Schmidt writes: "I knew him intimately, indeed, but with the feelings I entertained towards him, his name and character are something so sacred that I almost fear to speak of him. He was, in the strictest sense of the word, a Christian. Whatever other qualities he possessed, they were thoroughly pervaded, modified and controlled by the spirit of our holy religion, by consistent, practical Christianity. For me his character possessed attractions perfectly irresistible, and I loved him with an intensity that beggars description. Bitterly do I mourn his unexpected departure from among us." Dr. Reynolds says: "During the many years we have spent together, I do not now recall a single word of harshness or unkindness, a single act that was not that of a gentleman and a Christian. I seldom think of him otherwise than as one of the best and purest, as well as one of the most learned and eminently adapted to those posts of honor and responsibility which he so long occupied with no less honor to himself than profit to the numerous classes, both of the young and the old, whom he alike instructed and edified in the sacred desk and the Professor's chair." "My earliest and most pleasant recollections in the ministry," writes Dr. Lochman, "are associated with Dr. Krauth. Acquainted with him from my youth, I ever found him, in conversation, interesting and instructive; in the pulpit, earnest and devoted, and in his calling as Professor, faithful and diligent." "I have never thought of him," writes Rev. D. M. Gilbert, "except with an affection, mingled with respect, that amounts to veneration. His purity of heart, the tender kindness of his whole nature, his leniency towards the infirmities of others, his pleasant familiarity, tempered by a true Christian dignity, can never be forgotten. I have been trying to think over my past life, especially the six years spent under his roof, and I can honestly say that I have not one recollection of him that is not pleasant." "I have," says Rev. O. A. Kinsolving, of the Episcopal Church, "a most tender recollection of his earnest piety, his accurate knowledge, his genial good nature and simple, affectionate manners. In days gone by I knew and loved him dearly."

His mind was of the highest order, capacious, powerful in its grasp of subjects, active and discriminating. His analytic and reflective faculties were largely developed and strengthened by varied reading and diligent study. His perceptions were remarkably accurate and penetrating, so that whenever he undertook to investigate a question he was sure to attain the clearest ideas of it which its nature admitted. His mind was distinguished for the harmonious blending of all its powers. He was a man of mature, independent, sound judgment. He early acquired a love of research, a habit of thinking for himself, and his opinions were always formed with a deliberation, and in view of all the evidence he possessed. He was, also, gifted with a singularly retentive memory, in which were carefully treasured the results of his study and observation. He seemed to remember everything he ever heard, and often surprised his friends by the minute exactness of his knowledge. His attainments were much more extensive and varied, his erudition richer and more thorough than many persons imagined. He was a universal scholar, large-minded in his views, a man of the highest literary culture. He was acquainted with the best productions in the English language. The mathematics he read as another would an ordinary book. As a linguist he took the highest rank. The Sacred Scriptures he daily studied in the original. His intimacy with the Latin and Greek classics, which he read with almost the same facility as his vernacular, was maintained by frequent perusals to the close of life, and for the modern idea that would, in a course of liberal education, reject the study of these ancient authors, he entertained the most profound contempt. His knowledge of German literature and German theology was so general and thorough that a stranger would have supposed he had been educated at some German University. So conversant was he with the principles of Law and Medicine, so exuberant his information, that upon one unacquainted with his antecedents the impression was often produced that these subjects had been the exclusive studies of his life. He loved learning for its own sake. It was an absorbing passion, and he was never happier than when in his library among his treasured lore, or when discoursing with friends on his favorite topics. But, notwithstanding his acquisitions were so vast, and his resources so ample, his sense of propriety and æsthetic culture never allowed him to make a display of his knowledge. No trace of pedantry tinged his intercourse with others. "All sciolistic demonstration," says Dr. Morris, "was his abhorrence, and all pompous show, in the pulpit especially, was the object of his implacable disgust." A more unostentatious man, more modest and unassuming, never lived. This characteristic impressed itself upon everything he said and did, in public and private.

The honorary degree of Doctor of Divinity was, by a unanimous vote, conferred upon him by the University of Pennsylvania, in 1837.

In the pulpit Dr. Krauth was pre-eminent. It was the place where he loved to labor, where he especially excelled and wielded his great power. If he would have devoted himself entirely to the work, he would scarcely have had a rival in the country. Dr. Bittinger says: "Of his fluency in conversation, the lecture room, the pulpit—in the last rising to true Ciceronian eloquence —(and his face bore a striking resemblance to the great Roman orator, as witness the medals), it had to be heard and be compared with the stammerings and bogglings of other public and private talkers to be appreciated. Nor was it confined to his language only, his ideas were liquid. It seemed to make no difference what the topic was—Natural Theology, Metaphysics, Medicine, Chemistry or Anatomy." He had large intellectual resources from which to draw, and he would summon them to his aid as circumstances required. He always spoke to the purpose, never introducing anything irrelevant to the subject, or calculated to destroy its effect. His sermons were lucid, instructive and effective. There was, however, an inequality in his preaching, not so much in the matter presented as in the impression made. More than once he was heard to say that some of his more elaborate efforts were often received with less favor than a discourse preached from a text selected after he had entered the pulpit.

He was so full on every subject and so ready to communicate, that even when his preaching seemed to be extemporaneous it was not so; the matter had, perhaps, been carefully studied and laid on the shelf, as Cecil says, for future use, whenever demanded. He was often greatest as a speaker when called on without apparent premeditation to meet some special occasion. He was very much influenced by the inspiration of the hour or the state of his feelings. Dr. Morris refers to an interesting scene, which occurred ten years ago, in the Maryland Institute, whither he had accompanied him to a prayer-meeting, and where there were assembled not less than two thousand persons. The Doctor was, unexpectedly to himself, requested to speak; he, however, promptly responded to the invitation, and delivered, it is said, "one of the most thrilling and impressive addresses ever heard. The crowd, the place, the occasion, roused his inmost soul; the fire flashed in his eye, and the effect was powerful." When he had concluded the address, a Methodist clergyman arose and, with tearful eyes, praised God that, for the first time in thirty years, he, that day, was permitted to see the man who taught him the way of life and led his wandering feet to the cross of Christ. In prayer the Doctor was exceedingly happy. There was so much simplicity in his manner, so much humility and reverence, that you could not resist the impression he was speaking directly to the ear of mercy. One occasion we particularly remember. In the winter of 1837, when two, connected with him by the most tender ties, were under deep exercise of mind in reference to their spiritual interests, and he was called to lead the devotions of the great congregation; as with his warm, out-gushing heart, touched by the grateful fact, he thanked his Father in heaven "that bone of his bone and flesh of his flesh had been reached by the influence of the Spirit, the effect was thrilling. Many there are who will never forget that prayer, the impressions of that solemn hour. A gifted young man, a member of the Senior Class in College, reared in another Church, and, until that time, careless in relation to the salvation of his soul, was so completely overpowered that he shrieked out for mercy. That individual is now a prominent lawyer in the State, and an elder in the Presbyterian Church. Towards the close of his life, however, he sometimes expressed regret that he had not, to greater extent, made use of this medium for doing good. The contributions of his pen* were always received with favor and read with deference. "His Oration on the Study of the German," says Dr. Morris, " gave a fresh impulse to the study of that language among many of our young men, and to other students of literature in the country." His inaugural address, found among some old pamphlets in a country barn, arrested the attention of a young man, who gave his father no peace till he secured his consent to enter Pennsylvania College. He was graduated in 1844, and has since occupied prominent positions in the Church, and is most favorably known as a writer and preacher.

Dr. Schmidt observes: "His course was eminently irenic, but never at the expense of truth or principle. Honestly conservative and moderate in his views, he was just to all, and could meet and treat all who differed from him as brethren, even though they stood at opposite extremes." How often have we heard him say: "Uniformity of faith is attended with great difficulty. Let us cultivate peace, let us endeavor to be united and seek to do each other good. Let us endeavor to diffuse a spirit of concord and peace and God will bless us."

He studied the Scriptures constantly, earnestly, not merely as a source of theological knowledge, but as a means of spiritual culture. Under this influence his opinions were moulded, his spiritual life was matured. He loved the Lutheran Church. "As we grow older," he said, "we love it more, and whilst we sorrow for the apostacy of any of her sons, are horror-stricken when they treat her with disrespect, and we cling to her with increasing affection. She has been a good mother to us, and if within her walls we have been lean, it is our own fault. We expect to die in her service and honoring her virtues. Many have done excellently, but, *in our eyes* she excelleth them all."

---

* See a list of his writings in Bibliotheca Lutherana.

In his official discourse as President of the General Synod, delivered in Charleston in 1850, he says: "The desire for the Symbols of our Church, the attention that is paid to them, the admiration that is expressed for them, the candor with which they are viewed, the expressed willingness, on the part of many, only to dissent when it cannot be avoided, all indicate a new state of things, and are adapted to produce the conviction that the Church is disposed to renew her connection with the past, and in her future progress to walk under the guidance of the light which it has furnished." He was the warm friend of the General Synod. "His views in regard to the doctrines and cultus of the Church," says Dr. Lochman, "were always in perfect harmony with its position." He thought upon its basis, to use his own language, "the elements, somewhat discordant, of our Lutheran Zion could be held together." "Fidelity," he adds, "to the principle of the General Synod, is the only guarantee of a peaceful and prosperous Church." "The great question for our Church in this country is, can it be a unit, bound together in a common bond? If for unity, absolute agreement in all the minutiæ of Christian doctrine, government and ceremonies, is necessary, it is certain that it is not possible. But if substantial agreement in faith and practice is regarded as sufficient there can be no great difficulty. In most of our large denominations of Christians there is more or less diversity of opinion on doctrinal points." "If the Symbolism of any in the General Synod be so intense that they cannot tolerate those who differ from them, they can go to Missouri, to Buffalo, to Iowa, to Columbus. It is what we under similar circumstances would do ourselves—no disrespect is meant. If there are those whose antipathy to the Symbols is so great that they cannot endure those who venerate and *ex animo* subscribe them, they should look for some more congenial home. They have no right to say to the strict Symbolist, your position is *unlutheran*, your views are destitute of vital piety, you occupy untenable ground, you ought to be in some other Church. Mutual toleration is the correct principle. If this cannot be exercised, then let there be a peaceful separation and those unite who think alike and are prepared to act in perfect harmony. * * * We have no hesitation in affirming, that harmony is compatible with considerable diversity of opinion. Some concession in non-fundamental matters and forms of worship and a proper comparison of views on doctrinal differences would contribute much to smooth movement and peaceful progression.' He thought there was no excuse for "the heated strife," "the narrow bigoted spirit," "the condemnatory language," "the misrepresentation of views," "the wretched caricature," so often exhibited among members of the same Christian household. If we could not labor harmoniously together, then he deemed "separation necessary and profitable; in the end it might be conducive to the glory of God." His views were eminently conservative. He did not object to the use of the word. "The true position of the Lutheran Church," he says, "is conservative. It should hold fast the form of sound words it has received and display its doctrinal and ritual moderation. Occupying a middle position between prelatical Episcopacy and *jure divino* Congregationalism; extreme neither in one direction nor the other; conceding to utility all that it can ask without detriment to order, avoiding in doctrine the errors of Calvinism and those of low Arminianism and Pelagianism; repudiating a mere animal religion, while it shows no countenance to a morality, cold and religionless—these, its true position, its very essence and form, adapt it to exert an influence favorable to doctrinal soundness and religious purity. We do not claim for it too much when we ascribe to it a capacity to uphold a true, living system of Christianity, when we regard it as adapted to exert an influence opposed to extremes in the one direction or the other.

Dr. Krauth was a man of very attractive personal qualities. He was a model of integrity and propriety of the duties and graces he inculcated. In his daily walk, in his social relations, in the class room, the sanctuary and the pulpit, was seen the beautiful harmony between his teachings and his life. He was constituted with a large share of benevolent feeling. It shone in his countenance, it breathed from his lips, it found expression in his kind manners, it pervaded his whole nature. He cherished no resentments. His utter unselfishness ever prompted him to forget himself when there were opportunities offered of doing good. "His zeal involved no element of self." He seemed unconscious of his own interests. He was always ready to make sacrifices, and to confer favors with a cheerfulness and self abnegation rarely equalled. Although so kind and sympathetic in his nature, and so observant of the proprieties of life, he still had a strong sense of right and wrong, and when he was deeply impressed with the idea of evil-doing he knew how to give utterances to his feelings in solemn and indignant rebuke. Honor with him was a cardinal virtue. He abhorred meanness. He despised duplicity. His devotion to principle was a most prominent trait in his character. We never heard him charged, even in a whisper, with any unworthy conduct, with an attempt to accomplish a purpose by a circuitous route, or an equivocal course, with seeming to be intent on the attainment of one end, whilst his efforts were really directed to another. From all such manifestations his purity revolted. "In him," says Dr. Schmidt, "there was no seeming, no hollow pretence, not a particle of sham. Whatever personal peculiarities he had they were rooted in a sincerity so decided and transparent that distrust and suspicion in the minds of any who approached him were instantly disarmed, and confidence, unbounded, claimed and won. It was the fundamental property of a crystalline sincerity, which combined with the warm impulses of a generous and loving heart, made him so inestimable a friend." "Such," says Dr. Morris, "was my perfect confidence in the integrity of his character, the sincerity of his motives and the soundness of his judgment, that I would have taken it for granted, without ever knowing the circumstances of the case, that any one who had a quarrel with him was in the wrong." His love of justice and truth, of candor and fair dealing, and his hatred of injustice and falsehood, of deceit and fraud, were always manifest. His private life was without reproach. No shadow of suspicion rested upon it. No spot was left upon the perfect enamel of his character. Even malice could not stain its whiteness. He was a most instructive and genial companion. Although to strangers somewhat reserved, when in the society of intimate friends he would pour forth his stores of wisdom, kind feeling, apposite anecdote, rich illustration and quick repartee. "In an eminent degree he possessed that humor," says Dr. Schmidt, "which, never running into sarcasm, or ever indulging in ill-natured insinuation or offensive remark, 'illumines the feast of reason and the flow of soul' with unexpected sallies of pleasantry, and provokes the hearty laugh with witty sayings and Socratic questionings." There was nothing illiberal in his character or uncharitable in his temper; no affectation of austere rigor in his life, no narrowness of party or sect—"he knew no tinge of bigot bitterness."

But the secret of his attractive qualities, his beautiful life and eminent usefulness, lay in the depths of his religious convictions, in the power of the gospel to transform and exalt character, in his consistent, uniform and all pervading piety. Mind, heart and religious feeling were in unison. His whole life, since his first espousal of the cause of Christ, had been an uninterrupted course of devotion to its interests. Trained in daily duty, religion became the ascendant power of his soul. It was not a mere abstraction or a dogma, but a life nourished from an inward supply, and not by superficial, transitory causes. It had acquired the power of a habit and the force of a regulating principle. It pervaded his whole character. It was carried by him into every position, and his very presence was felt as an atmosphere of holiness and a rebuke to sin. In his conversation, in social communion, in casual and uninterrupted intercourse, he appeared the deeply spiritual and devoted man of God, in the habitual exercise of a living faith, an example of Christian piety and excellence, fruitful in good works, which it was refreshing to behold. To his mind there was nothing gloomy connected with the subject of religion. It hrd no dark side. It was associated with all that was designed to invigorate the intellect, elevate the affections and brighten life, to make the soul glad, and enable it to look with strong hope on all the events of this chequered life.

CHARLES R. DEMMÉ, OF PHILADELPHIA.

Dr. Demmé would have had a reputation as a pulpit orator equal that of any man in the country, if he had been a preacher in English. He had extraordinary gifts as a speaker, and then his matter was on a level with his manner; for he conscientiously studied and wrote out most of his sermons in full, and diligently studied the best models. He was far from being a handsome man, but, when in the full glow of excitement, his countenance was lighted up radiantly, and his strong features assumed a most pleasing appearance. His eyes flashed while he poured forth burning words, and the mere man seemed to be lost in the intense feeling of his heart. His theme absorbed him so completely that he saw nobody and heard nothing but his own sonorous voice as it rolled through the arches of the church and fell in impressive peals upon the ears of his audience.

His few published sermons are fine specimens of classic German writing and crammed with the soundest theology, but it was necessary to hear the man to appreciate his wonderful pulpit ability.

I have heard him preach on a hot summer day, and to a comparatively thin audience, with the same fervor as he would have done to a multitude, and he afterwards observed that he did not wonder that people would not come to church in such intensely warm weather.

He was a thoroughly educated man, and perfectly at home in the modern theology of the Church.

He enjoyed the high distinction of being a member of the American Philosophical Society, and was created a Doctor of Divinity by the University of Pennsylvania, in 1832.

He bore in one cheek the mark of a sabre stroke he received in the battle of Waterloo. He, with many other young Germans, volunteered to repel the invasion of Napoleon, and at Waterloo he was carried wounded and bleeding from the field. Intimate as I was with him for some years, yet he never alluded to his youthful military adventures. Indeed he seldom spoke of himself in any relation.

He was not friendly to the General Synod, more, I think, from personal feelings than peculiar views of church policy, and still the directors of the Theological Seminary of the General Synod elected him professor in 1840, which he, however, declined after a long and painful struggle. I well remember how he came to Baltimore to have a midnight conversation with me upon the subject. Strenuously as I advocated his election, yet I candidly told him the difficulties he would encounter on the ground of social relations in Gettysburg, and of associations with men who were differently trained and held intense American views of theology and church policy. I knew that he did not hold a few men in high personal esteem with whom he would have been closely connected.

He was greatly respected by the cultivated people of Philadelphia, and zealously co-operated with other denominations in the furtherance of benevolent enterprises and of the interests of education. He unsparingly denounced duplicity and every species of meanness, especially in ministers; but to honest men, whatever might be their convictions, and however they differed from his, he was courteous and forbearing.

He was a powerful debater on the floor of the Synod, and often had strong opponents. He wielded great influence, but never aspired to the place of demagogue, or even to the less objectionable honors of a party leader.

He was a man of strong impulses, and when excited he was impatient of contradiction, unless he was very politely opposed; then he was kind and even gentle. Whilst distantly respectful to those whom he did not esteem, or whose sincerity he suspected, he never led them to believe by word or action that he had any regard for them. He would praise modest merit discreetly, but he never flattered the charlatan, nor, for a moment, gave place to the insincere and presumptuous. Like other great preachers he had his imitators, but none came up to the grand original.

The last time I saw Dr. Demme was at the Synod of Pennsylvania, in Harrisburg, about the year 1857. He had already begun to fail, and he spoke freely of it. It seemed to mortify him that he called things by wrong names, and he gave some instances of it. Like a strong forest tree he began to fail at the top. That active brain was smitten, and part after part gave way, until he fell prostrate among the oaks that surrounded him.

Among his many other personal accomplishments, he was a thorough musician and splendid performer on the piano. He played with the skill of a master, and read the most difficult score at sight. I have put his facility in reading music to the test in my own parlor, and we were all surprised at the almost faultless accuracy of his performance, and yet he would say, "It's not very hard." See an extensive biographical sketch by Prof. Stoever in Ev. Rev., July, 1864.

to the Eastern States and his extensive correspondence with some of their learned men made him widely known.

He shaped and moulded the theological thought of most of the young men of the General Synod, which, unfortunately, I think, was not in strict accordance with the old Lutheran model. Like most professors of a peculiar system, some of his pupils went far ahead of him in one direction and became the advocates of the lowest Zwinglianism, whilst in others a reaction was created, and to his surprise and regret they became Old Lutherans.

Dr. Schmucker was an organizer and wrote nearly all the constitutions of Synods, Seminaries and of other institutions, which were required at that early day. He also well knew how to govern a certain numerous class of men. Some of them, however, refused to join the ranks, and others stepped out when they began to reflect for themselves. He was the most indefatigable man I ever knew—he never ceased work when at home and carried his work with him when he left. He was always busy on a liturgy, or constitution or something else connected with the Church, and would talk day and night about them without cessation. Even while sojourning at watering places during the summer, where he usually met some Lutheran ministers, he would draw out his manuscripts and expect that men who had come for recreation should submit to the discussion of the subject. A few of them impatiently shook him off. I once crossed the Atlantic with him, and I can safely affirm that not a day passed on which the everlasting theme was not introduced. Even when he was suffering from sea-sickness, it seemed to be a relief to him to talk about General Synod, Liturgy, Constitution, Seminary and certain men. It was not only talk, for that might have been endured, but it was discussion, controversy, scrutiny which required tension of thought to follow, and being at sea is not the place nor time for prolonged and logical thinking. I used to get rid of what really was an annoyance by looking out of the cabin window and exclaiming "whale!" "whale!" and rush up on deck to find my whale was nothing but a dark wave or a floating mast of some wrecked vessel, but it answered my purpose for the time.

As a theologian he had read many of the writings of our older authors, and was originally trained in the schools of Mosheim, Reinhard, Storr and Flatt, and others of the same modified type. He adopted their views on the Sacraments and strongly defended them in an "Appendix to the Doctrine of the Eucharist" on page 328, Vol. II of the first edition of his Storr and Flatt. He designated Reinhard's illustration of the Lord's Supper as "lucid and philosophical," and gives it his hearty assent. Dr. S. subsequently changed his views, and in his numerous writings labored to depreciate the old Confessional system of the Church, and even to disparage those sections of the Confessions themselves which teach the Lutheran doctrine of the Sacraments. He was all along a sturdy defender of the Church's interests as he understood them, and his influence on her progress was marked and decisive. He, with some others who did not know what they were doing, signed an appeal, which was sent to Europe in 1846, which disparaged the Lutheran doctrine of the Lord's Supper, and which strongly prejudiced the minds of many German theologians against him, and which they did not conceal during his visit to Europe in that year.

Never was a more senseless blunder committed. Whilst the Appeal may have been in conformity to the theological opinions of some in the United Church of Prussia, yet there were thousands of Lutherans who would not sanction it theologically. The United could not understand how men professing such doctrines or denying the fundamental principles of Lutheranism, could honestly call themselves Lutherans, for they have high notions of consistency abroad, and the Old Lutherans could not recognize men as such who had given up the distinctive points. The result was, to my personal knowledge, that when Drs. Schmucker and Kurtz went to Europe in 1846, not one of them was invited to preach in any pulpit on the Continent! This *I know* to be true, for I was with them. They were treated courteously enough, but neither Lutheran, nor Reformed, nor United, asked them into their pulpits. This appeal had been sent out before them, and had been extensively published. Tholuck and I had a conversation about it, and the worst he said of it was that before it was published in Germany he and some others rewrote it in pure and classic German. Dr. S. was aware of this, and said to me, "that he never in his life tried harder to write good German," but after all it sounded very much like a translation from English into German, which I presume it was, and it abounded in American Saxonisms.

When Dr. S. left Princeton Seminary he was the best educated young man in the Church, and had claims upon the most respectable pulpit, but there was no English pulpit vacant at that time. He could preach plain German, but there was no place in the central section of the church which needed his services. He took charge of an obscure pastorate in Shenandoah Co., Va., where his youthful appearance, his fluent speech, well prepared sermons and freshness of manner, secured for him a high popularity among the few cultivated people of that region outside of our church. Before his coming they had the poorest quality of preaching from ignorant Dunkers, bigoted Baptists, uneducated Methodists and untaught Lutherans. When young Schmucker came it was like fresh viands after a dreary winter of stale provision. A few days after his settlement he was invited to attend a funeral of some prominent man in the county. He had carefully prepared a sermon on "Blessed are the dead," &c. He was preceded by an old illiterate Baptist, who selected the same text and bungled through a very lame discourse. Schmucker was uneasy when he heard the announcement, fearing that the man would exhaust the subject and leave nothing for him to say; but he soon discovered that the man did not understand the text and made terrible work of the theme. He gained confidence as the man proceeded, and when the harrangue was finished the preacher announced that there "was a young man present who would add a few words." Schmucker arose and said, that the preacher *for want of time probably* had left some points of the text untouched, which he would supplement. He preached his whole sermon, and created an astounding sensation. He was an entire stranger, and every body asked who that young man was? From that day his reputation was established. I have often heard him tell this story with great glee. He never was pastor of any other church, and left this after a few years, when he was elected to the Seminary. Hence he never had much pastoral experience, and encountered none or very few of the difficulties of a long pastoral life.

Preaching was not Dr. S's. special province. He seldom preached from choice and never at night after he went to the Seminary. In the course of forty years he did not preach at night. Occasional sermons, and at special times, he rather delighted in, and has produced some excellent discourses of this character. He was clear and logical in his treatment of the subject, but his language is almost wholly destitute of figurative illustration or rhetorical beauty. He had no imagination, and all his discussions especially are dry, hard logic. Hence while he was pleasing as a speaker, no hearer was ever moved by his sermons.

As a teacher he was not interesting, though he had a complete mastery of his subject, yet he failed to awaken enthusiasm in his pupils. He was not socially inclined to them, and admitted few to intimacy with him. He was constantly at work and had no time for the amenities of life.

He was not always on cordial terms with his colleagues in the Faculty, and several resignations were the result.

It cannot be doubted that to Dr. Schmucker the Church is much indebted for the respectable position it assumed and the progress it made during the early part of his career. He had a noble ambition to elevate its character by the development of its resources, and he succeeded. He was indefatigable in his labors to promote what he conceived to be its best interests. I never knew a man more wholly given up to the prosecution of his plans. He read none of the popular books on science or literature, which most cultivated clergymen indulge in for recreation from more severe studies and to keep abreast of the progress of mind, but his entire time, day and night, at home and elsewhere, was devoted to his favorite pursuits of writing, planning, begging and talking for the Church.

As an author he was prolific. More than forty distinct publications have issued from his pen, besides ten or twelve articles in the Evangelical Review. Some of his later works are chiefly remodelings of the earlier, so that for the last fifteen years of his life he produced nothing absolutely new of permanent value.

His Appeal on Christian Union, published first in Andover, 1838, was republished in London, and contributed in no small degree in bringing about the World Alliance, held in London in 1846. I heard Dr. King, an eminent dissenting minister, openly declare on the platform in London that to Dr. Schmucker belongs much of the credit of originating and promoting that great movement.

When I was in Germany with Dr. S., in 1846, I was frequently asked by theologians, who was considered the most learned man of our native American Lutheran divines, and I invariably replied, "Dr. Schmucker." "Where was he educated?" "In the United States, at Philadelphia and Princeton." Now, when it is considered what they meant by a *learned* man, and knew little or nothing of our institutions, and, perhaps, rightly thought that no man could ever become *learned*, in their sense, out of Germany, no wonder they shrugged their shoulders and looked unconvinced. I followed it up by remarking that an American with less than half the book learning they had would be more efficient in the church and pulpit than a dozen of them together, at which they smiled incredulously.

Dr. S. deserves the credit of being the originator of Pennsylvania College, as he had been of the Gymnasium previously. For the "old academy," in which the latter was held before the college building was erected, he became personally responsible by either advancing the money or endorsing the notes. It was by his untiring efforts that the charter was secured from the legislature of Pennsylvania.

He was also greatly instrumental in arranging the complicated affairs of the Emmans Institute, and in a lengthy report displayed his acute business aptitude to a remarkable degree.

Of the hundreds of our ministers who have been partly or wholly trained for their work by Dr. S., I can claim the distinction of having been his pupil at an earlier period than any of them. After he had left the Seminary at Princeton, he took the temporary charge of the York Academy, and there it was that I received from him my final preparation for the Sophomore class at Princeton College. He was at that time a young man of twenty, of fair complexion, meagre visage, of vigorous health and of exceedingly staid deportment. Some people would have called his bearing dignified, but, young as I was, I set it down as ascetic, unsocial, recluse, and I was right. He was a laborious student and had no intimate companions. He did not frequent the society of young ladies, nor indeed of any class of people, and hence was not what is called a popular young man. Everybody regarded him as a model of perfection, as far as purity of morals was concerned, but nobody was intimate enough with him to regard him as a friend. He was considerably ahead of most, if not all, the young candidates for our ministry in theological and classical training of that day, for let not my readers forget that in 1819, or thereabouts, our whole list of ministers did not reach two hundred, and the number of students was very small.

At that remote day the cry for ministerial help was not as loud as it has since become. There were few vacant churches that were clamorous for a pastor. All the old districts were served and new ones were seldom formed. The idea of aggressiveness would have created dismay in the brain of these venerable fathers. They were content with things as they were, and a little more so. Hence when young Schmucker came home well furnished and ready for work there was no room for him. To employ his time he took charge of the York Academy until Providence would open an effectual door. I presume it was very mortifying to our young, and at that time, accomplished theologue, to be permitted to remain on the stocks so long after he was ready to be launched, but, gentle reader, remember this was fifty years ago. Things have changed a little since. Now most of our students are engaged to churches and otherwise *engaged* (unfortunately for some of them) to other people, before they leave the Seminary. Then our most promising young men had to wait until some old minister died or became too feeble to serve his ten or twelve churches before they could get employment.

Nicholas Schmucker, a godly, recluse old minister, the uncle of our subject, was pastor of a large district in Shenandoah and adjacent counties in Virginia. He preached only German, and was a perfect specimen of the old school of ministers. Exceedingly simple and even primitive in his habits, never going beyond the bounds of his parish, unknown to the outside world, yet his religious life, his ministerial fidelity and his blameless demeanor are to this day the theme of the people of that region. He relinquished the charge of four of his churches and prevailed upon the people to call his nephew as their minister. He accepted, and so we see the highly educated Princetonian, the classmate of men who afterward became Bishops McIlvaine and Johns, and of other eminent divines, tracing his steps to an obscure section of Virginia, to labor among a people not far advanced in intellectual refinement, of primitive simplicity and of exceedingly rural culture. A man of his mental endowment had never before ministered in that particular region. There were ministers and good men too, after their sort, but here was a young man, a handsome young man, a thoroughly educated young man, taking the pastoral care of churches who had never seen the like before. The same may be said of the minister; he had never seen the like before.

After he had been settled there several years he conceived the idea of establishing a sort of Pro-Seminary. This was in 1823, and it gradually led to the founding of the schools we now have at Gettysburg. Here, the second time, I became the pupil of S. S. Schmucker. There were five other young men who constituted the class, and a miscellaneous crowd it was. I mean that we were in every stage of preparation; one was a college graduate, another could spell but a few words of the Greek Testament, and a few others had the same difficulty with English. But they were all trained to be useful men. The mode of teaching was not very systematic, and we toddled along after a very remarkable fashion.

Our teacher was at that time engaged in translating the Theology of Storr and Flatt, which was published at Andover, and which reached a second edition with some alterations, as shall be noticed hereafter. He was a most untiring worker, and, being a widower, he had not the cares of a household, not even taking his meals in the parsonage. He thus devoted *his whole time* to his books. I never knew him to take a walk or do anything else for mere exercise. He did not seem to require it; at least I never knew him to suffer from severe confinement to head work. He had no visitors to annoy him, and was very impatient of intruders. His study was in a remote part of the house from ours, and I do not think one of us darkened the door of that sacro-sanctum in a month. So neither did he ever enter our workshop except once a day at recitation. He had no time for social intercourse, and we had none to hear a lecture on propriety.

During Mr. Schmucker's residence at New Market he accepted a call from a small number of people in Georgetown, D. C., to establish an English church in that place. It was a most auspicious time. Those of our people who had gone to other churches were ready to come home again if young Schmucker would become their leader. If he had done so we would now have a large church in that city. But what changed his mind? In the mean time a seminary had been spoken of. He was destined to be the head of it. After a hard struggle it was located at Gettysburg. He was chosen, and the acceptance to Georgetown was given up. He went to Gettysburg in 1826, and had a class of seven students the first year. Here, for the third time, I became his pupil for a very brief period.

His lectures were delivered in the old academy building until the seminary was built. Even at that early period he displayed an extent of reading and profundity of research that utterly astonished the raw youngsters, and would have called out the admiration of more intelligent men.

He here maintained the same retired and, what I would call, unsocial life of his earlier days, being exclusively given to his intellectual work. Once or twice a year, perhaps, he would accept an invitation to tea, but he regarded it as a bore, because it robbed him of a few hours of study. I am now speaking of the olden time. Whether he changed his ascetic habits in later times I do not know. He may have done so after he resigned his place in the seminary, but probably not before.

I never knew a man who needed and took less relaxation from severe mental toil than he. He never laid aside a subject he was working at because he had grown weary of it. He seemed not to require that variety or change of subject that so many other head-workers find necessary to quicken their brain or give it a pause. It is true that in later life he sometimes went to "the Springs," but he took his work with him and labored as hard as ever. One of our divines told me that he once met Dr. S. at Bedford. He was tinkering at the "interminable" Liturgy or some other Synodical machine, and insisted upon my friend hearing it read and helping him to "fix the thing up." He would annoy him by questions and bother him with difficulties, all the while as calm as an August morning, upon which my friend lost his patience and curtly said, "Dr. S., I have come here for relaxation. I want to lay aside all perplexing subjects, and I won't listen to you any longer." Now this was a state of mind of which Dr. S. had no conception, because he had no experience of it. With him it was work, work, all the time, without rest or cessation.

Dr. S. was the severest moralist I ever knew, and carried his principles, I think, to an extreme length. He objected to some amusements which a wiser age now sanctions, and opposed some recreations which the church now approves. He did not know one card from another. I do not suppose he ever had a dice box in his hand, even for amusement. He knew nothing of chequers or backgammon or chess. He never was in a theatre or circus; never heard an opera. He even doubted the propriety of Christians going to hear famous vocalists in a concert hall, especially if they had appeared on the operatic stage. He never used tobacco in any form. He never drank a drop of strong liquor as a beverage. He never conformed to any modern fashion in dress for fashion's sake, however neat and appropriate it might be.

He was the most imperturbable man I ever knew. Nothing could throw him off his guard. He would appear calm under the most violent assaults, and would repel an attack with an apparent mildness and unconcern which were remarkable. In the midst of the most excited debate, when everybody else around him was at fever heat, he was as cool as a frosty morning. This disposition gave him great advantage in debate, and he well knew how to use it to the best advantage. It is an old saying, that the man who first gets mad in a dispute is sure to have the wrong side; it is not universally true, for our friend was often wrong, and everybody knew it, and yet his very imperturbability would sometimes provoke his opponent to more violent language and manner than the occasion justified.

I never knew a man who had such perfect self-control. Associated with him for many years in Synods, meetings of boards, committees, conventions of every kind and degree, and sometimes under trying circumstances, when the discussion was warm and his positions were most vehemently, and, on some occasions, bitterly assailed, yet he never gave outward evidence that his temper was ruffled or his equanimity disturbed. I once was present when a violent assault was made upon his motives, and the severest objurgation hurled at him by a very influential man; yet Dr. S. did not even change countenance, nor did he retort in any other manner than by calmly observing that his assailant was no better than he was. This perfect self-possession gave him great advantage in animated discussion. Whilst everybody else around him was excited, he was serene and unmoved. Whilst his opponents spluttered and scolded and threatened, or ridiculed and sneered, he appeared to be as emotionless as an iceberg. The calmness of his reply often gained votes which his argument of itself would have failed to do. Men whose thinking he did for them voted with him because they thought he was badly treated.

He was a most ready and fluent debater. I never knew him to be at a loss for a word, and the right word also, and he seldom recalled one. He had a happy faculty of clearing up difficulties, and an equally dangerous one of sometimes holding back light when it was wanted. I merely mean that he did not tell all he knew when it was not necessary.

His unremitting devotion to his books and his love of undisturbed solitude did not interfere with the duties of hospitality.

On all occasions his house was open to his friends, and he dispensed the bounties of his table with gentlemanly grace and liberality.

On one occasion, during a visit of Dr. S. to Baltimore, he and I were sitting in Dr. Kurtz's study when the physician of our State Insane Asylum entered. He was introduced to Dr. S., but did not hear his name distinctly, and said to Dr. K., "I have come to inquire about a book on Psychology, by one of your ministers named Schmucker. I should like to see it, and I presumed you had it." I immediately said, "Dr. Fonerden, you have just been introduced to the author of it." Of course there was surprise and mutual gratification. Dr. S. was naturally much pleased, and from that time these two students of mental philosophy became good friends.

TRIBUTE TO DR. SCHMUCKER.

The following tribute to the memory of S. S. Schmucker, D. D., as an enlightened and consistent advocate of Christian Union among Protestants, constitutes the introduction of the address delivered by Dr. F. W. Conrad before the Evangelical Alliance on Interchange of Pulpits:

Dr. Schmucker commenced the study of the subject of Christian union more than half a century ago. The matured results of these studies were given to the world in his "Fraternal Appeal" to the American churches, which was first published in 1838, and subsequently passed through several editions in a revised and enlarged form. It was extensively circulated in England and America, awakened a deep interest in the subject, received favorable notice from the religious press, and numerous testimonials from many of the most distinguished divines of the different Protestant denominations. It is an admitted fact that the "Appeal" of Dr. Schmucker bore a prominent part in preparing the way for the organization of the Evangelical Alliance in 1846. He was present at its first meeting, and was even then designated as "the father of the Alliance," by Dr. King, of Ireland, in a public address delivered in London at that time. It was he also who moved already, at that first meeting of the Alliance, that its second meeting should be held in New York; and, although his motion was not adopted at that time, nevertheless it was carried out practically twenty-seven years later, as the present sixth conference of the Alliance here happily attests.

Dr. Schmucker took special interest in the subject of Christian union, and labored for its promotion, through the Evangelical Alliance, during the greater portion of his ministerial and professional life. As he approached the portals of eternity during his declining years his mind and heart were more and more absorbed by it, and he prepared a plan for the confederation of all Protestant denominations in an Evangelical Alliance of the entire Christian world. This plan was published, and favorably noticed by a number of religious journals of different denominations in this country during the past year, and a copy of it has been laid before the committee of the Alliance for their consideration. He looked forward to this meeting with ardent solicitude, and expected to be present to submit his plan of confederation before the Alliance in person.

The last letter I received from him had reference to the subject of Christian union, and contained a request that the speaker should, in his absence, take charge of his plan for the confederation of the churches of Protestant Christendom, and present it for consideration at the meeting of the General Synod of the Lutheran Church. But God, in his all-wise providence, so ordered that his strong desire to take part in this conference could not be gratified. On the 26th of July last, after entertaining friends at his house in the evening, he was suddenly seized with heart disease, and before midnight died, in the conscious hope of a blissful immortality. His last words were: "I have lived and am dying in the faith of Jesus."

DEATH OF DR. SCHMUCKER.

Last week's edition of THE OBSERVER announced to the church the sudden death of the most widely known and one of the most revered of her ministry. The funeral services of the deceased were attended in Christ Church, Gettysburg, on Tuesday evening, July 29th, at 5 o'clock. The church was appropriately draped in mourning, and a large number of personal friends and acquaintances of the deceased, and also a goodly number of the neighboring ministers, nearly all formerly his students, had assembled to do reverence to the memory of a distinguished and truly good man before his mortal body would be committed to the grave.

After an appropriate funeral chant by the choir, Rev. D. P. Rosenmiller, of Lancaster, read the Scripture, selected from I

Cor. xv, and I Thes. iv. Rev. Dr. Valentine offered prayer, and the choir sang "Rest, Spirit Rest."

Rev. Dr. Hay, pastor of the church, made the opening remarks. "A family bond was now broken. The church of Christ had now lost one of her most self-denying ministers; our own church one of her most distinguished members. He had been the first on the ground in establishing our Lutheran institution, and of the zealous and faithful band who labored so many years he was the last to pass away. Dr. Schmucker had frequent and unmistakeable premonitions of his approaching death, but found in them no occasion for alarm or distress. He died as he would have chosen—at home, in the bosom of his family. Though not disposed to place great importance on the last words of the dying, those of the deceased form precious testimony to his character—"I have lived and I am dying in the faith of Jesus." He needs no eulogy, but that noble witness which is on all sides, the traces of his life of successful work. The speaker then referred to the works of the venerable father for his own denomination, and to the efforts which continued through life to advance the desire for church union. Undoubtedly he has now no regrets for his labors to anticipate the union which takes place above."

Rev. Dr. Lochman, of York, for many years a friend, and in church work a noble associate of Dr. Schmucker, said: "The announcement of his death came like a flash of lightning in a clear summer sky. As once was said on earth in sweetest tones, so now we may hear the consoling utterance, "our friend sleepeth." We may reply as was done then: "Lord, if he sleepeth he shall do well." Cherished friends, cherished landmarks, may pass away, but never can the heart's cherished memory forget the revered names of Krauth, Baugher, Stoever, Jacobs, Schmucker.

"He did much to raise the standard of education, giving to the church men qualified for her ministry and equal to those in any church in the land.

"Though not the founder of the General Synod, yet when the effort of the fathers for its establishment had failed, his encouraging and persevering efforts effected its organization. Though dead, he is still laboring. To have left such a record as he has done was worth living for; to set up landmarks for all time, to utter sentiments that will thrill the hearts of thousands in the

Master's work. Death is a silent and powerful preacher, which here eloquently speaks to us through the departed friend."

Rev. Dr. Morris, of Baltimore, related several interesting reminiscences of his early and since then constant and intimate intercourse with Dr. Schmucker, first as his instructor in the York Academy, where Dr. S. taught shortly after leaving Princeton Seminary; then of the first year of Dr. S. as Professor in the Seminary at Gettysburg; the class numbered fourteen, of whom five are now alive. All who had known him could say, with a former fellow-citizen of Gettysburg: "The more I know of Dr. S. the more pleased I am with him." Though men might not agree with him in all things, yet they were compelled to respect and revere him. He filled a larger space in this country than any other Lutheran clergyman, and was everywhere the representative of our church, and a worthy one he was. Many years ago the speaker had heard Dr. King, an eminent dissenting clergyman of England, in a public address in London, ascribe the paternity of the evangelical alliance to Dr. Schmucker. The objects of this alliance Dr. S. ever held dear, and only a few weeks ago—speaking of the approaching meeting in New York—had said to the speaker: "I will go there to carry out, if I can, by God's help, my own sentiments." Who will be his biographer? To recount his life will be to give the history of the Lutheran Church in America."

As the successor of Dr. S. as chairman of the Theological Faculty, Rev. Dr. Brown, in a few remarks, bore witness to the kindly sympathy and hearty support which Dr. S. had ever given him in his official position, everywhere with cordial kindness, speaking even flatteringly of him, thus affording him much comfort and support in his laborious position." Rev. Dr. Baum, of York, chairman of the Seminary Board, in behalf of the board said: "We thank God for the life and ministry of Dr. Schmucker. During all the nearly forty years of the active connection of Dr. S. with the Seminary fullest harmony had existed between him and the board. Hardly a measure he had proposed but had met with their approval. Few had filled such a place as he had done."

The choir then sang "Asleep in Jesus," after which the body was borne to its last resting place, followed by a number of relatives and many friends. At the grave the solemn funeral service was read, and the last service of love for the body of Dr. Schmucker was performed, but his memory will ever be held dear to loving hearts. The pall-bearers were Revs. L. A. Gotwald and A. H. Sherts, of Chambersburg; P. Anstadt, of York; S. Yingling and G. Parsons, of Hanover, and C. L. Keedy, of Waynesboro.

E. S. B.

The following is from one of his earlier pupils:

"I first saw him in York, Pa., in 1825 or '26. He preached for his father in German in the morning, and in English at night. He was then a young man of very youthful appearance, and his preaching made a deep impression on my mind. But my intimate acquaintance with him properly began on the 28th of March, 1828, when I became a student at Gettysburg. He was then sole Professor of the Seminary, and Rev. David Jacobs was tutor of the old Academy. In 1830 I entered the Theological Seminary, and was under his instructions for nearly three years, and had a good opportunity of becoming acquainted with him as a man and a professor.

From 1828 to about 1845—some seventeen years—he occupied the highest position in the church, and during that time he had more influence in the Lutheran Church in the United States than any other man in it. He was a man of untiring industry, and being very methodical in his habits and accurate in his studies, he was able to accomplish much for the church. His lectures in the Seminary, and the sermons he preached at the meetings of the Synods, were models of neatness and accuracy. Everything was in place—nothing wanting—nothing redundant. Like Atlas, he seemed for a time to have carried the whole Lutheran Church on his shoulders. Nothing could be done without him; he had made his labors a necessity in the church. Thus he compiled its hymn book, and its liturgy, its formula of discipline—he prepared his Theology by request of the General Synod, and had the moulding of nearly all the ministers of the church in his own hands for over twenty years. And such was his influence, growing out of his elevated position, his talents and learning, and the urbanity and suavity of his manners, that he succeeded in forming very many of his students into his own model. He was a man of most exemplary piety and sincerity. His views on theology were clear and scriptural, and although he was devotedly attached to the Lutheran Church, it was doubted by many of his warmest friends, after 1845, whether he was true to the confessional stand-point of historical Lutheranism. His father, Dr. J. G. Schmucker, was a Pietistic Lutheran of the Spenerian School, and hence sent him to study theology at a Puritanical Seminary; this was, perhaps, a misfortune for one who was to have the training of not less than five hundred ministers in his hands.

He had his enemies in the Lutheran Church all along, and leading men in the Pennsylvania Synod, and in the New York Ministerium, and in Ohio and North Carolina, opposed his Puritanism, but he bravely maintained his position up to about 1846. About that time his Lutheran orthodoxy began to be suspected by some of his own students, and especially those who had charge of Pennsylvania College. An unpleasant state of things grew out of this want of confidence in his Lutheranism. By this time, too, the German and Scandinavian elements began to be more potent in the United States, and many, even of the Gettysburg men (*i. e.*, those who had studied there), began to lose confidence in him as the leader of the church. No one ever doubted his sincerity, his learning or his piety — his views in his "Theology," his "Patriarchs of Lutheranism," his "Lutheran Church in America," and other works, had been so fully and clearly expressed that there could be no mistaking them. He defended his views with great ingenuity and force, but all to no purpose, the tide set in against him, and he could not stem it. So he retired some ten years ago, and, in 1868, published his "Church of the Redeemer," which is little more than a kind of concentration of his former works; but the work attracted but little attention in the church, as the great work of its most excellent author had been fully finished before its publication. We do not state this fact to detract from the high and well-merited reputation of the author, for, as is well known, we were one of his most devoted friends, and firmly stood by him to the last. We were one among the few who endorsed his views, and cannot but regret that his clear, Scriptural and liberal views did not prevail in the Lutheran Church. We still hope and pray that his large and liberal views will, after some time be past, be endorsed by the Lutheran Church in America.

As a man and Christian we loved him. He stood high in the estimation of all the Protestant churches in the land, and did more toward raising the Lutheran Church in the opinion of the

Christian community of the United States than any other man among us. His labors will not soon be forgotten; his name and memory will be cherished with gratitude and affection by the many students who had the great pleasure of studying under him, and by none more so than by myself. R. W.

BENJAMIN KURTZ

exerted a more wide-spread influence over the laity of the church and many of the ministers than any man, and that was principally through the Lutheran Observer. He was an able preacher, a vigorous though, in his early life, a wordy writer. He stoutly maintained what was called the Evangelical stand-point, and was an ardent advocate of what, in his day, were called new measures. He was a hard man to preach to, and seldom listened to any other man's sermons with any degree of patience. I often charged him with this infirmity, and he never denied it. The only man whom I ever heard him speak well of as a preacher, that is, one whom he could listen to through a series of Sundays, was not of his own church. The result was that Dr. K., when he lived in places where he himself was not pastor, and where Lutheran churches existed, did not frequently attend divine service with his brethren of the same household of faith. Their preaching did not suit his taste, and he went elsewhere, but found it hard to be suited.

He was an able disputant with the pen and speech, and has gained credit in encounters with men distinguished for their controversial powers. A statesman and lawyer of distinction has said that if Dr. K. had turned his attention to politics or law he would have attained a wide-spread reputation.

He was cool in the fiercest debate, and not easily provoked by the severest attack.

His mind was metaphysically inclined, but he never profoundly studied mental philosophy.

He readily detected weak points in the argument of an opponent, and, like most men who love controversy, he often subjected himself to similar exposures.

He was not a man of original wit, though occasionally he wrote some smart things.

He was too profuse in his words to be a good narrator of stories, and, though a fair conversationalist, he was a bad listener.

He enjoyed the company of friends, but invariably practised the right of precedence in the conversation.

Dr. K. was not what we call a learned man or a profound theologian. He had no college training in early life, but he was uncommonly intelligent in all the ordinary affairs of life, and achieved more good in the ministry than many of far greater attainments.

He was diligent as an investigator, and never ventured upon any subject strange to him without thorough research into such sources that were within his reach. He would introduce the subject in conversation, in order to acquire information and ideas from others. I could give many instances of this, which is a practice greatly to be commended.

When Dr. K. came to Baltimore, in August, 1833, to assume the editorial charge of the Lutheran Observer, he was a widower and not in vigorous health. He had little experience in writing, and he had some difficulty in pruning his superfluous verbiage, but he acquired a vigorous, if not ornate style, and rendered invaluable service to the church in this position. He had no other employment, and was ambitious of success. He was not under the control of any Synod or Board, and pursued his own independent way. He maintained this position by himself for about fifteen years, until the establishment of the book and publishing office, principally through his own agency. He superintended that institution with great ability and success, for he had eminent business capacity. Some of his friends thought that he carried his extreme notions of economy too far, and blamed him for lack of commercial enterprise; but he carried into that business the same principles which governed him in his private affairs, and, never being imprudent in risks, he suffered few losses. He always lived within his income, however limited it may have been.

The foundation of the "Book Company" was the result of a conversation he and I had in my study in 1836. We both entered into it with earnestness, but the credit of getting it into successful operation belongs principally to him. He was the business man of the concern, and was well adapted to it. But of this institution I will speak at another place.

Mr. K. went to Germany in 1826 to solicit donations of money and books for the Theological Seminary about to be established at Gettysburg. He remained absent nearly two years, and brought home about $10,000 in money and a large number of books. Whilst in Germany he received many courtesies from all classes of men, and secured extensive popularity as a plain and impressive preacher. Immense crowds everywhere attended the churches in which he officiated.*

He went a second time to Europe in 1846 to attend the Evangelical Alliance in London in August of that year, and for recreation.

Ten years previous to this second voyage he had made preparations to visit the old world, but his design was frustrated by the death of his second wife. He was engaged by a railroad company in Georgia to go to Germany to secure the services of three thousand or more Germans to come to this country and construct that road. These emigrants were to labor several years for the money paid for their passage, and then to receive a portion of land. The enterprise was fiercely opposed by many influential Germans in this country, who, through the papers and circulars extensively distributed, warned their countrymen against accepting these offers. So vehement was the opposition made, and so violently were Mr. K's. motives and character assailed, that he found it expedient to come out in a public vindication of himself and of the managers of the enterprise.†

During the time when Mesmerism was rampant in this country he became a believer in the system; not in its lower, but in its higher manifestations, and was president of a club of intelligent gentlemen who prosecuted the subject as a matter of metaphysical research. I myself have seen him subject himself to an ignorant clairvoyant, who, under the alleged influence of the subtile fluid (or whatever else it was), pretended to inspect the condition of Mr. K's. lungs, and vowed that he saw tubercles and some other abnormal demonstrations!

In 1854 he was elected Professor of History and German Literature in Pennsylvania College, and Professor in the Theological Seminary, both of which he declined. He loved his work on the Observer too well to give it up for any other.

He died in Baltimore, December 29, 1865.

*See my History of the Seminary in Ev. Review, 1876, No. ...
†Luth. Obs. 1856. May 27, July 22.

For many of the particulars of Dr. Kurtz's life, see Ev. Review, January, 1867, and Hutter's Eulogy.

No man has died in the church for many years who more richly deserved, and whose life would furnish more interesting data for a full biography, than Dr. Kurtz.

SINCERE COMPLIMENT.

Dr. B. Kurtz was once riding to York in the cars, and fell in with a gentleman who soon announced himself as a Presbyterian minister, without, however, mentioning his name. Dr. K.'s name was equally unknown to him. The subject of baptism was discussed by them, and, as they were of one mind, every thing went on very pleasantly. The merits of various books on that subject were freely considered, and, in the midst of the animated conversation, the train stopped at York, and the passengers were summoned into the hotel, a few steps from the station, to dinner. Both our men sat down on opposite sides of the table. A number of the guests knew Dr. K., at least by name. The other gentleman recommenced the conversation on baptism, and said, "By the way, I wish to recommend a book to you, which, I think, is the very best of them all. It treats the matter more lucidly and popularly than any other I know. I have derived great benefit from it, and I recommend it to everybody." "Ah, sir, what book is that?" said K., looking over his plate of soup. "Why, it is a book written by a Lutheran clergyman in Baltimore, named Kurtz, and I repeat it is the best of them all. I advise you to read it." What did K. say? Not a word. He blushed a little, and proceeded with his dinner, perhaps, with better appetite than before. The others present who knew K. looked at him with smiles and anticipated some reply; but not a word escaped him, and K. did not manifest any emotion from which the stranger could discern the author.

REV. DR. B. KURTZ.

"The American Evangelical minister, Kurtz, was invited to dine with a merchant of this city upon a certain day last week. Mr. K. accepted the invitation, but soon after a messenger of the Crown Prince called upon him, and brought an invitation to dine with the Crown Prince on the same day on which Mr. K. had promised to dine with the merchant. Mr. K. excused himself saying, "I have promised to dine with merchant N. N., and consequently cannot accept of the polite invitation to dine with his Royal Highness." The messenger, to whom the like had never occurred, smiled and said, "It is customary to waive every engagement in consideration of a later invitation from great personages." Mr. K. declared, however, that His Royal Highness would certainly not require of a minister of the gospel to disregard a promise. The messenger, discovering that he had a singular person before him, appeared to be much mortified, and observed, "I cannot certainly bring His Royal Highness such an answer as I conceive you made. What shall I say?" "Say every thing as I have spoken, and, if you should be brought into any difficulty, I will make every exertion to apologize for you to His Royal Highness." The messenger departed and made report, upon which the Prince and Princess burst into laughter, and the Prince observed, "This must be an honest man who appreciates his word of promise so highly." Letter from Berlin, 1827, in Luth. Intell., Vol. II, July, 1827.

DR. B. KURTZ'S PREACHING IN GERMANY IN 1827.

The Rev. Mr. Kurtz, from North America, the important and benevolent object of whose mission is generally known, has at length visited Nurnberg, and delivered a discourse in the *Lorenzer* church on Exaudi Sunday. He spoke of the love of Christ, our Lord, from Ephes. III, 19. In the first part of his discourse he described the nature of this love, and in the second its excellency. The sermon was drawn from the pure fountain of the word of God, couched in the simple and powerful language of the spirit of God, and delivered in a most pathetic manner. Thousands of those who flocked to the church were edified and led to Christ, the Redeemer, by this truly evangelical sermon. A number of persons, lately confirmed, being present, were addressed in a most affecting manner, and encouraged to love the Lord. Not a few of the hearers declared that they could have listened to this man with extreme delight for many years. With such success is the heart addressed by the simple exposition of the gospel! May this worthy servant of Christ long continue to preach unto our brethren dwelling in America the name of Him to whom belongeth all honor and glory, for ever and ever." Extract of a German paper, quoted in Luth. Intell., Vol. II, Oct., 1827.

EMBARRASSMENT AND DELIVERANCE.

When the late Rev. Dr. B. Kurtz was in Europe, in 1826, in behalf of the Theological Seminary at Gettysburg, he was painfully embarrassed in London because his bill of exchange, owing to some informal item, could not be negotiated, and for some days he was without funds and much distressed. After describing his forlorn condition and deep despondency, he thus proceeds, in a letter to the *Lutheran Intelligencer*, of June, 1828:

One morning, after having made my breakfast on a bowl of water and a small slice of dry bread, I took my hat and sallied forth into the street, and, without having any particular object in view, strolled about from street to street until I lost myself; but He who has numbered the hairs of our head directed my steps. I was wandering in Bishopsgate street when I observed crowds of people issuing from different quarters and entering a large building called the "City of London Tavern." Perceiving a young gentleman and lady walking arm-in-arm towards the tavern, I was emboldened, by the mildness and sweetness of their countenances, to inquire into the cause of the meeting, and was told, in the most friendly manner, that the great "Sunday School Union" was to hold its anniversary, and that there would be many interesting speeches delivered. My mind was for a moment diverted from the gloomy subject that had been harrassing it, and I immediately resolved to attend the meeting. But the house was crowded to overflowing, and I could get no further than the door. After many fruitless attempts to gain admission, I resolved to withdraw, when that moment I espied a gentleman with a long staff in his hand and wearing a mark of authority upon his hat. I beckoned to him, and, telling him I was a minister of the gospel just arrived from North America, begged him to try and procure a seat for me. He kindly interfered, and obtained a place for me on the platform which had been prepared for the accommodation of those who were to address the assembly.

Here were about forty or fifty clergymen, a number of missionaries from different parts of the world, as well as nobility and members of the House of Parliament. I had not been here long before I was solicited to offer a resolution and support it with a speech. I declined, upon the ground of being entirely unprepared, and having come only with a view of being a spectator, &c.; but it was all to no purpose. I must rise and say something, and if it were only a few words on the state of the church and of Sunday schools in the United States. Finally, after much persuasion, I consented, and, though I had not one distinct idea arranged in my mind when I rose to speak, yet my tongue seemed to be suddenly loosed, and I was blessed with a train of thought and flow of feeling and freedom of language which altogether astonished myself. I had not spoken five minutes until an hundred voices exclaimed *hear him! hear him! hear him!* and then again there was such a clapping of hands and stamping of feet that I was several times obliged to be silent until the bursts of applause had subsided. It is in this way that the British teach and constrain their citizens, especially those who are young and timid to become public and extemporaneous speakers. If they hear a single good idea they will give the speaker credit for it the moment it is uttered by a loud expression of their approbation. If they perceive him to be embarrassed they will immediately come to his aid, and kindly relieve him by applauding his attempt. If he acquits himself well the very welkin re-echoes their shouts. This, indeed, renders their public meetings boisterous, but also more diversified and less tedious than ours. And hence a British audience will sit from 6 o'clock in the morning till 3 P. M., hearing and applauding public orators, without once manifesting a symptom of fatigue. And, whilst Americans would be gaping and yawning and sleeping, they will be acclaiming and cheering the orator; so that if he have one solitary latent spark of eloquence in his soul it will thus be called into action. When the gospel, however, is preached, they do not allow themselves such liberties, but observe the most respectful silence and solemnity. But I must return to my narrative. After the meeting was over a gentleman of respectable appearance approached me, and, laying his hand on my shoulder, said, in a most friendly manner, "My brother, will you have the goodness, in your way home, to call at the house of Mr. S.,* in Cheapside, No. 2?" "I presume, sir," said I, "you are under a mistake. There is no acquaintance whatever between Mr. S. and myself. I am a stranger and know nobody. Probably it is some other person whom Mr. S. is desirous to see." "Is your name Mr. Kurtz, and are you from the United States?" "Yes, sir, you have mentioned my name and my country." "Then, sir," continued he, "you are the person whom Mr. S. is desirous to see." I immediately repaired to Cheap-

---

* Mr. S. afterwards requested me not to make his name known.

side, and entered the house of Mr. S. I was conducted up stairs into a splendid drawing room, where I beheld a gentleman seated on a magnificent sofa, and engaged in reading a book. Here the following dialogue ensued:

Myself. I have taken the liberty, sir, to call on you at the request of a gentleman who is a stranger to me. I am apprehensive there must be a mistake; I beg you to pardon me if I am an intruder.

Mr. S. I am extremely happy to see you, sir; my name is S. Will you do me the favor to be seated?

Self. With pleasure, sir. It appears then my visit is not the result of a misunderstanding?

Mr. S. By no means. I was very anxious to form an acquaintance with you; I beg you to forgive me for presuming so much on your goodness as to ask the favor of a visit. I attended the anniversary of the "Sunday School Union" to-day, heard you deliver a speech there, and was delighted to find that you entertain the very same views on the subjects that I do. This was the more gratifying as we are inhabitants of different hemispheres, and live at least one thousand leagues from one another. If you had spoken from the very impressions resting on my mind you could not have more entirely given utterance to my ideas.

Self. Sir, it affords me much pleasure to learn that we coincide in the views which I endeavored to express at the meeting to-day.

Mr. S. I understood with the sincerest regret that your bill of exchange has been protested, and I can well imagine how unpleasant the situation of a gentleman in a strange land, and in an expensive city, under such circumstances, must be. I beg you to do me the favor of accepting this (holding out to me a handful of gold) as a small evidence of my gratitude for the delight your excellent speech afforded me.

Self. My dear sir, you are too kind. My bill has indeed been protested, but I still indulge the hope that it may yet be redeemed; and, in such an event, I should have to reproach myself for having received a present upon the mere supposition that my money had been lost.

Mr. S. I wish most ardently you may not be disappointed in your hope; the times, however, are precarious, the issue is doubtful, and I entreat you to accept this small sum not as a present, but as a well merited reward.

Self. Your disinterested benevolence quite overcomes me, yet it would not consist with my principles, under existing circumstances, to take advantage of it. But, as I am almost out of money, I would thankfully accept of your offer as a loan, and will pledge you my word as a Christian that it shall be honestly refunded to you.

Mr. S. I cannot lend you this money; but as I have also been informed that the object of your tour is to solicit donations for a Theological Seminary, and as I cordially approve of such institutions, and consider it the solemn duty of every Christian to support them to the utmost of his ability, you surely cannot object to receiving this trifling sum as my contribution.

Self. Sir, I receive it with gratitude, and tender you the thanks of the church, whose agent I am.

In the meantime a neatly dressed little man had made his appearance, and commenced taking my measure for a suit of clothes. Mr. S. hoped I would not object to this *measure*, and insisted on my submitting without saying a word. Having received an invitation to dine with Mr. S. next day, I departed, *praising God and rejoicing on my way.*

The next day I dined with him, and was treated by his pious and amiable family with every mark of attention and affection. In the course of the same day he sent me a fine and full suit of black clothes, which at that time my wardrobe loudly called for. During the residue of my stay in London I often visited and dined at the house of this gentleman, and spent some of my happiest hours with his family.

My purse being now replenished, I immediately settled my account at my boarding house and paid off several other small debts I had contracted, and still had six or seven guineas* left. I now bade adieu to the dismal garret, and took boarding in a more comfortable house. Not long afterwards Dr. Steinkopff returned rather unexpectedly, and from this time forward my prospects became brighter from day to day. But I have carried out my letter to a tedious length, and I will, therefore, forbear for the present.

I will only yet add that when in Kiel, about six weeks afterwards, I received a letter from the excellent and amiable Mr. Jackson, Secretary of the British and Foreign Bible Society, communicating the agreeable intelligence that my bill of exchange

---

* A guinea is worth about five dollars of our currency.

had been honored, and that the money was in his hands, subject to my orders."

He again visited Europe in 1846, and was absent about six months. He attended the Evangelical Alliance in London, and traveled extensively on the Continent; but theological opinion in Germany had changed considerably since his former visit in 1827, and Mr. Kurtz found few theologians who sympathized with him in his unconfessional views of Lutheran doctrine. Even the United and Reformed thought that a man calling himself a Lutheran should support the distinctive features of the Lutheran faith. Besides this, Mr. Kurtz had signed the famous "Appeal," which had been sent to Europe, in which genuine Lutheranism was repudiated, and this gave offence to all classes of theologians as an act inconsistent with a profession of that faith, and an assumption of the name.

JOHN CHRISTOPHER BAKER

was born in Philadelphia, May 7th, 1792, and in 1802 he was placed by his guardian at Nazareth Hall, a seminary of the Moravian church, where he remained five years.

Many years after some of his school companions write thus of him: Says one, "He was universally beloved by pupils and teachers, and, at that early day, he was piously inclined." Another says, "He was all the time of a meek, good natured and devotional temper, and endured injuries so meekly that he must have had truly pious parents, who, in early life, instilled into his mind the fear of God * * * * * and compassion for his fellow men."

At this period of his life, too, were manifested many of those personal peculiarities which were so striking, and which adhered to him through life. "I can still remember," says another, "many of his earnest expressions as well as his emphatic gestures. It was common among us boys in our plays, when some argument on any subject took place, to say, "Just look at young Baker! How he gesticulates!"

Although so steady a lad, and generally so correct in his deportment, he was, on a certain occasion, whilst at Nazareth, through the influence of some rebellious boys in the school, inveigled into a plot to resist rightful authority, and bid defiance to the rules of the institution. But he soon saw the wrong he had committed, and was the first voluntarily to come forward, acknowledge his guilt, and implore forgiveness and indulgence. So satisfied was he of his error that, selfmoved, he went to his companions, exposed to them in its proper light their insubordination, and earnestly and forcibly showed the consequences that must ensue from such conduct. The result was that, desperate as some of the characters were, they were all brought to submission by the force of his arguments and the influence of his example. The spirit of rebellion was at once crushed, and order in the school again restored.

Bishop Reinke writes, "One afternoon when, according to my custom, I withdrew from the noise and bustle of our play ground to the woods, to seek, in the deep anguish of my heart, the Lord in retirement, I saw my class mate, John C. Baker, sitting on a log, weeping bitterly, and reading, as I presently discovered, a small revival hymn book. On looking up and perceiving that I had likewise been weeping, he at once inferred that I had been praying, and said he thought I must be of the same mind with himself." These spiritual exercises continued for some time. He remained in this mental distress and under the bondage of sin so long, perhaps from a mistaken idea he entertained of the plan of salvation. But difficulties were subsequently removed, the cloud that rested upon him vanished, light beamed from the cross, and by the power of faith he was enabled to embrace the Lord Jesus as his Saviour.   *   *   *   *   *   *   *

In the year 1807 he was received as a member of Zion's church, Philadelphia, by Rev. John F. Schmidt. On leaving the seminary at Nazareth, in 1807, he soon after repaired to Lebannon, Pa., for the purpose of pursuing his theological studies under the direction of Rev. Dr. Lochman.   *   *   *   *   *   *

In the year 1811 he was set apart to the work of the ministry by the Synod of Pennsylvania, with which body he remained connected until his death. He immediately received a call as an assistant minister of the German Lutheran congregations of Philadelphia, which he accepted, and at once entered upon the duties of his appointment.   *   *   *   *   *   *   *

In the following year he accepted a unanimous call to the pastoral charge of the church in Germantown.

* * * * * * * *
Almost at the very commencement of his career the English language was introduced into the services of the sanctuary, and, although the measure at first encountered opposition, its adoption was fraught with important advantages to the interests of the church. * * * * * In the year 1818, under his auspices, the large new church edifice was erected, which still stands as a monument of the zeal and activity of the Pastor.
* * * * * * * * *
His remarkable faithfulness with respect to pastoral visiting, for which he was always distinguished, had its beginning here. Starting at the Rising-Sun village, his visits and labors included Nicetown, Germantown, Chestnut-Hill, Barren-Hill, Manayunk, Roxborough and Frankfort. Although it was no easy task to perform all this, yet, to say that he personally called upon every person in the long range, who belonged to or visited his churches, and that not only once or occasionally, but frequently and regularly, is stating only the simple truth, without any exaggeration. An amusing incident in reference to the Doctor at this period of his ministry is remembered, in which there was a display of more physical courage than many of his friends supposed he possessed. The great turnpike road leading from Germantown to Philadelphia was infested by robbers, who made it their business to stop and plunder market-wagons at the hill just below the village, which was, at the time, a dark, deep and narrow defile. One evening he reached the spot on his way to fill a preaching appointment at Nicetown, and found the road blocked up by eight or nine farmers' vehicles, the drivers of which were afraid to venture into the dangerous part of the road, lest an attack should be made upon them, and were eagerly waiting for some one to take the lead. This was finally done by the subject of our narrative driving in advance in his gig, followed by the *courageous* crowd. They all passed on without any hostile encounter. * * * * * In January, 1828, as successor to Rev. Dr. Endress, he assumed the pastoral care of the church at Lancaster. Here he labored with unwearied assiduity for twenty-five years. He introduced into his church the Sunday School system, which was yet a comparatively new thing in our country. For many years he served as President of the Board of Trustees of Franklin College, and as a Director of the Public Schools. He was fond of examining the children,

and threw into the work his whole soul. His visitations to the schools were frequent and systematic. He set apart one day every week to this business, and always entered the school-room so kindly with the familiar smile of a father, that he was ever a welcome and grateful visitor to both teachers and pupils. "I was often amused when a visitor at his house," says one who was intimate in the family, "to see little boys and girls come in for the purpose of having the Doctor write an excuse for the previous day's absence, or for permission to come home before school hours were over; these requests were never refused, but attended to on the spot; no matter who was present, or in what he was engaged, whether at his meal, or just ready to leave the house, the little fellows were never put off." * * * * * * * *

So heavy and incessant were the drafts that had been made upon Dr. Baker, that his physical constitution, naturally vigorous, began at length to yield. His health became impaired under the pressure of his manifold duties, and he concluded that it was advisable to resign the large field of labor which had long claimed his unwearied attention. He accordingly preached his Valedictory discourse, January 30th, 1853, and removed to Philadelphia; but, as he could not endure the idea of being idle, he was willing to take charge of a small Mission Church in the northern part of the city.

He died in May, 1859, aged sixty-eight years. His dying testimony was all of the most satisfactory and consolatory character. His children, whom he tenderly loved, and by whose presence and attentions he was soothed, he fervently commended "to the care and covenant-keeping of his Heavenly Father," and earnestly urged them to "abound in love and glory to God." On one occasion when asked if he was comfortable, he replied, "I might be more so," but added, "We count them happy that endure." The afternoon previous to his death, when apparently much distressed by difficulty of breathing, one of his children remarked, "Jesus said, My grace is sufficient for thee!" With a smile he replied, "Yes! Oh! I hope"—but he could say no more. * * * * * *

In looking at Dr. Baker's public character, the first thing that strikes us is the earnestness, the enthusiastic ardor with which he took hold of every subject that engaged his attention. He was scrupulously conscientious in fulfilling every known obligation, and labored with indefatigable zeal, untiring activity and self-sacrificing industry, constantly illustrating in his life the Saviour's motto, "I must work while it is day; the night cometh when no man can work!" He was emphatically a working man, battling on in the good cause to which he had consecrated his powers year after year, through good and through evil report, in season and out of season, eminently striving to be useful to his fellow men. Bishop Reinke, of the Moravian Church, who was, for a time, his colleague at Lancaster, once attempted to remonstrate with him in reference to his course, but without effect. "It was the doctor's custom," says the bishop, "to preach three times every Sabbath. I, therefore, took the liberty one day of reasoning with him on the propriety and necessity of diminishing these excessive labors, inasmuch as they would, if continued, break down his constitution before the time. But in reply he became quite warm and animated, and, hastily rising from his seat, pacing up and down the room, and throwing his long arms lustily around him, exclaimed, "No, I tell you, my dear brother, I *must* work while it is called to-day! I must spend and be spent in the cause of my blessed master!" *   *   *   *   *   *   *

Nothing could deter him from a mission of love and piety. Indisposition never interfered with the performance of any pastoral obligation. Physical infirmities were never presented as a plea for the neglect of duty. He was known to ride or drive miles in storms, through rain and snow, to hold a meeting for prayer or to attend to the ordinary services of the Lord's Day, when no one of all the congregation, not even the sexton, ventured out of doors. He had no sympathy with those who found it too hot or too cold or too stormy to attend church. He could go to preach, why not they to listen? He would notice those who were absent from the exercises of the sanctuary, and invariably called on them the following day, and inquired into the cause of their absence. The marriages he solemnized, the baptisms and funeral services he performed, are, perhaps, without a parallel in the history of any pastor. The Doctor also took a deep interest in the religious instruction of the children of the church, and, in addition to three services on the Lord's Day, whilst settled at Lancaster, he also attended the Sunday School. He also had a Bible class, composed of the teachers and older scholars, which he met weekly, and imparted careful instruction in the lesson for the succeeding Sabbath. In addition, during the week, two evenings were generally spent in lecturing, and sometimes, when he had classes of catechumens, which were formed regularly twice every year, four evenings were devoted to public services for the benefit of his people. The work never seemed to him irksome.   *   *   *   *   *

As a preacher Dr. Baker was plain, practical and edifying. He adhered closely to the text, and presented a simple exposition of God's word, a clear and full exhibition of the way of life. "Under his impressive and persuasive appeals," says one who often heard him preach, "I have seen the entire audience melted to tears." He never introduced anything flippant or irrelevant into the pulpit. In his preparations for the pulpit he was very laborious, particularly at that period of his ministry when he was in the habit of committing his sermons to memory. His texts were usually selected on Sunday night, after his return from the church, and the preparation was protracted till the close of the week; so that, in connection with the toil to which he submitted, he was often heard to say, "I have no pleasure of my life.   *   *

He was familiar with the best German and English writers in Theology, and was regarded as well read in the substantial literature of the day. The Bible was, however, the book which he carefully and faithfully studied. He also had some skill as a musician. He played very creditably upon the piano. He often played duetts with his daughters, and one of them received her entire musical instruction from him. He seldom wrote for the press. The only discourse he ever furnished for publication is a sermon on the death of Rev. Dr. Frederick D. Schaeffer. The Doctorate of Divinity was conferred upon him by Lafayette College in 1837.   *   *   *   *   *   *   *   *

He was a leading member of the Synod of Pennsylvania, and his power was felt among the members in private and on the floor in Synod.   *   *   *   *   *   *   *   *

At Synod he was always willing to work when others were disposed to ask a dispensation from labor. He was repeatedly elected by his brethren to offices of honor and trust. He served for many years as Treasurer of the Synod, and his accounts were kept with the most rigid exactness. As President of the body he was distinguished for industry and zeal, impartiality and vigor.   *   *

He was regarded as the life and the soul of the Synod. He generally expressed his convictions with great animation, and always secured the attention of the House. His speeches were with peculiar earnestness and characteristic vehemence, and, when there was any unpleasant excitement or acrimony of spirit manifested, he would usually restore good humor, and pour oil on the troubled waters. In Synod he had many an earnest contest in his advocacy of the General Synod. Several times he was defeated in his efforts to secure a re-union with that body, but he never despaired of ultimate success.

He was also often very absent-minded. Some ludicrous incidents are told of his going out with a torn coat, worn in his study, to make visits, and not observing his mistake until he was some distance from home, or had already entered the house of his host. He would frequently likewise pass along the streets, apparently absorbed in thought or some profound mental process, unconscious of what was transpiring around him, his hand all the time in constant action as he moved around with his long cane, his constant attendant. He disliked exceedingly to be called "old," and any allusion to "aged servant" in the public prayers of other clergymen was very annoying. When he was President of the Directors of Public Schools in Lancaster, Hon. James Buchanan was associated with him in the Board, and frequently, when speaking of him or addressing him, would playfully say, "the old gentleman," "the venerable Doctor," etc. But the thing was not relished by the subject of our sketch, who remembered it some years afterwards, and returned the compliment. When Mr. Buchanan became a candidate for the Presidency, his age, of course, transpired, and just after the election, the two old friends unexpectedly met in a Daguerreian Room in the city of Philadelphia. The Doctor seized the President by the hand, in his earnest, emphatic manner, and, by no means in a whisper, said, "Well, Mr. Buchanan, how are you, Sir? Well, Sir, when you and I used to meet in Lancaster, years ago, you often spoke of me as the "old gentleman," 'Sir, but I find now, Sir, that you are just one year older than I am, Sir!'" Mr. Buchanan laughed, and said it was a great mistake on his part to let his age become so public.

HE RECEIVES A COMPLIMENT.

We were present, on another occasion, when the topic of conversation was, the compliments, deserved or undeserved, which partial parishioners are prone to pay their ministers. "Well," said the Doctor, with characteristic simplicity and vehemency of gesture, "whether my people have been backward in the expression of their good opinions, or whether they have been [....] tery would spoil me, I know not, but it has, somehow, so happened, that my modesty has never been put to any severe test by over-many compliments. But I did once receive one, which I have never forgotten. On my way home from church, on a Sunday morning, after German preaching, Mrs. ....., a plain and very pious old lady, who for more than forty years had been a consistent member of the Lancaster church, walked a short distance by my side, and took occasion to say to me: "Well, Doctor, this morning you have once again faithfully expounded the Gospel of our loving Lord and Saviour, and most heartily do I thank you for it." "That," said the Doctor, "*that* was to me the most welcome compliment I have ever received, for I knew the old lady to be sincere, and that she meant what she said. She did not, you see, compliment me for my learning, or my eloquence, or for anything else I do not possess, but she gave me the nobler praise of being *a faithful Minister of the New Testament*, and higher ambition than that, in this world, I have none."

RT. REV. BISHOP BAKER.

He was, whilst Pastor in Lancaster, on the most intimate terms with Rev. Dr. Bowman, of the Episcopal Church, the present assistant Bishop of the State of Pennsylvania, and there existed a strong feeling of mutual attachment. They frequently interchanged visits and seemed to enjoy each other's society. But the Doctor could never endure the arrogant pretensions of those in the Episcopal Church, who were constantly asserting that *their* church was the only *true* Church, and *her* ministers the *only* genuine successors of the Apostles. "I have often heard him," says one, who often saw them together, propose the enquiry to the Bishop, "Do you know, Sir, who I am? I will tell you, Sir; I am the Rt. Rev. John C. Baker, Bishop of the Evangelical Lutheran Congregation of the Holy Trinity Church, Lancaster!" and, whilst saying this, he would rise from his chair and walk up and down the room with great earnestness, but he never exhibited any bitterness in his spirit, or unkindness in his manner.

He usually had, during the year, more weddings than all the other clergymen together. But in consequence of his cordial interest and active efforts in the Temperance movement, he alienated from him many of the landlords, all of them, too, respectable men, and consequently there was a great diminution in the number of his marriages, the tavern-keepers sending for other clergymen not favorable to the reform, or not prominent in supporting it.

UNPREMEDITATED PREACHING.

In a company of brethren, the conversation turned on the straits to which ministers are occasionally subjected when required to preach without having any time for preparation. In this connection, Dr. Baker related the following: "I was once called, on a Wednesday afternoon, to officiate at a funeral, a few miles out of Lancaster. The undertaker was painfully slow in his movements, and, quite unexpectedly to me, it was *night* before we got back to the city. Without having had time to take my tea, or even to return to my house, I was obliged to hurry to the church, to officiate at the Wednesday evening service. But, alas, I had no text to lecture, no skeleton, not even a subject. When I came to the church, the people had already assembled. I purposely gave out a long hymn (seven verses), that I might have time to select at least a text for my lecture. But the harder I tried, the greater was my perplexity. As a Scripture lesson, I selected one of the longest chapters in the New Testament, thinking, of course, I would hit upon a suitable verse, but failed. Then followed the opening prayer, and never did I so stand in need of God's forgiveness, because of my wandering and distracted thoughts, for I was thinking of my lecture. My second hymn was as long as the first, and again, during the singing, I employed my time in looking up a text. And now, my heart palpitated, and my knees shook. When, lo, just as the last verse of the second hymn was being sung—still conning over the leaves of my Bible—my eye fell upon Nahum, chapter 1, verse 7: "*The Lord is good, a strong-hold in the day of trouble, and he knoweth them that trust in him.*" On these words," continued the Doctor, "I began to discourse. At first it was an up-hill business, for when one sentence was out, I knew not what the next was to be. But, behold, I had not proceeded very far, when my Heavenly Father opened to me a door of utterance. Thoughts came into my mind unbidden. My tongue was loosed, and for three-quarters of an hour did I discourse on those words with a fluency and fervor such as I had never before experienced, and I could, without difficulty, have spoken on them twice as long, for the trouble with me now, was, to know *when to stop*. Best of all, after I had finished, two ladies, clad in mourning, approached me, extending their hands, and thanked me for the words of comfort I had spoken, saying, no doubt, I "had *prepared* that discourse expressly for *their* benefit!" The Doctor's answer was characteristically honest: "Ladies, if that discourse has proved a comfort to you, you are heartily welcome, for, I assure you, it was not studied or prepared at all." "And now," continued the Doctor, "does not this incident teach us, brethren, that God often leaves us to ourselves, that out of our weakness He may perfect His strength, and do we not perceive, that, without at all justifying indolence or indifference, our sermons would yet, as a general rule, be far more eloquent and effective, *if we depended more upon God, and less upon ourselves*." And, without controversy, the Doctor spake wisely.

BENJAMIN KELLER

was born in Lancaster, Pa., March 4th, 1794. He was confirmed by Rev. Dr. H. E. Muhlenberg, and soon after felt a strong desire to devote himself to the ministry. His classical and theological studies, in preparation for the work, were pursued at Frederick, Md., and Lancaster, Pa., under the direction of Rev. Dr. D. F. Schaeffer, and his revered and beloved pastor, Dr. Muhlenberg. On the completion of his course, in 1814, before he had reached his twenty-first year, he was commissioned by the Synod of Pennsylvania to preach the gospel, and, at once, entered upon the duties of the pastoral office. His first charge was Carlisle, Pa. Here he labored with zeal and fidelity for thirteen years, in serving eight congregations and performing an amount of service that seems almost incredible. In 1827 he received and accepted a call to the associated churches of Germantown, Barren-Hill and White-Marsh, where he continued for seven years. In 1834 he engaged in the service of the Education Society. But his preferences for the pastoral were so decided that after a brief and successful mission, he to resume the work, and accepted a call as Pastor of the Lutheran Church in Gettysburg. Here he continued to exercise his office for seventeen years. The relationship was terminated in consequence of the urgent desire of the Synod of Pennsylvania to secure his services in its effort to endow a German Professorship in the Institutions at Gettysburg. The funds required were procured and warm friends secured wherever his labors extended. The enterprise having been accomplished he settled in Philadelphia and devoted his time and energies to the German population in the northeastern part of the city. The effort was crowned with remarkable success, and the result was the organization of the large and prosperous congregation of St. James, and the speedy erection of a beautiful and substantial church edifice. But his physical strength was found inadequate for so extensive a field; he therefore withdrew, that another might enter into his labors. He did not, however, retire to rest. His active habits would not permit him to remain unemployed. He cheerfully yielded to the wishes of the Lutheran Board of Publication, and undertook a general agency and superintendence of its interests. His services, so faithfully rendered, have identified his name permanently with this Institution. He visited many of our churches, interested in the work pastors and people, whose confidence and affections he enjoyed in a high degree, collected funds, suggested and secured the publication of some of the most valuable and popular books the Society has issued, and continued its General Superintendent till his death, remained in the position by the unanimous wish of the Board, even when the state of his health allowed him to give to the work only his wise and faithful counsels. During the last two years of his life, when unable to travel through the Church, he was anxious to serve his Master by preaching the Gospel, and for a season, feeble as he was, regularly performed missionary labor for a German congregation, at Germantown. Until the last, the master-spirit of his life was strong; the desire of his heart was to be useful, to labor for the advancement of the great work, to which, in his early years, he had consecrated his powers. He died July 2d, 1864, in the seventy-first year of his age, and after a service of fifty years in the Gospel ministry. They laid his remains in the cemetery of St. Michael's Church, Germantown, once the scene of his active labors.

As a pastor he stood in the very foremost rank, a model of diligence, fidelity and wisdom, in the discharge of his diversified duties an example of earnest and laborious toil. He never filled a pastoral charge, or assumed any position with which a benediction was not connected.

As an agent he had also superior qualifications. This was seen in his good judgment, singular prudence, moderation and patience, as well as in the simplicity of his manners, the absence of every thing that looked like ostentation, his kindness and dignity, and his respect for all the proprieties of social life.

In private life there was much that was attractive in Mr. Keller's character. He was stern yet kind and gentle. He possessed great tenderness of spirit, a heart overflowing with the warmest sympathies. His life was marked by all the amenities which adorn the Christian character, beautiful and consistent, never, in his intercourse with others, conniving at wrong or indulging in the aimless jest or the idle word. Careful to a fault not to give the least trouble to his friends, always faithful to every interest committed to his trust, his example will never be forgotten. Among the more prominent traits of his character was his unswerving integrity; a rigid adherence to what he regarded as right, a steadfast maintenance of the truth. No considerations of present advantage, or expediency, or worldly prudence could carry him away from what he believed to be the path of duty. Nothing could tempt him, nothing appal him, nothing divert him from his purpose. However great the personal sacrifice, he would never abandon his honest convictions. He was a man of great intrepidity, quite above what, on a superficial acquaintance, might have been imagined. This was particularly seen when great principles were involved, or the interests of the church, as he supposed, were imperilled. He was distinguished for his habits of industry which led him to fill up his whole time with something useful, to "gather up the fragments that nothing should be lost." He allowed himself no vacant hours. He seemed always to be about his Father's business. Yet his labors were so methodically arranged, that he never appeared to be in a hurry, or at a loss to decide what subject should next claim his attention. He was most exact in fulfilling all his engagements. It was strange to find him a minute after time when an appointment had been made. Punctuality he regarded as one of the cardinal virtues. With his unfailing industry was closely connected great energy, a resolute will, an earnest and heroic perseverance that never yielded to any obstacle that was not absolutely insuperable. He was, also, remarkable for his benevolence. His heart and his hand were always extended to the relief of human suffering. Those who were brought into the most intimate relations with him were often struck with the fact, that he was constantly desirous of ministering to the comfort of others, of relieving human suffering and of subserving a good cause. There is no enlarged enterprise, or benevolent scheme in which the Lutheran Church has been engaged for the last forty years, in connection with which he did not occupy a prominent place and exercise a controlling influence. His devotion to the church was unfaltering and earnest. As a Director of the Theological Seminary, a Trustee of Pennsylvania College, a member of the Executive Committee of the Parent Education Society, as President of the Lutheran Board of Publication, or as Secretary, or President of Synod, he was always found at the post of duty, and prompt to render the required service.

But the crowning excellence of his character was his consistent, fervent and active piety. Religion was with him an all-pervading principle, exercising an influence over his whole life, his convictions, his feelings and his actions. He had no sympathy with fanaticism or extravagance, but in all his views and demonstrations he was calm, intelligent and decided; there was a simplicity, an earnestness in whatever he said or did that made it evident to every one that he was more than an ordinary Christian, a good man who daily walked with God and lived in charity with his brethren. "No man," says one* who knew him well, "could more thoroughly sanctify all his gifts: he lived and gave, as one who believed that all he was and all he had, belonged to Christ. Feeble in body, he was more abundant in labor than the strong; unpretending in all things, his steady light shone, while meteor after meteor dazzling for a while went out in forgetfulness; and when growing years increased his bodily infirmities, he still more than coped in toil and success with the young. Love and reverence waited on his steps. It is hard to prize such a man enough, but if a universal and enthusiastic affection on the part of our ministers and people could add anything to the joy of one who had, as he had, the approval of his conscience and of his God, he enjoyed it to the full. His Christian graces, his perfect geniality and amenity, his refined and unfailing consideration for the rights

*Rev. Dr. Krauth, of Philadelphia.

and feelings of others made him very dear to all who knew him. the aged and the young alike enjoyed his presence." "Thy life," adds another* who for several years sustained to him the relation of Pastor, "was not in vain! It was modest, active, careful, harmonious, symmetrical and consecrated to God. We would not call thee back. Thou hast fought a good fight; thou hast finished thy course; thou hast kept the faith. Thou art at rest, and we will hold thee in everlasting remembrance!"

SOME RECOLLECTIONS OF REV. B. KELLER, BY J. K. PLITT.

1. "Slow and sure." He was pre-eminently so. He neither talked, walked or drove at a break-neck rate; but he could generally be depended upon, and would come out all right in the end. If he had a journey to make with horse and buggy by a uniform "jogging along," he would make "good time." *Four* miles an hour was about his rate of speed. He was not exacting in his demands of his faithful beast. If he but "kept moving," the bill was filled. The result was generally "a good day's journey." Between himself and his beast there used to be "a perfect understanding," so that the proprieties of the relation were seldom outraged. The whip was not spared, however, when occasion required its use. "*Heat of style*" might easily have been charged to his "get up" for traveling purposes.

He *walked* as he drove, not at a "two-forty" rate. You never could see *his* coat-tail standing out in a horizontal line because of his rapidity of motion!

He *talked* deliberately too. I suppose he remembered *the solemn lesson* in the spelling-book, contained in the reason given for one having *two* ears and *one* mouth! He *thought* before he *spoke*. And when he had anything to say in Synod, in Church Boards, in Committee, &c., he would insist on being heard. You could not "choke him off" by any "previous question" or any "gag-law" arrangement. He was very tenacious of his rights, the right of speech especially. And his views, when expressed, were generally found to be worth something. He was very positive in his convictions, and firm when he took a stand.

2. *Punctuality* was a cardinal virtue with him. If he was not on hand according to arrangement something extraordinary was the matter. The congregation did not have to *wait* for him. Committee business did not lag for any failure of his to be present at

---

*Rev. Dr. Krotel, of Philadelphia.

the appointed hour. He could be depended upon for the fulfillment of an engagement. *His* promises were worth much more than those of many other men, even good men, too, for some of these latter, alas, are often "behind time." I owe a debt of gratitude to the "dear old father" for impressing on my own mind, in my student days at Gettysburg, the importance of the principle, "Pay as you go." At the beginning of my active life I began to conform to that rule, and, by keeping on in so doing through a quarter of a century, I have escaped many of the ills which worry many a poor fellow almost to death. To my *honored old uncle* I have been in the habit of ascribing much of the credit of the comfort I have thus enjoyed. I have not forgotten the advice given with so much earnestness and sincerity, nor will I ever forget it. "John, keep out of debt—pay as you go," are words of my uncle that have been ineffaceably engraven on my memory.

3. *Propriety in religious duty and service* he was ever careful to insist upon. His ideas of what was proper might seem old-fashioned sometimes, but they generally had a good foundation. I remember that he happened at my home once, when, having a babe to be baptized, we were glad to have him perform the service. In our own house, in a quiet way, the preparations were made; but they were only *complete* when the mother *put a bonnet on her head!* The idea seemed to be that a *woman* should not take part in a religious service with *uncovered head*. I also remember that when the *meeting of teachers* of his Sunday School was held at private houses, from week to week, during my student days at Gettysburg, it was necessary for the *female of the house to put on a bonnet*. The lady teachers all *kept theirs on*, and bonnets were *something* in those days! *The woman's head must be covered* was a regulation well understood by those who took part in religious services which he conducted. Any *improprieties* in the worship of the sanctuary were especially repugnant to his feelings. He had a stern, emphatic way of rebuking them. Few men could put more of the expression of righteous indignation into their looks than he. He could make a wrong-doer quail by his frown, aside from the word of reproof.

4. *He was scrupulously jealous of his good name.* He believed what Solomon says about *a good name*. He *had* such a name and he prized it highly. He was very prompt to follow up any imputations on his character. I remember that when he was canvassing

for the Publication Society at Easton and in the neighborhood, it came to his ears that a certain person had made some remarks reflecting upon his *honesty*. He was very much exercised about it. He spoke with much feeling about it whilst tarrying with me in my former home near Easton. And he could give himself no rest until he traced the thing up to its source, and compelled the offender to retract his charge, and to do all he could to repair the wrong. It was not a safe business for any one to take " undue liberties " with the name and character of the good old father. He was ever ready to vindicate himself, and, should it ever have become necessary, I doubt not he would have appealed to the law for defence. A slanderer of him would not be long in finding out that he had got into very " hot water." His good name was of far more account, in his estimation, than gold or silver.

5. *His perseverance was remarkable.* He had a great deal of that virtue which displays itself in " holding on." He took " a good grip," and he " stuck to it." When, amid many infirmities, and with not a little discomfort to himself, he traveled about among the churches, as agent for benevolent operations and works, he " kept at it " with such determination as not many of *our* agents, before or since, have shown. Impressed, himself, with a sense of the importance of his work, he felt that others must see it in the same light ; and it took a pretty " cute " fellow to get off without " coming down with the rhino." He had a way of presenting the claims of his cause which soon disarmed opposition. His suavity, combined with his earnestness and sincerity, procured many a contribution to our treasuries for benevolent purposes.

A little incident, to show how he " hung on," occurred years ago, at Easton. He had called frequently on a certain church member, whom he failed to find at home, coming either too soon or too late. At last the good wife of him whom he was seeking told him to call at six o'clock in the evening. By a remarkable combination of circumstances, he was a little later than *that hour*, and when he arrived at the house, lo ! *his man* had gone to bed ! The wife began to apologize ; but he soon interrupted her by telling her that it made no matter, that he would wait—that he supposed Mr. T. would not object to getting up, in order that he might see him ; and, in his mild, persuasive way, he broke in upon the domain of Somnus, aroused the sleeper, and got the contribution he expected.

6. *He was a prudent, cautious, careful man.* He magnified his office in his *outward life*, as well as in other ways. He saw well to it that he did not become a stumbling-block to others. Foolish talking and jesting did not enter into his speech. Gravity, sobriety, distinguished him. He would not join with us in our first alumni dinner at Gettysburg for fear of giving offence. He maintained a clerical appearance; and it was remarkable with what a slender and rarely renewed wardrobe he could do it. I have known the *same* coat to do duty *many* years! His outward man was almost a model of neatness, simplicity and respectability.

I mention here what I might have before said, perhaps in better connection, as illustrating his carefulness of his good name, that he would not ask a *female* to a seat with him in his buggy. He would *avoid occasion* for anything to be said, by the maliciously inclined, in such a connection. He knew how ready many people were to speak ill of ministers, and to associate their names disreputably with the other sex. No matter how tired-looking a woman might be whom he would overtake on the road, and how much his goodness of heart might prompt him to give her a little relief from walking, his sense of propriety was so keen that he would not invite her to a seat with him, *no matter who she might be.*

ABRAHAM RECK

was one of the holiest men I ever met. He was a plain, unpretending and zealous servant of his divine master, and was revered by all who ever knew him. Fifty years ago he was pastor at Winchester, and was one of the founders of the Seminary at Gettysburg. He subsequently served congregations in Maryland, and afterwards removed to Ohio, where he was unfortunate in some secular business, and he was made a poor man. But he never ceased preaching as long as he was able to stand.

In his early ministry he traveled as a Missionary in the western counties of Virginia, where he encountered some singular adventures.

He was associated with Krauth, Kurtz, Schmucker and others of less influence, in all the measures for the furtherance of the church; and a willing and industrious worker they found him to be.

He was not a man of brilliant mind, or extensive reading. He had been the pupil of a plain, village pastor, who had not much time to attend to his students, but Mr. Reck had the grace, the faith, the high spiritual qualification for his work among the people whom Providence committed to his pastoral care.

He was born in Littlestown, York county, Pa., January 2d, 1790, and died at Lancaster, Ohio, May 18th, 1869, aged seventy-nine years. He was licensed to preach in 1812, and accepted a call to Winchester in 1813. He was an ardent advocate of Evangelical measures, and an attempt made by some of his opponents to prosecute him before Synod, failed ignominiously. Some of these men afterwards became his warmest friends.

He did a large amount of missionary work in the earlier part of his ministry. He had one station thirty miles distant from his home, to reach which he had to cross a mountain road eleven miles in extent; the roads were desperately bad, and his sufferings in the winter were terrible. He also performed missionary tours, on one of which he traveled on horseback one thousand miles, and preached eighty-five sermons. As the result of his preaching at one place, it was said, "Young Reck has turned the whole neighborhood into fools, for they won't dance and frolic any more, but all go to prayer meeting." Dr. Stork, one of his successors at Winchester, says, "In our first ministry at Winchester, we heard so much of this good man from the people * * * * that he was enshrined in our affectionate remembrance." Rev. Dosh, another successor, says, "He was esteemed a man of devoted piety * * * * and his memory is still cherished with gratitude." Another minister who knew him well, says, "No one ever dared to breathe the slightest suspicion against his eminently upright conduct and unsullied character."

In 1828 he took charge of the churches in the Middletown, Md., pastorate. Here he remained nine years, and was greatly successful.

In 1836 he removed to Indianapolis, where he continued his missionary labors and established nine Lutheran Churches in the surrounding country. Here he purchased property, but misfortunes befel him and he lost all he had brought with him from Maryland, amounting to about $14,000.

In 1841 he went to Cincinnati, where he organized a church amid unparalleled difficulties. He preached "in a little open rickety place, over an engine shanty, the stairs outside and dangerous." Subsequently, "the little band rented the old college." Dr. Beecher and Prof. Stowe were his warm friends.

In 1845 he pitched his tent in Germantown, Ohio, where he remained three years.

We next find him in Tarleton, Ohio, where he also labored successfully. He finally settled down in Lancaster, Ohio, where he died.

All through his long life he was a model man. I never knew one who seemed to be more deeply imbued with the Spirit of Christ. He never had an enemy who was a true Christian. His bitterest opponents were compelled to acknowledge the unsullied purity of his life and the most established believer could learn profitable lessons from his conversation or his example. He was fearless in the defence of the truth and uncompromising in his opposition to wrong of every kind. He despised chicanery and meanness. Strongly attached to his own church, an enthusiastic admirer of Luther, yet he had a most catholic spirit and loved every body who loved Christ.

He suffered intense and protracted attacks of disease during every period of his life, and rejoiced in wonderful restorations; fearful accidents and remarkable deliverances; domestic afflictions and yet uncomplaining submission; diabolical opposition and yet most signal triumphs; seasons of the saddest depression and yet cheerful confidence in God; pinching poverty and yet unfailing trust in him who sent the ravens to feed the famishing prophet; alienation of former friends, but also reconciliation and affection of enemies; never despairing, ever hoping, because always praying.

He was a most laborious pastor and thoroughly instructed his young people in the faith of the church. "My ministerial experience," says he, "led me to appreciate the great wisdom of Luther in giving us his small catechism as one of the most successful methods, in judicious and pious hands, of indoctrinating and properly preparing candidates for membership in our good old Lutheran Reformation Church. Thereby God gave me the first Bible Revivals in the last century; I recommend the proper use of the catechism to all the younger brethren in our church and not to lay it aside as some have done."

He was repeatedly invited to prominent places, such as Chambersburg, Gettysburg, Lancaster, Charleston, but as he was useful in the position in which he was at the time laboring, he did not accept them.

The following incidents, with many more which I had not room to include in this sketch, were communicated to me by Mr. Reck towards the close of his life:

"Forty-seven years have elapsed since, at Synod in Cumberland, Maryland, upon warm, repeated solicitations of the brethren, I at last agreed to accept the appointment of home missionary for four months along the south and north sides of the Alleghanies. The brethren promised to supply my charge at W., but, am sorry to have to say, the promises were but poorly fulfilled. I passed through Hardy, Hampshire and Pendleton counties, and thence, after having to leave my excellent horse, who was injured and disabled, and borrowing another from a good friend, I proceeded in a bridle, or rather a former buffalo path, thirty miles over the mountains, without a house or even cabin on the route. I, at length, was overtaken by night, and it became exceedingly dark. And when I at length began to descend the spurs of the Alleghanies, amid grand oaks that both tore my clothes and skinned my face, my eyes also being in imminent danger, I had to hold one hand before my face and with the other try and guide my horse. At length I espied, at a long distance, a light before me. Now I tried to steer my way thitherward, and, about 10 P. M. in the long nights, I arrived at the first house I met all day and thus far in the night. I called loud several times. At length I heard a coarse, rough voice. "Who is there?" Responded I, "A stranger lost; can I tarry the night?" "If you put up with such as we have." "Willing to put up with anything." "Well, come in then." The family had retired for the night, and a big log fire blazed on the hearth. The rude mountaineer viewed me from head to foot, without asking me to be seated, and said, "Are you not a minister?" I replied in the affirmative. "What order?" "The Lutheran." "Never heard of them; what do you believe?" "The Bible." "But what do you believe about Baptism?" Now I took the hint and responded, "I believe it is an ordinance of divine appointment." "No," said he, "how do you baptize?" "With water." "No, don't you baptize by immersion?" "I think the mode unessential." Ah! that would not do at all with him. So, standing still, I said, "Well, I presume you believe what Christ said, John III, 'Ye must be born again of water and the Spirit,'" "Yes." "Well, I am tired and weary; I wish to have a little refreshment." "What will you have?" "A little mush and milk," as the family were all abed. With amazement he exclaimed, "Do you eat mush and milk?" "Oh, yes, I am very fond of it." So he attended to it himself, and then to my horse. Afterwards I asked if he would accompany me in a short evening service. "Oh, yes." So I prayed. I retired, rose early next morning to reach my appointments in Randolph county, Va. At the house of a brother-in-law of old Rev. P. Henkel, after service, made arrangements to return my borrowed horse. Bought of the family a young four year old, over seventeen hands high, a great swimmer. The Monongahela was quite high and rising, and they said there was but *one* place where I could ford without swimming the horse. But I was directed to kneel on the saddle, hold by the mane and let the horse have the bridle. But I could never learn to swim. The animal took me safely across, but the water ran over the horse both behind and before the saddle. I proceeded towards my next appointment, always made ahead. Now I came to where I had to recross the same river, but where it was much deeper. So I got with my horse into an old, rickety, leaking flatboat — a little more water in it might have sunk it — but, providentially, got safe across again. Indeed my whole tour of many hundred miles was throughout perilous. Preached at Wheeling, W. Va.; entered Virginia; filled appointments; had great danger in crossing Cheat river, filled with round bowlders of every size when it was rapidly swelling. The horse could not have any solid footing, all tripping and slipping from side to side. Passed and preached in the Greenglades, Preston county, Va.; thence to Cumberland, and, when I arrived at the North Fork of the Potomac, I found it furiously high and raging—no bridge. So I ventured to swim my horse, but was swept by the tremendous current, many rods below the landing place, against a very high and steep bank, all saturated. And every leap the horse made he was imbedded to his body in the wet sand and mud. Here I had a special interference of a good Providence to bring me safely over the nearly last and most imminent peril. Thank God for his goodness. Then arrived safely at my first charge in the old dominion, and found my little family as well as could have been expected. Found many destitute Lutherans who were glad to hear the word. Set in afresh to lead my sacred charge in the way they should go to attain to eternal life.

TRIALS OF EARLY TIMES.

When I moved to Indianapolis, thirty-three years ago, the name of a Lutheran was hardly known there. Then its population was three thousand, and mixed with a number of tolerably intelligent Yankees, one of whom asked me one day, "What new sect are you bringing in here? What do you believe, &c.? Why, sir, replied I, the Bible is our creed-book; but if you come to the court-house at such a day and hour, you can hear and judge for yourself." I and my whole family took chills and fever in the very worst type, notwithstanding, in less than six years, I organized nine congregations. Though small, they were the seed of Lutheranism in Indiana. I lived mostly out of pocket, with a very large and sickly family, and spent out of pocket three thousand dollars, and out of the balance left I was cheated by men who profess the christian religion; thus I was robbed in my old days."

"About twenty-eight years ago, on my return from my six and one-half month's collecting tour through the south and east, nearly dead with the throat disease, for my church at Indianapolis, Ind. I tarried over Lord's day in Cincinnati, at the Denizen house. Then there were thousands of persons viewing and watching a negro-mob; this continued over Sunday in despite of all the municipal and military authorities employed to quell it. Dr. L. Beecher and Rev. Blanchard's both abolition churches, were threatened with demolition. So I attended both, and three others the same day. And amid all this dreadful confusion God impressed most sensibly on my mind, "I must go to Cincinnati and organize an English Evangelical Lutheran Church. Synod met soon in my church at Indianapolis. I made known my determination. They consented with the English Synod of Ohio to give me four hundred dollars annually to support my large family. So I went."

The following paper was furnished by me to the Observer in 1869:

Our "ancients" are rapidly leaving us. Kurtz, Krauth, and ___ and others have gone before. These three were associated for years in the same Synod, and closely knit together in the bonds of sympathy and affection. They were "ancient men who had seen the first house, when the foundation of this house was laid before their eyes," Ezra III, 12, and they worked together for many years in building it up. There never lived more earnest, sincere and successful workers, and "their praise is in all the churches." Fitting eulogies have been pronounced upon the first two mentioned, and upon others, and affection has bound a wreath around the tomb of all, but "Father" Reck lived longer than any of them; he was their predecessor in the ministry by nearly a half a score of years; in "labors he was more abundant than them all;" and hence deserves special notice of the church biographer.

It is my good fortune to have before me an autobiographical sketch written by the lamented deceased less than a year before his death, and hence, I am able to relate facts, and identify dates, as they came from his own hand.

His grandfather came from Germany one hundred and fifty years ago, and settled near Littlestown, Pa. Soon after his family was sheltered, a Lutheran church was erected, and the descendants of those original settlers have grown abundant and strong. In speaking of his family, Mr. R. says: "All my progenitors were Evangelical Lutherans, and had inherited some of the Arndtian and Franckean spirit."

He was born in Littlestown, Pa., January 2, 1791. Died in Lancaster, O., May 18, 1869. At six years of age he was sent to school, and in eight months he learned to read his Bible "pretty well." In some remarks upon the expediency of using the Bible as a school book, he says: "I have known some young preachers, and graduates too, so poorly quote and misquote Scripture, that it mortified me, all owing to a want of acquaintance with the Bible in their youth." His "early religious impressions were received from the instructions and prayers of his parents, from hearing faithful preaching, and reading God's word, but chiefly from the catechetical instruction of Rev. John Grubb, a truly converted man." A severe accident from a scythe confined him to his room for four months, which turned out, as he says, to be the greatest blessing he had ever experienced. He spent the time in reading the Scriptures and praying, and was wonderfully favored with the Divine presence.

He taught school for several years and says: "I always added moral and religious instruction to my school efforts, and prayed with my pupils." Some years after, a relative once said to him, "Cousin A. you recollect when you taught school, you admonished us all to pray in private for a new heart; I did so, when but nine years old, and God heard and blessed me with a new heart." He observes, "that this lady was the most deeply pious person he ever knew."

He now resolved to study for the ministry, and was put under the care of Rev. F. V. Melsheimer of Hanover, who had several other pupils. Of his preceptor, Mr. R. says, "He was one of the most modest, retiring, humble *great* men I ever saw."

In January, 1813, he accepted a call from the church in Winchester, Va., where he labored successfully fifteen years. He states some very interesting facts in relation to his "revivals" and the bitter opposition he encountered. One party in a neighboring village even threatened to murder him, but he resolutely faced his wicked opponents and cowed them by his firmness. Though persecuted by the enemies of the truth, yet no man ever dared to breathe the slightest suspicion against his eminently upright conduct and his unsullied character. He was on most familiar terms with that eminent Presbyterian minister, the late Dr. Hill, of whom Mr. R. speaks in the most exalted terms of praise.

Among other interesting incidents which he relates concerning his fifteen years' residence at Winchester, is one which shows and demonstrates his zeal for God's house. He paid $100 to a master mechanic out of his own pocket to release an apprentice, whom he intended to train for the ministry. He took him to his own boarding-house and paid all his expenses for living, clothes and books for several years, until he was licensed. That minister, Keil, is still living in Ohio. Mr. R. estimates that he spent several thousand dollars in "fitting, in some degree, several pious and talented young men for the work of God."

In 1828 he took charge of the churches in Middletown, Md., and vicinity, after seven successive annual calls, where for some years he displayed the same untiring zeal and conscientious devotion to his pastoral duties. He found the spiritual condition of things very disheartening: "The work of the Lord," he says, "spread through my entire charge of nine congregations, and multitudes of the young as well as the old, dead formalists, professed conversion, and thus were my church members multiplied and greatly edified. * * * My self-sacrifice (though I say it myself) was great, and it is a wonder I did not fall a victim to my excessive labor, long rides and dreadful exposure to heat and cold, rain and snow, with severe pains in the chest and throat, all the time."

In speaking of his labors in the earlier part of his ministry, he says, " I had a congregation in Hampshire Co., Va., thirty miles from my home. I had to cross a mountain eleven miles from foot to foot. The roads were desperate — a part of it called 'The Featherbed' was covered with sharp pointed stones, fast in the beds of the rock, so that the poor horse could hardly venture to tread down. * * * I was obliged to leave home at three or four o'clock on short winter days to reach the place in time;—preached German and English and then catechized a class;—reached the first habitation on my return at ten at night;—sometimes literally frozen stiff, so that they were obliged to lift me from my horse and unbutton my coat and thaw me before a good fire. Then, I would have to roll on my bed during the greater part of the night from severe colic!"

Like some other good men, Mr. R. was sometimes tempted amid his severe bodily afflictions, to resign his holy office, from an overpowering sense of personal unworthiness. On one such occasion, he consulted his old pastor, Mr. Grubb, who in his usual abrupt but still tender way, said, "All this is from the devil,—he sees that God intends you for some good work, and therefore he tries to get you out of the way."

Our venerable friend was somewhat tenacious of his credit to certain well-meant innovations and says, " Bro. Heyer, then of Cumberland, claimed to have had the first Lutheran revival there in modern times. Others, lately, at the death of our very worthy Dr. B. Kurtz, wrote, that he had been favored with the first revival in our churches, but mine occurred several years before he was licensed."

The narrative which our friend has left of his ministerial life is not systematic, and hence he jots down events just as they occurred in his memory.

He gives an account of the opposition made to his measures in one of his churches and of the desperate efforts made to get rid of him. They even hired a lawyer to go to Synod and accuse him of irregularities, without showing him the respect of a legal notice. When the lawyer arose, Mr. R. strenuously objected to the proceedings as unconstitutional:—the lawyer was not even a member of the church, and the accused had not been notified of the charges, but he was allowed to proceed, and read "many pages of foolscap," the substance of which was, that the accused had departed from the good old way, and become a Methodist and fanatic, &c., &c.

"The sainted Dr. Lochman, of Harrisburg, volunteered to defend my holy cause, and did it most manfully, justifying me wholly. Then, Dr. B. Kurtz, the young pastor of Hagerstown, arose and clinched the nail that had been driven—and the work of the Lord still progressed."

Several instances of the extraordinary results of single sermons are given by him; the reformation in one neighborhood where he preached as a visitor was so thorough, that a member of another church remarked, that "young Reck had turned the whole neighborhood into fools, for they won't dance and frolic any more, but all go to prayer-meetings."

Mr. R. was animated all his life with an earnest missionary spirit, and in his earlier ministry visited many destitute places in Western Virginia, during the week, and exposed himself to perils of various kinds. He once sent word ahead that he would hold a prayer-meeting in a certain church, and when he arrived he found the house locked against him. A stout young fellow secretly raised long poles against the end of the house and adroitly entered the window unperceived, and unlocked it from the inside. He returned to the front, and carelessly leaned against the door as if to rest himself, when it flew open, and he fell in after it. The way was now clear, and the meeting was held. The young man himself was converted, and afterwards became a preacher.

In his early life our friend was on intimate and fraternal terms with that "family of preachers," the Henkels of Virginia. He was "always made a welcome visitor" at the house of old Paul Henkel, the father, with whom he often preached in company at Conferences, &c., and this intimacy continued until the Henkels took a decided stand against the General Synod. He relates several interesting facts in relation to this family, which for some years exerted a wide influence upon many members of the church in the Southwest.

Mr. R., during his long life, was invited to several prominent churches. He refused a call from Chambersburg just before Dr. B. Kurtz took charge of that people, and the reason was, that they would not sanction some popular measures which Mr. R. freely practiced, but which Dr. Kurtz afterwards successfully introduced. In the third year of his ministry, about 1816, he refused an invitation to Charleston, S. C., where Dr. Bachman has since labored with success for more than fifty years. He was called to Gettysburg, and invited to visit Lancaster, Pa., as well as other important churches.

In an account of a tour he made to North Carolina, he describes a visit to Rev. G. Stork. He says, "Of all ministers I ever met, Father Stork was the most interesting. A perfect scholar from the Universities of Germany, a perfect Christian gentleman, and of extraordinarily felicitous sociability, but withal a great sufferer from neuralgia. Of him, old Dr. Daniel Kurtz once remarked to me: Mr Stork was a very superior man, but so exceedingly humble, and modest, and self-diffident, that when he should have filled the first pulpit in any city, he settled in what was then the wild country of North Carolina."

In 1836 Mr. Reck was induced to remove to Indianapolis. He purchased property and immediately began to gather the scattered Lutherans of the vicinity. Always at work and always ready to sacrifice health, means and everything else to build up the Church he so dearly loved. Misfortunes of various kinds befel him; he lost his health and was cheated out of his property, after having spent over three thousand ($3,000) dollars of his own funds in sustaining our cause in that then destitute country. He was rendered utterly poor by the machinations of false friends, but was never forsaken by God or sympathizing brethren. A small legacy aided him in a slight degree during the last year of his life, and assistance was afforded from other sources. During his six years residence in Indianapolis he encountered "unparalleled sufferings in every way," "terrific, dark horrors seized upon him," but he was sustained by an Almighty arm amid all his severe trials. I dare not specify these exceedingly sore visitations, but there are few men who are called upon in a Christian land to undergo what Mr. R. did, and yet so submissively did he bear it all, that we are constrained to glorify God's grace in sustaining His servant amid fiery temptations.

In 1841 he removed to Cincinnati to attempt the organization of an English Church. He first preached "in a little, open, rickety place over an engine shanty, the stairs outside and dangerous." Afterward the feeble band "rented the old college." He gives a very interesting account of the conversion of an intelligent Catholic lady, who openly renounced Romanism in the church, submitted to re-confirmation, and had her only child baptized at the same time.

He remained there four years, and was succeeded by the lamented Harrison. During his residence in that city he secured the confidence of other Christian churches and ministers by his unwearied energy in the good cause and his blameless life. Dr. Beecher, and his son-in-law, Prof. Stowe, among others, were his intimate friends. Still, he was not without almost intolerable sufferings even here. After supporting his large family for six weeks on the poorest food, of which meat formed no part, a few friends from Germantown, Ohio, formerly residing in Maryland, came to his house and forced him to pack up at once and be conveyed bag and baggage in their market wagons to that place. Here he got into "a paper-war" with a self-styled Lutheran layman, who was a Universalist. Mr. R. proved from the Augsburg Confession, that no man, maintaining that doctrine, had any right to the name Lutheran, and his opponent was silenced. From the account of his work in that region he must have been eminently successful.

In 1847 he moved to Tarleton, and remained there three years. He was bitterly opposed by some of whom better things might have been looked for. He found himself "in a bad predicament, chiefly by the unfaithfulness of those who were pledged to stand by and sustain him." He also suffered extremely from ulcerated sore throat, but subsequently he was relieved from this painful and dangerous affliction, "as if by magic," in answer to fervent prayer.

1852 he took up his residence in Lancaster, O., but not in answer to any call from a church. Whilst living here he had numerous invitations to visit vacant churches as a candidate, but they were either too large for his impaired health or too small for his support. He tried raising vegetables for gaining a living, and failed in the enterprise.

Mr. R., in the "sketch" by his own hand, now before me, gives a chapter on his sicknesses and sorrows. It is an extraordinary chapter. Intense and protracted attacks of disease during every period of his life, and most wonderful restorations; fearful accidents and remarkable deliverances; domestic afflictions and yet uncomplaining submission; diabolical opposition and yet most signal triumphs over his enemies; seasons of the saddest depression and yet cheerful confidence in God; pinching poverty and yet trust in Him who sent the ravens to feed the famishing prophet; alienation of former friends and yet joyful attachment to Him who sticketh closer than a brother; never despairing, ever hoping, because always praying.

Mr. Reck was a model man. I never knew one who seemed to be more deeply imbued with the spirit of Christ. He never had an enemy who was a true Christian. His bitterest opponents were compelled to acknowledge the unsullied purity of his life, and the most established believer could learn something profitable from his conversation or his example. He was fearless in the defence of the truth, and uncompromising in his opposition to wrong of every kind. He never aimed at winning any man's favor by flattery, and despised chicanery and meanness of every degree. Strongly attached to his own church, and an enthusiastic admirer and almost a worshiper of Luther, yet he had a most catholic spirit, and loved everybody who loved Christ. He constantly practised the good old Lutheran custom of catechetical instruction, and often mentions Luther's catechism in terms of high admiration. As a preacher he was plain, fervent, impressive; as a pastor faithful, self-denying, persevering; as a friend constant, affectionate, forgiving. He was the pattern of a country Christian gentleman of the old school, without the tinsel embellishment of modern fashion, or the hollow-heartedness and duplicity of what is called polite and refined society. We cannot afford to spare many such men from our ministry, but his work was done and he was called home late. He lived seventy-eight years with faculties unimpaired; his memory retentive, his eye bright, his hand steady, and his faith growing. The manuscript before me, finished a few months before his death, shows the round, distinct and symmetrical hand of a youth.

No wonder that a man of such heart and faith should die calmly. His dying experience was edifying and consoling, and his redeemed spirit took its flight to heaven amid the plaudits of waiting angels and the "*Well done*" of a loving Saviour.

EARLY TRIALS OF MR. BECK.

Often when pious young ministers pant to enter the vineyard of their Lord, with the most buoyant expectations, they are sadly tried and crossed in the outset. Thus it happened with myself. I was sent by ecclesiastical authority to missionate three months up and down the valley of ....., with the privilege of locating wherever I chose. Eight of us were examined by the committee of ...... Synod, held at Carlisle, Pa. The first after licensure who was named by Synod was Mr. D. But he refused, so I was named second best, and, after reflection, I agreed to go. Well, when Mr. D. heard of my willingness, he withdrew his objection and offered to go. He was then told that he must go at his own charges, and he agreed. But I was the first appointee, and went and preached through the valley, and when solicited to accept a call from ...., I agreed in a verbal contract. But when Mr. D. afterward came along, he told the churches that I was not regularly sent, but he himself was. And as he pretended to a little more familiarity with the English than myself, the church council at .. .. broke their agreement with me. I was apprised of all this and went on a second tour over the same field, to make up my three months; and having acquiesced, as I thought, in the will of the Master, I stopped to feed in ...., and was seen by one of the elders, who asked me whether I would not now preach and take charge of them? I replied, "Why, you have a pastor in Mr. D." Then I was informed, although he had engaged to come, yet he never returned, nor even wrote to them. On having visited a number of vacant charges, and being solicited to take charge of several places, I felt a drawing to my first engagement at .... After this trial of faith and patience in the outset, I then re-contracted with the churches at .... Meanwhile a call had been prepared for me by the pastorate at Gettysburg, Pa. But I could not comply. I got Bro. A. Rudisill to go there, who soon died; my dearest fellow-student!! O! how long I must wander behind him here below! But God knows best what is good for us.

THE REV. DR. JOHN W. RICHARDS

was, during the whole period of his ministerial life, an influential member of the Synod of Pennsylvania. He was in advance of many of his fellow members in the advocacy of those measures which tended to unite the various sections of the church and to foster her modern institutions. He wrote a series of strong articles, in favor of the General Synod, for the Lutheran Observer, when his Synod stood aloof from that Union, and always supported every measure which aimed at improvement and progress.

He died suddenly at Reading in 1854, aged fifty-one. He was the great grand-son of Rev. Dr. Henry Melchior Muhlenberg, the apostle of Lutheranism on the Western Continent, and inherited a large portion of the spirit of that eminent minister.

For a biographical sketch see Sprague's Annals.

REV. FREDERICK RUTHRAUFF

was universally allowed to be one of the most Godly and devoted men that ever adorned our ministry. Those who knew him best bear the most unequivocal testimony to the uprightness of his life and the fervor of his spirit. He was born in Greencastle, Pa., October 25, 1796, and died at Worthington, Armstrong Co., Pa., September 18, 1859.

A brief autobiography is published in the Observer of October 14, 1859, in which he gives many interesting details of the early period of his life. He was a student at Washington College, Pa., for two years, but was obliged to leave on account of pecuniary embarrassments and began the study of Theology in 1820, under Dr. Lochman, of Harrisburg.

Dr. B. Kurtz, in a long obituary notice in Observer of Oct. 7, 1859, thus speaks of him:

"I think that I understood him thoroughly, and may be permitted to indulge in a few reflections. * * * In subsequent life he was constantly so immersed in the arduous duties of his vocation, that he had but little time left for study. When he first commenced his ministry, he wrote out every sermon he prepared, and read it *verbatim* to his audience. This was a ground of objection among his people, and I more than once chided him for *reading*, and urged him, while he studied his sermons thoroughly, to preach from brief notes at first, and gradually accustom himself to dispense with them also. He thought this impossible. But I continued from time to time to press the point, and referred to my own example as an incentive. I had at first written out all my sermons and delivered them from memory; I found this to be an intolerable drudgery; and driven by necessity, had learned to preach in my humble way from a prepared plan without any notes in the pulpit. He rejoined, that to preach *extempore* was a gift: that he possessed it not, and was sure that its attainment was utterly beyond his reach, and it was wholly in vain for him even to aim at it. I persisted, and he at last "with fear and trembling" made a trial, succeeded, tried again, and succeeded still better, and from that day until his death never, I presume, again read a sermon from the pulpit. He afterwards thanked me for my reproof and exhortations, and his people loved his more than ever.

Mr. R. was not a florid nor a fanciful speaker; but he was an earnest, impassioned, deeply spiritual and practical preacher. His sermons were systematic and thoroughly imbued with Gospel truth; his language plain, his manner solemn, his defence of the truth fearless, and his warnings and exhortations powerful and impressive, and often delivered with an ardor and eloquence that appalled the guilty, and caused the daring sinner to quiver with the barbed arrows that penetrated and rankled in his heart. His prayers especially were fervent and overpowering.

His life was such as might be expected from a man of his principles. It was consistent with the Gospel, and a practical commentary upon the Gospel's precepts. Conscientious, courageous in the discharge of duty, untiring in labor, candid in the expression of his sentiments, free and open alike with friend and foe, and habitually breathing a spirit of deep piety—I always felt stimulated by personal intercourse with him to become a better man and more devoted Christian. His ministry was repeatedly blessed with signal outpourings of the Spirit.

Bro. R. frequently changed his pastorate. This has furnished occasion for disparaging strictures. But I have been led to view those changes in a different light. It was peculiarly befitting that a man of such character should move to and fro in the church.

carrying with him wherever he went his remarkable energy and devotion, his deep spirituality and fidelity, imbuing the neighboring ministers, as well as his own charge with the same holy, God-consecrated spirit that animated himself.

Our brother had his frailties, probably fewer, however, than fall to the lot of many of us. Perhaps the chief defect in his ministerial character was the lack of adaptation in the matter and manner of his reproofs. He was too conscientious not to rebuke when occasion called for it. With him *duty* was paramount; and whether in private or in the pulpit, if he deemed it to be his duty to admonish, to warn, or to reprove, he was not the man to shirk out either for fear or favor. I am sure he never crooked the pregnant hinges of the knee, that thrift might follow fawning. But how to discharge this delicate and painful duty in the least offensive and most successful manner, was an art which he was slow to learn. More than once did I myself venture to take him to task for this failing, and more than once did he mourn over it and resolve to pray and study that he might acquire it.

Bro. R. was emphatically not "a dumb dog that could not bark:" he lifted up his voice like a trumpet, and the trumpet in his mouth never gave "an uncertain sound." Such earnestness and fidelity could not remain unproductive. No hazard is involved in saying that in every church committed to his charge he has left "seals to his ministry;" in every such church men and women may be found who loved and reverenced him, and will bear testimony to his worth. For myself, I knew no man on earth whom I would rather have had at my dying couch, because I am sure he would have dealt honestly with me in the momentous matter of my everlasting destiny, and prayed in living faith for my eternal salvation."

The Rev. M. J. Alleman thus speaks of him in the same paper:

"Mr. Ruthrauff was a fine looking man: tall and portly in person—erect in his bearing, dignified, yet easy in his manners, social in his habits, he always made a good impression upon the minds of those with whom he associated.

And as his body was erect, so was his soul sincere. He scorned hypocrisy, and despised the sycophant. He was no dissembler.—Himself honest and upright, he expected the same of others. And not only was this true of him in the ordinary transactions of this life, but likewise in the higher affairs of the spirit. He was as honest in things spiritual as in things temporal. If he saw any, in things ecclesiastical, ministers or laymen, making pretensions, or laying claims to more than justly belonged to them, he failed not to administer a withering rebuke, if opportunity offered.

For this reason, some have thought that Mr. Reffinaur was proud and haughty. Those not *intimately* acquainted with him might think so. Not so with those who were acquainted with the secrets of his heart. He was one of the humblest of men. The precept, "Think not more highly of yourself than ye ought to think," was fully complied with in his case. I have heard him, with tears in his eyes, lament his unworthiness—and freely acknowledge himself the *least* among his brethren.

As a preacher, in many respects he was a model. He aimed to awaken, instruct and edify. There was nothing of the bombastic in his efforts. His style was plain—a child could understand him —his statements clear and logical—his appeals powerful, and at times overwhelming. He preached to do good—not to please and captivate his hearers. He feared no man's face:—his exhortations were earnest, as his exposition of Scripture was evangelical. His rebukes of sin and sinners were withering, and sometimes gave offence; yet no man dared question his sincerity, though they might doubt his prudence.

Yet his crowning excellency was his piety—this was unaffected, deep-toned and progressive. I never heard his bitterest enemies (and he had these—Christ, Paul and Luther had them) ever express a doubt but that he was a good man, as he unquestionably was a good preacher. I had been associated with him in Synods, Conferences, protracted-meetings, prayer-meetings, and family devotions, ever since 1846, and he always exhibited the same devotional spirit, the same love to Christ and his kingdom, the same ardent longing for the salvation of sinners, and the edification of the flock of Jesus. Oh! how fervently and appropriately he used to pray, my heart often melted under his prayers—how heartily he used to sing, and how he loved to talk about Zion—how frequently he used to interrogate me in reference to news ecclesiastical. But he has gone to his rest, and his works do follow him.*

---

* I remember that I once showed Mr. R. an allusion to his name in a German book on "Pastoral Theology in Examples." It was an extract from an American paper, giving an account of a protracted meeting which he had held in Gettysburg, which, though nothing unusual in its results, was strange to the author of the book. Mr. R. was gratified, not so much at the fact of his own name appearing in a foreign book as that our over-the-sea friends should hear and appreciate such measures.

J. G. M.

WALTER GUNN

was the first missionary from our church to the heathen who died in the field. He sailed for India in 1843, and died in 1851. He was a graduate of Union College in 1841, and studied theology at Gettysburg. He was a man universally esteemed, and contributed immeasurably towards awakening a missionary spirit in our churches in this country. He was educated at the expense of a Female Benevolent Society of the Hartwick Synod; was licensed in 1842; ordained by that Synod at Johnstown in 1843.

The following letters from Sprague's Annals illustrate his character:

Rev. Dr. Pohlman writes: "The first time I ever saw the Rev. Walter Gunn was at the meeting of the General Synod in Baltimore, in 1843, when he was appointed the first Foreign Missionary of the Evangelical Lutheran Missionary Society of the United States. Shortly after this he visited me at New Germantown, N. J., where I had then my pastoral charge, and preached for me—the only time, I think, that I ever had the opportunity of hearing him. In 1845 I came into official relations with him as Corresponding Secretary of our Foreign Missionary Society, and continued in these relations for two or three years."

"Mr. Gunn was a very tall man, I should think somewhat over six feet, and proportionally slender. His appearance seemed prophetic of the approach of consumption, the disease which, I think, finally terminated his life. He was of light complexion, and had a light blue eye, with a general expression of countenance indicative rather of the milder than the sterner qualities. His manner in private intercourse was modest and retiring, and, though he conversed intelligently and appropriately, he seemed rather disposed to follow than to lead. As to his intellect I should be at a loss to say what faculty was the more prominent. His mind seemed distinguished rather for a symmetrical and equable constitution than for a striking development at any single point. I take it that his most prominent characteristic was that earnest and heroic devotion to the cause of Christ, which led him to give himself to the Foreign Missionary enterprise, and sustained him nobly in that work as long as he lived. A very slight acquaintance with him would reveal the fact that the great objects and interests upon which his heart was fixed lay beyond this world.

It was manifest that his whole soul was embarked in the effort to save the souls of the poor heathen, and that whatever stood in the way of this was either resolutely encountered or cheerfully sacrificed. The results of his labors show that he performed them in communion with the Lord his Strength. As the first American Lutheran Missionary who fell in the foreign field, his name will always remain fragrant throughout our Church."

FROM THE REV. CHARLES A. HAY, D. D.

Rev. and Dear Sir: As a fellow student of the Rev. Walter Gunn, in the Theological Seminary of the Lutheran Church at Gettysburg, I became somewhat intimately acquainted with him, and have always cherished his memory with peculiar pleasure. Naturally timid and reserved, and completely absorbed in the great work to which he had devoted his life, he did not seek the society of others, but rather shrank from their notice, and seemed to think no moment properly employed unless, in some way, it was made to facilitate his improvement in the essential qualifications for winning souls to Christ among the Heathen.

Perhaps the most striking feature of his character was his *singleness of purpose*. He gave himself up wholly and heartily to one controlling idea—the great idea of the Apostle to the Gentiles—" that I might, by all means, save some." Rarely do we meet with any one so regardless of all else, so indifferent to the opinions of those around him, so free from all desire for human applause, so eagerly intent upon doing only his duty. The work of Missions was to him the object of life. He thought and spoke of it by day, he dreamed of it by night. It was his meat and his drink. Nor was this an unintelligent enthusiasm or a romantic passion, but a true love of souls, embracing those near at hand with ardent affection, and seeming to glow with greater intensity as it expanded and included those far distant and far more destitute. It was a deeply rooted conviction of the duty of Christ's followers to be intently engaged in the great work of winning individual souls to Him. The preciousness of one soul was a theme upon which he delighted to dwell, and he seemed willing to undergo any privation and perform any amount of labor if he might but persuade a fellow sinner to be reconciled to God. From this it will be readily inferred that his influence upon his fellow students was highly salutary; and the records of the institution will probably was as perfect a man as I ever knew, and this is the testimony of all who were acquainted with him. The following letters from men who were better acquainted with him than I was give an unexaggerated picture of his character, and I will let them speak:

FROM PROFESSOR M. L. STOEVER.

His countenance indicated some degree of sternness, but there seemed beneath much tenderness of feeling, and great kindness and benevolence. His elevated tone of conversation and his dignified and sedate manner left an impression on my mind that was altogether agreeable; and the only effect of my being brought into more intimate relations with him was that the same impression was rendered deeper; especially I had a stronger sense of his great moral worth, and of the purity and force of his principles. He was at that time a member of the Junior class in Pennsylvania College, holding a high rank in the institution, and exerting an influence for good which it is seldom the privilege of a student to exert. He commanded the respect of all, and possessed the warm esteem of those who knew him more intimately. His very appearance was a check to levity and thoughtlessness. His Christian character seemed eminently consistent. He was regular in his attendance on all college duties, and faithful to every engagement that claimed his attention. The same traits of character he afterwards exhibited when he was called to act in more public stations.

Next to the devoted and all-pervading piety which, I should say, constituted the most prominent feature in Dr. Keller's character, or rather made it essentially what it was, I may mention his remarkable moral courage, which was adequate to any emergency requiring its exercise. He was fearless in the advocacy of such measures as he thought were right, regardless of the praise or the censure of his fellow men. "Not as pleasing man but God" was the great motto of his life, and to this he adhered with stern and unwavering fidelity. He had great force of character, which gave him more than ordinary influence over those with whom he was associated. He was remarkable for his untiring energy and indomitable perseverance. In youth he had formed habits of self-reliance which he carried with him through life. Whatever he undertook was almost certain to succeed.

As a preacher Dr. Keller possessed no small ability. He never failed to gain and hold the attention of his audience. His discourses were lucid, biblical, practical and weighty. They were remarkable for simple and pertinent illustration, and abounded in pathetic and touching allusions. He never attempted to explain what was inexplicable, never strayed off into the region of metaphysical subtlety, but contented himself with preaching the doctrines and precepts of the gospel in all their naked simplicity and purity. His manner was solemn and impressive, earnest and affectionate. The tones of his voice were clear, full and commanding, his enunciation easy and distinct, his gesture natural, while his personal appearance, and especially the expression of his countenance, served to aid, in no small degree, the general effect. In public prayer he was alike felicitous in his expressions and devout in his manner. No one who heard him could resist the conviction that the spirit which he breathed was imbibed in the closet, and that the petitions ascended from a heart in which the Sanctifier and the Comforter had his constant dwelling place.

Dr. Keller's services were much in demand in seasons of unusual religious interest, and they were on many such occasions attended with a manifest blessing. I heard him several times in the spring of 1843, when his preaching produced an impression not soon to be forgotten. His earnest expostulations, his tender and thrilling appeals, the deep concern he manifested in the sinner's welfare, excited an interest such as I have rarely witnessed, and crowded the place of worship with attentive and deeply affected listeners.

Dr. Keller was a very successful pastor. He kept a faithful watch over his flock. He was instant in season and out of season. He was equally at home in the sick chamber and the house of mourning, and knew how to speak a word in season to the doubting and the erring, the inconstant and the wayward. Kindness and firmness were blended in his character in beautiful propertions, rendering him everywhere at once acceptable and useful, and securing to him a warm place in the hearts of all with whom he associated.

I will only add that Dr. Keller possessed excellent natural abilities. His mind acted with great directness, clearness and force, readily grasping the strong points of every subject that engaged his attention. He possessed strong common sense, an accurate judgment and a penetrating foresight. Had he been spared to advanced life there is no doubt that he would have attained a rank among the most distinguished ministers of his day; and, notwithstanding his early death, he has left behind him a name that will long remain fragrant in many a circle.

FROM THE REV. SAMUEL SPRECHER, D. D., PRESIDENT OF WITTENBERG COLLEGE.

He was a man of strong passions, but, having by Divine grace brought them under the control of reason and conscience, he became one of the most calm and considerate, as well as one of the most determined and energetic men I ever saw. In the earlier part of his career, while struggling with poverty, it was connected with a tinge of severity bordering on moroseness, and a tone of austerity in his manner almost repulsive. Afterwards, when in more comfortable circumstances, that same great spirit went out among his followers with a peculiar generosity, kindness and tenderness. Sometimes there was, however, even in those early days, much playfulness in his sarcasm. At an entertainment given to his class on their graduation, he was sitting apart while the company was engaged in the trifling conversation which is too common on such occasions, when, on being accosted by one of them with the remark—"You must be pondering some great subject, Mr. Keller, as you are so silent." "Yes," he said, "I am wondering how intelligent young gentlemen and ladies can talk so much nonsense." I recollect, on one occasion, a report of most disgraceful conduct in a minister got into circulation, and, while his best friends in the neighborhood failed to inform him of it, Dr. K., though living at a distance, as soon as it reached his ear, wrote to that brother, who instantly demanded an investigation, which resulted in the most complete proof that the charge was a malicious slander. His firmness was so remarkable that an opponent of his once said to me in the way of complaint—" We have no remedy; when he says a thing we may as well give up; it will be done."

On the death of a very worthy youth, a student of Wittenberg College, he, as President of the institution, was invited by the father, who was an infidel, to pronounce a eulogy, but requested not to preach a sermon. Dr. K. positively refused to say one word unless he were permitted to declare what he believed to be the whole counsel of God. After much hesitation the father consented, but remarked:—"I hope you will spare us as much as you can." A congregation in his neighborhood was in a divided and distracted state, when he was invited by the Council to preside at a congregational meeting held for the purpose of electing a pastor. Though he knew that he should make for himself many enemies by the course which he would feel bound to take in the execution of constitutional provisions, he unhesitatingly performed the duty, and then wrote to the brother, who was elected in the midst of great opposition, in a tone of earnestness, nay, almost of command, to accept the post of difficulty and save, as he believed under God he could save, a church from ruin. And, induced in a great measure by his confidence in the wisdom as well as the firmness of Dr. Keller, that brother took the step proposed, and the result justified the expectations that were held out to him. The people were not only fully united in due time, but those who were most bitterly opposed to the interposition of Dr. K., and to the pastor elected, became the pastor's best friends, and afterwards, on his leaving his charge in a state of great prosperity for another field of labor, they were as loth to part with him as they had been to receive him.

And this great man, so strong in his determination, was as simple as a child in his confession of conscious error. In a literary contest with another student at college, he was led, in the chagrin of disappointed ambition (for, as I have said, his passions were strong), to utter charges against his rival, which he quickly discovered had no foundation in truth. He not only made full confession of the wrong to that individual, but availed himself of every opportunity to correct the wrong impression, and make all possible reparation for the injury.

My latest recollection of Dr. Keller is most tender and impressive. On his last visit to the East, only two months before his lamented death, he spent a few days with me, and made impressions on my mind which time cannot efface. There was a meek dignity, earnestness and tenderness, connected with an elevation, enlargement and benevolence of feeling, which I have never seen so fully exhibited in any other man. He preached to us on " doing good." It is not necessary for me to say that he was very eloquent; but as his was moral greatness, and as he was distinguished for his practical power, I may say that never did an audience realize more fully that doing good, in the very spirit of Jesus, was the characteristic of the preacher, and the soul of his eloquence. And though he seemed to be in good health, having become more fleshy than he was before he left the East, and though he spoke most confidently and gratefully of his strong and improved health, yet there was such a peculiar spirituality, such an almost superhuman solemnity about him, that I felt a reverence for him more profound than I have ever realized in the presence of a fellow mortal.

Among other things which I hope I shall never forget, is the following: — He seemed greatly concerned about the state of religion in our branch of the church, and deeply impressed with the idea that there was a decline in spirituality; that a reaction of error and formalism against the evangelical sentiments and the revival spirit, which had, for many years, been prevalent within the bounds of the General Synod of our Church, was coming down upon us. I had conducted him, in the course of our conversation, to a beautiful cemetery belonging to one of the churches of the place, and was pointing out to him, occasionally, some of the attractions of the grounds, when he requested me to be seated with him on one of the tombs; and then, alluding to the evidence which he had presented of the reality of the evils which threatened the church, he most solemnly charged me to be faithful to the truth and cause of God in the anticipated trial. Appealing to the fact that I, as well as he, had satisfactory evidence that the sentiments in which we had been educated were evangelical, and that the revival of religion with which a large part of the church had been favored for a quarter of a century was genuine, he charged me to be faithful to them, to be careful not to be seduced by the delusions which he thought were accumulating around us. Such seemed to be the habitual spirit of this devoted servant of God.

FROM THE REV. WILLIAM M. PAXTON, D. D., THEN PROFESSOR IN THE (PRESBYTERIAN) THEOLOGICAL SEMINARY, ALLEGHANY CITY, PA.

He was one of those men who impressed themselves upon my memory in boyhood, and, although many years have passed since, he comes up before me at this moment, in person and character, as distinctly as if I had parted with him but yesterday.

Ezra Keller was then a member of the Senior class of Pennsylvania College, and I, a little boy, receiving, under Frederick's cogent discipline, my first initiation into the mysteries of declensions and conjugations. To my youthful imagination a Senior was an object of no small reverence; but among the many men of mark in that class, there was no one who made so deep and abiding an impression upon my mind as Ezra Keller. There was something, even then, in his aspect and demeanor, that produced a solemn and inspiring impression, not only upon his own equals in age, but even upon men of mature minds and large experience. I can see him, even now, as he entered the College yard at the hour of morning recitation—his deliberate step, his self-possessed, impressive manner, his unusually genteel appearance, his ministerial air, his broad, heavy face and expansive forehead, his measured, solemn tones of voice, his deeply spiritual and devotional cast of countenance—all combining to foreshadow the very characteristics for which he was afterwards so much distinguished. He was perhaps the oldest, and certainly the most mature, student in the institution; and this, together with his superior mind, his accurate scholarship, and his manifest and acknowledged sanctity, rendered him a sort of oracle in the College. Among the pious students his influence was truly wonderful, his opinion on almost any question being regarded as decisive. In matters of practical religion he was looked up to as a model. His simple presence would repress all levity; his warmth of devotional feeling enkindled other hearts; his consistency exemplified the true law of the Christian life; his zeal stimulated every Christian enterprise; and the spirituality and earnestness of his daily life gave impression and tone to the religious circle in which he moved.

Among my most vivid recollections of that period was a literary contest in which he bore a conspicuous part. The rivalry between the two Literary Societies was, at that time, very strong, but strictly honorable. Keller was the champion of the Phrenakosmian Society, whilst the Philomathean was represented by a man of rare gifts and unusually popular eloquence. The prospect of such a literary rencontre awakened quite an excitement among the students, and enlisted the interest of the whole community. When the evening for the contest arrived, long before the chime of bells on the old Lutheran Church signalled the procession to start from the College, the church (with the exception of the seats reserved for the students) was filled to overflowing with an excited crowd, drawn from all classes in the town, and to some extent from the surrounding country. Both the combatants acquitted themselves admirably; but, as there were no judges appointed, no award of superiority was made, and, the audience being divided in sentiment, the public discussed the merits of the two speakers as warmly as *they* had discussed the merits of the question. The truth was that the gifts of the two debaters were so entirely different that they could not well be compared. Mr. Keller's portion of the debate was a masterly argument, characterized by that vigorous, massive, logical power of thought, which afterwards made him so able a Theologian and such a successful teacher. The other part of the debate was a splendid, eloquent oration, displaying such brilliant genius and rare powers of popular oratory as called forth the prediction (which has been fully verified) that the speaker would make one of the most eloquent and popular preachers in the Lutheran Church.

Another recollection, which I cannot omit to record, dates some years later. After Dr. Keller had been settled, for some time, in the ministry, he returned to Gettysburg, and preached in connection with the Rev. Mr. Conrad, in the College Church, during a protracted meeting in the winter of 1843. It was a time of wonderful religious impression. The preaching was blessed to the awakening of many persons in town; and such was the effect produced upon the College that I do not think there were more than two or three students who did not give evidence of some concern about the salvation of their souls. I was, at the time, a member of the Senior class, and well remember the preaching of Dr. Keller, and especially one sermon, which was among the first instrumentalities that led me to serious reflection. The sermon presented three vivid portraitures,—the sinner, first, in his carelessness; second, under conviction; and third, laying hold on Christ. The first picture, that of an impenitent, careless sinner, was so true to life, exhibiting so graphically the state of his thoughts and feelings, that I was alarmed, and felt as if I were myself the subject which the preacher was sketching. So deeply were my feelings wrought upon that, when he came to the second picture,—that of the convinced sinner,—I felt again that this was precisely my condition; and when he passed to the third, and described the sinner laying hold on Christ, he carried me along by a powerful constraint, and left me nearer the Cross than I had ever been before. The whole sermon was pronounced with great calmness and deliberation, but there was such clearness of statement, such an intimate knowledge of the workings of the human heart, such vividness of delineation and pungency of application, as showed that he was possessed of unusual qualifications for pulpit efficiency.

DR. LEWIS EICHELBERGER

was born in Frederick county, Md., on the 25th of August, 1803, so that at his death he had just entered upon his 57th year.

At the early age of ten or eleven years we find the subject of this notice in the school of Rev. Dr. Schaeffer, of Frederick, Md. Not a few of the clergymen of our church received their early training at that school. Subsequently he was removed to Georgetown, D. C., and whilst boarding in the family of a married sister, attended the classical school of the Rev. Dr. Carnahan, who afterwards became distinguished as the President of Princeton College.

From Georgetown he was transferred to Dickinson College, Carlisle, Pa., at which Institution he was graduated Sept. 27th, 1826. From the "order of exercises of that commencement, we see that the deceased was a classmate of the *Rev. Dr. Baugher*, President of Pennsylvania College, and of *George Buchanan*, brother of the President of the United States. The *Valedictory*, noted as the first honor, was taken by Mr. Buchanan; the *Latin Salutatory*, a second honor, was given to Dr. Baugher; and the *English Salutatory*, also a second honor, was assigned to Dr. Eichelberger.

From College he at once removed to the newly organized Theological Seminary at Gettysburg, and became a member of the first class formed in that Institution, and one of its first graduates. After spending two years in the study of Theology, he was licensed to preach the Gospel by the Evangelical Lutheran Synod of Maryland and Virginia, convened in Shepherdstown, Oct. 21st, 1828.

Whilst yet a student of Theology, he accepted an urgent invitation from the council of the Lutheran church of Winchester, Va., to visit them and preach for them. The result of this visit was his unanimous election as pastor of the congregation. Immediately after his licensure he repaired to his new field of labor, and at once commenced his duties.

His "ministerial journal" shows an amount of service and a degree of fidelity worthy of all praise. In connection with the church in Winchester, he served three congregations in the country. Having been vacant for a considerable time prior to his settlement over them, some of these congregations were much scattered and distracted, but in all of them great good seems to have been accomplished.

This connection continued until May 1st, 1833 (a period of four years and six months), when the charge of the church in Winchester was resigned, but that of the country churches retained. About this time Dr. Eichelberger opened a female school in this place known as Angevona Seminary, and shortly after became proprietor and editor of a weekly journal still known as "*The Virginian.*" In these several occupations he continued actively and usefully engaged until the year 1849, when he was elected to the Professorship of Theology in the Lutheran Seminary at Lexington, S. C. At first he declined the appointment, but was induced to change his decision, and he then removed from Winchester, after a residence of more than twenty years. As Professor of Theology he labored with the same untiring diligence and conscientious fidelity with which all his preceding duties had been discharged. He continued to serve the church in that responsible capacity until impaired health made it proper for him to ask a release. In the year 1853, his position and attainments were suitably recognized by one of the oldest and most influential literary institutions of our country. The honorary degree of *Doctor of Divinity* was conferred by Princeton College. He resigned his Professorship in March, 1858, and immediately returned to Winchester, warmly welcomed by many ardent friends. His time, however, was not without its appropriate employment. He eagerly seized the leisure at his disposal for the execution of a long cherished purpose to prepare for the press a compact and popular "*History of the Lutheran Church,*" for which he had made extensive preparation in the collection of materials, and the sketching of chapters, as other duties permitted, or other pursuits and studies furnished opportunities. Although frequently interrupted by illness and much disabled by bodily weakness, he yet lived to finish his last work of love to his church, of which he was ever an admiring, loyal son, and a faithful, self-denying servant. Death found him with the harness still on, ready to do or die as his Lord might order. His death was peace, was triumph. It was a privilege which shall never be forgotten to see his heavenly composure, and to hear his dying utterances. When he had but strength to whisper a few words at a time, he said to a brother in the ministry—"*Christ is a precious Saviour—he does more than he promises for his dying followers. Go, preach to sinners, Christ will save them all. Nothing but Christ will do in death.*"

He was very much beloved by all for whom and with whom he labored, and was universally respected and esteemed wherever he he lived. He was twice married, and left a widow and five children to mourn their loss, and cherish his memory.

Dr. Eichelberger was an eminently pious man, a devoted Christian, an able and faithful preacher and teacher, and an affectionate and sympathising friend and pastor. He always manifested great simplicity of character, exemplifying the humble virtues and meek adornments of the child of God.

HENRY LEWIS BAUGHER

was born in Abbottstown, Adams county, Pa., in 1804. His preparation for college life he received at the Gettysburg Academy, then under the care of Rev. Dr. McConaughy. He was graduated at Dickinson College in 1826, and entered the Theological Seminary at Princeton the same year. Subsequently, he became a student in the Seminary at Gettysburg. He was licensed to preach by the West Pennsylvania Synod in 1828. In 1829 he joined the Synod of Maryland and Virginia, and soon after became pastor of the church at Boonsboro, which was the only pastoral charge he ever had, except his connection with the college church at Gettysburg for several years.

He was called to Gettysburg in April, 1831, as classical teacher in the place of Rev. D. Jacobs, deceased, in the Gettysburg Gymnasium.

When Pennsylvania College was chartered, in 1832, Mr. Baugher was elected to the chair of Greek and Belles Lettres. This position he filled until the fall of 1850, when he was elected to the Presidency. He held this office nearly eighteen years. He died just as the senior year closed, April 14th, 1868. He was confined to his chamber only about a week, but his health had been declining for a year or two before.

His strong will continued to the last, and he thought he would recover his health, even on the morning of the day on which he died. When told of the opinion of the physicians, he replied: "The Lord's will be done."

Mr. Baugher received the degree of D. D. from Dickinson College in 1848, to which his name was proposed by a person who he never suspected would render such service to him.

One of my correspondents writes: "Dr. Baugher was a good man, and wanted to do good. He was very much interested in the college, and earnestly labored to advance its welfare. If his prejudices had been less strong, and his character less impulsive, he would, no doubt, have been a more useful man and more generally beloved by those who were brought in contact with him. He labored faithfully, and I often think of him now as resting. If he were now living, he would worry over matters which, after all, are of very little importance."

Dr. Baugher was a general reader, but his favorite reading, as it should be with all divines, was his Greek Testament. Homer was also read for recreation. His daily habit was, an hour before breakfast in private prayer and meditation and nearly an hour with his Greek Testament. After breakfast, study or college work all day.

After his graduation, he intended to study law with Frank Key, of Washington, but he began to think that if he did that it might endanger his spiritual welfare. His mother had made it a constant prayer that God would direct her youngest son to the ministry, and her prayer was heard.

He was a diligent writer of sermons, and one of his sons tells me that "he had stacks of them."

Dr. Baugher was a severe and exemplary moralist. He never

sanctioned among clergymen and Christian people what many regarded as innocent amusements, such as chess or chequers, and I doubt whether he would now sanction *croquet*, which has since become a popular clerical amusement.

He was a puritanic observer of what he called the Sabbath, and severely temperate in all things.

He was regarded by some as stern, or what is called "abrupt," and there is no doubt that he was an unsparing critic. Hence, he was not liked by some who did not intimately know him. He was, perhaps, a little too free in expressing his sentiments; he never disguised his opinion on any subject; he despised duplicity of every kind; and, on all measures and subjects, you could easily find out what he thought, if you wanted to know.

When he was elected President of the college, I was appointed to go to his house and inform him, and to receive his answer. He scarcely gave me time to announce my message, before he abruptly replied: "*I will not accept it.*" He had taken no time to deliberate, and I knew his manner too well to believe that this would be his final determination. He subsequently accepted the call, and presided over the college for nearly eighteen years with distinguished success.

He had administrative talent of the first class. As a disciplinarian he was stern, yet kindly considerate of the infirmities and temptations of young men.

He never aimed at authorship of the highest character, but his published sermons, baccalaureate addresses, Review and Observer articles, are forcibly written, and display an uncommon share of solid, good sense, without any rhetorical flourishes of style or affectation of what some call fine writing.

His Presbyterian training influenced the character of his Theology, although he was in no proper sense a Calvinist.

In the pulpit, he was instructive, solid, evangelical, and yet plain, and sometimes rising to impressive earnestness. He continued all his life to be a close reader of his sermons, and this detracted somewhat from his freedom of speech and the natural impulses of his disposition. If he had always preached as he spoke on the floor of the Synod or of other deliberative bodies, he would have been one of our most impressive pulpit orators.

Dr. Baugher had a vein of satire in his mental composition which, if cultivated and exercised, would have acquired him reputation as a writer, as well as more enemies than he had. It is known to very few of us that he was the writer of an article in "The Lutheran," entitled "The Lion Hunter," which gave serious offence in Gettysburg, and which was severely denounced by such amiable men even as Dr. Krauth; but nobody knew that the author was one of their own residents, and who, with a grim satisfaction, heard himself and his piece fiercely abused. He had projected a series of similar articles, but he concluded to abandon the idea of publishing them.

Dr. Baugher's hospitality was unbounded, and, though he had the name of being stern and too outspoken in his views of men and things, yet he had a kind and forgiving heart. His conversation among his friends was interesting and instructive, and his manners among strangers bland and courteous.

He died regretted by a large circle of friends, and in his death the church and the college sustained an irreparable loss.

REV. DR. EDWIN W. HUTTER.

The following sketch of Rev. Dr. Edwin W. Hutter is copied, for the most part, from the oration delivered at his funeral on September 27th, 1873, by Rev. Dr. Wedekind, to which I have appended some personal recollections of my own.

Dr. Hutter was born at Allentown, Pa., September 12, 1813, and was, therefore, at his death, sixty years and eight days old.

He received his education in the village school and the printer's office, that wonderful college from which some of the most celebrated men of our country have graduated. The want of a liberal college education was in a measure supplied by the home training under the supervision of his father, who was a man of more than ordinary attainments, and possessing a prodigious amount of energy, perseverance and application, features of character which have all been reproduced, and I may say even augmented by the subject of these remarks. Such were his application, industry and perseverance, that at the death of his father, when he was but seventeen years of age, he became the editor and proprietor of two weekly newspapers, one German and one English, supplying the editorial columns of both with his prolific pen, and supervising every department of the office work besides. It was here where he attained that marvelous facility with the pen that accompanied him through his whole life. Never have I known his equal in this particular. I have sat beside him in synods, amidst the most exciting debates, when he reported simultaneously for three different papers. And these reports were models for fairness, clearness and accuracy. His style as a writer was ornate, leaning a little to redundancy. His productions were always fresh and juicy, interspersed with historical facts and allusions of a striking character, for he had a *memory* that was marvelous for its capacity and retentiveness. It seemed to me sometimes that he never forgot anything that he had seen, heard or read. And his knowledge was not like a lumber yard of second-hand lumber, a chaos of confusion, where you can never get what you want without a world of trouble, but rather like an apothecary shop, where everything is labeled and in its proper place.

By reason of his position as editor he became acquainted with many of the politicians and statesmen of the country, who as friends cherished him, but as an antagonist dreaded him. For several years he resided at Washington as private secretary of Mr. Buchanan, then Secretary of State of the United States, and such was the estimate formed by that statesman of the ability and general character of brother H., that when subsequently elected to the presidential chair an embassy to a foreign court was tendered him. But God had meanwhile clothed him with an office infinitely above anything human. He had become an ambassador to the King of glory, and, like Nehemiah, he felt that he had a great work to do, and would not come down to serve earthly rulers. In God's providence he was called upon to follow the apple of his eye, his dear boy, to an early grave, amidst the saddest cries. But the death of the child became the life of the father. For whilst God smote him with his right arm, he emboldened him with his left, and drew him but the closer to himself. Over the marble-like corpse of little James he covenanted with his God and Father to serve him thereafter in a very different form from what he had done before, and, under the guidance of the Rev. Dr. Baker, of Lancaster, Pa., whom he afterward loved as a son loves a father, his thoughts were directed to the Christian ministry. Long and earnestly did he pray for light to decide that momentous question.

and when that light came, like Paul's, he consulted not long with flesh and blood, but promptly bade adieu to all political prospects and preferments, and moved to Baltimore, Md., where he studied theology under the direction of the late Dr. B. Kurtz. But, as usual, he did the work of two men there, applying himself earnestly to the study of theology, and discharging also the duties of the office editor of the *Observer*. In due time he took charge of St. Matthew's church, the only congregation he served. Here he stood, like a faithful sentinel, proclaiming fearlessly the whole counsel of God for twenty and three years, and many are the trophies here won for Christ, many the jewels here polished for the Redeemer's crown.

The personal characteristics of our friend and brother may be embraced in the comprehensive title, "A Christian Gentleman." He was firm without rudeness, and gentle without effeminacy. He dealt tenderly with the erring, and was "patient towards all." None could ever bring the charge of distance or coldness against him. His was a genial spirit. In the social circle he had few equals and no superiors. He was brimful of good nature, and had an inexhaustible flow of spirits and pleasantries, but nowhere and never did he forget his character as a minister. He was fervent in spirit, and, therefore, intensely practical in action. By original temperament and education he avoided all mere speculation on the one hand, and a mere striving for the beautiful on the other, and sought only to be useful. When he was "apprehended of Christ," he gave himself up to his Lord in strong confidence and hope, ever realizing that there was an Omnipotent arm lifted up for his support and deliverance. His also was an humble spirit. From his soul he abhorred pride and pedantry.

Whenever he alluded to his position as a minister he did so in the language of St. Paul, "As being the least of all apostles, as one born out of due time." In labors he was most abundant. Idleness found no quarters with him. Not only did he devote himself with the whole force of his being to the work of the ministry, but every other good work, in which he could honor his Master or serve his race, found in him a ready supporter and helper. The "Northern Home for Friendless Children" is in conjunction with his energetic wife, in a great measure his monument—a monument more eloquent in praise, more durable in nature, more truthful in character, than any marble column that may mark his final resting-place. And were I called upon to furnish an epitaph for his tombstone, I would inscribe upon it: "Here rests the friend of the friendless."

Dr. Hutter was emphatically a Bible student. With him the Bible was the one great book of study. He received its truths with all the confidence of a child, and bowed before it with a deep and holy reverence. Its teachings lay in his soul like a well of pure, deep waters, and during his protracted illness they would every now and then gush up with unrivalled beauty and accuracy, as I had abundant opportunity of witnessing when, last spring, I spent a day and night with him in his sick chamber. In prayer, especially, he brought in the Scriptures so appropriately and beautifully that it often seemed to me like weaving a cloth of gold, studded all over with brilliant diamonds. His sermons were very unlike many we hear of now-a-days, which contain almost everything except the simple message of salvation to man. His were plain, Scriptural, doctrinal, and therefore practical. Shielding himself behind the Cross, he ever held up the Crucified One as the only hope and help for a ruined world. From this pulpit Christ was never excluded, but He formed the sublime theme of all the preacher's discourses. Having himself experienced His saving grace, he never failed to recommend Him as the refuge of the sinner and the hope of the saint.

ADDENDA.

When Mr. Hutter was private secretary to Mr. Buchanan, at that time Secretary of State under President Polk (1846), I went to Washington to procure a passport for travel in Europe. This was, of course, easily got, but I wanted something more, which Mr. Buchanan, though I knew him well, resolutely refused to give me, and that was a private letter, over his signature as Secretary. He said it was unusual and undiplomatic, and he would not do it for his own brother, who, twenty years before, had been my room-mate at Princeton College. I told my difficulty to Mr. Hutter, with whom, at that time, I did not expect to be so intimately associated afterwards as a brother minister. He went to Mr. Buchanan and succeeded in getting what I had failed to do. I was afterwards told by a man of influence that, if I had belonged to the "right school of politics," as he expressed it, there would have been no difficulty. It may be so.

Mr. Hutter was an ardent supporter of Mr. Buchanan in his aspirations to the Presidency and of all his measures until the breaking out of the rebellion, when he turned against him, violently and openly denounced his prevaricating, and, as Hutter designated it, "unpatriotic" course.

When he came to Baltimore to aid Dr. Kurtz in editing the Observer, and to study Theology, he became a member of my church, and a lifelong intimacy sprang up between my family and his. He had lost his children, and needed sympathy. He and his wife secured the esteem of everybody who knew them. He was a warm admirer of Dr. Kurtz, and generally an advocate of his measures. He delivered a glowing eulogy upon him at Selinsgrove, and I happen to know that Dr. K. had the highest admiration of Mr. H.

St. Matthew's, in Philadelphia, was the only church he ever served, and he was pastor of that for twenty-three years. He was exceedingly popular among his people, and I presume no minister of our church ever received such valuable and numerous presents as he did, in testimony of their admiration.

He was a frequent contributor to the Observer, and many sermons on special occasions were printed in that paper.

REV. T. T. TITUS.

The following extract is from an obituary notice in the Observer, by Rev. J. Swartz:

From the journal before me I learn that Bro. Titus was born in Loudon county, Va., March the 4th, 1829. He was the son of poor parents, and the youngest of ten children. They dedicated him to the Lord in early baptism, and endeavored to rear him in the faith of the gospel. To the influence of his mother and her prayers in his behalf he traces, under God, his conversion in youth and his call to the ministry. He manifested an eager desire for learning when quite young, and, though living in a country where the schools were poor and the books were few, he managed to read a great deal, and acquired sufficient knowledge to become a competent teacher when about sixteen years of age, to which pursuit he devoted several years of his early life. He thus had opportunity, in some degree, to gratify his love of study and to procure books, which he read with great avidity. But being poor he was compelled to work hard, and often labored with slaves in the field, doing a man's work long before he attained full age and strength for such hard labor.

He dates his conversion from January, 1847. At a protracted-meeting, held by Rev. P. Willard, in his neighborhood, he was led to feel himself a lost sinner and to cast his soul upon Christ, in whom he found peace in believing. Not long after he united with the Lutheran Church, under the pastoral care of the favored minister who was the chosen instrument of his conversion. After much reflection and prayer he felt constrained to enter upon a course of study preparatory to the ministry. He went to Gettysburg in the fall of 1848, and commenced his studies in the preparatory department. He labored hard and succeeded well. He speaks of the great kindness of the professors to him, especially that of Prof. Stoever, and of the assistance afforded him by the beneficiary fund. But as the amount allowed him was altogether inadequate, he imposed upon himself the most painful economy, until, at last, driven by sheer necessity, he left college for a season, and this several times during his college course, either to engage in teaching, or to take an agency to sell books, until he accumulated a little money to prosecute his studies. Thus, with great perseverance, he worked along until he was graduated—receiving the honor of valedictorian—in 1853.

The next year, in order to procure means, he accepted the position of tutor in the preparatory department, and studied with the class in the seminary, reciting most of the lessons and keeping up with the class. But this double labor was too much for him, and soon began to tell seriously upon his health. He became pale and emaciated and began to suffer pain in his chest. He was compelled, after three full terms, to abandon his position as tutor and his studies in the seminary, and go abroad to recover his health. Not long after this he had a hemorrhage from his lungs, no doubtful symptom that the disease so fatal in his family had laid hold upon him. It may be believed, however, that whatever predisposition he had to take this disease, it was immediately induced by too much confinement and too much labor. Could he have been relieved of his double task and permitted, without embarrassment and harassing anxiety about money, to pursue his studies in the seminary, he might have completed his course with honor, as he did in the college, and escaped the early development of a disease which cut him down in mid-life, and which greatly impaired and too early arrested his usefulness.

He served in six different pastoral fields, Stoughstown, Lower Merion, Milton, Springfield, Ohio, St. John's and Trinity in Hagerstown. The latter was organized and built its beautiful edifice under his pastoral care. Preaching here until health and voice failed him, he reluctantly quit the pastoral work, which was ever the joy and delight of his heart, and removed to Hartwick Seminary in June, 1871, and took charge of that institution, which flourished under his care.

Here he labored with the zeal and energy that characterized him every where, until at last he grew so weak, and his voice so failed him, that he could not speak above a whisper. But even in this condition he continued occasionally to teach, until the last holiday vacation relieved him, when every whisper cost him pain, soreness of the throat and exhaustion, and only when his voice wholly failed him did he cease to labor. Then he pathetically writes, among the last things in his journal, "And now I am voiceless—cannot utter a loud sound—can praise God with my lips aloud never more; nor speak for him who bought me, in public. But it is all *perfectly right*, for the Lord did it."

For several years Bro. Titus had been anticipating the conclusion to which he felt himself to be rapidly hastening. Though death came to him early, it did not come unexpected nor unwelcome. On the 3d of January, 1871, he says: "This year may be my last. If it should be, and if I should die ere its close, may my family and all who read these lines, while the hand that is penning them is turning to dust, be assured that I died in the full confidence of eternal life through Jesus Christ my Lord. I am a poor, worthless sinner, yet, through grace, I hope to sing with angels. I die believing in the gospel with all its precious truths. I love my church * * * I love all who love Jesus. Yea, I love those who love him not, and would gladly pluck them as brands from the burning. * * * I ask all my friends and enemies to forgive me my faults and sins, as I forgive them, and as I pray God to forgive them and me. My hope is in Jesus, Jesus only, Jesus only; I have no other hope or trust.

'In my hand no price I bring,
Simply to thy cross I cling.'

This will be my dying motto, and this I desire inscribed on my tomb."

He speaks, too, of doubt and despondency which sometimes seem to brood heavily on his mind, but as death comes visibly nearer, he says: "My faith seems to rise with the occasion. I do not fear death. I can look forward, confidently believing that as my day, so my strength shall be. This promise is verified to me now. 'I know in whom I have believed, and he never leaves nor forsakes his people in the trying hour.'"

A dear friend and brother who attended his dying couch says: "Mr. Titus died in the triumph of faith. His decline was rapid, and his end peaceful. He talked of his departure as we would speak of making a journey. There was no uncertainty about the future. "All is bright," said he a few days before the end. "All is bright, there is not a cloud." Two hours before he died, taking the hand of the writer, he uttered these last words: "I am going through the dark valley." So we closed his eyes in death, fully assured that while we are one less, heaven has one more."

As a writer, Mr. Titus was favorably known. His contributions to the Lutheran Observer have been widely read. He has given to the church two very important relics of his usefulness, in the "Explanatory Question-Book" for Sunday-schools, the second volume of which has just been issued from the press.

As a preacher, he was instructive, earnest and impressive. He always sought to prepare his sermons with great care, and came to the pulpit with an evident impression of the seriousness and solemnity of his work upon his mind and heart. He spoke tenderly and lovingly, but boldly and fearlessly in the name of the Lord Jesus. He was a man of deep convictions and inflexible loyalty to what he believed the truth. His candor sometimes offended, and his pertinacity in argument, rather than to make easy concession for the sake of peace, sometimes worried his brethren, especially in deliberative assemblies, but he always showed clear discernment, sound judgment, and made upon all unprejudiced minds the impression that it was from a sense of duty and a love of truth, and not a desire of debate, that he contended earnestly.

He was very active in the temperance reform. As a teacher he was clear, patient and earnest, and accomplished, under the circumstances, what seemed scarcely possible for one so infirm in health.

REV. DR. T. STORK.

The following is an extract from a discourse delivered at the funeral of Dr. Stork in Philadelphia, April 10, 1874, by Rev. Dr. Baum:

For us who survive there is sorrow indeed. We mourn the departure of an able and faithful minister of Christ, of a skillful and accepted writer of Christian truth and morals, of a judicious and trusted counselor in the work of the church, and of a loving and sympathizing friend and brother. To his brethren in the ministry the death of Dr. Stork will be long and sorely felt. Kind and affable toward all, he enjoyed to an unusual extent the confidence and affection of all with whom he came in contact. His gentle spirit and earnest Christian character won for him a high place in the esteem of the laity of the church. Always a favorite in the pulpit—for he was born to preach the gospel—he was no less popular in synod, in society, and in the family. The charming sweetness of his spirit, baptized by the Holy Ghost, made him an ever dear and cherished companion and friend. Not the least of the pleasant anticipations of my removal to this city was the expectation of frequent and intimate association with him. His death is to me a personal affliction that will be long and sorely felt. And if thus to us, whose relationship is only that of friendship and associated labor, his death is so sad and grievous an event, how much more to those who stood connected with him in all the intimacies and endearments of the family and home. Empty and drear will that home be from which its head and ornament is thus taken. Of the strength and sincerity of the affection which was so worthily bestowed upon him, and as warmly returned, we need not here speak, except to offer sincerest sympathy and condolence to those who mourn his removal. It is the Lord; let him do what seemeth him good. There is left a remembrance that will sweeten even though it saddens every hour of life. His life was nobly and successfully given to the work of the Lord, and his end was peace.

As to its external facts and changes Dr. Stork's life may be easily told. Eternity alone can unfold the full extent of the work he did. The most useful and influential life is not always marked by the greatest changes or crowded with the most exciting incidents. Born in North Carolina, where his father preached the gospel with marked and blessed results, he was early brought to Christ, and became at once an open and pronounced Christian. His education was secured in the institutions of the church at Gettysburg, in which he took advanced grade, and where his memory is still fondly cherished. Entering the ministry about the year 1837, his first labors were given to Winchester, Va. Of the character and results of his first ministry I feel authorized to speak with confidence, as it was my good fortune, in after years, to occupy the same pulpit. Even to this day he is there remembered with undiminished confidence and affection, and his efforts spoken of in terms of highest praise. For long years his friends of that congregation maintained frequent communication with him, and consulted him freely upon questions of mutual interest.

During his ministry in that place the present church edifice was projected, and many of the most active and most zealous members of the congregation, who have ever since adorned the doctrine of God their Saviour in all things, were brought into the church. From Winchester he came to Philadelphia as pastor of St. Matthew's, and thus, for the second time, I have become his successor, entering into his labors. In this city his public ministerial life is known and read of all men. He was faithful in all things, and successful, in more than ordinary degree, in leading sinners to the Saviour. The additions to the membership, and the strong, undying attachments of those received, give full and satisfactory evidence of his power over men and of his fidelity to Christ. "The memory of the just is blessed," and we listen to-day, with a sad and chastened interest, to the unstinted praises and strong utterances of undying attachment from many sorrowing hearts of those who, in long years past, called Dr. Stork their pastor, and received the word of the Lord from his lips. "He being dead yet speaketh" in the words and works of a large and loving spiritual family.

Realizing then already the need of enlarged and advanced church accommodations, Dr. Stork proposed the enterprise of a new congregation in the rapidly increasing north-west section of the city. Leading the movement in person, he succeeded beyond expectation in building St. Mark's church, and establishing upon a firm basis St. Mark's congregation. As in each field of labor, so in this; his works do follow him. In all that St. Mark's has been and may yet become, the merit of its founding, as well as the wisdom of its timely inception, will be given to Dr. Stork. In this, as in all his movements, he showed genuine progressive courage and unfaltering childlike faith. He had faith in God and in God's word. He saw there was need and the ability to supply that need, and he unhesitatingly assumed the responsibility of guiding and consummating the movement; and, by God's grace and man's help, he succeeded. Let his success inspire many similar movements in this and in all the cities of our land, until all who need are supplied as advantageously as are those who followed him so readily in founding that now monument to his memory.

From the pulpit of St. Mark's Dr. Stork was called to the presidency of Newberry College, S. C. To this new field of labor he gave his maturest efforts, and very soon gave promise of being as acceptable as a teacher as he had been as a preacher. The hope of improving his impaired health exercised no little influence in deciding the question of his change of occupation and location. The milder winters of the South and the change of surroundings it was hoped would affect him beneficially. Not without hesitation, yet with much characteristic enthusiasm, he entered this new and untried work, hoping, if possible, in wider sphere, by educating the future educators of the church, to serve the cause he loved so well. But, ere he could become fairly engaged and interested, and his aptness or success become apparent, the disturbed condition of the country so far interfered with the conduct of the institution, and the prospect of an early adjustment of our civil difficulties was so unsatisfactory, that Dr. Stork very soon resigned and retired from the college, and once more held himself in readiness to serve his day and generation in the pastoral office.

Nor did he long wait for an engagement. St. Mark's, Baltimore, thankfully seized the opportunity, and urged his acceptance of their call to become pastor of their newly organized congregation. To this he readily acceded, and at once became a favorite within and without his charge. Under his faithful and affectionate care, St. Mark's, Baltimore, grew in every element of congregational strength, and now, under the charge of his son, is one of the most active and liberal congregations of our church.

Serving this people until his own son was prepared to assume charge thereof, Dr. Stork once more returned to this city, so dear to him by the most cherished associations. He was welcomed anew by hosts of devoted friends, who rejoiced in the prospect of long continued association with him.

Nor was he long disengaged. In this immediate locality he saw the need of a church, and began the unpromising work of establishing it. Circumstances interfered with the consummation of his original purpose, and the gradual failure of his health, attended at times with alarming symptoms, compelled a new line of engagements and a change of labor.

Gifted as a ready, ornate and acceptable writer, with strong literary tastes and long culture, he prepared his own productions for the press, all of which have met with a flattering reception, and served with untiring interest in the work of the Publication Society of our church. No one unacquainted with the difficulties and drudgery of that branch of church enterprise can form a just estimate of the unrequited service Dr. Stork rendered our Zion. Upon this his last days were engaged; his last hours were given to it. His last issue of the *Lutheran Home Monthly*, appearing about the same day with his death, contains his last literary labor, and, by a most singular and touchingly interesting coincidence, its leading editorial has this striking title, "*I am now ready.*" The article which follows breathes the spirit and has all the peculiarities of thought and style of its loved and now lamented author. He could not have written anything more appropriate for the occasion, nor can any one select a more fitting epitaph— "*I am now ready.*" Every line of that now sacred article might with eminent propriety be quoted here. Nothing better could be spoken.

The grace which enabled the aged imprisoned apostle to exclaim in triumph "*I am now ready*" was not withheld from him whose death we mourn. With fullest confidence we know he could say, as he did say, "*I am now ready.*" His time had come. His triumph through him who conquers for us was assured. In hope of a blessed immortality, he sleeps in Jesus. In his own words, "Who can look at the end of such a noble Christian life without some quickening of the soul, some kindling aspiration to be like Paul in our devotion to Christ—like him, in that calm peaceful assurance expressed in those parting and immortal words, '*I am now ready.*'"

We believe he was ready, awaiting Christ's coming. He was an humble Christian, that highest style of man, called, redeemed, pardoned and accepted in Jesus Christ.

He was a faithful Christian minister, devoted to his calling and "steadfast in the faith." He was an exemplary servant of Jesus

Christ, doing his Master's will with all alacrity, and seeking ever to advance his Master's interests.

Thus did he live and labor, and, in dying, could, with all meekness, say, "I am now ready to be offered, and the time of my departure is at hand."

REV. GEORGE A. LINTNER, D. D.

The following interesting biographical sketch of Dr. Lintner, by Rev. Edmund Belfour, we transfer from the Lutheran and Missionary:

Dr. Lintner was born at Minden, Montgomery county, N. Y., February 15, 1796, and spent his early childhood at the old homestead, which had long been in possession of the family, and which it was designed that he should own and occupy after the decease of his father. At the age of ten years he was sent to Cooperstown to attend school, and at that time understood not one word of the English language, the German being exclusively used in his father's family. He very soon manifested both inclination and capacity for study, and an earnest desire sprang up in his heart to qualify himself for the ministry. His father, though a very pious man, found it difficult to give up the cherished thought of having his only son succeed him on the farm. But his noble mother favored the praiseworthy ambition of the lad, and all acquiesced in the new purpose. He was at an early age admitted into Union College, Schenectady, N. Y., and there pursued the full course. After his graduation he entered upon the study of Theology, under the direction and guidance of his pastor, Rev. Mr. Domeier, a well-educated clergyman, and was licensed by the Evangelical Lutheran Ministerium of New York, in September, 1818.

In January, 1819, he accepted a call to the pastorate of the Lutheran Churches of Schoharie and Cobleskill, Schoharie county, N. Y., and was ordained and installed June 16 of the same year. He entered upon his work with all the zeal of an earnest and pious young man, and was heartily sustained by his people, and especially by his church councils, of whom he spoke in terms of admiration to the close of his life, as men of sterling worth and piety.

Among these were Judges Hermanns, Bouck, and Wm. C. Bouck, for a time Governor of the State. And, we need hardly add, he was eminently successful as a pastor, and his influence was very decided over the churches and ministers of a large district of country.

He was the recognized leader of the young men of his Synod, including Revs. Frederick Schaeffer and H. N. Pohlman, in their manly opposition to what he was wont to call the "Quitman Dynasty" of rationalism. But after a time he and others became so much dissatisfied with the character of the old Synod (which is *now* so thoroughly orthodox) that he initiated measures for the organization of a new Synod. A convention of all desiring to enter such an organization was called to meet in the church in Schoharie, in 1830. The convention met, and the result was the formation of the "Hartwick Synod," of which he was chosen the first president, an office which he often held and graced in after years.

In 1837 certain members of this Synod, who had become impatient of doctrinal and constitutional restraint, withdrew and formed the Franckean Synod, on the widest latitudinarian basis. The movement was thoroughly revolutionary, and led to the most vigorous controversies, and even to contests in the courts. In those stirring and exciting times, Dr. Lintner was the leading spirit in the Hartwick Synod, and courageously and successfully defended himself and his associates, and for this received much rough treatment.

But even these distracted scenes, in which he was the most prominent actor, did not draw his attention away from his pastoral work. His parish grew very rapidly, and new congregations were formed from time to time. He retained unimpaired the confidence and respect of his people and of the surrounding community as the years rolled by. He remained pastor of the church in Schoharie until 1849—thirty years. From the time of his resignation he was engaged in promoting the work of foreign missions and of the American Bible Society, and of any good cause which afforded him an opportunity to do something for his Master.

He was editor of the Lutheran Magazine from 1827 to 1831,

and contributed to various religious publications. And in his writings, sermons, and addresses, he was especially earnest, and almost bitter in his opposition to the use of all intoxicating liquors and wines; and we honor him for it.

Dr. Lintner had very clear perceptions and positive views of Christian doctrine. He was an earnest and enthusiastic admirer and advocate of the Augsburg Confession, and often stood side by side with the writer in defense of that great document where it was ruthlessly attacked. And his orthodoxy produced its legitimate effect—an earnest spiritual life.

He was a man of a strong and determined character. As his convictions were very positive, his resolution was firm. He seldom relinquished any purpose, but clung to it most tenaciously until it was accomplished, when that was possible. And, as may readily be inferred, he was a firm and constant friend and a most resolute opponent.

He was a gentleman of the old school—polite and affable in all the relations of life, dignified in his bearing, and chaste in his language. He was especially courteous to men holding official position, and, above all, to those of his own profession.

The writer knew him most intimately for many years, and for a long time was his pastor. And though a mere lad when he assumed that relation to this venerable minister, the latter uniformly treated him with the respect due to his office, and with fraternal cordiality. He was so tenacious of official honor and rights that he never volunteered advice to his young pastor, though always ready to give it when solicited. We can never forget the many hours which we spent with the deceased in our respective homes, and in our long rides on ministerial business, in which we were inseparable. His commanding personal appearance, his white hair, his courtly manner, his cheerful temper, and his readiness in conversation, all tended to make him an agreeable and valuable associate. And with perfect sincerity, and with deep and tender feelings, we here record our testimony to the distinguished ability and attainments and the noble character of our venerable and cherished friend, and can hardly keep back the struggling tear when we reflect on the painful fact that we shall see him no more in the flesh. But in God's own time the righteous shall meet again. May this thought inspire those of us who remain to strive more earnestly than ever for meetness for Heaven.

The following sketch of the late Dr. Lintner is from the Schoharie Republican of December 28th:

The funeral of the late Rev. Dr. Lintner, who died at his residence on the 21st instant, in the 76th year of his age, was largely attended on Sabbath afternoon last, at St. Paul's Lutheran Church, Schoharie C. H. The church had been beautifully decorated for the Christmas festival. The pulpit and altar were draped in mourning. A large number of the clergy were present and assisted in the solemn services. The sermon was preached by the Rev. Mr. Heck. It was an eloquent and peculiarly appropriate discourse. The Rev. Dr. Scholl, a lifelong friend of the deceased, made a touching and beautiful address upon the Christian virtues, scholarly attainments and successful ministry of the departed Father in Israel. Rev. Mr. Swope closed with a few remarks commemorative of the life and character of him who, for nearly sixty years, had preached the Gospel of Christ. The Rev. Messrs. Roe, Jones, Moot, Swope, Vedder, Scribner, Letler, and Porter, assisted by the venerable Mr. Osterhout, Sen., and others, acted as pall-bearers, and at twilight, Christmas Eve, the body of "the good man" was borne from the church in which he had preached Christ and Him crucified for over fifty years, to the beautiful cemetery on the hillside, and there, during the singing of a hymn by the throng of clergymen, laid in the grave, in the midst of those who had gone before him, and to whom he had been a faithful pastor and beloved friend. He waits the resurrection morning, and when the earth shall give up its dead, this minister of God shall rise in his glorified body, "bringing his sheaves with him."

George Ames Lintner was born in Minden, Montgomery county, N. Y., February 15, 1796. His parents were Albert and Elizabeth (Westerman) Lintner, both of whom were of German descent, and among the earliest settlers near the Mohawk river. At ten years of age George was sent to a school near the village of Cooperstown, and after his return home, in about a year, he remained in his father's family, working on the farm, until the fall of 1813. He was then placed in the Grammar school at Schenectady, under the tuition of the Rev. John S. Mabon, where he remained until the fall of 1815, when he entered the sophomore class in Union College, and graduated in July, 1817. While in college he took high rank, and had one of the highest honors upon commencement day. While in college he also took lessons in Theology from Rev. Peter Domeier, so that, in August of 1817, he preached his first sermon at Palatine. He continued his studies with the same divine until September, 1818, when he was licensed to preach by the Evangelical Lutheran Ministerium of the State of New York. After he was licensed, he preached occasionally in the village of Little Falls and other places. In January, 1819, he was called to the pastoral charge of the Evangelical Lutheran Churches of Schoharie and Cobleskill. On the 3d of March, 1819, he was married to Maria Waggoner; removed to Schoharie in May, 1819, and was ordained and installed as pastor of the Evangelical Lutheran Churches to which he had been called by a special meeting of the New York Ministerium, his ordination and installation taking place June 10, 1819. And then commenced a long and prosperous pastorate.

The Dietzs, the Lawyers, the Boucks, the Vromans, the Shafers, the Manns, the Bosts, the Hallenbecks, the Sternbergs, and other families who then belonged to the Lutheran Church, received the young minister with great cordiality, and over thirty years he had an influence in this community and the surrounding country few men have ever possessed. His wife died October 28, 1830, leaving him two children, a son and daughter. Her memory is still precious to those who knew her. He was married again May 30, 1832, to Mary Elizabeth Campbell. He received the degree of "Doctor of Divinity" from Pennsylvania College, September 17, 1835. He also edited the Lutheran Magazine, a religious monthly, from 1827 to 1831. He was President of the General Synod of the Lutheran Church in the United States in 1841 and 1843. May 1, 1849, he resigned the pastorate of the church at Schoharie.

He prepared the Liturgy of the Evangelical Lutheran Church of this country, which was published by order of the General Synod in 1832. He also published several sermons in the *National Preacher* and other publications. In 1853 he published the memoirs of Rev. Walter Gunn, the first foreign missionary sent out by the Foreign Missionary Society of the Lutheran Church in the United States. Mr. Gunn was a member of Dr. Lintner's church, and one of the fruits of his ministry. During his ministry at Schoharie he organized three new churches as the results of his work, one at Breakabeen, one at Middleburgh, and one at Central Bridge. In 1837 he was chosen President of the Schoharie County Bible Society, and held the position until his death. He was the first President of the Hartwick Synod, and often after he was called to preside over the deliberations of the Synod. After he had resigned, in 1849, his pastorate, he was called to work in his church for the Foreign Missionary Society, and for three years he was engaged in visiting the Lutheran churches in New York and New Jersey, and presenting the claims of the society, and collecting funds to aid in its operations.

In this work he took great delight, and was successful in awakening an increased missionary spirit in the churches which he visited. He also preached to the Germans, at their different settlements in this region, in their own language. He loved the work of his Lord and Master. He never laid aside the harness till, on the second of January last, he was paralyzed.

The reflection that he had faithfully endeavored to serve his Master afforded him great satisfaction in his last days.

FREDERICK HEYER

was, in my opinion, one of the most remarkable men of the period under consideration. Until his fiftieth year, he was a laborious pastor in several fields and then came to Baltimore on his own account to found a German mission. He is the father of St. John's Church, Biddle street. He had hard work but accomplished his purpose. He supported himself chiefly and advanced money from his own purse to uphold the cause.

He was the first missionary sent to India by the General Synod's Missionary Society. There was some plan proposed by which our missionary was to be in some way under the control of the American Board at Boston,* but he resolutely refused to go under such conditions. He was fifty years of age and we were advised by the Boston Board to send no man to India at that age. I voted against the measure, but was happily disappointed, for he lived in India in good health for 16 or 17 years, having returned twice to this country to recuperate and to rouse the churches to their duties in this enterprise.

*See General Synod of 1841.

On his final return he settled quietly down in Somerset, Pa., until called to the position of House Father in the Theological Seminary in Philadelphia, where he died in 1875.

He was at home in my family during his frequent visits to Baltimore and he never forgot a childish remark made by one of the little ones at the table thirty years before he died. The child asked in her simplicity who this stranger was, and upon being told it was Bro. Heyer, she exclaimed, "Isn't he pretty?" Everybody who knew him, is aware that only a child could form that judgment of him, but he enjoyed it exceedingly and often spoke of it to that same person after she had grown to womanhood.

Mr. Heyer was physically vigorous, though small of stature and lathe like in form. He endured the enervating climate of India without damaging discomfort and survived some younger men who labored with him.

He acquired the Telugu language with facility and translated Luther's Catechism for the benefit of the natives.

He was extremely simple in his habits and frugal in his diet, and could live where some other men would starve. On his first voyage to India he sailed from Boston in the same ship with some missionaries of the American Board. His salary was $600 and theirs over three times as much. He told me on his return, or wrote to me, that he was amazed to see the handsome, and, in his economical view, costly furniture which those men carried out with them, whilst he had nothing but a leathern sack which contained all his baggage. Much depends upon training, but Bro. Heyer had such apostolic notions of things that he thought that a bag and a staff were all a missionary should take with him. I doubt even whether he had "two coats."

In his latter years he allowed his beard and moustache to grow, which wonderfully changed his appearance. There is a fair portrait of him in the chapel of the Theological Seminary at Philadelphia.

One of our missionaries in India, on hearing of the death of Mr. Heyer, writes thus to the Observer:

A few thoughts, in his memory written among the scenes of his former labors, may probably not be thought out of place.

Father Heyer was the pioneer of our work here—the man, who with the weight of fifty years upon him, and a naturally delicate constitution, finding no younger man with courage enough to undertake the work, started for the other end of the world to found a mission, and, as we know, right bravely did he carry out his work. It may be interesting to know how he came to select Guntur as the center of his operations. The following, as far as I can ascertain, is the true story:

When he landed in India he was evidently not as well informed in regard to the prospects of the missionary enterprise as he might have been in 1842. And so landing at Colombo he commenced an irregular sort of search for a missionary opening, gradually finding his way northward. After a good deal of aimless searching, he did, what discretion, it would seem, should have dictated at first, went to Madras, and consulted with the missionaries there. Circumstances at the time seemed to indicate the Telugoo country as a promising field, and they advised him, if the stock of moral courage which he had brought along was sufficient, to commence his enterprise there. Now it was just in that very stuff, so absolutely essential to all decent success in life — simple moral courage — that the old gentleman pre-eminently abounded. There was none of the Pariah about him. So generous was the original stock that it lasted him eighty years, with enough left, I shall take it upon myself to say, to bear him unfalteringly through that ordeal which shall call for the divinest courage which the shrinking soul of man may ever know.

Accepting the advice of the missionaries, he bought an old palankeen, and set out for the Telugoo country. Passing on by Naidupett, Girdiur, Nellore and Ongole, he finally found himself among the palmyra topes of Báptula, some thirty miles south-east of Guntur. Here he resolved to establish the tabernacle. Selecting two contiguous trees he tied his palankeen up between them, out of the reach of prowling jackals and pariah dogs, and proclaimed the American Lutheran mission founded.

Mr. H. Stokes was then collector at Guntur, a godly, noble man, by the consent of all. He has returned to England long ago, but it will require many long years until the perennial fragrance of his fair fame shall have passed from the memory of the people of Guntur, Christian and heathen. We mean no detraction from the just merits of the early missionaries here, when we record that H. Stokes, the pious, godly collector of the Zillah, was the actual founder of the mission. The first converts in Guntur were from among his servants, influenced by him to accept Christianity. Old John, the first convert in the Palnud, where there are now upward of 2000 Christian adherents, told me one night as we sat in conversation under the stars, outside of his village, that it was through Mr. Stokes' influence that he, and the first Christians in the Palnud, were induced to cast their idols to the bats.

Shortly after Father Heyer had flung out his banner from the top of his old palankeen down among the palmyras, news came to Guntur, one day, that a little old padre had established himself down in the Báptula woods, asserting that he meant to stay there. Now Mr. Stokes, being a missionary himself, in his way, heard the news with rejoicing. It was for a fellow-missionary that he had long been waiting. He at once sent a peon with some coolies down to put the padre into his palky and bring him up; and that is the way, it is said, the mission came to be established at Guntur.

Now and then, though not frequently, God sends men into the world born pioneers, and Father Heyer was evidently one of them. He was a man peculiarly indifferent to those comforts and conveniences which most of us consider so essential to the proper enjoyment of life. Although I could never understand that a missionary was under greater obligation than anybody else to deny himself the poor little comforts which go to make his life — sad enough already, God knows — at least endurable. But the fact is Father Heyer cared nothing for them. Give him a dish of curry and rice, and a place to spread his blanket and mat, undisturbed by village dogs or pigs, and his catalogue of necessary comforts was complete.

A characteristic story used to be told of him by Gröning, one of his contemporaries here. Being on a missionary tour, he met an English official, and invited him to his headquarters to breakfast. Arrived there, he bade the Englishman be seated, and proceeded to extract a suspicious looking leg of mutton from the interior of an old boot, which, together with a pot of cold rice, he placed upon the table, and bade his guest to "lend a hand." The story goes that it suddenly occurred to his guest that he had some supplies in his bandy, hard by, and, holding out to the old gentleman that it was only fair that he should contribute at least something to the general stock, had them brought, and they made a joint affair of it.

He labored to carry on the mission on the most extreme principles of economy. And this is all right enough, too, within certain limits. The only difficulty was that he committed the error of supposing that everybody else could live as economically as he. One of the brethren once wrote him, asking his influence toward securing an increase of his salary. He replied that he thought the brother's salary quite sufficient, seeing that he himself managed to live quite comfortably on forty rupees per month.

He was singularly temperate and abstemious in his habits—the secret, no doubt, of his long and vigorous life. As far as practicable he conformed to the native manner of living. For he argued that it was most probable that, in the long run, the natives of any country would adopt habits of life most conducive to their preservation, and best suited to the physical circumstances around them. He had, no doubt, caught the true idea, and herein taught a lesson which all his successors would do well to remember, *i. e.*, that because a certain manner of living may be well adapted to the climate of America, it does not necessarily follow that every conceited peculiarity must needs be observed in a tropical residence ten thousand miles away.

Of a man who had risked his life as often as Father Heyer it would be most unwarranted to say that he had any morbid fears of death, but he seemed to be constantly anticipating it. The Christians at Poleipalli still point you to a little maryosa tree, at whose base he had commanded them to bury him, expecting soon to die. During an epidemic at Guogála he even went so far as to have his grave dug and coffin made. On his last trip to India he came by way of Bombay and Hyderabad, and joined Mr. Cully in the Palnud. Before he left him he gave him the address of his niece at school in Germany, with some others, directing him to write to the parties in the event of his death, which he thought would probably be very soon. Coming on to Guntur, he gave the same directions to Bro. Unangst.

He never made much progress in the Telugoo, but what he knew he put to the fullest use. He was an earnest, hard-working missionary. On his missionary tours he frequently traveled on foot, sleeping in the native huts or under a tree, with a simple dish of curry and rice as his only food. During his fifteen years' residence in India, he never had what, in any proper sense, could be called a home. Mr. Stokes presented to him a commodious bungalow at Gurgála, and requested him to make his headquarters there. A queer looking headquarters, it is said, he made of it.

A few old chairs, a rickety table and a dilapidated bedstead being the only indication that it was inhabited by a human being. He lived for years in an old lumber-room of the chapel in Guntur. He humorously called it the "prophet's room"—a title which it has ever since retained.

Well, he is gone now, and the tired old hands have been folded to rest. Surely it was a well-spent life. He is gone, but his work remains on two hemispheres — remains imperishably. And the little old padre, whose voice once resounded through these rooms in which I write, is, I doubt not, active to-day as he always was in life, only amid fairer scenes and infinitely nobler activities.

Another extract from the Observer:

QUITE A SURPRISE.

On the morning of July 10th I saw it announced that on the preceding day, Sunday, my venerated old friend Heyer had arrived in Baltimore from London. In the afternoon I was reading under one of my umbrageous oaks, when all of a sudden who should accost me but the veritable man himself. He had come out to spend the night, and our meeting was mutually joyous. Here stood that missionary patriarch, returned from his third voyage to India, with health as robust, spirits as cheerful, and heart as warm as thirty years ago. A very remarkable man, indeed! His strength has not abated, nor has his eye waxed dim, for he reads without spectacles. His facial appearance is improved, for he wears a gray beard and moustache, which cover his hollow cheeks, and which brought to my mind the likeness of Melanchthon. After congratulating him upon his vigorous health, he exclaimed, "This is my 79th birth day, and I have come to celebrate it in your house!" And we did. And such a time as we had of it! How we talked of old and recent times, and how rebuked I felt that nearly thirty years ago, at the General Synod in Baltimore, I obstinately opposed commissioning him to India, because he was then nearly fifty years old! But see him now after nearly eighteen years service in that climate, having never suffered severely from the fever of the country.

Father Heyer's career has been one of rare interest and unparalleled usefulness. He intends to retire to his home at Somerset, but not to spend his remaining days in idleness. If he carries out certain plans he has in view, the church will be vastly benefited; and he should be encouraged to write an autobiography, with reminiscences of Lutheran ministers of this country, as well as a book of mission sketches of his own rich experience.

There is not a man in our ministry who has made greater sacrifices, exposed himself to greater perils, encountered more difficulties, and secured the profound admiration of more friends than this venerable gentleman. Long may he live to enjoy his green old age, and to work for the church, which is already so deeply indebted to him for his self-denying labors!   J. G. M.

REV. DR. HENRY NEWMAN POHLMAN.

BY REV. W. D. STROBEL, D. D.

The subject of this memoir was born in the city of Albany, on the 8th day of March, 1800, and departed this life, in his native place, on the 20th day of January, 1874.

Dr. Pohlman's ancestors were all German. He bore the traces of his origin in every lineament of his countenance; looked like those men who in the fatherland initiated the great Protestant Reformation of the sixteenth century.

The boy grew up amidst the surroundings of a happy Christian home, confirming his baptismal vows early in life, and thus taking a decided stand with the disciples of our Lord. The influence of his sister, Mrs. McClure, a most devoted and excellent Christian woman, his own earnest desire to do good, with some peculiar circumstances connected with our church at the time, induced him to devote his life to the gospel ministry. His pastor, Rev. F. G. Mayer, had been one of the active agents in securing the property of the Hartwick Seminary, in 1816. The subject was one of much debate and no small excitement amongst the Lutherans of that day, ending in its present location, about seventy miles west of Albany. This was a great event in our infant church, struggling for existence. The professor of the seminary was a frequent visitor at his father's house. The conversations there heard had a great influence, and induced our friend, whilst comparatively a lad, to place himself under the guidance of good old Dr. Hazelius, thus becoming the first student in the first Lutheran Theological Seminary in the United States; and to his *Alma Mater* he clung through life.

In August, 1820, he graduated, before reaching his majority. According to the rules of the New York Ministerium, his license was not conferred until the following March, when the services took place in St. Peter's Church, Rhinebeck, being conducted by Rev. Drs. Quitman and Wackerhagen. In the following month of May, he was ordained in Christ's Church, in the city of New York, in company with Rev. Dr. G. B. Miller. When licensed, he had a call to two small churches in New Jersey, Saddle River and Ramapo, whither he immediately proceeded. But a larger and more important position soon presented itself. Within a year he took charge of the churches in Hunterdon county, New Jersey, over which he presided with great acceptance for twenty-one years. The pastorate was large, three churches, many miles apart, isolated, much neglected, demanding all the energies of a young man robust in health, just commencing his ministerial career. He proved equal to the situation, and lived to see his labors productive of such religious development that each of these congregations was able to have its own pastor, and to give him a more liberal support than was originally received from the united pastorate.

The great event of his ministerial life there was a remarkable revival of religion, which occurred in the village of New Germantown during the winter of 1839 and 1840. He had labored for years under much discouragement. The attendance at public worship was good, the Sunday-school flourishing, the moral tone of the community very high. I think that no intoxicating liquor was sold in the place; it was a rare thing to see an approach to the desecration of the day of rest. It was the model of a small, quiet, inland village. But there were few or no accessions to the membership of the church. In the hope of quickening the congregation, a series of week-evening meetings was introduced, of the simplest character, without any thing of what are technically called new measures. The interest increased from time to time until it became so absorbing, that meetings had to be held also in the day-time, when all places of business were closed during the hours of worship. According to my recollection, the persons who first gave evidence of decided religious impressions were an intemperate shoemaker and his wife, living on the outskirts of the village, whose conduct had rendered them very obnoxious to the community. After them followed in rapid succession many who took an open stand for Christ, until there was scarcely a house in the place in which the influence of the meeting was not felt. The number of conversions was about two hundred, of whom one hundred and twenty-eight joined the Lutheran church, which up to that period had a membership of only eighty-five. The revival seemed to be the result of seed long and faithfully sown, suddenly blooming into a rich harvest, the fruits of which are still being gathered in. The Doctor's name still remains a household word in that community, and after the lapse of thirty years, in his annual visits, he was always welcomed as a father returning to visit his spiritual children.

On the 7th of September, 1824, he was married to Miss Susan Cassidy, with whom he lived in the very happiest intercourse for thirty-nine years. She was the mother of five children, two of whom preceded both parents to the better land.

In the year 1843 he felt it to be his duty to leave the field in which he had been so very useful to take charge of the Evangelical Lutheran Ebenezer Church in his native city. He had then arrived at the full maturity of his powers, with large experience and vigorous health. The affairs of his new charge were not in a promising condition. The building was small, and much of the elements which once gave it strength had strayed off to other churches, whose pulpits were then occupied by an array of talent surpassed by that of few cities in the land. The prospect was far from hopeful. Things improved, but, with varying success, the most earnest efforts did not bring them up to the pastor's wishes or expectations. Having completed the labors of a quarter of a century, with the weight of advancing years pressing upon him, he retired from the pastoral office, but not to a life of inactivity. Preaching whenever an opportunity was presented, continually looking after the interests of the synod, engaged more or less in all of our benevolent operations, retaining his physical and mental activity to the end, it may be said that he died with his harness on.

The closing scene, though somewhat unexpected, was befitting one who had labored so long in the Lord's vineyard, and to whom rest would prove so welcome. For several years he had made his home with a beloved daughter, Mrs. Patten, where, surrounded by everything to make life comfortable and happy, his children, his books, the society of congenial Christian friends, he might have anticipated a green old age had not a latent affection of the heart exhibited symptoms of a dangerous character, to which he was not insensible. In closing the synodical meeting at Red Hook, in October, 1873, his mind was burdened with the thought that he would see the brethren no more in the flesh. In a farewell address he expressed this conviction in words the most touching, whilst there was nothing in voice or manner to indicate that the end was so near. He preached several times afterwards, and not until within a few weeks previous to his death were there indications of failing strength. On the day preceding he had a severe spasm in the region of the heart, which yielded to remedial agencies, but, within the next twenty-four hours, quietly sitting in his accustomed place, his head drooped upon his breast, and, without a struggle, he was asleep in Jesus.

The Doctor was a man of fine physique, commanding voice, chaste and impressive delivery. As a writer he was correct and forcible. Few who have heard him in the pulpit will forget his dignified bearing or lose the impression that he possessed not only great earnestness but more than ordinary force of character. At all general church gatherings a prominent place was allotted to him, and his deliverances were heard with pleasure. He did not aspire to the reputation of an erudite scholar. The time when he entered public life, and an isolated country parish for twenty years, did not offer many of the literary advantages now enjoyed. Still he collected a large and valuable library, of which he was a diligent student. He was well read on all subjects connected with his profession, an able rhetorician, a correct and graceful writer, and always ready and happy when called upon to make an impromptu address. As presiding officer of a deliberative body he had few equals. Prompt, decided, familiar with parliamentary rulings, he was always clear and courteous. All this, combined with the unbounded confidence reposed in his character, will make it not appear strange that he should have presided over the New York Ministerium for twenty-one years, and over the New York Synod from its organization to the time of his death, thus making him for twenty-seven years the presiding officer of the body with which he was connected. And it was but natural that he should have been chosen three times President of the General Synod, to every meeting of which, since 1836, he had been appointed delegate, failing in attendance but once. The merited title of Doctor of Divinity was conferred upon him by Pennsylvania College in 1843.

Dr. Pohlman was an active supporter of our Foreign Mission work and was for some years chairman of the Executive Committee.

There is a superb volume published by his daughter, Mrs. Patten, entitled "Memorial of the Rev. H. N. Pohlman, D. D." It contains a striking likeness of our venerated friend and a discourse by his life-long friend, Dr. Strobel; a Memorial Tribute by Rev. J. Z. Senderling; the Memorial Services observed at the meeting of the Synod of New York and New Jersey in St. James' Church, New York, with addresses from Rev. T. T. Everett and Dr. Wedekind, and remarks by Dr. Magee and others, concluding with an account of the Revival in the congregation at New Germantown, in 1840, of which he was Pastor at the time; and an address at the funeral of Mrs. S. C. Pohlman, in 1863, by Dr. W. B. Sprague.

REV. DR. D. F. BITTLE.

The following sketch has been abridged from Rev. Mr. Mann and others:

Dr. Bittle was born near Myersville, Maryland, possibly in 1811. Of his early years we have, at this writing, no intelligence. He was graduated from Pennsylvania College in the class of 1835, and had as associates in the recitation-room such men as Dr. Ezra Keller and Dr. Theophilus Stork, of blessed memory. He studied theology at Gettysburg, Pa., and on leaving the seminary was called to the oversight of a congregation in the vicinity of Staunton, Va. Here he labored for eight or nine years with the indomitable energy and self-sacrificing zeal that characterized his subsequent life. His efforts were eminently successful. Other congregations were organized and church buildings erected in Augusta and Rockbridge counties, which remain monuments of his zeal and devotion to the cause of Christ and humanity.

An ardent advocate of liberal education, he left no legitimate means untried to advance it, and interest all round about him in its benign and blessed influence. It was the *moral* as well as the intellectual faculties that he always aimed to develop and enlarge. He sought to reach the *heart* through the head. Education with him was enlarged power and influence, and that increased power and influence was beneficial *only when properly directed*, viz.: to the glory of God and the best interests of humanity. While preaching in Augusta county, Va., he established the "Virginia Institute," a classical academy, in which quite a number of young men received their preparatory training, and subsequently entered the ministry. Out of it grew Roanoke College. Early in the year 1845 Rev. Bittle resigned his congregations in Virginia, and accepted a call to Middletown.

In May, 1845, he entered upon the discharge of his duties as pastor of the Lutheran church in this place, and resigned in February, 1852. Here, as in Virginia, the church increased in numbers and efficiency. During his ministry here the parsonage, lecture-room, and Mt. Tabor church were built. Here, too, he aroused a spirit of education, and succeeded in establishing a classical school in which a number of young men now in the Lutheran ministry received their elementary training.

Notwithstanding the success that crowned his ministry here, he was characteristically modest, humble and unobtrusive. Recording the results of his abundant labors, as an item of church history, he simply says in the briefest space and in the most humble spirit—"The success of my labors will be determined at the great Judgment Day. I am only afraid it has been but little."

Leaving Middletown in February, 1852, his family resided in Hagerstown, while he engaged in an agency in behalf of female education. Successful in the collection of the requisite amount of funds, the institution was located at Hagerstown.

During all these busy years, Rev. Bittle found time for study; and his progress in scientific pursuits, and especially in theological attainments, gained for him honorable notice and commendation. It was possibly at the commencement of 1853 that the Trustees of Pennsylvania College conferred on him the honorary title of "Doctor Divinitatis."

About this time the church in Virginia was agitating the subject of the founding of a College. Dr. Bittle was urged to take the lead, and embark in the perilous enterprise. He consented to accept their call. The Institution was chartered with collegiate privileges, under the title of "Roanoke College," by the Legislature of Virginia, in 1853. Its first session closed with thirty-seven students enrolled. Gradually it pushed its way into public favor. Its thirty-seven students have increased to nearly two hundred. Its library numbers 14,000 volumes, and is one of the most valuable in the State. Its cabinet of minerals and relics bids fair to rival anything of the kind in the South. It has already graduated about one hundred and forty young men, nearly all of them occupying positions of honor and influence in the different professions and pursuits of life. A large per centum of its graduates, nearly one-third, are engaged in the active work of the ministry. Roanoke College draws her patronage from seventeen states in the Union. In point of patronage Roanoke College is now the fourth institution of its kind in Virginia.

The *Conservative* and *Monitor*, of Salem, speaks of him in his official character as follows:

As a President he was no martinet, least of all a tyrant, frequently, from humility and lowly-mindedness, failing to exercise even necessary authority. His was a gentle ruling, full of allowances for the frailties of "boy nature," and ever ready to try the chances of reform. The secret of his great influence over his student-realm was the strong appreciation every one felt of his earnest interest in his temporal and spiritual welfare, which, without relaxation, followed the student in all his ways.

As an instructor he loved his work, was happy in his lecture room, patiently labored to bring his own and the thoughts of his text-book home to the humblest conception. Any manifestation of interest in the subject taught, real or feigned, quickly won his attention, and in his estimation, like charity, "covered a multitude of faults."

He loved books. In his visits to the large cities he found out, as by instinct, the obscure stalls where old ones were for sale, and bore them as prizes to his own or the college shelves. During his sojourn he often substituted a rare book for a needed meal when the alternative was presented. The splendid library which he collected for the College is a monument both to his fine appreciation and tireless activity.

Physically Dr. Bittle had an iron constitution, built up by labor on the farm. A feebler body could not have sustained his labors nor afforded a basis for his will. Though sixty-five years of age at his death, a stranger, judging by his appearance alone, would have pronounced him ten or fifteen years younger.

As a scholar he was a man of extensive and varied learning. His attainments were remarkable, when his active life is considered. His mind was not quick to apprehend, but firmly retained its acquisitions, and by the diligent use of moments he attained his eminence in scholarship. He was well acquainted with geology and botany. Many of the rarest specimens of the splendid cabinet of the college were found by him. He was familiar with history. In addition to the ancient languages taught in the ordinary college course, he read Hebrew and the more popular modern languages. He was a fine metaphysician. He had investigated for himself all the great metaphysical questions, and while he could give a ready answer as to what others said, he was equally ready with his own opinions. His specialty was logic. He had a taste for antiquities, and was never more interesting than when discussing such things as the origin of man. His researches were directed to almost every department of literature and science, and, in the wide range of discussion encouraged in his class-room, we have never known one subject to arise with which he did not seem to be acquainted.

As a teacher he was successful. He laid the foundation and directed future study. His pupils generally have pursued metaphysical studies, as far as their opportunities allowed. Those who have prosecuted their course at the University of Virginia have all taken high rank in the school of Moral Philosophy.

He could not be regarded as a profound theologian. He did not seem to have worked thoroughly out any system. His judgments were often profound, but very frequently were not in harmony. We have heard him preach that which was consistent only with strict Calvinism; then again that which was Arminianism.

As a preacher he was plain, simple, practical and earnest. He was not a finished orator; but there was a simplicity and earnestness in all his sermons such as are found in few men, and "the people heard him gladly." His illustrations were always drawn from the Bible, and he was eminently a Biblical preacher. His language was that of every-day life, and often grammatically incorrect. He eschewed the flowers of rhetoric.

His arrangements often neglected all homiletical rules, and yet there was in every sermon a connection that gave it unity. His manner was to preach from short notes, mere heads. He rarely ever attempted to preach from manuscript, and then he always appeared to great disadvantage. He rarely ever wrote in full a discourse. He was a ready man. At Synod he said he was the "gap" preacher; when nobody else would preach, he was appointed. He was always willing.

One who was intimately associated with him said to us a few years ago, "The longer and better I know Dr. Bittle the more I admire the simplicity and deep moral earnestness of his character." He loved the Lutheran church, and he worked for Roanoke College only as a means of advancing the interests of the Church. We fully believe that if the relation of the college to the Lutheran church had been broken off he would have become indifferent to the destiny of the institution. He lived for Roanoke College, and loved and labored for it, because he loved the church which it was seeking to serve. He maintained an unblemished character in that section where he lived for almost a quarter of a century. The purity of his motive and his integrity were never called in question. He was above reproach.

He had a vein of humor that surprised and delighted. He relished an anecdote, and could relate it with effect. His sense of the ludicrous was quick and keen, and when a fit time had come to open its stores he was exceedingly amusing. He was always happy in his farewell addresses to his students, and never more so than at the last commencement. But his mirth was never ill-timed, nor his wit low. He seemed to find nothing laughable in the profane or indecent.

It was his unconquerable energy that distinguished him. He worked, and he pitied and condemned those who would not. He had succeeded because he won success by hard blows, and he thought that every man could. He met difficulties and surmounted them by bravely marching forward. He had no patience with men who whined about little obstacles. He would have men encounter seeming impossibilities, and by dint of effort and prayer remove them. He believed that men should make opportunities, not wait for them.

THE LATE PASTOR BROBST.

Rev. Samuel K. Brobst was born Nov. 16th, 1822, and licensed on the 4th of June, 1847, in Philadelphia, by the Ministerium of Pennsylvania. Notwithstanding the fact that he prosecuted the work of the ministry until within a few months of his death, the labors of his life were mainly devoted to the dissemination of the truth as it is in Jesus, through the medium of the press. He accordingly began the work of publishing and editing more than a quarter of a century ago.

In 1837 he went to Washington in Western Pennsylvania, to learn a trade, where he received deep religious impressions under the ministry of the Rev. Dr. Brown, the Presbyterian President of the college at that place. He did not like his trade and was anxious to devote himself to study. A severe attack of sickness in 1841 compelled him to return home; and in the fall he went to the Allentown Academy and also took private lessons in the German language. During the winter he taught school, and established Sunday schools in his native valley. When he fully determined to study theology, he was at loss to what seminary to go. He attended several schools, among them Marshall College at Lancaster and Washington College in Western Pennsylvania; in this place he preached German to a small congregation, and gave private lessons in that language. He became an agent to the American Sunday School Union to labor among the German in Eastern Pennsylvania, and rejected a splendid offer from that Institution to become its German Secretary and Editor.

He was licensed in 1847, but it was only during the last nine years of his life that he became a pastor. He never had robust health; but for thirty years he served the church principally as editor of German periodicals. He was confined to his bed but a few days, and died December 23d, 1876, deplored by all who knew him.

Realizing the value of Christian nurture, he first established the *Jugend Freund*, a German Sunday school paper which has attained a wide circulation. Nineteen years ago he founded the *Lutherische Zeitschrift*, which in due time became a good-sized weekly quarto, and attained a prominent position among its contemporaries. In 1868 he commenced the publication of his *Theologische Monat's Hefte*, a monthly theological journal, which, after six years, he was compelled to suspend for want of adequate support. He was likewise the publisher of the *Lutherischer Kalender*.

A Pennsylvania German by birth and of the sixth generation, he appreciated the German language as a medium of instruction and usefulness, and urged its study upon students, and its use in the preaching of the Gospel. He took a prominent part in the organization of the German Press Association of Pennsylvania, and presided over its annual deliberations, as president, from its origin, fifteen years ago, until his death. Apprehending the necessity of seminaries of learning and their usefulness to the Church, he agitated the subject of transforming the literary institution at Allentown into a denominational college, and lived to see his expectations realized in the founding and success of Muhlenberg College.

Nor were these the only agencies and instrumentalities through which he made himself felt in the Church. By his counsels in conference meetings, his speeches at synods, his efficiency on ecclesiastical committees and institutional boards, his visits to Sunday schools and churches, his special addresses, and his occasional publications for children and adults, he exerted a marked and wide-spread influence on the German portion of the Lutheran church, as well as upon the German population in America.

His talents and acquirements, although not of the highest, were, nevertheless, of a respectable character. He was endowed with more than an ordinary share of practical wisdom, which he constantly displayed in his publications and periodicals. His genius enabled him to form a true ideal of what a Sunday school paper or church periodical, or theological journal ought to be, and by his literary skill and editorial tact, he succeeded in adapting them, in a very high degree, to the attainment of their respective ends.

In the prosecution of the work of publishing and editing, he also established a printing office and book store, of which he took the entire management. He was enterprising in the projection of plans of usefulness, and energetic in their prosecution. In a word, his pastoral, editorial, and business life was characterized by constitutional industry, unwearied labor, indomitable energy, hopeful perseverance, and a self-sacrificing spirit.

He was born, baptized, reared, and consecrated to the Lutheran church. He was devotedly attached to her doctrines, usages, principles of government, and forms of worship. In the discussion of the confessional and practical standpoints, which have agitated the Lutheran church in this country during the last twenty-five years, he took a prominent part, and while he was decided in his convictions, and candid in his utterances, he was, at the same time, courteous and fair in dealing with his brethren who differed from him. He was a deplorer of ecclesiastical strife and division, a lover of peace, and an advocate of Lutheran union. While his constitutional temperament, as well as his Christian spirit, prompted him to avoid giving offence on the one hand, and led him to endeavor to please on the other, he, nevertheless, frequently failed to conciliate his opponents, and subjected himself to their criticisms. Some of the attacks thus made upon him by his contemporaries, were harsh and unjust, but in defending himself against them, he exhibited a commendable degree of moderation and forbearance. Candor on the other hand, constrains us to admit, that in his endeavors to become "all things to all men," in the church, according to the example of Paul, he sometimes erred and exposed himself to the charge of inconsistency, if not of vaccillation. On this account his influence as a leader became more circumscribed and the popularity of the *Zeitschrif* considerably diminished. But, notwithstanding all this, Pastor Brobst fulfilled his mission with such assiduity, sincerity, devotion, and fidelity, as to command the esteem and admiration of all who knew him, and exerted, notwithstanding his weakness and imperfections, a healthy and extensive Christian influence in the families, the schools and the congregations of the German Lutheran church in America.

MICHAEL JACOBS.

Michael Jacobs was born in Franklin county, Pa., January 18th, 1808. The ancestors of Michael Jacobs were Alsatians. Both his father, Henry, and his grandfather, Martin, were active in the church, and a strip of ground cut off from the old farm continues to be the site of what is still generally known in that region as Jacobs' Church.

For some years he attended the country schools in the neighborhood, where he was especially deficient in all taste for arithmetic until another teacher developed his faculty for mathematics, in which, subsequently, he became so proficient.

In the fall of 1825 he entered the preparatory department of Jefferson College, Canonsburg, Pa. During his connection with Jefferson College he made a profession of religion, and was received into the fellowship of the Presbyterian church. But the understanding was mutual between him and Dr. Brown, the pastor, that his connection with it was merely temporary until he would reside where there would be a Lutheran congregation, and that the act involved neither an acceptance of the distinctive doctrines of the Presbyterian church nor a rejection of the distinctive doctrines of the Lutheran church, to whose service he had determined to devote his life.

He passed through college without the least stain upon his record, and won the esteem and consideration of the faculty to such a degree that, on one occasion, they rescinded an act of expulsion of a class-mate under the condition that Michael Jacobs would receive him as his room-mate and exercise a guardianship over him—certainly a compliment to a boy not yet twenty years old. That, however, his college life was not entirely destitute of humor is manifest from a manuscript periodical, which he edited, that was privately circulated among the students, several numbers of which are in the possession of his family. In the vacations his brother David and himself started debating societies in the vicinity of their home, and taught the country school teacher grammar, which they then immediately communicated to their pupils. During one of his vacations he also made an extensive trip into Ohio, distributing tracts.

In 1828 he graduated with the second honor of his class and the valedictory. Shortly afterwards he visited Gettysburg, where his brother David had begun the Gettysburg Gymnasium, and was already suffering from overwork as a consequence of being the sole teacher. In a conference with Dr. Schmucker and his brother, he promised to take charge of the mathematical and scientific instruction of the school, but, as he had already promised to teach in a boarding school at Belair, Md., he could not enter upon his work until the following spring. In April, 1829, he accordingly moved to Gettysburg. When the Gettysburg Gymnasium

15

became Pennsylvania College, he was elected Professor of Mathematics and Natural Sciences. He read theology privately, and, in the fall of 1832, was licensed by the West Pennsylvania Synod. His labors at the college were very arduous. Three professors now occupy the field which he had to cultivate alone. The resources of the college were so limited that in order to do justice to his department he was compelled to manufacture the most of the chemical and philosophical apparatus which he used. He filled his regular appointments as preacher in the college church. He was repeatedly President and Treasurer of his Synod, and, for a time, was Secretary of the General Synod. He was for several years editor of the Linnean Record and Journal. In 1865 his department was divided and restricted to that of mathematics. In 1866 he withdrew entirely from the work of instruction. For some years his health had gradually been declining. He continued a student until the last, and was reading in course Carpenter's Human Physiology until within a few days of his death, which occurred on July 22nd, 1871.

In attempting an analysis of his character there are some traits we recall for which we believe that he was especially distinguished:

1. Quickness of perception, a quality which, perhaps, was developed by his scientific studies. He seemed almost by intuition to grasp at once any subject to which he gave attention. The most minute details were at once noticed at a glance. While walking the streets or along the roadside the smallest objects attracted his attention, and, while passing them rapidly, he would notice, in a manner that would surprise his companions, any peculiarity by which they were marked. Every stone and flower and weed seemed to be a familiar acquaintance, and every cloud and star spoke a language to him unheard by all beside. In the recitation room a mere glance was generally sufficient to detect any error in the most intricate mathematical operation; so as to give the students a foundation for their hyperbole that "Professor Jacobs could hear by the sound of the chalk as soon as a mistake was made." Nor was this the case only with objects of study, but in all his intercourse with the world. He was rarely deceived in men. He seemed at once to read them like a book, and attempts at subterfuge and hypocrisy were at once met. He had a piercing eye, and when it fell upon the offender it appeared to him as though there were nothing left but to at once confess his guilt.

2. With this was united a soundness of judgment no less remarkable. The people of Gettysburg regarded his predictions concerning the weather as almost infallible. In geology and mineralogy his judgment was constantly put to a similar test, and many, envious to gain a fortune by mining, found to their sorrow the folly of despising his advice. Early in the morning before the first days of the battle of Gettysburg he pointed out to a staff officer the strategic importance of Cemetery Hill, and urged its occupation as an almost impregnable position that commanded the country for miles around.

3. He was modest and retiring to a fault. He constantly underestimated his own attainments, and even feared to mingle with those eminent in his department. Shortly before his death, in referring to a paper read by him in 1846 before the American Association for the Advancement of Science, he remarked: "What presumption!"*

In the pulpit he was always somewhat embarrassed. In deliberative bodies he rarely spoke unless the importance of the subject, and his own relation to it, constrained him. He was only on one occasion prominent in controversy, and that was when an effort was made to abridge the college course of beneficiary students. For a short time he fought the entire Synod, and then carried the controversy into the church paper with success. When the degree of D. D. was conferred upon him in 1858, almost simultaneously by Wittenberg and Jefferson Colleges, those who knew him best can testify that he was much embarrassed by it. His excessive modesty was the chief reason why he did not publish more. His manuscripts cover almost the entire field of his extensive department. Of these his lectures on meteorology were of especial value, and his pupils constantly asked for their publication. But he was content simply with delivering them in the recitation room, and did not attempt anything in the line of authorship beyond his small volume of "Notes on the Battle of Gettysburg," and a number of review articles. He was also the inventor of the process of preserving fruit by canning; but was satisfied with imparting the invention to his friends.

4. He possessed very ready wit, which, however, he employed with the greatest caution and conscientiousness. It often served

---

*It was I who prevailed upon him to attend ... ; and I heard eminent meteorologists say that Prof. Jacob's paper ... "Indian ... was a most creditable performance, containing the ... that phenomenon they had ever heard.

to enliven the fatigue of the class room, or to check a student who was becoming presumptuous or disorderly; but, when its purpose was accomplished, was laid aside for more serious work.

5. His self-sacrificing devotion to what he was convinced was his duty, was also a prominent trait. His firmness and perseverance were inflexible, and all else was subordinate. His life might have been lengthened if he had spared himself labor which was often too much of a tax upon his health. But often he would rise from his bed to walk to the college, perhaps in a winter storm, and at the close of the hour return to take his bed again until the arrival of the next recitation hour, when he would again force himself out. Those too who had to deal with him knew that while he was very ready to acknowledge when he was in error, yet that when he had taken a stand in regard to the discipline of the college, or any other important matter, and his position could not be shown to be wrong, no motives of policy or threats of injury to the interests he was serving could deter him from his course. There was a vein of melancholy in his constitution, and he often apprehended the worst where others saw no danger; yet, notwithstanding this disadvantage, I never knew him to vacillate.

6. He was one of the most sincere and candid of men. Not indifferent to injury, but, on the contrary, somewhat sensitive, he had little to say concerning any whom he thought to have wronged him, but would seek the first occasion to at once tell the injuring one of the grievance, and to administer in private the needed rebuke. He knew nothing of underhanded movements, and the arts of chicanery and intrigue, but despised them from his inmost heart. His principles and intentions he was always ready to declare openly and directly. Notwithstanding his constitutional modesty in the private walks of life there was no one whom he feared to encounter, but was always prepared to argue by the hour with the very best and ablest of his opponents. Neither in such a discussion would any man's standing or position shield him from being severely condemned, in case the principles or the policy which he advocated were worthy of censure.

7. His æsthetic taste was highly cultivated. The beautiful in nature almost threw him into a rapture. A fine landscape, or an approaching storm, or a sunset, would afford him the greatest delight. He would remain up all night to observe an *aurora borealis*,

or sit for hours enjoying the blooming flowers in a garden. A few weeks before his death he walked to the end of Middle street, and looking out towards Seminary Hill, then in the glory of the fresh verdure of spring, he said to his companion: "I will not be here long, and it will be a happy exchange; but my great regret is to leave this beautiful world." And afterwards on his way to college he said: "This world is so beautiful, that it is hard to think of leaving it." He was also fond of music. He was himself a performer on the flute. He enjoyed the piano greatly; and was especially delighted when it accompanied the singing of some of the grand old German chorals of his childhood, of which he never grew weary. For other than sacred poetry, however, he had but little sympathy.

8. In his ecclesiastical position he was a strong and decided Lutheran. He constantly protested against the tendencies prevalent during the period of his maturity in the General Synod. The radicalism of the *Lutheran Observer* of that day was a great offence to him. The religious impressions of his childhood followed him throughout life, and these were derived from Lutheran sources. The Lutheran doctrine of original sin, denied then in some prominent places, he so clearly expounded, and so earnestly inculcated in his family, that one of them will never cease to be thankful for the foundation thus laid in early childhood, for the other doctrines of God's word. The Lutheran doctrine of the sacraments he accepted heartily, and preached where it required no little courage at that time to maintain it. The symbolical books he studied and endorsed, and was gratified during his later years by the higher appreciation in which they stood, and the many symptoms of the revival of a purer faith that were becoming manifest. It was his great regret that the multiplicity of duties connected with his department had absorbed so much of his time as to prevent him from giving more attention to the systematic study of theology. H. E. J.

JACOB MARTIN

studied theology under Rev. Father J. P. Schindler, of Sunbury, Northumberland county, Pa., (his native place) and entered the ministry in 1824, and served different pastorates as follows:

Danville, Livingston county, N. Y., was his first charge, serving there two congregations about eighteen months, when he was called to Williamsburg, Huntingdon county, Pa. Here his field of labor extended over a great portion of that county. Hollidaysburg, Frankstown, Martinsburg, Royer's Furnace, Cove Forge, &c., were some of the most prominent places. He remained at Williamsburg, Pa., some twelve years, and was next called to Greencastle, Franklin county, Pa., where he remained a little over a year, when he was called to Hollidaysburg, one of the dependencies of his former charge, Williamsburg, and to which he had promised a visit so soon as the house of worship that congregation was then erecting should be finished. Here he served, with Frankstown only two miles distant, acceptably for several years, when discord was sown, caused by "new measures" which he did not approve. Resigned and was invited to Mifflintown, Juniata county, Pa. At this place he remained some fifteen months, when he returned to Hollidaysburg.

He returned to Hollidaysburg, Pa., feeling assured, as his friends informed him, that common sense had predominated over "new measures." But in time the discord was renewed, and, therefore, gave up the charge in H. as hopeless, and withdrew from the contest.

He was next called to Berrysburg, Dauphin county, Pa., where he officiated in the German language altogether some two years.

Giving up his German charge, he went to Johnstown, Cambria county, Pa., where he remained two years, and then removed to Petersburg, Adams county, Pa. Here his field of labor was again extensive and his duties arduous. Four years from thence he went to Westminster, Carroll county, Md., and remained two years.

His last pastorate being Reisterstown, Baltimore county, Md., where he served three years, aiding in the erection of a house of worship there, and in the spring of 1871 returned to his native place, Sunbury, Pa., where he was permitted to enjoy the society of his friends and those of his youthful days who yet remained, but a few months, and then departed to reap the reward of his forty-seven years of ministerial labor, on the sixth day of November, 1871, being over sixty-eight years of age. G. M.

THE REV. SAMUEL FINCKEL, D. D.,

was born at Jonestown, Lebanon county, February 22d, 1811. In 1825 he commenced preparing for the ministry of the gospel under the direction of Pastor John Stein, in Jonestown.

In the spring of 1827, he says: "I repaired to Gettysburg, continued my preparation for the ministry under the direction of Rev. Prof. S. S. Schmucker and Dr. E. L. Hazelius."

"In July, 1831, I was called to Harrisburg, where I was employed as Tutor of the Dauphin Academy for several years, besides preaching at Greensburg and Middletown, and occasionally at Harrisburg."

"At the meeting, in the spring of 1832, of the Lutheran Ministerium of Pennsylvania, convened at Wommelsdorf (Pennsylvania), I was licensed to preach the gospel. At the meeting of the Synod at Pottsgrove, 1833, I was ordained, and commissioned as Pastor of the churches in Middletown and Greensburg, Dauphin county, Pennsylvania."

"I resided in Harrisburg, Pennsylvania, nearly three years; in Taneytown, Maryland, three and a quarter years; in Middletown, Pennsylvania, three years and one month; Germantown, Philadelphia, Pennsylvania, four years; at Cumberland, Maryland, two years and eight months, and have been twenty-three years of my ministry in Washington, D. C. December 27, 1869."

The years he spent in Washington were the most active and remarkable of his life. Taking charge of the German Evangelical Church when it was dwindled down to a membership of only fifteen, and a small house of worship, and no parsonage, and a mere pittance of a salary, in a few years the church was refitted, the congregation increased to a membership of nearly three hundred, a parsonage was built, and a few years more the church building was doubled in size.

During his ministry in his various charges he either built or enlarged every church he served.

After preaching for twenty-three years to the Germans in Washington, he resigned his German charge, it being too much for his advancing years to think out a sermon in English and transpose it into German; he then felt that it would not be right for him to give up preaching entirely, knowing he would have all eternity to rest in; he undertook the arduous work of gathering an

English congregation, and to this end St. Paul's congregation tendered to him very magnanimously the chapel of Memorial Hall, to which place, in a few years, he attracted about one hundred hearers, but the infirmities of age and overwork made such inroads upon his health that after two years he gave up preaching.

While he served his congregation in Washington he also held an office under the United States Government.

The following is from "The Daily National Republican," Washington, D. C., Saturday morning, February 15th, 1873:

THE LATE REV. S. D. FINCKEL.

"On the 14th instant the clerks of the Quartermaster General's Office assembled to take suitable action on the occasion of the death of their esteemed friend and fellow-clerk, Rev. Samuel D. Finckel, D. D.

General George C. Thomas was called to the chair, and Ira S. Allen was appointed Secretary.

On motion, John S. Gallaher, Esq., Major Thomas J. Abbott and Captain A. W. Lattimore were appointed a committee to report suitable resolutions. They submitted the following, which were unanimously adopted:

When a good man dies the grief of his family is, in a measure, assuaged by the reflection that he has been called to receive the reward of a well-spent and useful life.

He was appointed a clerk in the Quartermaster General's Office in 1848. In service he was the third in point of seniority in the office, and labored with unflagging industry even after disease preyed heavily upon his delicate frame and marked him for its own. Yet he was ever genial, courteous and kind, looking upon the bright side of life, and by example and precept impressing upon all the duty of fidelity to every trust assigned them by Providence.

Resolved, That we have heard with profound sorrow of the death of Rev. Dr. Finckel, and desire to add our tribute of respect and affection to his memory, and to attest our sense of his worth as a Christian gentleman and faithful public servant.

Resolved, That we shall cherish his memory as a bright example; and, as a further tribute of respect, will attend his funeral in a body.

Resolved, That a copy of this be forwarded to his widow."

The Quartermaster General himself, and excepting a few of the clerks, all the rest of the clerks attended the funeral in a body.

Lutheran Observer, February 21st, 1873.—"Just as we go to press we learn of the death of Dr. Samuel D. Finckel, one of the most widely known ministers of our church. * * * * He died at his residence in Washington city, * * * * quietly, trustingly, hopefully. He was only waiting for the coming of the blessed Master, whom he had endeavored to serve from his youth.

He was one of our earliest Gettysburg students. * * * * He was master of both the English and German languages, and read *Latin*, *Greek* and *Hebrew*. Several years since he resigned the church he served in Washington, and exercised his ministry for sometime in the Memorial Chapel, anxious to gather the anglicized people, whom he had served, into an English organization, hoping thereby to furnish a nucleus for the Memorial Church, in whose success he was deeply, prayerfully interested. He loved to preach Christ. His prayers were remarkably unctuous. He was broadly evangelical in his views of religious truth, and ecclesiastically of the pronounced General Synod School. * * * * * * * His life during his pastorate was a busy one, as must be the life of any faithful pastor, especially of a German church. He knew more thoroughly than any man in Washington the religious condition and wants of the German population. The gathering of them into our English churches as rapidly as they became anglicized he regarded as the true policy of our church." * *

See also "Letter from Washington, Lutheran Observer, February 28th, 1873."

He attended to his studies in the morning as long as I know anything about his literary habits. His library was small, but the best books and authors were his companions. But the Bible was his constant companion, a greater part of it he committed to memory. He could repeat whole chapters in several languages. His prayers were always replete with the inspirations of Psalmists, Prophets and Apostles. His manner of preaching was without manuscript or notes. Dr. S. S. Schmucker once said to me, when talking to him about my father, that "he was one of the best preachers in our Church, both in English and in German." I cannot criticise his manner of preaching, for I do not remember of hearing him in his prime in English. I have heard him preach the most thrilling German sermons, although I did not understand all he said; his action of body, his gesture of head and hand, his glowing eye, his face, now stern and then placid, as he proclaimed the law and the gospel, showed that his soul was set on fire by a coal from off God's altar. The visible effect upon the people showed that what he spoke was "Spirit and life." His voice was not the ore rotundo, in the lower chest deep tones, but that of the higher and more musical, very clear, very loud. His articulation was very precise, always certain sounds.

As a pastor, I think, yea, I know, he was a model. He knew where every parishioner lived; he knew the names of parents and their children, and wherever he went in Washington or Georgetown, or Capitol Hill, or in Uniontown across the river, wherever a Protestant, or even a Roman Catholic German family lived, he knew them and they knew him, and their children would run out and welcome Herr Pastor. The children all loved him; he always had something cheerful to say to them, and the old people loved him, for he could be old with them, and he could be young with the young. He liked happy and humble Christians, but he distrusted gloomy people. He would fear to trust a professor who did not show up the religion of the Lord Jesus as altogether lovely and desirable for man's peace and happiness.

In his family he was a thorough Lutheran. Singing and instrumental music were his delight. His children were brought up in the love of that science which gives quietude to troubled minds and drives away care. Sorrow and trouble will not stay by when harmonious voices of parents and children join in hymns.

REV. COL. J. J. LEHMANOWSKY,

COUNT DE BELLEVIEU—FORMER COLONEL OF NINTH POLISH LANCERS—LUTHERAN CLERGYMAN.

Many of our ministers of thirty years ago will remember Col. Lehmanowsky—a very remarkable man with a very eventful history. Some persons had doubts concerning him, but I believe he was an honest man, and was all that he gave himself out to be. No responsible person ever contradicted his statements, and there were Frenchmen enough who would have done so if they could.

He boldly challenged a refutation of his assertions, and no one ever accepted it. Levassear, the private secretary of Lafayette, and the historian of the General's tour in this country in 1824, speaks of having met the Colonel in Washington; and in his book calls him "the brave Polish officer who for twenty years fought in the ranks of the French army."

The following sketch, obligingly furnished by Rev. P. Rizer, gives many interesting facts in the Colonel's life:

According to the best information derived from personal intercourse and other sources, Col. John Jacob Lehmanowsky was born of Jewish parents in the city of Warsaw, in the year 1773. I am not sure that his mother was an Israelite; but his strongly marked Oriental features and familiarity with the Hebrew language, together with other circumstances, were satisfactory evidence to my mind that he was of the stock of Abraham. His father was a professional chemist, and this circumstance afforded the son ample opportunity for pursuing studies in natural science. Having received an education at the University, he directed special attention to the subject of christianity at a time when he felt deep concern about future retribution. His religious convictions resulted in his conversion to a firm faith in Jesus of Nazareth, the son of God. On announcing this fact to his father, on the following morning, after a night spent in great mental anxiety, he met with a decided rebuke. Subsequently, however, the old gentleman, who was an intelligent and learned man, bade him God-speed, and became reconciled to his religious change.

Soon afterwards he went to Paris, which city was then greatly agitated by the revolution, and the young and ardent Pole was induced by the repeated cry of "Liberté et Egolité," to join the Republican army. He accompanied the rising Napoleon, and was present at the siege and capture of Toulon, in November, 1793. Lehmanowsky remained faithful to his great Captain, and followed his fortunes from Toulon to Waterloo, a period of twenty-two years.

I have often heard him say that he had been engaged in two hundred and four battles. He was with Napoleon in genial Italy; amid the scorching sands of Egypt, and the drifting snows of Russia. In the campaign of 1812 he commanded a regiment of Polish Lancers; and during the disastrous retreat of the French Army from Moscow, subsisted for thirty-seven days on rotten horseflesh.

He was frequently wounded, the marks of which his person plainly showed. A very severe sabre wound near his mouth was received at the battle of Austerlitz in 1805; this occurred during the storming of a redoubt, when he killed two of three cavalry men, and escaped the third by bounding over a ravine after his pursuing enemy had slashed him with his sabre, which struck the chain of his cap, and was somewhat parried thereby.

Whilst Napoleon was at Elba, after the battle of Leipzig, Lehmanowsky occupied himself at Paris with the various clubs that were plotting for the Emperor's return. The picture of a violet with the sentence "*Reviendra aux Printemps,*" was well understood among the Imperial abettors. According to the Colonel's statement, Marshal Ney, with whom he was intimate, was deeply concerned in the plot. It is well known that this "bravest of the brave," who had been sent out by Louis XVIII to intercept the exiled Emperor of Elba, after he had landed at Cannes, joined with his command the invading army of Napoleon. The Polish Colonel was accustomed to maintain that Marshal Ney's promise to bring the exile to Paris like a caged lion was redeemed; for he did bring the lion and let him out of the cage at Paris. At the battle of Waterloo, in 1815, Col. Lehmanowsky was one of Marshal Ney's four aid-de-camps. Soon after that decisive conflict he was arrested and imprisoned in Paris about the same time with Marshal Ney. The latter was shot, whilst the Colonel effected his escape from prison in a remarkable manner. Cutting his bed blankets into strings and tying them together, he fastened one end to the iron grating of the window of his cell, which was in an upper story of the Bastile, he let himself down one night, but to his dismay he found the rope too short, and there he hung a considerable distance above the ditch surrounding the walls of his prison, which was filled with water. Feeling the desperateness of his situation, he let himself drop, and one of his feet was soon penetrated by a sharp spike, of which there were many projecting from the ditch. With much difficulty he managed to get loose, and after clearing the ditch, encountered an armed sentinel, to whom he said, "Do your duty." But the sentinel happening to be a soldier of his own regiment, recognized the well known voice of his commanding officer, said quietly, "Pass on Col. Lehmanowsky." He soon found himself at the house of a friend in the city of Paris, who returned with him and covered up the bloody tracks to a sufficient distance lest his retreat might be discovered. Here he was concealed for a number of weeks, until his wound was sufficiently healed to enable him to escape entirely from his enemies. In the meantime, the police were active in his pursuit, and handbills containing a full description of his person were extensively circulated; but all to no avail: for he succeeded in avoiding all their efforts to arrest him, and in due time found himself safely landed in the city of New York. When he reached the shores of this free country, he was so much overcome by his feelings that he prostrated himself upon the ground and heartily thanked God for the wonderful and benign providence which had brought him to the "land of the free and the home of the brave."

After sometime about the year 1819, he married a Swiss lady in the city of Philadelphia. By his first wife he became the father of four children, two daughters and two sons, viz.: Simonetta, Lewis, John Henry and Paulina. He resided subsequently several years in Eastern Pennsylvania at different places, and supported himself and family by teaching the art of fencing, at which he was an adept. He owned a sword which was of extraordinary elasticity. He also taught some of the modern languages, of which he understood quite a number; among them French, Spanish and Italian.

For reasons satisfactory to himself, he suppressed his real name, and for many years was known as Major Lehman. But in 1824, when General Lafayette was here on a visit as the guest of our nation, Lehmanowsky was appointed to lead a company of Poles and other foreigners as the escort of Lafayette into Washington city. On reviewing the military who had marched out to greet him, the illustrious guest recognized his old friend, and embracing him before the crowd of spectators, addressed him as Col. Lehmanowsky. By Gen. Lafayette he was persuaded to lay aside the name of Lehman, because, said he, "Should any of the Napoleon dynasty ever again ascend the French throne, it would forfeit your claims against the government." Accordingly from that time he resumed his legitimate name.

I have often heard him speak of George Washington Lafayette, son of the Marquis, as a fellow soldier in the French army, and as an intimate personal friend. Gen. Lafayette made a present of one thousand dollars to Col. Lehmanowsky through an attorney at Baltimore, for the purpose of enabling him to purchase a farm.

A lady at Nashville, Tenn., also presented him with a considerable sum for a similar purpose. Accordingly he purchased a small farm near Knightstown, in Henry county, Indiana, where he practiced medicine, being known as the Polish Doctor, and cultivated the land until the year 1837.

He was for some time employed as an agent by the Immigrants Friends' Society, and then had his headquarters at Cincinnati. During this time he married Miss Lydia Sieg, daughter of John Sieg, a respectable farmer living near Corydon, Ind. The Colonel had been previously, in October, 1836, in Boone county, Ky., ordained as a minister of the Gospel by the Evangelical Lutheran Synod of the West.

At the time of his second marriage he was sixty-four years of age, and his wife, Lydia, was twenty-two. By this marriage he came into possession of eighty acres of land, and soon after settled upon it.

About this time there came to Corydon a wandering Pole, who made some disturbance in the community by reporting that Col. Lehmanowsky was an impostor. Consequently, the Colonel called on some of his friends, who appointed a committee of three respectable citizens to investigate the charge and publish their report. The accuser appeared before the committee, but was not able to prove anything. The only point he made was that Col. Lehmanowsky could not speak the Polish, his mother tongue. On the other hand, Lehmanowsky produced an array of documents, well authenticated, which satisfied all reasonable people that he was justly entitled to respect. I shall never forget the castigation which the Colonel gave that loafer, in the French language, before a crowd of eager spectators. Dr. Mitchel, a prominent citizen and formerly a State Senator, was chairman of the meeting. Col. Lehmanowsky's mother resided in Sweden, at the city of Stockholm. I once saw one of her letters to him, written in beautiful style and full of maternal affection. It was in the German language. Bernodotte, the King of Sweden, once invited him to join the Swedish army, and offered him the command of all his cavalry. But Col. Lehmanowsky declined because he had no desire whatever for a renewal of military life. He likewise declined a similar invitation of Gen. Sam. Houston, before the battle of San Jacinto, in Texas.

Col. Lehmanowsky was a man of very strong passions. One of

his daughters told me that the way by which her mother could sometimes bring him to reflection and quietness, when greatly excited, was by dashing dishes on the floor at his feet. But he did not always suffer himself to be transported by sudden vexations and troubles. For one Sunday morning, when about to start to church with his father-in-law's family, his span of horses, which had been fastened to a hitching place, suddenly broke loose, ran away, and broke the wagon to pieces. The Colonel remained composed and calm as the summer morn, only remarking—"So goes my fortune."

Whilst residing in Washington city he wrote several letters to Joseph Bonaparte, then near Bordentown, New Jersey. Suspecting that his letters had been intercepted, he, Lehmanowsky, hastened in person to Bordentown to ascertain the truth. On arriving at the door of Bonaparte's residence, he was met in the hall by one of the officials, perhaps a private secretary, and informed that the proprietor was not at home. The Colonel immediately charged the man with intercepting his letters, and knocked him down. This raised a commotion, and Joseph Bonaparte soon made his appearance, and said with indignation—"Col Lehmanowsky, what does this mean?" "It means," said the Colonel, "that I solicited aid from you as one of your former soldiers now in need, and that this scoundrel has been standing between us. I now stand before you in person, and respectfully ask you to do me simple justice." "Ah," said Bonaparte, "first make me King of Spain again, and then come to me." "You need not wait for that," said Lehmanowsky, "when everybody knows you spend immense sums in sensualism." It is unnecessary to say that his mission was unsuccessful. I have often heard the Colonel say that all the brothers of the Emperor Napoleon were scoundrels. But he had unbounded admiration for the Empress Josephine, who, according to his opinion, was the beau ideal of loveliness and excellence.

As an agent of the "Immigrants Friends' Society," he solicited funds in some of the principal cities of the West. At first he would advocate the claims of the Foreign Immigrants, and then wind up with narratives of his personal adventures as a soldier of the great Napoleon. This plan he subsequently changed, and prepared a number of lectures, which he delivered for a certain fee of admittance. This proved more successful than asking for a voluntary collection, even from crowded houses. His lecture on "Josephine" was exceedingly interesting, and that on the "Destruction of the Inquisition at Madrid" has been made use of as a tract and published by the American Tract Society. For a confirmation of the truth of that narrative he referred to Col. Lelis, his former companion in arms, then an evangelical preacher in the city of Paris (1837).

I once asked him to explain why we do not find his name mentioned in the many histories of Napoleon. Said he—"There were too many others of greater importance than mine." But he continued—"You may find a prominent notice of me in a book entitled, 'Mémoires des Braves.'"

I have understood that on the accession of Louis Napoleon to the French throne, Col. Lehmanowsky went to Paris to seek payment for a large claim which he held against the government. He was arrested by the police as an adventurer, and had some difficulty in regaining his liberty.

J. Z. SENDERLING, D. D.

BY REV. P. PELTZ, D. D.

Last Thursday morning, Dec. 20th, 1877, almost the entire community of Johnstown, N. Y., was startled, as if a thunder-bolt had fallen from a clear sky, by the report that Dr. Senderling, a venerable and highly esteemed ex-pastor of St. Paul's Church, of this village, was dead. Only the day before he had been seen on the streets, in the apparent enjoyment of his usual health, and, as far as human eye could see, bidding fair to live yet several years, as his was a remarkably green old age. But in the council of Heaven his days were numbered, and thus suddenly he passed from earth to Heaven. As he was standing alone on his front stoop, the summons came that called him from his much-loved home below to his sweet and happy home above.

Concerning him, the universal testimony is that borne by the pen of inspiration of Barnabas, "he was a good man." He leaves an unblemished character, and in this, "although dead he yet speaketh." He was an earnest and instructive preacher of the Gospel, a faithful and sympathizing pastor, a devoted husband and a kind father. Although he was strong in his attachments to the church of his fathers, the church in whose service he spent his long and useful life, the church bearing the name of the immortal Reformer of the sixteenth century, yet he was no bigot, but was ready to co-operate with all evangelical churches, whatever their name, in every good work, and frequently occupied the pulpit of the various pastors in our village.

The deceased was born in the city of Philadelphia, November the 12th, 1800, and was, therefore, seventy-seven years, one month and eight days old at the time of his death. He was baptized and confirmed, according to the usage of the Lutheran Church, by Dr. Philip F. Mayer, who was above a half century pastor of St. John's church, Philadelphia. Having in early life a thirst for knowledge and a desire to be useful in the Master's service, he was advised by his pastor to prepare for the Gospel ministry. Without the least hesitation he accepted the advice, and at once entered upon the preparatory work. In the autumn of 1817 he entered Hartwick Classical and Theological Seminary, located in Otsego county, N. Y., where he remained seven years. Among his class mates were Rev. Jacob Berger, a very successful and eloquent preacher of the gospel; Rev. H. N. Pohlman, D. D., who was pastor of Ebenezer Lutheran church, Albany, for twenty-five years; and John Quitman, who afterwards became Gen. Quitman, one of the staff officers of Gen. Scott, who served with distinction in the Mexican war, and was the first to unfurl the Stars and Stripes of his country from the halls of the Montezumas. He subsequently became Governor of Mississippi and a Representative in Congress. Mr. Senderling was in the Seminary a diligent student, and graduated with honors. His Professor in Theology was the Rev. Ernest L. Hazelius, D. D., who sustained the reputation of being one of the ripest scholars in this country.

Immediately after graduating he was licensed to preach the Gospel and at once took charge of a small church in Clay, Onondaga county, N. Y. His salary here being inadequate for his support, the deficit was made up by teaching a common school. In 1826, two years after his entrance into the ministry, he received and accepted a call to Centre Brunswick, near Troy, where he spent twenty-five of the most eventful years of his life.

About this time he was married to the daughter of a Moravian clergyman, who, as to piety and culture, was well qualified for a pastor's wife. Unto them a large family of children was born, five of whom grew to manhood and womanhood, four of the number, three sons and a daughter, still living to mourn with their aged and feeble mother over this sad bereavement. May the great Comforter whom the departed father and husband so dearly loved and faithfully served, comfort them!

After his resignation of the church at Centre Brunswick he removed to the city of Troy, where he resided for three years, spending the greater portion of his time among the churches in efforts to create an interest in the Foreign Missionary cause. In him the benighted heathen had an earnest advocate, and a warm, sympathetic friend. For a number of years he was corresponding secretary of the Board of Foreign Missions of his church, and in this, as in every other station he was called to fill, he was a faithful and efficient worker.

In the spring of 1856 he received and accepted a unanimous call as pastor of St. Paul's church of this village, into which office he was installed May 28th of the same year. His pastorate here extended over a period of eleven years. The church grew not only numerically, but in spirituality and efficiency under his ministry. Never was pastoral work more faithfully performed than by him in this charge. He not only preached the Gospel from the pulpit, but carried it to the homes of the people, as, wherever he went, he had a word for the Master, a Gospel message to proclaim. He has left the record of three thousand three hundred and forty-nine pastoral visits during the eleven years of service in St. Paul's congregation. He organized the first Sunday-school held in this church, as well as the weekly evening prayer-service.

In the spring of 1867 he resigned this pastorate, and has, since that time, lived a retired life, occasionally preaching for the brethren of his own and of other churches. He loved to preach, and was always earnest and impressive in the pulpit. He loved the house of God, and, if not providentially prevented, was never absent. But no more will his genial countenance, his manly form, be seen in the sanctuary made with hands. He now worships with those in white before the throne. In his own language we would close this imperfect sketch of his life: "Home, home, at last with glorified millions, in the presence of Jesus, in the new and heavenly Jerusalem."

Dr. Senderling's funeral took place on Monday, December 24th. The services were held in St. Paul's church, the pastor preaching from John v. 35. Several pastors of the village churches, and others from abroad, assisted him in these solemn and impressive services. The attendance was large, and many a tear of affection moistened the eyes of the old and young.

CHARLES A. MORRIS.

BY REV. W. M. BAUM, D. D.

With feelings of no ordinary emotion do we record the death of this well-known and much-beloved friend and brother. For many years he had been one of the most active and most influential laymen of the Lutheran church, being intensely interested in her welfare and contributing largely to her efficiency. Everything connected with his life is of interest. He richly deserves a full biography. The church and the world would be benefited by an honest portraiture of his life and character. His example could not but stimulate others to worthy deeds.

What more eminently proper than for his only surviving brother and relative, for whom he ever entertained and showed the most touching and tender regard, and who has equal taste and talent in that direction, to expend his unwasted powers upon the preparation of a full memorial volume of this departed patriarch?

Although by no means in robust health for many years of his life, Mr. Morris nevertheless attained a good old age, being in his eighty-second year when he died. He was born and reared, and lived and died, in York, Pa., and was as extensively known as he was sincerely beloved by the entire community. A mere glimpse at his character is all that circumstances will allow at the present time.

Charles A. Morris combined so many excellencies of character, and showed so few of the ordinary weaknesses of human nature, that we believe no one who ever once knew him could fail to appreciate him. He was perfectly transparent, as easily read as any man we have ever known. He was the very soul of integrity and uprightness. No one ever doubted his perfect and entire simplicity and sincerity of Christian character, and of his success in "serving his day and generation according to the will of God," there is most abundant evidence.

He was broad and catholic as a Christian, but no less earnest and devoted as a Lutheran. Fully acquainted with the spirit and peculiarities of the church of his fathers and of his love, he was proud of her history and achievements, and untiring in his efforts and contributions for her advancement. In most marked and beautiful concert with his noble and gifted wife, who preceded him in death by a few years, he labored incessantly for the good of men and the glory of God. In all general objects, with other Christians, in church objects with his fellow-members, and in congregational objects with his immediate friends and associates, he was always doing and giving for the Lord Jesus. Using his pen, his purse and his voice with equal readiness and success, he was ever welcomed by all who needed judicious and discriminating help. In the Sabbath-school, prayer-meeting, church-council, synod or convention, he was equally at home.

It is claimed by those who can scarcely be mistaken, that he was at the time of his death the very oldest Sabbath-school worker, longest in service, in Pennsylvania. Beginning with the very earliest Sabbath-school movements, he continued unintermittingly, with increasing earnestness and fidelity, to the last Sabbath but one of his life. He was in full and successful service for more than half a century, preparing with conscientious faithfulness for every Sabbath. At Bible class and weekly congregational services he was a model of regularity and devout attention.

Uniting with the little band that organized St. Paul's congregation, in the early ministry of Rev. Dr. Oswald, he lived to see the consummation of his wishes in the completion of the present church edifice, of the cost of which he bore a very large proportion. Being successful in business, he was always able, and quite as ready, to contribute largely to all charitable and benevolent objects. His generosity was never exhausted. He gave constantly, even more freely and frequently than his friends knew or believed.

As a citizen, Mr. Morris was alike honored and useful. He

was especially interested in educational matters, and was consulted and enlisted in all questions of reform or improvement. For more than fifty consecutive years he served as a director of the York county academy, and was for many years the president of its board of directors. He was for a long number of years —perhaps through its whole history—a trustee of Pennsylvania College, in which he ever manifested an abiding interest, and to which he gave largely of his means.*

It may well be doubted whether ever an appeal was made to him for sympathy or assistance, that had any just claims upon him, without being carefully considered and liberally aided. In him the widow and the orphan, the poor and the needy, had an ever tender and sympathizing friend.

After a short but severe illness, induced, it is thought, by exposure, in going about among the unfortunate and suffering, he breathed his last on Friday morning, April 10th, surrounded by his friends and trusting with childlike faith in his Saviour.

THE LATE C. A. MORRIS—IN MEMORY OF A SUNDAY-SCHOOL TEACHER— BY ONE OF HIS EARLIEST SCHOLARS.

It is now just fifty years since I first attended Sunday-school in York, Pa., the school being held in the old parochial school-house back of the First Lutheran church, and was taught in German. C. A. Morris was the superintendent and often the only male teacher. The school was small, not more than twenty or thirty scholars attending. We used to sing the beautiful hymns in the German Lutheran catechism, some of which I then committed to memory and shall never forget while life endures. I remained in the school as a scholar until I became a member of the church, in 1826, and was confirmed with one hundred others by Dr. S. G. Schmucker.

As scholar, teacher, superintendent and pastor, I have been connected with the Sunday-school cause ever since. I have great reason to thank God for the Sunday-school, for I was a wild, thoughtless and wicked boy, exposed to many snares and temptations, and it was through the influence of the Sunday-school that my mind was directed to religion. C. A. Morris sowed the seed in my heart which afterward ripened into a tolerable crop. Never shall I be able to forget that good and earnest Christian

---

* $30,000 at one time and about $5,000 at other times to Pennsylvania College and about $5,000 to the Theological Seminary. During his long life, Mr. Morris gave upwards of $80,000 to religious objects.

worker. At that time working laymen were few, and pastors in our church had so many congregations that they could do nothing but preach. Even Dr. Schmucker, with one of the largest congregations in Pennsylvania, had to preach in some three or four other places. What a change! There are now six large Lutheran congregations in York, and from the little German Sunday-school in the alley have sprung four large and flourishing schools. "What hath not God wrought!" And much of this has under God been the work of C. A. Morris. In many respects Mr. Morris was far in advance of his age. Thus he was one among the earliest friends of the colored people, long before Garretson, May, Greeley or Sumner had commenced the great battle of humanity in behalf of the oppressed and down-trodden slave.

Mr. Morris was an active and intelligent Christian gentleman, and during his lifetime did as much for the Lutheran church as any other man. And although his gifts were large, often running up into the thousands, the half of his charities were never known. I know some of his private benefactions that are known to no other. It was through him that I went to Gettysburg. He took me by the hand when I was a poor boy, and with his counsel and his purse, he stood by me until I entered the ministry, and now since he is dead I feel it my duty, as one of his Sunday-school scholars, to bear this honorable testimony to his worth. R. W.

ADOLPHUS F. OCKERSHAUSEN.

No man who has taken an active part in our church within the last half century deserves a more prominent place than Adolphus F. Ockershausen. Born of Lutheran parentage, in the city of New York, on September 22nd, 1814, he became a member of St. James church on Easter Sunday, 1833, continuing his connection with it until his death, serving as one of the church officers for over thirty-five years. His benefactions to that church, of which we know nothing in detail, were by the thousands, and through that church the same might be said of other church institutions. He was educated in the Mechanics Society School, amongst the best in the city fifty years, and from his majority became one of its active members until the end. When comparatively a boy he went into his father's sugar refinery to learn the business. When but nineteen years of age both parents died within a short time of each other, leaving him to care for eight brothers and sisters. So mature in thought, so conversant with the business, so thoroughly trust-worthy, the executor on the estate left the business in his hands, with the entire support of the family — a responsibility which he fully met. The business grew and developed until *his* became one of the leading firms. In 1849 he met with heavy losses by a disastrous fire, which compelled him to make a compromise with his creditors for seventy-five cents in the dollar. In the year 1856, one of his first acts, after becoming successful in business, was to pay to his creditors the remaining twenty-five cents. Great prosperity attended him during the period of our civil war. From these results one of his first acts was the endowment, in October, 1864, of the Ockershausen Professorship at Gettysburg, and the pledge, which he was never called upon to redeem, of $10,000 to Hartwick Seminary (of which he was for many years a Trustee) as soon as the church should raise a similar amount. For fifteen years he was Treasurer of the General Synod. His courtesy, accuracy, and readiness to furnish funds when needed, are known to all who met him in that capacity. Other disastrous fires, losses in business, shrinkage in values, reduced his large estate most sensibly, enabling him in the end to leave his family only a small competency. But through a business life of nearly fifty years, his name was the synonym of integrity. A director of banks, insurance companies, benevolent institutions, he was regarded as a man whose opinion and judgment was always to be followed. The foster-father of his brothers and sisters, the mainstay of St. James church, an active business man for many years, he was distinguished in every relation of life for absolute fidelity, and carried with him to the grave a thousand memories of a well-spent life. W. D. S.

MARTIN LUTHER STOEVER

was born in Germantown, a district of Philadelphia, February 17, 1820. His preliminary education was received in the Germantown Academy, in his native place. But in 1833, at the age of thirteen, he went to Gettysburg, Pa., and entered the preparatory department of Pennsylvania College. In 1834 he was admitted to the Freshman Class in that institution. At the very beginning of his course he took high rank as a student, and maintained this until his graduation, in 1838, his graduation appointment being the Latin Salutatory. In the fall of 1838 he took charge of a school in Jefferson, Md., where he made many friends, and was looked up to as authority in all matters. At the earnest request of the Board, in the fall of 1839, he returned to Gettysburg, and assumed the charge of the Preparatory Department of Pennsylvania College. At different times, subsequently, he taught almost every branch of study in the college while exercising a general oversight as principal of the Preparatory Department. During the presidency of Dr. Krauth, Prof. Stoever lived in the college building, and acted as President *pro tem.* During the last ten or twelve years of his life, his attention was devoted to instruction in Latin, in the teaching of which branch he was entirely at home, and felt a deep interest in the progress of his pupils. He died July 22, 1870, in Philadelphia, at the close of a college year of excessive work, and at the end of the thirty-first year of his connection with the institution as instructor. Outside of college duties, his literary labors were almost entirely confined to the *Evangelical Quarterly Review*, in every number of which, from its inauguration in 1849, with the exception of two issues, one or more articles from his pen appeared. Associated in its editorship for several years with Drs. Reynolds and Krauth, he became sole editor and proprietor in 1862, and closed its life with his own with its twenty-first volume, in 1870. He published also memoirs of Revs. H. M. Muhlenberg, D. D., and P. F. Mayer, D. D., and several addresses delivered on special and public occasions. He received the degree of Ph. D. from Hamilton College, N. Y., in July, 1866, and that of LL. D. from Union College, N. Y., in July, 1869, both of which came unexpectedly to the recipient, his friends having secured these honors unknown to him.

Prof. Stoever was several times asked to take charge of female seminaries, but these he declined; also the invitation to the presidency of Girard College, in Philadelphia, and the Professorship of Latin in Muhlenberg College, Allentown, Pa., tendered to him in 1869. He was prominently connected with the Christian Commission during the late civil war, was well known among all denominations, and had many friends all over this country and in England, Scotland and Ireland. He was beloved by all his friends.

TRIBUTE TO PROFESSOR STOEVER—ACTION OF THE BOARD OF TRUSTEES OF PENNSYLVANIA COLLEGE ON THE DEATH OF PROF. M. L. STOEVER.

Dr. J. G. Morris, president *pro tem.*, having announced the death of Prof. M. L. Stoever, the senior member of the faculty of Pennsylvania College, a committee consisting of Rev. Drs. Conrad, Schmucker and Baum was appointed to prepare an appropriate testimonial respecting the character, worth, and services of the deceased. The committee subsequently reported the following minute, which was unanimously adopted, and ordered to be published and transmitted to his family:

WHEREAS, on the 22d of July last, in the city of Philadelphia, an all-wise Providence suddenly removed Martin Luther Stoever, Ph. D., LL. D., Professor of the Latin Language and Literature in Pennsylvania College, from the sphere of his active duties in this world; therefore,

Resolved, That we have heard the announcement of his death with deep regret and heartfelt sorrow, and that we bow to the will of God as manifested in his inscrutable Providence, with reverence, humility, and submission.

Resolved, That we recognize in Prof. Stoever a combination of natural talents and moral virtues constituting a Christian character of rare excellence. His integrity as a man, his attainments as a scholar, his faithfulness as a professor, his devotion as a husband and father, and his consistency as a Christian, won the esteem of all and endeared him to his relatives, pupils, and friends.

Resolved, That in every relation he sustained to this institution during the last thirty years, as student, alumnus, Principal of the Preparatory Department, and Professor of the Latin Language and Literature, he has exhibited diligence in study, aptness and ability in imparting instruction, firmness in government and discipline, thus reflecting credit upon himself, and rendering services of the highest value to the college.

Resolved, That as a layman in the congregation, secretary and historian of the General Synod, editor of the *Evangelical Review*, and biographer of deceased Lutheran ministers, he has evinced high literary culture, extensive knowledge, religious enterprise, and untiring devotion to the interests and progress of the Lutheran Church in the United States.

Resolved, That by his genial disposition, his pleasing manners, his ardent friendship, his considerate attention to strangers, his generous hospitality, his educational enthusiasm, and his catholic spirit, he became widely known and loved, and extended the sphere of his usefulness far beyond the bounds of his own denomination.

Resolved, That by his unselfish and varied ministrations of kindness and mercy to the wounded, the sick, and the dying, at Gettysburg and other battle-fields of the Republic during the late war, he displayed a patriotism and humanity which will be remembered by multitudes who were engaged in that great struggle, and who will cherish his memory with affection and gratitude.

Resolved, That we hereby tender his stricken widow and orphan children our sincere sympathy and condolence, praying that their present separation and bereavement may, by God's blessing, eventuate in their future reunion and eternal blessedness.

Resolved, That these resolutions be published in the papers of Gettysburg and of the Lutheran Church, and that the secretary be instructed to transmit a copy of them to the family of the departed. Respectfully submitted,

F. W. CONRAD,
S. S. SCHMUCKER,
W. M. BAUM.

THE LATE PROFESSOR STOEVER—ACTION OF THE STUDENTS OF PENNSYLVANIA COLLEGE ON THE DEATH OF PROF. STOEVER.

WHEREAS it has pleased our heavenly Father to remove from the number of our instructors our esteemed friend and professor, Dr. M. L. Stoever, who labored with untiring devotion in the various positions which he filled while in connection with Pennsylvania College; therefore,

Resolved, That, in this dispensation, we recognize the fact that God hath called him to himself to a nobler work on high, since by his life he gave evidence of his trust in Jesus as his Saviour.

Resolved, That while bowing submissively to the will of Providence, we also express our sorrow at our loss, and our deep sympathy with his afflicted family.

Resolved, That we, as students, desire to express our appreciation of his virtues, and shall ever remember with gratitude the uniform kindness shown to all his pupils, and the paternal anxiety which he ever manifested in their welfare.

Resolved, That a copy of these resolutions be sent to the family of the deceased, and that they be published in the church and town papers.

F. G. KNAPP,
E. F. BARTHOLOMEW,
GEO. M. MICHAEL,
JOHN BRUBAKER,
WM. S. FREASE,
Committee.

The Rev. Dr. Hay pronounced a memorial discourse on Prof. Stoever on Sunday, September 4th, 1870, in the College Church, Gettysburg, in which he eloquently improved the sad calamity.

I designated Prof. Stoever as "The Lutheran Plutarch of America." He wrote and published in the Review biographies and reminiscences of eighty deceased Lutheran ministers, and every person admires the impartiality and ability of these productions.

He once told me that he was gathering materials for a similar notice of me. It was said in a style of good natured banter, upon which I remarked, that though I was older than he, yet I might live to render a like service to his memory, which seemed for a moment to sadden him.

The resolutions quoted above represent his true character. They are not the usual stereotype complimentary utterances of a meeting hastily assembled and as hastily dissolved, but the deliberate and sincere expressions of men who knew him well and rightly estimated his exalted character.

I wrote to a mutual and life-long friend for a brief sketch of our dear departed brother, and he sent me the following, which characterizes him perfectly. Upon every one of these points much might be said in illustration.

"The distinctive traits of our much admired friend were:

1. His genial, kind-hearted, unaffected, and I may call it, *beautiful* disposition. 2. His open-handed, generous hospitality.

3. His accurate scholarship in his department. 4. His assiduity in keeping afloat the Review. In traveling in its interests he did much for Pennsylvania College by securing students. The church owes him a debt of gratitude by drawing out thereby so much valuable literary material. He rescued from oblivion many an important and interesting biographical and historical fact. 5. His extensive acquaintance in other churches where he favorably represented our own. 6. His persistent refusal to leave our church, though repeatedly approached with tempting offers from institutions in other churches. 7. His special efficiency during and after the battle of Gettysburg, and his untiring labors in the Christian Commission work for some months after the battle. 8. His original purpose to enter the ministry and his being deterred by his hesitancy of speech. 9. His habit of charitably construing the conduct of others—always putting the most favorable construction on their actions. This was a strong point of his character."

I have thus completed my gallery of portraits. Doubtless some of my readers will say that many more should have been introduced, and I will here state that not a few requests have been sent to me upon this subject. But I wish it to be remembered that I have not undertaken to furnish biographical sketches of all the ministers who have died during the last "Fifty Years," but only of some of those whom I personally knew, and who have left their impress upon the Church *generally*. To have introduced all would have enlarged this modest volume to greater proportions than are desirable. Many good men have died whose influence, though great, has been circumscribed, and my unpretending book does not claim to be a biographical dictionary of deceased Lutheran ministers, nor a complete history of the Church during this period. Another work is in contemplation which will embrace a notice of every one of our deceased clergymen of whom any account can be received, and of every other historical event in the Church from its foundation in this country. If Providence favors this enterprise, the nature of which will soon be made known, I am sure all our friends will be satisfied. Nothing will be omitted that will throw light upon our denominational progress, our biographical history, our church efficiency, our literary institutions, and everything else that concerns us as an ecclesiastical body.

GENERAL SYNOD.

I thought it well to give the following synopsis of the proceedings of the General Synod, which embraces only the principal events, that readers who may have occasion to refer to them might be saved the trouble of looking through all the distinct copies of proceedings. Here they have them at a glance. The transactions of the various societies are not given at large, because they will be treated with sufficient fullness under distinct heads. I thought the importance of the subject would justify such an extended chapter.

For a very interesting article upon this subject, entitled the General Synod and her assailants, see Evanglical Review, January, 1867.

History of the General Synod.[*]

The convention which organized the General Synod assembled in Hagerstown, Md., October 22, 1820. The initiatory step towards this union was taken by the Synod of Pennsylvania, convened in Baltimore in 1819.[†] At this meeting (1820) Rev. G. Schober, of North Carolina, presented the outline of a plan which was referred to a committee by which it was reported to the Synod with some changes, and which was adopted by a vote of forty-two to eight. A printed copy was sent to all the Synods in the church, with the understanding that if three-fourths of them approved the plan, the convention should be called. The proposition having been favorably received, Dr. J. G. Schmucker, the President, in accordance with the instructions given, published the proposed meeting at the time designated. At this convention delegates appeared from all the Synods except that of Ohio. From the Synod of Pennsylvania were present Rev. Drs. G. Lochman, F. W. Geissenhainer, C. Endress, J. G. Schmucker, H. A.

---

[*] See Evangelical Review, Vol. V., 239 et seq. Also minutes of General Synod. And an able article on the General Synod and her assailants in Evangelical Review, January, 1867.

[†] See Evangelical Review, April, 1861, p. 590.

Muhlenberg and Messrs. C. Kunkel, W. Hensel and P. Stichter; from the Synod of New York Rev. Drs. P. F. Mayer and F. C. Schaeffer; from the Synod of North Carolina Revs. G. Schober and P. Schmucker; from the Synod of Maryland Rev. Drs. J. D. Kurtz, D. F. Schaeffer and Mr. G. Shryock. Rev. Dr. J. D. Kurtz of Baltimore was chosen President, and Rev. Dr. Muhlenberg of Reading, Secretary. After two days of deliberation, a constitution was unanimously adopted. If three of the Synods represented should accept the constitution, the President was authorized to convene a meeting of the General Synod at Frederick, Md., on the third Monday of October, 1821. The President was instructed to address a fraternal letter to the Ohio Synod, prevailing upon it to unite in this important enterprise.

In expectation that the constitution would be approved, committees were appointed. 1. *To form a plan for a Seminary of Education.* 2. *To form a plan for a Missionary Institution.* 3. *To form a plan in aid of poor ministers and minister's widows and orphans.*

The constitution having received the approbation of three out of the five Synods then in existence—

The First Meeting of the General Synod was held in Frederick, October 22, 1821. Pennsylvania, North Carolina, Maryland and Virginia (at that time united in one Synod) were represented. New York and Ohio sent no delegates.

The subject of a Theological Seminary was discussed, but its establishment was deferred for several years, because it was presumed that the church was not yet ready for such an undertaking. Some suggestions relating to a more advanced theological training of candidates for the ministry were made, and a resolution to that effect was passed.

The subject of Home Missions was also brought up, and the Synods were recommended to send one or more missionaries into destitute parts.

It appears that a practice had prevailed to some extent of individual ministers ordaining candidates without the permission of their *ministerium*, which was disapproved in several Synods; also, the orders of deacons and candidates with power to administer the sacraments prevailed, which the Synod thought should not be retained longer than the exigency of the times might require.

A committee was also appointed to prepare an English Catechism, to report at the next meeting.

At that time the Synod of Pennsylvania was composed of eighty-five ministers; the Synod of Maryland and Virginia, which had been formed just one year before, and which was previously a part of the Synod of Pennsylvania, had fifteen ministers; the Synod of North Carolina reported thirteen ministers.

☞ This latter Synod reported that a committee from the Episcopal church attended their last meeting, with a view to confer on some plan by which friendly relations might be maintained between the two respective churches. The result of the conference was, that any minister in connection with the Synod should be entitled to a seat in the Episcopal convention of North Carolina, with the privilege of voting upon all subjects that did not pertain to the Episcopal church and *vice versa*. The committee on behalf of the Episcopal church also offered to the Synod to educate at their Seminary and prepare for the ministry gratuitously, any student the Synod might recommend. This fact, in connection with the proposition made by Bishop White to the Synod of Pennsylvania, to receive our ministers into the Episcopal church without requiring of them reordination, may be useful for reference in future controversies, as the question with regard to the ministerial ordination performed by other denominations is virtually conceded, and all claim for the divine authority of diocesan Episcopacy at once abandoned.*

The Second Meeting of the General Synod was held at Frederick, October, 1823. There were delegates from the Synods of North Carolina, of Ohio, of Maryland and Virginia, *but not of Pennsylvania*. There was also a deputation in attendance, appointed by a conference west of the Susquehanna, belonging to the Synod of Pennsylvania.

A resolution was passed expressing deep regret that the Pennsylvanians were induced by peculiar circumstances to recede from an institution which they aided in establishing.

The "peculiar circumstances" were the prejudices of the congregations, and the fear entertained by some of the ministers that the General Synod would exercise too much authority, and invade the rights of the districts; all of which was simple nonsense, and unworthy the men who pretended to entertain these fears. The fact is that some of those ministers were intimidated by the ravings of some fanatical foreigners who made the simple people believe that their civil liberties were in peril, and that church and

---

* I should like to know when this proposition was made by Bishop White!

state were about to be united through the agency of the Synod. Some of the ministers were afraid to assert their rights less they might lose their bread.*

The committee appointed on the Catechism at the previous meeting, reported, and their material was referred to another to report subsequently.

A committee on *Foreign Correspondence*, consisting of Drs. J. D. Kurtz, J. G. Schmucker and G. Schober, was also appointed.

The formula for the government and discipline of the church in Maryland and Virginia, prepared by S. S. Schmucker, was submitted for the sanction of the General Synod, and was unanimously approved.

At this meeting it was reported that there were five Synods, nine hundred churches, and one hundred and seventy-five ministers.

An elaborate address to the church, prepared by S. S. Schmucker and D. F. Schaeffer, was read and adopted.

The Third Meeting was held at Frederick, October, 1825. Delegates were present from North Carolina, Maryland and Virginia, and West Pennsylvania.

At this meeting the Theological Seminary was established, solicitors of funds appointed, and directors chosen.

It was determined that at an early period the directors should meet at Hagerstown to decide the location of the seminary.†

A committee was appointed to prepare a Hymn Book, Liturgy and Prayers in the English language, and another committee was authorized forthwith to publish the translation of Dr. Luther's Small Catechism, submitted by the committee previously appointed.

The Fourth Meeting was held at Gettysburg, October, 1827. Delegates were present from the Synods represented in the last convention.

Nothing of general interest was transacted. Resolutions of regret were passed in relation to the deaths of Rev. Drs. Lochman and Endress, who were among the founders of Synod.

The Committee on Foreign Correspondence reported letters from Rev. Dr. Planck, of Goettingen,‡ and Rev. Dr. Kniewel, of Dantzig.

---

*The Synod renewed its connections with the General Synod at Winchester in 1853, and severed it again at Fort Wayne in 1866.

† See my History of the Seminary in Ev. Rev., Vol. V, 413, for January, 1854, and my History in Ev. Quart. Rev., Vol. ...

‡ See Lutheran Intelligencer of this year.

Reports upon the Seminary and Rev. B. Kurtz's success in Europe were read.

The Fifth Meeting was held at Hagerstown, 1829. There were delegates present from the three Synods in attendance at the last meeting. At this meeting a Sunday School Union was formed.

The desire having been expressed for the publication of some good, practical work, under the sanction of the Church, a committee was appointed to prepare a devotional book for catechumens and Christians in general. This was the origin of my "Catechumens' and Communicants' Guide," published first in 1831, although it was not submitted to the Synod nor published under its sanction.

As objections had been made to the constitution of the General Synod, and misconstructions had arisen from the phraseology used, a committee was appointed to ascertain whether any changes were necessary. The committee reported several amendments, which were approved and subsequently endorsed by the District Synods.

A constitution for the government of the District Synods was also proposed and recommended for adoption.

A pastoral address was issued, defining the position of the Synod, and removing all objections to it on the ground of individual liberty and right of private judgment. It asserts that the Synod does not claim the right of calling to account the members of individual Synods for any offence in doctrine or practice, and could do no more than admonish the Synod to which the offender belongs, to take cognizance of the case. The several Synods constituting the General Synod are regarded as so many independent ecclesiastical polities, associated merely for the promotion of brotherly love, and for the concentration of their energies. * * *

The Sixth Meeting was held at Frederick, 1831. Hartwick Synod was now represented for the first time.

The want of a church literature seems to have been most felt, and the business principally related to this subject.

It was resolved that the publication of the following works would be encouraged: *The Lutheran Manual, The Lutheran Preacher,* a translation of *Arndt's True Christianity, The Lutheran Panoplist* or *Controversial Tracts,* an *English Liturgy, &c.* Fifteen members were elected as an editing committee, to whom any book prepared by another was to be submitted for examination before it was published.

17

The Lutheran Observer,* then issued in Baltimore, and the *Evangelical Magazine*, a German work, published in Gettysburg, were recommended.

The Seventh Meeting was held in Baltimore, 1833. The same Synods were represented as at the previous meeting.

The subject of union with the German Reformed Church was discussed, and a committee consisting of J. G. Morris, S. S. Schmucker and G. A. Lintner was appointed to report upon a basis of union. They subsequently reported that they could not come to any definite conclusion upon the subject, and, by request, were discharged.

At this convention a recommendation was passed that the district Synods adopt a uniform rule, requiring ministers and congregations to unite with the Synods within whose bounds they may be located.

Our ministers and churches were also recommended to celebrate the 31st of October in each year, in commemoration of the reformation. This measure had previously been adopted by the Synod of Maryland.

The Temperance Reformation was also warmly recommended, and the book committee reported the publication of a large edition of the Hymn Book. A collection of hymns for the Sunday schools, compiled by Dr. Krauth, was transferred to the Synod as its property, by Mr. Dull of Philadelphia.

The Eighth Meeting was held in York, June, 1835. Delegates appeared for the first time from the Synod of South Carolina.

The principal points of interest were *Missions* and *Beneficiary Education*. At this meeting the Parent Education was organized.†

The Pastoral Address presented an encouraging condition of the church.

The Ninth Meeting occurred at Hagerstown, June, 1837. In addition to the Synods heretofore represented, delegates were present from New York, which had assisted in the formation of the Synod at this place in 1820.

Nothing new of general interest was done at this meeting. The Pastoral Address reported two hundred and fifty ministers.

---

* The Observer was established by me in 1831, and I conducted it for two years. I gave it into the hands of Dr. B. Kurtz in 1833. The Evangelical Magazine was begun in 1829, and continued four years. Rev. J. Herbst was its editor the first year, and Dr. S. S. Schmucker the second, and Drs. Schmucker and Hazelius jointly the last two years.

† See article History of Education, *infra*.

The Tenth Meeting was held at Chambersburg. June.
The Synod of Virginia, which formerly constituted a part
Synod of Maryland, was admitted at this session.

At this meeting the power and influence of the General
the nature and authority of creeds and confessions, and the
ments of our church on various disputed points, were free
cussed, but no satisfactory decision was attained.

The feeling seemed to prevail that it was not the provi
the Synod to establish any theological basis or to propos
test of Lutheran orthodoxy. It is not the business of the
to inquire in reference to any Synod applying for adm
whether it gives only a qualified assent to the Augsburg C
sion, or whether it subscribes to every sentiment contained
Symbolical Books.

These discussions were interesting, but unfortunately they
not reported.

Drs. C. F. Schaeffer, S. S. Schmucker and B. Kurtz were
to open a correspondence with the companies recently arri
the United States from Germany, under the guidance of t
torious Stephan.*

The Eleventh Meeting convened in Baltimore, May, 18
which the Synod of the West was represented for the first
The arrangements connected with the *centenary celebration*
occupied attention, which will be treated as a separate artic

The numerical strength of the church was stated to be
four hundred ministers and one thousand churches.

The only college was that at Gettysburg. The Theol
Seminaries mentioned were Hartwick, Gettysburg, Columb
and Lexington, S. C.

The Twelfth Meeting was also held in Baltimore, in May,
Delegates at this meeting appeared, for the first time, fro
English Synod of Ohio. Alleghany Synod, Western Virgini
Synod of East Pennsylvania; making twelve in connection
the General Synod.

The *cent-a-week* plan for raising money for missions was r
mended to the churches, and which was practiced by som
a time, but it did not endure long. An agent was appointed
made considerable flourish, and he was affected with the si
delusion that, if he had the prefix of Professor to his
though only nominally, it would give him greater influence.

---

* See article, infra.

committee did not think so, nor was there any room or need for him in the college Faculty; nor would the trustees, even if asked, have consented to gratify the desire of an ambitious young man. He failed to secure the coveted title, and the much more valuable donations, also.

The importance of clerical education was considered, and the subject of the Liturgy, which was a standing theme for years, received attention.

Friendly relations were established with the General Synod of the German Reformed Church, and interchange of delegates determined.

The number of ministers in the church reported was four hundred and thirty; congregations, one thousand three hundred and seventy.

At this convention was organized the Historical Society, the object of which is to collect and preserve the literature of the Church and all documents pertaining to its history in this country.

The Thirteenth Meeting assembled in Philadelphia, May, 1845. Delegates from the Miami Synod were present for the first time.

Rev. Dr. B. J. Wallace appeared as a delegate from the General Assembly (new school) of the Presbyterian Church, upon which a plan of correspondence between our church and that was adopted. Dr. Pohlman was appointed our delegate to that body.

A memorial on Christian Union, by Rev. S. S. Schmucker, was adopted, and a committee was selected to take this subject into their special care.

The Committee on Foreign Correspondence was instructed "to prepare an address to the various ecclesiastical bodies of our church in Europe, setting forth the condition of our church in this country, and calculated to remove the false impressions which have been made there in regard to our doctrine and practice." This was designed to counteract the influence of the representations concerning our church which had been made in Germany the year previous by Rev. Mr. Wyneken, who was a member of the General Synod. He was not present when this resolution was passed, but when he appeared and heard of it he offered the following: "That the writings of Rev. Drs. Schmucker and B. Kurtz, as well as a volume of the Lutheran Observer and of the "Hirtenstimme," (then edited by Rev. Weyl, in Baltimore) and other books and papers in which the doctrine and practice of the General Synod are set forth, should be sent to Dr. Rudelbach, Prof. Harless and other editors of prominent Lutheran journals for examination, so that the orthodoxy of the General Synod might be demonstrated to the Lutheran Church in Germany.

Considerable excitement was occasioned by this resolution, and it was promptly laid upon the table, as Wyneken anticipated. He immediately after offered the following:

"*Resolved,* That the General Synod hereby disavow and reject the aforementioned writings of Drs. Schmucker and Kurtz, as well as the Lutheran Observer and Hirtenstimme, as heretical and as departing from the saving faith."

This demand was considered presumptuous, and was not entertained for a moment.

The address which was sent to Germany had a very unhappy effect; for, as it plainly expressed Anti-Lutheran sentiments, the people in that country who were not Lutherans themselves could not understand how men professing the sentiments of the address could still call themselves by that name. I have elsewhere alluded to this painful subject.

A committee was appointed to prepare and report at the next convention a clear and concise view of the doctrines of the Lutheran Church in America. They had the subject under consideration five years, and reported at Charleston, 1850, when the report was laid on the table and the committee discharged.

The church at this period numbered five hundred and forty ministers, and one thousand three hundred and sixty-seven congregations, and one hundred and thirty-five thousand communicants.

At this meeting the Home Missionary was formed, which will be treated in a separate article.

The Fourteenth Meeting convened in the city of New York, May, 1848. Fifteen Synods were represented. The Synods of Illinois, of the South West, and of Wittenberg, were admitted. Three years had elapsed since the last meeting.

Committees were appointed to correspond with Lutherans in Canada and Nova Scotia, and also with the Evangelical Synods of the West, for the purpose of establishing friendly relations with them.

A committee was also appointed to improve the small catechism, who, at a subsequent meeting, asked to be relieved from the duty.

Parochial Schools were recommended, and the thanks of the Synod were returned to the Book Company in Baltimore for an appropriation of nearly nine hundred dollars to the *Ministers' Fund.*

At this meeting, a correspondence was entered into with the Cumberland Presbyterian Church, and a delegate appointed to attend their assembly.

The Fifteenth Meeting was held in Charleston, S. C., April, 1850. The Olive Branch Synod was here admitted.

At this meeting, the General Association of the Congregational Churches in New Hampshire proposed to open a correspondence with us, and to maintain an interchange of delegates. A delegate was appointed.

A committee was authorized to publish a Lutheran almanac. This almanac was published for three successive years, when T. N. Kurtz issued it on his own responsibility.*

Resolutions encouraging Rev. Dr. Richards in his proposed translation of the *Hallische Nachrichten*, and the editors of the Evangelical Review, were passed.

Thanks were voted to Dr. Bachman for his liberal gift of a copy of his work *On the Unity of the Human Race.*

The Sixteenth Meeting was held in Winchester, Va., 1853. There were present one hundred and three members—fifty-eight clerical and forty-five lay—and fifty-eight visiting brethren.

At this meeting, the Synod of Pennsylvania renewed its connection with the General Synod after an interval of thirty years. The Pittsburg Synod, Texas Synod and the Synod of Northern Illinois were admitted, making twenty in all.

An application was presented on the part of the Synod of India, but it was not granted, because the constitution confines the union to District Synods within the bounds of the United States.

A committee was appointed to correspond with the professors of the various Lutheran Theological Seminaries for the purpose of ascertaining the probable causes which have indisposed young men to prepare for the ministry, and what means may be employed for increasing the number of theological students.

The Seventeenth Session was held at Dayton, O., June, 1855. The Synods of Kentucky, English District of Ohio and of Central Pennsylvania were admitted. There were no representatives from North Carolina, Synod of Southwest and of Texas.

* See article Almanacs.

Rev. Dr. Allen appeared as delegate from the General Assembly of the Presbyterian Church. Rev. Drs. Fisher and Gans, of the German Reformed Church, could not attend.

A committee was appointed to submit a plan for the organization and division of District Synods, and another to prepare a paper on the subject of the *Licentiate System* as it exists in our churches, which reported that it was inexpedient, at the present time, to take final action upon it.

The Liturgy Committee was continued, of course.

The proceedings of the convention held at Germantown, Pa., for the organization of a Lutheran Translation and Publication Society, were presented, upon which a committee reported that it is inexpedient to take any action in its favor until the constitution allows an official representation in its Executive Board on the part of the General Synod.

The establishment of a mission in Africa was reported favorably upon.

The subject of church extension engaged a considerable share of the Synod's attention, and the business of the various societies was, as usual, transacted.

This was the first meeting of the Synod west of the Alleghany mountains.

The Eighteenth Session was held in Reading, May, 1857. The Synods of Northern Indiana, of Southern Illinois and of Iowa were admitted. Present, one hundred and twenty members and eighty visiting ministers. It was the largest Synod that had met. Dr. Bamberger represented the German Reformed and Dr. Rowland the Presbyterian Church.*

A letter of Christian Salvation, from the Church Diet assembled at Lübeck in 1856, was received, with a copy of proceedings. A committee was appointed to represent the General Synod at the next meeting of the Diet, to be held in Stuttgart. Krotel, Stohlman, Krauth, Sear, C. A. Morris, and Dr. Luther, M. D., were appointed, but they did not go. The letter also

---

* This gentleman had evidently never been among Germans before, and expressed his gratified surprise that we were so far advanced in theology. Although he heard our Theological Seminary mentioned frequently in session, and our professors were sitting before him, yet he recommended us to send our students to Auburn Seminary! He betrayed such a deplorable ignorance of the history of the church, that Dr. Kurtz publicly advised him to read it again, a book he had probably never heard of. A neighboring Dr. remarked to him: "Advise him to read it for the first time; for it is plain he knows nothing about church history."

stated that an annual stipend had been placed in the hands of the Central Committee for the support of any young American, of the proper talent and attainment, who desired to attend the lectures of some Theological Faculty in Germany, with the view of afterwards serving the church in this country. A committee was appointed to receive applications and make selections, but I never heard that any students availed themselves of this offer.

Throughout the church there seemed to be an increasing interest evinced in all our literary and theological institutions as well as in our charitable societies.

The committee appointed at the last convention, to found in this country a school for the training of colored people to be employed as missionaries in Western Africa and to mature a plan for a mission in that country, reported that no officer had been appointed superintendent of the enterprise.*

Reports from fifteen of the Synods against any change in the present Licentiate System were received, and the subject was abandoned.

The Nineteenth Convention met at Pittsburg, May, 1859. All the Synods (26) were represented; one hundred and thirty-seven delegates present.

One of the most important questions considered was the application of the Melancthon Synod, of Maryland, for admission. It elicited an animated and protracted discussion. The application was conditionally granted.

A new constitution for the Pastors' Fund was adopted.

The African Mission claimed earnest attention. One officer was present and gave a history of his labors.

Delegates from the Presbyterian, Moravian and the Evangelical Church Union of the West were received.

A Report on Correspondence with the German Evangelical Church Diet was read by Dr. Mann.

The business of the various societies was transacted, the reports of which were generally encouraging.

The Twentieth Convention met at Lancaster, Pa., May, 1862.

The rebel war was raging, and there were no delegates from the Synods of Virginia, Western Virginia, North Carolina, South Carolina and Texas. It was stated that a communication had been received from the Texas delegate, who was in Europe, that he was desirous the Synod should know that "whatever traitors

---

* See African Mission, p. ...

and rebels in his State had done, the Synod of Texas had remained loyal to the government of the country."

The Synod of New Jersey was received.

A committee reported that the standing resolutions of all the sessions from 1820 had been collected and properly arranged.

At this meeting it was resolved that advisory members should not have the liberty of speaking as heretofore.

Dr. Schaff appeared as delegate from the German Reformed Church, and Rev. Kummer from the Moravian Church.

RESOLUTIONS ON THE STATE OF THE COUNTRY.

At an early session of the Synod a committee, consisting of one from each District Synod represented, was appointed to prepare a minute, expressive of the views of the body with regard to our duty as Christians and citizens, in the present crisis of our beloved country. The committee, through Rev. Dr. Passavant, subsequently submitted a report which, after a spirited and deeply interesting discussion, was adopted by an overwhelming majority. We give the resolutions in full for historical reference.

WHEREAS our beloved country, after having long been favored with a degree of political and religious freedom, security and prosperity, unexampled in the history of the world, now finds itself involved in a bloody war to suppress an armed rebellion against its lawfully constituted government; *and whereas*, the word of God, which is the sole rule of our faith and practice, requires loyal subjection to "the powers that be," because they are ordained of God, to be a terror to evil doers, and a praise to those who do well, and at the same time declares, that they who "resist the power" shall receive to themselves condemnation; *and whereas*, we, the representatives of the Evangelical Lutheran Synods in the United States, connected with the General Synod, assembled in Lancaster, Pa., recognize it as our duty to give public expression to our convictions of truth on this subject, and in every proper way to co-operate with our fellow-citizens in sustaining the great interests of law and authority, of liberty and righteousness, be it therefore,

1. *Resolved*, That it is the deliberate judgment of this Synod, that the rebellion against the constitutional government of this land is most wicked in its inception, unjustifiable in its cause, unnatural in its character, inhuman in its prosecution, oppressive

in its aims, and destructive in its results to the highest interests of morality and religion.

2. *Resolved*, That, in the suppression of this rebellion and in the maintenance of the constitution and the union by the sword, we recognize an unavoidable necessity and a sacred duty, which the government owes to the nation and to the world, and that, therefore, we call upon all our people to lift up holy hands in prayer to the God of battles, without personal wrath against the evil doers on the one hand, and without doubting the righteousness of our cause on the other, that He would give wisdom to the president and his counsellors, and success to the army and navy, that our beloved land may speedily be delivered from treason and anarchy.

3. *Resolved*, That while we recognize this unhappy war as a righteous judgment of God, visited upon us, because of the individual and national sins, of which we have been guilty, we nevertheless regard this rebellion as more immediately the natural result of the continuance and spread of domestic slavery in our land, and therefore hail with unmingled joy the proposition of our Chief Magistrate, which has received the sanction of Congress, to extend aid from the general government to any State, in which slavery exists, which shall deem fit to initiate a system of constitutional emancipation.

4. *Resolved*, That we deeply sympathize with all loyal citizens and Christian patriots in the rebellious portions of our country, and we cordially invite their co-operation, in offering united supplications at a Throne of Grace, that God would restore peace to our distracted country, re-establish fraternal relations between all the States, and make our land, in all time to come, the asylum of the oppressed, and the permanent abode of liberty and religion.

5. *Resolved*, That our devout thanks are due to Almighty God for the success which has crowned our arms, and while we praise and magnify his name for the help and succor he has graciously afforded our land and naval forces, in enabling them to overcome our enemies, we regard these tokens of his divine favor as cheering indications of the final triumph of our cause."

The action of the General Synod in the frank, fearless and unqualified expression of its views on the present national struggle, and its cordial support of the efforts now making to suppress the rebellion, is a deliverance, wise and noble, worthy of the occasion and of the first-born Church of the Reformation. The loyalty of the Church, through its representatives, has been expressed in the most unequivocal and decided manner. The discussion on the subject was able, conducted in a kind, serious and Christian spirit, and participated in by Drs. Passavant, Harkey, Sprecher, Stork, Hay, Hon. H. H. Van Dyke, Rev. W. G. Harter, Prof. Sternberg, Rev. T. T. Titus, J. J. Cochran, Esq., Prof. Eggers, Rev. B. M. Schmucker, Hon. C. Kugler, Rev. J. R. Focht, and others. Various substitutes and amendments were proposed, but they were all rejected. There was very little difference of opinion in the convention on the report of the committee, except in reference to the adoption of the third resolution, opposition to which was urged on the ground of expediency.

During one of the sessions of this meeting, Dr. Conrad came into the house, and in great excitement reported the news of a great Union victory; immediately all other business was suspended, and a motion made to unite in a service of thanksgiving. They did not give Dr. Kurtz, the President, time to put the vote, nor an opportunity to express his views, which I am sure would have been advice to wait until the report was confirmed, for there were so many false rumors afloat; but down upon their knees nearly the whole body fell, and Dr. Pohlman led in prayer. It afterwards turned out that the report was premature, or at least that the victory was not so great as stated.

These resolutions gave great offence to our Southern brethren, and they have all along declared that they will never reunite with the General Synod until the resolutions are expunged, which they never will be.

The Twenty-First Meeting was held in York, May, 1864. The Synods south of Maryland were not represented except Kentucky. The Synod of Minnesota and the Franckean were admitted. An animated debate ensued upon the subject of the latter, but it was finally voted in upon the condition that at its next meeting it declare in an official manner its adoption of the doctrinal articles of the Augsburg Confession.

STATE OF THE COUNTRY.

The most intense interest was manifested in reference to the state of our country. This was strengthened from the fact that our armies were then in motion and engaged in a fierce and sanguinary conflict. The sons of many of the brethren were in the field, and from nearly all our churches there were representatives, noble and patriotic men, mingling in the sad scenes, ready to make any sacrifice, or to meet death for the maintenance of our national life. At one of the first sessions of Synod a resolution was passed to set apart one hour, the succeeding day, for humble, earnest prayer to Almighty God, in the name of Jesus, for the forgiveness of our national sins, for his blessing upon our armies and navy in the opening campaign, for victory in the coming struggle, and for the speedy suppression of the rebellion and the restoration of peace to our distracted land. At the devotional services that were daily held in the church, fervent supplication on behalf of our country ascended to the mercy seat. All seemed to realize the importance of the contest and our need of the Divine blessing. A committee, consisting of one from each District Synod, was also appointed to prepare a minute on the state of the country and our duty, as Christians, in reference to it. The committee, through Rev. Dr. Passavant, subsequently presented a report which was unanimously adopted. We record the resolutions in full for future reference:

Resolved, That having assembled a second time, during the prevalence of civil war in our land, this Synod cannot separate without solemnly re-affirming the declarations adopted at our last convention in reference to the originating cause of the rebellion, the necessity of its forcible suppression, the righteousness of the war which is waged by the government of the United States for the maintenance of the national life, and the consequent duty of every Christian to support it by the whole weight of his influence, his prayers and his efforts.

Resolved, That we acknowledge, with profound gratitude to Almighty God, the various and important successes which have thus far crowned our arms; the merciful interposition of Providence in delivering us from the invasions of the enemy, and in protecting our homes, our churches and our institutions from the desolations of war; and the cheering progress which has been made by the government and the nation in the recognition of the laws of God and the rights of man in the measures which have been adopted for the suppression of the rebellion.

Resolved, That recognizing the sufferings and calamities of war as the righteous judgments of a just God, visited upon us for our transgressions, we call upon our pastors and churches to unite with us in the confession of our many and grievous individual and national sins, and in fervent supplication for the Divine forgiveness, that as a people we may break off sins by righteousness, and do justly, love mercy and walk humbly with God.

Resolved, That as persistent efforts are making among us, by professedly Christian writers, to prove from the Holy Scriptures the Divine institution of American slavery, the principal cause of this wicked rebellion, we, the delegates of the General Synod of the Evangelical Lutheran Church in the United States, hereby express our unqualified condemnation of such a course, which claims the sanction of the merciful God and Father of us all for a system of human oppression, which exists only by violence, under the cover of iniquitous laws.

RECEPTION OF THE FRANCKEAN SYNOD.

Although the debate was animated and earnest, it was in general conducted in a kind, fraternal and christian spirit. The discussion on the subject was thorough and able, and was participated in by Drs. Pohlman, Baugher, C. W. Schaeffer, Stork, Passavant, Harkey, Ziegler, Harrison, Sprecher and Rev. Messrs. Titus, Wedekind, Krotel, Hull, Welden, Bassler, Goodlin, Wenzel, Kunkelman, Senderling, Adleberg, Bolton, Neumann, Wieting, Van Alstine, Dr. Kemp, Hon. C. Kugler, J. J. Cochran, Esq., and others.

It was maintained, on the one side, that the Franckean Synod was Lutheran only in name, that it had a creed of its own, substituted for the Augsburg Confession, one that was inconsistent with the Church's doctrinal basis, and to which the Campbellites and other heretical sects in the West might subscribe; that this creed was evasive on points that were fundamental, that it contained nothing in its character that was distinctly Lutheran, and that it made no reference to the Confession of the Church. It was also stated, that the Synod had deliberately, at its formation, ignored and set aside the Confession, and that this action it had never yet repudiated. Allusion was made to a judicial decision given by Vice Chancellor Sanford of the State of New York, in which he expressed the opinion that the Franckean Synod was not a Lutheran body. It was maintained that a most dangerous precedent would be established, if Lutheran Synods were allowed to form new creeds; that the faith of the Lutheran Church was settled, and that the General Synod itself had no power to make changes or introduce innovations into it; that the Augsburg Confession was essential to constitute us Lutherans, and that, therefore, the Franckean Synod could not constitutionally be admitted as an integral part of the General Synod until it received the Confession as an exponent of the fundamental truths of the Bible, as taught by our Church.

It was argued, on the other side, that the Franckean Synod had complied with the requirements of the General Synod, that it had, in adopting its constitution, adopted its doctrinal basis, and that if there was anything in the creed which was at variance with the Confession it was by their recent action revoked or superseded. It was asserted that a direct recognition of the Augsburg Confession was not necessary for admission into the General Synod, as its constitution does not even mention the name of the Confession; that the Franckean Synod had as virtually adopted it as the General Synod itself had; that the Synod was not so much in fault as the Constitution of the General Synod was loose and indefinite. Their doctrinal views, it was said, should be compared with the Augsburg Confession; if they differ from it the Synod should not be received; if they do not, there could be no objection to their reception. The Synod, it was believed, did teach the fundamental doctrines of the Bible as they are taught by our Church, and its representatives, making application for admission, were sound in faith. It was argued that the principle which would exclude the Franckean Synod would cut off many of the District Synods which do not in their constitutions formally recognize the Augsburg Confession. Reference was also made to the origin and early history of the General Synod, to the views of the men who framed the constitution, and to the circumstances under which the New York Ministerium, the Hartwick and other Synods were received into the General Synod. The legal decision against the Lutheran character of the Franckean Synod, it was said, was entitled to no weight, inasmuch as Vice Chancellor Sanford was not a Lutheran, and no theologian, and that in the State of Ohio in one of the courts a legal opinion of an opposite bearing had been given, and that the civil authorities were not competent to determine questions that related to the Church. It was also stated that the Synod used the General Synod's Hymn Book; contributed its funds to the support of our Foreign Missions and other benevolent operations of the Church; educated its students at Hartwick Seminary; that it was represented in its Board of Trustees and Visitors, and interchanged delegates with the New York Ministerium and the Hartwick Synod. The delegates declared that they had presented themselves for admission with honest hearts, with an earnest desire to co-operate with their Lutheran brethren; that they desired to become a component part of the General Synod, that their usefulness as a Synod might be increased; that they were under the impression when their Synod adopted the Constitution of the General Synod they also adopted the Augsburg Confession as received by the General Synod.

All in the convention seemed anxious to admit the Synod if it could be done consistently with duty. The only difference was that some of the brethren desired to postpone the application until there was, in the constitution of the Synod, a distinct recognition of the Augsburg Confession, whilst others were willing, as the delegates were on the ground and supposed that they had complied with the conditions required, to receive it at once on the faith of the promise made, and with the express understanding that at the next meeting of the Synod, whatever informality there might have been in their proceedings, all room for doubt would be removed.

The Synod at first unanimously resolved that the Franckean Synod be admitted as an integral portion of the General Synod so soon as they shall give formal expression to their adoption of the Augsburg Confession as received by the General Synod. This action was, however, the next day, reconsidered, and the whole subject finally disposed of by the adoption of the following resolution:

Resolved, That the Franckean Synod be received into connection with the General Synod, with the understanding that, at its next meeting, it declare in an official manner its adoption of the doctrinal articles of the Augsburg Confession as a substantially correct exhibition of the fundamental doctrines of the Word of God.

Against this action of the General Synod Rev. Dr. C. W. Schaeffer and others felt it their duty to enter their earnest and respectful protest, disclaiming, at the same time, any disposition to impugn the motives of those who favored the application, and expressing high personal regard for the brethren of the Franckean Synod. The position assumed by the Protestants was: 1. That the General Synod provides for the admission of regularly constituted Synods, that a regularly constituted Synod is one that "holds the fundamental doctrines of the Bible, as taught by our Church," and that by universal consent these doctrines so taught are expressed in the Augsburg Confession; that the whole history of the Franckean Synod presents it as having no relation or connection whatever with the Augsburg Confession, and that in its official documents there is no evidence that it has ever accepted the Confession. 2. That the General Synod is forbidden by its constitution "to introduce such alterations in matters appertaining to the faith as might in any way tend to burden the consciences of the brethren in Christ," and that they felt their consciences burdened by holding Synodical relations with a body that had set up a new doctrinal standard. 3. That the General Synod, in the spirit of its constitution, requires and prescribes certain conditions as prerequisites to the admission of any Synod; that the Franckean Synod was admitted without a compliance with these conditions, and in doing so the constitution had been violated, and a precedent established which would be followed by the most lamentable results."

Dr. Schaeffer also presented a paper signed by the delegates of the Synod of Pennsylvania, announcing that inasmuch as the Pennsylvania Synod at the time of its re-union with the General Synod had resolved that, if the General Synod should violate its constitution and require assent to anything in conflict with the old and long established faith of the Evangelical Lutheran Church, their delegates be required to protest against such action, to withdraw from its sessions and to report to Synod, and as they regarded the admission of the Franckean Synod as a direct violation of the Constitution of the General Synod, they were compelled to retire and to report to the body they represented.

These papers were both entered upon the Minutes as well as the answer to the protest, prepared by a committee consisting of Rev. Drs. Baugher and Harrison, and Dr. Kemp, who subsequently reported, "that whilst they admitted that the Franckean Synod had not formally adopted the Augsburg Confession, yet they had formally adopted the Constitution of the General Synod, and their delegates had declared verbally, and in the most solemn manner in a written record, that they believed that, in adopting the Constitution of the General Synod, they were adopting the doctrinal basis required, which is the Augsburg Confession; what these brethren affirm they believed they were really doing they hesitate not to declare their Synod will do formally at its next regular session; and that for the purpose of securing the ends of truth and righteousness, and to satisfy the minds of the doubting and fearful, the resolution of the General Synod requires them to adopt in a formal manner the doctrinal basis of the Lutheran Church, viz., the Augsburg Confession, as containing the fundamental doctrines of the Word of God, or forfeit their connection with this body. The committee think (1) that, whilst confidence in the affirmed convictions of the Franckean Synod is conceded, the General Synod is secured against the introduction of a Synod into its body that is not Lutheran; (2) that the General Synod has not willingly or consciously violated the constitution, or set up a new doctrinal standard for the admission of new Synods; (3) that the Franckean Synod had really, although not formally, complied with the conditions required by the constitution. Inasmuch as the Constitution of the General Synod is indefinite, and a difference of opinion on the subject exists among the members of Synod, it was deemed best to yield the point, as had been done in the reception of other Synods, until the formal action required could be had, with the view of satisfying the consciences of some of the brethren, and more certainly harmonizing the whole Synod."

The withdrawal of the Pennsylvania Synod's delegates was greatly regretted, but there seemed to be no alternative, inasmuch as, in their judgment, the constitution had been violated and the instructions of the Synod on this subject were so explicit. We indulge the hope, however, that it is only a temporary separation, and that the discussion on this question and the subsequent action of the General Synod will have a tendency to bind together more firmly the whole Church, and deepen its affection for the venerable Confession.

The Twenty-Second Meeting was held at Fort Wayne, Ind., May, 1866.

At this meeting the connection of the Pennsylvania Synod with the General Synod was practically dissolved, before this convention was duly organized, by the following ruling of Dr. Sprecher, the President of the preceding meeting:

DECISION OF CHAIR CONCERNING PENNSYLVANIA SYNOD.

When the first eleven Synods had responded, the President decided as follows in reference to the Synod of Pennsylvania:

The Chair regards the act of the delegates of the Pennsylvania Synod, by which they severed their practical relations with the General Synod and withdrew from the partnership of the Synods in the governing functions of the General Synod, as the act of the Synod of Pennsylvania, and that consequently that Synod was out of practical union with the General Synod up to the adjournment of the last convention; and, as we cannot know officially what the action of that Synod has been since, she must be considered as in that state of practical withdrawal from the governing functions of the General Synod until the General Synod can receive a report of an act restoring her practical relations to the General Synod; and, as no such report can be received until said Synod is organized, the Chair cannot know any paper offered at this stage of the proceedings of the Synod as a certificate of delegation to this body.

CONCERNING FRANCKEAN SYNOD.

When the name of the Franckean Synod was read, the President decided that, not having any official knowledge whether the said Synod has complied with the conditions prescribed in the resolutions receiving that Synod, two years ago, into connection with the General Synod, the delegates from the Franckean Synod cannot, for the present, be received.

THE CHAIR SUSTAINED ON APPEAL.

An appeal being made from the decision of the Chair in regard to the Synod of Pennsylvania, that decision was sustained. A division of the house was called for, when the vote resulted in seventy-seven ayes to twenty-four nays.

CASE OF THE PENNSYLVANIA SYNOD.

The regular order of business was suspended to consider the reception of the credentials of the Pennsylvania Synod's delegation.

REFERRED TO A SPECIAL COMMITTEE.

On motion, the following was adopted:

Resolved, That the case of the Pennsylvania Synod, presented before the complete organization of this body, be now referred to a special committee of seven, whose duty it shall be to report on the subject at nine o'clock to-morrow morning.

DELEGATES REQUESTED TO REPORT.

On motion, it was

Resolved, That the delegates of the Pennsylvania Synod be now respectfully requested to report to this Synod by handing in their credentials and a copy of the minutes for each of their last two meetings, and that their documents be referred to the committee appointed to report on their case.

After several days' discussion, the following amended preamble and resolutions were adopted in place of what the committee had previously reported:

Your committee respectfully report, that in accordance with the public notice given in the church, they assembled at the specified time and place, to take into consideration the case of the Pennsylvania Synod, and any credentials or documents which the delegates of said Synod might, in accordance with the public invitation given by the President of the General Synod, see fit to present. Your committee regret to report that no credentials or other documents were communicated to them, and their only recourse was to the minutes of the Synod of Pennsylvania during the two years since the session of the last General Synod. After mature consideration of the case, your committee resolved *first*, to present to the Synod a statement of the facts in the case, as apparent from the minutes of the Pennsylvania Synod referred to, and from earlier minutes; and, *secondly*, on the basis of these facts to submit several resolutions.

It appears, then, that the Synod of Pennsylvania was one of the original Synods which formed the constitution of this body, in 1820, at Hagerstown; that they attended one meeting of the General Synod, in 1821, and in the spring of 1823 withdrew from this body, and resolved not to have any connection with it again until requested to do so by their congregations; that for thirty years thereafter they had no connection whatever with this body;

that when, in 1853, they re-entered into connection with it, they proposed only a qualified connection, specifying a contingency, on the occurrence of which their delegates were instructed, by a standing resolution, to withdraw from the sessions of this body and report to their Synod; that the admission of the Franckean Synod, in 1864, was, in the judgment of their delegates, such a case, and they therefore protested against said action, withdrew from the sessions of the General Synod, and reported to their Synod; that their Synod, after full discussion, approved the action of their delegates by a unanimous vote; that at their meeting, in 1864, they resolved "that the consideration of the future relation of this Synod to the General Synod be postponed until the time for the election of delegates to that body shall again recur;" that at the meeting of 1865 they elected delegates to this body, with the declaration that the "*Synod desires it to be distinctly understood that it has not ceased to approve of the protest and withdrawal* of its last delegation at the meeting at York," and also resolved that the Synod *now, as ever, reserves to itself the right asserted in the resolutions adopted at the time of the election of its delegation to the General Synod in 1853,* and which prompted the action of our delegation at the convention at York" in 1864; that the delegation thus elected made their appearance at this meeting, and tendered their credentials during and after calling the roll of Synods, before the election of officers and organization of the Synod, when the President gave this decision: "The Chair regards the act of delegates of the Pennsylvania Synod, by which they severed their practical relations with the General Synod and withdrew from the partnership of the Synods in the governing functions of the General Synod, as the act of the Synod of Pennsylvania, and that consequently that Synod was out of practical union with the General Synod up to the adjournment of the last convention; and, as we cannot know officially what the action of that Synod has been since, she must be considered as in that state of practical withdrawal from the governing functions of the General Synod until the General Synod can receive a report of an act restoring her practical relations to the General Synod; and, as no such report can be received until said Synod is organized, the Chair cannot know any paper offered at this stage of the proceedings of the Synod as a certificate of delegation to this body;" and, this decision being sustained by a vote of the house, their case was not taken up until after the organization, when they were called on to present their credentials, but declined to do so; that your committee was then appointed, to whom the matter was referred to report on.

Having thus detailed the facts, your committee present the following resolutions:

[Here follow the resolutions adopted, and as in part only those of the committee.]

1. *Resolved*, That this Synod regard the condition annexed by the Pennsylvania Synod to the appointment of the delegates as contrary to that equality among the Synods composing this body provided for by the Constitution of this Synod.

2. *Resolved*, That whatever motives of christian forbearance may have induced this Synod to receive the Pennsylvania delegates in 1853, with this condition, the unfavorable influences since exerted by it render it very desirable that said condition be rescinded by the Synod of Pennsylvania.

3. *Resolved*, That the General Synod hereby expresses its entire willingness to receive the delegates of the Synod of Pennsylvania.

After thus disposing of the foregoing, it was on motion—

Resolved, That the delegates from the Pennsylvania Synod be requested to waive what may seem to them an irregular organization of this body, and to acquiesce in the present organization.

It was, furthermore—

Resolved, That the Secretary be requested to present, in writing, to the delegates of the Pennsylvania Synod, the action just passed in reference to that body.

FRANCKEAN SYNOD'S DELEGATION RECEIVED.

In relation to the Franckean Synod, it was then—

Resolved, That, inasmuch as the Franckean Synod has complied with the condition of admission laid down by the last General Synod, its delegation be received.

In response to a suggestion made by a member, in view of the favorable disposal of the subject before the Synod during the last three days, the whole body rose and engaged in heartily singing the doxology.

When these resolutions were adopted, the delegates of the Synod of Pennsylvania retired, and that body has ever since remained distinct from the General Synod.

RESOLUTIONS ON THE STATE OF THE COUNTRY.

The following resolutions on the state of the country were offered, and unanimously adopted by a rising vote:

WHEREAS the last two sessions of the General Synod of the Evangelical Lutheran Church of the United States, convened, respectively, in the years 1862 and 1864, at Lancaster and York, in the State of Pennsylvania, were both held during the prevalence of a calamitous civil war; and

WHEREAS, at both of said sessions the General Synod, besides carefully enunciating its views in reference to the origin of said war and the great issues at stake, also offered fervent prayers to Almighty God for the speedy return of a peace based on the principles of his own truth and righteousness; be it, therefore,

1. *Resolved*, That we do hereby, as a General Synod, greatly rejoice that our present sessions are being held under circumstances, and amidst surroundings, which are in so grateful and happy contrast with those which at our two former sessions filled our hearts with so much anxiety and grief.

2. *Resolved*, That, not abating a jot or tittle of the declaration of principles then solemnly put forth, we do now join in ascriptions of praise, and power, and glory unto Him who is the Author of all our mercies, and the Source of all our blessings; that He has caused the desolations of war to cease in our land, and that peace once more sheds its benign influence over every part of our national domain.

3. *Resolved*, That in these our thanksgivings we include, as among the most obvious occasions of them, the final victory which he was graciously pleased to vouchsafe to our gallant army and navy; the preservation of our government and its associated institutions from meditated forcible overthrow, and the removal from amongst us of the curse of slavery, in whose interest, and for whose extension, the war was inaugurated and prosecuted.

4. *Resolved*, That the widows and orphans which the rebellion has made are the legacy of the nation, and that it behooves the church to unite with the States and the General Government in extending to them all possible sympathy, succor and support.

5. *Resolved*, That to the millions of bondmen, who by the vicissitudes of war have been so suddenly and strangely trans-

lated into a state of freedom, the country owes its most beneficent and paternal guardianship; that they suffer no detriment from neglect or abuse, but be strengthened, comforted and assisted, in which great duty the Church of Christ cannot and must not be found tardy or delinquent.

6. *Resolved*, That we share in the enlightened and spontaneous sentiment of the people of this land, in expressions of profoundest sorrow, because of the violent death of President Lincoln, whose memory as a patriot, a statesman and the highest type of a philanthropist we cherish and revere, and whose services to our nation and to the cause of the suffering and the oppressed we shall hold in grateful and affectionate remembrance.

PENNSYLVANIA SYNOD'S DELEGATION TO BE HEARD.

Resolved, That the delegation of the Pennsylvania Synod be heard to-morrow morning, at 9 o'clock.

RESPONSE OF PENNSYLVANIA SYNOD'S DELEGATION READ.

A communication from the delegates of the Synod of Pennsylvania was read by Rev. G. F. Krotel, D. D., one of their number.

When the reading was concluded, it was—

Resolved, That this paper be received.

FINAL PROPOSITIONS OF THE RESPONSE.

[A subsequent resolution of the Synod directs that the "final propositions" contained in this response be published in the minutes. They are therefore presented at this point as the proper place.]

The response was closed with the only terms on which its authors were willing to co-operate in the General Synod, viz.:

"Provided:

"That this body shall now declare that the Synod of Pennsylvania had, as it claimed to have, the constitutional right to be represented before the election of officers, and to take part in it, and might now justly claim the right of casting its vote.

"If the convention shall so declare, we are perfectly willing to waive the right of voting, will acquiesce in the present organization, and will take our seats in this body, equals among equals.

"Respectfully submitted,

(Signed,)   Joseph A. Seiss, *Ch. of Del.*
Charles P. Krauth,
G. F. Krotel,
C. W. Schaeffer,
S. K. Brobst,
Samuel Laird,
Louis L. Houpt,
Henry Lehman,
C. F. Norton,
Charles A. Heinitsh.

FURTHER ACTION IN PENNSYLVANIA SYNOD'S CASE PROPOSED.

Resolutions were offered for further action relative to the case of the Pennsylvania Synod. Before concluding the subject the morning hour expired. The afternoon being set apart for various societies, the Synod adjourned until to-morrow morning.

FINAL ACTION REGARDING THE SYNOD OF PENNSYLVANIA.

It was determined to suspend the regular order, and take up the unfinished business of yesterday, being the resolutions in regard to the Synod of Pennsylvania.

The following resolution was offered as a substitute for the first of the series:

ULTIMATE RESOLUTION.

Resolved, That, after hearing the response of the delegates of the Pennsylvania Synod, we cannot conscientiously recede from the action adopted by this body, believing, after full and careful deliberation, said action to have been regular and constitutional; but that we reaffirm our readiness to receive the delegates of said Synod as soon as they present their credentials in due form.

MOTION TO RECONSIDER MADE AND TABLED.

It was moved to reconsider the vote, and the motion was laid on the table.

Rev. Dr. J. A. Seiss, having asked permission, made a statement on behalf of the delegation of the Synod of Pennsylvania, of which he was chairman. He was requested to present the same in writing, to be entered on the record of the General Synod.

The President of the General Synod made a reply, which he also, according to request, reduced to writing, to accompany the statement.

STATEMENT OF DR. SEISS.

The delegates of the Pennsylvania Synod state to this convention that in retiring, as they now do, they distinctly declare that this their act in no sense or degree effects the relations of the Pennsylvania Synod to the General Synod of the Evangelical Lutheran Church in the United States.

REPLY OF THE PRESIDENT.

This body has not decided at any time that the Pennsylvania Synod was out of the General Synod. But having by its delegation openly withdrawn from the sessions of the General Synod, at York, Pa., the former President ruled that the practical relation of the Synod of Pennsylvania to the General Synod was such that no report could be heard from that Synod until the General Synod was organized. This ruling of the President was sustained by a very large majority, after an appeal had been taken. Immediately after its organization, the General Synod invited the delegates of the Synod of Pennsylvania to present their credentials and report; and has evinced its readiness at every stage to grant to the Synod of Pennsylvania every lawful privilege and every right. The General Synod hereby extend to the delegation from the Synod of Pennsylvania the assurance of its kindest regard.

PROTEST PRESENTED.

Rev. Dr. Passavant read a protest against the action of the Synod in the case of the Synod of Pennsylvania.

PROTEST.

The undersigned delegates of various Synods, connected with the General Synod, having cast their votes against the final action of this body, as regards the Pennsylvania Synod, respectfully ask leave to place on record the reasons which led them thus to vote, and at the same time, they solemnly, and in the fear of God, protest against this action, as, in their judgment, irregular, and contrary both to the constitution of the Synod and the law of equity as revealed in the word of God.

And, *First*, we protest against the decision of the retiring President, afterwards sustained by a majority of the delegates, by which the Pennsylvania Synod was declared as not being "in practical relations" to the General Synod, and consequently not entitled to any part in its organization, as *an unwarranted assumption* of power, because—

1. The name of the Pennsylvania Synod was on the official roll of Synods which had been furnished this body by the retiring Secretary, and after the withdrawal of the Pennsylvania delegates from the convention in York, the Synod itself is expressly recognized in an official paper as an integral part of the General Synod. In our judgment, therefore, the presiding officer was in duty bound to receive the credentials of the Pennsylvania Synod at the proper time.

2. Because the constitution and by-laws give him no power whatever to exclude Synods, or even to decide as to their relations to the General Synod, but merely make it his duty "to decide on the validity of the credentials of delegates."

3. The reason given by the Chair, and sustained by the majority, for such refusal to call the names of all the Synods on the official roll, that the Pennsylvania Synod, by the withdrawal of its delegation from the convention in York, placed itself out of governing relations to the General Synod—is not a valid one—*as such withdrawal from the sessions was merely the exercise of a right which was freely conceded by the General Synod to the Pennsylvania Synod at the time of its reception in Winchester, and which was never objected to, either before or on the occasion of its exercise.* The retirement of the Pennsylvania delegation from the further sessions of the Synod in York could not, therefore, affect the relations of the Synod to the General Synod—the sole object of this act being, as officially expressed, "in order to report to their own Synod at its approaching convention."

4. Even if the Pennsylvania Synod afterwards, by a formal act of separation, had sundered its connection with the General Synod, the President could not, by his own ruling, know this and act upon it until officially notified of such separation.

5. If such a principle is established, it is placed in the power of any future retiring President to rule "out of practical relations" any Synod or number of Synods he may deem proper thus to designate, and a majority of the remaining delegates, by sus-

taining him, may keep out such Synod or Synods until the convention is organized, and so long thereafter as they may deem advisable; or may even refuse to give them the rights which belong to all the constituent parts of this Synod, except on conditions which it was known beforehand could never be consented to without the setting aside of solemn compacts between brethren, or the sacrifice of christian principle.

And, *Secondly*, we solemnly protest against the final action of this body in the case of the Pennsylvania Synod, because, that notwithstanding the most satisfactory evidence officially communicated on the floor of this house, that the Pennsylvania Synod was, at the time of the organization, and continue to be, an integral part of this body, its original relations unchanged, and all its guaranteed rights intact, it has now finally been resolved that the previous action of this convention in disfranchising it, is "both regular and constitutional," a course of procedure which, in our judgment, is wholly without precedent in law and sanction in the Gospel of Jesus Christ. Its inevitable consequence must be a future fraught with the most serious results to the Church of God.

REPLY TO PROTEST.

Rev. Joel Swartz read, on behalf of the committee, a reply to the protest offered this morning.

Your committee to whom was referred the protest read by Dr. Passavant before this body, and signed by various members, against the action of the General Synod in the case of the Pennsylvania Synod, beg leave to submit the following answer:

The position of the protestants rests upon a mistake in regard to the nature and origin of the difficulty. They suppose that it has arisen from the exercise of the ordinary and legitimate rights of the members of an organized and representative body. Here is their capital mistake. What are those rights in such a body? They are evidently such only as can take place in the body, and compatibly with its existence; such as the right to speak, to vote, and, by calling for the ayes and nays, to have their votes recorded. If in the use of these rights they find themselves in a minority, the duty of loyalty requires them still to submit to the decisions expressed by the majority. If they regard the action as a violation of the constitution, then they have still another right—that of respectful protest, and the recording of such protest upon the minutes of the body, thus exonerating themselves from all responsibility for such action; but loyalty still demands submission. Beyond this, the integral parts of any organized and representative body cannot go, and still retain full and complete membership in it. If, however, they feel that they cannot submit even under protest, and, proceeding a step further, withdraw from the body, this act is incipient revolution, and of necessity disturbs the relations of such members with the body from whose sessions they secede, and forfeit their share in its governmental functions. When the body represented by such retiring delegates makes their action its own, the revolution is complete. This last step severs all relations, and forfeits all rights of future membership. In accordance with these manifest principles, the organizing President of the present convention decided that "the Synod of Pennsylvania was out of practical relation with the General Synod," as the delegates of the former body had openly, and without permission, seceded from the sessions of the last General Synod at York. Furthermore, he was assured by official documents placed in his hands, that the Synod of Pennsylvania had authorized her delegation in a certain contingency, of the occurrence of which she constituted them the judges, to protest and withdraw from the sessions of the General Synod; and having no official knowledge of the Pennsylvania Synod's subsequent action, he ruled that this body could not admit her delegates to participate in the organization of this convention, as no papers from such Synod could be examined and decided upon until the officers necessary to an organization could be elected. That is, this body could not entertain the application of delegates from a Synod having no practical relation to it until the General Synod had a formal existence. For the absurdity of a body being capable of receiving a report before its organization—that is, before it exists—needs scarcely to be pointed out, and the ruling of the President, based upon this view of the case, distinctly stated, was, upon appeal, taken to the undisputed delegations, sustained by an overwhelming majority. If anything further be necessary to illustrate the legitimacy of the President's ruling and its support by the convention, it may be seen from the absurdity of admitting a principle contrary to it. Suppose that any number of members of the General Synod could withdraw, without permission, for any cause, and yet be regarded as entitled to all the rights and privileges of full membership, what would be the consequence? Why, since the constitution requires a "majority of the deputies of a majority of the Synods attached to the General Synod" to "be present" before "business shall go on," then the very existence of this body might at any time be destroyed by the withdrawal of a majority of the members of the majority of the Synods, leaving the loyal minority without even the power of adjourning and appointing the time and place of a future meeting. Can it be possible that the General Synod is such a body? Is it credible that she has legitimated such a suicidal principle in her constitution, or in her official action? And yet this is what is practically contended for by the protestants. Nay, on the contrary, it is a principle of common sense, and universally admitted, that the rights and privileges of a loyal minority in a body cannot be destroyed by the defection from it of a disloyal majority. Upon the indubitable principle, then, that when the delegates of the Pennsylvania Synod withdrew from the sessions of the General Synod without its consent, they could not in such state of withdrawal be counted among its legitimate membership or be entitled to the benefit of undisturbed relations with this body. The arguments of the protestants are easily answered.

1st. The argument that the Pennsylvania Synod was officially recognized as a member of this body after the withdrawal of its delegates at York, because her name is found on the official roll made out by the retiring Secretary, rests upon a mistake, in regard to a point of fact. The roll in the possession of the President during the organization of this body was the list found recorded in the minutes of the last convention. The list contained the names of the delegates and of their Synods as reported in the organization of that convention, and as the Pennsylvania Synod was *then* in full relation to the General Synod, her name properly appeared in the list; just as being out of relations now, her name will not appear on the list or minutes of the present convention. No roll was made out by the retiring Secretary after the withdrawal of the delegates of the Pennsylvania Synod. If he had made such roll, it could not oblige the General Synod to be governed by it, for it was the mere act of the Secretary. To have bound the General Synod, it must have received her official sanction, which it did not. In like manner, the argument that the Pennsylvania Synod was officially recognized as in full membership in the General Synod after the withdrawal of her delegates at York, because she is so referred to in the "Report on the state of the Church," rests upon a misapprehension. It is simply said in that paper, that in view of the numbers, etc., represented in that Synod, the Pennsylvania Synod must ever enjoy a commanding place among the Synods of the General Synod. As the report was not upon the relations of the Synod to the General Synod, but upon quite a different subject, viz.: her numbers, resources, etc., the adoption of such a paper did not define those relations. As the chairman of your present committee was the chairman of the committee on that report, he may be permitted to say, that if the protestants suppose it was the design of the committee to go so far aside from their proper business as to express an opinion upon the subject in connection with which it is quoted in the protest, they are greatly mistaken. As well might a similar remark, made in a report a few years ago upon the extent and resources of Virginia, be quoted as defining the relations of that State to the American Union, against which she was then in rebellion. But since the protestants have referred to this report, it may not be inappropriate to attend to an argument which it incidentally furnishes, that the Pennsylvania Synod was, by the withdrawal of its delegates, put out of practical relations with the General Synod. Those who were present at the last Convention of the General Synod will, perhaps, remember that the chairman of the Pennsylvania delegation, who was also chairman of this very Committee on the State of the Church, delivered into the hands of the President of the General Synod the documents in his possession, with the remark, that he and his fellow delegates must be withdrawn from their places in the various committees on which they had been appointed. How could he have divested himself and his fellow delegates of the duty assigned them in the General Synod without its consent, if his Synod was still a governing power in the General Synod? Or by what right did the President of the General Synod substitute for the name of Rev. Dr. Schaeffer that of the chairman of your present committee, if the original chairman had, after his withdrawal, a right at any time to return and resume his seat in the General Synod and his place in said committee?

As to the second argument of the protestants, that, "Because the constitution and by-laws give no power whatever to exclude

Synods, or even to decide as to their relations to the General Synod, but merely make it his duty 'to decide on the validity of the credentials of the delegates,'" we have only to say that, having proved that the Pennsylvania Synod was out of practical relations with the General Synod, it was not competent to the President officially to know any paper or a credential of delegates from that Synod, and consequently not to receive it at that stage of the meeting even for examination. The third and further claim of the protestants, that the Pennsylvania Synod exercised only a conceded right in withdrawing from this body, and hence could not have violated her claim to full membership, is fallacious, because, if such right *was* conceded upon her reception into this body, at Winchester, in 1853, the retiring President in organizing the present convention could not officially know the fact; for it is not recorded in the minutes of this body. The General Synod can know only such facts as her official acts which have a recorded place in her minutes. The right alluded to as a concession, not being on official record, and consequently not binding on this body, the President could not, of course, respect the claim based upon its assumption. If the Pennsylvania Synod had, as she claims, secured such an unusual concession from this body, and one to which she attaches such an immense importance, and of which she now claims the right to avail herself, even at the peril of the life of the General Synod, it is her own oversight that it was not officially entered upon the minutes of this Synod, and the consequences of such neglect are of her own procuring. But if such a right as that claimed had received an official sanction by the General Synod, still, as it was essentially and necessarily revolutionary in the very nature of the case, this body could have consented to it only as she consents the other integral parts of this and every organization have the ultimate right of revolution whenever the contingency justifying its exercise actually occurs. Of course, then, she expected to regard the Pennsylvania Synod as occupying that necessary relation of practical withdrawal whenever the latter body choose to exercise the right claimed to have been granted.

As to the remaining argument upon this point, that "the principle upon which the retiring President acted, places it in the power of any future retiring President to rule out of practical relations any Synod or number of Synods, etc.," it may be answered, that it presupposes what is contrary to common sense, viz., that future Presidents shall not be capable of distinguishing between the delegates of Synods that remain in loyal obedience to the body and those who disloyally and violently sever themselves from it.

Finally, in regard to their solemn protest against the final action of this body in the case of the Pennsylvania Synod, we have only time to say that it was announced by the retiring President that an opportunity would, no doubt, be given, to present a report or credentials from persons claiming to be delegates of the Pennsylvania Synod, immediately after the organization, by the election of officers; that this body did immediately after its organization ask for such a report, and invite those brethren to present their credentials; that she has repeated this invitation in her last action; and that consequently there is no ground whatever for the pathetic complaint and the doleful prophecies which the protest concludes.

All of which is respectfully submitted.

     JOEL SWARTZ,
     CHAS. A. HAY,
     LEVI STERNBERG,
     D. A. BUEHLER,
     W. F. WAGENSELLER,
        Committee.

CONSTITUTIONAL AMENDMENTS.

(ADOPTED.)

1. Amendment to Article II, in relation to the ratio of representation. Strike out the second paragraph of said article and insert the following:

"Each Evangelical Lutheran Synod containing eight ministers may send one; if it contains sixteen, two; if twenty-four, three; if thirty-two, four; if forty, five; if fifty-five, six; if seventy, seven; if eighty-five, eight; and if it contain one hundred and upwards, nine delegates of the rank of ordained ministers, and an equal number of lay delegates. Each Synod at present connected with this body shall be entitled to at least one clerical and one lay representative."

2. Amendment to Article III, Section 3, in relation to the admission of Synods. Strike out Section 3 and insert the following:

"All regularly constituted Lutheran Synods, not now in connection with the General Synod, receiving and holding, with the Evangelical Lutheran Church of our fathers, the Word of God, as contained in the Canonical Scriptures of the Old and New Testaments, as the only infallible rule of faith and practice, and the Augsburg Confession as a correct exhibition of the fundamental doctrines of the Divine Word, and of the faith of our Church founded upon that Word, may at any time become associated with the General Synod by complying with the requisitions of this constitution and sending delegates to its convention according to the ratio specified in Article II."

The *Twenty-Third Meeting* was held at Harrisburg, Pa., May, 1868. The proposed amended constitution was adopted and submitted to the District Synods for their "decision."

A resolution was passed relative to the World's Evangelical Alliance, and a committee was appointed to attend it, whether the next meeting be held in Europe or America.

The following paper on the Jubilee of the Reformation was adopted:

Your committee appointed to prepare a plan for the prosecution of the work of the Jubilee, beg leave to present the following:

WHEREAS the Reformation of the Sixteenth Century, inaugurated by the nailing of the Ninety-five Theses on the door of the Castle Church, by Martin Luther, on the thirty-first day of October, 1517, was an event of such magnitude and of such importance to the Christian Church as to deserve perpetual commemoration; and,

WHEREAS the Lutheran Church has heretofore celebrated both Centennial and Semi-Centennial Jubilees; and,

WHEREAS the year commencing on the thirty-first of October, 1867, and ending on the thirty-first of October, 1868, is the Seventh Semi-Centennial year since the Reformation; and

WHEREAS the exigencies, wants and interests of the Lutheran Church in the United States call for large donations of money to meet these exigencies, supply these wants and advance these interests; therefore,

Resolved, That the history of our beloved Church, from the time of her planting by the Reformers up to this Jubilee year, calls loudly upon us to acknowledge with devout gratitude the Divine goodness which has been so signally displayed in her perpetuity and prosperity, the maintenance of her pure faith, the development of her distinctive life, and her unexampled growth.

Resolved, That, encouraged by the past and present of her history, we look hopefully to her future triumphs, and especially rejoice in the indications that this Jubilee year is to make a new era in her spiritual life and benevolent labors;

Resolved, That we call earnestly upon all the pastors and churches in connection with this General Synod to celebrate this, our Jubilee, with thanksgiving to God and renewed consecration to Christ and his Church; and, as a substantial expression of their gratitude, to contribute largely of their means to the Jubilee offerings for the treasury of the Lord.

Resolved, That the historic Church year now passing be celebrated by all the churches of the General Synod as a Jubilee unto the Lord, and that it be characterized by religious offerings, commensurate with the ability of the members of the church and the demands made upon them as the stewards of the Lord.

Resolved, That, to secure the important ends designed to be attained, we recommend the following plan, viz.:

1. That the Secretary of the General Synod be authorized to have prepared and printed .... cards in the following form, and that these cards be sent to each pastor connected with us in such numbers as may be ordered:

I, A. B., agree to give as a Jubilee offering the following sums, as annexed, for the purpose designated. (Here follows a list of all our benevolent societies and the names of our institutions.)

2. That this Synod recommend that the pastor of each charge in connection with the General Synod, sometime during the present Jubilee year, present to each of his congregations the special work of the several benevolent societies connected with the General Synod; and that after such presentation a Jubilee offering be solicited for the support of these societies, and for the support and endowment of the theological and literary institutions of the Church, &c., &c.

3. That the subscriptions be continued until the next meeting of the General Synod, and that at that meeting each Synod be requested to make a full report of all its Jubilee offerings.

The Twenty-Fourth Convention was held at Washington, 1869. Twenty-two Synods were represented.

At this meeting the Order of Public Worship, as now practised by many of our eastern churches, was adopted, as well as the improved Formula of Church Discipline and Government.

The Twenty-Fifth Session was held at Dayton, June, 1871. Nothing requiring special mention in these "reminiscences" was done at this meeting. The regular business was transacted, and encouraging reports of the progress of the church were made, but nothing of an *extraordinary* character was done.

The Twenty-Sixth Meeting was held at Canton, Ohio, June, 1873. The Synod of New York and New Jersey was admitted.

ROMISH BAPTISM.

The committee on Romish Baptism would report that this subject has engaged the attention of the Protestant Church without reaching a unanimous or definite conclusion. It is impracticable to lay down any general rule that will apply to every case; and we can therefore only present a few general principles:

1. The Evangelical Lutheran Church has never in general denied the validity of baptism, as administered in the Roman Catholic Church, holding that the validity of this sacrament does not depend on the moral or spiritual character of the administration, nor that of the subject, but upon divine appointment, and upon the right application of water in the name of the Father, Son and Holy Ghost.

2. The Evangelical Lutheran Church does not encourage or sanction the repetition of this sacrament, believing that if once rightly administered, it should not be repeated.

3. So much must depend on the circumstances under which baptism may have been administered, and so much is due to the conscientious convictions of the parties concerned, that individual cases must be left largely to the discretion of the individual minister and the subject applying.

CENTENNIAL CELEBRATION.

The Committee on the Centennial Celebration report that the paper submitted to their examination is a circular addressed by the United States Centennial Commission to the clergy and religious associations of the United States.

This circular informs us that, "Occupying a prominent place in the Grand Centennial Exhibition of 1876, is Group 95, comprehending the general subject of religious organizations and systems, and subdivided into classes as follows:

"1. Origin, nature, growth and extent of various religious systems; statistical and historical facts.

"2. Religious orders and societies, and their objects.

"3. Societies and organizations for the propagation of systems of religion by missionary effort.

"4. Spreading the knowledge of religious systems by publications.

"5. Systems and methods of religious instructions and training for the young."

It thus appears that we, along with the other churches, are invited to present at the great Centennial an exhibition of our progress as a church for the last one hundred years in this country.

The committee therefore offer the following:

WHEREAS the Lutheran Church, and especially the English portion of it, has lost much prestige by failing to bring itself prominently before the world when occasion affords; and

WHEREAS we are now invited, with our sister denominations, to make an exhibit of our progress—national, intellectual and spiritual—during the last century, and our standing at its close; therefore,

Resolved, That this whole subject be referred to the *Committee on Statistics*.

Resolved, That this committee be instructed to report the progress that they have made to the next meeting of this General Synod, in order that they may be further instructed and assisted in making the illustration of our standing as a church a success, and in order that we may take our appropriate place among the denominations of the country.

The Twenty-Seventh Meeting was held in Baltimore, May, 1875. The number of districts now united is twenty-three; three were added at this meeting.

The interests of the various societes were attended to, which as was before remarked, I have not room to specify, and which must be looked for in the printed proceedings.

The question on ministerium was discussed for several days, and the friends of that ancient institution gained their point.

The proposed *colloquium* was defeated.

The Twenty-Eighth Meeting was held at Carthage, Ill., in May, 1877. Twenty-three Synods were represented. The Synod of Wartburg was admitted.

One important item of business is the following:

Your committee would also report the reception of a communication from Rev. S. A. Repass, of Salem, Virginia, together with copies of the minutes of the ninth and tenth conventions of the Evangelical Lutheran General Synod in North America, from which it appears that the said General Synod has commissioned Rev. S. A. Repass as a delegate with fraternal greetings to our body "*on condition that any existing* resolutions of the latter (*i. e.*, our General Synod) body compromising the christian character of the ministers and churches represented by this General Synod be rescinded."

Rev. Repass is not in attendance at our present meeting, but awaits our action, and asks a copy of the minutes detailing our action upon this communication.

Your committee would respectfully report that they have given this whole subject a very careful examination, and submit the following conclusions:

The only resolutions of any of our General Synods, known to your committee, which would be affected by this requirement of the General Synod South is found on page 31 of the minutes of the meeting at Lancaster, Pa., in 1862. In the deliberate judgment of your committee, the language of this resolution does not, by either fair or forced interpretation, compromise the christian character of our Southern ministers and churches, and therefore the way to the completion of the friendly relations contemplated by the Southern General Synod is rendered not only possible, but also highly desirable.

We offer the following:

WHEREAS in the judgment of this General Synod, the action of former General Synods was not intended to compromise the christian character of the ministers and churches of the General Synod South, and is not so interpreted by us; and whereas, if there be anything found therein that can rightfully be so construed (*i. e.*, as compromising the christian character of said ministers and churches), we hereby place upon record our belief that such is not the sentiment of this body; therefore,

Resolved, That the duly commissioned delegate from the Southern General Synod be officially informed of this action, and be cordially invited to consummate the object of his appointment by appearing in our midst, and by presenting his credentials in person.

Resolved, That the officers of this General Synod be and they are hereby authorized to appoint a delegate to return our most cordial fraternal greetings to the Southern General Synod, should the way for such appointment be opened by the acceptance of this overture.

Respectfully,

W. M. BAUM,
A. W. LILLY,
J. B. BALTZLEY,
I. MAGEE,
R. A. FINK.

The General Council of the Evangelical Lutheran Church
IN NORTH AMERICA.

WRITTEN EXPRESSLY FOR THIS WORK BY REV. DR. SPAETH.

The General Council of the Evangelical Lutheran Church in North America consists chiefly of Synods which were formerly connected with the General Synod of the Evangelical Lutheran Church. These Synods, in 1866 and 1867, left the General Synod and formed a new general body, the General Council. The formal occasion which led to this rupture and the consequent organization of the General Council was the following:

At the meeting of the General Synod held at York, Pa., A. D. 1864, the Franckean Synod was admitted into the General Synod. As the relation of the Franckean Synod to the Confession of the Lutheran Church had never been defined in a satisfactory manner, objection was made to its reception. The delegates of the Ministerium of Pennsylvania united with delegates from other district Synods in a firm and earnest protest against the action of the General Synod in admitting the Franckean Synod, as being in violation of its constitution. In addition to their protest, the delegates from the Synod of Pennsylvania withdrew from the sessions of the General Synod in order to report to their own body. This was done in accordance with their instructions based upon the resolutions of the mother Synod, adopted A. D. 1853, when the Ministerium of Pennsylvania, which had taken an active part in the establishment of the General Synod, but had afterwards seceded from its connection, resolved to return to its former place in the General Synod. In renewing this connection the Ministerium of Pennsylvania had taken good care to secure some guarantees that this union should not endanger the faith or oppress the conscience of those who had long resisted the resumption of an active connection with the General Synod, principally on the ground of doctrinal difficulties. It was, therefore, "resolved, that should the General Synod, as a condition of admission, or of continuation of membership, require assent to anything conflicting with the old and long established faith of the Evangelical Lutheran Church, then our delegates are hereby required to protest against such action, to withdraw from its sessions, and to report to this body." In the judgment of the Pennsylvania Synod's delegates, the admission of the Franckean Synod in 1864 was such a case, demanding not only their protest, but also their withdrawal from the sessions of the General Synod in order to report to their body.

With this action of the delegates, however, the connection of the Synod of Pennsylvania with the General Synod was not dissolved. And as the convention at York, after the withdrawal of the delegates from Pennsylvania had united on certain resolutions, which appeared to indicate an earnest desire to do more justice to the Confession of the Evangelical Lutheran Church, and to prevent in future the reception of any Synod which would not stand on a decidedly Lutheran basis, the Ministerium of Pennsylvania retaining its old relation to the General Synod, elected the usual number of delegates to represent it at the next convention in Fort Wayne, A. D. 1866. In order to afford an opportunity to these delegates to attend this convention, the time of the regular annual meeting of the Ministerium of Pennsylvania was even postponed.

But at the organization of the General Synod in Fort Wayne, May 17th, 1866, when the time had come for the delegation from Pennsylvania to present their credentials, and take their seats as members of the body, the President refused to receive those credentials, and declared "that the Synod of Pennsylvania was out of practical union with the General Synod up to the adjournment of the last convention, and that she must be considered as in that state of practical withdrawal until the General Synod can receive a report of an act restoring her practical relations to the General Synod." This decision of the chair was sustained by a large majority, and the protracted discussion on "the case of the Synod of Pennsylvania" had no other result but to affirm that this deliberate action had been "regular and constitutional." There was no alternative left to the delegates from Pennsylvania but to withdraw again in order to report to their Synod. After they had left Fort Wayne, a protest against the action of the majority was entered, signed by twenty-two delegates belonging to eight different district Synods.

The serious results of this action at Fort Wayne appeared soon enough. Only a few weeks afterwards the Ministerium of Pennsylvania, at its convention in Lancaster, Pa., formally declared its connection with the General Synod dissolved, because it has been "unjustly deprived of its rights by the late convention of delegates at Fort Wayne, and because of the conviction, that the task of uniting the conflicting elements in the General Synod has become hopeless, and the purpose for which it was originally formed has signally failed." It was also resolved to prepare and issue a fraternal address to all Evangelical Lutheran Synods, ministers and congregations in the United States and Canadas, which confess the *unaltered* Augsburg Confession, inviting them to unite in a convention for the purpose of forming a union of Lutheran Synods.

In pursuance of this call, a convention of Lutheran ministers and laymen met in the same year at Reading, Pa., from December 11th to 14th. The following Synods were there represented: The Ministerium of Pennsylvania, Joint Synod of Ohio, English District Synod of Ohio, English Synod of Ohio, Pittsburgh Synod, the Synods of Michigan, Wisconsin, Minnesota, Missouri, Iowa, Canada, the Ministerium of New York and the Norwegian Synod. A series of Theses prepared by Rev. C. P. Krauth D. D., containing "fundamental principles of faith and church polity," was discussed, and after their unanimous adoption it was resolved to proceed to the organization of the "General Council of the Evangelical Lutheran Church in North America." The first convention was held in November, 1867, in Fort Wayne, Indiana, the following Synods appearing on the official register: Ministerium of Pennsylvania, Ministerium of New York, English Synod of Ohio, Pittsburgh Synod, Synod of Wisconsin, Iowa, English District Synod of Ohio, Synod of Michigan, Scandinavian Augustana Synod, the Synods of Minnesota, Canada and Illinois. There were also present delegates from the Joint Synod of Ohio, though this body had not adopted the constitution and was not ready to enter into an organic union with the General Council. Their reason for declining to do so was "the unlutheran doctrine and practice, which, despite the reception of the confession or doctrinal basis" they "found to exist in some Synods." At the same time they laid before the General Council four questions on its relation to chiliasm, altar and pulpit-fellowship and secret societies, which have ever since played an important part in the history of the General Council as the famous "four points." Several of these points were also laid before the Council in a paper from the Iowa Synod, desiring the General Council expressly to acknowledge what, according to their understanding, was virtually acknowledged in the fundamental articles, viz.: Rejection of all church-fellowship with such as are not Lutheran. It was also demanded in the same paper that church discipline be exercised especially at the celebration of the Holy Communion, and against members of secret societies; and that the resolutions of representative bodies (Synods, General Council) should not be legislative but only advisory in their power over congregations. As the General Council in its official answer to this paper declared itself "not prepared to endorse the declaration of the Synod of Iowa as the correct logical deduction and application of the negative part of our Confessional Books," and referred the matter to the District Synods, the delegates from Iowa in obedience to their instructions declared that their Synod could not, under these circumstances, complete the contemplated connection with the General Council, but that they had to withdraw to the position of merely advisory membership with the privilege of debate.

Thus it became manifest, at the very first meeting of the General Council, that, after all, those had not been altogether wrong, who, after the rupture with the General Synod, hesitated to proceed at once to the organization of a new body, and preferred correspondence and conferences between the different Synods as the better way to the formation of a thoroughly united General Body. The history of the Synods which, once against the old General Synod, desired to represent a genuine Lutheranism and to attain a union on a thoroughly Lutheran basis, had been a very different one. There were great differences between the East and the West, between the newly immigrated and the Americanized elements. Important questions of doctrine and practice, which had been fully discussed on the one side, had hardly ever been touched by the other. It cannot be denied that there were many, and some of them prominent members of the General Council, who, whilst honestly subscribing to its Confessional basis, were not fully aware of all the consequences implied in this step. It was, therefore, perfectly honest and strictly in accordance with the facts when the answer to the paper of the Iowa Synod declared that the General Council, as a body, was not prepared to endorse the declaration of the Iowa Synod, etc.

If, in the face of these facts, the leaders of the General Council still preferred to proceed at once to a permanent organization and to maintain it in spite of disappointments; they did so, not only with a sincere wish to prevent a further disintegration of our Lutheran Church in this country, but also with a confident hope that upon the good foundation which had been laid a solid structure might safely, though slowly, be built, and that the pure confession of the fathers, having once been honestly and unreservedly adopted, would virtually prove itself the power of moulding the whole life of the Church, wherever its principles would be fully understood and faithfully carried out. The work thus undertaken was, however, not an easy one. Elements, in many respects not at all homogeneous, were to be kept together in an organic union. Principles, which, though generally adopted as fundamental, had not been so generally appreciated in all their bearings and logical consequences, had to work out convictions in all patience and firmness. And this was to be done under a constant pressure from outside, which would give neither time nor rest for dispassionate, quiet consideration, and for the healthy growth of solid and sober conviction. The history of the General Council consequently shows abundant evidence of the difficulties under which it had to labor. It is, to a great extent, the history of the four points, or rather of the one point of church fellowship, on which a declaration had been asked for at the very first Convention. One declaration followed another: At Pittsburg, 1868; at Lancaster, O., 1870; at Acron, 1871; at Galesburg, 1875. All these official utterances, from the earliest to the latest, acknowledge, with more or less decision, the Confessional principle involved in the question of pulpit and altar-fellowship, and in spite of the laxity of some with reference to the *application* of the principle. There has been a steady growth in the fuller appreciation of the principle itself and its practical application, culminating in the famous Galesburg declaration, which approves of the decided testimony of the Augustana Synod and against unionistic practices, pronounces the rule, " Lutheran pulpits for Lutheran ministers only, Lutheran altars for Lutheran communicants only," as according " with the word of God and with the confessions of our Church." If the delegates meeting at each convention are to be considered as the real exponents of their respective Synods, with their congregations, it may be said that, at the present time, a small majority of the General Council has come to a full conviction of the correctness of the Confessional Principle in the Church fellowship question, and is prepared to carry it out consistently.

This position has been reached in spite of the hasty withdrawal of those very Synods which from the beginning claimed to be the representatives and champions of the "confessional principle." The Wisconsin Synod left the General Council in 1869. The Synods of Minnesota and Illinois followed in 1871, because the declarations on church-fellowship were to them unsatisfactory. On the other hand the Synod of Iowa has maintained its friendly relation to the General Council, partaking in its debates, though not entering into full union with it. The same position is held since 1871 by the Norwegian Danish Augustana Synod. The Synod of Texas entered the General Council in 1868; the Indiana Synod in 1872, and the Holston Synod in 1864, making the number of ministers in the General Council, including the two Synods with privilege of debate, 724, with 1396 congregations, and 201,174 communicants. Of these there are about 120,000 German or German-English, 44,586 Scandinavian, and 36,588 English.

During the ten years of its existence the General Council has bestowed the greatest care and attention on the production of books of worship in English and German for the use of its members in the family, the school and the church. In this work it has been most successful. The Sunday school books and the church books, published in both languages by authority of the General Council, may well be said to be models of their kind. They are based upon the most careful and thorough studies in liturgies and hymnology, and in their preparation the very best and most reliable sources have been used. They are pure in doctrine, and complete in the material which they contain. They breathe throughout that spirit of devotion and unction which has always characterized the Lutheran Church above all others. With their confessions, prayers, scripture lessons, psalms and hymns, they form an inexhaustible treasure, which must become ever dearer to the pious heart the more they are known and used in spirit and in truth. Wherever they have been introduced they are a powerful bond of union not only between distant congregations, but also between the German and English element of our Church in this country.

The General Council has also been active on the field of missions. Its Home Mission Work, it is true, cannot thus far boast of great results, for the simple reason that the different District Synods have always had their hands more than full of this work in their own respective fields. But the Immigrant Mission at Castle Garden, New York, which was commenced in 1864 as the joint work of the Ministeriums of Pennsylvania and New York, and afterwards transferred to the General Council, has proved a great blessing to our Church in this country by taking care of the stranger on his arrival, and showing him the way to the word of God and to the church of his fathers. This mission work is now connected with the Emigrant House, 16 State street, New York, which offers to the traveler all the comforts of a well-conducted boarding house, together with the spiritual blessings of a Christian home. In the Foreign Mission field the General Council thus far has only two missionaries amongst the Telugoos, in India, but the lively interest which has lately been shown in this mission justifies the hope that the work amongst these Gentiles will be a blessing to many souls.

Ten years is a short time in history, and in the life of General Church bodies. The soberminded observer will not expect to see great and far-reaching results in so short a time. So we find in the history of the General Council for the present only beginnings. But these beginnings we believe to have sprung from good and healthy seed. With the help of God they will grow and prosper, and bring their fruit in due season, if only the sowers will show themselves faithful to their calling.

More than any other Lutheran Body of this country the General Council represents the peculiar mixture of our American Lutheran Church of German, Scandinavian and English elements, and that critical period of transition from the church of the immigrant to that of the native English-speaking American population. Its great work is to transfer into the sphere of the English tongue a genuine Lutheranism, sound in doctrine, government and form of worship (cultus). For this peculiar and difficult work God has endowed it with gifts and faculties, such as were never before united in the Lutheran Church of this country. By the grace of God it will accomplish its task in proportion as it remains and ever more grows faithful to its own " confessional principle " as laid down in its fundamental articles.

OUR CHURCH LITERATURE IN THE UNITED STATES.

Every church has its denominational literature; its own peculiar writers who defend its doctrinal position, or write its history, or prepare its books of devotion or morals suited to its own people, and though the public in general may be and is profited, yet the fame of these writers is reflected on the church to which they belong, and the church is proud that she has produced such men.

By the literature of our church I do not mean our libraries and collections of valuable historical manuscripts, whether public or private, but our own literary productions, the writings of our own ministers and laymen.

There were many difficulties in the way of our ministers becoming authors in the early periods of our church in this country. Though most of the prominent men of that day were thoroughly educated at foreign Universities, yet here they had but little time to study or write; they were obliged to spend more time in the saddle than in the study; their mission fields were vast and laborious; besides this, our people were not generally extensive readers, as but few primitive settlers any where can be; they could not afford to buy books even if books had been furnished, but above all, there was no great necessity for new books, for the ministers brought libraries with them from Europe, and the people had their Bibles and Arndt's *Wahres Christenthum* and a few other religious books. These reasons have some force even to this day, and our transition state is not favorable to the cultivation or encouragement of the highest style of literary production, but still we have done something, and it will be my aim to state what has been accomplished.

In the second volume of the Lutheran Intelligencer, in 1828, I published the first list of Lutheran writers in America that was ever made. It contained only the chief productions, but still the number was few. In 1840 a list of our American authors was appended by Professor Schmucker to his "Portraiture of Lutheranism." The number had increased considerably between 1828 and 1840, but still the Professor's list did not embrace all the publications. A third list was published by Professor Stoever in the Evangelical Quarterly Review for October, 1856, and a fourth by the same gentleman in April 1861. In 1876 I published the Bibliotheca Lutherana, containing the names of five hundred and forty-four authors, to which work I refer all readers who are desirous of further information.

We all know and highly value Prof. Stoever as an untiring and successful gatherer of Lutheran Statistics and an eminent Lutheran Biographer. I have named him the Plutarch of the Lutheran Church, and he eminently deserves the title. The man who devotes his time to gathering historical facts concerning the church, and rescuing from oblivion many names of precious memory, to restoring broken monuments and dilapidated tomb-stones and freshening up with his skilful chisel the nearly effaced inscriptions, as that gentleman has done, deserves the everlasting gratitude of the church, and will receive it. But for his indefatigable industry and unwearied patience, many an interesting and important fact would have been lost for ever, and many a name fragrant with apostolic piety would have perished from the memory of men.

It would be too laborious and perhaps impossible to ascertain the number of articles furnished by our ministers to the various monthly journals that have appeared in our Church, and utterly out of the question to ascertain the authors of the thousand articles in our religious papers. But there are several other publications of a more substantial character than the Monthly Magazine or Weekly Paper, which are properly mentioned here. One is the "Lutheran Preacher," conducted by the lamented Eichelberger. To this twenty-two of our ministers contributed sermons, six of whom never published anything else. And the other is the "Lutheran Pulpit," conducted by Rev. C. A. Smith, for which seventeen of our ministers furnished sermons, three of whom never published anything else.

There is another interesting question connected with this branch of our subject, and that is, how many of our ministers have contributed to the Reviews and kindred publications of other denominations? As far as I have been able to ascertain only thirteen,[*] and the publications for which they have written are the "Bibliotheca Sacra," the "Congregational Quarterly," the "Mercersburg

---

[*] Rev. Drs. Krauth, Sen., Reynolds, Hay, C. F. Schaeffer, Prof. Stoever, Rev. F. M. Bird, Prof. Jacobs (father and son), Spaeth and Rev. Dr. C. P. Krauth, Jr., Bachman, **Brown, Morris.**

Review," the "United States Service Magazine," "Appleton's Encyclopedia," "McClintock's and Strong's Cyclopedia," "Johnson's Cyclopedia," "The Presbyterian Review," and some "Scientific Magazines" of this country and of Europe.

The books on theology are the most numerous, the specific subjects of which embrace a wide range. The remainder are on science, history and education. The pamphlets are for the most part sermons. The others treat the subjects of literature, science, temperance and education.

We never had amongst us a poet of the highest reputation. The only volumes of poems ever produced by us are two in the German language, one by a German minister in a Western State—and that was a posthumous publication—and one by Rev. Dr. Swartz. These display very considerable poetic talent.

The list of publications I have spoken of is creditable to our ministry. It shows that amid pressing pastoral labors over five hundred of them have had time to write something, and courage to trust themselves to the press. I will not say that we have all done wisely, and no doubt some have wished that they had waited a little while longer and pondered their thoughts more maturely before committing them to print. But in this country many things are done unadvisedly, and many a man is in a hurry to publish crude and undigested stuff, which exposes him to severe and well-merited criticism, and occasions grief to himself and his friends. This is true, particularly of many of the communications in our weekly press.

But it is not only the book makers and pamphleteers who deserve honorable notice. The Review writers are equally and, perhaps, more entitled to favorable mention than the writers of fugitive pamphlets. No man with a decent sense of propriety will commit himself to a Review who has not thoroughly investigated his subject. He knows that few except the most intelligent and best educated of our clergy and people read Reviews, and that his article will undergo the keen scrutiny of competent critics. He therefore lays out all his strength on his article, and it costs him more labor than a mere popular sermon, and hence he deserves the more credit. Yet book making, pamphleteering and Review writing are not to be considered the only tests of scholarship. There are not a few men who have never been inconsiderate enough to write a book, publish a pamphlet or contribute to a Review, who are known to be better general scholars and more learned theologians than many who have inflicted their writings on an indulgent public. Cases of this character will occur to every intelligent mind.*

It will, perhaps, surprise some to hear that of the several thousand publications less than one-third are in the German language, and very few of these are more than occasional sermons and controversial tracts. There are a few devotional volumes and some illustrations of Luther's Catechism. But this fact need surprise no one. Our German churches were better supplied with a church literature than the English churches; neither were they, in general, readers of other books than two of the best ever published, viz., the Bible and Arndt's Wahres Christenthum; neither had most of our German ministers encouragement or time to write.

There is one fact which, in this connection, is worth mentioning. There is no church in this country in which the Gospel is preached in as many languages as in our own. We have German, English, Swedish, Norwegian, Danish, Icelandic, Bohemian in several dialects, and have had French and Low Dutch, so that eight languages have been employed by our ministers in proclaiming the glad tidings of salvation. Whilst we have periodicals published in other languages besides the German and English, no book has been published by us in any other language in this country except Luther's Catechism, a Hymn Book and a few sermons in one of the Scandinavian tongues.

These publications have been received with varied success and approbation. Many of them, such as sermons particularly, were designed for private circulation, and are not extensively known. Some of the more ambitious productions have had a wider circulation and have been several times republished.

A few of our writers have been handsomely compensated for their labor, yet few books pay. Not over one in a hundred ever pays expenses, and, if any money is made at all out of the ninety-nine, the publisher gets it all and the poor author is left dry. Authorship is a very poor business, and yet not a few are ambitious to invest presumed or real talent in it, and some are not a little vexed when Committees on Publications and professional book publishers do not accept their manuscripts and put them in print at their own expense and risk.

Nothing is more certain, and encouraging, too, than that our

* See my Bibliotheca Lutherana.

people are fast improving. They buy and read more books now than ever before, and every really good book furnished by our ministers is purchased by many. And yet there is good reason to complain that our writers are not sufficiently encouraged.

Only three of our church productions have ever been republished abroad, and they are Dr. Schmucker's book on "Christian Union," which appeared in London in 1845; his translation of "Storr and Flatt's Biblical Theology," in London, and Dr. C. P. Krauth's translation of "Tholuck's John," in Edinburg. Rev. Dr. Krauth's sermon before the General Synod, in Charleston, was translated and published in "Rudelbach und Guericke's Zeitschrift." This is a well deserved compliment, and shows the high appreciation of them by foreign Christians.

Not a few of our clergy have received titular dignities. We have sixty-six who flourish the title of D. D., and surely, if these honors are any real test of theological scholarship, we have made wonderful advancement. But a D. D. at the present day is not expected to be a learned man. The question with those sagacious college trustees who confer these cheap degrees is not always how many books has the candidate read or written, what attainments in theological science has he made, what learned articles has he contributed to the Reviews, what great books of other times has he edited with improvements, but how many students can he secure for the college, how many votes can he influence for a certain measure, how many particular friends has he among the trustees. It is not so in all cases; there are some exceptions, but we are Americans and a very fast people. Besides, we have five who have the honor of Ph. D.; three of LL. D. It is said that some means, in certain cases, not very creditable to the actors, have been employed to secure this cheap distinction. The report is, and it has never been contradicted, that seven or eight of a certain board of trustees abrogated a rule which was in the way of their receiving the honor, and, after they had "doctored" themselves, they reinstated the rule!

None of our men, as far as I know, have received theological honors from abroad. Foreign universities are not quite so lavish of college dignities as we and they, simple people, think that a man should be learned before he is called so, and that a man should be a divine before he is styled a Doctor of Divinity. Whilst no theological honors have been bestowed upon us from

Europe, I know two of our men who have received diplomas from scientific societies of high distinction, and one of these has been twice thus honored. A few of our men have been elected honorary members of distinguished scientific, philosophical and literary associations in our own country, but there is only one who has had the honor of membership in that most learned and exclusive of all our American societies, the Oriental.

There is one class of literature that has been successfully cultivated among us, and that is translation, and mostly from the German. This is supposed by some to be an inferior department of literature, requiring no research, and very little preparatory knowledge. It is true to some extent, and yet not every man who understands two languages is necessarily a good translator. It requires taste, tact, judgment and a copiousness of language to do it well, and all good scholars do not possess these qualifications.

I have heard more than one of our ministers regret that we have left so many good Lutheran books to be translated by men of other denominations. Nearly all the theological books translated in this country have been Lutheran, and some of our ministers affirm that we should be ashamed not to have done this work ourselves, for it is our literature, and we should have secured the credit of furnishing it to the English reading community. I am not of that opinion, for in the first place, few of our men have the requisite time to devote to literary pursuits, for I boldly affirm, that no clergymen of any church are more laborious in the discharge of pastoral duties, and few, if any, have as much pastoral work to do, as ours. Instead of being ashamed that our ministers have not rendered more service of this character, I hold that we should congratulate ourselves that our English reading community so highly appreciate the German productions of our church as to spend so much time and labor in translating them. Credit is reflected on the church which furnishes such writers, and that church are we.

But our periodical literature demands attention, and in this department we have succeeded well. The first Lutheran Magazine ever published in this country was, Das Evangelische Magazin, commenced in Philadelphia, in 1811, and was edited by Drs. Helmuth, Schmidt and others. It was published at intervals in 8vo. form and was discontinued in 1814. From that period until 1826, the church was destitute of a religious journal. In March,

1826, the first number of the "Lutheran Intelligencer" was issued in Fredericktown, Md., under the editorship of Drs. Schaeffer and Krauth, the latter of whom at the time resided in Martinsburg, Va. It was a monthly publication, 8vo. size, and each number contained about 26 pp. It was the first English Lutheran periodical published in this country. It originated in what was then known as the Synod of Maryland and Virginia, and was published at its expense. Its duration of life was five years. In February, 1831, the last number was issued, when it had less than five hundred subscribers and was $800 in debt. After a vigorous attempt to collect the dues, there still remained a balance of $500 against it, which the Synod of Maryland was compelled to pay. The Intelligencer, though not highly valued in the last several years of its existence, performed good service, even if it did no more than prepare the way for other more popular journals. A sturdy pioneer in a good work always deserves respect. The chief editor was an active and laborious pastor of a large parish, and received no compensation for his editorial work.

The next periodical in the order of time was the "Lutheran Magazine," published in monthly numbers at Schoharie, New York, and edited by an association of clergymen, but chiefly by the Rev. Dr. Lintner. The first number appeared in February, 1827, just eleven months after the birth of the Intelligencer. At the termination of the third volume it was transferred to the directors of the Domestic Missionary Society, but it was not continued.

The next which appeared was "Das Evangelische Magazin," published in monthly numbers, in German, and was edited at first by Rev. J. Herbst, but subsequently by Drs. Hazelius and S. S. Schmucker. Its first number was issued in September, 1829, and its last in April, 1833.

The "Lutheran Intelligencer" and the "Lutheran Magazine" having been discontinued, there was no English paper published in the church from January, 1830, to August, 1831. On that day No. 1 of the "Lutheran Observer" was sent forth. It was "a little one," a modest, unpretending monthly 8vo. of 30 pp., but it has grown to be a power in the church. It has had more friends, and, I may say, more enemies, too, than any paper ever printed in the church, and has exercised a commanding influence for over thirty years. It was begun in Baltimore, but afterwards transferred to Philadelphia, and was first edited by a very young man, who had no subscribers, no capital, and no experience. He was injudicious enough to assume the responsibility, at the earnest solicitation of some influential men of that day, and the implied understanding was that the church was to receive the profits and he himself to pay the losses! He has the satisfaction of having heard more than one man of judgment declare that the earlier volumes of the "Observer" are to this day very interesting and readable documents. But every man likes to hear his first-born well spoken of, especially where there is good ground of admiration! The prospectus of the "Observer" was issued at Gettysburg, where it was intended to be published; but before No. 1 appeared, it was transferred to Baltimore, and the aforesaid ministerial stripling was induced to undertake it. The reason of its being transferred to Baltimore was simply this: in those days of extreme undenominational liberality it was feared that a paper issued at Gettysburg, with the name *Lutheran* as significant of its character, would give offence to the Presbyterians in that place, and hence it was brought to Baltimore, where no such apprehension existed. The second volume of the "Observer" was issued in 4to. form, and continued thus for one year, when the editorship was conveyed to Rev. B. Kurtz, in 1833. It may just do well here to say, that the first editor never retained a cent for his services, but gave the profits to the poor. Mr. Kurtz removed to Baltimore, in August, 1833, and entered upon his duties with energy. The "Observer" was then converted into a weekly 4to. sheet, and continued to be published in this form for six months. In April, 1834, it appeared in an enlarged form, of usual newspaper size. For twenty-five years Dr. Kurtz conducted the paper with varying success, and since his retirement its history is too recent to be written.*

In 1848 the "Missionary" was started by Mr. Passavant, in Pittsburg, which has been merged into the "Lutheran and Missionary," now published in Philadelphia. The "Lutheran Standard" was begun in New Philadelphia, O., in 1842, and is still continued, though published at the present at Columbus, O. The "Evangelical Lutheran" first appeared in Springfield, O., in 1853, and was discontinued after a few years.

During this period other journals, edited by Lutheran gentle-

* For a full history of the Observer, see that paper for January, 1877, and my Bibliotheca Lutherana, 131.

men, appeared, but have ceased to exist, such as the "Frederick Visitor," the "Olive Branch," of Illinois, the "Linnæan Journal and Record," the "Lutheran Pulpit," the "Lutheran Preacher," the "Monthly Magazine of Religion and Literature," the "Lutheran Home Journal," the "Eclectic Magazine." The "Sunday School Herald," published at Philadelphia, commenced in 1860, and is still vigorously conducted and extensively patronized.

In July, 1849, appeared No. 1 of the "Evangelical Review," and has ever since maintained a high standard for excellence. This is the *Luna inter minora sidera*. The German papers have increased in larger proportion than the English, though their circulation is not so extensive. I should be pleased to give the history, as far as practicable, of every periodical ever published in our church, but the detail would be dry, and must be reserved for another occasion, and in a form different from a public address.*

Our periodical literature presents some striking and encouraging facts. Some of us remember when we had but one English paper and one German, and now there are seventy-five journals especially devoted to the interests of our church—twenty-two English, thirty German, five Swedish, seven Norwegian and one Danish.

The earliest Lutheran book written in America, though not printed here, is a translation of Luther's Catechism in the language of the Delaware Indians, printed in Stockholm, in 1696-8, and the next is the journal of the proceedings of the Salzburg emigrants, who formed the settlement of Ebenezer in Georgia. It is entitled Ausführliche Nachrichten von den Salzburgischen Emigranten die sich in America niederlassen haben herausg. von Samuel Urlsperger, Halle, 1734. 4th. This journal was continued from year to year until 1752, forming eighteen parts. Another was commenced in 1754, which is entitled Americanisches Ackerwerk Gottes, oder Zuverlässige Nachrichten den Zustand des Americanish-Englischen und von Salzburgischen Emigranten erbauten Pflanzstadt Ebenezer in Georgien betreffend, &c., Augsburg, 1754. 4th. The second volume was published in 1755, the third in 1756, with a supplement in 1760, and a fourth in 1767. These Salzburgers appear to have been as industrious with their pens as with their plough; the printed books relating to their little colony, would form a small library. There are a

* See a list in the Lutheran Almanacs and in my Bibliotheca Luth., 131 seq.

few of these volumes in the Seminary library at Gettysburg. The Hallische Nachrichten, begun in 1744 by the Patriarch Muhlenberg and his associates, are of the same character of publications and belong to our Lutheran literature.

The "Bibliotheca Lutherana," published by me in 1876, will give a better view of the progress and present condition of our Lutheran literature than whole pages of description, and to that book I respectfully refer the reader.

List of Books on Lutheran Church History in America.

The following works are indispensable to the writer of our Church history in America.

I can divide my list into three classes: 1. The originals. 2. The second-hand. 3. Modern.

I. THE ORIGINALS.

I. *Acrelius Israeli*, Beskrining om de Swenska Forsamlingars Forna oetnarawan de Tilstæna uti nya Swevige sedan nya Nederland, Stockholm, 1759, 4to. Description of the present and former state of the Swedish congregation in New Sweden (so called), since New Netherland, &c.

Acrelius was provost of the Swedish churches in America, and pastor of the church at Christina, (Wilmington). He returned to Sweden in 1756, and became provost and pastor at Fellingbro. He died in 1800.

Copies may be seen in the New York State Library at Albany, and in the Astor Library, city of New York. There is a translation of part of it, entitled New Sweden or the Swedish settlements on the Delaware, N. Y., 1840, by Rev. Nicholas Collin. There is a copy in the Library of the American Philosophical Society, Philadelphia. See also, New York Historical Collections, vol. series II., p. 400.

II. *Records of the Dutch Colonial Government.* These will be found in the office of the Secretary of State at Albany, and are indispensable to a correct history of our church. They contain many curious and interesting facts concerning the difficulties which our Church ancestors had to overcome. The future historian must use these records, if he finds it necessary to travel to Albany, and spend weeks in the study of them.

III. *Thomas Campanius Holmiensis*, Kort Beskrining om Provincien nya Swesige, &c., Stockholm, 1702, 4to. This is a very scarce work, relating to the establishment of the Swedes in New Sweden, afterwards Pennsylvania. In some American catalogues its author is erroneously called *Holm*. There is a translation of it entitled "Description of New Sweden, with Notes, by Peter S. Duponceau, Philadelphia, 1834," 8vo. See, also, Historical Society of Pennsylvania, Mem. vol. III.

IV. *Falkner, Prof. D.* Nachrichten von Pennsylvania. Frankfort, 1702.

V. *Geiser, E. G.* Svenska Folkets History III. This is said to be a capital book, and it must be highly esteemed, for a translation of it, by J. H. Turner, was published in London as late as 1845.

VI. *Loccenius, Joh.* Historiæ Rerum Suecicarum. Upsal. This book is quoted by Campanius, 1662, 4to., and is original authority. The author was Professor of Law in Upsal, and died in 1677.

VII. *Ausführliche Beschreibung* von der unglücklicken Reise der Jüngsthin aus Deutschland nach Carolina und Pennsylvania Wanderden Pilgrim. Frankfort, 1711.

VIII. *Hallische Nachrichten, Halle.* This important work consists of reports from Muhlenberg and other early German missionaries to the society at Halle. They begin in 1745 and end in 1785. [Indispensable to a historian.]

IX. *H. Melchoir Muhlenberg.* Journal of a voyage from Philadelphia to Ebenezer, Ga., in the years 1774-75, translated by Rev. J. W. Richards, and published in the *Evangelical Review*, Vols. I, II, III, IV.

X. *Ternaux Compans:* Notice sur la Colonie de la Nouvelle Swede. Paris, 1843. This work will be found in every good public library; it embraces "Notices" upon all the Colonies.

XI. *A Memorial of the Case of the German Emigrants* settled in the British Colonies of Pennsylvania, and in the back parts of Maryland, Virginia, &c. London, 1754. I never could get a sight of this publication. Colonel Aspinwall, a great collector of curious American books, had a copy, and there is another in the British Museum. It must contain some strange facts.

XII. There is another Swedish book, which I do not see quoted by Reynolds, or other American writers on this subject. I will give a translation of the title: "A short account of the present situation of the Swedish Church in America, with incontrovertible thoughts (oförgripheliga tankar) on its future progress, drawn up by Andreas Hessel, late its pastor and priest in Pennsylvania." Norkioping, 1725, 4to, pp. 23. Andreas Hesselius, the author, was minister at Christina, from 1711 to 1723, when he was recalled home to Sweden, and died in 1733. I have seen no other notice of this book than in Rich's Bibliotheca Americana Nova.

XIII. *Pastorius, Melch. A.* Beschreibung von Pennsylvania. Frankfort, 1704.

XIV. *Urlsperger, Samuel.* Ausführliche Nachrichten von den Salzburgischen Emigranten, die sich in America niedergelassen haben, &c., &c. Halle, 1735, 4to. There is a copy in the Gettysburg Seminary Library. This journal of the proceedings of the Salzburg emigrants who formed the settlement of Ebenezer, in Georgia, was continued from year to year to 1752, forming eighteen parts. Another work on the same subject was commenced in 1754, and is called Americanischer Ackerwerk Gottes, &c., &c. Augsburg. This is a continuation of the book noted above; the second volume was published in 1755; the third in 1756, with a supplement in 1760; the fourth volume was published by Johann August Urlsperger in 1767. The honest Salzburgers appear to have been as industrious with their pens as with their ploughs; the printed books relating to their little colony would form a small library.

By the SECOND DIVISION I do not mean *second rate*, but those writers of history who have used the *originals* in the composition of their books, with numerous references and quotations, and by *the modern* I mean those who for *the most part* are indebted to the *second-hand* for their facts, because the *originals*, or most of them, were not within their reach.

Under my second division belong such books as:

1. Documentary History of New York, to be found in every public library.

2. O'Callaghan's History of the New Netherlands. This important work dare not be overlooked by the historian.

3. Munsell's History of Albany will furnish some interesting details.

4. Brodhead's History of New York must be consulted, and so may Dunlap's.

5. Bancroft's United States, though containing some errors with regard to our Church, must be on your table.

6. Coming down to Pennsylvania, you will find Hazard's Annals

indispensable, as well as the volumes of the Colonial Records of Pennsylvania.

7. Williamson's History of North Carolina, though meagre and unsatisfactory, contains some facts.

8. Ferris, Benjamin. History of the original settlements on the Delaware. Last edition, Wilmington, 1846. You cannot get along without this, and the same may be said of Clay, J. C. Annals of the Swedes on the Delaware.

The above comprise the most important works of class II., but if any readers or writers do not desire to extend their researches quite so far, I will give them a few names under class III., THE MODERN.

1. Reynolds, W. M. The Swedish Churches on the Delaware. See Evangelical Review, I, 161.

The Lutheran Church in New Netherlands and New York. Ibid., VI, 303. Both capital articles, and thorough with full references.

2. Schmucker, S. S. The Lutheran Church in America.

3. Hazelius, E. S. History of American Lutheran Church. 1846.

4. Schaeffer, C. W. Early History of Lutheran Church.

5. Stoever, M. L. Evangelical Lutheran Church in the United States. Evangelical Review, Reminiscences of Lutheran Clergymen—in Evangelical Review, Life and Times of H. M. Muhlenberg. 1856.

6. Strobel, P. The Saltzburgers and their descendants. 1835.

7. Muhlenberg, F. A. Memoir of H. M. Muhlenberg. Evangelical Review, III, 151.

8. Krauth, C. P., Sr. The Lutheran Church in United States. Evangelical Review, II, 1.

9. Lintner, G. A. Early History of Lutheran Church in State of New York. 1867.

10. Pohlman, H. N. The German Colony in Maine. Evangelical Review. 1869.

11. Harkey, S. W. Early History of Lutheranism in Illinois. Evangelical Review, XVII, 526.

12. Bernheim, G. German Settlement and the Lutheran Church in the Carolinas.

Several of our men, as Diehl, Harbaugh, Focht, Harkey and others, have published histories of individual churches, which are important to a historian, and it would be well if printed or unprinted records of that character were carefully preserved.

Everything connected with our history must be studiously examined, and hence I would commend to the notice of our future historiographer, a series of articles in the "Kirchliches Informatorium," Detroit, 1870, upon the Rise, Emigration, Settlement and Church Development of the Prussians, &c., now known as the Buffalo Synod.

Herzog's Encyclopedia also furnishes some facts, under various articles, which the student can easily find, and among others, that one giving an account of the earlier history of what is now called the Missouri Synod.

Some interesting papers on the history of the Church in the city of New York, which appeared in the Lutheran Observer, by G. P. Ockerhausen.

The following is an appropriate sequel to the preceding. It is kindly furnished by Rev. Mr. Sheeleigh, who is one of our most industrious and successful collectors of Lutheran Literature among us. This collection is precisely what the future historian of our church will want, and I esteem it a privilege to insert it here. He says:

In my library, consisting of about three thousand volumes, there are publications of Lutherans in America about four hundred volumes, large and small.

Add to these bound volumes of collected Lutheran Sermons, Addresses, &c., twenty-three volumes, containing about seven hundred pamphlets.

Catalogues of Lutheran Colleges, Seminaries, &c., eight volumes, containing over three hundred pamphlets.

Lutheran Almanacs, four volumes, about one hundred.

Specimens of Lutheran Periodicals, in pamphlet form, near one hundred.

Minutes of Synods, about twelve hundred.

Of Lutheran Papers, &c., I possess files of the greater part, many bound.

Have nearly all our Lutheran Hymn Books—English, German, &c., large and small, for church and Sunday school.

Have seventy-five different American issues and editions of Luther's smaller Catechism—English, German, Swedish and Norwegian.

Have gathered nearly one thousand American Lutheran publications, exclusive of minutes, catalogues, &c., in the last twenty-five years.

Of translations of Luther's Hymn Ein' feste Burg, I have as follows:

English, produced in this country and Great Britain, upwards of fifty.

In twenty-two other languages, from one to six in each, gathered from the greater part of Europe and more distant parts; making the aggregate number of copies almost one hundred.

Besides these, I have several imitations and parodies, also several pieces of music written for the hymn.

I estimate that we have thus far had over five hundred authors in this country, and about fifteen hundred distinct productions.

MARTIN STEPHAN AND THE STEPHANITES.

The object of this article, which is abbreviated from a paper by Dr. J. B. Kummer, of Dresden, is to give my readers the benefit of the clear and important light which it throws upon the nearly unknown origin, early history, and real attitude and animus of a class of co-religionists among us, much praised by some and much censured by others. We refer to those who are best known by the name of Missouri Lutherans—a body which has now become large and influential, particularly among the German population. Some of their most distinguished leaders are named in the article, which fully, impartially and authentically explains under what circumstances and to what intent they came among us. The history, we are sure, is a very different one from what is generally supposed, and it gives the true and natural key to the right understanding of some of the more marked and extraordinary characteristics of a body with which the Lutheran Church, in general, has, *and will have*, more or less to do. It is but just, therefore, that it should be known whence they sprang, how they came hither, and what the nature is of that root from which they have grown and derived their life.*

The name of Stephan is connected with a too important and far-reaching movement in the church history of our time not to deserve a place here.

Martin Stephan was born at Strausberg, Moravia, August 13, 1777. His parents were originally Roman Catholics. The father, a weaver, became a member of the Lutheran Church, while the mother, with the children, remained Catholic. Afterwards, however, she also joined the Lutheran Church. His father destined him for his own trade, but, with his pietistic tendency, he took particular care of his Christian education, so that Martin, already in early youth, became pretty familiar with the Bible. But, as both his parents died already at an early period, he spent his childhood and youth in sorrow and want, and under the Austrian

---

* See Herzog's Encyclopedia, Vol. XV, 41-61; Ev. Quart. Rev., April No., 1870; Kurtz's Church History; Kostering Auswanderung der Sächsischen Lutheraner, im Jahre 1838, St. Louis, 1867; Schieferdecker Geschichte d. ersten Deutschen Ansiedelung in Altenburg, Perry co., Mo.

"edict of toleration." His education was, under these circumstances, a very limited one. In his twenty-first year he came, as a journeyman weaver, to Breslau, after having been subjected at home to the persecution of the Catholics. In Breslau he immediately joined the Pietists, and attended their devotional meetings, indulging in polemics already at that time with an inflexible mind and an imperious character. With the ardent desire of the newly awakened to preach the salvation also to others, and supported by Christian philanthropists, he entered, in the year 1802, the Elizabeth Gymnasium at Breslau.

He was already then very familiar with the German Bible, since he had improved even the nights for reading the Scriptures as well as other religious books. At the age of twenty-five years, a member of the fourth form in school, he naturally had to encounter a great deal of ridicule on the part of his younger school-fellows, which, to be sure, was partly repressed by his extraordinary strength and size (he measured six feet three inches), but which, nevertheless, contributed towards more and more confirming him in his natural bitterness, asperity and imperiousness, as also in his strong self-reliance. In spite of his strong will, he was unable to retrieve what he had neglected, and, more on account of his age than of his maturity, he gradually advanced to the first form, where the office of amanuensis of the Rector gave him a sort of legal authority over his fellow-students, which he not unfrequently, with arbitrary tyranny, extended beyond its proper bounds. At that time he is said to have procured for himself an old gown, and to have preached in a loud voice for hours in his cell. After having learned only the most necessary Latin and much less Greek, he entered, in 1804, the University of Halle, still aided by support which he received from Breslau, and, after an interruption from 1806–1809, the University of Leipsic, where he attended some philosophical and theological lectures, without making great progress in the learned studies, which he rejected as "carnal sciences." In everything that did not date from *antiquity* he discovered infidelity or heterodoxy. Here, too, his principal studies were devoted to the ascetics, especially from the period of *Spener* and *Francke*. His dogmatic theology he owed, next to the symbolical writings, to Freylinghausen's fundamental theology, his knowledge of homiletics to Scriver's "Seelenschatz." Of ecclesiastical history he had a thorough, though one-sided, knowledge, which he also knew how skilfully to apply to instruction or conversation. The deficient extent of his knowledge was made good by its intensity, to which a good memory and a great amount of serious experience was added. Thus his sermons and conversations were never tedious.

Stephan had hardly finished his studies when he received a call as pastor to Haber, in Bohemia, and, after one year spent in this "school of abstinence," another call as pastor of the Bohemian congregation of exiles, and German preacher at St. John's church in Dresden (1810), mainly through the vigorous intercession of the court-chaplain, Dr. Doering, since he then was considered a Moravian. He had declined a call to Rochsburg as court-chaplain. In Dresden his sermons, in which the strict Lutheran-biblical spirit prevailed, met immediately with great approval on the part of the small number of susceptible persons, and before long a large audience gathered around him at the *German* service, while the *Bohemian* congregation, at that time, numbered hardly more than three hundred members. Besides, he continued, in the manner of Spener, the devotional exercises, "which had been kept up for nearly half a century by all his predecessors, especially by Pastor M. Petermann. Every fortnight Pastor Stephan instituted on Sunday evening, after singing and prayer, a "recapitulation of the sermon;" on the alternate Sundays he had a sermon read; Mondays and Fridays, from 8–10 P. M., there were devotional exercises; on the first Monday of every month there was "conversation" for men, to which, however, also boys were admitted; and, at other stated times, various other religious meetings were held. During the "conversations," which, however, were instituted only at a later time (about 1830?), to gratify the wants of the many in search of advice and instruction, every member was entitled to anonymously write down questions regarding matters of faith and conscience, as also domestic affairs, and deposit them into a box, or to orally propound them; and the pastor afterwards answered these questions generally with great precaution, pastoral wisdom and rare knowledge of human nature. On Friday evenings there was a *Bible-lesson* for both sexes, when the Bible was read, chapter by chapter, together with the Tubingen Summaries; these, too, were seldom attended by Stephan himself. When, during these devotional exercises, any prayers were said, they had always to be *read* by the laymen, as he did not allow any free, extemporaneous prayers on these occasions.

But what secured to Stephan, in so short a time, such a number of followers, "aside of his vigorous, tall, though somewhat clumsy form, he possessed *nothing* that could have attracted the world—neither declamatory nor gesticulatory excellence, nor fiery or fluent eloquence, nor a pure pronunciation, nor any artistic skill in the arrangement of his sermons, nor any rhetorical aid whatever. With a Bohemian accent, a hollow, monotonous voice, and defective German, this man ventured to preach the "divine folly of the gospel" to one of the most highly cultivated cities of Germany." And yet the two-edged sword of the Spirit, managed by an apparently unskilled hand, entered with an almost irresistible power deep into the hearts of all his hearers, so that they either suffered their wounds to be bound up by him with the consolation of divine mercy, or, at least, for the most part, took home a sting of conscience.

The powerful impression produced by his sermons caused him soon to appear to many as a "dangerous man." Stephan's activity in Dresden, by his sermons and his zeal, was at that time, until about 1825, undeniably *blessed* by the Lord in many respects! In his personal intercourse he was extremely amiable, attractive and interesting, nay overpowering and winning the hearts "with magic force;" there was hardly a trace perceptible of any zealotical disposition; his nightly walks in the woods, of which he had always been very fond, and in which he generally indulged in company with a friend only, or with his Bohemian chorister, were still of an entirely harmless character.

The sensation produced by the fidelity of the strictly Lutheran preacher to his faith, and by the extraordinary success of his activity, increased the number of the curious, and gradually changed into hatred and contumely among the masses.

The clergy of the church of the cross ("*Kreuz-Kirche*," the principal church of the old city Dresden), submitted to the church-superintendents on the 13th of March, 1820, a well supported complaint against him. But in spite of the admonition which he received from his superior, and in spite of his promises, everything remained as before, and his encroachments even increased. But now soon the first public attack appeared on the part of an anonymous writer in the "correspondent from and for Germany" of the 25th of August, 1821, in which Stephan was called a "misguided mind, lying preacher and fanatic, with a misleading doctrine, apt to undermine the state, who endeavored to found a sect; while his congregation was called a miserable band of weak-minded, short-sighted and crazed fanatics. These criminations of a "malignant slanderer" Stephan refuted by a "correction" in the "national Gazette of the Germans" No. 47 (Nov. 21, 1821), in which he said among other things: "I am neither a founder nor a leader of sects; I hate all sectarianism and fanaticism. I am an Evangelical Lutheran preacher;—my religion is neither *above* nor *below* the Bible, but written *in* the Bible and leads to Christ;—the recapitulations of my sermons I hold in my parsonage *with the doors open;*—in my congregation neither insanity nor murder has taken place, &c."

Since busy rumor now involved him more and more, by circulating scandalous reports and denouncing him to the police, he found himself compelled to submit to his superiors an "explicit well-founded declaration," which seems to have given complete satisfaction (L. Fischer, page 19). But to the inhabitants of Dresden he addressed in the month December, 1823, a preface to two of his sermons "*Herzlicher Zuruf an alle evangelischen Christen,*" in which he defends himself especially against the accusation of fanaticism and sectarianism. Still more important was in the year 1825, the publication of one year's sermons. Already the title of this work, "*The Christian faith*, in one year's sermons," &c., shows that he intended to give here something complete, the Christian faith, such as he was teaching it, his open confession. Pernicious, however, and not to be justified in this way, are the assertions of miracles which even now are taking place and to be expected (Part II page 331). Connected with many objectionable expressions is a very awkward quarreling with those of different opinions [of this Stephan was especially fond in his hours of devotion, according to the testimony of all witnesses] and particularly very harsh criticisms of those teachers whom Pastor Stephan considered as infidels. With such defects these sermons might easily foster fanatical belief in miracles [as it *actually was* to be found here and there among the Stephanites] superstitious ideas of God's judgments and intolerant tendencies.

Adversaries among his hearers, though bearing witness to the purity of the Lutheran doctrine he preached, assured that *he accused as heretics all who were not his followers,* and invited them in the main to believe blindly. His own followers are all more or less distinguished by *a stubborn adherence to the letter of the Bible and of the symbols, which they are far from correctly understanding,* and by great zeal for the doctrine preached by Stephan, &c.

Thus reads in the main the corresponding passage in the report of the commissaries, who, since November, 1839, had been charged with the examination of the complaints against Stephan. The publication of these sermons, we are told by one well informed ("The emigrants and the Lutheran Church"), proved to be "a very decisive turning-point for Stephan." That time was "the period of his bloom, for he then enjoyed the undivided respect and love of more than one thousand persons, among whom there were many families of rank; within the sphere of his activity there reigned an active Christian life; his position with regard to the outside world could hardly be called a hostile one; in spite of many calumnies and his preceding unpleasant experiences, the number of his friends had increased; in his heart there dwelt an apparent serenity on account of the many mercies which God had granted him in his calling," &c. But for the mass of his hearers his stock of sermons became now "as it were, a symbolical book."

"Many who had listened for years to his lengthy sermons, which were rarely logically arranged, without being plainly conscious of his doctrine, became so by means of this book; those more accustomed to reading received in it a standard, by which to decide all dubious cases and religious disputes, so that Stephan now also not only on Sundays, but every day and at any time, became their spiritual adviser, teacher, and comforter. This book gave likewise a special impulse and aid to his later adherents, to secure authority to Stephan's name *in the province.* In general the absolute devotion of the "*Stephanites*" to Stephan's doctrine and person grew more and more; "it turned more and more into a carnal *attachment to, and dependence upon, the creature, without Stephan's trying to prevent it,* as it would have been the duty of a minister and experienced Christian, and thus detracted from the Lord's glory" (Pastor Blucher). It did good to his heart which was naturally inclined to pride, nay he fostered it at least indirectly, by often emphasizing the dignity of the ministry in a manner touching the priesthood of the Old Testament, as also by assuming the authority of God's interpreter, when asked for his advice in domestic affairs, *and almost claiming infallibility.*

Thus he became for his followers more and more an indispensable spiritual adviser who enslaved their consciences and *influenced the manner of thinking and acting of his parishioners as any Catholic confessor.*" His declaration ended all hesitation, all disputes. *He gave divine oracles from the tripod, by identifying his word with the word of God.* And indeed he pronounced everything with such a wisdom and knowledge of human nature, and with *such an assurance,* that simple minds especially necessarily considered his sayings and his advice as equivalent to God's word. No doubt he has in this manner given good advice to many and prevented them from many follies; yet on the whole he very much hindered the souls in their Christian course by so doing, nay even often frustrated in them the beginning work of grace; for many thought it now sufficient for being good Christians, to strictly follow Pastor Stephan's advice and prescription, or even only to be in outward alliance with him, and as it were to touch the hem of his garment. The former produced a *legal* (or judicial) manner of acting, the latter an external, secular (worldly) one, which now principally led to the frequently mentioned and ill-reported *nightly* promenades and meetings, in and outside of the city.

Before discussing these more at length, we must, indeed, in justice to truth, call attention to the fact that there were very different degrees of Stephanites. Some only attended his sermons, perhaps even the confessional, but kept aloof from the "hours" (of devotion) and from intercourse with him. The middle class attended the sermons *and* the "hours," honored in Stephan more the teacher than the minister proper, and thought to be permitted to listen also to other faithful preachers. "The Stephanites" proper, for there were many who did not go with him to extremes, at last not only *exclusively* attended Stephan's church and devotional exercises only, but owned him as their minister and spiritual father; many, in later years, *as him on whom alone the salvation of their little band and of the Lutheran Church depended.* These formed a circle close around the master. They principally attended the "conversational hours" (*Sprechstunden*), went everywhere in quest of him, accompanied him on extensive, mostly nocturnal, walks and short excursions on foot, and celebrated the day as a holiday when Stephan made them happy by a personal visit. Among these were also the most decided Christians and men of the best civil respectability, yet also people of very unclean minds, uncharitableness and dubious reputation.

In order to meet the social wants of Christians of the lower classes (especially of artisans, for whom there were not then, as now, all kinds of "associations"), Stephan *caused the formation of clubs* ("*geschlossene Gesellschaften*"), which originally served, in an entirely lawful manner, only the purpose of recreation, not of edification, and were moving within the bounds of order and of decency. This club was invited by the pastor once a month, on some Sunday evening. On a joyful feast-day it was permitted to bring the wives and daughters. In consequence of his unfortunate habit of lucubrating, however, Stephan never made his appearance before 10 P. M., which therefore turned the perfectly innocent evening gathering into a lucubration, which was generally protracted until after 1 A. M., and gave so much the greater offence to the world, as Stephan's return home led him through one of the most suspicious streets of the city, and several of his followers, with their wives, used to accompany him.

With these evening parties soon also summer parties were connected, which, likewise, ended only late at night, often even on the next morning. Stephan was *completely deaf* to all friendly representations regarding the indecorum of these nightly meetings and regarding the offensive accusation which they made in the world, justifying himself on the ground of *his* dietetic welfare, and could not even then be dissuaded from them, when they involved him and his family in actual vexations, besides producing the saddest consequences in other families (disturbance of domestic peace, suits for divorce, &c.)

In truth, *Stephan, by acting thus, gave great offence.* If any of his followers expressed their disapprobation, they made themselves liable to be excommunicated. The more considerate withdrew from all *personal* intercourse, but still continued to attend his sermons. The excitement in the city against Stephan and the Stephanites continually increased. Boundless opprobrium and bitter scorn were lavished upon them. The most romantic tales were circulated and found credence. But they became more and more insensible to the hatred of the world. They bore "the cross for Christ's sake," "the disgrace of Christ!" At last the authorities were compelled to interfere, when, in 1835, the news of the Koenigsburg hypocrisy ("*muckerei*") and alleged (scandalous) 'developments" (*Enthuellungen*) were circulated and produced the profoundest moral indignation. The police succeeded in ascertaining one of the secret meeting places, and surprised the pastor in the midst of his flock; yet the suspicion of "Muckerei" found no sufficient support. But, to obviate any further offence, Pastor Stephan was, in the same year (1835), prohibited by the authorities from holding any nocturnal meetings, *i. e.*, such as were protracted until 10 P. M. Stephan promised to abide by this decision, and actually conducted himself for a while more cautiously. Yet soon he resumed his nocturnal doings more boldly and in a worse manner still.

The year 1830, with its political movements, had deprived the Bohemian pastor of the direct protection of his poweful patron, the privy-minister Count Einsiedel (1861); also other influential men of high rank, who were well disposed toward him (Minister von Geobig, President of the Consistory, von Ferber and others) had died or resigned.

To the most exasperated attacks, the most violent invectives and abuses, which filled the public prints now to excess, and often in the most unworthy manner, Stephan opposed complete silence in public. To again answer them, "the dear minister considered as beneath the dignity of his holy office." (Confession, page 6). But one of his most faithful disciples, candidate Poeschel, a perfectly pure and pious, humble soul, but entirely taken with Stephan's imposing mind, who afterwards, in reward for his confident, unlimited devotion to pastor Stephan, was excommunicated by the latter, *on account of an alleged difference of doctrine*, and still he says: "*Pastor Stephan is a conscientious, honest man; he is what he pretends to be, an old-Lutheran preacher.*"

With the Prussian Old-Lutherans Stephan stood always, until after 1830. in intimate communion; with the fanatic dissidents in Wurtemberg and Baden he remained closely connected until the time of his emigration. But in Saxony the number of his followers had (especially since 1827) greatly increased. Many of the "Lutheran" ministers who formerly were on friendly terms with him, he now denied, and uttered calumnies and condemnations. He, no less than his people, assiduously speaks of heretics, blasphemers, despisers of the Bible, &c. *The young ministers, who were devoted to him with blind confidence, and who formerly, as candidates, had been under his spiritual care, worked entirely in his service, and with his zealotic, hierarchical means, especially pastor Keil, in Wiederfrahne and the brothers Walther* (both the pastor and substitute), *only they lacked his prudence.* Stephan visited them every year and preached to an immense concourse of people in their churches. He had, as it were, his "stations" throughout the land, which were waiting for his wink.

Discord, severe differences, the most bitter enmities broke out in numerous congregations among the parishioners, between the pastor and his flock, as also with the neighbors, in consequence of the *usurping, zealotic and condemnatory conduct of the only orthodox "ecclesiola."* At the same time the Stephanites and their head, nevertheless, *complained of persecutions and oppressions, saying that God's word was bound, and the Lutheran Church in danger.* And yet both secular and ecclesiastical authorities practiced the greatest possible and wise clemency and forbearance, whilst *they were bent upon martyrdom!*

The doing of the Bohemian pastor on the one hand, which became more and more bold and provoking, and, on the other hand, the power of excited public opinion, which became still more excited by the zealotic conduct of Baron Uckermann, a Stephanite, with his fulminating invectives against all neologists, heretics, infidels, demagogues, servile persons, &c., in his *Epistles to Prof. Krug* (Sondershausen, 1837), *compelled* the authorities to interfere. Even the Diet ("*Landtag*") of 1837 took the affairs of the Stephanites into consideration, treated them very thoroughly, and the sharpest speeches were heard regarding them; yet, they also found warm champions. The minister of religious matters ("*cultus minister*") von Carlonitz, felt it his official duty to defend them in the Chamber.

On the 8th of November, 1837, the police, charged with the strictest vigilance in their investigation, succeeded at last in discovering a number of Stephan's friends in the vineyard-house at Hollösswitz, which had often been frequented by them in the dead of night, and, early on the morning following, the pastor, who had followed them with his usual suspicious female companion, and concealed himself in the vineyard, and arrested them. The question, whether religious *conventicles* were being held here, was most decidedly answered in the negative by both Stephan and his friends. The pastor was summoned to make his appearance in Dresden early on the next day (November 9th), against which he protested most solemnly. Immediately afterwards he was *suspended*, and so remained until the time of his departure. *Judicial proceedings* against Stephan were instituted at the Royal Court of Justice, during which he did not recede from his *obstinate and stubborn* manner, and, which is much to be regretted, *took recourse even to falsehood and denial of facts*.

Some time after the Bohemian congregation (1838) handed in (April 17th) a written complaint against their pastor, which they still further sustained by an addition under date of July 5th of the same year. In the former, Stephan is charged with the following facts: 1. Carnal and unchaste conduct (an accusation founded upon statements which most grievously shock every better sentiment); 2. The dishonest management of the pecuniary interests of the congregation, and 3. Manifold neglect of his official duties, especially with regard to church, school, the sick and dying. (Among other things, they complained of his lying in bed until towards noon, in consequence of his lewdness, of his commencing the Bohemian service, out of laziness, one or two hours after the appropriate time, &c.) In conclusion they apply for his final suspension from office and the appointment of another pastor. They pray, first, for the institution of proceedings against pastors, on account of unfaithful administration of funds, peculation and fraud; second, they protest against granting him a pass for emigrating to America, as long as he shall not have settled his accounts, delivered the correct balances of the funds and inventory, and refunded the embezzled and peculated amounts of money, as also the amount of one hundred thalers, borrowed from the property of the congregation against his note of hand, but *for which he had, during a period of twenty-eight years, not paid any interest*, including interest and cost; finally, they asked for the confiscation of valuable vessels, documents and other parts of the inventory still withheld by him.

In the spring of 1838 he definitely *declared it to be his will that they should start on their emigration voyage;* and then a deliberation committee was appointed, and installments were paid in to the "credit-fund."

In the summer of 1838 Stephan had again taken up his residence in the town of Radeberg; the nightly scenes in the wood and meadow were repeated, and consequently also the measures of the police to suppress them, and since his secret escape, even without a pass, was feared, a judicial expedition was sent after him; but early in the morning only two girls, asleep, were found in his residence, while he himself had departed during the night to Dresden with the two other girls (according to documentary evidence). Here now he was kept a prisoner in his own house from October 15th to 24th; yet he knew cunningly how to evade the practical efforts of this measure.

Every one awaited the issue with the greatest suspense; the Stephanites, who, ready for emigration, had partly started already, the remainder waited anxiously for their leader and shepherd, in compliance with a most humble direct supplication of Stephan to his majesty the King, (dated October 20th), the two pending judicial proceedings against him were *quashed* under date of October 23d, 1839—provided that Stephan would give bail to the amount of five hundred thalers for the security of the Bohemian congregation. His private imprisonment was immediately relaxed. In the hour of midnight, between October 27th and 28th, Stephan clandestinely, and without taking leave of his family, left the city with post-horses, in order to join the emigrants in Bremen. There the "ecclesia pressa" ("six clergymen with about seven hundred souls, among whom there were ten candidates and four teachers") had gathered; there *songs of the exiles* ("*exulantenlieder*") were published: "to such an extent as here the disgraceful worship of men's persons had never yet been carried, and the actual *idolatry* of Stephan was rapidly developed upon the sea toward its worst disgraceful completion in St. Louis." (Dr. Vehse).

Stephan followed the ships which had preceded him (there were five in all, of which the "Amalia" was lost) with his "*staff*," on the 18th of November, continued his lewd debauchery after having passed through sea-sickness, showing himself cowardly and timid during the dangers of a storm, preached very seldom during the voyage, which lasted sixty-four days, "partly from laziness, partly to make himself rare," but becoming strikingly more and more exhaustid, he caused his vicar to preach a series of sermons. Knowing how to silence his legal counsel, and fearing a separation of the secular and spiritual power, he caused the *office of a bishop* to be offered to himself five days before their arrival in New Orleans. Shortly before their arrival in St. Louis, Stephan had the ill-reputed *declaration of submission* drawn up upon the steamer "Selma," and had it signed, *by way of an oath, by all the men and women of the company.* In St. Louis itself, where Stephan, to the great injury of the emigrants, permitted more than two months to pass unimproved, the bishop had his own way without any interference whatever; the vestments of the bishop, consisting of an extremely heavy golden chain, crook and mitre, were made; a real "rioting" was carried on in the "house" of the bishop, into which, to the general scandal, more and more young women were introduced.

At last, 1839, April 26, the bishop departed with a part of his company to the colony "Wittenberg," Perry county, on the Mississippi, which in the meantime had been purchased; there, on rogation-day (May 5), several girls made the first disclosures, in the first place, to Pastor Löber, of indecent intimacies which "the grey-haired sensualist, with wicked abuse of God's holy name and word, had made to them already during the sea-voyage," and afterwards confirmed them by oath.

On May 30th, the *deposition* and excommunication was pronounced upon one who had deceived at first himself, and then, for so long and disgracefully, hundreds of our co-religionists. On the next day, with a compensation of one hundred piasters and the necessary equipment, he was exported to the opposite State of Illinois, whither afterwards his concubine, Gertrude, who remained faithful to him unto death, followed him. There he died according to the official certificate "on the last day, or during the last days of February, 1846, in Randolph county," nearly seventy-two years old. The rumors of his return to Europe are without foundation. Another rumor says that he has again returned to the bosom of the Catholic church. [Kurtz, in his Church History, so affirms.]

Now the emigrants had, for some time, to pass through hard struggles of physical want and internal dissensions. The clergymen would not very soon divest themselves of the hierarchical principles which Stephan had imparted to them. At last, 1840, November 22d, the congregation at St. Louis held an extraordinary fast-day, when their richly endowed pastor, O. Herm. Walther, made a sincere, profound confession of repentance. Gradually also the external condition of the newly founded, now well regulated, congregations was much improved.

Dr. C. E. Vehse, who, as is well known, was on most intimate terms with Stephan for a long time down to his fall, says, among other things, "Stephan is a psychological enigma; as clever a man as he was wicked. I must say even now, after having been so fearfully undeceived, that in my whole life I have never heard anything more magnificent than his addresses in the devotional exercises on Sunday afternoons. Yes indeed," adds Dr. Vehse "on the other hand, *after all nothing but a clerical impostor*."

Pastor L. Fischer, in his "The False Martyrdom," while denouncing him as an apostate, yet speaks in appreciative terms of his "firmness of conviction, strength of character, unbroken courage, indescribable zeal, connected with energetic straightforwardness and Luther-like sturdiness. And even such a man as the learned, pious *Franz Delitzsch* writes a glowing panegyric, after having, in 1836, dedicated his first work, "Contributions to the History of Jewish Poetry," &c., to Pastor Stephan as to his revered teacher and parental friend out of grateful love. With reference to this, the forementioned L. Fischer now, however, says, (p. 14, "The False Martyrdom"): "*Stephan's spirit is and remains a sectarian and partisan spirit*, who, during the latter part of his career among us, *had no longer any idea of* (the martyr) *Stephan's wisdom and joyfulness of faith, nor of Luther's simplicity, but who only, in self-assumed clerical dignity, went around to capture and enslave innocent souls*; and, although branded by public opinion and abandoned by the members of his own household, yet did not cease, in his unchristian heedlessness, to scorn Christian freedom and give room to the scoffer." (p. 52): "Not so much the *doctrine* as the *conduct* of Pastor Stephan was it that brought about his fall in Saxony." (p. 29): "Stephan's last departure from his family (*in which he was a real tyrant*) is crushing, pitiless, accomplished with cold, rigid eyes, and a bold, insolent face."

We conclude with the opinion of von Polenz ("Public Opinion," p. 17 *sq.*): "Stephan's faith, firm as a rock, in the Lord and his mercy *was more objective than a subjective, transforming one*. In his constant external struggles he lost more and more that inwardness ("*Innerlichkeit*") so necessary for the Christian, and became accustomed to the torch of the gospel more outwardly than inwardly. He gradually lost all that he always, perhaps even shortly before his fall, had, in so rich a measure, given to others; and, in fine, he was more a *servant* than a *child* of God." (p. 77): "He presents, as it were, the type of *proud solitariness, of one sided, rude separation.* And accessible as he was only to his own people, who almost worshipped him as an idol, he would have had to be an angel if *the idea of his own infallibility had not taken root in him.* THIS IDEA THEN NECESSARILY PASSED OVER INTO THE MINDS OF HIS FOLLOWERS TO SUCH AN EXTENT THAT THEY BELIEVED THEY EXCLUSIVELY REPRESENTED IN THEMSELVES, NOT ONLY THE LUTHERAN, BUT ALSO THE CHRISTIAN CHURCH, AND ADMITTED OF NO SALVATION OUTSIDE OF THEIR CIRCLE."

This is the origin of that powerful and influential church organization, which, in less than forty years, has erected not less than one thousand places of worship, numbers over six hundred ministers, established three colleges, two theological seminaries, numerous academies and parochial schools, and orphan houses.

THE DEFINITE PLATFORM.

In the early part of September, 1855, most of the *leading ministers* connected with the General Synod, received through the post-office a neat pamphlet of forty-two pages, issued as was announced by Miller and Burlock, printers in Philadelphia, and bearing the name of "Definite Platform, doctrinal and disciplinarian, for Evangelical Lutheran District Synods, constructed in accordance with the principles of the General Synod." The author's name was not mentioned, neither was there any intimation given by whom it was sent. Those who were thus complimented were requested in the preface to return it to the printers, if they did not desire to keep it, but if they did, to remit twenty-five cents to the firm in Philadelphia!

The pamphlet had a mysterious air about it. It was a child thrown upon the Church of whom nobody was willing to acknowledge the parentage.

I distinctly remember that one of the unknown authors of it was in my study when it was received. I naturally enquired as to its origin, and, in evident confusion, he replied, "Oh! you know well enough where in all probability any attempt to change the Confession would come from." Of course I did. To the credit of this gentleman, I will here add, that he was the first of the triumvirate of its authors, who had candor enough to admit the fact after the lapse of several weeks. He felt humbled at the idea of fighting from behind a tree and openly avowed that he took part in preparing it. The other two never made a public avowal, though they were well known.

The introduction to this "Platform" says, "The following *American Recension of the Augsburg Confession* has been prepared by consultation and co-operation of a number* of Evangelical Lutheran ministers of Eastern and Western Lutheran Synods belonging to the General Synod, at the special request of *Western* brethren, whose churches particularly need it, being intermingled with German Churches, which avow the whole mass of the former

---

* Only *three* were ever known to have anything to do with its preparation either by "consultation or co-operation."

symbols. In this revision not a single sentence has been added to the Augsburg Confession, whilst those several aspects of doctrine have been omitted which have long since been regarded by the great mass of our Churches as unscriptural and as remnants of Romish error."

"The only errors contained in the Confession (which are all omitted in this Recension) are—

1. The approval of the ceremonies of the mass.
2. Private confession and absolution.
3. Denial of the divine obligation of the Christian Sabbath.
4. Baptismal regeneration.
5. The real presence of the Body and Blood of the Saviour in the Eucharist.

"With these few exceptions we retain the entire Augsburg Confession, with all the great doctrines of the reformation."

Among other resolutions contained in this introduction and recommended to be passed by the Synods, was this:

"*Resolved*, That we will not receive into our Synod any minister who will not adopt this platform and faithfully labor to maintain its discipline in his charge."

No sooner had this pamphlet been thus secretly distributed than the war began, which continued for several months. Nearly every issue of the Observer from September 21, 1855, to May, 1856, contained several articles either in opposition or vindication of it. "The American Lutheran" party, headed by Dr. S. S. Schmucker and the editor of the Observer, employed their best talent in its defence, and exerted all their power in the Synods to have it adopted, and yet, with all their influence, only three Synods at that time in connection with the General Synod, and these were the Synod of Ohio, the Olive Branch Synod of Ohio, and the Synod of Wittenberg, (Ohio), the leading man of which was one of the triumvirate who built the Platform, ever adopted it. This protracted controversy covered the whole ground of the subscription to creeds, as well as of the doctrines which the Platform rejected. Some able men on both sides participated in it, but, besides these, there was a large number of immature scribblers and half educated fanatics who inflicted their undigested nonsense upon the Church. The unhappy editor often complained to me of the annoyance occasioned by the reception of such articles, most of which he was obliged to publish for prudential reasons.

No doubt the projectors of this measure were amazed at the opposition which it encountered from some quarters. Where they expected sympathy they received stern rebuke. I remember that the late Dr. D. F. Bittle was one of its fiercest opponents, and he was before that presumed to be on "the *American* Lutheran" side.

If any person were now to undertake the task of going over this whole controversy as I have been compelled to do, he would be astonished at the *extremely* unlutheran and unchurchly, and even rationalistic positions assumed by some of the disputants on the one side, and the moderate and yet firm churchly tone of opposition on the other.

The following resolutions unanimously passed by the Synod of East Pennsylvania, at Lebanon, 1855, represent the general sentiment of all those in the Church who would not stand on "the Platform." They were written by Rev. Dr. J. A. Brown, at that time pastor in Reading:

WHEREAS an anonymous pamphlet, entitled "*Definite Synodical Platform*," has been very widely circulated in the Church, and has been transmitted to the members of this Synod generally; *and whereas* the inevitable tendency of this production is to agitate, distract and divide the Church by the introduction of changes of the gravest character in the confessional position and ecclesiastical and fraternal relations of the various sections of the Lutheran Church towards each other; *and whereas* this Synod most deeply deprecates such an agitation, and recoils with mingled alarm and abhorrence from the intolerant and proscriptive principles here avowed and proposed for introduction into the organic structure of our Church by the adoption of such a creed, and its arbitrary enforcement upon pain of exclusion from church-fellowship of all who will not sanction the system thus proposed. Therefore,

Resolved, That we hereby express our most unqualified disapprobation of this most dangerous attempt to change the doctrinal basis and revolutionize the existing character of the Lutheran Churches now united in the General Synod, and that we hereby most solemnly warn our sister Synods against this dangerous proposition, express our most earnest hope that none of them will either engage in or countenance such an agitation, but will use increased diligence "*to keep the unity of the spirit in the bond of peace*" with their brethren in all parts of the Lutheran Church who hold to the great Evangelical doctrines of the Reformation, that we may, if possible, be daily drawn more closely to each other in faith and love, and thus be prepared to labor more efficiently in all those high and holy enterprizes for the edification of the Church and the conversion of the world, to which the providence of God and the plain teachings of the gospel direct us."

These resolutions occasioned alarm in the minds of the "Platformists," who vainly believed that the personal influence of their leaders would ensure it a general acceptation, but never were men more painfully disappointed.

After it was discovered that the Eastern Synods universally rejected the measure, it was given out in the Observer (October 19th, 1855), that the "Platform was prepared *chiefly* for the use of our Western Synods, though Eastern ones may adopt it if they like." Thus they were willing that the Church should have two Confessions to suit different latitudes. It was asked if this were so, "Why was it sown broadcast over the East? why was there no intimation that this was its main object? why were *Eastern* men employed as its principal constructors? why was it printed in the *East* and commended so carefully to the Synods in connection with the General Synod?"

But they were still more accommodating. One of the authors of it openly acknowledged before the Synod of Maryland the same year, "that it was intended only as a temporary expedient, which might after while be changed." Immense personal efforts were made at that meeting to adopt the new Creed. Two of its originators were present and employed all their personal influence and argument in vain. Even some of the men who sympathized with them in their theological views and general church policy, and whom they thought they could influence in almost any measure, could not be moved to mutilate the old Confession, and their disorganizing attempt ingloriously failed.

For nearly two months, during which time the Observer contained several articles on this subject in every issue, the editor said not a word, but finding that his lighter troops were being fast demolished, at length himself entered into the conflict. He employed all his acknowledged skill in argument, all his wit and sarcasm in several long columns, for three successive weeks, in vindication of his favorite project. Some of the Synods were yet to meet during that autumn; but not one of them which met after the appearance of these able papers was convinced by their logic, and only two had adopted it before this time.

On December 7th, the editor informed us that "he had intended to write one or two more editorials on the subject, but as another brother has commenced a series he gladly yields the field to him."

These new articles were signed by S. S. S., and this is the first time that gentleman appeared in print upon the subject. In five successive Observers he published seventeen columns of defence. The articles displayed his well known acuteness and extensive acquaintance with the history of the Church and of her creed. Every candid reader gave him credit for the ability with which he handled the exciting subject, and, although he may have confirmed some of the wavering in their anti-confessional tendencies, yet he did not secure votes for the Platform.

After S. S. S. had finished his long articles, the editor found it necessary once more to come to the rescue, and this time not so much in favor of the new creed as against some of his over-zealous friends. They began to talk of dividing, "setting up for themselves," "getting rid of the old, musty, worm eaten" Symbolical Books! The editor, with his usual astuteness, saw that this spirit of secession must be rebuked, and hence, on January 25th, 1856, came out in a two column editorial severely denouncing such language and ideas. He knew well enough that his cherished cause would be endangered by such proceedings, and therefore called in his skirmishers, who were imprudently exposing their cause. It had the effect.

On February 1st, 1856, he begs his correspondents to "stay their pens and direct their attention to other subjects," and yet tells his readers that he intends to publish the Platform in the Observer, which accordingly appeared in full in the number for February 29th, 1856.

At this stage of the controversy, several compromises were proposed—a sort of armistice during which the belligerents should lay down their arms and cease from the conflict. Out of them grew what was called "A Pacific Overture," which first appeared in the Observer of February 29th, 1856. It was signed on its first appearance by twenty-three ministers, who pledged themselves to "the doctrinal basis of the General Synod" and deprecated the further prosecution of the controversy;" but even this did not terminate the war. Numerous other articles appeared until both parties retired from the battle ground from pure exhaustion, but never since that day have any attempts been made to foist a new creed upon the Church.

Various articles appeared in the Evangelical Review upon this vexed question, or extended allusions to it, and two small books were written in opposition to the Platform; one by Rev. John N. Hoffman, then at Reading, which he called *The Broken Platform*. It contained many strong arguments and damaging facts, but the book was crudely put together, hastily prepared and carelessly composed. It was not equal to the acknowledged talents of the author. He was a man of mental vigor but of imperfect education and most bilious temperament.

The other book was by the Rev. Dr. Julius W. Mann, of Philadelphia, entitled *A Defense of the Augsburg Confession*, a most admirable production, which powerfully demonstrated the true doctrine of the Church and exploded the vaunted pretensions of the new Creed.

An occasional sportive allusion is still made to the Platform in the papers by men who were active in the Church twenty-five years ago (1876), but it has made so little impression upon the Church, and it is now almost universally forgotten or remembered only to excite compassion for good men who were guilty of the stupendous folly of trying to force it upon our Synods. *Requiescat in Pace.*

In the book notices of the Evangelical Review, Vol. VII, p. 293, we find the following:

"This (the Definite Platform) is an attempt to bring into practice and give reality to the principles set forth in Dr. Schmucker's 'Manual.' *There* it is declared that the Lutheran Church has rejected certain parts of the Augsburg Confession and other Symbolical Books, and *here* is a form in which it is proposed to do this! It seems to us that this process is rather awkward. The Synodical action ought to have preceded the authoritative announcement of such an expurgation ('*recension*,' as it is here called) of the Augsburg Confession. In fact, this proposition is an admission of the utter groundlessness of the assertions made in the 'Manual' as to the present position of the Lutheran Church in connection with the General Synod. Although so small an affair in form, this brochure of forty odd pages may become a most serious matter—may serve as an entering wedge for splitting and dividing the Lutheran Church in America, not only from her confessions, which stand upon an immovable rock of truth, and from the reviving Church in Germany, which begins once more to gather around and endeavor to take its stand upon this rock, after the floods of infidelity have passed over it, but may also be the means of splitting the gradually uniting church here in America into ten thousand scattered fragments. It is a proposition, not merely to adopt Dr. Schmucker's emasculated Augsburg Confession, but to pronounce heretical and separate from and anathematize every one who does not do so and who will not unite in a wholesale rejection and condemnation of all the other symbols of the church—symbols prepared and believed by so many sainted heroes of the Church; the great testimony of Protestanism against Romanism, and of the Lutheran Church against various forms of error; and its solemn testimony to the great truths of the gospel! It is the introduction into the Lutheran Church of 'The Act and Testimony' of the old school party in the Presbyterian Church, by which that body was first agitated for years, and finally divided into two hostile parties, whose heart-burnings may be handed down from generation to generation. Only it differs from that movement which was intended to preserve the Presbyterian Confessions in their integrity and purity. But we have neither time nor space here to go into any analysis and proper characterization of this movement. That will doubtless be done by clearer heads and stronger hands than ours. We only give our simple impressions as to the nature and tendency of this strange proposition. We trust, however, that no Lutheran Synod will be beguiled into the awful movement here so abruptly yet so confidently proposed to them—to revolutionize their whole previous history and declare separation from the whole Lutheran Church of the past and all their brethren in the present who hold to the faith of the fathers, 'the faith once delivered to the saints' at Augsburg and Schmalkald, and reiterated by almost every church in Germany in the Form of Concord, we trust no Synod connected with the General Synod will be prepared to adopt the rescinding process proposed by this pamphlet, and especially set forth in these words: Resolved, That we will not receive into our Synod any minister who will not adopt this platform and faithfully labor to maintain its discipline in his charge."

The Rev. Dr. Lintner, in an able article on Church Government, published in the July number of the Evangelical Review, 1856, thus expresses himself in a note, page 1·9:

"A pamphlet has lately appeared among us, entitled, 'Definite Platform, &c.,' purporting to give the views of a number of our ministers who 'desire a more specific expression of the General Synod's doctrinal basis.' It has been circulated through the Church with a view to its adoption by the churches connected with the General Synod instead of the present basis of that body. It is indeed strange that an overture on a subject of so much importance as *changing our doctrinal basis* and introducing a *new standard* into the Church, should come to us without any names or ecclesiastical authority to recommend it. When changes are proposed, 'doctrinal or disciplinarian,' affecting the interests of the whole Church, they are generally recommended by Synods or conventions who are duly authorized to do so. But here is a project, got up by a few individuals in secret conclave, and then thrown out upon the Church, like a torpedo, to make an explosion, without any one being willing to assume the responsibility. Perhaps it was deemed the wisest course by those who were engaged in the plot. But it looked suspicious on the very face of the platform. It showed that its projectors lacked confidence in the undertaking, and it was regarded by many, perhaps most of the readers of the pamphlet, as *prima facie* evidence that there was something wrong in it. The Platform professes to be a review of the Augsburg Confession, to adopt it to the circumstances of the times and make it more acceptable to the churches. But it looks more like a labored attempt to stigmatize it and make it odious. It does not treat the subject fairly. It takes isolated passages, separates them from their connection, and puts constructions upon them which are not warranted by the general sense; and, by this *dissecting* and *mutilating process*, it presents us with a *caricature* to bring that honored and sacred instrument, which has so long been regarded with veneration, into disrepute and contempt. The attempt, however, if such has been the design, has failed, and may teach a useful lesson to others who, in future, might be disposed to engage in similar attempts to break down the hedges which the wisdom and piety of our fathers have placed over Evangelical Zion."

On page 140 of the same number of the Review, Dr. Lintner relates the following story in a note:

"Ministers sometimes involve themselves in difficulties by attempting to introduce new expedients which have not been used and approved by the Church. To illustrate this, I will relate the following incident which occurred not long since in one of our churches: An honest, conscientious old elder, well instructed in the doctrines of the Lutheran Church, and cherishing a high regard for the Augsburg Confession, was, one day, told by his minister, that he was going to introduce a new *Platform*, which would do away the necessity of adhering any longer to the Augsburg Confession. The elder asked him to explain the new *Platform*, and show wherein it was so much better than their old confession of faith, which it was to supersede.

"'I cannot now enter into the subject as fully as I wish,' said the minister, 'But if you will come to my house on the day before our next communion, I think I shall be able to convince you that we need something different from the Augsburg Confession, and that the proposed change will remove the difficulties under which we have hitherto labored.'

"On the day appointed, the elder repaired to the house of the minister, who labored hard to persuade him that the Augsburg Confession was an old relic, that had grown out of date, and that in this enlightened age and advanced state of theological science, we needed something more adapted to the spirit of the times to keep pace with the improvements going on all around us. The elder listened attentively to all this, and then asked, 'What *is* this new Platform you are speaking of, and how will it *work* in our congregation?' 'O!' replied the minister, 'It points out all the errors of the Confession, and it will have the good effect of relieving us from the imputation of holding to those errors. Besides, it will show us what parts of the Confession we reject, and what we believe.'" "'I consider the Augsburg Confession correct in all fundamental points of doctrine, said the elder—I always regarded it as scriptural and evangelical. Under this impression I was received into the Church. I believe so still. Such is the belief of the body of our Church. You were called to be our pastor with this belief, and if you are going to introduce a new Platform, and throw away the old Confession, I must frankly tell you, though it grieves me to say so, you had better throw up your call and leave us.' 'I did not know' said the minister, 'that you were such a strong old Lutheran. I am sorry now, that I said anything to you about the matter. But let us leave it where it is, and prepare to go to the communion to-morrow without having our minds disturbed by it; for on the day of judgment, it will not be asked of us whether we have stood on the *old* or the *new* Platform.'"

There is one aspect of this Platform subject which has never been fully considered, or I may say, even looked at. The General Synod requires its members—that is, the District Synods, to stand upon the unaltered Augsburg Confession of 1530, and hence those which adopt the Platform stand upon a different basis, and rule themselves out of the General Synod! This result is inevitable, and yet one or two Synods which have adopted it are still in connection with the General Body, and apparently very ardent friends of it. This inconsistency has been permitted to exist for years, but as the Platform is really defunct, and is rarely mentioned, and then only in derision, it has been thought best not to provoke a controversy upon that subject. It is not a pleasant thing to exhume a decomposed corpse.

From the Evangelical Review, Vol. VIII, 1857, April.

"The attempt to introduce a new confession of faith into the Lutheran Church of the United States, has already been noticed in this journal, in various ways. The author of the work to which we are now about to direct attention, has displayed great literary, as well as personal activity in this effort. From the appearance of his 'Popular Theology' (in 1830), to the book now before us, all his publications bearing upon the Lutheran Church have had this tendency, either directly or indirectly. The whole of this, however, culminated and took its most distinct and proper form in the '*Definite Platform*,' which, although endorsed by others, was properly his work, both in design and execution. The opposition with which the '*Platform*' met, not only from our theologians, but from the great mass of the Church, except by a few Western Synods, and a few of our Eastern ministers, trained under peculiar influences; this almost unanimous opposition to the 'Platform,' we say, necessitated not only reiterated apologies and defences of the Platform, by its authors and advocates, but even a very considerable modification of the Platform itself. The Platform as originally prepared, not only contemplated, but almost in so many words, proposed a division of the Lutheran Church, professing to be written in the spirit and in the interest of the General Synod of the Lutheran Church, and to be only a legitimate and consistent application of its principles, 'constructed in accordance with the principles of the General Synod,' says the title, ('perfectly consistent with the doctrinal test of the General Synod'— Preface to Definite Platform, page 2) or rather, the proper explanation and application of them (Platform page 4), it was here proposed (by resolution III) to ostracise all who would not unconditionally receive the Platform, and its interpretations and misrepresentations of the Augsburg Confession and other symbols of the Church; in a word, to divide the General Synod, by refusing fellowship to a certain part of its members. So prompt and decided was the rejection of this feature of the Platform, by the great mass of the Church, lay as well as clerical, wherever it was understood, that the leader in this movement found it necessary to disavow the project, and it was declared that this was not the design, or the proper sense of the article, and that it was only intended that ministers should receive all the doctrines set forth in the altered confession, but that their adherence to the unaltered Augsburg Confession should be no bar to Synodical-fellowship! And yet one of the prominent reasons urged for adopting the Platform was, that the Lutheran Church was rendered odious by being represented as holding certain doctrines of the Augsburg Confession, and other symbolical books, and that they wished to have no connection with so called 'Old-Lutherans.'

"To meet this, a revised edition of the Platform was soon published, with some verbal alterations and notes, which only rendered its inconsistencies the more glaring. Thus, for example, whilst it is said in the last paragraph of the 'Preface' that 'Part II of this Definite Synodical Platform is not a part of the pledge or doctrinal basis to be individually subscribed,' &c., the preceding paragraph tells us that, 'any District Synod connected with the General Synod may, with perfect consistency, adopt this Platform, *if the majority of her members approve of the Synodical disclaimer contained in part II,*' showing very clearly that the second part is essential to the whole plan. The clause which we have italicised, is also added to the revised edition, as the absurdity of expecting a District Synod which received the Augsburg Confession entire, to adopt the Platform, was palpable. But as this was not sufficient, in the work before us, we have not only another defence of the Platform, but a third edition, and a new metamorphosis of the 'Definite Platform,' which thus, after all, appears to be very indefinite, and to need more alterations than the old Augsburg Confession and the other '*former Symbolical Books*,' so much decried by this chameleon-like document. Here, in an appendix, we have a 'Definite Platform, being the doctrinal basis or creed * * * constructed in accordance with the principles of the General Synod.' To say nothing of the new Preface, which is, however, a very different thing from both its predecessors, we only observe that all traces of the ostracising and exscinding process, so zealously and definitely urged in the two editions preceding, are here carefully removed. Part second is omitted bodily, and the whole is razed down to a simple avowal of belief in certain articles, altered and unaltered, of the Augsburg Confession, together with the presentation of some motives for this alteration of the long established faith of the Church."

We cheerfully admit that this is some improvement so far as regards, not only the style and language of the article, though these are not yet rendered by any means faultless, but still more the matter, of which the less we have the better. And, in view of these facts, we should think that few will regard the omens of permanence in this new Confession as by any means promising.

" But our main object at this time is briefly to examine the new reasons here urged in defence of this somewhat fluctuating Platform, which seems to have been called '*definite*' upon the principle of the Roman etymologist, who says that '*lucus*' is derived '*a non lucendo.*'"

MODE OF WORSHIP—CULT—LITURGY, &c.

Until about the year 1830, the liturgical services at the ordinary worship in our Churches were exceedingly simple. A few of our old German ministers had a very brief altar service, which consisted usually of an invocation and the reading of the scripture lesson, but there was no general confession of sins, and the creed was not recited. The large majority of our ministers had nothing of this character, and practiced the mode of worship common among Presbyterians and Methodists. In baptisms and communions most of them read or recited the form prescribed in the liturgy, and, a few of them, also at marriages and funerals. But there was no uniform practice, and each man did as he liked. In many churches the choir sang a preliminary anthem, and that even was not considered by all ministers a part of the worship, for I have heard men after the choir had finished their performance rise and say, "Let us *begin* our worship by singing the ...... hymn."

Many of our men were anxious for a change, and maintained that the people should take a more active part in the service than merely listening to the preaching or joining in the singing, which many did not do. They held that our service was too bald and uninteresting,—that worship did not consist in merely going to church and hearing a sermon,—that the sanctuary itself should in its inner decorations present an appearance different from a plain school-house or a large room filled with benches and a pulpit. Thus, by degrees, our churches came to be carpeted, which was entirely unknown in most houses of worship fifty years ago, and even some of them twenty-five years ago, ventured upon stained glass for their windows, which was severely objected to by some who claimed to be "spiritually minded" above their fellow members. Gradually figures of saints and bible scenes and crosses were represented on the stained glass, and these gave offence to some, and soon crosses made of flowers were erected in the chancel on Christmas Sunday-school celebrations, and soon after crosses made of various materials were introduced as permanent fixtures. People soon get accustomed to these things, if they are brought in *by degrees.* I remember the time when flowers on the communion table or on the pulpit would have been considered popish, but now that ornament to a well ordered church is very common.

When chanting was introduced about thirty years ago, it was violently opposed by the Observer, which gave tone to the sentiment of a large number of ministers. When our little chapel at Lutherville was consecrated, the editor of the Observer and several other men of like mind were present, and when the choir chanted the Lord's Prayer, these men looked at each other with evidence of painful uneasiness, and I would not have been surprised if they had abruptly left the house, but those of them who yet survive have happily changed their minds.

The Sunday morning liturgy as it is now embodied in the General Synod's Book of Worship, was by slow degrees introduced, and it is not yet universal. It was proposed and adopted by the Synod of Maryland in 1864. Some of us at first *recited* the confession only—that was tolerated, and to diversify the service, we wrote other confessions and used them, coming back however to the old confession about once a month—and then we would occasionally *recite* the creed and the *Gloria Patri* as a part of the prayer, until the people became accustomed to it, and then every few weeks, we would *read* the whole as it is set forth in the book. The difficulty was to have the choir chant the *Gloria in Excelsis* without disturbing the pious equanimity of some of our saints, but they admired the music, and we took occassion to gratify them nearly every Sunday, until at length the whole service was introduced, and, now most of them like it. But a still greater difficulty was to be met, and that was the *response* from the congregation, but even this was overcome by their consideration of its manifest propriety, and especially by their being told that the people should exercise their right of participating in the service to a greater extent than merely hearing a sermon and feebly singing the hymns, and especially by hearing the Sunday school in an impressive responsive service. Many of our ministers have not yet been able to introduce the liturgy. I know several who recite it in part by mingling it with other portions of the service, and I know one whose church permits him to use it all *excepting the creed.*

The pity is that we do not all use the same prescribed liturgy. That of the General Synod differs to some extent from that of the General Council. That of the latter is more complete, although theirs, like ours, is far from being universally used. Very few country churches in either body use the Sunday liturgy, but it is by degrees working its wholesome way.

Many of our good people have the erroneous idea that *liturgik* and *symbolik* are necessarily concomitant. Facts disprove that assumption. Not a few of our General Synod men who are not suspected of strong confessional leanings are still ardent supporters of the liturgy, and the Missourians, who are distinguished for their symbolism, have little or no liturgy as we understand the word. Their altar service is more simple than that of most of our own unliturgical churches.

This whole subject was fully discussed in the Observer twenty-five years ago, and sometimes in a spirit not the most amiable. The argument of the opposition was for the most part grounded upon the assumption that the use of the liturgy and strong adherence to the confession were evidences of a decline of piety. This must be admitted, if by piety was meant the extravagance and fanaticism which were so popular at that day, and which presumptuously arrogated to itself an exclusive right to that sacred name.

THE USE OF THE CLERICAL GOWN

has not become general, and the most of those churches in which it is worn by the minister, introduced it with their origin. There are very few indeed which have adopted it as a new element, after they had been in existence for some years without it. It is an innovation which few would sanction, and it has never been considered of sufficient importance to awaken much interest in the Church.

There is no *established* mode of worship among us. There is no judicatory that would assume the right to do it. Every minister consults his own inclination or taste, but it is not every one whose taste is gratified. There are some who would like to introduce the full liturgy, but they are opposed; and there are a few who would like to abolish it, but they are not permitted to do so by the people. The habit of reciting the Lord's prayer at the end of the sermon is common, but I know of but one minister who has introduced the " new measure" of having the doxology sung at the beginning of the service instead of the close, which is the old and almost universal custom.

Under this head may properly be introduced the subject of

PRAYER-MEETINGS,

which are at present much more common than they were fifty years ago. It was seldom, at that time, that lay-men were called upon to pray in public, and yet it was not unknown. When I was a boy, Dr. J. G. Schmucker held a meeting of this kind every week, and I presume there were others, in which lay-men led in prayer.

The subject of

WOMEN PRAYING IN PROMISCUOUS ASSEMBLIES

was made a matter of discussion only about thirty years ago. The Observer contained numerous articles upon it, and even until as late as ten years ago some zealous advocate of the cause would occasionally insist upon being heard in its defence. But the subject has been laid aside, probably never to be revived again.

There was a singular practice in vogue in a few of the old time German Lutheran Churches, and this was that at the meeting preparatory to the Lord's Supper, (*Die Beicht*), the minister called upon some one in the congregation to confess the sins of the people, and as few of the men felt themselves competent to do it, it usually fell to the lot of some pious old woman. I have witnessed this scene myself in old Zion's Church, in Baltimore, when Dr. D. Kurtz was pastor. We all knelt, and this mother in Israel led us in a fervent acknowledgment of sin, and this was done in the Church when the minister was present, and upon his invitation. I thought it very singular and have never heard it repeated.

There are still many subjects which merit notice, and some of them to a greater extent than my space will allow, but I will briefly state them, and those who hereafter continue these Reminiscences may enlarge upon them.

THE METHOD OF PREACHING

has changed considerably within the past fifty years. *Reading* sermons in the pulpit was almost entirely unknown forty years ago. A few ministers who preached English read from the manuscript; but it was unknown among the German preachers. The practice was introduced with the establishment of our Theological Seminaries and by the influence of Puritan theology and example. I will not say that it was affectation and a weak imitation of distinguished preachers, but it has gradually gained popularity, and many congregations now patiently endure what would have been a heavy yoke to their fathers. Many of our young preachers now read their sermons, and, I presume, that the practice will grow, so that afterwhile among our young English ministers it will become almost universal. Some of our old-fashioned churches, however, will not suffer it, and insert in their calls for a pastor a condition that he is not to read his sermons.

Some of our men commit their discourses, which is a slavish business, of which they soon grow tired ; others do not even prepare skeletons but trust to their fluency of speech and strength of their lungs, but they soon degenerate to the baldest superficiality and unedifying repetition. I believe, however, that our conscientious men who do not read in the pulpit carefully write out an extended skeleton, and take it with them into the pulpit or commit it to memory.

This is not the place for a discussion of the relative merits of various styles of preaching, but I do not regard the growing prevalence of reading their sermons by our ministers as an evidence of their increasing usefulness, to say the least.

As to the *matter* of preaching of the present day, compared with the olden time, I would decidedly say that it is not as solid, nor as well elaborated, and of course, not as instructive as was that of the pious and orthodox Fathers. There is much good preaching at present ; more in quantity than there was fifty years ago, for there are ten times as many ministers; the preaching of the present day is, for the most part, more ornate, and highly polished, but it is not more methodical or systematically arranged, nor so fully illustrated by Scripture. Many of our modern sermons are mere homilies—essays—dissertations on a given theme, without unction or religious force, and very little Scripture.

SACRED OR CHURCH MUSIC

has made a decided progress in these last days. The German singing, years ago, was anything but artistically refined or scientific. In most places it was a slow, dragging, unmusical utterance of notes, led by a school-master or an elder without taste or knowledge, and followed by a congregation of whom every one seemed to try at out-singing his neighbor.

In the English Churches or in English singing there was a little improvement, but not much, especially where they had the

German leader or organist. In most of the country churches the hymns *were lined out*, which is destructive to all devotional and edifying singing. Many of the German churches had organs, but these were for the most part most shockingly played, and did nothing but contribute to the horrible din and confusion of the singing. There were few scientific performers in our Churches, and the instruments were generally of a very inferior character.

Everybody knows what church music is at present—the superior musical training of many of our young people—the employment of competent leaders and organists, the vast improvement in church instruments, and the introduction of a higher style of music, have contributed unspeakably to the advantage of that important part of public worship.

THE EMBELLISHMENT OF THE CHURCH WITH FLOWERS,

now so common, was altogether unknown fifty years ago. Whether it was owing to a lack of refined taste or dread of an approximation to popish worship, it would be hard to tell, but flowers were never seen in any of our Churches until about twenty years ago. I do not know where they were first introduced and whether the practice owes its origin to Sunday School celebrations or to the congregation. It is now firmly established, and will never be abolished. There is an evident propriety and beauty in it, and nobody objects to it.

THE INTRODUCTION OF STAINED GLASS

into the windows of our Churches was unknown until within twenty-five years ago. It was regarded as *popish*, and more so when it had any figure of the cross or of angels or saints upon it. Now it is very common, and scarcely any new church is built which has not stained glass, more or less ornamental, in its windows. It is no longer considered popish. I distinctly remember when its introduction first began, that the Observer, ever jealous of all other new measures except The Anxious Bench, warned the Churches against all such innovations, and represented it as confined exclusively to the Old School, High Church, Anti-Revival Lutherans. The Observer was horrified and trembled for the Ark of the Lord, when he heard that a new church, recently built by one of his most attached friends and advocates, had not only stained glass in every window, but that the glass bore figures of Christ and saints, and, above all, *seven crosses* in the various windows!

Inscriptions upon the walls and the Lord's Prayer and Ten Commandments were not so uncommon in the olden time, and I wish they were more frequently met with at present.

FRAMED PICTURES OR SCRIPTURE SCENES

upon the walls were only occasionally seen, and are not usual now, although appropriate and edifying. The old Church at York, before it was demolished to make room for the present building, had a Scripture scene painted upon every panel of the gallery, but they were horrible caricatures as productions of art. Some Churches, built within the last twenty-five years, have large Scripture scenes painted on the wall behind the pulpit, which have a very wholesome effect.

The Missouri Lutherans have crucifixes on the altar and lighted candles during the Sacrament.

There were

NO COAL FURNACES

below, nor large coal stoves in the body of the Church fifty years ago, and the result was that places of worship were imperfectly heated, which kept many old and weakly people away. I remember seeing, in my boyhood, some pious old ladies carrying a hot brick wrapped in a piece of carpet, to church, to put their feet on, and those who came from a distance would first put the brick on the hot stove to heat the brick thoroughly before using it. Nothing but wood consuming stoves were used, and they were usually placed as high from the floor as possible. The result was that the floor was never heated, and the feet of the people always cold. The sexton would regularly go round and stir the fire, whilst the minister was preaching, and make as much fuss as possible to show his earnestness in duty.

In the olden times it was the practice in many churches to gather the pennies in a *little black bag* attached to a long black pole. At the lower part of the bag there was a little bell, and you can imagine the noise when three or four were tinkling at the same time. It was said that the bells were intended to rouse up the sleepers. When the bag became heavy with pennies, another deacon would follow the collectors and empty the bag into his hat, and thus relieve the collector.

There was no

GAS LIGHT

in those days, but the Churches were imperfectly lighted with candles or odorous fish oil. Twice during the service the sexton would consider it his duty to top the candles, either hauling down the chandelier with a rope or stand upon a step-ladder. He would even ascend the pulpit, which was usually high, and perform the duty. Everybody of course looked at him, and when he would top one out, as was often the case, there was an audible expression of merriment or wonder, or it may be of sympathy, over the whole house.

The custom of the men *standing and holding their hats before their face* while offering a short prayer, when arriving at their places in Church, was very common fifty years ago, but is now almost abolished in the town Churches. You sometimes see it in the German Churches, but it is not common.

KNEELING AT THE COMMUNION

is a modern innovation among us. It was not practiced in the olden times. I do not know when it was introduced, but it was not simultaneous. It gradually came into fashion, and has not yet become universal. I do not think, although it may be so, that the practice came in with our advanced views of the Sacrament which have arisen within twenty years. It cannot be this entirely, for I know men who have very low conception of the real presence who also kneel at the Lord's Supper.

Not very long ago a country minister, in whose church the Synod was held, rebuked me for kneeling at the altar, in which all the ministers followed me, of course. He said his people had never seen it before. Some of them would be offended at it, whilst others would like it, and perhaps practice it themselves, and thus confusion would be created.

WAFERS

were generally, though perhaps not universally, used in the Sacrament by our fathers. I have not been able to find out when or why leavened bread was first used. I presume that few, or perhaps none of our English churches, established within forty years, use the wafer; neither do all the German. Some have bread and wafer on the same plate, and leave the communicants take their choice. This is the case in churches of which some members have been brought up in the Reformed Church. They prefer the bread and accommodation to their preposessions as practiced. This practice is severely condemned by orthodox Lutherans among us; not because there is leavened bread upon the plate, but because there are both wafer *and* bread. It seems to them to be a sort of compromise between Zwinglianism and Lutheranism, which is not just; they are satisfied with either one or the other, for the kind of bread is nothing essential, and the true Lutheran can discern the Lord's Body in either, but for a Lutheran pastor to have both is regarded as a dangerous indifference to the true doctrine, and something more than a sanction of the Zwinglian error.

This has never been a subject of discussion in the Churches of the General Synod. Ordinary bread, for the most part, has been used ever since the establishment of English churches. There may be a few exceptions, but I am not aware of them, but I am certain that bread and wafers were never used at the same time, giving the privilege to the communicant to take which he preferred. The first time I ever saw this practiced, was in the German Lutheran Church in Baltimore, at that time served by the Rev. Mr. Haesbaert. The design was to accommodate those members, of which there were many, who had been reared in the German Reformed Church, and who had prejudices against the use of the wafer. This practice was abolished by Mr. Haesbaert's successor, who retained the wafer alone.

I am not sure whether all the old German Churches of Pennsylvania, especially in the country, use the wafer exclusively, but it is the practice of some, at least, of the English Churches belonging to the General Council, but none of them regard it as essential to the Sacrament. They consider fermented bread as equally appropriate.

At the meeting of the Synod of Pennsylvania, in 1877, it was discovered that some of the ministers still used both the bread and wafer at the Sacrament, in accommodation to the views of their German Reformed neighbors, who usually communed with them. The subject was brought up and referred to a committee, who present it in such a plain, liberal and evangelical spirit, that I have inserted it below. In the discussion which ensued, some of the country ministers boldly took the ground that it was perfectly proper to use the two kinds of bread, out of regard to the weakness, prejudice, or scruples of the Reformed. They thought they were doing less harm, by practicing this accommodation, than by pertinaciously retaining the wafer, exclusively, and thus driving them from the Lord's Supper. The committee takes a different and more correct view.

Some persons look upon this as a very unimportant question, and not worthy serious consideration, but I beg all such to read the following report carefully. The question is not, Shall we use bread or wafer? (that is, unfermented bread). That is plain enough—one or the other, and it matters not which, but the question is, Shall both be placed, at the same time, upon the plate, that the communicant may have the privilege of choosing?

This presupposes the fact, however, that the administrator hands the plate around without touching the bread himself, and in this case, the communicant might choose, but suppose that the minister gives the element with his own hand, as is usually done, how could he discriminate? But read the report.

REPORT OF THE COMMITTEE ON THE QUESTION IN REGARD TO THE BREAD IN THE COMMUNION.

The committee appointed to consider the question in regard to the simultaneous use of two kinds of bread at the Communion, believing that the judgment of the Ministerium would be more useful, if accompanied by a statement of the principles on which it rests, would submit the following:

1. In the Lord's Supper, bread is one of the divinely ordained elements, which cannot be omitted, and for which nothing can be lawfully substituted; but it is a matter of indifference, fully committed to the liberty of the Church, of what kind this bread shall be. Any real bread, whether in the form of wafers or in some other form, may be employed.

2. The existing rite, in things indifferent, if all other things are equal, should have the preference, as this tends to peace and order in the Church.

Augs. Conf., Art. xv.

3. The distribution of bread in two forms at the same Communion, is an offence against the law of order and of Christian charity, for these and other reasons:

i. There is neither necessity, sufficient reason nor historical warrant for more than one kind of bread at the Supper. Of this, beginning with our Lord's Institution itself, to this hour, there has been a general recognition.

ii. The use of a second kind of bread might be used to justify the introduction of the unfermented juice of the grape for those who have scruples about any use of wine in its ordinary forms.

iii. It would either make separate tables of communicants,

classified according to the kind of bread they receive, or would destroy the possibility of the ministers making an individual distribution of the bread, giving it to each communicant, in accordance with the example of our Lord himself, and of the universal usage of our Church, and of Christendom, at large, throughout all ages.

iv. It would suggest scruples of conscience where there ought to be none, would give life and distinctness to differences unworthy of the prominence thus given them, would disturb and divide the attention of communicants at the very moment when it should be permanently fixed upon the Lord of the Supper, and thus for the discerning of His precious body would be substituted a discerning of the bread. The outward element, instead of being an aid of faith, would become a disturber of it.

v. Those who claim that a second form of bread should be used, because they prefer it, do so on one of two untenable grounds. If they say it is a *concession*, which should be made on the ground of their weakness, they desire not that the Church should make them strong by resisting their weakness, but should make them weaker by yielding to it, and should further weaken and give offence to her trusting children at the urgency of those who choose her altars as the place at which to show their doubts as to her being a safe guide. If they say it is a right, which they claim, because they have the true view in the case, they are judging and condemning the Church and their fellow communicants at the table of the Lord. Thus two classes of communicants are created, a spirit of disputation and of obstinate scrupulosity is aroused, and the Sacrament of love and unity is perverted into a fomenter of dissension and faction.

vi. The use of bread in the form of wafers is a mark of the Lutheran Church only when it is maintained in her Christian liberty, as a part of free preference for established usage over against all attempts at civil or moral coercion or false attempts to make a matter of conscience of that which our Lord has left as a matter of freedom. Our Church therefore neither condemns the free use of any form of bread which her own congregations or any part of the Christian world may prefer, provided that use be free from false doctrine, and from all violation of the law of good order and Christian charity.

vii. Where mistaken views on this subject have prevailed, it is the duty of pastors, sustained by the sympathy and coöperation of their faithful officers and members, in all gentleness and wisdom to assert and teach the truth to those who are in error, but to be unyielding in their refusal to conform to the unsound doctrine.

C. P. KRAUTH,
A. SPAETH,
Committee.

The following incident, closely connected with the preceding, is related of Rev. Mr. Wyneken, when he took charge of the German Church in Baltimore, previously served by the Rev. Mr. Haesbaert:

On the Sunday immediately following his installation, the Lord's Supper was to be celebrated. The preparation of the altar had been intrusted to the sexton. Wyneken's consternation may be more readily imagined than described, when, in the confessional service, he appeared before the sacramental table and instantly perceived, that in this place the Holy Supper had assuredly never yet been administered after the manner of the truly Lutheran Church! There was the wine in a huge earthen jug, and on the plate were *wafers and bread side by side.* What was to be done?

He immediately called the deacons into the sacristy and explained to them, that the congregation is not Lutheran at all; that in extending a call to him he had been deceived; that he could not distribute the sacrament! The good people were filled with surprise and confusion, declared that they had not been aware that they were not purely Lutheran, and requested him to act in the case in accord with his conscience as a Lutheran Pastor. They thereupon urgently entreated him to distribute the Sacrament once more in the manner to which the people had hitherto been accustomed, for the purpose of avoiding the very great dissatisfaction that would otherwise arise among the communicants who were present.

Under existing circumstances Wyneken likewise regarded this as the better course, and acted accordingly. After the sermon, however, he requested the congregation to remain in the church for a short time after the close of the service. And now he declared in the presence of the people, *that he had not found them to be a Lutheran, but much more a unionistic congregation, and that therefore the best course for them to pursue would probably be, to* dismiss him immediately; that, in case he should remain among them, he would certainly occasion many disturbances and dissatisfactions in the midst of such a mixed multitude.

The congregation, however, would not consent to his going away, but was decided in its desire that he should remain. "Well, then," said Wyneken, "I will begin on next Sunday to take both the Lutheran and Heidelberg Catechisms with me into the pulpit, and will read from and explain both; then each one will have the opportunity of knowing and judging for himself as to which side has and confesses the complete truth of the divine word!"

This, accordingly, was the course that Wyneken subsequently pursued. He explained from both catechisms the distinction between the Lutheran and Reformed doctrines; he rebuked the practice hitherto observed in administering the Lord's Supper, and showed from the Scriptures, that Reformed and Lutherans cannot possibly be members of one and the same congregation, inasmuch as every congregation that desires to act with true Christian candor and uprightness cannot adopt and adhere to more than one confession.

This course resulted in a fearful storm in the congregation. The Reformed maintained that they had been betrayed, and the greater number of them did not even have the forbearance patiently to hear Wyneken's explanations; and among the Lutherans also, they found erring friends who criticised the course of the new Pastor, and desired to have the former state of affairs retained. Not in the congregational meetings only, but also on the streets and in the homes of the people, lively and often bitter disputations took place. Many children of Reformed parents had become Lutherans; others were intermarried with Lutherans; accordingly daughters stood opposed to their mothers and husbands to their wives. It was a time of visitation; but the truth gained the victory. The Reformed left the congregation (on a single Sunday more than eighty names were announced from the pulpit of persons who severed their connection with the congregation) and built a German Reformed Church on Calvert street. It was self-evident that they regarded Wyneken as their enemy, and quite a length of time elapsed before the excitement that had arisen subsided.

NAMING CHURCHES.

It is only of late years that many of our new churches are named after some saint, or that some other distinctive title is given them. At the present time we have all the apostles and evangelists, and sometimes even duplicated, for there are two Lutheran St. Marks and St. Pauls in Baltimore. Such designations as The Church of the Reformation and Church of the Holy Communion, which are the names of two of our city Churches, were almost unknown in the olden times. Many of our country Churches are called after a family name, such as Hofacker's, Quigal's, Wolf's, &c., &c., probably, because the ground was given by such family. Some are known from the district or township in which they are located, as Tulpehocken Church, &c. Some Churches in the same city are designated numerically, as the First English Lutheran Church, the Second, the Third, as is the case with three of the Churches in Baltimore. Those subsequently built are distinguished by the names of saints. This practice is becoming very common, and the reason would be an interesting subject of inquiry.

THE BURIAL OF NON-MEMBERS OF THE CHURCH, OF SUICIDES, &C.

I have never heard that any of our ministers have refused to perform the funeral service at the burial of the worst class of sinners, or that they have refused to attend a funeral as Christian ministers, because a rationalist or heretic was to officiate. I have heard of one man who would not take part in a funeral service with a Unitarian minister, because, he said, his presence would seem to sanction the validity of the Unitarian's claims as a Christian clergyman. We have all heard that some Episcopal ministers have declined to officiate at the funerals of deceased actors, whilst others are not so scrupulous, and we know that the Church of Rome forbids her priests to perform such service, but there are very few ministers of any denomination who positively refuse to attend the funeral of any class of men who die unconnected with the Church. I presume most of them perform such functions with the hope of instructing and comforting bereaved relatives, and, especially, of benefitting those at the funeral by plain gospel preaching, which many of them seldom hear. Besides, it has the appearance of heartlessness to refuse Christian services on such occasions. But I think that a difference should be made between Christian *service* and Christian *burial*. I may preach and pray at the funeral, but I may or may not recite the liturgy for the dead over a deceased drunkard, gambler, suicide or other wicked man.

I once buried a man out of a low tavern, who had been killed in a street broil. I was surrounded by a crowd of his companions, who seldom or never heard the gospel. I preached to them in a side room, but I did not pronounce the "dust to dust," nor commit to the grave our "deceased brother," nor did I express any hope of a "glorious resurrection at the last day," and yet, by all this, I did not intend to determine the future destiny of the man. I only meant that I could not give him what we call *Christian burial*.

The Synod of Pennsylvania, at its meeting in 1877, had a committee on this subject, who presented the following report. I insert it here, because it is really a valuable and interesting document, which very few of my readers would ever see otherwise:

THESES ON BURIAL OF SUICIDES.

1. Church burial is that interment of the dead, at which a regularly ordained minister of the Church officiates, the changing or entire omission of individual parts of the usual burial service creating no difference.

2. By Christian burial, which, expressive of love and honor to the dead, is granted to the dead and not to the living, the Church indicates: that the deceased was connected with her in life, and that she recognizes him as one belonging to her.

3. Inasmuch as Christian burial is the public recognition on the part of the Church of the fact, that the deceased during life, or at least at the time of death, belonged to the Church and was by her recognized as a member; therefore the Church cannot grant Christian burial to such deceased persons, who during their lifetime have never according to the recognized order confessed themselves as belonging to her, or have publicly and designedly separated from her, or on account of their unbelief or open sinfulness have been excluded, and have departed from this life in a state of impenitence.

4. The granting or refusal of Christian burial can evidently take place only in the name of the Church and in accordance

with the principles publicly recognized by her; therefore, the decision thereof may not depend upon the subjective opinion of a pastor or even of a congregation, but must be done according to the principles recognized by the Church.

5. The Church, on her part, in granting or refusing Christian burial, does not express an opinion as to the salvation or damnation of the dead, but she simply testifies "that the deceased was or was not a member of her fold."

The Church may not express a hope for the salvation of any one in death for whom she does not express this hope whilst he is living.

6. Aside from official participation in the burial of a person, not belonging to the Church during life, the pastor can, and shall, especially when requested by his family or relatives, render them every service of love and mercy; e. g. preach the Word of God to them, comfort them, pray with them, etc. But, in connection with such service, even the appearance must be avoided, as if such person, not belonging to the Church, had now received a Christian funeral.

After these general principles and instructions concerning Church burial, there now follow those which have special reference to the deportment of the Church in cases of suicide on the part of Church members.

1. Since the Church, in early times, refused her burial, without distinction, to every suicide, even if he was by her regarded as a member until death, the Church of the present day can, at least, not take an entirely opposite course, by granting Christian burial, especially in its more solemn form, to all suicides, without distinction.

2. According to the more recent decision of the Church, burial in its less solemn form may be granted to those who have committed suicide in a state of irresponsibility (Unzurechnungsfæhigkeit) not caused by guilt of their own.

NOTE.—More solemn burial consists in being held at the usual time with all the usual ceremonies; less solemn burial is distinguished by the intentional omission of certain of these ceremonies, or by its taking place at an unusual time.

3. Suicides who put an end to their own lives in order to avoid the expected punishment of crimes which they have committed; those who end their lives during an attack of delirium-tremens;

gamblers, who end their lives when they have lost heavily; debauchees, spendthrifts, misers, etc., who in consequence of their vices are plunged into despair, and commit self-murder; such persons the Church shall under no circumstances bury.

4. The Church cannot readily draw a certain line of demarcation between cases of irresponsibility—not caused by personal guilt, or partially so caused—particularly when the positive proofs of open unbelief, of wicked contempt of the Word of God and the Sacraments, are wanting. In such cases the less solemn form of burial may be allowed.

5. No pastor, belonging to our Synod, shall be allowed to bury a suicide who was connected with another denomination, which, according to its order, refused him Christian burial; no matter from what causes or in what mental condition the deed was committed.

6. In the case of suicide on the part of a member of a congregation, the minister, together with the elders and deacons of the congregation, are to decide whether, according to the above principles of the Church, Christian burial in its less solemn form shall be granted or refused.

PRESENTS TO MINISTERS AND DONATION PARTIES—PAYING FOR PASTORAL SERVICES.

From the earliest times many of our American born Lutherans have had the laudable habit of sending gifts of various value to their ministers. They usually consisted of provision for man and beast, fuel and sometimes clothing; money very rarely. Indeed, were it not for these extra gifts, many of our men would find it hard to get along. Some men are very handsomely remembered; others, slenderly. It is unfortunate for a minister to have the reputation of being well off in this world's goods; people are apt to think that he does not need presents, or would not accept them, forgetting that such a man would not value a gift according to its worth in money, but as an evidence of their esteem for their pastor; but, unhappily, they do not take such a refined view of the subject. I know a successful minister of a large city church who in many years did not receive a hundred dollars worth of presents, merely because his people thought that he did not stand in need of them, which might have been true, but still, I am sure, he would have appreciated the smallest donation as a demonstration of their regard for him.

Every country pastor expects such demonstrations, and many are not disappointed. At certain seasons of the year, provisions rush in at a superfluous rate. I know one man who had enough to open a meat and sausage store if he had wanted to; indeed, he did sell the superabundance, which was fair enough. I have heard of one old man in Pennsylvania who was never satisfied with the gifts he received. The young men of his church determined to stop his complainings and send him a sausage some yards in length. He gloated over it triumphantly, and as he transferred it from the tub in which it was sent to his own, he would exclaim, at every turn, "beautiful!—grand!—glorious!—enough for all winter!" and when he got to the end of the serpentine convolution, he muttered, "Yes, all nice enough, only if *there had been more of it!!*"

Some of our men are occasionally imposed upon. I have seen more than a dozen people stop at the parsonage and dine there on Sunday after church in the country. This would be all nice enough if they had sent in the provision on Saturday, but this was not often the case, and the parson's larder suffered, and the patience of the poor parson's wife was sorely tried.

I have heard of the following case; a minister bought a turkey of a parishioner for a dollar; the said parishioner knew that the turkey was to be on the table next Sunday, and he invited himself, wife and five children to dinner! he got his price for the bird and helped to eat it besides!

DONATION PARTIES.

The *Donation Parties* of which we see so much in the Observer, have not become a fixed institution as far South as Maryland. Occasionally, we hear of one, but they are not common. I am told that they occasion much bother to the minister's wives and that in many instances, nearly as much is consumed by the crowd as is brought. But still, it is a social meeting, at which the young folks have a gay time, and the old ones renew their youth.

I know some people who are mischievous enough to smile suspiciously at some luminous expression of thanks in the Observer to a "generous congregation for their distinguished liberality" to their minister, when it is well known that there are not three subscribers to the Observer in the parish! These mischievous people strongly suspect that the design of said thanks " was to let other people know how popular the aforesaid minister is!" The world is full of suspicious people!

In old times it was an almost universal custom, which in many places, is happily not yet abolished, to compensate the minister for baptisms and funerals, as well as marriages. In some congregations, at present, many parishioners give him nothing for the two former. Why the good old custom has been abolished I do not know: perhaps it is the increased subscription to the minister's salary, but that does not apply to all cases, for unfortunately those who have not added to their pew rent or subscription, follow the bad example of those who have and do not pay the parson for those special services.

Marriage fees, as they are erroneously called, are supposed to be universal, but I could fill pages with interesting, and in some cases, ludicrous incidents, showing the contrary. Every minister has more than one story to tell of forgetfulness, neglect, and even downright deception in this matter.

CRAPE AT FUNERALS

is not so common as it was fifty years ago. Then every man who attended the funeral had his hat bandaged with a long streamer, and gloves were given to the pall-bearers, but the women were overlooked, and why, it is hard to say. I remember when white scarfs were given to the clergy, and a cheap white stuff was tied round the hats of the carriage drivers at funerals in Baltimore. This latter custom has been long since abolished. Black crape is still common, and gloves for the minister, but it is a useless expense, and for the last twenty years I have refused them. It gave offence at first, but after an explanation, the people were satisfied. I had heard so often from undertakers and store keepers that a certain class of people in imitation of those socially and pecuniarily above them, and with the vain idea of showing respect to their dead, had gone into debt for coffin and funeral carriages and hearse and crape and gloves, far beyond their ability to pay, that I resolved not to countenance such unwarrantable extravagance and have ever since refused to accept crape from rich or poor.

WHY WE LOSE SOME MEMBERS.

Our Church in this country during her transition state has lost a large number of members, and even at the present time pastors are sometimes heard complaining of the secession of some of their flock. I do not mean to intimate that other denominations have no reason to mourn over the same misfortune, or that they all gain by secessions from us alone. On the contrary, every one of them has nurtured children for other families, and dismissals from one to the other is a common event. But we, as a people, have probably had more separatists from our communion than most others, for reasons that shall presently be given. Whilst it is true that we have lost many, yet we have also gained; for every member of our Churches with an English name is a positive gain either from some other denomination, or from families not *originally* connected with us. These names are numerous, so that the loss and gain probably counterbalance each other. This would be an interesting subject for inquiry, which, however, could only be prosecuted within a limited district and time; but if all the ministers of a Conference or Synod would perseveringly conduct the investigation, interesting results would be reached. I am sure that in some congregations the gains from non-German families and other churches are greater than our losses, whilst in others the converse would be the case.

The principal reasons that have led some people to leave us are:

1. *There was no Lutheran Church in the place where they settled.* This applies particularly to new settlements in the West, or places elsewhere founded by people of other denominations. Some of our people settle there, and finding no Lutheran Church, and seeing no speedy prospect of having one, they attach themselves to other denominations. Some hesitate a long time, in hope of relief sooner or later; but others, not so firm or so patient, and es-

pecially when courted and flattered by strangers, sever their original church connections and are lost to our communion. Such people are found in every city and town in the West, and some also in the East, where there are Lutheran churches, but who reside at too great a distance from the Church for a Sunday walk. Whilst the introduction of street cars removes the objection to some extent, still the expense of a whole family riding to church, even once on a Sunday, is a considerable item, especially to poorer men.

2. *Marrying persons of other churches* is also a source of loss to some degree, though it may also be said it is a source of gain—but we are speaking only of the former at present. It is sometimes said that the husband should follow the wife, but it is not laid down as a law, and even if it were, it is not universally obeyed; but there is no doubt of the fact, that many a young Lutheran gentleman and Lutheran lady, marrying "out of the church," has followed "the party of the other part," and left their church home. In some cases they alternate, and go to one church in the morning or one whole Sunday, and the next to the church of the other party; but even this mutual accommodation loosens the ties, and in frequent instances it does not require much to sever them altogether.

When a Lutheran young man marries a Romish lady, he may be counted among the "lost" from the day of the marriage; and when a Lutheran lady marries a Romish young man, her name might as well be stricken from the roll, for it will not be long before she is wheedled away by bribery, intimidation, threats, or flattery.

3. *Prospect of professional gain or business advantage* has led some of our young men away. I once met a schoolmate of mine in a western city, who was a physician, and who, besides, kept a large drug store. He had been reared strictly to the church in his native place, but was not deeply rooted in principle. He went West, and although there was an English Lutheran church in the city, yet he joined the Presbyterians, and frankly told me that the only reason was, that he could secure more practice and sell more goods among that people, and he went where his worldly interests lay. This case will illustrate many others, and I presume every minister could recite many similar ones.

Under this head may be mentioned an analogous motive; for instance, a young man *has an eye to an advantageous matrimonial alliance*, and finds the object of his amatory pursuit snugly domiciliated in another church, in which *papa* may be a ruling elder, or at least an influential, and most probably a wealthy member, and *mamma* the leader of the sewing and missionary society. It is so pleasing to them to gain a new convert, and the daughter would be so much gratified, that the poor love-smitten young Lutheran soon finds it so convenient to ask his pastor for a letter of dismissal!

4. Some simple people expect to *secure higher social position* by joining a more fashionable and influential church. Nobody will deny that in many places the Episcopalians and Presbyterians have generally the most refined and cultivated people, and the Methodists in some instances have the advantage in numbers and popularity. Some of our people, who have been successful in business, and become ambitious of display, look for a wider field for family demonstration; and abandoning their plain Lutheran associates, unite with those of a higher rank in society. This is most frequently the case in Lutheran families which have ambitious daughters, who seek for more fashionable company than they find in their own church. They expect, of course, to be visited and caressed by the ladies and young gentlemen of the church which they join, and to be invited to the grand parties and other social demonstrations, and thus to begin a new and exciting career of fashionable life. But some of them are destined to disappointment. I could tell some interesting cases of mortified pride and painful disappointment. The recusant families were not visited nor caressed nor invited by the *haut ton* of the church which they joined, and rose no higher in the social scale than they maintained in their old home. No doubt, some do improve their manners, if not their morals—some do gain a position which they would not have secured at home; but this is not owing to their merits, but to circumstances, and hence not laudable. Improvement in piety does not enter into the question. They were probably furnished with more wholesome spiritual food at home, but it was not served in silver dishes, and the caterers were not dressed in lawn and silk.

5. There are some who leave us *because their piety is so far in advance of ours*, that they can find no religious enjoyment among their old fellow-members. They love strong religious excitement and high-wrought emotion, which they do not find among us, and of which they themselves soon weary in their new positions. They are not satisfied with the nourishing Gospel Manna on our

table, and go elsewhere to feed on the more stimulating but less substantial food of strangers. Some of them soon find that they do not grow in spiritual strength, as they expected, and get homesick and return; whilst some others, ashamed of their apostacy, and having lost all zest for purely emotional religion, stray away into the camp of the Philistines.

6. I have known some to leave us because, as they maintained, *they were not appreciated by* the Lutherans. As far as concerns some ministers who have left us for this alleged reason, I have treated the subject, under "Ministers who have left us," elsewhere; but I now speak of private members particularly. "Not being appreciated," simply means that these people, regarding themselves so far ahead of others in piety, intelligence and general worth, that the distinguished consideration to which they were entitled not being awarded to them, they retired in disgust, and sought and sometimes secured church offices and influence elsewhere.

A man left my church, years ago, because I would not allow him to exhort and conduct the private meetings as often as he thought he should. He was ignorant, though well-meaning; ungrammatical in his language, and ludicrously imperfect in his pronunciation of Scripture names. He excited merriment in some, pity in others, and dissatisfaction in all. He joined the German Methodists, and became a preacher among them.

But there are others of a higher rank who fancy they are overlooked in the church, and wonder that other people do not think as much of them as they do themselves; there are some who find that they are behind most of their fellow-members in intelligence and influence, and they naturally drift among those of their own level, and "forsake us." Some of them have their ambitious longings gratified by being elected to subordinate offices; others are grievously disappointed, and after awhile are seen lingering about the old church door of a fine Sunday morning, and with subdued emotion, say, as one did to me not long ago, "I find my old friends truer than my new ones, and I'll come home again." Thus many would say, if they were not ashamed.

7. One of the principal causes of loss some years ago was *the services in German exclusively*. Young people, not understanding the German well enough to be profited by the preaching, of course left the church; and superadded to this was their association

with other English-speaking young people, with whom they would naturally prefer going to church. This cause does not operate so influentially at the present time as in the past, for English Lutheran Churches are established; but still there are large cities, of which more than a dozen might be named, in which German Lutherans abound, but where there is no English Lutheran Church. In such places, the well-disposed German young persons, who prefer English services, join other denominations.

These are the chief causes of our losses; probably there are a few others.

There is one aspect of this subject which is particularly unpleasant. Why is it that the children of some of our ministers forsake the Church, even, as in some cases, during the lifetime of their fathers? Most probably one or the other of the above causes may be assigned in relation to those sons of our ministers who have not adopted their father's profession; but I know several of our men whose sons are in the ministry of other churches! One of them I know tried to dissuade his son from that step, and another I know rather encouraged his son, because the father himself was not very successful in our ministry, and never had a very desirable place. He did not wish to subject his son to the same mortifying experience, and advised him to seek his bread elsewhere; but it is doubtful whether he has succeeded better than if he had staid at home.

I am sure that some of the daughters, at least, have gained nothing by their "departure." One, whose father is deceased, and who is now an Episcopalian, applied to me some time ago for my influence in securing for her a position as a teacher in a Lutheran school! And when I mildly asked her why her *new* friends did not take better care of her, she blushed!

There is still another subject closely connected with this which must not be overlooked. Why is it that comparatively so few young foreign Germans, who speak English better than their native language, join our English Lutheran Churches, even where they have the opportunity? This question has been extensively discussed in some of our church papers. Various reasons have been assigned, such, for instance, as their lack of religious interest; but this is not universal, and hence not the only or even a very good reason. Others have said it is owing to an indisposition to any changes of importance natural to the German, which simply means German obstinacy. Some account for it on the ground of their love of home; but this cannot be the reason because thousands of them do not stay at home, but wander away, not to other churches, but further still from home. Some have said that the young Germans are so backward and modest, and many of them are poor, that they would not feel comfortable among Americans. This cannot be true, because many of them associate with young American people. I heard a German minister say that in most of our English churches genuine old Lutheranism is not preached, and that is the reason why young Germans do not come to our churches! This is not true, for various reasons. First, the good old faith *is* preached in our English churches. Here in Baltimore, for example, there is an old Lutheran English Church "of the straitest sect," served by a minister of irreproachable character, and on terms of close fraternal relationship with some of the German ministers, and yet he receives very few young persons from the German churches. There are similar instances in other cities. And, secondly, the young Germans are not so thoroughly indoctrinated in old Lutheranism as to be a barrier to their connnection with an English church, if they desired it. Another one accounted for it on the ground that our English service was too bald, and that our English ministers did not wear the clerical gown. Neither of these is true; for it is a fact that in most of our English churches the liturgical service is longer, and the singing is better than in German churches, and some of our ministers do wear the gown: and yet even they do not admit more of this class than others.

After spending considerable reflection upon this subject, I have come to the conclusion that the *fault principally lies* with the German ministers themselves, who discourage their Anglicized young people from joining the English Lutheran Churches. Some of these ministers are candid enough to acknowledge it. I boldly charge some of them with a more grievous offence than that; some of them do not even advise their young people, who are leaving the German churches, to prefer an English Lutheran church above any other communion!

Dr. Bachman, in an anniversary sermon preached in 1858, in which he gives a sketch of the history of the church in the South, among other things, says of the earlier times: "Our ministers, with very few exceptions, performed service exclusively in the

German language. This was a great error, inasmuch as it excluded from the church the descendants of Lutherans, who had, by education and association, adopted the language of the country. "Our doctrines were not objectionable to them, but they could not understand the language in which they were promulgated. Thus the progress of the Church was greatly retarded in consequence of the bigoted attachment of our ancestors, and *especially their clergy*, to a foreign language. Since the introduction of the English language into our ministrations the church has made rapid progress."*

Many other men would bear the same testimony, and among them even some German ministers.

From the Lutheran Observer.

WHY DO SO FEW OF OUR FOREIGN GERMANS JOIN OUR ENGLISH CHURCHES?

This question was discussed to some extent a few years ago, but by no means exhausted. Though its agitation now may elicit some facts, and lead to results, far from being pleasant to some worthy brethren, yet, it is high time to bring it before the public mind and sift it thoroughly, without regard to private feeling or individual prejudice. No man who loves truth will shrink from investigation, however much the consequence may affect his present interests or previous opinions. With all proper respect, then, for the professions and religious character of many of our German clergy, I will proceed calmly and truthfully to discuss this question.

No one will deny the *fact* that many, very many, of our German young people, who understand English as well as their native tongue, do not join our English churches, *although they have left their own*. Occasionally a few are rescued, but the vast majority wander away from their maternal fold and are lost to the Lutheran church. I would not have any respect for the intelligence or the candor of any man who would deny this well established *fact*.

It is not, however, true that all our Anglicized young Germans, or old ones either, leave their own church, on account of the language; very far from it. Mingle with almost any German congregation as it issues out of church on a fine Sunday morning, and you will hear many of them speaking English before they

*Bernheim's German Settlement, p. 420.

have descended the church steps, and yet they remain with the German church. Neither is it true, that all our Anglicized, and even Americanized old Germans, join the English churches in their vicinity. This fact is apparent in every place where there is an English branch of the old German congregation. We observe in the latter, not a few old people, who do not speak German in their families, and very little in their business, who still adhere with unyielding pertinacity to "the old church," in which they have worshipped for years, which they have helped to build, and in the graveyard of which their deceased children lie buried. I respect their feelings, and will not blame their action. They say, "let our children go to the English church, as for us, we will stay with the old hive, and send out another swarm after a while."

Neither is it true that none of our young Germans attach themselves to our English churches. Many of our pastors admit a few every year, and in many instances they make the most consistent and useful members of the flock. I, myself, belong to a congregation in which, at nearly every communion, a few of this class are received, but after all, the number is comparatively small.

Neither is it true that many of this class join other denominations. Now and then, we hear of an instance, but it is not often. Other denominations have succeeded much better in gathering in German Germans, than English speaking Germans, as every body knows. We hear of Methodist, Episcopalian, Presbyterian and even Baptist *German* churches, but nobody can tell us of any congregation of these sects composed of Anglicized foreigners. I admit there is a slight mixture of this German element in some of their churches, but it is not enough to affect the complexion or appearance of the purely American mass. I think it would not be hard to prove that more of our American Lutheran people join those churches than Anglicized German.

But the question at the head of my paper still remains to be answered. I will give you my solution of it, and allow me to say:

I. The reason is *not* because these Anglicized Germans would not hear in our churches the same doctrines which they have heard in their own. We all hold the same essential system, and very few Germans are so wedded to any distinctive phase of orthodox Lutheranism as to make it an objection to their joining any Lutheran church. The extreme "Missourian" might, but I know a few, even of them, who are now among the best members of an American Lutheran church, and, strange to say, they are native Americans and not at all familiar with German.

II. The reason is *not* that they would not find in our English churches an appropriate and impressive liturgy. I have heard this reason given by a worthy German minister, but I am satisfied there is no force in it whatever, *for most of our city English churches have a more extensive altar service than the Germans have.* There is no doubt of this, and hence the reason for not joining us on this ground is futile. Besides this, every body knows that nearly every Province in Germany has a different altar service, which is generally more simple and not near so impressive as ours. This, then, cannot be the reason.

III. The reason is *not* that our English ministers, generally, do not wear the gown.

It is said by some, that the association of minister and gown in a German's mind, is so close and strong, that he can scarcely recognize the man as a minister without his clerical robe in the pulpit. Now, admitting the force of this prejudice, and I can easily conceive of its existence, and could account for it on very natural grounds, yet it will not explain the difficulty, for in two of our largest cities most of our ministers do wear the gown, and do they receive into their churches more of this class of Germans than those who do not wear that very appropriate clerical vestment? Do St. John's, St. Mark's, St. Stephen's, and St. Michael's in a certain city, receive more than St. Matthew's, St. Andrew's, and the Messiah? Even if it be the case, yet, I am satisfied that the gown, however becoming as a distinctive ministerial uniform, is not the prevailing reason.

IV. The reason is *not* because our congregational music, and our church comforts are not equal to those of the Germans. The reverse is the fact. We do not sing quite so loud, but our music is equally artistic and more impressive and refined, and our pew cushions are usually a little softer than theirs. These things they will themselves admit.

I have thus far discussed what may be called the *negative* side of this question, and showed what were *not* the reasons for the course of which we complain. Let me now treat it *affirmatively*, and exhibit directly why it is that so few of this class of persons continue their connection with us as a church.

In the place where my observations are most direct, and in which I cannot be deceived, about four hundred young persons were confirmed in the German churches at Easter, one year ago, and I venture to assert, that not more than one hundred and fifty of them all have been at the communion since, or even go to church.

This may be regarded as a bold venture, but I make it and challenge a refutation! Where are the remaining two hundred and fifty? Some may have moved to other places—a few may have married out of the church (although none of the boys and very few of the girls are old enough for that condition of life),—a few may be at service in non-Lutheran families and are cared for by them—a few may have died—a few, very few, may have joined other churches;—a few, *very few* have joined English churches;—but allowing all this, and more too, at least two hundred are not accounted for. Where are they? Evidently not in the German churches, nor in our English Luthern churches, and *why?* That is now the question.

I. The first reason I give is, that these young people have been but superficially taught religious doctrine and duty, or that they are for the most part too young fully to comprehend them. I do not intend to charge most of our German ministers with lack of fidelity in instructing their catechumens. Some of them meet their classes several times a week, for six months together, and their pupils learn the Catechism, and all the proof-texts by heart, and it is interesting to hear them, on examination-day, most fluently reciting all they have learned. But still it is painfully manifest, as their subsequent course demonstrates, that, for the most part, it is a mere school lesson, learned as they have done their geography and history. They seem to regard it as a necessary part of their school education, and when it is over, that is, when they have been confirmed, they think it no worse to leave their church than to leave their school after they have finished the scholastic course. The fact is, they are regarded as pretty much the same thing. When they receive their school certificate, they, of course, leave school, and when they get their confirmation certificate and have paid their fees, they leave church. It is distressing to say these things, but in a discussion of this kind the truth must be told, though the *whole* truth need not be uttered. A *part* is enough for our purpose. What does all this show?

Plainly, a superficiality of teaching and an almost necessary failure in impressing upon the *heart* a proper sense of religious *obligation* founded upon a proper understanding of religious *doctrine*. In a word, *true piety* is absent, and I fear this, for the most part, results from imperfect and heartless teaching. If it were not so, the majority of these young people would not leave their church immediately after their first communion. If their hearts were right, they would crowd into the sanctuary—but they are not there, and there is no better evidence that they have no piety. I have heard pious German ministers themselves complain of this, but they plead old church customs, national prejudice and the *fear of offending parents*, as good grounds for the continuance of this mischievous system. Some have not hesitated to say, that a large portion of their support depends on the number of their catechumens, and hence they confirm all, with an exception now and then, who come. From this results the practice of receiving to communion, little boys and girls, who give no evidence whatever of steadfast religious principle, and who do not understand the doctrines and duties which may have been faithfully taught them. But the ignorant parents desire it, and even strenuously insist upon it. The minister derives a considerable income from it. He is anxious to report a large number of additions to the Synod, and his pride is gratified with the attendance of a large class upon his instructions. I am strongly tempted to enlarge upon this head, but will forbear, unless I am contradicted, and then you may expect some strange revelations.

II. Another reason is that *that a love for the church* is not properly instilled into the minds of these young persons. I do not mean to say that they are not told to go to church regularly, and to attend to other outward religious duties. I know the contrary, but that strong, unwavering attachment to Zion, which the Germans happily express by *Kirchlichkeit*, is not properly impressed upon them. They have very imperfect ideas of the church universal. The claims of their own congregation upon them, they may, perhaps, superficially, understand, but their relations to the Kingdom of Christ as an universal, divine institution they do not recognize. Hence, the majority of them, when they leave their own congregation, do not *feel bound* to join any other. They cut themselves off entirely, and would be surprised, and perhaps indignant, to be told that their confirmation vows bind them to the church all their lives. If they were taught, *as they should be*, that when, by reason of language, or distance, or some other good cause, they should leave their own congregation, they should feel it their duty to join an *English* Lutheran church, the result would be very different. To the honor and religious zeal of some German ministers, let it be said, that they *do* this, but it is to be feared that but *few* are of this character. This is to be deplored, but there is no doubt of the fact.

III. Another reason is, that the parents of these young people do not set them a better example. There are many exceptions, but alas! how is it with the majority? They are satisfied that their children are confirmed, and there it ends. Most of them do not go to church themselves, except on the holy days, and no wonder their children, superficially indoctrinated, follow their example. They absent themselves from their own church, and with such irreligious examples at home they are not influenced to join any other. They are not called to account for a neglect of their confirmation vows, for they fear the terrible retort: "Physician, heal thyself."

IV. Among the minor reasons are: First. The English speaking Germans of the poorer classes are backward in associating with Americans. They feel awkward in our society, and are afraid of being laughed at. Second. The German is slow in forming new social connections; he is timid and with good reasons, perhaps, in some cases, thinks that the American is proud and regards himself his superior. Third. He fears the affected hauteur and ridiculous self-sufficiency of many Americans, as well as the presumed greater cost of worshipping in an English church. Fourth. Our pew system may keep some away, though the reason is futile.

These, and a few other reasons, groundless as they are, may have some influence in deciding the great question. But even if they were tenable, they would not be strong enough to keep young Germans out of our English churches, if they were true Christians and loved God's House as they should.

V. Finally, *the German ministers themselves* are severely at fault in this matter. And yet not all. I know a few who encourage the efforts of English Lutheran missionaries in their churches, and advise their English speaking young people to cast in their lot with them. It would be absurd and unnatural, however, to expect German ministers to advise such of their young people to go, who still understand German well enough to be profited by German preaching, and who prefer staying at home. This we do not ask, but we do complain that these brethren seem to take no pains in directing their straying sheep to an English Lutheran fold. I know this to be the fact from painful experience, and I have heard of others which I am slow to believe and will not record. I directly charge them with dereliction of duty in this respect. Most of them are culpably negligent in not endeavoring to keep their young people within their own congregation, and much more so, in not using their influence in retaining within the sanctifying bounds of the Lutheran Church, the large number who wander away.

I have pretty thoroughly discussed this question, and have given the principal reasons why our English pastors do not receive more of our semi-Americanized Germans into their churches. It has, this moment, occurred to me, that an additional reason might be given, and that is, because so many of this class would not be received, even if they applied. That might be, but the fact is, so few apply, that we have no opportunity of rejecting them, and we had better wait until they come before we talk of testing their religious character. I would state (in a whisper, however), that there are some, and not a few, of our Americans admitted into our churches, who do not bear a better religious character than many of the Germans. We had better not say anything more on that part of our subject.

My experience is, that very few German ministers like to talk on this matter. They evade it, if possible, and very naturally, for they feel self-condemned. They are aware that the Church is suffering from the course they pursue, and yet they will not change it. But there are exceptions. I know one who has been recently reasoned into an acknowledgment of his error, and he is now willing to have English preaching in his church, to prevent his young people from straying away. He deplores the result of his former practice, and now wishes to begin a new career.

But our German ministerial brethren are not alone to blame for this unhappy condition of things. Let us be candid and take a large portion of it upon ourselves. How can this be made out? Very easily.

We have kept too far aloof from these people, and have not

cultivated their acquaintance, nor sought them out in their wanderings. We have not tried to get their young men and maidens into our religious societies, nor invited their co-operation in our benevolent undertakings. We have not sought to elevate their social position, nor tried to convince them that we do not think ourselves above them. We have not enlisted the services of our young men and women to draw back these sheep straying from the Lutheran fold. We have not been anxious to distribute our publications among them, and thus show them, what we really believe and teach. In a word, we have "passed them by on the other side," until some of them, at least, were cared for by a Samaritan, not of our family. All this is true, and let us be willing to confess and lament it.

That man has but little acquaintance with the German character who does not know that German parents are gratified when their children are kindly noticed and treated by young Americans, and that these young Germans themselves regard association with Americans as a badge of higher respectability. Let us, then, promote social relations with them, as far as is proper, and we will gain many.

I would propose that in every city church there be formed a society of young persons with this special design in view. It would accomplish more than some of the benevolent societies already in existence. Most young men and ladies know some young Germans of the class under consideration, whom they could influence. They could easily find out many others. Let them go to them and earnestly represent the case, and every pastor would soon have reason to rejoice in the happy results. It is a most inviting and promising field of Home Missions. I presume that every church has among its members some of this very class. They are the persons best adapted to the work, but others need not be idle. I will suggest this course to my own pastor, who, I know, will cheerfully give us his influence, and we shall soon have an "*Inner Mission Society,*" whose exclusive aim will be to save the thousands of young Germans from wandering away from the church of their fathers, after they have been received into it, in a way of very equivocal propriety.

I should like to see the whole English church roused into action, and it will require very little to do it, if we proceed deliberately, intelligently, prudently.

MINISTERS WHO HAVE LEFT US AND THOSE WHO HAVE COME TO US.

During this period of fifty years some ministers born and educated among us (and some of them at our expense) have left us and joined other communions.

There are some who have obtained tickets of leave, because they have utterly failed among us, or have rendered their ministry undesirable to any of our churches. A few have gone because, not attaining to the position to which they thought their distinguished talents entitled them, have concluded they were not "appreciated," and have abandoned us in disgust. Probably there are a few now in our ministry who are of the same opinion, but remain with us because they have no prospect of bettering their condition, and because no other denomination holds out any inducements to them, or "appreciates" them more highly than their own people do. A few have gone because advantageous positions and a higher salary were offered them by other churches; and a few more, because by that step they expected to secure a higher social standing by living among more influential and wealthy people. A few have gone because they have exhausted their stock of sermons among us, and go to a denomination which orders a general change of ministers every few years, and thus their ministers may turn up the under side of the scanty bundle and start on a fresh round. A few more have gone with the hope of increased patronage for their schools, and a few to make sure of a desirable matrimonial alliance.

I do not believe that more than three or four have bid us farewell because of dissatisfaction with our doctrine or government. With all the rest it was a matter of expediency and convenience, and hence they say that their theological views are precisely now what they were when they were members of our synods.

I will first give a list of those who have gone away from us, as far as their names could be ascertained, after diligent search. I cannot give these "departures" in chronological order, nor name the synods to which they all belonged, nor the date.

It would be interesting to trace the subsequent history of these men, and their successes among their new friends. Probably the least said concerning the outward prosperity and fate of some of them the better.

It is a question often spoken of among our men, have we as a church received any benefit from these accessions of *outside* ministers? There is very little diversity of opinion, and yet there are synods who will eagerly snatch up any starved-out, dissatisfied or incompetent minister from another denomination. Now, it is true, some of these "comers" are true and useful men, but it is also true, what a blunt Western correspondent of mine says, whilst furnishing me a list of "comers and goers." "Some of these," says he, "are good men, and some are regular soft heads. A fellow not dyed in the wool, cannot make a good Lutheran." Why then do you admit such fellows?

MINISTERS WHO HAVE LEFT US.
To the Protestant Episcopal Church.

George Streibeck, of N. Y., in 1805; R. J. Miller, N. C., in 1821; Goodman, Phila., in 1828; Cruse, N. Y.; Rumpf, Hartwick; Scull, Va.; Koehler, Md.; W. M. Reynolds, W. Pa.; E. Myers, N. Y.; F. M. Bird, Pa.; C. W. Knauff, Pa.; H. L. Ziegenfuss, Pa.; Wiles, E. J. Koons, Pa., in 1876; L. Riedel; J. C. S. Weills; C. Steck (returned).

To the Presbyterian Church.

Goertner, of Hartwick; C. A. Smith, Hartwick; J. F. Smith, F. W. Brauns, Md.; A. Essick, Pa. (returned); H. Bishop, Md.; Sprecher, Ohio; Olmstead, Wilson, Crofts, N. Ill.; J. S. Cook; Black, Cent. Ill.; Shaver, Cent. Ill.; English, Hartwick; Axline, Ohio; Trimper, Kansas, in 1876 (returned); Willox, N. J.; Fenner, Hartwick; Sternberg, J. K. Kast, Pa.; J. A. Keiser, H. K. Hennig, A. Bartholomew, E. Lubkert, C. Steck (returned), W. H. Hyman (returned), St. John, G. W. Wilson, T. Hill, J. Post, J. O. Hough.

To the Methodist Church.

Miller of Cent. Ill.; Haigler, N. C.; T. T. Everett, Ohio, in 1877; P. Schmucker, W. A. G. Emerson, G. Wohlschlegel, W. Bauermeister (returned), S. B. Hyman (returned).

To the Congregationalists.

M. Officer, of Ohio; T. Hill, Billman, St. John, N. Ill.; Kutz, Pa.; C. Sparry (returned), J. K. Eckman, Kloss.

To the Baptists.

Hopkins, of S. Car.; Whittle, of S. Car., in 1858; Winder, G. Schmidt.

To the Campbellites.

McChesney, Hoshour, of Md.

To German Reformed.
F. Kuckerman, W. B. Rally, L. Richter.

To United Brethren.
C. Nussbaum, H. Gathers.

To Moravians.
Ricksecker.

To the Universalists.
Bosserman, of Ohio.

To the Swedenborgians.
Brickman, of Pa.; E. A. Fünfstuck.

To Rome.
Oertel, of Missouri; Preuss, of Missouri; Schnurrer, Brandt (returned), H. Baumstark.

LIST OF THOSE WHO HAVE COME
From the Romish Church.
Peixoto, and F. von Badenfield, to the Pennsylvania Synod; Gustiniani, to the Maryland Synod; J. E. Freggang (left or dropped), C. Maier, C. E. Raymond.

From the German Methodist Church.
Winder, to the Maryland Synod.

From the Methodist Protestant Church.
Hunt, Appleby, Jennings, to the Maryland Synod; J. Rolliston (left), J. Schoeffer, C. Becker, J. H. Honour.

From the Presbyterian Church.
Ewing (left again) and Bradley (left again), to the Maryland Synod; Rankin, to the Tennessee Synod; McDonald, to the Southwestern Virginia Synod; H. Gans (left again), F. R. Tompkins, J. Wolf, J. King, J. B. Morris, A. Gans (left), F. F. Friedgen.

From the Methodist Episcopal Church, and other Methodist Branches.
Bell, Smith and Jones, to Southwestern Virginia Synod; J. Wolf and Emerson, to English Synod of Ohio; Vogelbach, to Pennsylvania Synod; Short, to Southern Illinois Synod; Krack, Lavender, Tignier and Julian, to Synod of Georgia; Gibson, Mallinson; Sweitzer and Whittaker, to Synod of New York; Dorsey and Forsyth (1876), to Synod of Maryland; Anthony, Crist, Grabill, Hicks (left), to Synod of South Carolina, H. Wells, J. Fry, J. D. Chapman, A. C. Frick, M. A. Hockman,

W. J. Leslie, G. Battersby, E. E. Berry, J. Diefendorf, N. W. Cummins, J. C. Myers, J. K. Booker, W. Eckermeyer, R. Maze, W. H. Buttner, G. Dreher, — Williston, G. W. Lewis, J. Kimball, A. Buhrman, L. L. Bonnell, J. W. Miller, Emerson (2), J. J. Miller, E. W. Erick, F. W. Flemming, W. R. Faris, C. Sink (expelled), J. A. Beidler, L. Rice, J. Fleming, J. Shafer, James Williams, to Wittenberg Synod, 77; J. R. Sykes, D. H. Snowden, to Kansas Synod.

From the Protestant Episcopal Church.

Muller, to Synod of Maryland; Behringer, to Synod of New York and New Jersey; Marriott, to Synod of Pennsylvania (suspended); Atkinson, E. V. Thorn, J. C. Bell, J. Gorden, Edwin Potter, from Reformed Episcopal Church, to Hartwick Synod.

From the Baptist Church.

Blessene, to Synod of Northern Illinois; Sparry, to Synod of New York; Barnes, to English Synod of Ohio.

From the Congregational Church.

Collins, to Synod of East Pennsylvania; D. M. Hoyt, S. Kelso.

From the German Reformed Church.

Mehrwein, to Synod of Pennsylvania; Herring, E. S. Hernsey, A. Steffens, to Wartburg Synod; Eckert.

From the Dutch Reformed Church.

Emerick, to Synod of New York.

From the Moravian Church.

Eberman, to Synod of Pennsylvania (left again).

From the United Brethren.

J. Surface, L. Richter (left), G. W. Hussey (dropped), C. Linn, J. H. Bratten, C. F. Eckert (left), A. Oberlander, J. W. Shreeves, P. B. Shirk, W. D. Trover, J. Hall, C. F. Malzahn, Tobias, M. S. Morrison, C. Caskrey, J. M. Smith.

These are all of both classes whose names I could get. It appears from the above lists, that during the last fifty years the Lutheran Church in this country has lost *seventy-three* ministers by withdrawals into other denominations, and during the same period has gained *one hundred and one* ministers, who have entered it from other churches. The lists may be somewhat defective, both as to accessions and losses, and some few may be credited to wrong denominations.

REVIVALISM AND NEW MEASURES.

About the years 1833-'40 nearly all the churches in the country were affected by an extraordinary religious interest, which was especially manifested by holding frequent meetings, which in some instances were continued several weeks, and even longer. Usually, as long as any special interest was displayed by the numerous attendance or an increasing number of "inquirers" appeared, the meetings were protracted. Sometimes they were closed from pure exhaustion of the ministers and their helpers. The constant strain and excitement of several weeks hard work, in many cases both day and night, wore out the strength of the most vigorous and compelled them to desist.

There were men of other churches and a few of our own who had the reputation of being successful "revivalists," and these were sent for when any unusual excitement was evident, or when an attempt was made to rouse up an inactive and decaying congregation. These men usually attracted large audiences and awakened what seemed to be an extraordinary interest in religion. The conduct of the meetings was usually left to them entirely, the pastor being but a subordinate and treated as such. When the "revivalist" left and the pastor resumed the chief command, having neither the preaching ability, nor the reputation, nor the tact of the man whom he had invited, he soon found that he could not keep up the interest, nor attract the crowd, and he accordingly suffered. In many instances divisions ensued, and the pastor was compelled to leave. This result did not occur so frequently among us as among others I could mention, for we had no men who were distinguished as "revival" preachers, no men who were invited to the cities or large towns to "get up a revival" and conduct it exclusively, and few or none of our men called in the services of those professional evangelists who were in great demand elsewhere, among people who could afford to pay them well for their labor. Hence few or none of our ministers were obliged to leave their churches as the result of a "revival" conducted by a stranger; some of them gained a surer footing by their own unaided efforts, although some, for want of discretion, lost the confidence of their churches and found it convenient to move.

I remember one incident connected with an expiring church (not one of ours, but of our first cousin's), which had invited one of the most famous and really strong itinerant "revivalists." The church was in a large city, but it had been preached almost to death, and a sad state of things existed. The pastor thought that if he could get a crowd in his house of worship through the agency of the preacher who was at that time followed by multitudes, and "have many converted there," the converts would probably "join the church in which they had been converted," and thus build up his decaying establishment. He invited the popular preacher and he went. The house was crammed as usual wherever he preached. The pastor was in the pulpit, and in his first sermon the preacher turned half round to the pastor and gave him such a lecture on pastoral unfaithfulness and church deadness, which he attributed to the pastor, as he had never heard before, and for which he had not bargained. There were not many meetings held in that church and "converts did not stay there." It was not exactly polite in the preacher to treat the pastor thus in his own pulpit, but that man claimed and exercised "sovereign sway" wherever he went.

Many of our ministers in all sections of the Church earnestly engaged in this revival work. In some places the services were conducted with becoming propriety, but in others unallowable extravagances were practiced. The "anxious or mourner's bench" was introduced in imitation of the Methodists; disorders in the meetings, such as shouting in some places, and groaning, and members praying at the same time, women praying in public, clapping of hands, singing of hymns of doggerel verse to the most frivolous tunes and in protracted repetition, whilst the minister and other members, and sometimes women, were speaking to the "mourners;" these and other "exercises" were not only sanctioned but encouraged.

All the usual methods of rousing the feelings of the audience were employed, sometimes by portraying the terrors of hell, the recital of affecting stories, allusion to deaths in families, violent vociferation, the singing of "lively" tunes, and other arts. These had the desired effect, and the minister would invite "these mourners to the altar or bench." If any appeared, several brethren would go and speak to them, not in a whisper, but in audible tones, and when several were speaking thus at the same time, the minister meanwhile addressing the audience, or going up and down the aisles and pews, urging other people to come, who had a serious aspect; then some person, and sometimes a woman, while all this was going on, commenced singing some exciting hymn, uninvited; and probably before the hymn was finished, some zealous brother would exclaim—"Let us pray," and all would kneel down, and many would pray nearly as loud as the leader, and others would heartily respond, amen! to every petition, and often too, most inappropriately. When they rose, some one else would commence singing, in which all would join if they could; and during all this time the brothers and sisters would continue speaking to the "mourners." This series of exercises was continued night after night (but never on Sunday mornings) and protracted sometimes to a late hour. There was preaching, but that seemed to be a subordinate part of the performance. The main dependence was upon the singing, praying and anxious bench.

Every one who has witnessed these scenes as they were enacted thirty years ago, will acknowledge that this is not an exaggerated statement.

Some of our plainer people also adopted what I would call the religious slang of the day, and used the vulgar phrases of "getting religion," "getting through," and others of like character. The results of many of these meetings were large additions to the churches. In some places from eighty to one hundred and more were admitted at one time. Many of these had received little or no previous religious instruction, and did not long retain their church connection, whilst others more thoughtful, have maintained their Christian integrity to this day. I know many of our most efficient church members, whose profession was the result of this revival system.

Other results at some places were disastrous to our Lutheran time-honored practice of Catechetical instruction to Catechumens. Many people conceived a distaste for this slow process, when they could go to a revival meeting and "get religion" in one evening. Even at this day, when another class of ministers has come in, they find it hard, and in some places impossible, to introduce the system of the fathers.

Another consequence was, a dissatisfaction with the use of the ordinary means of grace, and a constant, unwholesome longing after excitement. Two or three "lively" meetings a year were essential to what they considered their Christian life.

Many also became weary of their ministers if they did not by their preaching and other efforts, labor to keep "the fire burning," by which they meant, exciting and sometimes boisterous, meetings.

Some of our ministers who favored this system, also lost a most disheartening number of their members. The latter, upon the slightest pretext, went over to other churches given to such measures. They saw no difference between their own church and that of these neighbors as far as their proceedings were concerned, and the step was easy and short.

The name "New Measures," was given to these operations, and fierce was the discussion in the Observer upon their scriptural lawfulness and expediency. Numerous articles appeared on both sides, and more acrimony than was becoming was displayed in the controversy. The editor, Dr. Kurtz, was a vigorous advocate of the system, and for sixteen successive weeks he had a standing heading, "New Measures," in his editorial columns. He sanctioned many of the extravagancies and wielded his powerful pen in defence of them.

During this period of religious excitement, a very remarkable little book entitled, *The Anxious Bench*, from the pen of Rev. Dr. Nevin of the German Reformed Church, appeared, which gave fresh vigor to the controversy, and which was violently assailed by the Observer. Dr. Nevin replied in the German Reformed Messenger, and the contest was carried on for several months.

The extreme measures, once so popular, are now practiced by very few. Moody and Sankey's labors show that strong religious interest may be awakened and sustained without violence, and this has had a tendency to moderate the old school revivalists and to shake the confidence of the people in the old system.

RELIEF FUND FOR SUPERANNUATED MINISTERS, WIDOWS OF MINISTERS—INSURANCE LEAGUE.

As far back as 1831 the General Synod laid the foundation of a relief system, but it was insecure. At that meeting, held in Frederick, Prof. S. S. Schmucker moved that one-half of the profits of those works to be published, with the sanction of the General Synod, * * * shall be paid into the treasury, to constitute a fund for the relief of superannuated ministers belonging to the General Synod, and their widows and orphans.

25

A committee, of which Dr. B. Kurtz was chairman, was appointed to draft a constitution for the management of this fund.

It was not until 1837 that a regular system was adopted and trustees appointed. The revenue was to be derived from the sale of hymn books and catechisms, and $50 were to be appropriated to those entitled to it. (See Proceedings of Gen. Syn., 1837, at Hagerstown). C. A. Morris, Dr. Gilbert, Isaac Baugher, Rev. B. Kurtz and Prof. Schmucker were appointed the first trustees.

At the subsequent meeting of the Synod, held in Chambersburg, 1839, the system previously adopted was repealed, a new constitution was adopted, and the name of "Lutheran Pastors' Fund" was given to the organization. It was a cumbersome document, consisting of not less than *twenty-five* sections. There was too much *government* about it, besides it was complicated and not easy to understand, and hard to be carried out. It contemplated raising funds by "voluntary donations, subscription, legacies, &c." besides having some features of a mutual insurance society. But it was adopted. Frederick Smith, of Chambersburg, was elected President; J. G. Morris, Secretary; Dr. Gilbert, Treasurer. Two years after, at the meeting in Baltimore, Dr. Gilbert reported *sixty-three dollars and ninety cents* in the treasury. In four years the fund was not increased *one cent* by donations or any other means, except $36 interest on a mortgage. In six years there was no addition to the fund from other sources. In eight years the fund amounted to $1,184,28, which arose from accumulated interest and a donation of $500 by the Synod. In ten years it increased $136 from interest.

But in the course of time a deeper concern was awakened, and at the meeting of the Synod at Carthage, 1877, active measures were adopted.

PASTORS' FUND OF MARYLAND SYNOD.

This is an institution chartered by the Legislature of Maryland, and has accomplished much good, cheering the heart of many a disabled or superannuated minister, and ministering to the relief of many a widow and orphan.

It was established at the session of Synod held in Frederick in 1856, and has been in successful operation ever since. It does not confine its benefactions to members of that Synod only, but extends them to all who are in need without regard to synodical territory.

The capital invested now amounts to $4,546.73, which was derived from the following sources:

A small amount was subscribed by various members of Synod, but the principal sum, $200, was received from the sale of the Lutheran Observer, which at that time belonged to the Synod, and from a donation of $804 by the stockholders of the "Book Company" when that institution was dissolved, which, with the accrued interest, amounts to the sum specified.

The appropriations are annually voted by the Synod, which are carried out by the trustees, who meet soon after the adjournment of Synod, when the report of the Treasurer is received and the general business transacted, all of which is reported to the Synod at its subsequent meeting.

Usually not over $100 are voted to any one person, and never less than $50, and on no occasion has over $450 been appropriated at one time.

The number of claimants has never exceeded five, and of the beneficiaries for the last several years not one was a member of the Synod of Maryland, nor was the husband of any of the widows aided a member of that body when he died.

***

LUTHERAN MINISTERS' INSURANCE LEAGUE.

A member of the Synod of Maryland had thrown out some suggestions relative to a more efficient method of benefiting the widows of deceased clergymen, and after having explained and discussed the subject in the Observer, and secured the interest of some friends, a meeting of gentlemen was held in Baltimore in the late summer of 1870, when the "Lutheran Ministers' Insurance League" was formally established. The corporators were John G. Morris, John McCron, William D. Strobel (at that time a resident of Baltimore and the efficient agent of the Maryland Tract Society), Charles A. Stork and Philip Hennighausen.

The object of the corporation is "the exercise of mutual benevolence and the mutual insurance of relief to the families of its deceased members."

The initiation fee was in the beginning one dollar, but graded subsequently according to the age of the applicant, and no "one over fifty years of age" is now admitted.

The League is governed by Trustees elected annually, and for convenience sake the annual meeting is held during the week of the session of the Synod of Maryland.

The "League" encountered severe and persevering opposition in our church papers, but when the most formidable opponent acknowledged his error and joined the association, all controversy ceased.

Four hundred and seventy of our ministers have been or are members, of whom eighty-seven have died, and to whose families nearly $19,858 have been paid. The number of living members, according to the last report, is four hundred and twenty-four. The highest amount received by any one widow was $894.

The relief which the League has furnished to these widows has rescued some of them from dependent poverty, by enabling some of them to open small stores, purchase a small house in the country, pay debts, clothe their children or lay in a stock of winter fuel and provisions.

It has been silently pursuing its career of usefulness, and there are many who rise up and call its founders and supporters, blessed.

STATE OF THEOLOGY.

Fifty years ago, when there were less than two hundred ministers in the Church, neither the Augsburg Confession nor any other creed was regarded as obligatory upon them. The large majority of them, however, were orthodox in the usual acceptation of the term; that is, they accepted the evangelical system of Christian doctrine, and a large proportion of them preached it faithfully. But many of them were not strictly Lutheran on the dogma of the Sacraments, or at least they did not attach much importance to it. It never was a subject of discussion among them, and hence there was a great diversity of sentiment. Many of them were not thoroughly educated men, and they gave themselves no trouble concerning the distinguishing features of our faith. They were sturdy Lutherans in name as a party signal, but sadly latitudinarian in their theology.

To so little extent was distinctive Lutheran theology discussed, that it may, perhaps, surprise some of my readers to learn that in the three volumes of *Das Evangelische Magazin*, the first professedly Lutheran periodical published in this country, the subject of our doctrine on the Sacraments is not even alluded to.

This magazine was issued in Philadelphia, in 1811–14, and edited by Drs. Helmuth, Schmidt and Schaeffer. Many of the influential ministers of that day had been trained by these men, and they were all very moderate in their Lutheranism. Dr. J. G. Schmucker, of York, one of their pupils in 1790, was the only man I knew who was pronounced in his Lutheran orthodoxy; but I am not certain that he learned it from his Philadelphia teachers. In my intimate intercourse of over twenty years with Dr. J. D. Kurtz, I do not remember that he ever gave a decided expression of his views. I am certain, however, that he was not what we now call a doctrinal Lutheran on the Sacraments.

Dr. Endress, in Lutheran Intelligencer, January, 1827, p. 265; Dr. Lochman, in his "Principles of the Christian Religion," p. 33, 34; Dr. Hazelius, in "Discipline, &c., of the Synod of South Carolina," p. 20–23; Dr. Miller, in sermon before the Ministerium of New York, 1831, p. 8; Dr. Bachman, in sermon on Doctrine and Discipline of Lutheran Church, 1837; Dr. B. Kurtz, in "Why are you a Lutheran?" p. 148, and some other influential ministers, have expressed such views on the nature of the Lord's Supper, which do not entirely agree with the teachings of the Symbols nor with the expositions of our standard Lutheran divines.

Before the establishment of Gettysburg Seminary, some of our ministers took private pupils. Rev. David F. Schaeffer, of Frederick, Md., was the only man with whom I was intimately acquainted, of the older class of ministers, who taught his pupils the true Lutheran doctrine of the Sacraments. Several of them, who have since become authors, resolutely defend the system which was maintained by him, whilst a few others, of very superficial preliminary training, though good men in general, were not zealous in the defence of the cause.

But there was another school of men in our ministry fifty years ago, who had not only departed from the Lutheran faith as such, but who were strongly suspected on good grounds of entertaining principles at variance with the plain teaching of the gospel. One of the leaders denied the doctrine of justification by faith alone, and of course the total depravity of man and the divinity of Christ. Another openly taught Universalism, and a few others were what was then called Rationalists. None of them ever published their unlutheran sentiments. Happily, the number of this school was not large; but they were men of some influence in their limited circle, and infected others with their heresies who had not the moral courage openly to express their views. I have heard several of their cotemporaries say, such as Drs. J. G. Schmucker and J. Daniel Kurtz, that in private circles, during the meeting of Synod (for they seldom saw each other at other times), the discussions on these fundamental doctrines were protracted and earnest. The end of three of these men, whom I now call to mind, was disastrous.

I remember once traveling to a Synod as a mere looker on, before I was licensed, with one of the youngest of that generation. He was the only man in our section of the country who was suspected of unsoundness, and he was very cautious about expressing his opinions, for he was well aware that the Synod to which he belonged would call him to account. But, as we were jogging along in an old-fashioned gig, he hinted at Universalism as a very consoling doctrine. Inexperienced as I was in the wiles of cunning men, yet still I suspected he was trying to shake my faith. He did not quote Scripture in defence of his views, but argued from the goodness of God and from nature, and uttered a great deal of pretty nonsense. In illustration of Final Restoration, as he called it, he pointed to a fallen tree lying by the road side. "See; from that fallen tree," he said, "a good table may yet be made." I knew what he meant, and, before he had time to continue, I quickly retorted—"and yes, and after the table falls to pieces it may still make good *fire* wood!" He knew what I meant, laughed at my reply, and said no more on that subject.

Reports, very unfavorable to the orthodoxy of some of our ministers in a certain section of the Church, had been spread. Before I was licensed I once met the Rev. Dr. Alexander, of Princeton, in Augusta county, Va. I had often heard him preach when I was a student at Princeton College, and, as we both stopped at the same hotel, I introduced myself to him. He asked me whether it was true that most of the Lutheran ministers of that section of Pennsylvania were Unitarians. I was too young to know much about it, but I hoped it was not true; was sure it was not true of all, and of none of the city clergy. I made all sorts of explanations and extenuations, which were neither satisfactory to him nor to myself.

Until that time theological instruction had been given almost exclusively in the German language. A few of our ministers who had students taught in the English language, but they were very few.

The German text books used were orthodox, but the instruction given was rather superficial, and not because all the teachers were incompetent men, but because most of their students were not prepared by elementary training to receive or appreciate higher instruction. Hence many men were hurried into the ministry with inadequate preparation and immature theological views. They were not bound to the confessions, and a rigid Lutheran orthodoxy was not required of them. Most of them, however, adhered to the Evangelical faith as commonly understood, and some of them were godly preachers and pastors.

There were some well educated theologians and first-class scholars among the men of that generation, but they were foreigners who had been trained in the Universities of Germany. No native American of fifty years ago had attained to any grade of theological scholarship above a respectable mediocrity. A few who were licensed about or shortly before that period, have since acquired some reputation, outside of our own church, as men of extensive and solid learning.

Before fifty years ago, our men had no opportunity of a thorough theological training in their own church, for we had no seminary, and our few learned men who did devote some time to teaching had for the most part inferior material to work upon.

There was no book on systematic divinity in the English language published until 1826, when Rev. S. S. Schmucker's translation of Storr and Flatt's German work was issued. It was published at Andover and had considerable circulation in New England, for it was recommended by some distinguished divines of that school. I remember that a box of these volumes arrived at Princeton Seminary when I was a student there, and they were examined by some of the pupils, who pronounced them unorthodox, meaning that they did not teach the calvinistic doctrine of predestination.

A theological work of this size and claims was an event in

those days, and the publication secured a wide spread reputation for the author. Some of our own men, especially the pupils of Dr. Schmucker, studied it with great advantage. It was a thoroughly Lutheran book, and it was hoped by the advocates of a sound Lutheranism that it would become the means of establishing the wavering, enlightening those ignorant of the faith, and reclaiming those who had departed from the old scriptural system of doctrine. Independently of the high Lutheran ground which the original work takes, the translator in his notes and addenda had strongly vindicated the Lutheran faith, thus superadding his own testimony to it. In the appendix to his translation, he gives eleven pages of extracts from Reinhard's Dogmatik, and Mosheim illustrating the Lutheran view of the Lord's Supper, interspersed with notes of his own. Any one desirous of seeing what Dr. Schmucker designates as a "lucid illustration" of this doctrine, should read this appendix.

Notwithstanding this exposition of the true faith, the Doctor, who was called to the seminary about the time of its publication, was not known to be ardent in the defence of the doctrine in his lectures. A second edition of this work appeared a few years after, from which all the appendix on the Lord's Supper with his notes *was left out!* And from that time forth his instruction became decidedly more anti-Lutheran on the sacraments. The result was what might be expected. While on the one hand the majority of his pupils left the seminary with undisguised anti-Lutheran tendencies, there was on the other hand a goodly number who assumed the opposite extreme, the result, as they declared, of the Professor's lax views on the Sacraments. They pursued an independent examination of the subject, and adopted the teachings of the confessions.

Since the resignation of Professor Schmucker, the theology taught at Gettysburg has been more confessional. There is nothing said to depreciate the system as was formally done, and which, as I have said, had a reactionary influence upon some students, but both sides of the question are fairly stated, with a strong leaning to the right side.

Most of the best educated and most influential theological alumni of Gettysburg Seminary are outspoken in their Lutheran orthodoxy, and many more are sincere in their adoption of the true faith without any decided demonstration.

The publication of an English translation of "Schmid's Dogmatik," emanating from Gettysburg, is regarded as a happy sign of reviving orthodoxy. Krauth's "Conservation Reformation" has also contributed much to promote the progress of true Lutheranism. Indeed, the appearance of these two great books, may be regarded as an era in the history of our Dogmatics.

No book or article in the Evangelical Quarterly, directly assailing the sacramental doctrines of the church at the present time, would meet with any favor or defence. Even those articles of this character published ten or more years ago were coldly received by the few, and fiercely attacked by the many. The authors of both are no longer of us, one having been discharged by his Synod, and the other having gone to the Presbyterians.

All the German and Scandinavian Seminaries, with the more decidedly English ones at Philadelphia, Columbus and Salem, are stringently Lutheran, whilst Gettysburg and Selinsgrove belong to the moderate school, at which nothing is said or done to depreciate the doctrines of the church, as was formerly the case, at one of them, at least. At both the church is exalted and her ancient doctors are held in due veneration. Wittenberg and Hartwick have given no public demonstration of a decided Lutheran *Richtung*, but it is well known that their pupils, from which fact alone we may judge, do not generally maintain an advanced churchly position.

Our religious journals have not for years contained any articles worth noticing and proceeding from respectable sources antagonistic to our peculiar doctrines. I do not mean to intimate that the latter are universally adopted, but that the opponents of them are aware that they would assail them in vain, and they prudently hide themselves from public observation. There was a time when their articles were welcomed in the Observer and other papers, but that time has happily gone by.

OUR STUDENTS AND MINISTERS IN THE UNION ARMY.

In obedience to the urgent appeal of President Lincoln and of Governor Curtin for troops to repel the invading rebel army under General Lee, a call was posted up at Buehler's drug store in Gettysburg, on June 16th, 1863. About sixty college students, and four from the Theological Seminary, together with several citizens, assembled in the College Campus and organized by electing F. Klinefelter, captain (who had been the only student who had responded to the *first* call and served under General Patterson in Virginia in the three months' campaign); W. F. Hinkle, first lieutenant; L. M. Slater, second lieutenant, H. C. Frey, H. C. Shindle, S. D. Schmucker, W. H. Rupp, and O. L. Fegley, sergeants; and D. H. Yount, T. C. Pritchard, D. F. Rank, J. C. Koller, J. C. Dizinger, E. J. Wolf, J. Irrgang, corporals.

They immediately offered their services to Governor Curtin and were ordered to report in Harrisburg. Early next morning they were in line, and after a brief address from Prof. F. A. Muhlenberg they left for Camp Curtin, there reporting to Gen. D. H. Crouch.

In consequence of some dissatisfaction with the terms of muster, several thousand troops already in camp refused to be sworn in until the terms were changed. The college recruits waiving these objections, manifested their faith in the government by a large proportion of the company mustering into the service on June 17th, without any limitation, the same as volunteers for the war. They thus secured the honor of being the first company mustered into the service under that call. Next day, the terms having been changed to a service for the existing emergency in the Department of the Susquehannah, others were sworn in, including several who joined their number at Harrisburg, among them some who had formerly been students at Gettysburg, but whose names I could not obtain. General Crouch hearing that the majority of this company were students, drew upon their number for clerks, and for "The Signal Corps." In this latter department some remained after the company was mustered out.

The regiment to which this company of students belonged was commanded by Col. Jennings; and McKnight, one of the students, was adjutant.

The regiment hastily and imperfectly armed, was ordered to report at Gettysburg. It was delayed by a railroad accident and encamped about six miles from the town, awaiting further orders. This was a week before the battle of Gettysburg, and but two days before the advance of Lee's army entered the place. There were no other Union forces within fifty miles, save two small bodies of cavalry.

On the night of the 25th one hundred picked men were ordered to proceed toward the mountain and cut off the rebel pickets, who were gradually approaching the town; but the heavy rain of that night caused them to be detained until the arrival of the regiment in the morning, and they were thus saved from capture or destruction, for the rebels were advancing in force. The regiment marched to the distance of several miles, encamped and threw out pickets. In the afternoon the rebels made their appearance and captured forty of the pickets. Col. Jennings seeing himself vastly outnumbered, and knowing that his seven hundred or eight hundred new recruits could not stand an attack, ordered a retreat, which was conducted with singular skill. They were pursued for miles, but Jennings managed the affair so adroitly and deceived the rebels so successfully by various manœuvres, that he brought his fagged-out regiment safely to Harrisburg with the loss of only one hundred and twenty men, most of whom were picked up as stragglers by the enemy. These young men, unaccustomed to exposure or work, marched fifty-four out of sixty consecutive hours.

The remainder of the term of service, ending July 30th, was spent mainly in Fort Washington, opposite Harrisburg. Their whole term of service was not over six weeks.

The following is a list of those students in this company who afterwards became ministers of our church: F. Klinefelter, H. C. Shindel, T. C. Pritchard, J. C. Koller, J. C. Dizinger, E. J. Wolf, M. H. Richards, T. C. Billheimer, M. G. Boyer, H. S. Cook, Phil. Doerr, G. W. Frederick, F. B. Wolf, H. W. McKnight, J. W. Finkbeiner, W. H. Golwald, S. Henry, A. McLaughlin, W. E. Parson, F. Richards, T. L. Seip, J. D. Schindle, W. A. Steck, W. C. Schaeffer, J. C. S. Weils, H. L. Ziegenfuss, J. A. Clutz and others.

The sons of Lutheran ministers in the company who did not become ministers, are S. D. Schmucker, J. M. Krauth, F. W. Baugher, W. O. Bishop and C. A. Heilig.

There were others in the service who are now, or have been ministers, and among those whose names I could procure are L. M. Heilman, D. H. Geissinger, both of whom were wounded: T. F. Dornblaser; Rev. McConaghy fell in battle.

Captain McCreery of Gettysburg also raised a company, of which the following students were members: G. W. Hemminger, L. W. Dietrich, L. W. McKenzie (now Rev.), H. C. Grossman (do.), H.

W. McKnight (do.) He joined Captain McCreery's company after Captain Klinefelter's was mustered out, and this accounts for the appearance of his name in both lists. H. J. Wortz, Dr. Wm. McKnight.

The Rev. Mr. Lingle, a licentiate of the Illinois Synod, entered the army of the Union early in 1861 as a private, but by his bravery and attention to his duties, he rose through the various grades until he became a captain. He was in the midst of many hard-fought battles, but always came out unscathed. He remained in the service until after the close of the war. After the death of the president, Captain Lingle was detailed with a squad of men of his own company to guard the tomb of the great president. So he pitched his tents at Oak Ridge Cemetery, and there for six months, night and day, like Rizpah of old, he watched the remains. That this precaution was necessary is evident from the well-known fact, that quite recently a most daring attempt was made at Oak Ridge Cemetery to carry off the bones of the martyred president, but for what purpose is not known; perhaps with a view of extorting money from the government for the recovery of his remains! After Captain Lingle's services were no longer needed at Oak Ridge, he returned to his work in the ministry and is now (1877) the efficient pastor of a Lutheran church in Southern Illinois.

Some of our men labored faithfully in the Christian Commission work, and the following are the names of chaplains in the field or in hospitals, and some of them in both: Prof. J. A. Brown, S. W. Harkey, J. H. W. Stuckenberg, R. F. Delo, D. S. Truckenmiller, W. G. Emerson, A. R. Brown, F. Springer, D. S. Altman, G. Pile, Jer. Shindle, A. R. Howbert (who also served two years on Gov. Tod's staff); P. Rizer (was present in the first Bull Run battle, afterwards served in the navy in the steamship Vanderbilt, and was present at the bombardment of Port Royal, Nov. 7th, 1861, under Commodore Dupont); J. G. Butler, F. B. Wolf (army of the Rio Grande); Rev. S. A. Holman, chaplain of 48th Regiment, Pennsylvania Volunteers.

There were also some Gettysburg students from the South in the rebel army. I remember hearing Prof. Stoever say that one called on him. Another named Dinkle, from near Winchester, was killed at Fairfield, eight miles from Gettysburg, and another, name not recollected, was killed in the battle there and is buried in the National Cemetery.

Some of our ministers were rather roughly treated during the war. The Rev. Dr. Hay, then of Harrisburg, was arrested by order of General Wool, who commanded here in Baltimore, and whose department embraced Pennsylvania. The whole affair is so interesting that I give an account of it as it appeared in a Harrisburg paper.

THE ILLEGAL ARREST OF THE REV. DR. HAY—ITS CAUSE—THE HEARING—HONORABLE DISCHARGE.

We have already announced that the Rev. Dr. Charles A. Hay, minister of the First Lutheran church in this city, had been illegally taken from his home on Tuesday morning, on the strength of a telegraphic dispatch from Gen. Wool to Gen. Wilson, asking the Provost Marshal to secure Dr. Hay and bring him at once under guard to his headquarters in Baltimore. In obedience to this dispatch, Marshal Kleckner arrested Dr. Hay on Monday evening, placing a guard inside of his residence, and also one on the outer door. The Rev. Dr. had been engaged to perform the funeral services of one of our oldest and most respectable ladies, Mrs. Judge Hummel, on Tuesday morning, but he managed to send word to Mr. William M. Kerr, president of the Harrisburg bank, and son-in-law of the deceased, that he would be unable to attend, and that he was held a prisoner. Mr. Kerr, who is well known to every man in this city as one of the most upright and loyal men in the country, made an attempt to have an interview with Dr. Hay, but he was not permitted to see him, nor would the guard accompany him so that he might hear all the conversation. Dr. Hay was treated worse than a criminal guilty of a high offence.

The writer of this article saw Dr. Hay but a few minutes before the cars started, and upon examination of the paper on which the arrest was made, it was discovered at once that the whole proceeding was illegal, since, by an express order of the War Department, it has been ordered that no person should be arrested unless by authority from the War Department direct, or the Judge Advocate, General Turner. Dr. Hay, however, perfectly conscious that no offence had been committed, and acting as a loyal citizen, who would suffer any privation for the sake of supporting the government, submitted to this tyrannical proceeding and accompanied the guard to Baltimore.

Before, however, we give the proceedings had before Gen. Wool, we will narrate the offence which Dr. Hay committed, in the judgment of the General, and for which he was summoned hence to answer.

During a late visit to Baltimore he met with the wife of one of the leading merchants in that city, who boastingly told him how those who openly sympathise with secessionists in Baltimore were permitted to take sick rebel prisoners captured in battle, to their homes, and quarter them among their friends, and that quite a rivalry existed among them to honor the rebel sick and wounded. This, of course, mortified Dr. Hay most extremely. It was almost too much for a man who had devoted day and night to the care of the sick Union soldiers, to hear; and knowing the lady intimately as truthful, he left that city with a sad heart, deploring that it could be possible that secessionists of Baltimore can nurse the sick rebels while our own Union soldiers are left to the tender care of hospital nurses.

Dr. Hay found upon reaching home, that Rev. Dr. Lochman, a highly respectable and loyal clergyman of York, had made several applications to the Surgeon General, asking for the transfer of a loyal sick soldier from Camp Curtin Hospital to the hospital at York, so that his friends and relatives might minister to the sick soldier at home. This reasonable request had been denied to a loyal man who had been fighting and bleeding for his country. Feeling indignant at this contrast between the treatment of rebel and loyal soldiers, he wrote the following card:

EDITOR OF THE TELEGRAPH:—I have just returned from Baltimore. Whilst there I fell in with a lady of well-known secession proclivities, who boasted of having brought away from Fort McHenry, by *permission of General Wool*, four of the wounded prisoners lately transferred from Frederick. I inquired if they were in any of the Baltimore hospitals. "No; they are in the hands of OUR FRIENDS. A dozen ladies scrambled for them, but I had already promised them to others, and they are well cared for."

Now I wish to call public attention to this fact, which speaks for itself. Would the same General allow similar privileges to loyal ladies in behalf of loyal soldiers?

CHARLES A. HAY.

Harrisburg, October 24, 1862.

Dr. Hay arrived at Baltimore at one o'clock, and was ushered at once into the headquarters of General Wool. After waiting some time, the General appeared, seemingly very much excited, and, after examining several papers lying on his table, he accused Dr. Hay with being the writer of different articles published in the *Baltimore American*, remarking at the same time that " they were all a pack of lies."

Dr. Hay replied coolly that he had never written anything for that paper.

Gen. Wool then remarked that an article had been published over his own signature, at the same time still hunting in great excitement over his papers, but unable to find the article in question.

Dr. Hay then stated that he had published an article in the Harrisburg paper, at the same time handing him the article cut from the *Telegraph*.

Gen. Wool took the slip, read it, pacing up and down the room, and stating that " it was a pack of lies."

Dr. Hay answered coolly that he was not in the habit of telling lies.

After this conversation Dr. Hay gave a full history of the transactions at Camp Curtin and of his visit to Baltimore, giving the author of the fact that secession prisoners had been taken from the fort and quartered among the secessionists of Baltimore.

Gen. Wool stated that he had an official account of the transactions at Fort McHenry before him, but insisted that Dr. Hay had been wrong in stating that *he* had given permission to take these secession prisoners from the fort, at the same time not denying that this had been done by the commander of the fort. Gen. Wool read from the official report of Gen. Morris concerning the disturbances there, which corroborated many of the statements of Dr. Hay's informant, and satisfied him that the General to whom the lady referred was not Gen. Wool.

Dr. Hay saw, after this explanation, that the deed had not been directly committed by Gen. Wool, yet it was done under his command and he was responsible for it. He told the General at once that he had no hesitation in saying publicly that he had been in error in regard to the person granting such permission.

This seemed to satisfy the General, who had no doubt heard of some in connection with the affair, and he thereupon discharged Dr. Hay without condition.

This illegal arrest and examination has ended in failing to disprove the fact that some one under the *control of General Wool* had permitted four secession prisoners to be taken from the fort and quartered among secessionists in Baltimore, which privilege has been denied to Union soldiers. We are therefore glad that an opportunity has been given to investigate this matter, and we have no doubt that the illegal arrest of Dr. Hay will bring about the discharge of incompetent officers (to use the mildest term) and arrest abuses in the department of Gen. Wool, which have grown almost insufferable to loyal men.

Gov. Curtin telegraphed at once, when he ascertained the arrest of Dr. Hay, to the War Department, asking his immediate release. Secretary Stanton answered promptly that no authority had been given for such arrest, and desired to know by whom it was ordered. This shows clearly that the whole responsibility rests upon Gen. Wool, and that he will have to answer for his conduct to a higher power. The administration is not in the least to blame, as it was done without its knowledge. The whole matter will be laid before the War Department, and somebody discover that, however they may act the tyrant over a sick soldier and discharge rebel prisoners, they will not be permitted to drag loyal and better men from their homes with impunity.

The Rev. Mr. Stirewall, of Virginia, was one night ordered out of his bed and was told to prepare himself for death by hanging. He demanded the order for his execution from the rebel savages, and succeeded in setting so clearly before them the civil and military wrong of putting him to death without order, and the terrible consequences to themselves as murderers, that they finally left the premises without doing him any harm.

A similar event is related concerning the Rev. Mr. Jenkins, of Tennessee, the particulars of which I do not know.

MURDER OF REV. MR. GLENN.

Rev. Mr. Glenn was the pastor of a Lutheran church at Corydon, Indiana. He was a strong Union man but too old for service in the army. He resided in the country, not far from Corydon. His family consisted of his wife and children, among which were two full grown daughters. One evening just as they had eaten their supper, a number of soldiers on horseback made their appearance at the parsonage. One of the soldiers, quite gentlemanly in his appearance, came into the house and inquired whether they could give them something to eat? The pastor said, "Yes, certainly, if there are not too many of you." "Well there are only ten of us, and we are very hungry." The women commenced getting the supper. The ten men, who consisted of the rebel Col. Morgan and his staff, then came into the house, and each man had his liquor in his canteen—and they took pretty heavy drafts, so that by the time the supper was ready they were all pretty well intoxicated. Of course Mr. Glenn did not know who his obstreperous guests were. At the supper-table the wife and daughters were most grossly insulted by those men. Mr. Glenn could bear it no longer and began to remonstrate with the men for their rudeness. But they only laughed at him, and said, "Old fellow, you evidently don't know who we are, or you would not talk so to us." "Well, I supposed that you were gentlemen, and would so far respect the rights of hospitality, and in the presence of ladies as not to act so rudely." Morgan replied, "To hell with your preaching!" and drawing his revolver, he said, "Now, old fellow, you had better shut up, or you will get yourself riddled." At that moment Mr. Glenn arose, perhaps to leave the room, and one of the men cried out, "Shoot him!" Morgan fired, and the pastor fell with a bullet in his brains. As soon as the family saw this they fled and hid themselves in a thicket not far from the house, and thus escaped the brutality of those infamous rebels.

As soon as they had finished their supper, they set fire to the house, and when they saw it well under way they mounted their horses and continued their daring raid. The house was burned, and the body of Rev. Mr. Glenn with it. This was one of the sad results of Morgan's raid into Indiana and Ohio, and this was one of the scenes that awakened the people to a sense of their danger, and raised an army of indignant men, who followed these daring outlaws, and at last captured them in Columbiana county, Ohio. Morgan himself was captured and put in prison at Columbus. He broke jail there and made his escape, but died afterwards, and has gone to settle his long account of misdeeds before the Judge of all the earth.

LEGACIES AND DONATIONS.

Rev. Mr. Hartwick's legacy to found an institution of learning, and Mr. Frey's, a layman, for the establishment of an orphan house at Middletown, Pa., are events which occurred before fifty years ago, and in regard to them I will content myself with pointing out the sources of information to those desirous of investigating these subjects.

In Sprague's Annals, Dr. Pohlman's address at the semi-centennial anniversary of Hartwick Seminary, 1867, and Stoever's Reminiscences in the Evangelical Review, the student will find everything necessary; and concerning Frey, he may consult the Lutheran Observer, October 7, 1838, and April 28, 1838; Evangelical Review, XII, p. 574, and the proceedings of the Synod of East Pennsylvania of the same period.

The largest legacy made during the fifty years was one of $20,000, made to Pennsylvania College by Charles A. Morris, of York.

Mr. Thiel, a wealthy German, bequeathed a larger amount to found a college, which was named after him, and which is located at Greenville, Pa.

Mr. Jacob Straub, of Danville, Pa., left a legacy of several thousand dollars, to be divided between several Synods for literary and benevolent purposes.

Mr. Davis Pierson, of Philadelphia, bequeathed to Pennsylvania College a certain amount of stocks in coal mines, valued at $20,000, but from which only $12,000 were realized.

The *donations* to Pennsylvania College were $20,000 by Messrs. A. F. and G. P. Oekershausen, of New York; C. A. Morris gave $5000 at various times, and the following persons gave $1000 or more to the same institution: Samuel Appold, Rev. Dr. F. W. Conrad, Jacob Garver, Martin Buehler, Thos. Baumgardner, O. E. Shannon, E. Roehm, C. Yeager, F. and H. Baumgardner, Edward G. Smyser, John Eyerman, J. Donald Cameron, M. B. Spahr, Weiser, Son and Carl, William Smith, &c., &c.

Thaddeus Stevens gave $1000 towards the erection of the building for the Preparatory Department.

The whole amount of the college endowment is (1877) $110,201.32. The liabilities amount to $8750.

The cost of the observatory of Pennsylvania College was $4750, to the erection of which Samuel Appold, of Baltimore, contributed liberally.

The *legacies to the Theological Seminary* were $200 by Mr. King, of Adams county, Pa.; $2500 by Mrs. Thorn, of Carlisle, Pa., the widow of a Lutheran minister, formerly an Episcopalian;

C. A. Morris bequeathed $1000; Miss Motter, of Frederick, Md., $500; Mr. Stroup, $500.

The Graff family, at Pittsburg, *gave* to the Gettysburg Seminary $10,500.

The following persons have given each $500: C. W. Humrichouse, Mrs. C. Hager, David Artz, Mrs. E. Heilman, D. P. Ramsay, C. C. Mason, J. Westley, J. C. Bridges, Dr. T. Stork, Wm. Auspach, John Rouzahn, Rev. Dr. F. W. Conrad, Samuel Garver, Jacob Garver, Samuel Bireley, G. M. Dove, Rev. Dr. Hay. It is proper to state that these gifts have been received during the term of the present Treasurer, Daniel Kraber, of York, who informs me that he holds notes to the amount of some thousands, which he does not consider "good," and which are not noticed in this account.

There is one note for $1000, payable after the death of the giver, which is considered "good," and another obligation which is estimated at $5000 of the same condition.

A short time ago (August 1877) Dr. Brown handed to the Treasurer $5000, the proceeds of the Jubilee Fund.

The endowment of Gettysburg Seminary is at this time, in round numbers, $100,000, which produced by interest last year $5146. The salaries of the professors amount to $5000, and contingent expenses from $300 to $500 annually, so that the endowment is not sufficient to support the institution.

The following persons have given each $1000 to Roanoke College: Michael Miller, Geo. Miller, Samuel Hulbert, Jacob Miller, Miss Sallie Miller.

To the Philadelphia Seminary, Mr. Norton, of that city, gave $50,000 to found a professorship, and Mrs. Burkhalter, of the city of New York, an equal amount.

George Lefler, of Philadelphia, bequeathed $1000 to the same institution.

Henry Muller, of Platt's Springs, Lexington county, S. C., gave $4000 at one time to the Theological Seminary, then located at Lexington, and subsequently a second donation of $2000.

West Caughman made a donation of $1000 to the same institution.

David Ewart, of Columbia, S. C., gave $10,000 in stock of Columbia Bridge Company, to the Seminary.

Charles Courter, of Cobleskill, N. Y., has given $20,000 towards the erection of a Lutheran church in that village

The only person that I know who has given more than $1000 to Foreign Missions, is the widow of a Lutheran minister, whose contributions now amount to upwards of $4000.

Obadiah Ware bequeathed $2000 to the Lutheran church in Butler, Ill., in 1876, the interest to be applied to the support of the minister.

Rev. J. Wolf, who came to the Synod of Northern Indiana, bequeathed his farm of eighty acres, worth $75.00 an acre, to Wittenberg College.

John W. Cooper, of Savannah, Ga., (not a Lutheran) bequeathed $1000 to the Lutheran church of that city.

Frederick Seyler, of Baltimore, bequeathed $1000 to the First English Lutheran church of that city.

George Lefler, of Philadelphia, bequeathed $4500 to the Synod of Pennsylvania, and the one-fourth part of the remainder of his estate after the death of his widow.

Miss Adelaide Sager, of Philadelphia, bequeathed $6000 to St. Matthew's church, Philadelphia, and $20,000 to Pennsylvania College, Gettysburg.

It was exceedingly difficult to collect reliable information upon this subject of legacies and donations, and no doubt many have been undesignedly omitted.

POLITICAL OFFICE.

Very few of our ministers have ever aspired to political distinction, or, at least, have succeeded in attaining it. Henry A. Muhlenberg was a member of Congress and Ambassador to Austria, and John A. Schultz, in his early days a minister of our church, was Governor of Pennsylvania.

I know a few in Pennsylvania who were candidates for Congress, but they were defeated in the election, which was better for them and the country.

Rev. Dr. J. G. Butler is the only Lutheran minister who was ever elected Chaplain to the House of Representatives or the Senate.

CHURCH TRIALS IN CIVIL COURTS.

***

No doubt there have been more cases of this character than have come prominently before the public, and which I have failed to notice. They are not pleasant subjects, and usually do not excite much interest beyond those immediately concerned. The following are well authenticated cases, and grew out of the formation of the General Council, and all occurred in Pennsylvania:

1.—THE LEECHBURG CHURCH SUIT.

The decision of Judge Logan in the Leechburg church suit was filed in the court of Armstrong county. By that decision the petition of the seceding portion of the Hebron Evangelical Lutheran congregation, of Leechburg, to have an amendment granted to the charter of said congregation, transferring it and its property to the General Council, has been rejected. An injunction restraining the General Council minority from holding the church building, and putting its lawful owners, the organization faithful to the General Synod, into possession thereof, was issued at the following September court.

As this case has excited a great deal of interest, not only in this and adjoining congregations, but throughout the greater part of the Lutheran Church, and amongst other denominations, a brief resume thereof, and of some of the leading facts therein connected, may not be out of place at this time.

Under the ministration of Rev. L. M. Kuhns, which continued for about eleven years, the Hebron Lutheran congregation was one of the most flourishing in the whole church. Whilst he was pastor, in 1864, an amendment was granted to the charter, by which the congregation and the academy, which was built in that year, were brought into connection with the General Synod—or rather, the congregation was required to be in connection with the General Synod, for prior to this it belonged already, indeed, to that body, but only by virtue of its connection with the Pittsburg Synod. Rev. Mr. Kuhns ceased to be pastor of the congregation April 1st, 1866. He was at once succeeded by Rev. J. Sarver, who still serves the General Council organization. During the first year of his ministry, when the church troubles first began in this region, Mr. Sarver made some efforts to have a change made in the charter, but for certain reasons he soon desisted. Near the close of his first year he announced that unless the charter were changed he could not remain as pastor, inasmuch as he had resolved to follow the fortunes of the General Council. By a *compromise*, however, it was resolved to retain him a second year, but as a *supply* merely. In this compromise it was agreed that there should be no unnecessary doctrinal discussion. Despite this arrangement, however, the peculiar doctrines of the General Council, as held in its "Fundamental Principles of Faith and Polity," were preached from time to time; so that, early in 1868, the members of the congregation faithful to the General Synod, having become alarmed, desired that a minister of the General Synod might also be allowed to preach in the church, so that their side might have a hearing also. This desire they expressed, but their reasonable request was refused. There was, therefore, no alternative but to seek another place in which to have the gospel preached to them. They found a shelter, for a brief time, in the Presbyterian building, and subsequently in that of the Methodists. Soon after they adjourned to the academy building, which was under their control, having previously called Rev. H. H. Hall as their pastor. And while here four members of the board of trustees of the academy, all General Council men, and among them the pastor, snugly occupying a church not belonging to him, *solemnly protested against their holding service even there.*

On the 5th of March, 1868, a congregational meeting was held, and a vote taken for and against a change of charter. The vote stood fifty-seven for and forty-two against a change. Subsequently seven persons, who had not understood the merits of the question, and who had voted *yea*, changed their votes to *nay*, making the vote stand fifty for and forty-nine against a change. Rev. Mr. Sarver and council refused to permit Messrs. Salem Hill, David Kuhns and Andrew Sober to vote, although they were entitled to vote, as Mr. Boggs clearly demonstrated in his argument before the court, from the church record kept *by Mr. Sarver's own council!* So that in reality the nays were in a majority. In this condition of things the General Council-men applied to court for a change of charter. A remonstrance on the part of the General Synod-men duly followed. On application of the petitioners, a commissioner to take evidence was appointed by the court. F. Mechlin, Esq., was the person chosen. Many witnesses were then called on both sides, among them C. P. Krauth, Jr., D. D., Dr. Passavant, Rev. S. Laird and others for the petitioners, and J. A. Brown, D. D., Rev. L. M. Kuhns and others for the respondents. Those for the petitioners sought to show in brief that the General Synod had departed from the Lutheran faith, whilst those for the respondents *did* show that the General Synod is a Lutheran body, and that the Hebron congregation had remained true to it and to the principles on which it itself was founded. The testimony was taken at different times and at different places, and months passed by ere it closed. After this the case hung in court a long time, his honor, Judge Buffington, being too unwell, was unable to hold an argument court. But finally Judge B. resigned, and Judge Logan was appointed in his place. Before the latter, with Judges Beatty and Nulton as associates, the case was argued on the 27th, 28th and 29th of July. E. S. Golden appeared for the petitioners. He spoke some six hours altogether, a good part of which he devoted to Dr. Brown. He laid out his strength in trying to show that the three brethren above mentioned had no right to vote. There his only hope lay. Messrs. Boggs, of Kittanning, and ex-Senator Cowan, of Greensburg, attorneys for the respondents, followed him. The former vindicated Dr. Brown completely. Mr. Cowan made a compact, powerful argument. Mr. Cowan maintained that it was not a question of *faith*, but of *law*, that was here to be decided; that the petition for a change of charter should not be granted, because, first, the application was irregular; second, this part of the charter cannot be changed except by unanimous consent; and third, there are as many remonstrants as petitioners, if not more. All of these, together with other points, he elaborated fully and forcibly.

The Kittanning bar manifested much interest in the debate. The unanimous opinion among them seemed to be, when the debate closed, that there would be no change of charter. So, in good spirits, we of the General Synod returned home and confidently awaited the issue. The news was brought to us that the change of charter asked would not be granted, and that the petitioners are directed to pay the costs.

II.—FREEPORT, ARMSTRONG COUNTY, PA.

This case was similar to the Leechburg case, only that the church was not, by its charter, expressly bound to the General Synod, but only to some Lutheran Synod. The General Council-people being in possession of the property, the General Synod-people brought suit to recover the property from them. By mutual consent the testimony in the Leechburg case, so far as it related to the history, doctrines and usages of the Lutheran church, was accepted. The case was given into the hands of a master in chancery, and, after a long delay, was by him, in 1876, decided in favor of the General Council-party. From this decision no appeal was taken. The fact that the charter failed to bind the congregation to the General Synod lost us our Freeport church property.

III.—VENANGO, CRAWFORD COUNTY, PENNA.

This case was like the Freeport case in its essential features. The General Council-people held the church and parsonage, and the General Synod-people brought suit to gain possession thereof, for their money had largely built them. Rev. Gaumer, pastor, was the principal witness on the General Council side, and Rev. I. J. Delo on the General Synod.

This case, too, was decided in favor of the Council-party. In the last two cases *possession* was everything.

IV.—BEAVERTOWN, SNYDER COUNTY, PENNA.

In this case the General Synod-party gained the suit.

V.—ALLENTOWN, LEHIGH COUNTY, PENNA.

The General Synod-party held possession of St. Paul's, Rev. W. G. Mennig, pastor. A minority of the congregation, dissatisfied with the usages of Rev. Mennig, which were those of the General Synod churches, brought suit against the pastor and that part of the congregation faithful to him, for the possession of the property. Here again Dr. Brown was the principal witness for the General Synod-men, and Dr. Krauth, Jr., for the General Council-party.

After a patient and full hearing of this great case, second only to that of Leechburg, the court decided it in favor of Bro. Mennig.

A full account of the proceedings and testimony in this case may be seen in the Quarterly Evangelical Review for January, 1878.

NORTH CAROLINA.

A case of some interest was tried as far back as 1821 in North Carolina, between the Synod and a body of Lutheran ministers composing the Tennessee Synod, known as "Henkelites," though that designation was given them by their enemies.

It was charged that the latter party took forcible possession of what was known as "The Organ church" in Rowan county. The suit resulted in the ejectment of this party by order of the court.

The Tennessee Synod claimed that the North Carolina Synod had departed from the Confessions of the Lutheran church, and hence that it had no right to hold property which had been acquired by Lutherans. The court decided differently. The facts concerning this trial can be learned from the records of Rowan county court, Salisbury.

FRANCKEAN SYNOD.

The next case which I have to record, is that between the Franckean Synod, or some members of it, and the Hartwick Synod of N. Y., in 1844. It was Philip Kniskern and others vs. Philip Wieting, the Evangelical Lutheran churches of St. John's, at Durlach, and St. Peter's, at New Rhinebeck, in Sharon, and others.

These churches, together with that in Cobleskill, were in existence as one church in 1787. In 1789 they were designated by the name of *the Lutheran congregation of Cobleskill and New Durlach*. In the same year, one hundred and fifty acres of land were conveyed to them in fee *forever*. In 1798 a church edifice was built at New Rhinebeck, and one at Durlach the next year. These churches had distinct acts of incorporation. The land was amicably divided between the three churches, Cobleskill, Durlach and Rhinebeck. They were first attached to the New York ministerium. This body afterwards united with the General Synod. In 1830, the Hartwick Synod was formed, and these churches became a part of that Synod. In 1831, the Hartwick joined the General Synod. Mr. Wieting, as pastor of these churches, participated in the organization of the Hartwick Synod and its union with the General Synod, and continued in connection with them until 1837.

In 1837, Mr. Wieting, with a number of other members, separated from the Hartwick Synod and the General Synod and formed the Franckean Evangelical Lutheran Synod, and adopted a declaration of faith and a system of church government and ordinances, in some respects deviating from the Augsburg Confession. The two churches, St. John's and St. Peter's, continued their connection with the Franckean; the complainants, who are members of these churches, adhere to the Hartwick Synod. They bring suit to recover the property out of the possession of the Franckean.

The trial was held in Albany, January 13, 15, 16, 1844, and the judgment was rendered by Justice Sanford at New York, July 17th of the same year.

The opinion of the learned chancellor makes a large 8vo. pamphlet of sixty-nine pages, in which the whole subject of the law relating to church property, with numerous decisions of other courts and many references, is lucidly set forth.

The Franckeans admitted that they denied some of the teachings of the Augsburg Confession, but still claimed the property which was granted to and possessed by churches professing the faith of that Confession. They were founded and established as *Evangelical Lutheran churches*, and the property in controversy was bestowed for the support of the *doctrines* and *tenets* of the Evangelical Lutheran church.

The question then was, "What were the essential or cardinal doctrines and tenets of the Evangelical Lutheran church when this property was bestowed upon these trusts, and by what standard or symbol were they declared?" The inquiry is limited to the belief and doctrines of those who, in 1789, and subsequently, were the *donors of this property*. The unbelief of the congregation, thirty or forty years afterwards, can be of little or no weight in the scale.

It was proved that the creed of these churches in 1789 was the Augsburg Confession, or that the doctrines of that famous declaration were taught to them, and that by name they were *Lutheran* churches, and believed in the faith, practice and doctrines of that church as expressed and declared in the Symbolical Books.

One of the conclusions to which Justice Sanford comes is the following, and that would be enough to settle the question:

"It is therefore established that the Augsburg Confession was accepted and received by the churches in question at the time of their endowment, and by the members thereof as their confession of faith; and the churches were founded for the purpose of having the faith and doctrine expressed in that Confession taught and inculcated therein, and that, in respect of the doctrines in this suit, there never had been any established or even known dissent from the Augsburg Confession in this or any of the Lutheran churches."

It was shown on the other hand that the Franckeans no longer recognized the Augsburg Confession as their symbol or doctrinal standard. Their constitution makes no allusion to it. Mr. Wieting, a leader among them, gave from the pulpit of one of these churches his reasons for separating from the Hartwick Synod, and stated that he did not believe the Augsburg Confession; that it was an antiquated thing, unfit for the present age. In view of this and several other similar utterances, Chancellor Sanford says: "I cannot doubt, therefore, but that the defendants have abandoned the Augsburg Confession of Faith in these churches, and that in some essential articles they have repudiated it." The judge also mentions "the palpable Unitarianism of the Franckean declaration of faith adopted in 1837," and of their amended and improved declaration of 1838. Judge Sanford says "that the Franckean article is *capable* of a Trinitarian construction, but merely equivocal, accommodating itself to the consciences of both Trinitarians and Unitarians." He then proceeds to point out numerous other deviations of the Franckean Declaration from the Augsburg Confession.

Without taking up more space with this most interesting case, I will only state that the chancellor's decision was in favor of the complainants.

CHURCH SUIT AT MARVIN'S MILLS

Some years ago a difficulty grew up in the St. Paul's congregation at Marvin's Mills, Crawford county, Pa., through the dismissal of its pastor, by a majority of the members, at a regular meeting.

The congregation had been in practical connection with the Joint Synod of Ohio and under its ecclesiastical jurisdiction. After the dismissal of the pastor, the majority called different members of the Pittsburg Synod to serve them. The majority separated themselves from the body of the church of which they were members, formed an organization, elected officers, were served by pastors of the Joint Synod of Ohio, and recently brought suit for the church property on the ground mainly that the Pittsburgh Synod was not a Lutheran body.

In his report, filed January 13, 1873, and which the Court of Common Pleas of Crawford county approved, the master, J. Newton M'Closkey, Esq., says:

"There does not appear to be an appreciable distinction between the religious tenets and doctrinal basis adopted and taught by both the Evangelical Lutheran Joint Synod of Ohio and the Evangelical Lutheran Synod of Pittsburgh. In fact, their faith and worship are identical. * * * * * *

"We can therefore, from all the evidence cited in this case, discover no radical change of faith and doctrine by the respondents, who compose a majority of the original congregation, 'or succession of associate owners,' and have not by their acts, professions, practices, charter of incorporation, ceased to be a Lutheran congregation, and become alienated and estranged from the ancient faith, discipline, usages and customs of the founders of the Evangelical Lutheran St. Paul's church; and moreover, that the respondents, by uniting or connecting in any way, for the spiritual and temporal welfare of the congregation, with the Evangelical Lutheran Pittsburgh Synod, a genuine Lutheran Synod of the same church denomination, have not thereby forfeited their right to the possession and control of the church property." * * *

The conclusion to which we have arrived, from an application of the principles enunciated in the foregoing authorities to the evidence in this case, is that there has not been such a departure by the respondents from the faith, discipline and worship of the genuine Lutheran church as to work a forfeiture to the title and possession of the church property granted to the Evangelical Lutheran St. Paul's church, in "trust for said church," but that, so far as the right of the property is concerned, they are the legitimate, continuous church organization, whose possession of the property ought not to be disturbed, and that, therefore, the complainants' bill be dismissed.

ROEDELSHEIMER'S AND STREIT'S LEGACIES.

Although this subject is not embraced properly within my "Fifty years," yet it is one that has been hitherto almost entirely unknown; the history of these legacies has never before been traced, and it was only after numerous inquiries and considerable research that I have been able to procure any reliable information.

Every year the Presidents of Pennsylvania and West Pennsylvania Synods report the receipts of certain interests derived from these two legacies invested in Europe, amounting to about $500.

This sum is divided between those two Synods, who appropriate it as they please, and yet nobody knew who these legatees were and no pains were ever taken to ascertain their history.

The amounts are now voted by these Synods to benevolent and literary purposes, but in the early history of the Pennsylvania Synod, or as far back as 1820, running through a series of years, they were distributed among the members, on some occasions each man receiving as small a sum as $5. I remember hearing old Dr. Schaeffer, of Philadelphia, saying that he proposed to invest the amount of interest for some religious purposes, but his enlightened proposition met with no encouragement, and he was told by some of the "leaders" "that every man could do with his share as he liked."

I am now able to throw some light upon this matter. In section ten of the Preface to the twelfth continuation of "The reports from some Evangelical churches in America, particularly in Pennsylvania, edited by Dr. Johann George Knapp, professor, &c., and director of the Orphan House at Halle, 1771," I find the following statement:

"First of all I cannot refrain herewith from publicly expressing the most profound gratitude to the noble reigning Count in Germany, who has been induced by reading the hitherto published narratives of these churches and their pastors, to bestow a legacy of thirteen thousand ducats, and ordered this to be paid whilst he is still living. He has been graciously pleased to forbid the mention of his distinguished name in these reports, but he will surely not take it amiss that we here praise the goodness of the Lord who has stimulated his heart and made him willing to perform this kind deed, and that we at the same time stir up the churches in Pennsylvania and their pastors to gratitude towards God and their unknown benefactor, and to intercession for his temporal and eternal welfare. The following statement of the noble donor sets forth the object and aim of this munificent grant:

"Our purpose in forwarding some time ago thirteen thousand gulden through Mr. N. N. to Prof. Knapp, D. D., at Halle, was that this sum should be appropriated for the benefit of the United German Evangelical Lutheran congregation in Pennsylvania and their churches and schools, in such manner that three thousand ducats should be paid towards the liquidation of the debt on certain church buildings for which Pastor Muhlenberg has made himself responsible, and that the remaining ten thousand ducats be securely invested and the interest of the same be applied to the support of several pastors and school-masters, such as are regularly called by the Directors of the Orphan House at Halle, or at least such as have been recognized by them as regularly called faithful pastors and teachers, and who are most in need and most deserving of this aid."

"In order, however, that this object and aim of the last mentioned ten thousand ducats may be the more certainly attained, we request the Directors of the Orphan House at Glaucha-Halle, viz., Rev. Prof. I. D. Knapp, D. D., and after his death his successor in office, as Directors of the said Orphan House, forever, to act as administrators and trustees, in such manner that they shall have power alone to dispose of this endowment and its revenues as alone indicated, and especially to designate those pastors and teachers whom they shall recognize as deserving of aid from these revenues, and also that they shall be at liberty to execute this their trusteeship through a duly empowered agent. We are all the more inclined to confide in the said Director and his successors, that they will conscientiously and to the best of their knowledge care for the well-being of the churches and schools among the German Evangelical Lutheran congregations in Pennsylvania, inasmuch as these are mainly indebted to the Orphan House at

Glaucha and its Directors for their original foundation and establishment."

"In case it may be considered needful and useful that a conscientious co-trustee and co-administrator in England should be appointed, we hereby authorize whoever may be the Director of the Orphan House for the time being, to appoint the person in whom he may have the highest confidence as such a co-trustee and co-administrator in England, and in connection with him unitedly superintend the application of this endowment. And as the present Director of the Orphan House, Dr. Knapp, has requested the Royal British Chief Court Preacher in the German Court Chapel at London, the Rev. F. M. Ziegenhagen, who has faithfully and paternally interested himself in these united congregations and been their greatest benefactor hitherto, to continue his affectionate care for them, and especially to aid in the management of this our endowment, we approve of his nomination as co-trustee and co-administrator, and authorize the Director of the Orphan House hereafter, for the time being, after the death of said co-trustee, to select and appoint another in England.

"Done under my hand and seal. N. N., *Count of N.*"

This Count was Roedelsheim.

My obliging friend, Rev. Mr. Sheeleigh, writes to me:

I have just happened to meet the following in a book called, "History of Montgomery County, &c." In noting the Barren Hill church, the writer, Mr. Wm. I. Buck, says:

"This church owes its origin to a division in the Germantown congregation, and was built in 1761. The Rev. Henry M. Muhlenberg laid the corner stone, and gave towards it, out of a certain legacy, twenty-four pounds, and preached in it before it was roofed, in which state it had cost five hundred pounds, and on its completion cost upwards of five hundred pounds more. It appears that the congregation had subscribed but very little towards its building, for they were in debt upwards of one thousand pounds ($2,000.00) when the church was finished. Hearing of the pecuniary embarrassment of this church, the chaplain of the king of England authorized Mr. Muhlenberg to draw on him for one hundred pounds sterling. After the most clamorous of the creditors were paid off, the church, school-house and lot were, by indenture, conveyed to the German Lutheran congregation of Philadelphia. But what principally enabled the sureties to meet their engagements was a legacy of thirteen thousand gulden ($5,200) from the Count of Roedelsheim, in Germany, which he bequeathed to the German Lutheran congregations of Pennsylvania, three thousand ($1200) of which was expressly given towards the payment of the indebtedness of this church. Having become much in want of repair, the congregation objected to making it unless the church was again restored to them by the Philadelphia congregation, which was accordingly done by an act of assembly passed February 25th, 1801."

From the proceedings of the Synod of Pennsylvania, held at Womelsdorf, 1832, I translate the following:

"The President appointed a committee, consisting of I. Miller, Demme, Krauth, Baetis and Probst, to investigate the affairs of the European legacies more carefully, and to present the most complete report possible.

"The committee reported that both legacies are designed for different objects, and should be regarded in that light by the President for the time, and a distinct account of each should be kept.

"According to Dr. Niemeyer's instructions, it must be left to the discretion of the President to appropriate the funds of the *Roedelsheim legacy*, but still it is the opinion of the committee that the Synod may recommend to the President worthy indigent ministers and school-masters.

"Agreeably to the will of the testator, *Streit's legacy* was to be devoted to the support of the poor of churches and of schools of the United Evangelical Lutheran congregations in America. Last year applications of a three-fold character were made to the President:

"1. For the support of students of theology.
"2. From schools, through German papers.
"3. From congregations who were erecting new churches.

"The committee are of opinion that applications of this character are in perfect accordance with the design of the deceased testator.

"Dr. Niemeyer's instructions must determine the manner in which the object of this legacy is to be carried out. It is plain to the committee that Dr. Niemeyer regards the President as the instrument by which the Synod acts, and hence their opinion is that all applications for support from this legacy should be examined and determined. Further, it appears from Streit's testament that the accrued interest should be appropriated to these purposes, and should never be loaned as new capital on interest. The committee is of opinion that the moneys which have been thus invested should be called in by the President.

"On reading Streit's will, the committee discovered that he designed his legacy for the United Evangelical Lutheran Churches in that section of North America subject to the dominion of Great Britain (Ebenezer and its dependencies excluded), and that his will is dated Halle, October 15, 1753.

"It is true that Dr. Niemeyer, in a letter dated November 14, 1825, declares that he regarded the funds of this legacy invested in Europe as belonging to the *Pennsylvania* churches, and Dr. Knapp, in a letter of May 15, 1825, that the deceased Streit had designed this legacy exclusively for the support of Pennsylvania churches.

"The committee has high respect for the opinions of men who always speak according to their convictions, and yet, as claims have been made upon this legacy by other Synods, and we believe that our Synod does not wish to be the curator of funds which do not belong to it, we have thoroughly investigated this subject, and give the following as our deliberate opinion: Every congregation which can prove that it existed as a congregation on October 15, 1753, and at that date belonged to the United Evangelical Lutheran Churches, has a valid claim upon this legacy; and, although the claims of that character may be few, yet that the Synod should recognize every one in case any person would give himself the trouble to make it.

"In relation to the affair with the corporation of the Philadelphia congregation, as growing out of these European legacies, we believe that it could be amicably adjusted if the President would refer the matter to the judgment of ex-Governor Shultz, of Pennsylvania."

The Synod of Pennsylvania, in 1876, resolved to expend a sufficient sum of money to procure a copy of certain documents in Halle relating to these legacies, and until they shall be received we must be content with the meagre information we now have.

In anticipation of the receipt of these documents, I am able, through the kindness of correspondents, to give the following biographical sketch of Streit, which was copied from a work somewhat rare. It may be seen in the library of the German society of Philadelphia, and is entitled, Bülau, Geheime Geschichte und Rathselhafte Menschen Sammlung verborgener oder Vergessener Merkwürdigkeiten, Leipzig, 1856.

Sigismund Streit, born in Berlin, April 13, 1687, was the son of David Streit, a smith and brewer, and of Eva Maria Melzon. His father intended him for a profession, and hence sent him to the gymnasium; but not feeling inclined to study, he resolved after his father's death to abandon school and to devote himself to trade and to seek his fortune in a foreign country. In 1701 he carried out this resolution, and acquiring knowledge of mercantile and industrial pursuits in various business establishments, he finally traveled on foot all the way to Venice amid the severest privations, where he arrived towards the close of the year 1709 in a very destitute condition.

From this period until 1715 he must have been employed on small wages, for in that year he established himself in business on a small capital and without credit, but by industry, perseverance and thrift, he gradually rose to commercial prosperity and high social position. In 1749 he retired from the headship of the establishment, but still held an interest in the then celebrated house of Wagner, in Venice, to the end of his life. From that time, on account of his health, he lived eight months of the year in Padua, and from 1754 entirely in that city, where he died December 20, 1775, and was buried in the Protestant cemetery of Venice. He remained unmarried all his days.

In 1724, upon the occasion of a journey to England, he tried to discover his relatives in Berlin to ascertain whether assistance to any of them would lead to favorable results. But they did not come up to his expectations. Yet he took under his care the children of his brother Benjamin, who had also left his native country, notwithstanding he had, at an earlier period, wronged him out of one-third of his small patrimony. He gave to this brother's daughter, who was married in Hamburg, four thousand marks, and a son, who was serving an apprenticeship in Berlin, was sent by him to Hamburg, London, Amsterdam and Paris, for the purpose of improving in the knowledge of mercantile affairs. He then took him to Venice, where he intended to make him his heir and successor, if he had not been deceived in him, so that he finally discharged him with the interest of a capital of two thousand dollars. From that time he determined to devote his property to benevolent institutions, and for years gathered information respecting their designs and mode of government, corresponded with Rector Bodenburg and Court Counsellor Wackenroder in Berlin, with Professor Francke in Halle, and others, and arranged his plans to the minutest particular, and had everything secured in the most careful manner. In 1752 he was able to give the sum of ten thousand dollars, the interest of which was to be spent during his life time for the benefit of the teachers and pupils of the Berlin Gymnasium, and five thousand dollars for the widows of teachers. Subsequently he appropriated to the same institution a number of books and beautiful pictures, and in 1760 the further sum of fifty thousand dollars, which, however, was not to be expended for the benefit of the objects designated, until the sum was trebled, which occurred in 1786.

In addition, in 1753, he appropriated to the Evangelical Lutheran churches in North America, fifteen thousand florins, which sum was to be administered by the Director of the Orphan House in Halle, and in 1754 he gave a similar amount for the Evangelical Mission in East India. Both these institutions received, in 1756, an additional sum of seventeen hundred and forty florins.

The above is all the information I could collect on this interesting subject, and this is the first time that the principal facts have been brought together.

There is no doubt of one thing, and that is that some other Synods, besides those of Pennsylvania and West Pennsylvania, are entitled to a portion of the proceeds of *Streit's* legacy. The "North America" of 1753, mentioned above, was then composed of the thirteen colonies of Great Britain. No other "North America" was known or recognized, and that included some *original* states or territories which do not receive any benefit from this fund. For some years the Synod of Maryland, which was an *original* colony, drew her share, but it was so small in proportion that, more than thirty years ago, it was resolved to direct the President of West Pennsylvania Synod to appropriate the Maryland Synod's small share to the seminary at Gettysburg. It was done for several years, but the Presidents of later days are, perhaps, not aware of this provision, but the Maryland Synod is more to blame for not insisting upon her rights.

STATISTICS, FUNERALS, &c.

The Difficulty of Securing Correct Statistics has always been felt in our church. Our various almanacs differ greatly, even to the extent of thousands in the number of communicants. The number of ministers, Synods, institutions, &c., can be ascertained with moderate correctness, but of regular church members, and the amount of contributions to benevolent and literary objects, we have never had an exact account. This can be accounted for in several ways. Every year not a small number of ministers fail to report, and some others report incorrectly. I know some men who, instead of giving the number of distinct individuals who have communed during the year, count every individual as often as he communes, and this is why some of them who have three hundred members report twelve hundred, because each of these three hundred has communed four times in the year! This is unfair and delusive, and yet I know some German ministers who do it every Synod.

Kurtz's Almanac for 1877 gives us fifty-eight Synods, two thousand seven hundred and ninety-five ministers, four thousand eight hundred and twenty-two churches, six hundred thousand three hundred and fifty-three communicants. The other almanacs differ, so that no estimate of the number of members is reliable.

But other churches have the same difficulty. Two Episcopal almanacs differ twenty thousand in the number of communicants, and the Campbellites do not know whether they have three hundred thousand or four hundred thousand members. I believe that the Methodists, Presbyterians and Congregationalists are more accurate, though even the latter, at least, must include some errors in their totals, if we can judge from such a report from the Yale College church, which offers the following curious statistics: "Male members, 491; female members, 39; total, 530; *absent*, 428.

FURNISHING WINE AND CAKE at funerals was the universal custom in the towns, at least, of some sections of Pennsylvania, many years ago. After the burial all those present were invited to the house of the family to partake of these refreshments, just as it is yet the custom in the country to invite all present to return and take a meal. The wine, or that which had that name, was freely dispensed, and the consequences were not always happy. Rev. Dr. Mayer, the German Reformed minister, was the first man who attacked the custom in York, and it was gradually abolished.

We have never tried to gather the COLORED PEOPLE into churches. Nearly all our churches in the South have always had a few colored members, but we never had an exclusively colored congregation that was permanent. A colored man named Jehu Jones, some years ago, was rather notorious, and made an effort to raise a congregation in Philadelphia, and perhaps elsewhere, but failed. We have never been able to get a man of color, who was a Lutheran preacher, to go to Africa to work in our mission.

Bishop Payne, now of the Methodist church, was reared a Lutheran by Dr. Bachman, of Charleston, and studied for a while at Gettysburg; but there was no field for him among us, and he was advised to go to the Methodists, among whom he has become quite distinguished.

SEMI-CENTENNIAL JUBILEE IN 1868.

In 1867, and perhaps a short while before, numerous articles appeared in the Observer and other church papers, recommending a grand celebration of the semi-centennial of the Reformation. As usual, great swelling words were employed and glorious results predicted. It was proposed to raise large amounts of money for the purpose of endowing the colleges and seminaries and societies already in existence, and to found others in various sections of the church.

Those of my readers who desire to see what was proposed may consult the proceedings of the General Synod of 1868. Those who have preserved copies of the Observer of that period will be amused, if not instructed, in looking at the numerous recommendations and glowing promises made. Considerable amounts of money were raised, but not much of it was appropriated to the *general* purposes originally designed; but yet I believe that the results of this noisy demonstration were productive of some good, intellectually at least, as will be seen from what follows.

I presume we shall never know the precise or even proximate amount of money raised for the benefit of the church during the Jubilee year. Much of it has never been reported; much has been expended for local objects, such as repairing churches, paying debts, building new houses of worship, buying church furniture and some, but too little, in donations to the minister or in replenishing the Sunday-School library. If all that has been given to general and local objects could be summed up, it would be a much larger amount than any of us imagine.

But whilst we shall never find out how much money has been contributed as the special result of the grand occasion, yet there is one department of the Jubilee effort on which I am happily able to give very specific information. It is not the department of *dollars* but of *brains*, and this I am sure will be of some interest to those of my readers who have brains. The *Literature of the*

Jubilee year is no unimportant item in its history, and this, with the help of another, who has picked up, like myself, loose waifs floating on the church sea, I can furnish complete.

This list of titles I give below embraces every publication, I believe, relating *directly* to the Reformation, that appeared in our church during the Jubilee year. If any has been omitted, it is because it has not been noticed in our papers or did not otherwise come under my observation. But, I presume it is complete, for that which might escape my vision, though aided by artificial means, would be sure to be caught up by the keen and searching natural eyesight of my friend, the poet laureate of the church.

I have no doubt that several other publications which have been announced, such as the new translation of Arndt's True Christianity and several of Dr. Seiss's books, and probably others have been *occasioned* by the Jubilee, but as they do not *directly* refer to the Reformation, they are here omitted.

Now, when we reflect that these publications have been read by thousands, and that hundreds of our ministers have preached special sermons on this subject, which have been heard by thousands more, we may form some conception of the amount of information spread abroad. Even presuming that many were familiar with the facts in general, yet the occasion, the united purpose, the re-animated zeal, the growing church-love, the revival of the true doctrine, the consciousness of eminent church position and destiny, the higher appreciation of Luther's work and of his teaching, all combined to impart fresh interest to the glorious theme, and tens of thousands now feel a stronger attachment to the church, and are virtuously prouder of their church pedigree than ever before. We see evidences of it in our church papers; we discover it in our Synods; we hear it in the social circle. The interest is growing, and let any minister announce that next Sunday night he will preach on the Lutheran Reformation, and he will have a full house.

It is very likely that hundreds of the unprinted sermons were better than anything here noticed, but we can take cognizance of that only which has been given to the public in this form.

List of the Jubilee Publications in the Lutheran Church of the United States from October 31, 1867, to same date, 1868.

1. Brobst, S. K. Haupt Gottesdienst Ordnung am 350 jährigen Jubilaeum der Reformation. (Sheet). Allentown, Pennsylvania.
2. Fick, C. H. Lieder zum viertel halb hundert-jährigen Reformations Jubilaeum am 31 October 1867·

    Gottes Wort und Luther's Lehr,
Vergehen nun und nimmermehr.

3. "Sechs Reformations Lieder—St. Louis. St. Louis, Mo., 1867. Pp. 16.
4. Fry, J. Catechism for the Jubilee. Reading, Pa. Pp. 8.
5. Fry, J. The privileges and obligations connected with the great Reformation, a Jubilee sermon preached in Trinity Church, Reading, Dec. 29, 1867. Pp. 20.
6. Gotwald, W. H. Jubilee Catechism. Lancaster, Pa. Pp. 8.
7. Greenwald, E. The Lutheran Reformation in a series of discourses. Rev. E. Greenwald, D. D., Lancaster. Philadelphia. 12mo. Pp. 392.
8. Hinterleitner. Ein Baustein zu Luther's Denkmal, errichtet im Herzen unseres Lutherischen Christenvolks, bei der VIIten Jubelfeier der Reformation. 1867. (A poem). Allentown. Pp. 8.
9. Krauth, C. P, Jr. Ein feste Burg (with music). Luther's Battle Hymn, translated. (Sheet, on the back, Reformation events and dates). Philadelphia.
10. Krauth, C. P, Jr. The Jubilee Service: An order of divine worship for the Seventh Jubilee of the Reformation. 12mo. Pp. 24.
11. Morris, Jubilee Tract. Pp. 4.
12. Müller, J. A. H. Jubelfest Büchlein: das ist, Fragen und Antworten über die Geschichte d. Evang. Luth. Kirche, Pittsburg. St. Louis. Pp. 32.
13. Rath, J. B. Catechism for the Seventh Jubilee of the Reformation. Bethlehem, Pa. 1867.
14. Riis, H. N. Kurzer Unterricht ueber Luther u. d. Reformation in Fragen u. Antworten. Allentown. Pp. 7.
15. Seiss, J. A. The Jubilee. Phila. Pp. 4.

16. Seiss, J. A. Ecclesia Lutheranna: a brief survey of the Ev. Luth. Church. Philadelphia. 1868. 12mo. Pp. 276.
17. Seiss, J. A. The Lutheran Church. (Reprint with amendments). Baltimore. Pp. 19.
18. Sheeleigh, M. Hymns for the Seventh Semi-centennial Jubilee of the Reformation. Philda. 1867. 16mo. Pp. 18.
19. Jubilee Hymn, with music. (Sheet).
20. Stork, T, Sr. Two Hymns for the Jubilee of the Reformation. Philadelphia.
21. Stork, C, Jr. The Reformation God's Work. A sermon. Nov. 5, 1867. Baltimore. Pp. 16.
22. [Stuckenberg.] Ninety Five Theses for the Seventh Semi-centennial Jubilee of the Reformation. Balt. 1868. Pp. 68.
23. Strobel, W. D. Jubilee Tract, No. 2. The Lutheran Church, why should I love it? Baltimore. Pp. 4.
24. Vogelbach, S. Zur Errinerung an die 350 Jährigen Jubelfeier der Reformation. Phila. Pp. 8.
25. Weiser, R. Lutheran Jubilee. A Synodical sermon. Pp. 20.

The following are anonymous:

26. The 350th anniversary of the Reformation, at Plymouth church, under the auspices of the Young Men's Christian Association of St. Matthews Evangelical Lutheran Church. Programme. Pp. 4. Brooklyn, N. Y.
27. 350th anniversary of the Reformed Lutheran Mission. Wheeling, Pa. Pp. 4.
28. Pittsburg Jubilee Service. 1867.
29. Die Feier des 350 Reform. Jubilaeum in Addison, Ill. St. Louis. Pp. 15.
30. Luther's Photograph. Lutheran Publication Society. Philadelphia.
31. Harrisburg Lutheran Jubilee, Nos. 1, 2. Publisher of Lutheran Sunday-school.
32. Seventh Semi-centennial Jubilee of the Reformation in St. James' Lutheran church, N. Y. Programme. Pp. 4.
33. Sunday School Jubilee of 1st Evangelical Lutheran church, Harrisburg, May 6th, 1868. (Sheet).
34. Photographs of members of General Synod. Harrisburg, May, 1868.

35. Jubilee Card, published by General Synod.
36. Jubilee Medal. Milwaukee.
37. Jubilee Medal. Philadelphia. With bust of Luther and inscriptions.

I here insert a few articles taken from the Observer, to show the spirit of the times relating to this subject. The Observer of those days is crowded with communications of a similar character.

THE JUBILEE—TO THE MINISTERS AND CHURCHES OF THE SYNOD OF EAST PENNSYLVANIA.

In compliance with the request of Synod, I desire to call your attention to its action in reference to the celebration of the approaching Semi-centennial of the Reformation. As this action has not yet been published, and may be needed as, to some extent, the basis and guide of operations in the proposed celebration, it is proper that I should here bring to your notice the principal resolutions adopted:

1. *Resolved*, That this Synod heartily rejoices in the prospect of such a celebration by the churches of the General Synod, and herewith earnestly exhorts all our people to unite in the same.

2. That the main features of the celebration should be the presentation, from the pulpit and otherwise, of the great doctrines of the Reformation, and the contribution of funds for the various benevolent operations of the church.

3. That we will endeavor to raise for benevolent purposes, during the year, at least $100,000 within the bounds of our Synod.

4. That the following objects be specially commended to the attention of our people, every one selecting from among them according to his individual preference, and giving liberally according as the Lord hath prospered him: Foreign Missions, Home Missions, Education, Church Extension, Publication Society, Pastor's Fund, Theological Seminaries, Colleges, Orphans' Home at Loysville, Perry county, Pa., Memorial Church at Washington, D. C., and General Benevolence.

These resolutions, with this schedule of benevolent objects, were followed by resolutions requiring pastors to send to the President of Synod monthly reports of contributions made, and the President to keep a full account of such contributions, and publish monthly the amount contributed to each object.

THE JUBILEE IN YORK, PA.—ITS OBSERVANCE INAUGURATED.

An interesting and spirited meeting of members of the four Lutheran churches of York, Pa., was held in St. Paul's, Rev. W. M. Baum, pastor, on Monday evening, October 7th. The exercises were opened by the choir, rendering that noble anthem, "*Mighty Jehovah*," with fine effect. The sixty-second chapter of Isaiah was then read by the pastor, and prayer offered by Rev. C. J. Deininger. The choir and congregation sang with great earnestness that grand old hymn 845: "All Hail the Power of Jesus' Name."

The object of the meeting was then very happily stated by Rev. Dr. Lochman, pastor of the First Lutheran Church. The necessity for a Reformation of the Church, the manner of its accomplishment, and the blessed results flowing in an ever increasing stream through all of Protestant Christianity, were very handsomely presented. Those present were then asked whether they would unite with the great body of the Lutheran Church in the United States and Europe in celebrating the Seventh Jubilee of this event. It was desirable for our four congregations, between whose pastors and members there are perfect concord and harmony, to act in *concert*, and seek, by *united* effort, to make the occasion memorable and blessed.

Rev. W. M. Baum followed in an earnest address, claiming a high position for the Lutheran Church, and predicting a glorious future, when her own members shall awake to the full consciousness of the blessed inheritance bequeathed them in the history, the doctrines and the services of their church.

The following questions were then put directly to the audience: "*Shall we unite in this commemoration of the Reformation?*" "*Shall we signalize this occasion by trimming our churches, having special services and by asking a grand Free-Will Thank Offering of our means to the Church?*"

To these questions the response was hearty, unanimous and emphatic. The pastors were not a whit in advance of their people. Every proposition was eagerly received and cheerfully endorsed.

Mr. Charles A. Morris, a layman of St. Paul's, but as well known in the church as the great mass of our ministers, was the next speaker. Seldom have we heard a better or more pertinent address. Clear, impressive and whole-souled, the fire of early years flashed forth anew in the utterances of this tried and faithful veteran of seventy-five. Nothing but the sacredness of the place and the solemnity of the occasion prevented a hearty endorsement of his sentiments by rapturous applause.

Rev. C. J. Deininger, pastor of several congregations in the immediate vicinity of York, expressed his fullest sympathy and heartiest endorsement of the objects of the meeting, and declared his intention to inaugurate similar services in the churches under his care.

Rev. J. H. Menges did not quite endorse the proposition for church-decorations, but was heart and soul for everything that would elevate our church and extend her usefulness.

LECTURESHIPS AND PRIZES

In the year 1865 the Rev. Samuel A. Holman, of the Synod of East Pennsylvania, placed in the hands of the Directors of the Theological Seminary at Gettysburg the sum of $2000, the interest of which is to be paid to a person appointed by the Board to deliver a lecture at Gettysburg on some article of the Augsburg Confession. There is one lecture every year, and it has heretofore been delivered on some evening during commencement week, when usually many visiting ministers are present. But of late years the audiences have been small. The ministers know they can read it afterwards in the Review, and the laity feel no interest in what they falsely call a dry theological lecture. This induced the Board (at its last meeting, 1877) to change the time and place of the delivery of the dissertation. It is not to be public, as heretofore, but in the Seminary, before the professors and students, and such others who may choose to attend.

The *first* lecture on the First Article of the Confession, which treats of *God*, was delivered by Rev. Dr. James A. Brown, in 1866, professor in the Seminary. The *second*, of *Original Sin*, by S. S. Sprecher, Wittenberg College. The *third*, of *the Son of God and of the Holy Spirit*, by S. S. Schmucker. The *fourth*, of *Justification*, by M. Valentine. The *fifth*, *of the ministry of the Church*, by Rev. Dr. Charles A. Hay, a professor in the Seminary. The *sixth*, of *New Obedience*, by Rev. Dr. Chas. A. Stork. The *seventh*, of *the Church*, by Rev. John G. Morris. The *eighth*, *What the Church is*, by Rev. Henry Ziegler. The *ninth*, on *Baptism*, by Rev. F. W. Conrad, D. D. The *tenth*, of *the Lord's Supper*, by George Diehl, in 1875. The *eleventh*, of *Confession*, by Rev. A. C. Wedekind, in 1876. The *twelfth*, *of Repentance*, by Simeon W. Harkey, in 1877. The next lecturer is Rev. Dr. Baum. All these lectures have been published in the Evangelical Quarterly.

In 1871 Mr. John Rice, of Baltimore, founded a lectureship on "Methods in Ministerial Work," with special reference to developing and directing the benevolence of the church, the care of the young, and the development of lay work, and placed $1000 in the hands of the Directors of the Seminary, the yearly interest of which is to be paid to the person appointed. Mr. Rice has retained the privilege of nominating the lecturer, but he is really appointed by the Board. Those who have been appointed are Rev. Drs. J. G. Butler, in 1872; C. A. Stork, 1873; L. A. Gotwald, 1874; A. C. Wedekind, 1875; G. H. Wenner, 1876; Tyng, of N. Y., 1877, who failed to appear.

In 1876 the Rev. Dr. F. W. Conrad offered a prize of $30 to that student in the Seminary who, in the judgment of the faculty, excelled in elocutionary ability or reading of Scriptures, Hymns and Liturgy; but the students, apprehensive that it would tend to excite unfriendly competition and rivalry, begged leave to decline the well intended offer.

Mr. C. W. Hassler, then of the U. S. Navy, gave, in 1866, $250, the interest of which to be expended annually for the purchase of a gold medal to that student of the Junior class in college who shall have shown the greatest proficiency in the Latin language.

John Graeff, of Philadelphia, annually authorizes the Professor of English Literature in Pennsylvania College to have a gold medal prepared, at a cost of $30, for the best essay in that department.

"A Friend" (Dr. H. H. M., of Reading) gave $500 in 1856-61, the interest of which is given to that student in the Freshman class who excels in general scholarship.

CELEBRATION OF REFORMATION DAY.

It is only about thirty years ago that it was first proposed in the *Maryland Synod* to recommend to the churches the celebration of the thirty-first of October as *Reformation Day*. It was suggested that, on that day or the Sunday nearest to it, special sermons be preached upon the subject, information be diffused, and the interest of the churches be awakened. For the first few years it was not extensively observed, but at the present time hundreds of ministers in every section of the church preach upon the glorious theme. Even some superintendents of Sunday schools have taken it up, and are instructing the pupils in the grand historical fact. The result has been the publication of several good books and many sermons on the Reformation in general and Luther in particular. We have the proud gratification of knowing that, as one of the results of this measure, Luther's character is more clearly developed, his mighty work more highly appreciated, and his influence upon the destiny of mankind more distinctly felt than ever before, and that not only by our own people, but by those of all other Protestant churches. Luther's name is more frequently mentioned in discourses and writings than ever before. More books relating to him have been written and published by persons outside of our church than on any other man connected with the Reformation, and every year the number is increasing.

LUTHERAN MINISTERS

Who have served as Professors or Tutors in Colleges of other denominations or who have been elected to such positions.

Aughey, Samuel. Professor of Science in Nebraska University.

Bachman, John. Professor of Natural History in South Carolina College. The Presidency was offered to him.

Breidenbaugh, Edward. Assistant Professor of Chemistry, Yale College.

Butler, J. G. Professor of Chemistry, History and Homiletics, Linwen University, Washington.

BUTLER, G. Professor in Howard University, Washington, D. C.

Cruse. Professor of Greek, University of Pennsylvania, Philadelphia.

Eggers, H. Professor of Latin, Western University, Pittsburg.

Endress, C. Tutor in University of Pennsylvania.

Ernst, W. Tutor in University of Pennsylvania.

Haverstick, H. Professor of Languages, High School, Philadelphia.

Hazelius, E. L. Elected—Lafayette College and Princeton.

Heilig, W. Professor in Baltimore City College.

Helmuth, J. C. H. Professor of German and Oriental Languages, University Pennsylvania.

Hubbert, W. E. Professor of Ancient Languages and Literature, Blacksburg, Virginia.

Knauff (Layman). Professor University Pennsylvania.

Krauth, C. P, Jr. Vice Provost and Professor of Moral Philosophy, University of Pennsylvania.

Kunze, J. C. Professor of Oriental Languages, University Pennsylvania, afterwards same in Columbia College, New York.

Lehman, W. Professor of Modern Languages, High School, Pitsfield Massachusetts—elected to Franklin College, Georgia,

Mayer, P. F. Elected Provost, University Pennsylvania.

Morris, J. G. Elected Professor of Natural History, University of Maryland.

Muhlenberg, F. A. Professor of Greek, University of Pennsylvania.
Parson, W. Professor of English, Imperial University, Japan.
Richard, J. W. Professor of German, Lafayette College, Pennsylvania.
Sadtler, S. (Layman). Professor of Chemistry and Mineralogy, University Pennsylvania, Philadelphia.
Schaeffer, F. C. Professor of German, Columbia College, New York.
Schmidt, H. I. Professor of German, Columbia College, New York.
Schmidt, F. Lafayette College.
Schwartz, J. C. Assistant Professor of Languages, Charleston College.
Sihler. Fellow and Professor of Greek, Johns Hopkins University, Baltimore.
Sihler. Biology, in Johns Hopkins University.
Uhler, P. R. (Layman.) Assistant Professor of Natural History.
Uhlhorn, J. Professor of Greek, University of Maryland.
Wynn. Professor, Western College.

Doctors of Divinity and LL. D. in the Lutheran Church.

Names.	Source.
Albert, L. E	Pennsylvania College.
Auspach, F. R	Franklin and Marshal.
Aughhey, S., LL. D.	
Bachman, J	Pennsylvania College.
and LL. D.	University of Berlin.
Babb, A	Pennsylvania College.
Baker, J. C	Lafayette College.
Baltzly, J. B	Wittenberg College.
Baugher, H. L	Dickenson College.
Baum, W. M	Pennsylvania College.
Bernheim, G. A	Pennsylvania College.
Bikle, L. A	Pennsylvania College.
Bittle, D. F.	Pennsylvania College.
Bowman, J	Pennsylvania College.
Brown, J. G	Pennsylvania College.
Brown, A. J.	Pennsylvania College.
Butler, J. G	Pennsylvania College.
Conrad, F. W	Wittenberg College.
Crouse, J	Wittenberg College.
Davis, J. B	Wittenberg College.
Demme, C. R	University of Pennsylvania.
Diehl, G	Pennsylvania College.
Diehl, M	Wittenberg College.
Domer, S	Roanoke College.
Dosh, F. W	Roanoke College.
Eichelberger, L	Princeton College.
Endress, C. F	University of Pennsylvania.
Ernst, W	University of Pennsylvania.
Felts, P	
Finckle, S	Irving, Md.
Fink, R. A	Pennsylvania College.
Fry, J	Pennsylvania College.
Geissenhainer, F. W	University of New York.
Geissenhainer, F. W., Jr	University of Pennsylvania.
Gotwald, L	Pennsylvania College.
Greenwald, E	

Names.	Source.
Harkey, S. W.	Wittenberg College.
Harrison, W.	Wittenberg College.
Hauer, D.	Irving, Md.
Hay, C. A.	Pennsylvania College.
Hazelius, E. L.	University of Pennsylvania.
Helmuth, A.	University of Pennsylvania.
Henkle, S.	North Carolina College.
Honour, J. H.	North Carolina College.
Hutter, E. W.	Pennsylvania College.
Jacobs, M.	Jefferson and Wittenberg.
Jacobs, H. E.	Thiel College.
Keller, E.	Jefferson College.
Krauth, C. P., Sr.	University of Pennsylvania.
Krauth, C. P., Jr.	Pennsylvania College.
Krotel, G. F.	
Kunze, J. C.	University of Pennsylvania.
Kuhns, L. M.	Wittenberg College.
Kurtz, D.	University of Pennsylvania.
Kurtz, B.	Washington College.
and LL. D.	Wittenberg College.
Lintner, C. A.	Pennsylvania College.
Lochman, J. G.	Alleghany College, Meadville, Pa., and University of Pennsylvania.
Lochman, A. H.	Pennsylvania College.
Magee, Irving.	
Mann, W. J.	Pennsylvania College.
McCron, J.	Roanoke College.
Mayer, P. F.	University of Pennsylvania and Columbia College.
Miller, J.	University of Pennsylvania.
Miller, G. B.	Union College.
Mohldehnke, Edward.	Germany.
Morris, J. G., LL. D.	Pennsylvania College.
Muhlenberg, H. M.	University of Pennsylvania.
Muhlenberg, H. E.	University of Pennsylvania.
Muhlenberg, F. A.	Pennsylvania College.
Ort, S. A.	Wittenberg College.
Oswald, J.	Wittenberg College.
Passavant, W. A.	Pennsylvania College.
Pohlman, H. N.	Pennsylvania College.

Names.	Source.
Quitman, F. H.	Harvard University.
Reinmund, J. F.	Wittenberg College.
Richards, J. W.	Jefferson College.
Sadtler, B.	Pennsylvania College.
Schaeffer, F. D.	University of Pennsylvania.
Schaeffer, F. C.	Columbia College.
Schaeffer, D. F.	St. John's, Md.
Schaeffer, C. F.	Pennsylvania College.
Schaeffer, C. W.	Wittenberg College.
Schmidt, H. J.	Pennsylvania College.
Schmucker, J. G	University of Pennsylvania.
Schmucker, S. S	Jefferson College and Rutger's College.
Schmucker, B. M	Pennsylvania College.
Schock, G. L	Pennsylvania College.
Scholl, W. N	Pennsylvania College.
Seiss, J. A	Pennsylvania College.
Senderling, J. Z	Pennsylvania College.
Seyfarth, G	Pennsylvania College.
Smeltzer, J. P.	Pennsylvania College.
Spaeth, A.	
Sprecher, G	Washington College.
Spangenberg, J. A	Germany.
Steck, D	Wittenberg College.
Steck, J	Wittenberg College.
Sternberg, L.	Union College.
Stelling, G. F	Wittenberg College.
Stohlman, C. F. E	Capitol University, Columbus, Ohio.
Stork, T	Wittenberg College.
Stork, C. A	Pennsylvania College.
Strobel, W. D	Hamilton College.
Swartz, J	Wittenberg College.
Thuemmel, C. B.	
Valentine, M.	Pennsylvania College.
Wackerhagen, A.	Union College.
Wedekind, A. C	Union College.
Weiser, R.	Pennsylvania College.
Wiles, H. L.	Jefferson College.
Wolf, E. J.	Jefferson College.
Ziegler, H.	Wittenberg College.

MEMBERS OF FOREIGN LEARNED SOCIETIES.

The following are the only ministers of our church whom I could ascertain as having been elected members of foreign societies :
Dr. Henry Ernst Muhlenberg, of Lancaster (1770–1815).
    Member of the Naturforschende Freunde, Berlin. Member of the Philosophical and Physical Societies of Goettingen.
Rev. John Bachman, D. D., Charleston, S. C.
Rev. John G. Morris.
    Member of the Royal Ante-Columbian Society of Northern Antiquaries, Copenhagen.
    Member of Die Naturhistorische Gesellschaft zu Nurnberg, Bavaria.

Members of the American Philosophical Society, Philadelphia.

Rev. Dr. H. E. Muhlenberg.
Rev. Dr. C. R. Demme.
Rev. Dr. C. P. Krauth, Jr.
Prof. S. B. Sadtler.

    Dr. C. P. Krauth is also the only Lutheran minister who is a member of The Oriental Society, and of The American Committee co-operating with the Revisers of the Authorized Version, and of The American Bible Society's Committee on Versions.

LUTHERAN MINISTERS AND LAYMEN

Who have written on various Departments of Science.

Our theological and purely literary writers are well known to all the church. Those departments are in one sense, professional, but there is besides this, a field that has been to some extent cultivated by our men, and to show at a glance what we have contributed to science, I have here brought together all their names and the abbreviated titles of their principal writings.[*] I am sure it will be gratifying to many to see this distinct group.

---

[*] For a full catalogue of our Lutheran Literature in America, see my Bibliotheca Lutherana. Philadelphia. 1876.

AUGHEY, SAMUEL, Ph. D.
> The Geology of Nebraska. 1873.
> Catalogue of the Plants of Nebraska. 1874.
> The Superficial Deposits of Nebraska. 1875.
> Catalogue of the Land and Fresh Water Shells of Nebraska.

BACHMAN, JOHN, D. D., LL. D.
> The Doctrine of the Unity of the Human Race.
> A Notice of Nott and Gliddon's "Types of Mankind."
> An Examination of Agassiz's "Natural Provinces of the Animal World."
> An Examination of the characteristics of Genera and Species.
> Catalogue of the Phaenogamous Plants and Ferns of South Carolina.
> Experiments on the Habits of Vultures.
> Monograph of the Genus *Sciurus* (Squirrels).
> The Changes in the Colors of Feathers in Birds and of Hair in Animals.
> The Introduction and Propagation of Fresh Water Fish.
> Controversy with Dr. Morton on Hybridity.
> Dr. Bachman had a principal hand in the writing of Audubon's great work on our Birds and Quadrupeds, and has also contributed numerous other scientific articles to various Journals.

BIKLE, P. M.
> Parody, the Scientist and Christian. Quart. Rev., No. 420.
> Our present knowledge of the Sun. Ib. VII., No. 387.

BREIDENBAUGH, EDWARD.
> Various articles.

BROWN, JAMES A.
> Christian Anthropology, Amer. Presbyt. Rev. 1869.
> Review of Tyndall's Address, Quart. Rev. V. 68.

DAVIS, J. B.
> Various articles in Reviews and Journals.

DUMLING, H.
> Illustrirtes Thierleben. 1875. 8vo.

DUMLING, F. F. H.
> Arithmetisches Exempel Buch. 1876.

FOCHT, D. H.
> The Geology in the vicinity of Bloomsfield. 1860.

GILBERT, DR. D.
    Five Introductory and Valedictory Addresses to Graduating Classes of Medicine.

HOUPT, GENL. H.
    General Theory of Bridge Construction.
    Improvement of the Ohio River.

HOUPT, L. L.
    Conversation on Engineering.

JACOBS, PROF. M.
    Consistency of Geology and Revelation. Ev. Rev., 1363.
    Unity of the Human Race. Ib. II, 451.
    Relation of the Animal to the Vegetable World. Ib. XI, 256.
    Meteorology. Ib. X, 161.
    The Indian Summer. Linn. Journ.

KEMP, DR. W. M.
    One Thousand Cases of Obstetrics.

KUNZE, J. C.
    New Method of Calculating the Eclipse of June 16, 1806.

LINDEMANN, J. C. C.
    Lehrbuch der Arithmetik, Astronomische, Unterredungen.

MELSHEIMER, F. V.
    Catalogue of the Insects of Pennsylvania.

MELSHEIMER, DR. E. F.
    Catalogue of the Coleoptera of the U. S.
    Author of numerous articles on Entomology.

MORRIS, JOHN G.
    Von Leonhard's Lectures on Geology—Translated.
    Address on the Study of Natural History. 1841.
    Address at Dedication of Linnaean Hall. 1847.
    Catalogue of the Described Lepidoptera of U. S. Published by the Smithsonian Institution. 1860.
    Synopsis of the Described Lepidoptera of U. S. Smithsonian Institution. 1861.
    Contributions to the History of Entomology in the U. S. Silliman's Journ. Numerous shorter articles.

MUHLENBERG, HENRY E.
    Descriptio Uberior Graminum.
    Catalogus Plantarum.
    Flora Lancastriensis.

SEYFARTH, G.
    Amerikanischer Kalender.
    Die Wahre Zeitrechnung der Alt. Test.
    An Astronomical Inscription Concerning the Year 22 B. C.
    Rudimenta Hieroglyphica.
    Systema Astronomiae Aegyptiacae.
    (Many other writings on Astronomy, Chronology and Aegyptiology.) See Rev., VIII, 34.
THOMAS, C.
    Zoology of Colorado in Hayden's Expedition.
    (Several other scientific treatises.)
WALTZ, E. L.
    Erklaerung des Kalenders. 1830.

LUTHERAN COMMENTATORS OF THE SCRIPTURES

IN THE UNITED STATES.

Schmucker, J. G.
    Prophetic History of the Christian Religion; or, Explanation of the Revelation of St. John. 2 Vol. 8vo. 1817. (German.)
    Die Vornehmste Weissagungen der Heiligen Schrift. Hagerstown. 1807.
Krauth, C. P., Jr.
    Commentary on John. By Tholuck. (Translated.)
J. G. Morris and C. A. Smith.
    Explanation of the Gospels. Baltimore. 2 Vols. 12mo.
Seiss, J. A.
    Lectures on the Epistle to the Hebrews. Baltimore. 1846. 8vo. Pp. 408.
    The Gospel in Leviticus. Phila. 1860. 12mo.
    Lectures on the Gospels. Phila.
    The Apocalypse. A Series of Lectures. Philadelphia. 1866.

Books and Articles in Reviews Concerning Luther,

BY NON-LUTHERAN WRITERS, PUBLISHED IN THE UNITED STATES.

I have thought that the following list would be at least interesting to some of my friends. It is probable that my list is not complete, but it shows the popularity of the Reformer. Indeed, all good books on the subject are eagerly read.

D'Aubigne. History of the Great Reformation. (Various Editions.)

Chronicles of the Schoenberg Cotta Family. 1864.

Watchwords from the Warfare of Life, from Dr. Martin Luther, translated by the authors of Chronicles of the Schoenberg Cotta Family. 1868.

History of the Reformation, extracted from Milner's Church History. 2 Vol. 12mo.

Robert Montgomery. Luther, a Poem.

Henry Mayhew. The Boyhood of Luther. Harpers. 1864.

Villers, C. An Essay on the Spirit and Influence of the Reformation, by Luther. 1867. 8vo.

Child's Life of Luther. American Tract Society.

Martyn, W. C. Life and Times of Martin Luther. American Tract Society.

Sears, B. Select Treatises of Martin Luther. Andover. 1846.

Sears, B. Life of Martin Luther. Philadelphia. 18mo.

Audin, G. M. History of the Life, Writings and Doctrines of Martin Luther. Philadelphia. 1841. 8vo. (Roman Catholic.)

Bunsen, Chev. Life of Martin Luther, with an estimate of Luther's Character, by T. Carlyle. New York. 12mo.

Koenig. Life of Luther, with fifty historical engravings. New York. 1857. 4to.

Michelet. Life of Martin Luther, gathered from his own writings. New York. 1846. 12mo.

Hare. Vindication of Luther.

Labouchere. Illustrations of the Life of Luther.

Adams, Charles. Words that Shook the World, or Martin Luther his own biographer. New York. 1856. 12mo.

Luther's Christ Baum mit Sechs Schoenen Bilder. Steiger. New York. 1855. 8vo.

Luther and the Reformation in Germany, with an Introduction by Rev. Dr. T. Stork. Philadelphia. 8vo.

Luther and His Times. Philadelphia. 12mo.

Carlyle, T. Hero Worship.

Hazlitt's Table Talk of Luther.

Magazine and Review Articles on Luther.

Luther, Michelet's Life of. North Amer. Rev., LXIII, 433.

Luther, Martin. Christian Examiner, XXX, 148; XXXII, 19; XLIII, 98. Southern Literary Messenger, IV, 596.

Luther and Melanchthon. Southern Literary Messenger, IX, 641.

Luther and Zwingli. Christ. Exam., XLV, 170.

Luther at Worms. Princeton Review, VIII, 445. Methodist Quarterly Rev., IV, 528.

Luther, Cell of. South. Lit. Mess., IX, 746.

Luther, Childhood and Youth of. Amer. Bib. Repository, 2nd Ser., III, 594.

Luther, Correspondence and Character of. Living Age, VI, 325.

Luther, Funeral Oration of. Living Age, VIII, 164.

Luther Incognito. South. Lit. Mess., II, 699.

Luther, Last Days and Death of. Amer. Bib. Repos., 2d Ser., I, 195.

Luther, Life and Times of. Christian Exam., XXVIII, 402.

Luther, Religious Experience of. Bibliotheca Sacra, V, 519.

Luther, Sear's Life of. Princeton Rev., XXII, 437.

Luther, Sear's Life of. Bib. Sac., VII, 600.

Luther, Table Talk. Amer. Bib. Repos., 3d Ser., III, 553.

Luther, Writings of. Amer. Bib. Repos., II, 191; 2nd Ser., XI, 241; XII, 1.

Lutheranism and the Reformation. Amer. Bib. Repos., 3d Ser., I, 119.

Sears, B. The Fathers and Founders of the Lutheran Church. Bib. Sac., XX, 636.

Frequent Notices of Amer. Repos. I, 425–463.

Martin Luther and the Old Church. National Quar., XVI, 108.

Luther's Correspondence and Character. Eclectic, Sep., 1845.
Luther as a Preacher. Dr. Waterbury's Eloquent Preachers.
Luther, a Man of Soul. Dr. Hazen's Inaugural Address.
The Reformation: Its Spirit and Influences. Christ. Spectator, 1854.
Luther and his Principles. Bancroft, U. S., I, 457.

WRITINGS OF LUTHERAN MINISTERS

IN THE UNITED STATES ON LUTHER AND THE LUTHERAN CHURCH.

I have no doubt it will surprise many who have not looked at my *Bibliotheca Lutherana*, that so many of our ministers have written on these subjects. The matter is of such absorbing interest, and most of these writings are so creditable to their authors, as well as showing their Lutheran zeal, that I have thought it would be acceptable to give a list of them. This list embraces only *book* and review articles; there are many others of our ministers who have written equally well for our church papers on the same subject, but not being in book or review form, I could not collect them. For size, date and place of publication see the Bibliotheca Lutherana.

ALBAUGH, W.
 Life of Luther. Translated from Meurer.
BACHMAN, J.
 Defence of Luther and the Reformation.
 Sermons on the Doctrines and Discipline of the Lutheran Church.
BAUGHER, H. L.
 The Counter Reformation.
BERNHEIM, G. D.
 History of the German Settlements and of the Lutheran Church in North and South Carolina.
BORELIUS.
 The Lutheran Augustana Synod and its Mission.
BRANDT, C. A.
 Stimmen der Kirche am Reformations Feste.

Brobst, S. K.
> Der grosse Mangel in der Kirche.
> Ein Wort für die Deutschen in d. Luth. Kirche.
> [Nearly all Brobst's numerous publications have reference to the Church].

Brown, Abel J.
> Vindication of the Lutheran Synod of Tennessee.
> The Lutheran Church built on the only true Foundation.

Brown, James A.
> The Reformation the work of God.
> The General Synod and its Assailants.
> The Lutheran Church in the United States.
> Union in the Lutheran Church.
> Dr. Hodge on the Luth. Doctrine of the Person of Christ.
> The Ministerium.
> Augsburg Confession and Second coming of Christ.
> The General Synod.
> The Four General Bodies, wherein they agree, &c., &c.

Butler, J. B. (Layman).
> History of the Lutheran Church, Hopeful, Ky.

Buttner, G.
> Geschichte d. Reformation.

Conrad, F. W.
> The Confessors and Confession of Augsburg.
> The Lutheran Doctrine of Baptism.
> The Church.
> Characteristics of the Augsburg Confession.

Diehl, G.
> Historical Discourse on the Church in Frederick.
> Holman Lecture on the Ninth Article of Augsburg Confession.
> Martin Luther.
> The Human and Divine Factors in a Call to the Ministry.

Domer, S.
> The Jubilee of 1865.

Drees, P. J.
> Beiträage zur Mission d. Luth. Kirche in New York.

Fick, C. I. H.
> Das Martyner Buch.
> Das Luther Buch.
> Lieder zum Jubilaeum d. Reformation.

FINCKEL, S. D.
   Luther and the Reformation.
FOCHT, D. H.
   History of Grindstone Hill Church.
   The Lutheran Church.
   The Church between the Mountains.
FRANK, C. A.
   Chemnitz's Examen Concil. Trid.—translated.
FRITSCHE, G.
   (Various articles.)
FRY, J.
   Catechism for the Jubilee.
   The Church Book Explained.
GOTWALD, W. V.
   Jubilee Catechism.
   History of St. John's, Lancaster.
GRAETZ, R.
   Ob l'apsthum in d. Luth. Kirche, &c.
GREENWALD, E.
   The Lutheran Reformation.
   The True Church.
   True and False Spiritualism as Taught by Our Confession.
GROSSE, PROF.
   Katachese über d. Symbolischen Bücher.
HARBAUGH, D.
   History of Hopeful Church, Ky.
HARKEY, S. W.
   Mission of Lutheran Church in the United States.
   Mission of the General Synod.
   Importance of Developing the Resources of the Lutheran Church.
   Early History of Lutheran Church in Illinois.
HAY, C. A.
   The Ministerium.
   Schmid's Dogmatik—translated.
   The Castle of Wartburg.
HAZELIUS, E. L.
   Life of Luther.
   Augsburg Confession.
   History of American Lutheran Church.
   Discipline, Articles of Faith of, Synod of South Carolina.

HENKEL, C.
    The Reformation.
HENKEL, A.
    Luther on the Sacraments—translated.
    Book of Concord—translated.
HENKEL, D. M.
    Mission Work of Luth. Church.
HILL, R.
    The Luth. Church and its Mission.
HINTERLEITNER, G. A.
    Ein Baustein zu Luther's Denkmale.
HOFFMAN, J. N.
    The Broken Platform.
    The Lutheran Church.
HOLMAN, A. P.
    The Conflict in the Church.
JACOBS, H. E.
    Lutheran Doctrine of the Lord's Day.
    Lutheran Doctrine of the Ministry.
    Lutheran Doctrine of the Sabbath.
    Compend of Lutheran Theology—translated.
    Schmid's Dogmatik—translated. See Hay.
    Day of Augsburg.
    Melanchthon.
    History of the Lutheran Church in the United States.
KAUFFMAN, J. C.
    Home Mission Work in General Synod.
KAEHLER, C. W.
    Jubelfest Büchlein.
KEYL, E. W. C.
    Lutherophilus.
KÖSTERING, J. F.
    Auswanderung d. Sächsischen Auswanderer in Jahre 1838.
KRAUTH, C. P.
    Works of Melanchthon.
    General Synod.
    Early History of the Lutheran Church
    Schmid's Dogmatik.
    The Lutheran Church in the United States.
    Present Position of the Lutheran Church.
    Contributions to the History of Church.
    Luther and Melanchthon.

KRAUTH, C. P., JR.
- Discourse on the Burning of the Old Lutheran Church in Wisnhata.
- The Ev. Luth. Church.
- Jubilee Service.
- The Reformation
- Translation of Augsburg Confession.
- Origin and Result of the Ninty-five Theses.
- New Translation of the Ninty-five Theses.
- The Conservative Reformation.
- The Relation of Confession to the Reformation.
- Unity of the Lutheran Church.
- The Luth. Church and the Divine Obligation of the Lord's Day.
- Bibliography of the Augsburg Confession.
- The Reformation.
- The Lutheran Church.

KROTEL, G. F.
- The Lutheran Church and the Denominations Around Us.
- Life of Melanchthon.
- The Lutheran Church.
- History of Trinity Church.
- Fest Predigt in Zion's Kirche.
- Luther and the Swiss.

KURTZ, B.
- Why are you a Lutheran?
- Year Book of the Reformation.
- Lutheran Prayer Book.
- Predictions concerning Luther.
- Passages in the Life of Luther.

LARSEN, L.
- The Literal Meaning of the Words of Lord's Supper.

LINDEMAN, J. C. C.
- Luther, als Erzieher d. Iugend.

LINTNER, G. A.
- Augsburg Confession, with notes.
- Early History of the Lutheran Church in the State of New York.

LOCHMAN, J. G.
- History, Doctrines and Discipline of Lutheran Church.

Loy, M.
>Life and Deeds of Luther.
>Luther's House Postil.
>The Lutheran Cultus.
>Lutheran Doctrine of Ordination.

Luther, D.
>The Lutheran Church and the German Language.

Mageres, S. M.
>Translator from the Danish of the Articles of Faith of the Lutheran Church.

Mann, W. J.
>Plea for the Augsburg Confession.
>Lutheranism in America.
>The Great Reformation.
>Theses on the Lutheranism of Our Church Fathers in the United States.

Miller, Clemens.
>Declaration in regard to Difficulties in the Church.

Miller, G.
>Discourse on the Fundamental Principles of the Reformation.
>Doctrine and Discipline of the Lutheran Church.

Mohldehnke, E. F.
>Theologie vom Luth. Standpunckte aus.

Morris, J. G.
>Year Book of the Reformation.
>Sermon on the Reformation.
>Blind Girl of Wittenberg.
>To Rome and back again.
>Catherine De Bora.
>Quaint Sayings and Doings Concerning Luther.
>Address on Reformation Jubilee.
>Luther's Visit to Rome.
>The Theses of Luther.
>Luther as a Pulpit Orator.
>The Literature of the Lutheran Church.
>Bibliotheca Lutherana.
>Necessity and Blessings of the Reformation.
>John Reuchlin.
>John Calvin.
>The Augsburg Confession and the Thirty-nine Articles.

MUHLENBERG, F. A.
  Centennary Jubilee of Trinity Church.
  Theses upon the Church.
MULLER, J. A.
  Jubelfest Büchlein.
MULTANOWSKY, E.
  Ist Methodismus u. Lutherthum einerlei?
PEIXOTO, E. P.
  Leitfaden zu Erklaerung d. Kleinen Catechismus.
POHLMAN, H. N.
  Address at the Semi-Centennial of Hartwick Seminary.
  The German Colony and Lutheran Church in Maine.
QUITMAN, F. A.
  Sermon on the Reformation.
RATH, J. B.
  Catechism for the Seventh Jubilee.
RICHARDS, J. W.
  The Walk about Zion.
RITZ, S.
  Dialogue, Luther and the Reformation.
RUHLING, J. C. (Layman).
  Das Eche d. 300 Jähriger Jubelfeier.
SADTLER, B.
  Effect of the Adoption of the Formula of Concord upon the Lutheran Church.
SCHAEFFER, D. F.
  Address on the Reformation.
SCHAEFFER, F. C.
  The Blessed Reformation.
SCHAEFFER, C. F.
  Sermon at the Centennary Jubilee at Lancaster.
  The Lutheran Doctrine of Election.
  The Confessions of the Lutheran Church.
  Flaccus Illyrius and his Times.
  Maurice and the Emperor.
SCHAEFFER, C. W.
  Fiftieth Anniversary of Lutheran Church at Harrisburg.
  Early History of Lutheran Church in America.
  Luther's Preaching.
  The Lord's Supper, from Luther.

SCHICK, G.
    Luther's Anweisung zum rechten Studium d. Theologie.

SCHIERENBECK, J. H. C.
    Lebensbeschreibungen von Luth. Predigern in Amerika.

SCHMIDT, H. I.
    Lutheran Doctrine of the Lord's Supper.
    Meurers' Life of Luther.
    The three Saxon Electors of the Era of the Reformation.
    Condition of the Church.
    The Ambuscade; Night and Morning.

SCHMUCKER, J. G.
    Reformations Geschichte.

SCHMUCKER, S. S.
    Discourse on the Reformation.
    The American Lutheran Church.
    The Peace of Zion.
    Lutheran Manual.
    American Lutheranism Vindicated.
    Portraiture of Lutheranism.
    Retrospect of Lutheranism in the United States.
    Vocation of the American Lutheran Church.
    The Primitive Church and that of the Early Reformers.

SCHMUCKER, B. M.
    State of the Church in Norway.
    Divine Worship as held by the Lutheran Church.

SEISS, J. A.
    Reflections on the Lutheran Church.
    Jus Ecclesiasticum.
    Our Temple.
    Digest of Christian Doctrine.
    The Lutheran Church.
    How shall we order our Worship.
    Church Forms; Ministerial Acts.
    Address in behalf of the New Lutheran Church, Phila.
    Brief Survey of the Lutheran Church.
    The Lutheran Church; The Jubilee.
    Ecclesia Lutherana; The Javelin.
    Misunderstandings and Misrepresentations of the Lutheran Church.

SEVERINGHAUS, J. D.
>   Formel Buch; Denkschrift Zeugniss für den Luth. Charakter d. General Synode.
>   The Relation of the Sermon to the Church Year.
>   The German Language in the Institutions of the Lutheran Church.

SHEELEIGH, M.
>   Hymns for Sunday Schools of the Lutheran Church.
>   Lutheran Almanac; Ecclesiad; Jubilee Poem.
>   Relation of the Sunday School to the Church.
>   The Conservation of our Church's History.
>   Historical Society of General Synod.

SHOBER, G.
>   History of the Lutheran Reformation and of the Lutheran Church.

SPIEKER, G. F.
>   Hutten's Compend of Lutheran Theology: Translated.

SPRECHER, S.
>   Article II. of Augsburg Confession; Holman Lecture.
>   The principle of the Lutheran Reformation.

SPRINGER, F.
>   Lutheranism in the United States.
>   The Lutheran Church in Illinois.

STEIMLE, F. W. T.
>   Die Reformation ein Werk Gottes.

STOEVER, M. L. (Layman).
>   Life and Times of Henry Melchior Muhlenberg.
>   Sketch of the Lutheran Church in this Country.
>   Discourse before the General Synod.
>   Life and Correspondence of Dr. Quitman.
>   Martin Luther at the Diet of Worms.
>   Lutheran Church in the United States; General Synod.
>   Patriarchs of the Lutheran Church, from Halle.
>   [Numerous Sketches of Deceased Lutheran Ministers, printed in Evangelical Review.]

STOHLMAN, C. F. E.
>   Ich bin auch in Lutheraner.

STORK, T.
>   Life of Luther and of the Reformation.
>   Luther's Christmas Tree.
>   Luther at Home.

STORK, C. A.
>   The Reformation God's Work.
>   Liturgical Forms in Worship.

STRAEFFER, J. M. (Layman).
>   Lutheranism and Lutherans.

STROBEL, W. D.
>   Jubilee Tract.

STROBEL, P. A.
>   The Salzburgers and their Descendants.

STUCKENBERG, J. H. W.
>   Ninety-five Theses.
>   History of the Augsburg Confession.
>   The Authority of the Augsburg Confession.

TITUS, T. T.
>   History of St. Paul's Church, Lower Merion.

TORGERSEN, J. Z.
>   Translation of Bp. Pontopopidau's Catechism.

VALENTINE, M.
>   The Reformation.
>   Education in the Lutheran Church.

VOGELBACH, J.
>   Leben Dr. M. Luther.

WALTHER, C. F. W.
>   Warum hängen wir so fest an d. Luth. Kirche?
>   Warum sind d. Symbol. Bücher ...... unbedingt zu unterschreiben?
>   Die Luth. Kirche d. wahre sichtbare Kirche Gottes auf Erden.
>   Jubels fest Predigt.
>   Warum sollen wir unser Luthers, denen Namen wir tragen, nicht Schämen?
>   Die Kirche d. Reformation.
>   Warum sollen wir den bekanten Schriften unserer Luth. Kirche auch noch fest halten?
>   Predigt am Reformations Fest.

WEDEKIND, A. C.
>   Sacramental Ideas of Lutheran Church in Relation to Practical Piety.

WEISER, R.
    Life of Luther.
    Lutheranism before Luther.
    The Delivery of the Augsburg Confession.
    The Missionary Institute.
    The Lutheran Jubilee.
WYNEKEN, F. C.
    Die noth d. Deutschen Lutheraner in Amerika.

THE COLLOQUIUM AND THE DIET.

For several years before 1875 the subject of holding a general convention of our church in this country, for a free discussion upon the points which we did not all hold in common, was extensively discussed. These points related chiefly to the Sacraments, and to Pulpit and Altar Fellowship. Others of minor importance, such as secret societies, &c., would also have been introduced if such a meeting had been held.

The church papers were crowded with articles on the subject for some months, and the advocates and the opponents of the measure were not divided by party lines. There were friends and foes in every school.

It was argued by its advocates that a large assemblage of our ministers in friendly discussion for some days would of itself have a beneficent effect, even if nothing definite were settled; that social intercourse, mutual acquaintance and fraternal greetings would lead to harmonizing results. They also hoped that those in alleged error upon either of these points might, perhaps, be brought to change their minds, or, at least, to relax the severity of their views, and that this would prepare the way gradually for a final reconciliation and universal agreement.

Overtures of a fraternal character were made by the General Synod to the Council, but they resulted in nothing permanent. The former body discussed the subject at length at its meeting in Baltimore in 1875, where it was voted that it was not expedient to hold a Colloquium, and from that time the question has not been agitated. The opponents of the measure in the General Synod would not entertain the idea for a moment of going into convention with men who they apprehended would not recognize their Lutheran orthodoxy nor, perhaps, admit their claim to the name of Lutheran, which I think was unfounded.

(a.) Because, on account of the expense and distance of residence of many, even from a central point of meeting, there would not be a full or even partial representation of all the Synods.

(b.) Presuming that there might be a meeting of several hundred, there was no place in the central section of the church which offered to entertain so large a number of men, and few could afford to come, paying both the expense of travel and of board.

(c.) It would require at least one or more months' time to discuss, with any degree of thoroughness, the subjects proposed, and few of our men can ordinarily remain away from home longer than a week, even at their Synod. It was felt that the discussion of one or two, or even three points, would result in no permanent benefit.

(d.) The Missouri Synod refused to join a colloquium except upon such conditions which could not for a moment be recognized, and it was apprehended that some others would also propose such conditions of membership, which would occasion controversy, even at the beginning, fatal to the intended design.

These and some other reasons determined a majority vote against the measure in the General Synod, and the project was abandoned.

Defeated in the hope of a general colloquium, I did not give up the hope of accomplishing some good by drawing our men together in some other way, and I began by throwing out hints in the Observer about the expediency of a more limited Diet. I matured the matter privately, named the men who were to take prominent parts and selected some of the subjects for essays to be read. The plan was sanctioned by those to whom I communicated it privately, and then I laid it before Dr. Seiss and solicited his co-operation. He promptly entered into it and we divided the arrangement of the affair between us. I undertook the correspondence, and I wrote over fifty letters before the work was completed. Secrecy was enjoined upon all, for we desired to avoid discussion in the papers, which might have occasioned confusion. We thought it best to assume all the responsibility ourselves—appoint essayists, officers, time, place and everything, believing that if these were left to the decision of a public meeting or to newspaper settlement, nothing would ever have been done. No special time, place, men, subjects would have suited all, and hence, to cut the matter short, we took it upon ourselves to arrange the meeting.

We expected that various changes would be suggested and complaints made, and no sooner had the announcement been made than they began to be heard. A few complained that they were not invited to read a paper; others that the West had been left out; change of time and place was proposed but it was too late for any alteration. Some thought that if Prof. Repass was invited to represent the South, others from places equally remote should have been equally honored, but it was thought proper to call in the South as an act of Christian comity, inasmuch as their Synods belonged neither to the Council nor to the General Synod; and again, it was thought that men living at a distance from the centre would not attend the Diet in mid winter; and finally, that the distant sections of the church would also hold Diets as the central section proposed to do.

It was hard work to make arrangements for a meeting as it was, without going farther out of the way, and as this was the first and a doubtful experiment, we concluded not to spread out too far in the beginning. Hereafter it will be differently arranged, and other men can learn from our experience.

Objection was made to the time, but we presumed that inasmuch as about half of the essayists were professors, it would be well to hold the Diet during their vacation. Philadelphia was chosen as the place, because we could there secure a larger attendance of our ministers at less expense and trouble than at any other place, for there are three hundred within three hours distance from that city, besides those students of the Seminary who might be there during the Christmas vacation.

The following was the first announcement, made in November, 1877, and which appeared in the Observer and in the Lutheran the same week:

A LUTHERAN CHURCH DIET.

A Free Diet of the Lutheran church to discuss living subjects of general worth and importance to all Lutherans has been arranged to be held in the lecture room of St. Matthew's church (Dr. Baum's), in Philadelphia, beginning at 10 A. M. on Thursday, December 27th, 1877, to continue in session several days.

The chief business of this Diet will be the reading of essays on given topics by men engaged for the purpose, and the free discussion of the subject of each essay after its presentation. The essayists engaged, and with whom is the responsibility for the calling and character of this Diet, are:

1. "*The Augsburg Confession the Source of the Thirty-nine Articles of the Church of England, and incidentally, of all other Protestant Confessions.*" Rev. J. G. Morris, D. D., LL. D., of Baltimore, Md.
2. "*The Relations of the Lutheran Church to the Denominations around us.*" Rev. Prof. C. P. Krauth, D. D., LL. D., of Philadelphia, Pa.
3. "*The Four General Bodies of the Lutheran Church in the United States, wherein they agree, and wherein they might harmoniously co-operate.*" Rev. Prof. J. A. Brown, D. D., of Gettysburg, Pa.
4. "*The History and progress of the Lutheran Church in the United States.*" Rev. Prof. H. E. Jacobs, D. D., of Gettysburg, Pa.
5. "*Education in the Lutheran Church in the United States.*" Rev. Prof. M. Valentine, D. D., of Gettysburg, Pa.
6. "*The Interests of the Lutheran Church in America, as Affected by Diversities of Language.*" D. Luther, M. D., of Reading, Pa.
7. "*Misunderstandings and Misrepresentations of the Lutheran Church.*" Rev. J. A. Seiss, D. D., of Philadelphia, Pa.
8. "*Characteristics of the Augsburg Confession.*" Rev. F. W. Conrad, D. D., of Philadelphia, Pa.
9. "*Liturgical Forms in Worship.*" Rev. C. A. Stork, D. D., of Baltimore, Md.
10. "*Theses on the Lutheranism of the Fathers of our Church in this Country.*" Rev. Prof. W. J. Mann, D. D., of Philadelphia, Pa.
11. "*The Divine and Human Factors in a Call to the Ministry, as viewed by Lutheran Theologians.*" Rev. G. Diehl, D. D., of Frederick, Md.

12. "*The Educational and Sacramental Ideas of the Lutheran Church in Relation to Practical Piety.*" Rev. A. C. Wedekind, D. D., of New York.

13. "*True and False Spiritualism.*" Rev. E. Greenwald, D. D., of Lancaster, Pa.

The Diet was an acknowledged success, one hundred Lutheran ministers having been in attendance, and has created so marked and favorable an impression as to warrant the belief that a very large edition of *The Proceedings* will be called for. Ten thousand copies should be sold. The volume should be in the library of every Lutheran. It is one of the most important Lutheran books that has ever been published in America.

As the publication of *The Proceedings* involves considerable expenditure of money, the publisher would earnestly request the recipient of the enclosed to reply immediately, whether ordering or not ordering the book. By this means, when the MS. is ready for the press, some idea can be formed of how large an edition should be published.

J. FREDERICK SMITH, Publisher,

January, 1878. 42 North 9th Street, Philadelphia.

No essay is to exceed forty-five minutes in length, and no speech in the general discussion shall exceed ten minutes. The essayist shall always have the right of making the closing speech on the subject presented by him.

No subjects other than those of the essays will be discussed, and no vote will be taken on any of the subjects considered.

No essay will be received which has already appeared in print, and the manuscript of each essay is to be furnished for publication; also a synopsis of each speech in the discussion.

The peculiar difficulties of the situation and the hazardous uncertainty of calling an unorganized promiscuous convention have induced the determination of all the arrangements in advance, as above given, and no proposed changes for this Diet will be entertained. If others should follow it, the method of procedure may be according to what is thought best after the experience in this case.

Though all these things have been, as only they could be, privately arranged, there is every reason to believe that there will be a general interest in what is thus proposed, and that our ministers and laymen will heartily second what has been done and favor the Diet with their presence and participation.

P. S.—As this convention is not a Synod, or other organized body called by authority or by vote, the ministers and congregations in Philadelphia have not been engaged to make general provision for the entertainment of those in attendance; but timely conference with friends in the city will no doubt secure free accommodations to those members of the Diet who desire it while in attendance.

The Diet was held in St. Matthew's church, Philadelphia, December 27–28, and was attended by the precise number of *one hundred* Lutheran ministers.

The meeting was characterized by the spirit of fraternal confidence and mutual regard, and so favorable was the impression made that a committee was appointed to make arrangements for another at a suitable time. Mr. J. Frederick Smith, of Philadelphia, assumed the responsibility of publishing the essays.

Most of our church papers spoke favorably of the Diet, and all were compelled to acknowledge that the conception was good and that the result may ultimately be beneficial.

Visits of Foreign Lutheran Ministers to the United States.

Whilst numerous American clergymen pay a short visit to Europe every summer, and not a few extend their tour to Egypt and Palestine, there are comparatively few European ministers, Germans especially, who visit our country for recreation. The reasons are that very few of those Germans can afford the expense; secondly, they would find it difficult to secure leave of absence for so long a period from their official superiors; and thirdly, they have not the roaming disposition which we Americans have. They are hard to move. Although multitudes of their parishioners come over here to settle permanently, yet clergymen have no motive, and they are content to stay at home.

Some scientific and literary Germans of high distinction have traveled through our country, a few of whom I have met. *Koch,* an eminent conchologist, spent some time in Baltimore, whom I had the pleasure of seeing and of rendering him some service. But the only other one I shall here mention is the great historian, *Von Raumer.* He came here accompanied by his son. The Professor was a small, lithe, active man, of about sixty years of age at that time, who experienced no inconvenience whatever in ascending the Washington monument, the view from which he thought was one of the finest he had ever seen. I showed him all the sights worth seeing in this city, but he seemed more interested in our political than in our artistic or literary condition. He had no high opinion of the state of art among us, and I will never forget his criticism upon that group of sculpture on the east front of the Capitol at Washington. He said that Columbus with the globe in his hand looked precisely like a fellow who was about trying to make a ten strike in a ball alley, and I dare not record here what he said of the Indian group of the same place. When I tried to apologize by telling him that these figures were designed and sculptured by a foreigner, he shut me up by retorting that the committee of Congress who had the affair in charge, and the whole country, whose money paid for them, were to be blamed for accepting such monstrosities from the pretended artist!

After I had gone the rounds with the Professor, he said there was one thing more he wanted to see, and what do you think that was? *A negro revival meeting!* The eminent German historian, the philosopher, the diplomat, wanted to see an exhibition of fanaticism! He had read of those wonderful demonstrations, and that which to us is an almost every day occurrence, and of no interest, because of its frequency, was to him a matter of intense curiosity. He regarded it in a physiological aspect, and philosophized about it wonderfully. The shrieks, the distortions of face, the rolling on the floor, the confused mingling of praying and singing, the unearthly yells, the indescribable confusion created by clapping of hands and stamping, and other religious gymnastics of these deluded people, amazed him at first, and then by turns amused and saddened him. He had seen the dancing Dervishes in the East, and every form of fanatical worship, but this exceeded all. He was satisfied, and expressed his regret that such disgraceful exhibitions should be made in the name of Christianity. What was wonderful to him, also, was that the *Government should allow such demonstrations of insane fanaticism!*

But I wish to speak particularly of German clergymen. In 1849, Fliedner of the Kaiserswerth Deaconness Institution was in this country. He had letters to me, but not finding me in Baltimore, he followed me to York, where I was sojourning for a few days. It was the day on which General Taylor passed through that place on his presidential tour, and of course there was a popular demonstration. The President made a clumsy speech from the platform of the railroad car, and the crowd shouted vociferously. To my surprise and amusement, Fliedner waved his hat and was as noisy in his applause as any of them. He said he was completely carried away with the enthusiasm of the people, never having witnessed such a scene before, and especially admiring the simplicity and patriotism of a Republican people, who could thus greet their Chief Magistrate, whom they themselves had elected, and who, unattended by soldiery and undistinguished from them in dress, could thus travel through the country receiving the homage of the sovereign people. It was to Fliedner a sublime, moral spectacle.

I should judge that he was about fifty years of age, but very active in movement and sprightly in conversation. He saw many things to admire in our manners and culture, and much to be grieved at in our exhibition of the charities of Christianity.

I took him with me to Baltimore and put him in the way of visiting our penal and eleemosynary institutions. I remember one day he came home deeply dejected, and upon inquiring into the cause, he told me that he had just come from the city prison, where he conversed with an unfortunate young girl who had been committed for some petty crime, and that she had not been visited by some Christian female to instruct and reform her. In his impulsive nature, he exclaimed, "My God! have you no Christian women here who visit their sinning or sick sisters in prison? What is the character of your American Christianity?" I was compelled to confess that generally it did not assume that feature. I had no doubt that many Christian women would freely contribute money to the rescue of the fallen, but as to "visiting them in prison" it was not considered *genteel!* He could not appreciate my lame apology, nor could I.

He left us with exalted esteem for our thrift, energy and prosperity as a people, but with rather moderate appreciation of our *practical* piety. *His* Christianity was love to God *and* men, manifested in works of kindness and relief to all classes and doing good by the exercise of self-denial to the poor, the lowly, the sinful and the forsaken.

Some years ago, an accomplished and fine looking young man, a brother of Prof. Olshausen, of Berlin, visited us. He had some sort of commission from the Prussian government, whether diplomatic or ecclesiastical, I could not find out, but he was very diligent in his inquiries about the religious condition of the Germans.

I never knew what impressions he carried away concerning us, but he witnessed some sights which were not calculated to impress him very favorably. He was unfortunately present at the meeting of one of our Synods in Pennsylvania, during which the humiliating spectacle of the settlement of a difficulty between two ministers was enacted. The mutual recriminations were anything but amiable, and these were conveyed in German, that was far from being classic. The well-bred young foreigner went away disgusted.

"The alliance," in 1873, brought over a number of German celebrities. It was my privilege to meet most of them at a social reunion in Baltimore, after a public religious meeting in one of our German churches, at which three or four of them delivered stirring addresses, more in our American style than is usual with freshly arrived Germans. They were all first class men; sociable, refined, and truly pious. Our reunion was an event; it was after the good old German style and we kept up our spirited conversation to a late hour. There were nearly twenty of us together, and the intellectual and social enjoyment was superb.

I am indebted to a friend for the following sketches of four of the men here named:

1. THE REV. J. A. DORNER, D. D., *Professor of Theology in the University of Berlin*. I mention him first, because of his seniority in years; secondly, because of his official position—*Ober-Consistorial Rath*—and thirdly, because of his deserved reputation as one of the ablest speculative divines of the age. His Christology—*Entwickelungs Geschichte der Person Christi*—has attained a classical position among theologians of all denominations. His *Theme* at the Evangelical Alliance held in October 2-12, 1873, "THE INFALLIBILISM OF THE VATICAN COUNCIL AND NOMINAL PROTESTANTISM," was an exhaustive discussion of *fallible* men, making an *infallible Pope!* It was an unwise arrangement by

which his powerful Paper lost much of its influence at the time of its delivery, to induce him to present it in very broken and defective English. As it now stands in very accurate and beautiful English dress given to it by *Dr. Schaff*, in the *Alliance Volume*, it will be of permanent value to all who desire to investigate that subject thoroughly.

Dr. Dorner is small of stature; of childlike simplicity of manner; very genial and unpretending. He resembles Dr. Tholuck somewhat in appearance, has the same benevolent disposition, which occasionally has led him, in his official position, to yield concessions to the rationalistic element around him, that have pained the more rigid orthodox party in the German Empire. But his earnest Christian spirit, combined with his profound learning, critical penetration and power of generalization, has exerted a most salutary influence on Evangelical piety throughout Germany. He expressed great willingness to assist us in securing rechglaübige Prediger, for the many thousand Germans that had come and were continually coming to us from the "Fatherland."

2. THE REV. W. NOEL, *Counselor of the "Ober-Kirchenrath," First Pastor of the Louisa Parish Church at Berlin, and Secretary of the German Evangelical Church Diet*. His subject was: *The Evangelical Alliance; its Objects and Influence in Promoting the Universal Priesthood of Believers to the Communion of Saints*. This was a theme for the heart more than for the head. Not that it lacked profundity of thought, or keen critical analysis; for it possessed both in an eminent degree; but the entire subject and its development was baptized with a spirit of love. Indeed, Counselor Noël could, with propriety, be styled the *John* of the German delegation. And a happy day will it be for the Church, when his theme and his spirit will not only be regarded as *pium desiderium*, but as the universal *practice* of all believers.

On the last evening of the Convention Counselor Noël delivered an address in the Cooper Institute, to at least four thousand Germans, on *Missions of the Evangelical Church of Prussia among German Protestant Congregations abroad.*. It was an intensely interesting discourse, and many of us opened our eyes and ears as we were told of the German congregations in the Danubian Principalities, in Turkey, in Jerusalem and Bethlehem, in Alexandria and Cairo. We hardly could believe our ears when we were informed of the many flourishing congregations in South America: in Buenos Ayres, two thousand five hundred souls; in Montevideo, three hundred and fifty souls; in Porto Alegre (South Brazil), one thousand two hundred; with at least fifty other places scattered through that empire. We more than smiled when we heard of the *Hamburger-Berg*, in Brazil, with two hundred and eighty families, and in *New Petropolis*, with one thousand one hundred souls.

We felt like shouting when we were told that Luther was preaching in *Rome* by his translated Bible and his catechism to two hundred and fifty souls every Lord's day, and in Florence to six hundred, and in Venice, Milan, Leghorn, Naples and Messina. Could the intrepid Reformer have imagined, even in his most sanguine moments, any such results? Sure enough, Melanchthon was right when he said—

"Gottes Wort und Luther's Lehr
Vergehen nun und nimmermehr."

3. THE REV. W. KRAFT, D. D., *Professor of Church History in the University of Bonn*. His subject was—"*The Vatican Council and the Old Catholic Movement.*" Such a theme from such a pen could not but be exhaustive. With a master hand he laid open the inner working of that council. Step by step he traced the monstrous assumption of Papal Infallibility, and poured such a flood of historic light upon his theme that the blasphemy of the odious dogma become absolutely disgusting. In no paper read at the Alliance Convention were the wily machinations of the Jesuits made to stand out in such bold relief as in this. They had every thing their own way, because everything had been pre-arranged. The high hopes entertained by Dr. Kraft of the Old Catholic Movement have not been and will not be realized, simply because no reformation within the Romish Church is possible. Reformation there means destruction. Battering to pieces certain abuses of Popery is doubtless a great work, but, unless the vital truths of the pure Gospel be substituted in all their fullness, it is the mere taking of the outer trenches; the citadel remains intact; it remains mere head work, for which the masses have little taste and less heart. Luther understood this much better; for whilst he smote with a giant's arm the former, he supplied with a shepherd's care the latter, and so was successful.

Dr. Kraft is in the prime of life, a sound theologian, a ripe scholar, a sincere Christian, and a noble specimen of a Teuton.

4. THE REV. THEODORE CHRISTLIEB, D. D., *Professor of Theology and Chaplain in the University of Bonn*. His subject was—

THE BEST METHODS OF COUNTERACTING MODERN INFIDELITY. He was undoubtedly the great man of the Convention, *the* giant among giants. He had the decided advantage over all his associates from Germany, that he spoke the English language as fluently as "if native to the manor born." Whenever and wherever he spoke, he chained his audience as if by magic. With a pleasing *personnel*, he unites a musical voice, a vivid imagination, an animated manner, and a mental force and freshness that charms whilst it convinces and pleases whilst it instructs. Youthful in appearance, he has the scholastic attainments of a veteran. Never were the rich stores of knowledge brought to tell with such overwhelming power upon the self-complacent theories of infidelity. Never did Emerson's vaunted declaration that "Christian faith had better take an inventory of its effects, since it was nearly over with it," appear so contemptible, for never seemed Zion's bulwarks so impregnable. Even the infidel press was awed into silence, if not brought into submission.

Synodical Visits to Presidents of the United States.

During the meeting of our Synods of Maryland in Washington, it is our custom to wait upon the President in a body. Our intention is communicated to him, and he appoints a time to receive us.

I remember our visits to Presidents Pearce, Polk, Buchanan, Johnson and Grant. I believe that the General Synod once paid their respects to President Lincoln, but I was not present.

It so happened that I was either President of our Synod, or at least, was appointed to address him whenever we visited him, and I always emphasized ourselves as representatives of that numerous and influential class of our fellow-citizens, the Germans, well knowing that his Excellency would seize the occasion to glorify the Germans in his reply, for our addresses were always fully reported, and it pleased them to hear themselves well spoken of by the President, and, perhaps, it was no disadvantage to himself.

We once paid our respects to General Grant before his election, and while he was General in chief of the Army, but after his nomination, I said to him, that for myself I hoped that the next time the Synod of Maryland would visit him we would find him in a larger and *whiter* house than he then occupied, for he lived in a brick front. The only reply he made was, that "he was perfectly satisfied with his present position." Of our *German* character, which I prominently mentioned, he said not a word. After his election we visited him again, and then I reminded him of what I had said on our previous visit about the larger and the *whiter* house, and brought in the Germans again, extolling their thrift, energy and patriotism during the war, and thought I would bring him out on that subject, but he made no reply of any kind, and all that he said was, "Gentlemen, I am glad to see you," and shaking his hand the interview was over in five minutes. He wouldn't praise the Germans.

At our last meeting we did not wait on President Hayes. He had not time to receive us; but I am sure he would speak in high terms of the Germans.

MINISTERS' SUMMER VACATIONS.

It is only within the last twenty-five years that our ministers asked for or were allowed a summer vacation, which has now become so common, and, I think, eminently proper.

Fifty years ago, and even much later, it never occurred to them to take a month's recreation as a matter of course; first, very few could afford to go to the "springs," or the seashore, or the mountains, and perhaps very few had relations to visit who were able to keep them and the madam and a couple or half a dozen of juveniles of all ages and temperaments; secondly, their people were opposed to their long absence, and thought that ministers were in no more need of holiday than themselves, which was true of many; and, thirdly, facilities of travel and proximity of seashore enjoyments, and the renovating influence of mountain air, were not so attainable, nor fashionable, nor so necessary as at present.

I remember long ago, that one summer I proposed to be absent from my church two consecutive Sundays. There was decided opposition to it, and not because my Council did not think I needed recreation, but it was true I did not need it—in those remote days we did not need many things without which we could not now get along—but because they knew I would be compelled to invite to my pulpit Rev. Mr. Sartorius, who kept a clothing store round the corner, but who gratified himself and amused his hearers by trying to preach on Sunday, for unemployed educated ministers were not so numerous as at present—and because, as my church was a struggling enterprise, some stranger would drop in to hear me and would be disappointed at my absence; and, thirdly, because they did not want to hear any other preacher (this was a sly appeal to my young vanity, but after a few years they were glad enough to have an occasional change, and so was I); and, fourthly, who would bury the dead, if any should die in my absence, and marry the living, if any should venture upon that enterprise (and just here let me mention that I seldom left home without the occasion of a death or of a wedding, much to my regret on account of both)! The result was that for the first ten or fifteen years of my ministry I was not out of my pulpit for two consecutive Sundays more than once or twice. It was not necessary for my health that I should go; I could not afford to make long journeys or "recreate" at the springs; it was not customary for ministers to be absent during the summer.

The idea of closing the church for a month to give the pastor and the people a holiday never entered the minds of the people, and would have been deemed preposterous if it had been suggested, and I think they were right. It is true that at present many of our city families leave town, and the summer congregations are rather thin, and the night service is usually intermitted, but a sufficient number remain at home to be preached to by somebody, even if the pastor be absent—and people get sick and some die. I have known men who have gone to the residences of half a dozen ministers to secure their services for a funeral, but they were all gone.

No slight difficulty is sometimes encountered by the absentees in securing substitutes. So many other pastors are also absent, and those ministers not pastors, if there are any about, are already engaged by absentees, so that it is hard to have the pulpit supplied. The result is that they are often compelled to invite men to preach who are not desired by the congregation. The supplying is sometimes left to the Church Council, who have little time or inclination to attend to such business. They are tempted to put it off until the end of the week, and then you hear of them running all around town hunting a preacher, and ready to accept of almost any one who has the prefix Rev. to his name. The people are aware of this, and hence many of them do not go to church as long as the pastor is absent.

But in the olden time comparatively few of our people left home during the heated term; but now, since many have grown rich, and influential, and fashionable, they follow the crowd. It is this class particularly who think that the over-worked minister should also have a vacation, which is all right, but not because these people think so. On the part of many of them it is mere selfishness; they are absent themselves, and for that reason they think that the minister might as well be.

And this leads me to remark that it is wonderful how few comparatively of these summer sojourners at the springs or the seashore attend church on Sundays. I live in a village where all summer there are over one hundred summer boarders; and, although many of them are regular and devout attendants at church when at home, they seldom attend the services of our village churches. They prefer staying at home on Sundays, although they are within three minutes' walk of a house of worship. They seem to give their religion a holiday as well as themselves. I once asked a very earnest Lutheran lady, who never misses church at home, "Why do you not come to our church here? We belong to the same Synod that your minister does, we have the same liturgical service, we have very good preaching, and yet you have not been in our church but once the whole summer. Does not every toll of the church-bell reprove your carelessness?" "Oh," said she, "I came to the country to enjoy the fresh air; I want holiday; it is not worth while to dress to go to church here." I told her I would report her to the minister, but she begged me not to say anything about it to the "dear, good man." But the next Sunday she was in church.

Taking a trip to Europe for pleasure was quite unknown among our men thirty years ago; but since that time many of our clergymen have enjoyed the agreeable but expensive recreation, and I wish that more of them had the time and the means to do it. It is now comparatively cheap and convenient, but still not many of our men can afford it. I know a few of our men who have borrowed the money to enable them to make this fashionable voyage, but they have not paid it all back yet, and they will utter many a poignant groan before it is all repaid. Few of them have such generous church members as one of our city ministers in Maryland has. This summer (1877) one member offered to pay his pastor's expenses to Europe, but the liberal offer was declined on account of sickness in his family.

I believe it is usual when a minister goes to Europe "for his health," that his salary is generously continued during his absence, and that kind friends contribute liberally towards paying his expenses. I know this has been the case with some; but I am not so certain whether the absent minister pays out of his own pocket for the supply of his pulpit. When I went abroad, my salary went on, but I paid my substitute. A few friends gave me some money, and several sent me a lot of smoked tongues and hams, a barrel of apples, and some canned oysters; for I went on a sailing vessel, and not a steamer, and it was presumed that the ship's fare would not be the best. Well, one Sunday morning I told the officers of the ship, who took their meals in the cabin, that I would treat them at dinner upon American tongue and ham and apple-dumplings. The captain ordered the cook to get my provisions out of the hold, in which they had been stored, and boil the tongue and make dough for the dumplings, and we would have a royal Sunday dinner in mid-ocean. The cook soon returned and reported that neither meat nor apples could be found, that the barrels were empty, and we would have no dumplings for dinner. I fear that the captain swore at somebody in Platt Deutsch for stealing his passengers' stores.

Some innocent indulgences are now allowed to ministers which were formerly forbidden, especially in the more densely settled sections of the church, or in those which consider themselves the more pious. Fishing, hunting, skating, croquet, and chess, were forbidden, and only enjoyed by stealth by ministers who loved these sports. I know one man, and perhaps there are others, who was mortally offended at his minister for playing croquet; and yet this man did not pay his debts, and was otherwise unsymmetrical in his Christian character. At the present time all these amusements are freely participated in by ministers, and they are the better for it; and at almost every watering place or seaside resort you will find numbers of our most godly preachers enjoying some sort of amusement. It seems to be regarded almost as a matter of course that these men, who have worked hard incessantly for eleven months, should have one for recreation. More of them would avail themselves of this recognized right if they could afford the money necessary. Is this an evidence of advancing civilization, an acknowledgment of a right long withheld, an increased physical deterioration among our clergy requiring cessation from protracted labor, or a compliance with the loud call of fashion and conformity to the world without? It is growing every year, and it is not uncommon now for ministers to make provision for a month's summer vacation in their engagements with their churches. It is all perfectly proper, even if they do not take advantage of it. I have seen grave Presbyterian and other Doctors of Divinity, even at so public a place as Saratoga Springs, rolling ten-pins, with their coats off, and enjoying the sport hugely. This and similar recreations have now become very common, which, thirty years ago, would not have been sanctioned by public opinion.

This matter of public opinion is not steadfast or reliable, but very changeable. There is a story told of a gentleman who was once a student at a celebrated Puritan college. He visited the college some years after leaving, and was conducted round by a professor to see the improvements in buildings, libraries, apparatus, room furniture, and other conveniences made in the meantime. After they had gone the rounds, the professor remarked, "Now, let us wind up with a game of ten-pins." "What!" exclaimed the visitor. "Do you allow ten-pins here? Don't you know that I was dismissed from this very college ten years ago for playing that game?" Times have changed and men with them; and thus it is in many other things.

In our new settlements, where the churches are still poor and the salaries small, our ministers cannot afford to take a summer's holiday if expense is involved; but hunting and fishing are freely allowed them, for they are universal amusements, and I presume contribute considerably to the support of the family. Every country minister, at least, ought to have his rifle and other implements, of which he should make generous use.

Camping out on the banks of some lake or river well with fish is becoming rather common among be an enjoyable recreation where the company is good-natured, in good health and capable of some endurance, and when they can persuade themselves that they are really comfortable, which it usually requires a great deal of philosophy or self-deception to do. It is hard to feel comfortable when attacked by hordes of mosquitoes and ticks—to try to sleep upon a bed of hemlock boughs—to protect yourself against rain and storms—to do your own cooking and washing and wood-gathering, and all this sometimes during a soaking shower—to expose yourself to malaria, and to endure the grumbling of some dyspeptic fellow-sufferer; and yet amid all these sylvan inconveniences, there are some men who tell you they were comfortable—very, but you seldom hear of them repeating the experiment. One summer's camping out seems to have restored their impaired health to a degree never requiring a second cure.

HISTORY OF FOREIGN MISSIONS.

It was about forty-five years ago that Foreign Missions first engaged the attention of our ministers and people. Our own children were stretching out their hands and begging for bread, and our wants at home first received our attention; and yet it is true that the very idea of sending missionaries to the heathen was suggested in connection with efforts that were made to supply the destitute of our own land with the means of grace.

The first time the subject was brought directly to the notice of the General Synod was at Baltimore, when, at the motion of C. A. Morris, Esq., a committee was appointed upon this subject, and it was likewise determined to hold a missionary meeting at the next meeting of the General Synod, and D. Lintner was appointed to preach a sermon on the occasion.

Before this, however, several of the District Synods had organized societies in reference more particularly to the wants of feeble and destitute churches, and collections were also taken up in some of the parishes on behalf of the heathen and forwarded to the American Board.

At the eighth convention of the General Synod, held in York in 1835, the committee appointed at the former meeting presented a valuable report, which was signed by Rev. Drs. J. G. Schmucker and D. F. Schaeffer. It enters most fully into the discussion of the subject, and gives the causes which have retarded missionary efforts in the church. The committee propose various good resolutions bearing mainly, however, on the cause of missions at home, and "as soon after as possible for the churches to extend their care and labors to the conversion of the heathen."

It was also moved (by J. G. M.) that a missionary convention of Lutheran ministers be held in October, 1835, at Mechanicsburg, Pennsylvania, at the time of the meeting of the West Pennsylvania Synod. One of the resolutions of the series was, that it be recommended to the District Synods to give at their ensuing meetings an expression of their sentiments and feelings respecting *the establishment of a Foreign Mission* by the Evangelical Lutheran Church *in the United States*.

A pastoral address was ordered at this meeting of the General Synod, which was subsequently issued, and is signed by Rev. Dr. Bachman and Rev. J. Z. Senderling.

The convention was held at Mechanicsburg in the autumn of 1835, which resulted in the formation of the Central Missionary Society, whose object was "to send the gospel to the destitute portions of the Lutheran church in the United States * * * *and ultimately to co-operate in sending it to the heathen.*" The obligation of the church to send the gospel abroad was every day more and more felt, and the feasibility of the work was discussed in different sections of the church.

Just about this time, when our members seemed gradually to have been prepared for the work, letters were received from Gutzlaff in China, and from Rhenius in India, appealing to the German churches in this country for assistance. These appeals made a deep impression upon the church. The conviction was general that Rhenius must be sustained.

In the spring of 1837, the General Synod met at Hagerstown, when a committee was appointed on this absorbing subject. The report which was made was signed by Rev. Drs. B. Kurtz, H. N. Pohlman, S. S. Schmucker, Rev. B. Keller, and L. Medtart, Esq. One of the resolutions recommended was that we regard the calls of those distinguished and devoted German laborers,

Rhenius and Gutzlaff and their associates, as specially providential, * * * * * and another was, that the plan adopted (for aiding these men) ought * * * * * *to embrace in it a connection with the American Board of Commissioners for Foreign Missions.*

A convention was then held embracing all ministers present and not merely members of the Synod (May 30, 1837), which resulted in the organization of a society called *The German Foreign Missionary Society*, and designed to *embrace all churches and individuals of German descent, or association, in the United States.* The title German F. M. S. was adopted, as the co-operation of all the churches of German extraction was expected and desired. A circular-letter signed by J. G. Morris, H. L. Baugher and A. H. Lochman, was addressed to the German Reformed and other German churches, inviting them to co-operate with us in this work.

At this meeting it was also resolved to sustain Rhenius and his companions in the Palamcotta Mission, provided satisfactory reasons were given in reference to the wants of the mission and the causes of its separation from the society in Germany, and the secretary was directed to open an immediate correspondence upon the subject with the missionaries in India, and also the London Missionary Society.

At the meeting of the General Synod at Chambersburg, 1839, several young men were mentioned as willing to go to India as missionaries.

No response to the appeal previously made for a union with the German churches was received. Another effort was made on motion of Dr. B. Kurtz to enlist the co-operation of the German Reformed Church, but the proposition was declined. The title of the society was then changed by dropping the word German at the beginning.

About this time intelligence of the death of Rhenius was received, but our society still resolved to sustain his associates, but when we learned that these men had renewed their connection with the English Church Missionary Society our aid was withdrawn.

In the spring of 1840, Rev. C. F. Heyer was appointed missionary. After consultation with the American Board, it was determined that our operations should be directed to the Telugu country in Southern India. At a meeting of the society in May, 1841, it was resolved to transact its business through the American Board, and a plan of union was adopted. This measure was strongly opposed, and the proposed union was never consummated. (See my report to General Synod, Baltimore, 1843.) Mr. Heyer expecting that it would be, resigned his appointment, upon which the Synod of Pennsylvania, which had maintained its distinct missionary organization, resolved to appoint him. The South Carolina Synod also preferred independent action, and stood by that of Pennsylvania. Mr. Heyer having received his instructions at a public meeting in Philadelphia, sailed from Boston October 14th, 1841, and arrived in India in the ensuing spring. He soon planted a mission at Guntoor, and thus the oldest Synod of our Church in this country enjoys the distinction of having sent the first Lutheran missionary from the United States among the heathen.

The General Society, however, did not relax its efforts, although it is true that the ardor of many cooled.

At the meeting of the society at Baltimore in 1843, the executive committee was instructed to send a missionary as soon as possible, and, if expedient, in co-operation with the society of the Synod of Pennsylvania.

In obedience to these instructions, Rev. Walter Gunn, of the State of New York, was appointed May 25th, 1843, with directions to proceed to Southern India to labor among the Telegu in conjunction with Heyer, provided an arrangement to that effect could be made with the Society of the Pennsylvania Synod. Such an arrangement was made, and continued until the entire control of the mission was transferred by the Pennsylvania Synod to the General Society.

The missionary was publicly set apart to the work in Philadelphia October 24th, 1843. I, as corresponding secretary, read to him the instructions of the committee, and Dr. B. Kurtz gave the charge. He sailed from Boston on November 18th, with his wife, and on June 18th, 1844, he arrived at Guntoor. He immediately entered upon his duties. Some time after Mr. Heyer received permission to return home. The whole superintendence and government of the mission was then transferred to the General Society, the Pennsylvania Synod expressing a willingness to continue its contributions to its support.

In 1847 Dr. Heyer, on the resuscitation of his health, again offered his services for the work, which were gladly accepted. He embarked for India on December 4th.

During this year (1848) the committee appointed Rev. J. C. Martz as missionary, who arrived on the ground sometime in 1849.

In 1850 the committee received into their service Rev. C. W. Groening of the North German Missionary Society, and subsequently accepted from the same society the offer of their mission at Rajahmundry, with the buildings and two missionaries laboring there. Rev. Messrs. Valette and Heise were, therefore, added to the laborers under the care of our society. The following year Mr. Valette was permitted to return to Germany, and also the succeeding year Mr. Martz to the United States. The mission, however, soon received a reinforcement in the Rev. Messrs. W. J. Cutter of Ohio, and W. E. Snyder of New York, who sailed with their wives August 11th, 1851, and reached India the beginning of next year.

In the month of January, 1853, the first meeting of the Evangelical Lutheran Synod of India was held at Guntoor. The following ordained missionaries were present, viz., Rev. C. F. Heyer from the Palnaud, Rev. A. F. Heise and Rev. W. J. Cutter from Rajahmundry, and Rev. C. W. Groening and Rev. W. E. Snyder from Guntoor. Its first officers were Rev. C. F. Heyer, President, and Rev. W. E. Snyder, Secretary. A committee appointed to give an historical and statistical relation of the mission stations reported as follows:

Guntoor. Began 1842; missionaries in charge from 1842–1846, C. F. Heyer; from 1846–1851, W. Gunn and G. Martz; at present, C. W. Groening and W. E. Snyder; one congregation; baptisms from 1842–46, thirty-two; to '51, twenty-four; to '52, twenty-two; total, seventy-eight; communicants, sixteen; marriages, eight; deaths, twelve; day schools, six; scholars, one hundred and sixty-five; boarding school, one; scholars, five; teachers, nine; expenses last year one thousand seven hundred and forty-six rupees.

Rajahmundry. Began 1845; missionaries in charge from 1845–50, Valette; from 1846–49, C. W. Groening; from 1846–52, A. F. Heise; 1852, W. J. Cutter; one congregation, thirteen baptisms, ten communicants, eight day schools, two hundred and twenty scholars, eight teachers; expenses last year, eight hundred rupees.

Palnaud. Began 1849; missionary, C. F. Heyer; five congregations, two hundred and forty-three baptisms, forty-four communicants, five marriages, one death, two expulsions, six day schools, seventy-four scholars; one boarding school, twenty-one scholars; seven teachers; expenses last year, eight hundred and sixty rupees.

At the meeting of the Foreign Missionary Society at Reading, in 1857, the following missionaries were reported as having left the mission field on account of impaired health. Rev. A. F. Heise, Rev. W. E. Snyder and Rev. W. J. Cutter. In the spring of 1857, Rev. C. F. Heyer also took his departure, followed in 1858 by the Rev. C. W. Groening, who was permitted, after twelve years of active labor, to return with his family to Germany for needed rest and change.

In 1857 Rev. A. F. Heise returned again to his post at Rajahmundry.

On the 21st of November, 1857, Rev. Adam Long, in company with W. E. Synder and Rev. E. Unangst, and their wives, sailed for India, and entered upon their mission work April 1st, 1858.

In 1861 Rev. C. W. Groening returned again to India, and remained until September, 1865, when he was obliged on account of impaired health to leave the mission and return to Germany.

In 1859 the mission in India sustained a sore bereavement in the death of Rev. W. E. Snyder.

On the 12th of March, 1862, Rev. A. F. Heise, completely broken down by work and sickness, withdrew from the mission and returned to Germany.

On the 5th of March, 1866, Rev. Adam Long departed this life at Rajahmundry, India. His widow returned to America on the 4th of May, 1867.

In 1871 Rev. E. Unangst, accompanied by his family, left India for America.

On January 6th, 1872, Rev. E. Unangst, accompanied by Rev. J. H. Harpster of the Theological Seminary at Gettysburg, set sail for India, leaving his family in America.

On the 7th of December, 1872, Rev. L. L. Uhl of Wittenberg College, accompanied by his wife, took their departure for India. They were followed in September, 1874, by Rev. A. D. Rowe and wife—Mr. Rowe being known as the Children's Missionary.

On the 22d of March, 1876, Rev. J. H. Harpster, on account of throat disease, left India for America.

On the second Sabbath of 1877, two native pastors, the Revs. B. John and M. Nathaniel, were solemnly ordained to the work of the gospel ministry.

The statistics of the field in India at present (1877) are as follows: Communicants, 1,263; backsliders, 103; baptisms since the commencement of the mission, thirty-five years ago, 4,084; candidates for baptism, 320; villages where native christians reside, 111; school or prayer houses, 53; chapel, 1; high school, 1, boarders, 51; caste girls schools, 3; pupils, 101; ordinary mission schools, 29; pupils, 429. The entire working force of this field embraces five ordained ministers, of whom two are native pastors; catechists, 3; itinerant teachers, 29; Bible colporteurs, 2; tract colporteurs, 2; female missionaries, 2; together exclusive of the High School at Guntoor. The expense of this agency for the last two years has amounted to $20,847.16.

The history of the African Mission is as follows: The General Synod having resolved at its session in Pittsburg in 1859 to establish a mission in the territory of Liberia, Rev. Morris Officer and Rev. Mr. Heigerd set sail from Baltimore on the 22d day of February, 1860, and reached the Liberian coast on the 5th day of April following. A site for a mission was selected on St. Paul's River, about thirty miles inland from Monrovia. A mission farm of one hundred acres was received from the Liberian government, upon which the mission buildings were erected. Two hundred acres were also given as a reservation. A mission school of forty children was at once organized, these children having been selected from a captured slaver in the latter part of August, 1860. On the 17th of February, 1861, a small church was organized. In 1861 Rev. Officer left the mission in care of Rev. Heigerd. In 1864 Rev. Heigerd returned to America, having been preceded by his wife, who, on account of ill health, was obliged to abandon the work.

In 1863 the mission was reinforced by the arrival of Rev. J. Kistler and wife. In 1864 Rev. J. M. Rice and wife were commissioned as missionaries to Africa, but after a sojourn of seven months only, returned to their native land July 26th, 1865.

In September, 1866, Mrs. Kistler, the wife of the Rev. J. Kistler, died at the Muhlenburg mission. This was followed soon after by the departure of the Rev. Mr. Kistler from Africa and his return to America in the latter part of the month of April, 1867.

Both Mr. Rice and Mr. Kistler were compelled to leave the mission on account of their impaired health. The mission being left thus practically without a head, its affairs were entrusted temporarily to a lay-brother, by name David Kelly.

On the 25th of January, 1869, Rev. S. P. Carnell sailed for Africa, reaching the mission March 14th, 1869.

Brother Carnell's missionary life was of short duration; he soon fell a victim to over-work and undue exposure.

On the 26th of May, 1873, Rev. J. G. Breininger and wife started to reinforce the African mission. Their work was of short duration, Mr. Breininger being soon deprived of his companion by death, and he himself returning to this country in 1874. His place, however, was speedily supplied by the Rev. David A. Day, a graduate of the Theological Department at Selinsgrove, Pa. In September, 1875, Rev. B. B. Collins and wife embarked for Africa, where they arrived in November following. But scarcely had one month passed over them when Mr. Collins was smitten down by fever, which greatly prostrated him. His wife, soon after, was taken down by the same disease, and her life was greatly endangered. A return home was imperatively demanded. They re-embarked for America in April, being accompanied also by Mr. Day, whose wife, for special reasons, had previously sailed for home. Mr. Collins' health rapidly improved, while his devoted wife, after having been one week at sea, died, and was buried in mid-ocean. The missionaries landed at New York in June, 1876. In the fall of the same year, Rev. David A. Day and wife again returned to Africa, where, at this present writing, they are still laboring. Truly this mission has been one of arduous toil and heroic sacrifices. Its present condition is hopeful and prosperous.

For the first eighteen years the society received $38,220.60, and expended $38,021.03, and in the last twenty-two years the expenses of our foreign missions have been very large.

Mr. Gunn died after a residence of seven years in India on July 5th, 1851, aged thirty-seven.

The mission in India was composed of Rev. C. F. Heyer, M. D., Rev. W. J. Cutter and his wife, Rev. W. E. Snyder and his wife, with the widow Gunn, from the United States; Rev. Messrs. Groening and wife, and Rev. A. F. Heise from Germany, and at present Rev. Messrs Unangst and Rowe from the United States.

The General Council also supports a mission in India, with Rev. H. C. Schmidt at the head of it. His field of labor is Rajahmundry.

IGNORANCE CONCERNING OUR CHURCH.

Although the Lutheran church is the largest protestant communion in the world, and her contributions to theological science vastly more profound, scholarly and useful than those of any other—although her great authors are recognized the world over as superior to all others, and her universities are frequented by students from all Christian countries—although even in the United States we have upwards of two thousand ministers and numerous colleges, theological seminaries and church journals, yet there exists even among some otherwise intelligent persons a pitiable ignorance of our condition, character and work.

This is owing in part to the prevalence of the German language which was formerly so extensively employed, but more particularly, I think, to the undemonstrative character of our ministers and people. We have not sought notoriety as some others have—we have not, until recently, mingled much with other people in what are called the general benevolent enterprises of the day—we have not coveted platform glory, and hence neither the names of our church and of our principal ministers have flourished in the religious papers.

But there are other and more proximate reasons for this ignorance concerning us. Even otherwise well instructed men have not regarded a knowledge of church history as an important part of their education, and hence some of them make monstrous blunders when they write about us.

Some of their people affect a contempt for the "Dutch" as they call us—they look upon our ministers and people as uncultured and irreligious, and hence in places where our people are not numerous and not socially influential we are not treated very respectfully.

When I was a student in Princeton Seminary, in 1826, a very zealous young man proposed in the missionary meeting that special efforts be made for the conversion of both ministers and people among the Germans of Eastern Pennsylvania—he said that no section of the country stood in greater need of evangelization than that, and plead lustily for some of the students to offer themselves as Home Missionaries for that benighted region.

I admitted that there was probably room for improvement, but held that the sending of English Presbyterian preachers, who could not speak a word of German, was of questionable utility, to put it in the mildest terms.

He looked upon that people precisely as he did upon the heathen, among whom it was eminently proper to send the gospel, and that it would be no interference with the rights of others who had preoccupied the ground. He was supremely ignorant of the character, wants and circumstances of the people, but not more so than many other persons since that day.

When Dr. Reynolds lived at Columbus, Ohio, as President of the college, he was most painfully mortified at the want of courtesy shown him by the Presbyterian and other ministers of that city. Probably a better scholar than any of them, he felt himself entitled to some social attention, but he did not receive it, and it was because he was associated with an institution and with men who were "Dutch," and of course who could not be respectable. Poor Reynolds was also grievously disappointed in another expectation. He went out there under the full conviction that he could persuade the Ohio Synod to join the General Synod, but he encountered such fierce opposition that he gave up the idea in despair.

Their opposition to his measure was transferred to his person, and he soon became so unpopular that he was compelled to resign. He could not speak German, and the majority did not want "einen Irischen," as they called him, to be at the head of their college. He paid them back by calling them "Black Dutch," and left in disgust.

This ignorance of our denominational peculiarities has been the occasion of many ludicrous blunders. Even in such a respectable paper as the New York Observer we occasionally find ourselves confounded with the German Reformed, betraying a pitiable unacquaintance with church history. The church item editor of that paper does not seem to be familiar with denominational distinctions, and hence nearly every week we see the Dutch Reformed church and the German Reformed church incongruously intermingled, and both made to pass for one. No Lutheran editor would ever make such unpardonable blunders. Our men are too well educated to be guilty of such nonsense.

One of our ministers was once asked whether the "Lutherans were not a branch of the Methodists?"

A Methodist minister once told me he had recently read a life of Martin Luther, of whom he had known nothing before, but he now looked upon him as a rather remarkable man.

It is surprising with what pertinacity even some intelligent men will reiterate the charge that Lutherans believe in consubstantiation, which has been shown to be false over one hundred times, even in our own country, but still every now and then the same erroneous statement is made.

But of late years people intelligent in general church affairs have become better acquainted with us as a christian communion. They often see our name mentioned in their church papers, and sometimes, too, not in the most favorable light. They also hear of the literary or theological productions of some of our scholars, and respect them. I now, of course, speak of those people who live in places not settled by Lutherans, and where there is no Lutheran Church, and yet I once knew a Presbyterian minister who was pastor in one of the largest inland towns of Pennsylvania, in which there were four large Lutheran Churches, who reported to his Presbytery that he lived in a German town, but he had no doubt that before long many of the people would join his church! Evidently he did not know what the Lutherans were!

But of what advantage is it to be widely known? We have our own peculiar field to cultivate, and should have no ambitious aspirings after notoriety. While many of our men at the present day are known by name to everybody, and highly respected, too, let the rest of us be content to work on in humble retirement.

THE MARYLAND SYNOD QUESTION

This name was given to a subject which some years ago excited general interest, and which is deemed of sufficient importance to give it a place in my book. It will be observed that it involves deep principle as well as momentous practice, and was the occasion of leading to a result mutually satisfactory. I am indebted to Dr. Diehl for this important paper.

In the spring of 1853, Rev. J. Winter applied to Rev. J. A. Seiss, President of the Maryland Synod, for an honorable dismission from the Synod without intending to apply to any other Synod or any other ecclesiastical body for admission.

At the next annual meeting of the Synod, October 21st, 1853, the President, Mr. Seiss, stated his action in his report, thus:

"During the sitting of the General Synod at Winchester, Va., I received a letter from Rev. John Winter, requesting of me 'a letter of honorable dismission' from the Synod of Maryland, and stating that he was 'compelled to this by feelings of self-respect.' I immediately wrote to him urging him to reconsider and withdraw his application. His reply was, that 'after cool and calm reflection,' he found he could come to no other conclusion, and insisted upon compliance with his request. I accordingly gave him a certificate of honorable dismission. But as Mr. Winter has put his present withdrawal upon the ground of improper treatment from a member of this body, whom he names in his communication, it might be well to have this correspondence referred to a committee to report thereon to the ministerium, and thus furnish an opportunity for a proper investigation of the charges alleged. A committee consisting of Rev. G. Diehl, Dr. H. L. Baugher and Rev. J. Heck was appointed to report on the President's report. On the item referring to the dismission of Rev. J. Winter, they proposed the following, which was referred to the ministerium:

"That the action of the President in giving an honorable dismission to Rev. J. Winter, cannot be considered as final, inasmuch as an honorable dismission cannot constitutionally be given by its presiding officer to a member *who remains within the bounds of the*

Synod. The committee therefore propose the following resolution:

Resolved, That the Synod do not confirm the dismission given to Rev. J. Winter, which it is understood is still in his hands, and consequently under our control, but that Brother Winter be requested to return it."

Minutes of 1853, pages 6 and 25.

The Synod adjourned on Tuesday, 25th October, a little before twelve o'clock. At twelve M. the ministerium held a session, at which this item was called up for action. The published minutes read thus:

The second item of report on President's report (referring to the case of Rev. J. Winter) as amended, was adopted.

Revs. Seiss and Kurtz gave notice that they would offer protests against the adoption of this item of the report. But Synod having adjourned before they were received, the provisional acts relating thereto in the by-laws, (sec 16) exclude these documents from the present minutes.

At the Synod, 1854, at Clearspring, Rev. F. R. Anspach, President, reported on this case.

"On the 10th of November, the Secretary of this body forwarded to me two papers which had been sent to him to be incorporated with the minutes, one from Dr. B. Kurtz, and the other from Rev. J. A. Seiss, both protesting against the action of Synod in relation to the case of Rev. John Winter. As this is a novel feature in our ecclesiastical affairs, and as I had no precedent by which my judgment could be guided, the Synod will indulge me in a brief statement of the reasons which determined me to rule the protests out of our minutes, and in which opinion the other officers concurred. It is moreover due to the brethren who protested as well as myself, to show why their papers were excluded from the record, and more particularly since I understand that it is their intention to test the justness of our decision."

An able argument sustaining the exclusion of the protests from the record follows, the strongest point being, that the section sixteen of By-Laws goes on the presumption that the protest should be offered to the Synod during the convention, as it provides for a reply to the protest, which could not be had if the Secretary were allowed to receive a protest after adjournment, and enter it upon the record. This would give the minority the privilege of recording their reasons for their vote in the negative, and deny to the majority all opportunity of giving their reasons for their affirmative vote, as the majority could not reply to the protest."

This action of the President was referred to a committee consisting of Rev. J. F. Campbell, Rev. G. Diehl and Mr. G. Strauss. They offered this report:

"That the action of the President in ruling out the protests of Dr. Kurtz and Rev. Seiss, in the case of John Winter, deceased, from the proceedings of this body, was under the circumstances not only justifiable, but highly proper, and is hereby sustained."

No action was taken on this, but the chairman was allowed to withdraw it. The following was subsequently passed:

Resolved, That the remark of the Secretary on pages 33 and 34 of last year's minutes, respecting the exclusion of the protests of Revs. Seiss and Kurtz, be stricken out."

The Synod thus left it an open question whether a protest can be offered after adjournment and entered by the Secretary on the record.

At a session of the ministerium during this convention, October 16th, 1854, "Rev. Seiss moved a repeal of that part of the report of the committee on the President's report for 1852-3, recorded on page 25 of the minutes of 1853, and adopted by the ministerium at the conclusion of its final session of last year; the matter sought to be repealed being marked item No. 2, with the appended resolution in the words following, viz.: (See resolution.)

This subject was again discussed at some length. After which the following resolution offered by Rev. Anspach was passed:

"*Resolved*, That the subject of repealing the action of the ministerium, in relation to the dismission of Rev. J. Winter be postponed for consideration until the next Synod."

Rev. John Winter having departed this life March, 1854, some seven months before this convention of the Synod, his widow, under an impression that the action of the Synod in 1853 reflected unfavorably upon the conduct of her husband, addressed a communication to the Synod, which was put into the hands of a committee consisting of Rev. G. Diehl and Rev. J. G. Butler, who reported that no aspersion was intended or was in reality cast upon the conduct and character of her late husband.

The discussion of the subject was now transferred to the columns of the Lutheran Observer. In the issue of November 17, 1854, a short communication, over the signature "H.," under the heading—"*The Maryland Synod—A Question for the Church,*" called attention to it. The writer said—"The question is, *whether a man in good standing in the Synod, and wishing to discontinue his membership, though announcing no intention to join any other Synod, is entitled to an honorable dismission?*"

To this Dr. Kurtz, the then editor, replied at some length. He said—"It involves the first, the plainest and fundamental principles of rational liberty. Synods do not constitute ministerial character, but merely recognize and proclaim it. It is God who makes ministers, who calls them into his service, qualifies and ordains them. And when he thus creates no human power can destroy; what he makes man cannot unmake. If the examination of a candidate for licensure and ordination, and the scrutiny of the Synod result in the conviction that God has called and qualified the man, the Synod recognizes and receives him as a member, and thereby proclaims the fact that they acknowledge him as a minister of Jesus Christ. If he subsequently desires to withdraw from Synod, may he not do so? His entrance was voluntary, and may not his withdrawal be equally voluntary?" The doctor said a man may be "a minister at large," that it is an inherent right that a man entering a Synod with a good character, and deporting himself properly for a term of years, may withdraw, and is entitled to testimonials of his Christian and ministerial character."

He continues—"We are assured that both in Virginia and in Pennsylvania, and no doubt in other sections of the church, ministers have been honorably dismissed without their intending to join other clerical organizations. He had also heard of similar cases in the Presbyterian Church." He adds—"Let it be borne in mind that, having withdrawn from all ecclesiastical connection with us, he is no longer a Lutheran minister, and we are no longer responsible for his conduct."

To this editorial and its leading position Rev. G. Diehl replied in a communication under the heading—"*The Maryland Synod's Question,*" in the Observer of December 1, 1854. He first defined the import of a certificate of honorable dismission. "A certificate of dismission to a minister, given by a Synod or its presiding officer, is a testimonial of his Christian and ministerial character, and an expression of the consent of his Synod to transfer his membership to another clerical body."

The article maintains that the church is a congregation of believers, among whom the Gospel is preached and the sacraments administered according to the Gospel (Augs. Conf.) That while an individual church may be independent, and independency and congregationalism come within the definition of the church in our standards, congregations and ministers in primitive times were united in occasional Synods. That this harmonizes with the symbolic representations of the church in the New Testament—a tree, branches of the vine, a kingdom, &c., an organized body. The Lutheran Church in this country has adopted Synodical government, and all loyal Lutheran ministers should conform to the established order; therefore, to dismiss with honorable testimonials a minister, unless the dismission be the mere transferrence of membership to another body, would be to dismiss to the world. That the Synod cannot sanction the departure of a good minister from the church to the world. Moreover, the dismissal of a minister to no body, neither to an individual congregation nor to a ministerial body, would place him in a position in which he would be separated from the communion of saints, and could not, without a violation of church order, obey Christ's dying command—"Do this in remembrance of me." Nor would the minister in such a position be amenable to anybody for discipline. This would be a kind of apostasy from the church to the world, and a Synod could not sanction such withdrawal from all church discipline and church fellowship. If a minister should ask to withdraw, to take his position as a layman in a congregation or to become pastor of an independent congregation, the ends of Christian fellowship and church discipline would be answered. But this is not the case before the Maryland Synod."

In the Observer, December 22d, 1854, Rev. J. A. Seiss defended the honorable dismissal of Rev. Winter, and replied to G. Diehl's article as follows: "This is a question that must be decided by the New Testament alone. The New Testament Church is republican—a free state in which, if the individual citizen but observe the simple, common laws of the founder, there is no earthly, rightful tribunal to interfere with him. Obedience to Jesus invests a man with an inviolable standing before God, and guarantees to him all his ecclesiastical rights in defiance of all Synods, bishops, patriarchs, conclaves, popes and grandees of ecclesiastical office, that the vanity, or the pusillanimity or the wisdom of mortals have ever set up in christendom. Are Synods any part of the original, divine, essential constitution of the church? Not a whit more than the national conventions of political parties are a part of the constitution of the great American Republic. Synods are mere human contrivances, the creatures of human expediency. We read of no Synods in the New Testament. God has not said a word about Synods, therefore they have no peculiar, special, divine power. Synods are nothing more than voluntary associations of ministers and churches who consent together to exercise jointly what they each have a divine warrant and commission to exercise separately. If a faithful minister of Jesus, under the responsibilities to which he stands to his Lord, should be forced to decide against the expediency of this combination, and feel conscientiously bound to recede from it and carry on his ministry in the way God originally gave it, who has the authority to hinder him? Hundreds of holy, active and sound ministers belong to no Synod, and yet on the plain principle of the word of God, suffer no detriment in their ministerial authority."

In the Observer, January 12th, 1855, Rev. G. Diehl replied, "That all Mr. Seiss's representations did not touch the question involved before the Maryland Synod, but constituted merely a defence of congregationalism, and congregational independency. In this form of church polity, the minister submits to church discipline, holds himself amenable to the congregation, partakes of the sacrament of the altar, and is in the communion of the saints. But in the case before the Synod, the minister was honorably dismissed out of the church into the wide world, a position in which he was not entitled to church fellowship, or amenable to discipline."

February 2, 1855, Mr. Seiss rejoins—"The ministry is a thing of God. A minister cannot be constituted except as God has ordained. And when the ministry has once been legitimately conferred upon a man, it cannot be taken from him except on grounds which God has indicated. God has not made validity of ministerial authority dependent on Synodical connections. Ceasing to hold membership in a Synod does not dissolve ministerial authority; and that to depose a man on such ground alone is to act without divine sanction, to make human expediency set aside the clear statements of inspiration, to exalt human enactments above the laws of God, and to assign to Synodical regulations power to repeal the ordinance of Christ."

In the April (1855) number of the Evangelical Review, there is an able article by Dr. Baugher in defence of the action of the Synod in not sanctioning the dismissal of a minister without connecting himself with some ecclesiastical or clerical body. In the number of July 1855, Rev. J. A. Seiss pulished an elaborate reply.

At the Synod of Maryland at Washington, October, 1855, a paper drawn up by Dr. Baugher and Mr. Seiss was presented and adopted.

"Whereas certain proceedings of the Synod of Maryland touching the honorable dismission of Rev. John Winter, now deceased, which were passed in Baltimore, 1853, have caused serious trouble among some of the brethren; and whereas it is desirable that we should agree upon some settled basis with regard to the questions involved, therefore—

"I. *Resolved*, That the following statement be adopted as the sense of this Synod upon the subject.

"1. That we view Synodical organizations not as of absolute divine institution, but as early and wisely introduced into the Christian church for the more satisfactory and efficient administration of its general affairs, but possessing no specific divine powers beyond or above those resident in the ministers and churches of which they are composed.

"2. That fraternal association for mutual consultation and advice, and for the joint exercise of God's gifts to his individual ministers and churches, Synods are vital to the operations of the church as it exists in this country; and that the wisdom of our Lutheran fathers in adopting and incorporating them into the government and discipline of our church claims our highest commendation.

"3. That it is rightfully expected of all who claim to be accredited ministers of our church, as constituted in this country, that they seek connection with some one of our District Synods.

"4. That a minister in good standing in the Synod may withdraw from his connection with it, and may receive testimonials of his good standing up to the moment of his withdrawal; but that after he has thus withdrawn he will no longer be regarded by us as an accredited minister of the Lutheran church until he has again secured membership in some one of our regular Synods.

"5. That the power of giving the testimonials above alluded to shall not lie with the President *ad interim*, but the Synod itself in regular session assembled.

"II. *Resolved*, That the proceedings of the Synod in 1853, which relate to the honorable dismission of the Rev. J. Winter, so far as they are inconsistent with the above statements, be and are hereby rescinded: that the resolution of the Synod in 1853 has respect only to the constitutional powers of the President, and that if there be any reflection on Brother Winter's character in that act we hereby disclaim and repeal it."

Dr. Diehl has stated this subject very fairly. Since the period above announced only two applications from dissatisfied ministers have been made for dismission from the Synod without the intention of joining any other. They were promptly refused, but both these men are no longer members of any Synod by their own acts.

ENGLISH LUTHERAN HYMN BOOKS.

BY REV. M. SHEELEIGH.

The "Hymn and Prayer Book" of Dr. Kunze, published in 1795, was the first work of the kind prepared expressly for the public worship of English Lutheran congregations. He was one of our apostolic laborers in this Western world—a contemporary and successor of the great Muhlenberg, as well as one of the most learned men who assisted in laying the foundation of our American Institutions after the Revolutionary war. It is doubtful whether he had in him enough of the poetical element for the work of writing or compiling a strictly Lutheran Hymn Book in the English language. But apart from this, his knowledge of the English language was too limited to admit of the possibility of success in such an undertaking. Hence he took as his basis the translations of the Psalmodia Germanica, and the Moravian Collection of 1789, without any material alterations. In his preface he says, "All except those in the appendix are taken from printed books, particularly the German Psalmody, with which many serious English persons have been greatly delighted; and from a collection of the Moravian Brethren, printed in London,

1789." This latter book contained some hymns of Watts, Newton, Erskine, Kenn, &c., but all the rest are wretchedly poor. The Rev. Messrs. Strebeck and Ernst were Dr. Kunze's assistants, but they had no poetic talent, their English was imperfect, and their original contributions, as well as those of Dr. Kunze, would not be endured at the present day. They are full of barbarisms, and the imperfections are simply intolerable.

The book never took a firm hold upon the church; plain people could not understand the hymns, and educated people were shocked at their coarseness of versification.

In 1797 another book was issued in New York, which, like the former, was an individual enterprise. Its editor was Rev. George Strebeck, then pastor of the English Lutheran Church of that city. The volume embraced two hundred and ninety-seven hymns, a Liturgy, the Gospels and Epistles, and the Augsburg Confession.

A third book was published in New York, six years later, in 1806. The compiler was Rev. Ralph Williston. The book is furnished with a certificate by Dr. Kunze, showing that it was designed to be regarded in a synodically official light. The hymn division comprises three hundred and nineteen pages, followed by one hundred pages of liturgy.

The next hymn book was compiled by Drs. Quitman, Wackerhagen and Mayer, first published in 1814. This is what is commonly known as "The Old New York Hymn Book." It almost entirely rejects the German element which so fully pervaded Dr. Kunze's book, and draws its hymns from sources almost exclusively English. But some of the most beautiful and old-fashioned orthodox hymns are mutilated or perverted.* Some of the cardinal doctrines of the New Testament are barely hinted at or ignored. The distinctive Lutheran teachings on the sacraments are not recognized.

To the volume was added a liturgy, which probably sustained the book among the people of some of our English churches in New York, New Jersey and Pennsylvania, for a longer time than the hymns alone would have done. The preface was signed by Frederick H. Quitman, D. D., as President, and Augustus Wackerhagen, as Secretary of the Synod. In 1834 the book was issued with a larger number of hymns and prayers. The "Additional Hymns" ran the whole number up to seven hundred.

* See Evangelical Review, October, 1859, 189-90.

Rev. Dr. P. F. Mayer was chairman of the committee charged with the work of improvement.

There is more unction and a higher tone of literary merit in these "Additional Hymns," but there is no clear recognition of the orthodoxy of the church, unless we except the benediction, in which we find the trinity at least by implication. The book contains nothing that is distinctively Lutheran.

The first edition of the General Synod's Hymn Book was published in 1828, and down to 1841 twenty-nine editions had been printed. That year the General Synod instructed the Hymn Book Committee—then consisting of Rev. Dr. S. S. Schmucker, Rev. Dr. J. G. Morris and Mr. C. A Morris—to prepare a selection of a few additional hymns to be appended to the book. The thirtieth edition, dated 1842, accordingly appeared with an appendix of one hundred and ninety-nine hymns, making the whole nine hundred and sixty-five. Only two hymns were substituted in the body of the book.

In 1848 the General Synod appointed a committee of fifteen—one from each district Synod—to revise the book. A sub-committee of three, residing in Gettysburg, was finally specially charged with the work—namely, Profs. Reynolds, Baugher and Schmucker. Two years later, the book appeared with numerous changes. In the body of the collection there were about fifty substitutions, together with many verbal changes and omissions of stanzas, while the appendix was wholly rearranged and enlarged. The whole number of hymns was now one thousand and twenty-four, embracing a considerable number of translations from the stores of German hymnology. With this revision appeared the first attempt to present the authors of hymns. The list was prepared chiefly by Rev. M. Sheeleigh, but it was first unhappily confused in the printing.

The type of the 24mo. book being considered too small for the eyes of the aged, it was, in 1852, issued also in 12mo. form, suitable also for the pulpit. In 1854 it appeared in 48mo. form, so as to be more conveniently carried.

In 1858 the publishing of the Hymn Book was transferred to the Lutheran Publication Society, Philadelphia, where numerous editions appeared until the year 1870, when this book was wholly displaced by another that had been authorized.

The General Synod, in 1866, again appointed a committee to

revise the Hymn Book. The result was a book wholly new in arrangement. Many new hymns were introduced, many old ones were cast aside, and the whole number was reduced to six hundred and one, and sixteen doxologies. The selection, as a whole, will bear a more rigid criticism than its predecessors. This volume is entitled, "The Book of Worship." There are embodied in it an Order of Public Worship, Family Prayers, Luther's Smaller Catechism, The Augsburg Confession, The Formula of Government and Discipline, and the Constitution of the General Synod. The authors of the hymns are given in the index of the first lines. The compilation of hymns was made by the Rev. Drs. S. S. Schmucker, M. Valentine and C. A. Stork.

In 1845 the Joint Synod of Ohio issued a book at Zanesville, with the title, "A Collection of Hymns and Prayers for Public and Private Worship." This work was made to conform, in arrangement and contents, to the General Synod's book, as nearly as permitted by the objects which suggested the compilation. The number of hymns it contains, including doxologies, is four hundred and fifty-eight. The names of the committee who prepared the book are not given. There are seventy-nine pages of prayers for the use of families and individuals added.

A second book, published by order of the Joint Synod of Ohio, appeared in 1853, at Columbus. The names of the committee of compilation are not given; but report ascribes the prominent part of the labor to Rev. Prof. M. Loy. The number of hymns is three hundred and fifty-four, and seven doxologies. The arrangement is distinct from that of the former book. Many of the hymns are translations from the German. This book contains hymns alone.

The Tennessee Synod published an English Hymn book, entitled, "Church Hymn Book in 1816." It was compiled, and largely composed, by Rev. Paul Henkel. It contains five hundred and forty-six pages.

In the year 1838 a new book of five hundred and twenty-seven pages appeared by the same authority. Though called a second edition, it was in some of its features a new book. It was prepared by Rev. Ambrose Henkel, a son of the former. The preface informs us that though this book varies in some respects from the former, it was founded upon the same basis, and comprised essentially the same matter. Many hymns were added. A third and a fourth edition appeared, respectively, in 1850 and 1857. In each case there are a few additions of hymns. The whole number is now six hundred and seventy-nine, and the book is published at New Market, Virginia.

The Evangelical Psalmist is the name of a book issued in 1860, from the house of Lindsay and Blakiston, Philadelphia. It is substantially the General Synod's Hymn Book of that time (with some omissions and additions), together with tunes. It was the joint work of Drs. Seiss, McCron and Passavant. The hymn and tune part of the book contains four hundred and thirty-eight pages. Ninety pages of church forms are appended. It was introduced into very few churches.

The late civil war having separated the Southern Synods from the General Synod, they organized a Southern General Synod. A new hymn book was prepared, the first issue of which appeared in 1867. It was called the Book of Worship. It contains four hundred and sixty-five hymns and thirteen doxologies, a Liturgy, Scripture Lessons, Confessions, Prayers, Formula of Government, and the Constitution of the Southern General Synod. The book was prepared by Rev. Prof. Wm. D. Roedel, chairman of the committee. It is published at Columbia, S. C.

Another compilation, called The Church Book, appeared in Philadelphia in 1869, by order of the General Council. There are here five hundred and eighty-eight hymns and eighteen doxologies; also Forms of Service, Prayers, Confessions, etc. The authors' names appear in connection with the hymns. The compilers of the hymns were Rev. F. M. Bird and Rev. Dr. B. M. Schmucker.

SUNDAY SCHOOL HYMN BOOKS.

BY REV. M. SHEELEIGH.

The first hymn book for English Lutheran Sunday Schools made its appearance in 1833. Although anonymous, it is known to have been prepared by the elder Rev. Dr. C. P. Krauth, while pastor of St. Matthew's church, Philadelphia. Its title is, "Hymns, Selected and Arranged for Sunday Schools of the Evangelical Lutheran Church," etc. The hymns were numbered to two hundred and seventeen. An edition of 1838 has in it ten additional hymns.

Ten years later, or in 1843, another book appeared in Baltimore. The selection was the work of Rev. Dr. W. A. Passavant. No compiler's name, however, appears. As the book was designed to fill the place of the former, which had gone out of print, it bears the same title, excepting that for the word "Arranged" the word "Original" is substituted. It contains altogether three hundred and four hymns, the last forty-two forming a Supplement for Infant Sunday Schools.

The publisher of the latter, Mr. T. Newton Kurtz, desiring to extend the usefulness of the book, secured its enlargement and improvement. The hymns as far as number two hundred and fifty-one were left standing intact, to which an appendix was compiled by Rev. M. Sheeleigh, running the number up to four hundred and thirty-five. Then follow thirty-nine pages occupied with forms for opening and closing Sunday Schools, The Lord's Prayer, The Ten Commandments, The Creed, etc. The book is in 32mo. form, and contains four hundred and sixty-seven pages. It was printed at Baltimore in 1860.

A supplement was prepared for the last by Rev. M. Sheeleigh. The title is "Hymns, Selected and Original, for Infant Sunday Schools in the Evangelical Lutheran Church." The number of hymns is one hundred and thirty-two. Following these are The Lord's Prayer, The Ten Commandments, The Creed, etc., together with a little Catechism adapted to infants, prepared for the book by the compiler. This infant book is often found bound up with the larger volume.

In the same year with the last, 1860, the Lutheran Board of Publication, Philadelphia, issued a book, entitled, "Hymns for Sunday Schools," published by order of the General Synod of the Evangelical Lutheran church. It was compiled by Rev. Dr. L. E. Albert and Rev. Prof. T. T. Titus. There are in the body of the book three hundred and forty-six hymns and fifteen doxologies, covering two hundred and eighty-six pages.

To the above is added an appendix of fifty hymns for infants, or forty-six pages, also issued separately, as in the former case. It was prepared by the same hands that produced the larger book, and at the same time.

A little manual of select hymns, compiled expressly for the use of the Sunday School of St. John's Evangelical Lutheran Church,

Philadelphia, was printed in 1864. It contains seventy-five hymns, gathered from the popular music books used in Sunday schools at the time.

In 1873, by order of the General Council, a book appeared in Philadelphia, with the title, "Sunday School Book for the use of Evangelical Lutheran Congregations." There are in it three hundred and nine pages, embracing two hundred thirty-three hymns, accompanied by tunes. These are preceded by an "Order of Service, The Catechism, and Chants and Canticles." The book was prepared by a committee of which Rev. Dr. C. W. Schaeffer was the chairman.

BRIEF SKETCHES OF LUTHERAN COLLEGES.

PENNSYLVANIA COLLEGE.

When the Theological Seminary at Gettysburg was established, in 1826, it was soon discovered that another institution was necessary, in which young men, destined for the ministry, might receive academic training. Accordingly, in June, 1827, a classical school was established, under the direction of D. Jacobs, A. M., and in 1829 a scientific department was connected with it, under the care of his brother, M. Jacobs. In the summer of 1829, the plan of the institution having been enlarged, the name was changed to that of the *Gettysburg Gymnasium*. After the death of David Jacobs the classical department was vacant except by temporary supplies, until April, 1831, when Rev. H. L. Baugher, A. M., was appointed to take charge of it.

It was soon deemed expedient to place the school on a more permanent basis by enlarging its operations, and organizing the Gymnasium into a Collegiate form. A charter was obtained from the legislature in April, 1832, and on the 4th of July of that year, the institution was organized under the title of *Pennsylvania College*. The Hon. Calvin Blythe delivered an address on the occasion. On the same day, the Patrons[*] of the College selected the following *Board of Trustees*:

[*] This was the title given to those who were chosen from the number of contributors to the support of the school, and to whom its government was given before the college was chartered.

Hon. Calvin Blythe, President; John G. Morris, Secretary; J. B. McPherson, Esq., Treasurer; Hon. A. Thompson, L. L. D., J. G. Schmucker, D. D., D. F. Schaeffer, D. D., J. C. Baker, D. D., B. Kurtz, D. D., S. S. Schmucker, D. D., E. L. Hazelius, D. D., C. P. Krauth, D. D., Hon. D. Sheffer, Rev. C. F. Heyer, Rev. A. Reck, R. G. Harper, Esq., Hon. T. C. Miller, J. F. McFarlane, Esq., Rev. F. Ruthrauff, Rev. J. Medtard, Rev. Emanuel Keller, Rev. A. H. Lochman.

On the same evening the Board met and organized the following faculty:

S. S. Schmucker, D. D., *Professor of Intellectual Philosophy and Moral Science;* E. L. Hazelius, D. D., *Professor of the Latin Language and Literature;* Rev. H. L. Baugher, A. M., *Professor of the Greek Language and Belles Lettres;* M. Jacobs, A. M., *Professor of Mathematics and Natural Science;* J. H. Marsden, A. M., *Professor of Mineralogy and Botany.*

In consequence of their duties in the Theological Seminary, Doctors Hazelius and Schmucker, who agreed to serve only until other arrangements could be made, withdrew from the faculty in 1833, and Rev. C. P. Krauth of Philadelphia was elected to the Professorship of Intellectual and Moral Science. In the spring of 1834 he was appointed to the Presidency of the college, and was inducted into office at the commencement of the winter session. Subsequently, the corps of instructors was filled by the appointment of William M. Reynolds, A. M., who had, for some time previously, been acting as Principal of the Preparatory Department, to the chair of latin language and literature.

During the winter of 1833-34, through the efforts of Hon. Thaddeus Stevens, a member of the legislature, an appropriation of eighteen thousand dollars was secured for the college from the State.

This appropriation enabled the trustees to erect an edifice more suitable than the old "Academy," in which the instructions had heretofore been given. The building was commenced in 1836, and in the autumn of 1837 it was sufficiently advanced to admit of its occupancy by a part of the students.

The annual appropriation of one thousand dollars by the State to this and other colleges, enabled the trustees to extend its operations by the appointment of additional instructors. Accordingly, in the autumn of 1838, Rev. H. I. Schmidt, A. M., was elected

Professor of the German Language and Literature, History and French. He resigned in 1843; M. L. Stoever, A. M., who, for some time before, had been at the head of the Academical Department, was elected Professor of History, and instruction in German was given by one of the other Professors, until the winter term of 1844, when Rev. C. A. Hay, A. M., entered upon the duties of that chair. In the spring of 1845, H. Haupt, A. M., was appointed adjunct Professor of Mathematics. In the fall of 1847 Professors Hay and Haupt resigned, the former that his time might be entirely devoted to the Theological Seminary, and the latter to accept a more desirable appointment elsewhere. In 1850 Professor Reynolds withdrew to accept the Presidency of the University at Columbus, Ohio, and the department of Latin Language and Literature was assigned to Professor Stoever. The Presidency, during this year, also became vacant by the election of Dr. Krauth to a Professorship in the Seminary. Dr. Baugher, who had been a Professor in the College from the time of its organization, was chosen his successor, and F. A. Muhlenberg, A. M., was elected to the vacant Professorship of the Greek Language and Literature. In 1850 Dr. D. Gilbert was appointed Lecturer on Anatomy and Physiology, and H. Montanus, Instructor in German and French.

The "Franklin Professorship" was founded the same year with the funds received as the Lutheran interest of Franklin College, Lancaster, chartered by an act of the Legislature in 1787, with special reference to the wants of the German population. This institution was designed for "the citizens of the Commonwealth of German birth or extraction, and for others not thus descended, that they might be carefully instructed in the principles of the Christian religion, the English, German and Classical languages, science and literature, to qualify them for taking an intelligent and active part in the management of the affairs of this State or of the General Government, or of being useful to the learned professions or the mechanic arts." By a provision of the charter the Board of Trustees was to consist of not less than forty-five, of whom fifteen were to be forever selected from the members of the Lutheran Church, fifteen from the Reformed or Calvinistic Church, and the remaining fifteen from any other denominations of Christians. With the consent of all the parties interested, an act of the Legislature was secured, in 1850, by which one-third of the funds (upwards of seventeen thousand dollars) were transferred to Pennsylvania College for the permanent endowment of the "Franklin Professorship," the first incumbent of which was to be Professor of Ancient Languages, and appointed by the existing Lutheran members of the Franklin Board. The right of nominating the subsequent incumbents was invested in the Synod of Pennsylvania. By the same act the Lutheran Trustees of Franklin College were to be united with the Trustees of Pennsylvania College. The names are F. A. Muhlenberg, M. D,, J. C. Baker, D. D., Rev. Wm. Baetes, J. G. Schmucker, D. D., S. S. Schmucker. D. D., A. H. Lochman, D. D., C. R. Demme, D. D., Rev. B. Keller, H. H. Muhlenberg, M. D., John F. Long, Christopher Hager, George Musser, G. Mayer, Adam Keller, and George Krug. Several of these gentlemen were at the time also Trustees of Pennsylvania College, and others had served at previous periods in this capacity. Professor Muhlenberg, who had been for twelve years connected with Franklin College as an instructor, was transferred to this Professorship.

In 1851 the Synod of Pennsylvania determined to endow a Professorship of the German Language and Literature, with the mutual understanding that the Synod should always have the power of nominating the incumbent. The resolution was subsequently modified so that the Professor might also impart theological instruction in the German language in the Seminary. Through the indefatigable and successful services of Rev. Benjamin Keller the requisite funds were collected, and the Rev. Charles F. Schaeffer, D. D., a graduate of the University of Pennsylvania, was, in 1855, unanimously selected for the Professorship. Dr. Schaeffer continued to occupy the position until the fall term of 1864, when he resigned to accept a call in the recently established Theological Seminary in Philadelphia.

The endowment of these two Professorships was very important to the interests of the College. The relief, too, came very opportunely, at a time when funds were much needed to meet the necessary expenses of the Institution. Of late years there had been a considerable reduction in the number of students, in consequence of the multiplication of Colleges and Preparatory Schools in all parts of the Church.

In addition to the two Professorships mentioned, the College has funds invested to the amount of $17,000 (1865), secured principally by the sale of scholarships, which have rendered more than an equivalent in the gratuitous instruction furnished.

LINNAEAN HALL.

Linnaean Hall was erected in 1846 under the auspices of the Linnaean Association, aided by the Board of Trustees. The corner-stone was laid with appropriate ceremonies, August 23, 1846. It was completed the following summer, and dedicated September 14, 1847.

The *President's House* was built in 1860.

The two *Professors' Houses* on the College Campus were erected in 1868.

The *German Professor's House* on Chambersburg street was purchased and forms part of the endowment of the Professorship of the German Language and Literature.

The *McCreary-Gymnasium*, ninety feet by forty-eight feet, was built in 1872. A large part of the money was collected by the students, and the building was named after John B. McCreary, in recognition of his contribution of one thousand dollars to it. It was opened for use October 17, 1872.

The establishment of the Preparatory School was contemporaneous with the founding of the College itself—1832. Until 1846 the work of the Preparatory Department was carried on in the College building in which the students also lodged. After the erection of the Linnaean Hall in 1846, the first story of that was formed into recitation rooms for this department. The new *Preparatory Building* was begun in 1867, the corner-stone being laid August 8th. An address was delivered on the occasion by M. Russell Thayer of Philadelphia. It was completed—the centre building only—in 1868. No dedication exercises were held. The name Stevens' Hall was given to it.

PRINCIPALS OF PREPARATORY DEPARTMENT.

M. L. Stoever, A. M., 1842–1856.

C. J. Ehrehart, A. M., 1865–1869.

Rev. S. Sentman was *Superintendent*, 1870–1871, the teaching being done by Tutors.

Hart Gilbert, A. M., 1872–1873.

Since 1873 the teaching was done by Rev. P. L. Harrison, A. M., and Hart Gilbert, A. M., as Co-ordinate Instructors, Mr. Harrison being *Superintendent*. In the interval (1857–1864) between the principalship of Profs. Stoever and Ehrehart the instruction was given by Tutors.

The *Astronomical Observatory* was erected in 1874 under W. F. Weber of Baltimore as architect. It is forty-eight feet long by sixteen wide at centre—consists of central building sixteen feet square, with two wings, each sixteen by twelve feet—central part surmounted by hemispherical dome for Equatorical Telescope. One wing contains Transit Instrument, Chronometer &c., and the other Calculators' rooms. Built of corrugated iron. Cost $8000. The money collected by Dr. Valentine.

```
Whole number of Students, about..............2,100
Graduates.....................................577
Ministry (including partials)................450
(For ministry of the graduates)..............320
Professors in Colleges........................54
Presidents of Colleges........................12
```

CHIEF GRANTS AND DONATIONS.

```
From the State...........................$24,500
From Franklin College.....................17,169
Messrs. A. F. and G. P. Ockershausen......20,000
John E. Graeff, Philadelphia..............20,000
Davis Pearson.............................12,000
C. A. Morris, York........................25,000
John Eyerman, Easton.......................3,000
```

Each of the following contributed $1000, viz.: Martin Baehler, Philadelphia; F. W. Conrad, D. D., Philadelphia; Hon. Simon Cameron, Harrisburg; E. Rahm, Pittsburg; C. Yeager, Pittsburg; Wm. Smith, York; Weiser, Son and Carl, York, Pa.; M. B. Spahr, York, Pa.; J. D. Cameron, Harrisburg, Pa.; Hon. Thad. Stevens (legacy), S. Appold, Baltimore; E. G. Smyser, York, Pa.

Besides this subscription by Mr. Appold, he gave several years ago, $1000 for the use of the Department of Chemistry under Prof. Sadtler, and subsequently a liberal sum for the purchase of meteorological instruments. Sums of $500 have been contributed by various persons—in some cases repeated. Total endowment $142,076.48.

FACULTY.

Dr. S. S. Schmucker, Professor Intellectual and Moral Philosophy, 1832–1833.

Dr. C. P. Krauth, Professor Intellectual and Moral Philosophy, 1833–1834.

Dr. C. P. Krauth, President, and Professor Intellectual and Moral Philosophy, 1834–1850.

Dr. E. L. Hazelius, Latin Language and German Literature, 1832.

Dr. H. L. Baugher, Greek Language and Belles-Lettres, 1832–1850.

Dr. H. L. Baugher, President, and Professor Mental and Moral Philosophy, 1850–1868.

Dr. M. Jacobs, Professor Mathematics, Chemistry and Natural Philosophy, 1832–1865.

J. H. Marsden, A. M., Professor Mineralogy and Botany, 1832–1835.

Rev. H. I. Smith, A. M., Professor German Language and Literature, 1838–1843.

M. L. Stoever, A. M., &c., Professor History, 1843–1850.

M. L. Stoever, Latin Language and Literature, 1851–1870.

Rev. C. A. Hay, A. M., Professor German Language and Literature, 1844–1847.

Rev. W. M. Reynolds, D. D., Latin Language and Literature, 1834–1849.

Herman Haupt, A. M., Adjunct Professor Mathematics, 1845–1847.

F. A. Muhlenberg, D. D., Professor Greek Language and Literature, 1850–1867.

Rev. W. H. Harrison, A. M., Assistant Professor Languages, 1845.

C. F. Schaeffer, D. D., Professor German Language and Literature, 1857–1863.

A. M. Mayer, Ph. D., Ockershausen-Professor Natural Sciences, 1864–1866.

Rev. V. L. Conrad, A. M., Ockershausen-Professor of Natural Sciences, 1867–1870.

S. P. Sadtler, Ph. D., Ockershausen-Professor Chemistry and Natural Sciences, 1871–1874.

L. H. Croll, A. M., Professor Mathematics and Astronomy, 1866.

Rev. E. Ferrier, A. M., Graeff-Professor English Language and Literature, 1866-1873.

Rev. H. Louis Baugher, A. M., Pearson-Professor Greek Language and Literature, 1869.

Rev. H. E. Jacobs, A. M., Franklin-Professor Latin Language and Literature, and of History, 1872.

Rev. J. F. Wilkens, Professor German Language and Literature, 1867.

Rev. F. W. A. Notz, Ph. D., Professor German Language and Literature, 1868–1869.

Rev. A. Martin, A. M., Professor German Language and Literature, 1869.

John A. Himes, A. M., Graeff-Professor English Language and Literature, 1873.

Rev. P. M. Bikle, A. M., Ockershausen-Professor Physics and Astronomy, 1874.

Ed. S. Breidenbaugh, A. M., Conrad-Professor of Chemistry and Mineralogy, 1874.

H. L. Baugher, D. D., President, 1850–1868.

M. Valentine, D. D., President, and Professor Intellectual and Moral Philosophy, 1868.

D. Gilbert, M. D., Lecturer on Anatomy and Physiology, 1837–1851.

Rev. Dr. J. G. Morris, Lecturer on Zoology, 1844–1874.

H. S. Huber, M. D., Lecturer on Anatomy, 1852–1865.

These names are not put in their proper order of precedence as to the time of their entrance or their professorships.

WITTENBERG COLLEGE, SPRINGFIELD, OHIO.

ORIGIN OF THE INSTITUTION.

This institution originated in the educational and in the religious want of the Lutheran Church in the West, then so-called.

The members of the English Synod of Ohio, at a convention at Washington, Guernsey county, in the month of November, 1842—

Resolved, "That in reliance upon the triune Jehovah, and alone for His honor and glory, we now establish a Literary and a Theological Institution."

The design of its founders combined its literary and its theological departments under one management.

The first President of the College was the Rev. Ezra Keller, D. D., a graduate of Gettysburg College, Pennsylvania, and a member of the class of 1835. At the time of his call to the institution March 1844, he was pastor of the First English Lutheran Church of Hagerstown, Md.

Dr. Keller opened the Grammar School of the College on the 3d day of November, 1845, in the lecture-room of the First English Evangelical Lutheran Church of Springfield, Ohio. The attendance, on the first day of the session, was eight students and a faculty of one Professor and two Tutors. This was increased to seventy-one before the close of the first year, and to one hundred and forty-three during the second year. Three years of steady progress passed away without any unusual occurrence in the history of the institution, but the fourth year opened with an event which filled the minds and hearts of the friends of the infant college with deep anxiety and profound sadness. After a brief illness, the summons of death came to the first President of the institution, in the midnight hour of the 29th day of December, 1848. He was called away from the midst of his arduous labors, and when in the vigor and prime of life. *He died in the thirty-seventh year of his age.*

A friend of Dr. Keller has observed that his decease was brought upon him by excessive labor, there remains but little doubt, for he performed at least as much work as two men should do.

The Rev. Samuel Sprecher, the second President of Wittenberg College, was, at the time of his election, pastor of the First English Lutheran Church of Chambersburg, Pennsylvania. He was publicly inducted into the chair of christian theology in the Seminary, and President of the institution on the 14th of August, 1849. The subject of his inaugural, being: "What Wittenberg College should be and do in her Theological Relations." And under the masterly leadership, morally and intellectually, of her second president, and in harmony with the spirit of her constitution, all such measures as are promotive of experimental piety and christian intelligence have been steadily maintained in the institution.

The labors of Dr. Sprecher have been prolonged and arduous in the institution, and during the term of his presidency the congregations in connection with the institution have increased ten fold in membership, and more than twelve fold in churches or houses of worship. Twenty-four classes were graduated from the college, aggregating two hundred and sixteen members during the presidency of Dr. Sprecher; and also during the same period there were sent into the churches from the Theological Department of the College, one hundred and forty-one ministers, making, from both departments of the institution, three hundred and fifty-seven. Some are occupying professors chairs in Colleges and Theological Institutions. Thirty-four have entered the legal profession, and a still larger number have become Principals and Superintendents in our Academies and Public Schools, while not less than four hundred have been engaged in teaching.

Dr. Sprecher resigned the presidency of the College on the 10th day of June, 1874, after a quarter of a century of most faithful and successful labor, both in relation to the institution and in its influence upon the churches connected with it. Dr. Sprecher is devoting his time chiefly to the Theological department of the institution, still, however, retaining his classes in the department of Mental Philosophy in the College. At a regular meeting of the Board of Trustees, at which time also the Rev. J. B. Helwig, then pastor of the First English Lutheran Church of Dayton, Ohio, and a member of the class of 1861, was chosen to the Presidency of the College, (1874).

GRANTS AND ENDOWMENTS.

The citizens of Springfield, at the founding of the institution, partially donated to it seventeen acres of ground; and the friends of the College abroad have enabled the Board of Trustees to purchase nineteen acres additional, to which a grant of four acres has also been added; and from individual benefactions the institution has thus far received a productive endowment-fund of one hundred and twenty-five thousand dollars.

In grounds, buildings and endowment-fund the assets of the institution may be fairly estimated at one hundred and seventy-five thousand dollars.

This does not include the value of the libraries, the cabinet and the philosophical apparatus.

The institution has no indebtedness.

FACULTY.

Rev. J. B. Helwig, D. D., President, and Professor of Moral Science and Political Economy.

Samuel Sprecher, D. D., L. L. D., Professor of Mental Philosophy.

H. R. Geiger, A. M., Ph. D., Professor of Natural Sciences.

Isaac Sprecher, A. M., Professor of Ancient Languages.

B. F. Prince, A. M., Professor of Natural History and Assistant Professor of Greek.

S. F. Brackenridge, A. M., Professor of Mathematics.

Professor of Belles-Lettres and English Literature. The duties of this Professorship are now performed by Professors Helwig and Prince.

Professor of German Language and Literature. The duties of this Professorship are now performed by Prof. J. H. W. Stuckenberg.

The average attendance in the College, for twenty-five years past, has been one hundred and fifty-two. About one hundred from abroad, and fifty-two home students, or within Clarke county.

The institution was opened at Wooster, Ohio, for a few months only. No buildings erected there.

The first session was opened with Dr. Keller as President and Principal Teacher, and Joseph Welty, now of New Philadelphia, Tutor.

The first catalogue for 1845-47 gives the following as the faculty:

Rev. Ezra Keller, D. D., President, and Professor of Mental and Moral Science; Rev. T. Stork A. M., Professor (elect) of Belles-Lettres, Logic, &c.; Rev. M. Diehl, A. M., Professor of Languages; H. R. Geiger, A. M., Professor of Mathematics; Jno. A. Ruhl and Morris Officer, Tutors; J. F. Reinmund, Teacher of Penmanship.

The next catalogue, 1847-48, has Rev. J. G. Harris in the place of Dr. Stork, and T. A. Burrows, Principal of Preparatory Department, and J. W. Goodlin, Teacher of Penmanship.

The third catalogue, 1848-49, has Dr. Sprecher's name in place of Dr. Keller (deceased), and then same as before, with William J. Cutter, Teacher of German.

The fourth catalogue, 1849-50, has Dr. Conrad's name instead of Rev. Harris as Professor of Belles-Lettres, Homiletics, &c.

In 1851-52 I find Professor I. Sprecher as Assistant Teacher, and who became a year later Professor of History and Principal of Preparatory Department; then there was a Commercial Department with E. Harrison as Professor. Rev. A. J. Imhoff was also

Tutor for a time. So also, Wm. B. Youce and Morris Kirby. In 1854-55 Rev. Essick was Professor of Natural Science. In 1858-59 Rev. Charles Ehrenfeld was Assistant Teacher in Preparatory Department, and in 1859-60 George Sprecher was teaching in that department, son of Dr. S. In 1864-65 Dr. Swartz was Professor of Church History, Homiletics, &c., and Professor Ort Tutor. In 1869-70 Professor Sprecher was elected to chair of Ancient Languages. Professor Diehl (deceased) and Professor Prince Assistant Professor of Greek and Principal of Preparatory Department, and Professor Ort Assistant Professor of Mathematics, and that was the Faculty until the present, according to the catalogue of 1876.

COLLEGE OF SOUTH CAROLINA.

When the Theological Seminary of this Synod was established, in 1831, at Lexington, arrangements were made for the opening of a classical school under the name of The Lexington Institute, and in 1848 efforts began to be made to elevate it to the rank of a college, and for ten years there was a vigorous contest between several villages in which of them the institution should be finally located, for it was conceded that Lexington was not the proper place. In 1859 both the college and seminary were removed to Newberry. At the meeting of the Synod soon after, Rev. Dr. J. A. Brown was elected Professor of Theology in the seminary and Professor of Latin in the college. Rev. Dr. T. Stork was elected President of the College, Rev. C. A. Stork Professor of Greek, Mr. Garlington Professor of Mathematics, Rev. M. Whittle, Principal of the Preparatory Department, and Mr. A. P. Pifer Assistant. Early in 1860 the college went into actual operation, and the inauguration services were held in October, 1860, at a church six miles east of the village! The beginning was hopeful and encouraging, but early in 1861 circumstances occurred which led Dr. Stork to resign and leave in March. Soon after Prof. C. A. Stork also left, and his place was supplied until the end of the session by Rev. C. F. Bansemer. Dr. Brown was then elected, but he left in 1862, owing to the breaking out of the rebel war. Rev. J. P. Smeltzer succeeded him. Rev. F. R. Anspach had been previously elected, but declined. An over-zealous advocate of Mr. Anspach's election represented him as "one of us, being born in Virginia." The young men went into the rebel army, and the college degenerated to a village school. The building had been carelessly erected and of bad materials. The walls cracked and it soon became a heap of ruins. All the funds were lost in confederate bonds and broken banks, and the prospects were gloomy.

Walhalla, a German settlement in the north-west corner of South Carolina, was the unsuccessful competitor with Newberry for the location of the College, and in 1868, when the institution was almost extinct at the latter place, President Smeltzer, representing the college, removed to Walhalla, the people of which offered the institution "a temporary home" bearing the name of "Newberry College at Walhalla." In 1876 it was transferred again to Newberry. In 1877 all the faculty resigned and new professors were elected. A correspondent writes thus:

"When Newberry was originally established several persons each gave $1000 for the erection of buildings. The college became involved in debt, and the building was defective and was injured by the federal troops during the war. The institution was removed to Walhalla, S. C., and the sheriff sold the college property here. This was, I think, in 1868.

"II. The property did not pay the fourth of the debts. In September, 1876, the parties holding claims released them as follows: Maj. J. P. Kinard assigned his claim to South Carolina Synod, amounting to $13,700, exclusive of interest; Mr. W. A. Cline $3800, exclusive of interest; Capt. A. P. Pifer $1,644.65, exclusive of interest; Capt. J. P. Aull $300, exclusive of interest; Mr. W. Johnson $36, exclusive of interest.

"III. Our college has again returned to Newberry. The old building was taken down, and a new one is now being erected on the same grounds. One man, Mr. John D. Cash, gives $1000 towards the building, others less, &c. We are raising an endowment for Newberry College; have an agent in the field—Rev. S. P. Hughes; have about $12,000 in bonds.

ANSGARI COLLEGE.

Ansgari College is the name of an institution established for the benefit of the Swedes mainly through the influence of Rev.

C. Anderson. It was commenced at Keokuk, on October 1, 1875, and then was known as the Swedish Evangelical Lutheran Mission Institute. It was incorporated in June, 1875, and removed to Knoxville, Ill., because of its more convenient and central position.

The citizens of Knoxville offered the institute fifteen thousand dollars, of which amount the Hon. James Knox gave at various times twelve thousand nine hundred and fifty dollars. He died October 9, 1876, and although his residence was near the building which his liberality so essentially helped to erect, he was never known to have been inside of it.

The College has no endowment whatever, but depends upon the fees of students and the contributions of the church, for its support. It is said the prospects for doing good are encouraging, but it needs the fostering care of our people, for the Swedes are generally poor.

The present corps of teachers is:

Rev. C. Anderson, Principal Latin and Theology.
Rev. John Anjou, Greek, Theology and Swedish.
Rev. J. Angus Lowe, Mathematics and English Literature.
Miss Sophia Larkee, assistant teacher in Mathematics and English Branches.

These teachers receive from three hundred dollars to four hundred dollars a year. There are now (February, 1877) fifty-three students, of whom fifteen are destined for the ministry. The present Theological Class consists of eight.

Eight beneficiaries are supported at an expense of five hundred dollars.

There is only one Swedish Synod in connection with the General Synod, called Ansgari, organized in May, 1873, consisting of fifteen ministers, which is double the number that there was two years ago.

There are twelve congregations in the Synod.

ROANOKE COLLEGE, SALEM, VA.

In the year 1842 Rev. C. C. Baughman located himself in Augusta county, Va., where he founded, in connection with Rev. D. F. Bittle, a classical school. Rev. Bittle was at that time in charge of Mt. Tabor congregation and others of the county.

Rev. Baughman was to devote all his time to teaching, Rev. Bittle two days in the week. The school was called the "Virginia Institute." It flourished, and established thus by individual enterprise, soon claimed the attention of the Virginia Synods. Pennsylvania College, to which it was an avowed feeder, realized no mean supplies from the institute in the way of students. In 1844 Rev. Bittle removed to the Middletown, Md., charge, and J. Edward Herbst, a graduate of Pennsylvania College, was appointed his successor in the institute in 1846. On the 30th of January, 1845, the school was incorporated by the State Legislature under the name "Virginia Collegiate Institute." The Synods now began to agitate the removal of the institute to a more central point and in 1847, this removal was effected to Salem, Roanoke county, its present location. In the year 1848 the erection of buildings began, exercises being carried on meanwhile in buildings proffered by the citizens of Salem. The central part of the main building was erected first. In 1851 the west wing was built. Meanwhile grounds were laid out and trees planted. The Campus is now very beautiful. In 1853 the charter was obtained changing the "Institute" into a College, and Rev. Bittle was called to its presidency. Rev. Baughman having removed to Hagerstown Md., Prof. S. C. Wells was placed in the chair of Mathematics, and Prof. Henri G. Von Hoxar in that of Ancient Languages. This was the first Faculty.

The buildings and grounds were at this time worth about ten thousand dollars, with liabilities of about eight thousand dollars.

The buildings have all been erected and other improvements made by donations from abroad, none of which ever amounted to over one thousand dollars from any one party. The institute has no endowment. The Library, collected by the active energies of Dr. Bittle and the kindness of friends, now amounts to between ten thousand and fourteen thousand volumes, mostly well-selected reference works. Included in this is the Library of Dr. S. S. Schmucker, of Gettysburg, purchased by subscription.

Apparatus is increasing in value. Mineral Cabinet is very valuable, next to that of the University the most valuable in the State.

Students have increased in number constantly from the foundation of the institution, commencing at the number sixty and reaching now one hundred and eighty. This has been effected by wide-spread agencies and advertisements throughout the South.

Out of one hundred and thirty graduates forty-eight have entered the ministry. A large proportion of those who did not finish the course have entered the sacred office, what proportion I could not say.

MUHLENBERG COLLEGE.

Muhlenberg College commenced as such in the fall of 1867. First class graduated in summer of 1868.

The Faculty was originally constituted as follows: Rev. Dr. F. A. Muhlenberg, President; Rev. E. J. Koons, Vice-President; Rev. M. H. Richards, Latin and English; Rev. H. N. Rüss, German; Rev. T L. Seip, Principal Academic Department; Luther A. Swope, Tutor.

Rev. W. Notz afterwards took the place of Rüss in German. He was succeeded by Rev. G. F. Miller, as German Professor.

Mr. Seip soon became Professor of Latin in the college proper, and still holds the position.

Davis Garber was early chosen as Professor of Mathematics, and still occupies the place.

Rev. R. F. Weidner, an alumnus, served for two years as Professor of English Department, closing with last college year.

Rev. Dr. Sadtler was recently called to the Presidency as successor of Dr. M. Rev. M. H. Richards was recalled as Professor of the English Department after an absence of three years from the institution.

Rev. R. Hill has been doing some teaching since beginning of present college year.

T. J. Yeager, M. D., has also served as Professor of Chemistry. He was son of Rev. Joshua Yeager. He is now deceased.

W. A. Beates has been for several years at the head of the Academic Department.

The Faculty is now constituted thus: Rev. B. Sadtler, D. D., President; Rev. T. L. Seip, Latin, &c.; Rev. M. H. Richards, Greek, &c.; Davis Garber, Mathematics; Rev. G. F. Miller, German, &c.; W. A. Beates, Principal of Preparatory Department.

The number of students at this time scarcely reaches one hundred, due largely to the "hard times." An average yearly attendance from the beginning would be about one hundred and thirty or one hundred and forty. Another consideration that has influenced the *number* of students is that it could not be determined exactly what *kind* of an institution was wanted. Some of the Germans preferred more of a *church* school; most of the English wanted a *college* in the proper *American sense*. The conflict of *language* has had a damaging influence likewise. The Germans would have *too much German*, the English *too little*, and so some German pastors sent their students elsewhere.

It is hard to tell exactly how many of the students are looking towards the ministry. I think a safe estimate would be about *one-fourth* of the whole number.

I learn from one who has a good deal to do with the finances that the present endowment is $58,000, and that the largest donation from any individual is $1000. Of this latter class the number is considerable, and Prof. Seip, who has been collecting for nearly a year, has added considerably to this. He has raised upwards of $20,000 since he commenced his operations. His mission among the churches has been highly successful for these times.

The college library contains about twelve hundred volumes; each of the literary societies has a similar number.

The apparatus is said to be quite respectable for a young institution, but cannot give you any particulars.

A movement has recently been started to endow a *German-Probst Professorship* as a memorial of Rev. S. K. B., recently deceased, and to whose labors the college owes much.

The college has been heavily burdened with debt for some years. Too much money was put into brick and mortar. But the success of Prof. Seip seems to be an augury of better days.

WARTBURG SEMINARY.

Wartburg Seminary was founded in 1854, at Dubuque, Iowa, but removed to Mendota in 1874. The present (1877) number of students is thirty-one, but about one hundred and twenty have been connected with it from its beginning. Eighty-two of them have entered the ministry. The amount of endowment does not exceed $8000.

The Professors are Rev. Sigm. Fritschel, Rev. Gottfr. Fritschel and Rev. F. Richter.

In connection with Wartburg Seminary there is a classical school, called Evangelical Lutheran Collegium, which was founded in Galena, Ill., in 1868, and moved to Mendota in 1875. There are at present twenty-five students, and there have been about eighty from the beginning. Twenty-one of the present number are preparing for the ministry.

Faculty, Revs. J. List, C. H. Thilo, Sigm. Fritschel, G. Fritschel, F. Richter.

LUTHER COLLEGE.

Luther College is now a Swedish institution, and was founded at Decorah, Iowa, in 1861, under other auspices. The present number of students is one hundred and seventy, and from the beginning about seven hundred and eighty-eight. Fifty-seven of these have entered the ministry, and nearly one hundred of the present number are preparing for it. Mr. Beck, of St. Louis, gave $1000 for the support of the institution, and various other donations of smaller sums have been made.

Faculty, Prof. L. Larsen, President; Rev. N. Brandt, Pastor; Professors J. D. Jacobsen, L. Siewers, Th. Bothne, L. S. Reque; A. Bredisen and C. Norvesen, Assistants.

CARTHAGE COLLEGE, ILL.

An educational convention was held at Dixon, Ill., in the autumn of 1869, to harmonize and marshal the elements that had been somewhat conflicting and scattered. The Synods of Northern, Central and Southern Illinois, and the Synod of Iowa, co-operated in the movement, and resolved to unite their efforts to establish one institution in lieu of the colleges they had striven to maintain independently. Carthage College embodies the remnants of three or four other institutions. The coming together was by the law of "elective affinity." The Kansas and the Nebraska Synods have joined the Union, and the other territories will by and by be admitted. Carthage, therefore, claims to be the General Synod's educational capital of her territory west of Indiana.

Our endowment is $45,000.

We have about two thousand volumes; apparatus worth $600—good as far as it goes. We have a *very choice* collection of rarer minerals, which I bought from an amateur mineralogist for $500—half-price.

Largest gift—Dr. Kitzmiller's estate, with consent of his daughter, through the kind offices of Dr. Conrad—$12,500. Dr. Conrad personally subscribed $1000; Wm. P. Miller subscribed $1000; several, $500 each.

Average number of students two hundred.

Have had five hundred students.

Our first graduate is just ready to enter the ministry. About forty preparing in different classes.

Buildings and grounds worth $50,000. The main building is a large, four-story, brick edifice—all parts of it devoted to school purposes. The dormitories are separate, flanking the college building, and contain fifty rooms.

FACULTY AND INSTRUCTORS

Rev. D. L. Tressler, Ph. D., President, and Professor of Mental and Moral Science.

L. F. M. Easterday, A. M., Professor of Mathematics and Astronomy.

Rev. J. W. Richard, A. M., Professor of the Latin Language and History.

Rev. E. F. Bartholomew, A. M., Professor of Chemistry and Natural Sciences.

Rev. E. F. Giese, A. M., Professor of the Greek and German Languages.

Rev. John Brubaker, A. M., Professor of English Language and Literature.

P. M. Fasold, A. B., Tutor.

Mrs. M. B. Fry, Teacher of Music.

THIEL COLLEGE, GREENVILLE, PA.

This institution derives its name from Mr. A. Louis Thiel, a liberal German gentleman who has been its chief patron. As far back as 1866 he placed four thousand five hundred dollars in the hands of a few friends who had contemplated the establishment of a Lutheran school in Western Pennsylvania. In that year, a property was purchased in Philipsburg, Beaver county, Pa., for four thousand five hundred dollars, and a few months later an adjoining house and lot were bought at one thousand dollars, and an edifice was erected which was called "Thiel Hall." A school was opened under the instruction of Rev. Prof. Giese. Mr. Kopp was added to the list of teachers in the course of a year. Mr. Giese left for New York, after which Prof. H. E. Jacobs, now of Gettysburg, and Prof. Feitshans, conducted the school for two years. It was incorporated as a college in 1870. The two gentlemen just named resigned, when Rev. Messrs. H. W. Roth, W. F. Ulery and D. McKee took charge of it. The college was removed to Greenville in 1871, where a fine building has been built and where the college has flourished to a very encouraging extent. It is the most thoroughly Lutheran *English* College in our church.

Before Mr. Thiel died he placed in the hands of trustees securities which realized the sum of twenty-five thousand dollars, and the residue of his estate, after the payment of some legacies, is eventually to be transferred to the college.

The present Faculty are Rev. H. W. Roth, A. M., Rev. H. Gilbert, A. M., Rev. D. McKee, A. M., Rev. J. R. Titzel, A. M., and Jno. E. Whitteker, A. B., Tutor.

Within a year or two the farm of Mr. Samuel Ridgway, adjacent to the college grounds, consisting of forty acres, having thereon erected two good dwelling houses, a large barn, and all other necessary outbuildings, well watered, and having an excellent orchard, was purchased at a cost of nine thousand five hundred dollars. Four thousand dollars paid April 1st, 1876, the remaining four thousand five hundred dollars payable in two annual payments from April 1st, 1876, with interest at six per cent. per annum.

The reasons influencing the Board in this purchase were:

1st. That by having control of the land adjacent to the college grounds, they could control the uses to which it could be put, and thereby prevent the projection of any improvements deemed hurtful or undesirable, or disadvantageous to the institution.

2d. That at a nominal expense, the main house could be fitted up to answer the purpose of a boarding-house, and thus the immediate and pressing want of the college could be supplied; and,

3d. That it was safe and judicious.

With this last purchase the college has become the owner of sixty-three acres of land.

Rents and subscriptions for the year past have been $2,476.00.

The Treasurer's books show that there were received on interest of the Thiel Endowment Fund, $2,105.40.

There were in attendance, the past year, seventy-five students; of these five were Seniors, three Juniors, five Sophomores, seven Freshmen, seventeen Senior and thirty-five Junior Academicians.

About six hundred students have been in attendance from 1866 to 1876. Twelve are in the ministry, twelve studying Theology, and twelve in college looking towards the ministry.

CONCORDIA COLLEGE.

Concordia College, in St. Louis, was founded in Altenburg, Mo., in 1839, and was removed to the former place in 1849. Connected with this there is a theological school (Prediger Seminar) which they designate as "Theoretisch" in distinction from the "Praktische" at Springfield, Ill. These are badly chosen distinctive terms, which the Missourians themselves acknowledge.

The Seminary at St. Louis furnishes a thorough theological course similar to that of a German University, and only such who have gone through the Gymnasium, and are well versed in Latin and Greek, and have made a beginning in Hebrew, are admitted.

The following are the Professors who are or have been connected with it:

C. F. W. Walther, since 1849; J. J. Goenner, died 1864; A. Biewend, died 1858; G. Seyfath, from 1857 to 1863; E. Preuss, 1870-71, (an apostate and now editor of Roman Catholic Political Journal, "Amerika," in St. Louis); R. Lange, from 1858 to 1860, now pastor in Chicago; A. Schmidt, Norwegian Professor, 1873-76; G. Schaller, since 1873; M. Günther, since 1874; A. Crämer was in St. Louis 1860-74, but in the Practical Seminary.

PRACTICAL SEMINARY.

The Practical Seminary, now in Springfield, is designed for students who have not received a thorough preliminary training, and who are prepared to preach without pursuing a full course.

They are not taught any ancient language except Latin. It is equivalent to the Missionary Institute at Selinsgrove. It was first opened in Fort Wayne in 1846; was removed to St. Louis in 1860, and, in 1874, was transferred to Springfield, Ill.

THE GYMNASIUM.

The Gymnasium, at Fort Wayne, was also founded in Altenberg, Perry county, Mo., in 1830; was removed to St. Louis the same year, and, in 1860, was finally located at Fort Wayne.

DAS SCHULLEHRER SEMINAR.

The Seminary for training teachers (Das Schullehrer Seminar) was founded in Fort Wayne in 1846, and removed to Addison, Ill., 1864.

PRO-SEMINAR.

The Pro-Seminar is a preparatory school for those not qualified to enter the Seminary.

None of these institutions have any endowment. The highest salary paid is twelve hundred dollars per annum, ranging down to nine hundred dollars, with free dwelling.

The College and Seminary edifice at St. Louis is one hundred and forty feet long; that at Fort Wayne one hundred and eighty; that at Addison, two hundred and six.

COLUMBUS UNIVERSITY, OHIO.

I made several efforts to get the history of this institution but no attention was paid to my requests.

Beneficiary Education and the Parent Education Society.

Beneficiary education received no attention *systematically* from our church in this country until the establishment of our institutions at Gettysburg. In this good work, as in most others, we find the Synod of Maryland taking the initiative. As far back as 1831, and earlier in her history, we find this Synod active in her collections for missions and education.

No formal action was had by the Church until the meeting of the General Synod in 1835. During the sessions of Synod a convention, which had been previously called, was held, and resulted in the formation of the first General Society, which then received the name of *The Parent Education Society of the Evangelical Lutheran Church.* The constitution which was adopted was signed by the delegates from the Synods of South and North Carolina, Maryland, Virginia, West Pennsylvania and Hartwick. The operations of the Society were to be conducted by a Board of Directors, composed of one member from each of the Synods.

The framers of this constitution proposed, by the distribution of directors over the whole Church, to secure the co-operation of all, and emphatically make the society general. The object was good, but the mode of securing it was a remarkable failure. The nearest directors lived fifty, and several of them three hundred miles apart, and the result was that, under the first organization, they never held a meeting. Such was the extremely deficient and even culpable management of some church operations of that day. This was not the only one that displayed a lamentable degree of foresight in the men who controlled the Church.

I remember giving great offence to an old minister by objecting to having men put on important committees, requiring meetings during the year, who lived "over the mountains." I had no direct reference to him, but he rebuked me severely and said that some "beardless ministerial boys were a little forward." I meekly submitted, but everybody soon found out that I was right.

As the organization of 1835 was found to be impracticable, a reorganization was effected in 1837, at the meeting of the General Synod in Hagerstown. An improved constitution was adopted, according to which the administration of the affairs of the society was placed in the hands of an executive committee, composed of twelve. The provisions for the education of indigent young men for the ministry were complete and liberal.

During the first two years ending in October, 1837, the whole number received on the funds was forty-one, and the receipts into the treasury were $4449. In 1839 the number was fifty-three, and the amount collected was $6722. In 1841 the number receiving aid was sixty-seven, and the receipts $6810. In 1843 the number of beneficiaries was fifty-seven, the receipts $5011. In 1845 the number aided was forty-four, the receipts were $6198, leaving a debt of $2504. The next step we take covers three years and reaches to 1848. The society began to decline. The whole sum paid in was $8394, and the number sustained was only seventeen. But the interest in the society seemed to revive in 1850, when the number on the funds was forty-two and the receipts $2956.

From this time on, individual Synods assumed the control of beneficiary education within their own bounds, and the Parent Society necessarily expired. It accomplished much good in its day. It has been instrumental in introducing into the ministry about one hundred and twenty men, many of whom were useful and faithful pastors.

I have no means of determining precisely the number of beneficiaries supported by the various Synods, but it is safe to calculate that more than three-fourths of the theological students were of that character.

The cause has undergone various fluctuations. Owing to some failures and some secessions on the part of students, many persons have withdrawn their support, although the proportion of such failures has not been large.

The cause itself will always remain a good one, but the mode of prosecuting it as we have practiced it may not have been the best, and yet it is not easy to suggest a better one.

ORIGIN AND HISTORY OF THEOLOGICAL EDUCATION

IN OUR CHURCH IN THIS COUNTRY.

Dr. Kunze arrived in America in 1770, thirty-two years after the coming of the elder Muhlenberg, and it was only then that the first successful efforts were made to establish a school of a high order for the benefit of our German population. Muhlenberg and his few fellow-laborers devoted all their time to the active duties of their sacred office, and had no means and no encouragement to found any school for advanced education.

Kunze gives a disheartening account of the condition of the Germans in a letter to the Orphan House at Halle, (Hallische Nachrichten, p. 1377), when he says: "The Germans here are, in general, not very desirous of acquiring any scientific knowledge, as they see very little opportunity before them of deriving any worldly advantage from it, and hence they have little conception of more extended education. The English among us judge of all Germany from this low standard set up by our people." He accounts for this condition of things by adding, "The Germans are composed, *for the most part*, of those inhabitants of the Palatinate, Wurtemberg and Alsace, who, in their native country, belonged to the lower classes, and were oppressed with extreme poverty." No enlarged views on the subject of education or of any other could be expected of such men, and although some of the German preachers were men of extensive theological training, they could do nothing more towards establishing a high school than gradually educating the people up to the idea.

Dr. Kunze was indefatigable in his efforts to lay the foundation of a school which should be permanent and elevating in its influence on the Germans. He writes that he "has discovered in himself a peculiar proclivity to be engaged in a school in which the languages and sciences are taught, and that, notwithstanding his multiplied duties, he is burdened with the conception of establishing an institution of this description among the Germans of Pennsylvania." He thought that if he could, by any honest means, become the possessor of twenty pounds, he would purchase the first German student who was encumbered with the debt of his passage to this country, and commence a Latin school in an upper chamber of his dwelling." (Hallische Nachrichten, 1575-1580). The next day a Mr. Leps, a student from the University of Halle, unincumbered, but poor, presented himself. The proposition is at once made that he open a classical school, and notice to that effect is published in the papers of the city. No sooner did this appear than one of the most respectable members of the Lutheran congregation came to the assistance of Kunze, who, with another of similar spirit, obtained the requisite number of subscribers. An association is formed with the title, "The Society for the advancement of Christianity and all useful knowledge among the Germans in America." Mr. Leps was employed, and the school was opened in the presence of the subscribers, with singing and prayer, on February 17th, 1773. The beginning was small (with only fifteen scholars), but the conception was worthy of a lofty and christian mind.*

Out of this association was to grow an orphan and an almshouse, the seat of a mission to the Indians, and, before them all, in point of time, a *University* in which were to be taught the higher branches of science, English law, medicine and theology. Freylinghausen, of Halle, expressed his warmest approbation of this enterprise. (Hallische Nachrichten, pp. 1504-10).

The war of the Revolution in 1776 interfered seriously with Kunze's plans and temporarily suspended his efforts. The school was, however, in existence in 1779. During this year the University of Pennsylvania was established in Philadelphia under the auspices of the State, and Kunze was elected a trustee. He was one of a committee of five to report a plan for the University. He had sufficient influence to secure the appointment of a German Professor of Theology, with a Tutor as Assistant, while the German students enjoyed the privilege of daily instruction in the English language (Hall. Nachr. p. 1421). Kunze was elected Professor, and in a short time had the satisfaction of witnessing the attendance of upwards of thirty students. About this time he accepted an invitation to settle in the city of New York, influenced chiefly by the hope of there advancing the interest of Theological education in the Lutheran church. The Legislature

* See Evangelical Review, vol. I, pages 20-26.

of New York had passed an act for the establishment of a University, in which act it was proposed that if any congregation or individual would secure the annual payment of two hundred bushels of wheat, there should be elected in the University a Professor of Theology of the denomination to which the donors belonged, or some person whom they might designate (H. N. 1510). Kunze wrote immediately to Germany on this subject, and hoped that the way was opened for the endowment of a theological professorship for the Lutheran church. He writes to Freylinghausen as follows: "In my letter to Mr. Pasche I stated the contents of an article in our University act, by which authority is given to establish a theological professorship, as soon as a fund shall have been collected, which will yield annually two hundred bushels of wheat or eighty pounds of our currency, and, as I added, this article particularly influenced me to accept of the invitation to New York. Such an institution, by which men can be prepared for the sanctuary, our church in North America needs, where the harvest is great and the want of faithful laborers is yet greater. I came here (he writes from New York) in the hope that God would from time to time awaken those who would promote the welfare of our Evangelical church in this part of the world. The institution in Philadelphia might, by degrees, send us students, especially if it pleased the Lord to found certain benefactions (scholarships) for those who would devote themselves to the work, but whose parents are too poor to sustain them in the University, as we can in an especial manner depend upon the poor. My eyes are here directed to the Lord." H. N. 1504-5-10. It was the fond hope of Dr. Kunze that many poor and pious men would receive their preparatory education in the University of Pennsylvania, sustained by patrons in this country and in Germany, and then, by the endowment of a theological professorship in the University of New York, they could then receive their theological training. Mr. Schmidt succeeded Dr. Kunze as preacher, and Dr. Helmuth succeeded him as Professor of German in the University of Pennsylvania. The prospects of education in the church became brighter. "Nothing," writes Mr. Schmidt (H. N. p. 1516), "lies nearer the hearts of us preachers than a German educational institution, in which the youth can be prepared for the peculiar service of the church. We have, it is true, a share in the University here, which we improve. The German section of the University, which receives from the Trustees annually six hundred pounds Pennsylvania currency, is not without hope for the future. Helmuth, who superintends this department, teaches seven hours daily, giving instruction in Latin and Greek to the German youth, and in German to the English students * * * * * * * We two preachers, in Philadelphia, propose, in the approaching winter * * * * * to impart instruction in the different parts of theology * * * * *"

Thus we see what were the feelings and views of the leading ministers of our church in the first half century of her existence in this country. Nothing of permanent value to the church grew out of the effort either in Philadelphia or New York. Their experience and ours shows most clearly that in one respect they failed in foresight. *They conceived of nothing but German churches and German preachers.* It seems that it never entered into their minds that the rising generation of Germans would grow up in the language and manners and tastes of the people with whom they daily associated, and that, therefore, their church policy, so far as these things prevailed, must be adapted to them. Here was a great and fatal mistake, from the melancholy effects of which the church has not recovered to this day.

No further efforts were made to found a distinct theological school, but Dr. Schmidt and Helmuth for some years had private pupils whom they trained for the ministry. Most of the men who entered our ministry between 1800 and 1815, were taught by one or the other of these men. After their death, Dr. Lochman of Lebanon, and afterwards of Harrisburg, took students of theology. Rev. D. F. Schaeffer of Frederick, Md., had some students almost constantly. Rev. S. S. Schmucker of New Market, Va., also, and thus other ministers devoted a portion of their time to the private instruction of divinity-pupils until the establishment of Gettysburg Seminary in 1826.

Before this period Hartwick Seminary had trained a number, but after the Gettysburg school was opened, Hartwick declined.

I have at another place in this book given sketches of our several Theological Institutions, to which the reader is referred for the progress of Theological Education in our Church in the United States.

LUTHERAN ALMANACS.

The first distinctively Lutheran Almanac in this country was printed at Troy, N. Y., in English, for the year 1835. The next attempt was made in the same language at the Lutheran Publication Rooms, Baltimore, for 1842 and 1843. One number, for the former year, appeared at the same place in German. After an interval of seven years, the present series was commenced for 1851, in Baltimore, by Mr. T. Newton Kurtz, in whose hands it is still continued. Consequently, the present number, for 1878, is the 28th. At the end of ten years, the form was changed from the quarto to the duodecimo. This number is the 17th in the smaller form, and the 7th by the present editor. In 1853 Rev. S. K. Brobst, of Allentown, Pa., began his Lutherischer Kalender, for the German people, which is still continued. A Norwegian Almanac was issued for three years, from 1857 to 1860 inclusive, at Madison, Wis. An English calendar, called the Church Almanac, was begun at Allentown in 1866, and has been continued since 1871 in Philadelphia. A small Lutheran Almanac, in English, was published for the years 1867 and 1868, by Duffie & Chapman, successively at Newberry and Columbia, S. C. In 1870 the Amerikanischer Kalender für Deutsche Lutheraner made its first appearance at St. Louis, and is issued annually. The last enterprise of this kind is the Kirchenfreund Kalender (German), for 1876, by Severinghaus & Co., at Chicago, Ill., which is to be continued. Thus, so far as the writer knows, *ten* series of Lutheran Almanacs have been introduced; and of this number *five* continue to appear.

THEOLOGICAL SEMINARY AT GETTYSBURG.*

Nothing definite was attempted towards the establishment of a seminary until the meeting held at Hagerstown, September, 1820, when the constitution of the General Synod was adopted, at which time a committee was appointed to draft a plan of such a school. The committee reported a year after that they could not agree upon a feasible plan, and were discharged.

In 1823, at the monthly conferences of the Synod of Maryland and Virginia, composed for the most part of young and religiously active men, the subject was frequently discussed, but nothing positive was done.

In 1824 Rev. S. S. Schmucker, of New Market, Va., preached a sermon before the Synod at Middletown, in which he recommended the enlargement of his private theological school into a general institution. Several months afterwards, Rev. B. Kurtz, of Hagerstown, informed Mr. Schmucker that Prof. McLelland, of Dickenson College, had told him that the trustees of that college were anxious that the Lutheran Church should establish a seminary at Carlisle. This proposition was not accepted, but Mr. K. proposed another plan which had been laid before the conference at Martinsburg, February 9th, 1825,‡ which was that the seminary should be located at Hagerstown, that the church school-house would be offered as a lecture room, that the professor should serve several country churches, and that the *Pastor loci* should be one of the professors. The plan was not adopted, upon the ground the Synod alone was the proper body to elect professors, but, by this arrangement, the professors would elect themselves, for it was understood that Mr. Schmucker was to be one, and Mr. Kurtz was the pastor. At the meeting of the Synod in October, 1825, at Hagerstown, Messrs. Schmucker, Krauth and Kurtz were appointed to draft a plan for the immediate establishment of a

---

* For a full history, see my address at the semi centennial celebration, June, 1876, published in Quarterly Review, October, 1876.

‡ This meeting was composed of Messrs. Kurtz, Krauth, F. Ruthrauf and Winter; a collection taken up which amounted to six or seven dollars *was the first money ever contributed to this purpose.*

seminary, which, with the additional articles, was subsequently adopted by the General Synod. A month afterwards the General Synod met at Frederick, when the plan which was proposed by the Synod of Maryland and Virginia was adopted, and immediate measures were taken to collect funds for the support of the institution, and Mr. Kurtz was commissioned to go to Europe to solicit contributions for its benefit. Mr. Kurtz accepted the trust. He was instructed to assure the people abroad that their contributions should be appropriated to the support of a German professorship. He sailed for Liverpool, from New York, April 1st, 1826, and was absent twenty-two months. For many particulars concerning his European agency, see my History of the Seminary in Quarterly Review, and sketch in this work, p. 137. After Mr. Kurtz's return, in 1827, an outcry against the seminary was made by many German ministers and others in this country, that the fund collected abroad was not appropriated according to agreement, that the directors had not kept their word, and that no German professorship was employed. I happen to know that Mr. K., himself, was extremely dissatisfied with this failure on the part of the directors, and frequently expressed his mind plainly and forcibly upon the subject.

The first Board of Directors was elected at this meeting,* and Rev. S. S. Schmucker was elected first professor, at a salary of five hundred dollars for the current year.

On March 2d, 1826, the Board met for the first time, at Hagerstown, when the location of the seminary was to be determined. The following proposals were received:

Hagerstown offered $6635; Carlisle, $2000 in money, a professor's house for five years, and $3000 towards erecting a seminary building; the trustees of Dickenson College offered the use of a room in the college for the lectures of the professor, a lot of ground one hundred feet square, the use of the college library, and gratuitous access to the lectures of some of the professors, on condition that our professor should become a member of the faculty, and teach Hebrew, &c., in the college; Gettysburg offered $7000 in money, and the use of the academy. Upon the second ballot, Gettysburg was selected much to the chagrin of many friends of the seminary. York made no proposal.†

The institution was opened on the first Tuesday of September,

---

* See their names. Quarterly Review, October, 1876.
† See sketch of J. G. Schmucker, p. 11.

1826. The professor was installed,* and his first class consisted of William Artz, David Jacobs, Jonathan Oswald, David P. Rosenmiller, Jacob Kaempfer, J. S. Galloway (Presbyterian), Lewis Eichelberger, Henry Haverstick, Daniel Heilig, Benjamin Oehrle, N. R. Sharrets, George Yeager, S. D. Finckel and J. G. Morris. Five of these yet survive. (1878).

The seminary was incorporated by the Legislature of Pennsylvania in 1827.

At the second meeting of the Board, September, 1826, a committee reported that $17,513 had been *subscribed*, of which only $1674 had been *collected!*

A classical school, in connection with the seminary, was opened in 1827, of which David Jacobs, a theological student, was appointed teacher. A scientific department was added in 1830, of which Michael Jacobs was the teacher. David Jacobs died in 1830, and Rev. H. L. Baugher was appointed his successor.

On May 14th, 1828, Prof. Schmucker obligated himself to pay one thousand dollars in ten annual installments, to aid poor young men to prepare for the ministry.

In 1829 a committee was appointed to procure plans for a seminary edifice. A contract was made with Mr. Pierce, of Chambersburg, for $7750, but considerable sums were paid subsequently for extra work as usual. The corner stone was laid on May 26th, 1831.

On May 17th, 1830, Dr. Hazelius† was chosen Professor of Biblical and Oriental Literature, who entered upon his duties in the September following. He remained three years and accepted a call to the Seminary in South Carolina.

At the spring meeting of the Board 1831 it was announced by letter from Rev. C. Shober, of North Carolina, that the late Rev. C. A. G. Storch, of the same State, had bequeathed to the Seminary a number of books, of which a catalogue was sent. A committee reported that they would be of no use to us and the books were never sent.

At this session, fifty volumes from the library were presented to the Seminary of the Synod of Ohio, but the donation was not appreciated, consisting for the most part of "Predigt und Andacht Buecher" as Prof. Schmidt once expressed it to me.

Candor as a historian compels me to state, that the Board about this time most injudiciously and wrongfully appropriated money

---
* See Minutes of the Board, p. 6, and my History of Seminary, *supra cit.*
† See sketch, p. 66.

to the payment of the building which had been collected for the endowment of the Second Professorship, and *which has never been paid back!*

By resolution of the Board, Rev. Mr. Krauth, of Philadelphia, was requested to prepare an Address on the Importance, Utility and Necessity of Studying the German Language, which was delivered in May, 1832, and published at the expense of the Board.

At this time five additional acres of land were purchased, one of which was to be laid out as an ornamental garden, which was never done.

In 1833 contracts were made for erecting dwelling houses for the Professors.

When Dr. Hazelius retired in this year, temporary provision for instruction in German, Hebrew and Greek, was made, and at the next meeting Rev. Mr. Krauth was elected professor.

At this time it was announced that a bequest of five hundred dollars had been made to the Seminary by Mr. Scholl, of Frederick.

A donation of fifty volumes was made to the Seminary of the South Carolina Synod.

At the spring session of 1834 the Rev. B. Kurtz was appointed temporary Professor of German Literature and Church History, which he declined.

About this time, several rooms in the Seminary were furnished by individuals or congregations, for the use of indigent students.

The shade trees, which a number of years subsequently adorned the front campus, were presented by the editor of the Lutheran Observer (J. G. M.) out of profits arising from that journal.

During this period the Board heard that Rev. G. Shober, of North Carolina had bequeathed a tract of land situated in that State. It has never been of any benefit to us.

In 1836 Prof. Schmucker reported that he had received subscriptions to the amount of about four thousand dollars in New York and New England.

In 1837 nothing of importance occurred in our history. In 1838 Dr. Krauth, who had been elected President of Pennsylvania College, resigned his professorship in the Seminary.—Another gentleman (J. G. M.) was elected in his place, who declined the position. Dr. Krauth kindly consented to withdraw his resignation, and continued to give instruction in some branches of his department.

In 1839 Rev. H. I. Smith, who had previously been elected a member of the College Faculty, was elected Professor of German Literature in the Seminary.

In this year the first catalogue was printed with the constitution.

In 1841 it was announced that Mr. Schroeder, of Hamburg, bequeathed some money to the Seminary, but it was never received. This whole affair was so indefinite, that I could never arrive at any satisfactory knowledge of it. It was said to have fallen into other hands and to have been appropriated to an institution of another church.

In the winter of 1842–43 an epidemic prevailed in the Seminary, and some of the students were dangerously affected.

In 1843 the *Alumni Association* was formed, which has continued to exist to the present day. It has undertaken to establish a professorship, but it has not yet succeeded.

At the September meeting of 1844, Rev. Charles A. Hay, of the Synod of Maryland (who had previously spent two years at several German Universities), was elected Professor of Biblical Literature and the German Language.

In April, 1845, a letter was read from a committee of the Methodist Protestant Church in reference to supporting a professor of their church in our Seminary, but nothing resulted from it.

In the winter of 1846–47 a virulent fever broke out in the Seminary, causing the death of several promising young men.

About this time Mr. Koenig, of Adams county, gave over to the treasury the sum of four hundred dollars, on condition that the sum of twenty-four dollars be annually paid to him during his life, and after his death the same amount to be paid to a beneficiary. This amount was afterwards increased by similar donations from Mr. K. in 1865 and '66, and after his death, in 1872, the whole, amounting, with some interest, to two thousand five hundred dollars, was by the Board made to constitute the KING SCHOLARSHIP for the support of a needy student.

In April, 1848, Prof. Hay resigned his professorship.

In 1849, a proposition was made by Mr. Spitler, Patron of the Missionary Institute at Basle, to send young men to our seminary.

The result was that for several years some students came over and received instruction in our school.

In 1848 measures were adopted to secure the co-operation of the Synod of Pennsylvania in the support of a second professor. The result was that the Synod resolved to pay three hundred dollars a year towards his support. Dr. Demme was thereupon elected professor, but he declined.*

In 1850 Dr. Krauth was elected to the second professorship and accepted it.

In 1851 it was reported to the Board, that our seminary was to have part of the services of the German professor supported by the Synod of Pennsylvania in the college, in teaching theological branches in the German language. Dr. Mann was nominated but he declined. Four years after, Dr. C. F. Schaeffer was elected, and resigned to enter the Faculty of the newly established Theological Seminary in Philadelphia.

For several years nothing requiring special notice was done, but at the meeting of August 11, 1863, this resolution was passed:

Resolved, That the Board has heard with proud satisfaction of the heroic conduct of those students of the seminary who have rushed so promptly to the defence of their country during the late rebel invasion, and that their course is approved.†

For several months after the battle of Gettysburg, the seminary building was occupied as an hospital by the government. It was resolved by the Board at a subsequent meeting, "that from motives of patriotism and gratitude to God for the glorious victory vouchsafed to our arms at Gettysburg, during the first three days of July, 1863, no compensation should be solicited from the government for damages sustained to the buildings, but will look to the free-will offerings of the churches for the means necessary to repair the same." Four thousand two hundred and ten dollars were raised for this purpose, and yet in the proceedings of the Board a year later, August, 1864, I find that six hundred and sixty dollars and fifty cents were received from the government for the use of the seminary as an hospital.

At this meeting (1863) Dr. Schmucker resigned his professorship, after a service of nearly forty years. His name was continued on the catalogue as *Professor emeritus*. Dr. James A. Brown was elected in his place.

* See Biographical Notice of Demme, page 119.
† See p. 397.

At the August meeting of this year (1865) the following gentlemen, Revs. Grahn, Kohler and Mr. L. L. Haupt, presented themselves as Directors from the Synod of Pennsylvania, and claimed admission, which was refused upon the ground that that Synod had placed itself without the pale of the General Synod by its action at the meeting of the latter body at York, and that it had established a seminary at Philadelphia, to which its entire support and patronage were devoted, and withdrawing the German professor without giving the constitutional notice, and forbidding his successor to impart instruction in the seminary, according to the conditions of his appointment, thus placing itself in direct antagonism to our institution.

The gentlemen who were refused seats, together with Dr. H. H. Muhlenberg, a member previously elected, presented a protest against this action and withdrew.

At this session Rev. M. Valentine, of Reading, was elected Professor of Biblical and Ecclesiastical History, and a fourth professor was chosen in the person of Rev. Dr. C. A. Hay, of Harrisburg.

In this year, 1865, the Rev. Samuel A. Holman, then of Altoona, Pa., informed the Board that he had subscribed two thousand dollars "for the purpose of securing an annual lecture on one of the twenty-one doctrinal articles of the Augsburg Confession," the interest of which sum shall be paid to the lecturer annually chosen by the Directors.

Dr. Krauth died May 30th, 1867.

Dr. Valentine resigned September, 1868, and Rev. C. A. Stork, of Baltimore, was chosen in his place, but he did not accept.

Dr. Krauth's library was purchased by the Board at one thousand dollars.

In 1871 Mr. John Rice, of Baltimore, gave one thousand dollars, the interest of which is to be paid to a minister, annually selected by the Board, to deliver a lecture on "Ministerial Work."

At a special meeting, November 9th, 1871, Rev. E. J. Wolf, of Baltimore, was elected professor, but declined the call. In June, 1872, Dr. Sprecher was chosen, who also refused to accept.

In June, 1873, Dr. Valentine was elected to the third ship in full, expecting to resign his place as President college, but subsequently, he felt it his duty to d call.

Dr. Schmucker died August, 1873.

At an adjourned meeting, in 1873, Rev. Dr. L. E. Albert was elected to the position declined by Dr. Valentine, who also refused, and at a special meeting, December 2d, 1873, Mr. Wolf was again elected and accepted.

At the meeting, in June, 1875, measures were adopted for celebrating the semi-centennial year of the seminary, and in the following summer, 1876, the following programme was carried out:

Exercises at Christ Church, Tuesday, A. M., Dr. Brown, "A Congratulatory Address;" Dr. Conrad, "The Influence of this Seminary on the Church;" Dr. Harkey, "What the Church owes in return to this Seminary."

Tuesday, P. M., Dr. Davis, "The History of Theological Seminaries;" Dr. Sadtler, "The Advantages of Seminary Training." Tuesday night, Seminary Graduation Exercises; Alumni Association Meeting.

Wednesday, A. M., Dr. Morris, "This Seminary's History and Statistics;" M. Sheeleigh, "A Poem;" R. Weiser, "The Necrology of this Seminary."

Exercises at the Seminary, Wednesday, P. M., Grand Reunion; Dr. Albert, President of the Board, "Address of Welcome;" Dr. Scholl, "Response to Welcome;" Dr. Baum, "What Memorial shall we rear to-day?" Volunteer speeches.

In fifty years our ministry has grown from two hundred and fifty to two thousand and eight hundred, of which number five hundred and forty have been in whole or part educated at Gettysburg, an average of ten a year.

Besides the three houses for professors' dwellings, and the Seminary building, we own twenty acres of land in the vicinity.

The present invested fund is about $100,000, most of which is productive.

The library contains more than ten thousand volumes.

The largest donation ever made by one person is $5,000; the largest bequest, $3,000.

The professors were: Rev. S. S. Schmucker, 1826–64; Rev. E. L. Hazelius, 1830–33; Rev. C. P. Krauth, 1850–67; Rev. H. I. Smith, 1839–43; Rev. C. A. Hay, 1844–48; Rev. C. F. Schaeffer, 1855–64; Rev. J. A. Brown, 1864; Rev. M. Valentine, 1865–68; Rev. C. A. Hay, 1865; Rev. E. J. Wolf, 1873.

Rev. H. L. Baugher and Dr. Valentine, both professors in Pennsylvania College, were temporarily employed in the seminary. When the latter withdrew, in 1872, Rev. C. A. Stork was appointed in his place, but retired after a few months' service on account of pastoral engagements in Baltimore, where he continued to reside. J. G. Morris, for the last several years, has spent several weeks of the winter in giving instructions in Sacred Rhetoric and the connection between Science and Revelation.

The persons elected to full professorships, but declined, are J G. Morris, B. Kurtz, C. R. Demme, J. W. Mann, C. A. Stork, S. Sprecher and L. E. Albert.

Nine of the students have gone as missionaries to the heathen; thirty-nine have served as Presidents or professors of colleges and classical academies; forty-three have received the title of D. D.; three, that of L. L. D., and one has received diplomas from two learned societies in Europe.

The number of those who abandoned the ministry altogether, after having served several years, is six. The number of those who never entered the ministry is six; the number of those who abandoned our church is eleven.

We never had but one colored student, and that was Daniel A. Payne, who afterwards became a bishop in the Methodist church.

Of the five hundred and forty who have been students here, one hundred and thirty-seven have published books and pamphlets of their own writing.

SEMINARY OF SOUTH CAROLINA.

The first steps taken towards the establishment of a Theological Seminary, by the South Carolina Synod, were sundry resolutions passed at the meeting of Synod, held in Savannah, Ga., November 20th, 1829,[*] but the fate of the institution was not fully decided until the next year, when the subject was thoroughly discussed by Dr. Bachman, in his annual address, as well as in his Synodical sermon. Various committees were appointed, and considerable interest was awakened in the proposed institution. Additional resolutions were passed by this meeting (1830), and provision was made for the appointment of directors, and the elec-

[*] Bernheim, German Settlement, &c., 489.

tion of a professor. The Rev. J. G. Swartz was accordingly elected, who although only twenty-three years of age, was said to be eminently qualified for the position.*

The permanent location of the seminary was postponed to some future time; however, as Prof. Swartz had taken charge of several churches in Newberry District, which he was unwilling to resign until another year had expired, and he gave notice "that for the year 1831 his residence will be in Newberry District, * * * * and, that, he will be prepared, in February, to receive theological students."

The seminary opened with very flattering prospects; so many students came, that the Professor expressed his fears, that if more would come, they could not be accommodated.

He began his labors in February, 1831, at his residence, and in less than seven months afterward he was numbered with the dead. He died August 26th, having just reached his twenty-fourth year. Dr. Bachman delivered a funeral discourse, in which he portrays in eloquent language the exalted character of this promising young man.

During an interim of two years, Lexington Village was selected as the final location, and earnest efforts were made towards the endowment of the professorship, and the erection of buildings. In 1833, the Rev. Ernst L. Hazelius,† of Gettysburg, was elected Professor of Theology, and Rev. W. Muller, Principal of the Classical Academy.

Dr. Hazelius went to Lexington in the fall of 1833, and commenced his labors in January, 1834, and remained there for nearly twenty years, to the close of his life in 1853. Rev. C. B. Thuemmel was an assistant to Dr. Hazelius in 1841 to 1844. Rev. W. F. Leppard was also assistant for some time.

In 1850 the Rev. William Berley was elected the second professor of the seminary, and principal of the preparatory department. Mr. Henry Muller has been the most liberal benefactor of the seminary, having on one occasion pledged himself for the sum of four thousand dollars, and besides having erected a dwelling for the second professor at a cost of two thousand dollars, and presented it to the Synod.‡

In 1849 Rev. L. Eichelberger, of Winchester, Va., was elected

---

* Ibid, 494, 500 502, 513.
† See sketch of Dr. H., p. 66.
‡ Bernheim, 540.

second Professor of Theology,† but declined the offer. In 1852 Dr. Hazelius resigned on account of age and infirmity, when Mr. Eichelberger was again elected to fill the vacancy, and accepted. He resigned in 1858 and returned to Winchester, his former residence, where he died.

In 1859 Rev. Dr. J. A. Brown was elected Professor, and left in 1862.

The seminary was afterwards removed to Salem, Roanoke county, Va., of which Rev. Dr. Repass is, at present, Professor.

This institution has had singular adventures. It has been in operation in Newberry District, S. C., under the care of Professor Swartz; then at Lexington, S. C., under the care of Drs. Hazelius, Eichelberger and several assistants; then at Newberry C. H., S. C., under the care of Dr. Brown, and now at Salem, Va.

MISSIONARY INSTITUTE.

This school originated with Benjamin Kurtz, D. D., late of Baltimore, Md.

In 1854 or 1855, he brought it before the Maryland Synod and secured the appointment of a committee on the subject, which consisted of B. Kurtz, W. Jenkins, Chas. Witmer and George Hickman.

This committee presented its report to the Synod at its convention held in the city of Frederick, in October, 1856, (See Mins. pp. 22-26.)

In this report the committee argues the necessity of an institution in addition to our regular colleges and theological seminaries, in which to educate for the gospel ministry by a shorter course, and without going through the curriculum of an eight or ten years' course of training, pious, common-sense, practical, earnest men for the ministry.

The Synod appointed a Board of Trustees, which proceeded at once to adopt "*Statutes for the Government of the Missionary Institute,*" and which appeared twice in the Lutheran Observer in 1856 and 1857.

† See sketch, p. 189.

The Executive Committee appointed by the Board of Managers rendered its first report to the Synod (Md.) in October, 1857, at its convention held in Baltimore.

It reported "encouraging progress made toward the establishment of the Institute" as the appointment of a superintendent, the reception of various proposals for the location of the Institute, the appointment of Rev. H. Ziegler as agent to solicit subscriptions, and the preparation of a constitution to be submitted for adoption after maturer deliberation.

At the request of the Board of Managers, and in view of the probability that the Institute would be located outside of the State of Maryland, the Executive Committee proposed the following resolutions, which were adopted:

"*Resolved*, That the Board of Managers of our contemplated Missionary Institute, is hereby constituted a self-perpetuating body, having all the right to fill by its own vote, its own vacancies, arising from death, resignation, or otherwise."

"And, whereas, it is thought probable that the institute will be located within the bounds of another Synod than that of Maryland, and such Synod should have the principal management of it, therefore, to remove all impediments."

"*Resolved*, That this Synod hereby abolish its existing relations to said institute, and dissolve its present special connection with it."

The Board, at its meeting held in Baltimore, May 5d, 1858, located the institute at Selinsgrove, Pa., the subscription for its location being $15,012. At this meeting several members resigned, and vacancies were filled by the election of others residing in Selinsgrove.

After this, the Board met regularly at Selinsgrove. At one of its first meetings, the statutes were so amended as to increase the Board to thirty members.

The first session of the institute was opened on the 7th October, 1858, in two rooms belonging to the second Lutheran Church of Selinsgrove.

The faculty was: B. Kurtz, D. D., Superintendent; Rev. H. Ziegler, assistant Professor of Theology; and Theophilus Weaver, A. B., Principal of the Classical Department.

The second school year was opened, in the autumn of 1859, in the Institute building, erected on a lot of ground containing six and two-thirds acres, adjoining the town of Selinsgrove. The building is brick, eighty-six by forty-three feet, and is four stories, including a basement for cellar, kitchen and dining-room. This was paid by the subscription already named.

A charter was procured conferring university   We have, however, confined our work to a classical and a   department. The former prepares students for the Junior and Sophomore classes of college; the latter embraces, in a three years course, the branches usually taught in our theological seminaries.

Our plan is (in the theological department) to have all the students in one class, formed, according to their time of entering, into three divisions. They all attend the same studies, except in Hebrew, so that each division completes the curriculum in three years. It works admirably. Besides, it is a great saving of time to the professors, and of money to the church.

The present teachers are: In the Theological Department, H. Ziegler Superintendent and Theological Professor, and P. Born, Assistant, giving two recitations per week. In the Classical Department, P. Born, Principal since 1859, with three assistants.

The classical department sustains itself. For some years the theological department was sustained by voluntary contributions. That plan was gradually abandoned. We have now a funded endowment of about sixteen thousand dollars, besides some six or seven thousand in unpaid subscriptions and notes. In addition we know of bequests amounting to from twelve to fifteen thousand dollars, which will be available some time in the future.

We have also erected on the grounds of the institute five double houses for the use of married students, each half house having a lot of one hundred and seventy-five feet by thirty feet. The cost of the buildings is $7,090.67, all received by voluntary contributions except about $1,500. Ten families occupy these houses, at a rent of $12 each, yearly.

The number of classical students averages from one hundred to one hundred and thirty. The present theological class numbers seventeen.

The library contains about three thousand volumes, many of them being choice and valuable works, and to which all the students have access free of charge.

The number of students sent out, and licensed or ordained, is seventy-five, to which may be added seven more who will be applicants in a few weeks. Total eighty-two.

Of this number *two* have died; *four* are no longer in the ministry; *one* on account of ill health, and *three* on account of moral delinquency; *one* is with the Synodical Conference; *three* are connected with sister churches; and all the others (leaving seventy-two) are in connection with the General Synod.

AUGUSTANA COLLEGE AND THEOLOGICAL SEMINARY.

Augustana College and Theological Seminary has had a very small beginning, but has also had an unusual growth and development. To God alone belongs the glory, for through his grace and help this institution has progressed and become what it is.

Already at the organization of the Augustana Synod, or at its first convention, which was held at Clinton, Rock county, Wis., June, 1860, a resolution was passed to establish a school for the education of pastors and parochial school teachers. To this was given the name of Augustana Seminary, which was temporarily located at Chicago. Rev. L. P. Esbjorn, who during nearly two years had been Scandinavian Professor at Illinois State University, Springfield, Ill., was chosen the first professor. He occupied his position until the summer 1863, when he returned to Sweden. During this time the number of students ranged from fifteen to twenty. At the synod held in Chicago, June 23d–29th, 1863, the Institution was incorporated under the general law of Illinois; but afterwards, by a special act of the Legislature of Illinois, approved February 16th, 1865; and amended by the same body by a supplementary act approved March 10th, 1869. At the same convention of the Synod it was resolved to remove the school to Paxton, Ford county, Illinois. Rev. T. N. Hasselquist, pastor of the Swedish Lutheran Congregation in Galesburg, Ill., was elected professor in place of Rev. L. P. Esbjörn. The Board of Directors purchased an old school-building, and, during the summer, erected a new one (the "boarding-house") upon the lot donated by Rev. T. N. Hasselquist. During the first school-year the number of students was only seven Swedes and three Norwegians, and Rev.

T. N. Hasselquist was the only instructor. At the meeting of Synod in Rockford, 1864, Rev. Wm. Kopp was elected English Professor. During the school-year 1864-65 the attendance was only fifteen, but during the year 1865-66 there were about forty students. In 1868 the teaching-force was increased by the election of Prof. A. Weenas, who had recently arrived from Norway, and Dr. A. R. Cervin, from Sweden. Owing to failing health, Prof. Kopp resigned, and Rev. S. L. Harkey was elected, and served about one year. He was succeeded by Rev. H. Reck, who has continued to the present time.

In 1870 an important change occurred, by the separation of the Norwegian pastors from the Augustana Synod, with the view of organizing a Synod for themselves, and the consequent withdrawal of the Norwegians from the school. Notwithstanding this, there were during this school year, about fifty persons in attendance, which number was increased to eighty during the last year (1874-75) in Paxton; and the instruction was imparted by six teachers—four regular professors and two assistants—viz.: Rev. T. N. Hasselquist, D. D., Dr. A. R. Cervin, Prof. H. Reck, Prof. C. O. Granere, Rev. F. Lagerman and Mr. Albert Wihlborg.

The expectation that a large Swedish population would settle in the South or South-west was not realized, and the desire to relocate this school at a place more central for the mass of the Swedish people was often expressed, and resolutions upon the removal of the institution were passed at the Synodical Conventions held at Moline, 1869, at Andover, 1870, and at Chicago Lake, Minn., 1871; but only during the Convention at Galesburg, September, 1872, did the Board of Directors receive authority to remove the institution to Moline or Rock Island. In March, 1873, eighteen and seventy-five hundredths acres of picturesque bluff-land in eastern Rock Island were purchased of H. P. Hull, Esq., for ten thousand dollars. At the Synod held in Paxton, June, 1873, the Board of Directors was authorized to erect upon the new site, suitable school-buildings. Without a "building fund," and with a very considerable debt for the land, the Directors, in reliance upon God, undertook the work. In the fall of 1875 the library and other effects of the institution were removed to Rock Island, and on the 22d of September, the first session was opened in the new and beautiful edifice, which was solemnly dedicated to God and the church, on the 14th day of October, 1875.

Augustana College and Theological Seminary had now entered upon a new stage of development, and, notwithstanding many and great obstacles, rapidly increased. The attendance of pupils during the Academic year 1875-76 was one hundred and twelve, and the corps of instructors was strengthened by the arrival of Prof. P. E. Melin, who had been called from Sweden, and of Rev. Prof. W. F. Eyster, from Nebraska.

The present faculty is composed of Rev. T. N. Hasselquist, D. D., President and Professor of Systematic and Pastoral Theology, Exegesis, &c.; Rev. Olof Olsson, Professor of Church History, Ethics, Catechetics, &c.; Rev. H. Reck, Vice President and Professor of Natural and Mental Philosophy; Rev. A. R. Cervin, Ph. D., Professor of Mathematics, Greek and German; Rev. C. O. Granere, Professor of the Latin and the Swedish Languages; P. E. Melin, Ph. Cand., Professor of the Greek and the Hebrew Languages; Rev. Wm. F. Eyster, Professor of the English Language and of History; Albert Wihlborg, Assistant Instructor in Latin, Swedish and German; Prof. T. A. Frey, Instructor in Bookkeeping and Penmanship; M. P. Oden, Assistant in Swedish.

LIBRARY AND MUSEUM.

The library of the institution was established at an early day, by a valuable donation of books in the Swedish, Latin, French, German and other languages, made by Charles XV. (now deceased) King of Sweden.

A society of ladies in Upsala, and other friends of our cause, also made valuable contributions; and additions have been made from time to time, especially by the Bureau of Education at Washington, so that the library now contains about six thousand volumes.

The museum contains interesting and valuable specimens of Mineralogy, Natural History, Botany and Ancient relics.

The philosophical apparatus is yet limited, and we earnestly desire to make additions, so as to increase facilities for making illustrations and experiments in Natural Philosophy and in Chemistry.

Thanks are expressed to Julin Dannfelt, Esq., Commissioner General of the Swedish part of the Centennial Exposition, Philadelphia, for valuable contributions of philosophical apparatus, botanical charts, school furniture, etc.

Ninety-nine students, of whom eighty-six ………………, teen Norwegians, have been trained in the ………………… of this institution, all of whom have been ……………

There are at present (1877) nineteen ……………… total number in all the departments, one ……………… seven.

NORTH CAROLINA COLLEGE.

This institution was chartered January, 1859, and commenced its first session in September following. It was founded by the Lutheran Synod of North Carolina, and sprung originally out of Western Carolina Male Academy, which had been in operation for four years previous under the Principalship of Rev. W. Gerhardt.

Though established by a Lutheran Synod, and still under its fostering care, it is subject to no ecclesiastical restrictions, being altogether catholic and free in its arrangements and discipline.

The college is located at Mount Pleasant, an incorporated and growing village, in Cabarrus county, nine miles from Concord, the county seat and nearest railroad station. It is in one of the most healthy sections of North Carolina, and is surrounded by an industrious, thrifty and moral population. The seclusion of the place is to some extent compensated by its healthfulness and by the absence of those allurements of vice and extravagance which generally beset institutions in more accessible and public localities.

The college buildings are three in number. They are beautifully situated on an eminence overlooking the village and surrounding country, and afford ample accommodation for students and professors. The centre and main building, which is seventy-five feet long by forty feet wide, is a plain, substantial brick structure, three stories, and contains the chapel and the students' rooms. The north and south wings, each sixty feet long by thirty feet wide, are two story buildings, also of brick, and contain the professors' rooms and the halls and libraries of the two literary societies connected with the institution. In addition to these buildings, there is within the campus a convenient and commodious residence for the use of the President.

The endowment of the college was originally twenty thousand dollars. It was collected in 1859, and invested in North Carolina State Bonds. Of this amount, nine thousand dollars were appropriated in 1863 or 64 to the payment of the debt incurred in putting up the two wings. The eleven thousand dollars, still on hand, are considered worthless; have been no source of income for years.

Four years ago, an attempt was made to secure another endowment of twenty thousand dollars, but it was not successful. The agent appointed to prosecute the work of endowment abandoned it after several months of canvassing. Less than five thousand dollars were realized.

The faculty is constituted as follows: Louis A. Bikle, D. D., President; Rev. S. S. Rahn, A. M., Professor of Ancient Languages and Literature; H. T. J. Ludwick, A. M., Professor of Mathematics and Natural Sciences; Paul A. Barrier, M. D., Lecturer on Anatomy and Physiology.

The number of students in attendance on the exercises of both departments of the college, during the academic year ending June 20th, 1877, was seventy. Of this number, fifteen were in the collegiate, and fifty-five were in the preparatory department. The graduates were three.

The library is small, but contains some valuable works. As there is no invested fund for the purpose, the additions to it are not regular, nor numerous, nor always of the best publications.

The chemical and philosophical apparatus is an excellent one. Care was taken in its selection. It is nearly new, and is extensive enough for all experiments in the natural sciences.

The cabinet of minerals is limited, but sufficient for necessary illustrations in the class-room.

ANECDOTES AND QUEER DOINGS

OF LUTHERAN MINISTERS.

I have been earnestly solicited to incorporate with my reminiscences the following anecdotes and facts concerning some of our ministers. I have carefully avoided mentioning names where proper, but all the facts are authentic. Many more in my possession might have been inserted, but these will suffice to give some idea of the condition of things during this period, and will serve to enliven the duller portion of this volume.

"Anecdotes of the pulpit" and "of the ministry," are not rare in literature, but all the following relate exclusively to Lutheran ministers, and for that reason will be more acceptable to the readers of this book.

INTERRUPTIONS DURING WORSHIP.

When the late Dr. B. was pastor at B., in his early life, the gravity of the congregation was considerably disturbed one Sunday, after he had given out the hymn. A very good man lead the singing, and to do things properly, he stood near the altar. His voice was harsh, unmelodious and exceedingly unpleasant. As he was going on with his discordant tones and unmusical clatter, a dog in the church, posted himself right in front of the precentor, and looking up in his face, began the most awful, prolonged howls, just as though his whole nervous system was shaken to pieces. Some one near at hand gave him a kick, and this brought out a succession of terrific yelps. He sneaked under a bench, but as soon as the second verse was begun, out came the dog and recommenced his lamentations. He was finally put out with much trouble. The good brother singer was very much embarrassed, not knowing exactly whether the dog was complimenting him or suffering from nervousness.

One day during service in a country church, whilst the minister was very earnestly exhorting the people, a man stood at the door, and in a loud voice, exclaimed, "Sister Scott, your mar's loose!" Of course, Sister Scott went out to catch and secure the animal.

The loud exclamation of the rude boor, and the hurried departure of Sister Scott in pursuit of her *man*, upset the dignity of all present, and it was sometime before order could be restored, that the service might proceed.

A similar incident occurred in a country church, near Philadelphia. Whilst the services were going on, a man made the general proclamation, "Somebody's horse is loose!" Of course, everybody who had come to church on horseback, rushed out, presuming it was his horse, and during the commotion the minister was compelled to stop.—F. A.

I was once preaching on the repentance of Peter, and quoted the passage, "Peter *went out* and wept bitterly," and added, "The Saviour *saw* those tears of his penitent disciple." A man in church, who was a stranger, rose and exclaimed, "Sir, did you not say, that Peter *went out* and wept? How then, could the Saviour, who remained in the hall, *see* those tears?" I merely replied, "The Lord Jesus is omniscient, but this is not the time or place to discuss the point with you, call on me after the service and I will talk to you."—J. C. D.

A well dressed young man, with an intelligent face, entered my lecture room one Wednesday night, after the service had commenced. I knew him as a candidate for the ministry, and the son of a respectable Methodist minister, but I was not aware of his being at large, having previously heard that he had been a patient in an Insane Asylum. He conducted himself with perfect propriety for half an hour, when, all of a sudden, as I was preaching earnestly, he exclaimed, "Give it to them, Doctor; pitch into them hard!" The consequent confusion may be presumed. Mentioning his name, I entreated him to be quiet, and in a subdued tone, told my hearers his mental condition. I had not proceeded five minutes, when, in an excited voice, he cried out, "Doctor, let me come up there and I'll drive the devil out of them in no time!" With much beside of a similar character, this speech terrified the ladies and aroused the gentlemen, several of whom rushed to him and violently laid hold of him. He rose and clung with the strength of an insane man to one of the columns. By that time, I had approached him, and observing that his eyes flashed and every nerve vibrated with excitement, indicative of a violent paroxysm, I begged my men to release their grasp upon him, and began to speak calmly and kindly to him. By this time, many of the ladies had fled from the room in terrible alarm, and the men were anything but composed. The poor young man promised that he would go with me, if the men who were holding him would release him. He quietly submitted, and I led him out through rows of ladies who had remained to witness the end of the scene, but, who from fear, had mounted the settees, and shrunk backwards as we proceeded to the door. I conducted him to his boarding-house and gave him over to the care of some friends.—J. G. M.

A minister, during the celebration of the marriage service in church, asked the usual question, "If any one present objects to this marriage, let him now speak." An old lady rose, and in a squeaky voice, exclaimed, "I object, sir." "What is your objection, madam?" "Why, they're both too young, sir." The minister did not consider it a valid objection, and proceeded in his duty.—D. H.

S. R. was once preaching at .... the time the canal was being dug through Ohio. An Irishman, no doubt led by curiosity, entered the church and quietly took his seat. R. took his text from Isaiah, "The bed is shorter than that a man can stretch himself on it, and the covering narrower than that he can wrap himself in it." He went on to show that morality was too short and too narrow, that universalism was ditto, &c. In the midst of his sermon two dogs began fighting in the church, and he stopped until the deacons had put the intruders out. He then said, "My brethren, I have often noticed that whenever I am interested, and think I am doing some good, the devil is sure to make some disturbance. My thoughts have been so distracted that I scarcely know what I was talking about." Here Pat arose and said, "Your riverence was saying something about the blanket being too short." There was first a suppressed titter, and then an explosion followed that forbid any further service.
D. H. B.

One of our ministers was once holding forth one Sabbath evening in his lecture-room. Some cats in the yard had a terrific rumpus. It sounded, I am told, as if all the cats in the neighborhood had congregated there for a general fight. The young people tittered, the old ones tried to look grave, and the preacher was compelled to stop, not, perhaps, so much on account of the discordant noise just outside the door, as from an irrepressible fit of laughter which seized him. His fat sides and cheeks shook, and when he had recovered some degree of composure, he said in a most imploring tone, "Will not some of the brethren go out and drive away those cats!" Too many were glad of the opportunity to vent their feelings, some of wrath and others of mirth, and out they went. Then, the fracas was redoubled, for the men cried "*Skat;*" some of them threw stones which struck heavily against the fence, one of which smashed several domestic utensils standing in the yard; the cats which escaped scrambled over the fence with a rush, and those which were wounded uttered terrific yells. After scattering the enemy, the victorious combatants returned to the lecture-room to be greeted with a suppressed laugh of all present, preacher included, who thought it about as well to conclude his services for that evening.—O. T.

One Sunday, a minister of our church who was not at the time a pastor, was attending worship near his own residence in the country. Among other means of procuring an honest livelihood, he cultivated bees and sold large quantities of honey.

One Sunday, one of his children came into church in a great hurry, and rushed up to his father's pew, and in evident alarm whispered something to him. The old gentleman suddenly seized his hat and hastened out of the house. The attention of every body was diverted from the sermon, and every body thought that something terrible had happened. The people were impatient and painfully awaited the conclusion of the service, deeply sympathizing with their unfortunate neighbor. When they came out of church, they learned that the cause of all this confusion was, *the swarming of a hive of bees*, which it was necessary to prevent from escaping. They saw the ex-parson and his whole family industriously engaged in securing the fugitives, which had taken refuge on a neighboring tree!

Dr. D., when pastor at B., preached on the parable of the Ten Virgins. His sexton had been exceedingly unfortunate with his lamps that evening. Some of them went out. D., in making his application, pointed out many delinquencies on the part of his members, and closed every series of remarks to the different classes, by the words "You have no oil in your lamps." The old sexton stood the charge (supposing it personal) as long as he could. It was repeated again, and the old man jumped up and said, "Either the oil was good for nothing, or the devil was in the lamps. He had done his best, and if D. was not satisfied, he might get another sexton."—D. H. B.

NO FEE.

A wedding party of ten or twelve folks of the colored persuasion once drove up to my door in fine style. I took them into the parlor, arranged them in proper order and form, and went through the ceremony as provided. When all was done, I observed some anxious and significant whispering among them, and heard the groom say to another, "O, tell a' Boss! tell a' Boss!" He straightened himself with dignity, and in a pompous tone said, "Boss, de woman have come off and forgot de money! Yes, I sware if she didn't—won't you trust till to-morrow?" Of course I did, but this time *de man* forgot it.—J. C. D.

BAPTISMAL NAME.

I once baptized an infant, and the mother named it *Larry*, which is the usual abbreviation for *Lawrence*, and when I asked her the date of her *boy's* birth, "Oh! my!" she exclaimed, "'tis not a boy; 'tis a gal." "But did you not say the name was *Larry?*" "Yes, but it's a gal for all." After a good deal of talk I found that the kind but ignorant woman meant *Laura!* I told her how to spell and pronounce it, but I doubt whether she profited by my instructions.—J. C. D.

ANOTHER.

I was called to baptize the twelfth child of Mr. N., and when I asked the name, the father responded "*Harry Clay*." "But, Mr. N., Harry is a nick name, why not say *Henry* Clay at once?" "Because," he replied, "I have one Henry already in the family." So I baptized the infant Harry Clay, in honor of the great statesman.—J. C. D.

DR. BEECHER'S OPINION OF LUTHER.

During my residence in C., our Christian Protestant Association appointed Dr. C. Stowe, Theological Professor of Lane Seminary, and son-in-law of Dr. Beecher, President of the Seminary, and also at the same time pastor of the Second Presbyterian church of C., to lecture one whole winter, once a week on Dr. Luther and the reformation. Dr. S. had traveled all over Germany and Europe in search of works on the Lutheran reform, both by Romanist and Protestant authors, in different languages, which he could read off in English as though it were a translation. He was named the walking library. And he honored me several times by supplying my pulpit. Dr. B., in whose church the lectures were delivered, and myself, were in the pulpit, when Prof. S. gave the characteristics of Dr. M. L. in the highest style of truthful oratory. At the close of this lecture, Dr. B. jumped up and embraced me most cordially, saying aloud, " Mr. R.! Dr. Luther was a greater man than Paul." I assented (inspiration excepted) in my own mind, but, also, that I had rather you, as a Presbyterian, should thus compliment him, than I, as a Lutheran. The whole course was one continuous feast for intellect and heart. What sublimity of moral heroism both repeatedly manifested!! I think two such men *now* would find work!!—A. R.

ANECDOTE CONCERNING DR. HELMUTH.

I was providentially favored, when I was licensed to preach, in having some of the most prominent and pious ministers of the old mother Synod to be my *special friends*, who, like fathers, took me under their fostering wings; among them, were Drs. J. G. Schmucker, Helmuth, Lochman, Dr. Daniel Kurtz, &c. The latter of whom, took me, many years ago, to pay a special visit to Dr. Helmuth, of Philadelphia, who, then, was *bitterly slandered* and *persecuted;* and, that by his own members of old Zion's church. We felt a deep interest in his case; so we ventured, but very remotely, to *hint* at the matter—and a hint to the *wise* is always sufficient, and so it proved here. The old Doctor silently walked to another room and brought in his hand a manuscript of poetry (for he was a poet), and read in reference to the accusation of *moral delinquency, &c.*, and, then without another word on that subject, returned his manuscript. It referred to a remarkable providential intervention in his behalf, when quite a youth of about fifteen years. It ran thus: When he left his gymnasium for a university, he being poor and entirely out of money, was about to be left behind by the post stage; so he quickly retired behind a *large oak*, knelt and prayed in his dilemma, and getting manifest comfort, he arose and went to overtake the departing coach—when lo! an unknown person met him, handed him a paper, and when he looked, it contained some gold coin. So he paid his way, and was enabled to accomplish his good and great end.—A. R.

DR. HELMUTH.

During a visit to the country, he preached for a brother minister. The audience was large, and seemed deeply interested. The Doctor intending to impress the truth more deeply upon their minds, turned to the fathers and said, "*Nun, stellt euch vor!*" literally signifying, *now, present yourselves*, but metaphorically, *now, imagine a case*, or *suppose*, &c. To his astonishment, the old men, taking the words in their literal sense, absolutely rose from their seats and *presented* themselves at the altar. Not at all disconcerted by the result, and ever ready to turn anything to good account, the good Doctor addressed them earnestly and affectionately, and then told them to take their seats. By this time, the feeling in the congregation was most intense. Unwilling to let pass such an opportunity of doing good, he next turned to the mothers. "*Jetzt ihr mütter stellt euch vor!*" Now, you mothers, present yourselves, which they did, and, after that, in the same way, he called up the young women and the young men.

REV. S...... R......

Many of our readers will remember this good man. He was converted under the ministry of Rev. William Yeager, often called the "Apostle of the Mountains," as his labors were pretty much confined to the Eastern spurs of the Alleghanies. Solomon had been rather a wild boy, and of an ardent and impetuous temperament, and when after a terrible struggle with sin and the devil (for like Luther he believed in a personal devil, and like the greater reformer at the Wartburg, he had his own difficulties with his satanic majesty). Well, after a terrible conflict he became converted, and of course carried his ardent and impetuous temperament with him, over into the kingdom of grace. About that time (1831) there was a great religious excitement all through Western Pennsylvania. Rev. John Winebrenner had kindled the fires of fanaticism, and the Albrights, and United Brethren, and the Tunkers, or River Brethren had also caught the infection. The mode of worship of these sects was anything but orderly. S. R. was heart and soul in this fanatical current. He immediately commenced holding meetings on his own account. And as he had a good voice to sing and talk, he soon became very popular as an exhorter. However I think in the fall of '31 he went to Gettysburg, and remained there several years, but his studying did not cure him of his injudicious zeal. He left Gettysburg the same Solomon, only with a little more knowledge. He was instrumental in the conversion of many souls. He was full of zeal and energy—he could preach for a whole month every day and night, and he always measured his success in preaching by the wetness of his under clothes when he was done. If they were dry he reproached himself for not having "cried aloud." Among others he was instrumental in the conversion of Rev. J. S. This man had been a hard case before his conversion; he was fond of frolic and other objectionable acts. But to proceed with Solomon's case. After he left Gettysburg, I think, in 1835, he settled at Mount Vernon, Ohio. Whilst in Ohio he was very active in promoting revivals, or what he called revivals. Although he no doubt did some good, his ministry cannot be called a success. He was too eccentric, and too impetuous to be extensively useful. He was unquestionably a truely pious man, and labored for the glory of God in the salvation of men. He was a man that thought some, but his thoughts were generally disjointed and crude. He had naturally a good mind with no little originality, but it was undisciplined by proper study. Hence his preaching was nothing but ranting, and yet that kind of preaching was popular in those days. I have heard him make some of the most powerful appeals I ever heard. He had the knack of moving a congregation that I have rarely seen excelled. He could pour scorching hot fire, like burning lava, on the hearts of wicked sinners. He always preached with all the physical power God had given him.

He once rebuked me with his sharp, adder-tongue, most unmercifully, and I afterwards convinced him that he had done me a great wrong. But I always respected and loved him because I knew he was honest and true. I can say of him as Cicero said of his friend Cato Major, "Ille vir, haud magnus cum re, sed plenus fidei."

In order to give some idea of the man and his manner of doing things, the following may serve as an illustration:

On one occasion, while on his way to Synod in company with two or three of his ministerial brethren, they came to a small village, in some part of Ohio. Solomon was full of holy fire, and having learned that there was no preaching in that place, he was determined there should be preaching there that night. So he went out into the kitchen and talked with the woman of the house about it. She at once consented. He then applied to the landlord, but he refused. But Solomon was not the man to be bluffed off in a matter of such moment. Preach he would, and preach he did, and, that too, in the bar-room where all the drunken loafers in the village used to meet. The landlord, when he found there was no other way, gave a reluctant consent. So the people were invited in, and a good many came. The opposition Solomon had encountered and overcame, only increased his energy, and imparted new zest to his zeal. His text was, "We must all appear before the Judgment seat of Christ," and he out did himself. He called up the different classes of sinners to the bar of Judgment; the drunkards, and the landlords who made the drunkards he stript them naked, and dissected them. Before he was done preaching the desired effect was visible and audible, the women were crying out for mercy, and the men were quaking like aspen leaves. The mourners bench was called into requisition, and the machinery, which Solomon knew so well how to handle with effect, was put in motion. Quite a number presented themselves for prayer and conversation. The meeting was continued until after midnight; many professed to have been converted, and among the rest, the landlord and his wife. Solomon, who wanted people to be truly converted, seems to have had some doubts about the genuineness of the landlord's conversion. So, after the meeting was dismissed, he said to the landlord, "Now, sir, if you are really in earnest about your soul's salvation, you must quit selling liquor." "Oh, yes," says the man, "of course I will quit when I shall have sold what I have on hand." "No, sir, that will not do; you must quit now; your liquor must be poured out into the gutter, and your sign-post must come down, or you will surely go to hell!" It was then agreed that the liquor should be poured out, and the sign-post should come down. In the morning, when the people had again come to see the great preacher, Solomon put his hands on the bottles and poured the liquor into the gutter. He then asked the landlord to get him an ax. He brought him one. Solomon took his coat off and went to work, and continued until the post and sign came down, amid the shouts of applause of the women. It is said that he visited that place afterwards, and organized a Lutheran congregation that is still in existence, and in a prosperous condition.—R. W.

ABRUPT INTERFERENCE.

One of our young ministers (G. D.) was once leading family worship in the house of a worthy widow, who, in her youth, had a good voice, and prided herself in singing the old-fashioned tunes of the church. Our young friend struck up an unusual tune, somewhat of the fandango order, which the good old lady tried to follow, but in vain. At the end of the third line, while the others in the room were devoutly singing, she all at once exclaimed, "Good heavens! Mr. D., what sort of tune is that?"

TRIALS OF SOME OF OUR MISSIONARIES IN THE WEST AS LATE AS 1846.

Rev. Jacob Scherer, whom some of our ministers will remember, states in his diary, of February 1846, when he had located near Olney, Richland county, Ill.,

"We moved into one of Mr. S......'s houses   Our furniture is truly sucker;* no table; three stools; scarcely bed clothes enough to keep us warm. Our bedsteads consist of rails let into the cracks of the wall at one end, and tied up at the other by withes to rails set up between the joist and floor. We have a few books with us. This is to be our best accommodation for a time. We live in a little one-story house, all in one room. The rest of the week I was engaged in fixing little matters in the house, getting up firewood, making up a school, etc., etc.

DR. KUNZE.

He held a newspaper controversy on the Gregorian period of the century 1800. It is well known that the discussion enlisted much feeling among the astronomers, both abroad and at home. Kunze, after mature deliberation, addressed a communication on the vexed question to the editor of the New York Gazette, John Lang. He had adverted to the Gregorian style in his letter, and incidentally referred to Pope Gregory. The faithful Gazette printed the name *Tom* Gregory; the venerable Doctor hastened to his friend and remonstrated on the injury he had done him, and requested an *erratum* to specify, instead of *Tom* Gregory, Pope Gregory XIII. Only one more attempt at correction was made,

* A nickname for Illinoisians.

when the compositor had its typography so changed that it read Tome Gregory the Pope. The learned divine, with a heavy heart, in a final interview with the erudite editor, begged him to make no further improvements, as he dreaded the loss of all the reputation his years of devotion to the subject had secured to him. Dr. Francis in Sprague's Annals of Lutheran Pulpit, p. 56.

It was only in the German language that Dr. Kunze was capable of preaching with any degree of facility. He, once, for a short time, attempted to preach in English, but with such poor success that he was induced quickly to give it up. Some wild and wicked young men went to the church door, on one occasion, when he was trying his hand at English, and his text happened to be, "God is not willing that any should perish," &c. In order to ridicule his German pronunciation of English, they went away and reported that the Doctor had said, in his pulpit, that "God is not a villain." The report soon reached his ears, and he never afterwards attempted to preach, except in his native tongue. Dr. Mayer in Sprague's Annals, p. 58.

DANGER OF IMITATION.

Mr. Baetes used to tell a story in reference to a Lutheran minister, who wanted to take as a model the distinguished Whitfield, who, on a certain occasion, was compelled to remain over night at a country inn, where he found a large number of men engaged in drinking and indulging in most offensive imprecations. Stepping up to the bar, he called for a pitcher of water, and, handing it to the most profane man of the party, urged him, in tones peculiarly his own, to take a hearty drink *now*, for the time would soon come, when in the next world, he would cry in vain for a single drop of water to cool his parched tongue. The truth, together with Mr. Whitfield's manner, made a deep impression upon the sinner's heart, and the result was his conversion. The Lutheran minister, on a similar occasion, having remembered the incident, concluded to employ the same remedy, but without success. To his surprise, personal violence was offered him; he was most severely handled.

WOULDN'T SAY AMEN!

One of our ultra revival men, after having preached some time in his new charge, said to the people, "You sit here like stupid blocks and say nothing. I know not whether I preach good sermons or indifferent ones. Where I came from I could always tell this, for whenever I said anything that pleased the people, or that was particularly good, a number of persons would say, 'Amen.' This would encourage me, and I could preach better. But here I never get any such encouragement." He then began his sermon, and was soon in full swing. He waxed louder and louder, and eloquence was at its height, when he vociferated, "We are all cold and dead. We all, minister and people, need a revival. Your sons and your daughters are on the road to hell." "Amen," shouted out one of the audience. The preacher suddenly stopped, gave him one look, and then scolded the poor fellow more severely for saying "Amen," than he had some time before for not saying it. The old fellow muttered, as he came out church, "He may say amen himself next time."—D. H. D.

Being at Synod, in a Maryland village, I, with some other ministers, was invited to dine at the house of the purse-proud and conceited nabob of the place. He was lord of the manor, and a country magistrate of great self-consequence. He was never contradicted, and claimed the right of saying what he pleased. He handed me the celery, which he pronounced *salary*, saying, in a sneering tone, "Mr. M., take a piece of *salary*, for I believe most preachers like *salary!*" "Yes," retorted I, "They love celery, but hate bad puns! Your dinner is better than your joke, and your wine is better than your wit!" He lost his appetite after that, and never forgave me.

A MODEL REVIVAL.

An old-fashioned minister found his young people attending a Methodist revival, and some leaving him. Upon this, he made an appointment in the following language: "To-morrow evening we will *hold a revival* in this house." The evening came, and the house was crowded. A young man preached the sermon. At the end of the sermon, the old pastor arose and said, "Now let all the young gentlemen, who wish to be prayed for, come forward and kneel around the altar." Some dozens of young men obeyed the invitation, and the old man kneeled down and prayed, not forgetting "God's ancient people, the Jews," in the course of his supplications. He then arose and said, "The young gentlemen will now go to their seats, and the young ladies will surround the altar." Some scores of young ladies obeyed the summons, and the good old man went through the same long, tedious prayer, not forgetting the "ancient people." He then arose, remanded the young ladies to their seats, and *appointed a revival* for next evening, and dismissed the congregation. The next evening came, but all the young men and young ladies were at the Methodist church, and remained there.—D. H. B.

A JUVENILE PREACHER.

Many years ago, I repeatedly met Rev. R. S. We preached together at special Conferences and Synods. I had always respected him for German integrity and honesty. When his elder son was about half a dozen years old, being *smart*, the father got him into his pulpit to deliver *little, short* sermons, which he had memorized. He acquitted himself pretty well as a *child;* and this caused the elated parent to boast of it. And, lo! it came to the ears of our very venerable President of the Maryland and Virginia Synod, the Rev. Daniel Kurtz, D. D., while Synod met at Cumberland, over sixty years ago. The worthy President was much displeased, and publicly reprimanded the father for desecration of the holy office. This influenced him to leave our Synod and attach himself to another. I was sorry for him, but it could not be avoided. —A. R.

THE TWO STUDENTS.

In the early history of the institutions at G., two students came there from the same neighborhood at the same time. The one had seen some little of the world, and thought he knew more than he did, but had no brains. The other was very green, and had a poor opinion of himself, but had a splendid mind in its raw state. The "Brotherhood" was then in full blast, and I had the honor of being at the head of the establishment. So Prof. S. sent the two new men to me, to see if I could make room for them. Mr. G. had brass enough in his composition to make a lawyer, whilst Mr. B. was very modest. So when they came to my room, I asked Mr. G. who came with him? He replied, "Oh, nobody but this dumb fellow." Well, the dumb fellow sat back in the corner, and had nothing to say. I made room for them in the "Brotherhood," and they set into study. Mr. G. had no mind, and nothing could be made of him. He nibbled on through the Latin Grammar, but Greek remained Greek to him. Mr. B. studied successfully, and few students could keep up to him. Mr. G. was admitted to the ministry somewhere in the West, but never accomplished anything. Mr. B. graduated in the college with honor, passed through the seminary, entered the ministry, was a very efficient pastor, and is now a D. D., and at the head of an institution of no mean position.

We are often deceived by appearances, and we can learn from this, that the bold and forward, are not always the most talented.—R. W.

THE TRIALS OF BENEFICIARIES.

In the beginning of our educational operations, most of the young men at Gettysburg Seminary boarded in clubs. They bought their own provisions, and employed some woman to cook them at her own house, where the students went to take their frugal meals. One morning, the coffee had a peculiar and unusual taste. Each man swallowed a portion and made a wry face. They looked at each other, and every visage bore evidence of disgust. One's face was elongated, another's nose was wrinkled, another's cheeks were distended, another's eyes were closed, another's jaws hung down, and all presented a most lugubrious aspect. One declared that the cook had boiled unroasted or green coffee, another thought that verdigris had gathered in the coffee pot or water kettle, and one was sure that poison had been put into the beverage. At this annunciation, several began to feel uneasy below, and betrayed symptoms of vomiting, and all turned pale. A few concluded it was all over with them now, and how could the church get along without them? They began to think of adjourning the breakfast to a prayer-meeting, and preparing for a sudden end. One of them, who has since become a Doctor of Divinity and the President of a college, bethought himself of examining the vessel, in which the coffee had been brought upon the table, and after pouring out the nasty liquid, discovered at the bottom a *huge plug of tobacco* boiled to leaves, with loose portions floating all through the abominable stuff. The cook could not account for it, but it cured some of them, and they henceforth foreswore the use of coffee and tobacco, especially as an ingredient of their customary morning potation.—R. W.

THE VITALITY OF LUTHERANISM.

Lutheranism is a hardy plant. It thrives in all climates, and under all circumstances, and is hard to exterminate. It is of God-planting, and cannot be plucked up. We give the following as one of many instances. About forty years ago the Rev. S., a most pious and excellent young Lutheran minister, was called to the pastorate of the Lutheran church at M. He was full of life and fire. His preaching took effect upon the hearts of the people. An extensive revival followed. Many souls were awakened, and there was a very great excitement. Poor Bro. S. was himself made of very excitable material, and contrary to the convictions of his better judgment, he was also carried away in the maelstrom of physical excitement. His members became fanatical, and, under the pressure of excitement, ran every thing into the ground. Some few of the older, and more grave and intelligent members of the church, resisted this new style of Lutheranism, and contended for the good old ways of their fathers. The church split, the great body of the members going with the new party, leaving the few firm old Lutherans in a hopeless minority. The new party, as they supposed, with the wealth, the members, and all the piety on their side, would no doubt carry away the palm. They built a new church; they were not going to remain in the old rat hole—no not they! They were going to have a purer and a holier church, a church in which every man would be converted. Well, they built their church, and went out from the old rat hole, and set up for themselves. But alas! they soon found that some of their members were not as perfect as the angels. Like all the sects that have gone out of other churches for the sake of having a perfectly pure church, they found that the good and bad must exist together in this imperfect world. Poor Bro. S. was driven away. The brethren thought it would go better with a new pastor, one that did not know them so well. But alas! it still went down, down, down, until their congregation was scattered to the four winds! The last we heard of those reformed Lutherans, was that they had become Millerites, and were among those who had their ascension robes ready to go up to glory! The church is long since among the things that were. Like Moses, it is dead, and buried, but no man knoweth unto this day where it is buried. Mr. S. has long since seen the errors of his youthful zeal without knowledge, and has been and is still laboring faithfully, and with acceptance and success, in the old Lutheran vineyard that hath not been destroyed by the wild boar of the forest.

And now for the old rat hole. Few cases have occurred where

Lutheranism had a better opportunity to give the world an exhibition of its vitality. Here it was an old dilapidated building, surrounded by a fanatical atmosphere, with nearly all its young material driven off—only a few old people left—the prospects were indeed dark and gloomy. But their motto was:

> "Gottes Wort, und Luther's Lehr,
> Vergehen nun und nimmermehr."

They raised the old Lutheran standard, and the friends of Bible religion clustered around it. It is now a large flourishing and efficient congregation. What hath not God wrought?

True Lutheranism never dies; it is immortal. Two hundred years ago it was planted on the frozen shores of Iceland, and it is still there in a flourishing condition. It was planted nearly a century ago on the burning plains of India, and is still there, bearing like the palm tree, its precious fruit. Where it once gets a foot hold it remains.—R. W.

DANGEROUS IMITATION.

One of our most eminent ministers, at present, some years ago preached in W......... His peculiarity of gesture was the subject of conversation next day in a store. A young Methodist preacher, who was present, said he would "take him off," and, mounting a stool, began to imitate his wild gestures. By a singular mischance he slipped, and falling in a particular way, broke his leg. This was told to our preacher next morning. He remarked "he was lucky, very lucky; it is a wonder he did not break his neck. The foolish fellow might have known that any attempt to imitate me would end disastrously."—D. H. B.

A SINGULAR TEMPTATION MET.

Some years ago, a very active and worthy lady member of the Lutheran Church became quite prepossessed in favor of the Episcopalians. Why, she could not exactly tell; but she could not rid herself of the notion that she ought to become an Episcopalian. Her surroundings were such that there were very strong considerations in her way, which she did not feel quite at liberty to disregard to such an extent as the change would require. Neither had she any objection to the Lutheran Church, or its confession. She had always worked cheerfully in it, brought up her children in it, and, indeed, knew no gospel but that which the

Lutheran Church had taught her, and which all her relatives and connections heartily accepted. Still, she was pursued and haunted with the idea that she ought to be an Episcopalian.

Meeting her pastor one day in the presence of her family, she recounted her feelings and her trouble in this respect, and at the end, said: "Do tell me, what is the reason that the devil tempts and torments me in this way?"

The minister gravely answered: "I do not know, madame, unless it is that he wishes to make an Episcopalian of you."

The lady blushed, the family laughed, the subject was changed, and the transfer has not been made.—J. A. S.

The sainted Rev. F. V. Melsheimer, my most worthy professor, had several peculiarities. He was a great linguist, theologian, &c., &c. He had been President and Professor of our Lutheran and German Reformed College, at Lancaster, Pa., then pastor of the Hanover Pastorate. Here he attended to as many students of theology as he could board. Myself was one of the last classes, nearly sixty years ago. He was a *very good* preacher, but he could not look his auditory in the face, from great timidity, and hence he always fixed his eye on one spot on the facing of the gallery. When a thunder-storm occurred, if practicable, he would lie down between two feather beds, as nonconductors. His son John inherited the same infirmity. This was evident in the fact, when he was to preach a funeral sermon at Kreutzkirch, his first attempt. He rode up in sight of the church, when his courage failed him; he dismounted at a farmhouse and watched until the folks, after waiting a considerable time for his arrival and promised service, began to disperse after burying the dead; then only he mounted his horse and galloped up to the church—and lo! they were all gone. On his return his father asked him how he got along in his *first attempt* to preach; he replied, to the great surprise and chagrin of his father, that they were all gone when he arrived. His father never got at the secret until a few years after, when he happened to stop at the same house. This both aggravated and amused his father. And then he, after his licensure, was sent to Shepherdstown, Va., as Pastor; he soon resigned his pastorate, from timidity, and went to the practice of medicine, until his father died, and he was called to Hanover, filling his father's place. "The fear of man bringeth a snare."—A. R.

AN EMBARRASSED HEARER.

A minister of our church was in the habit, some years ago, of translating his German sermons, and then preaching them in English. There was in his charge a numerous family by the name of Ritter, one of whom was called Sammy. He preached a sermon in German on the subject of "Der Gute Samariter," which he pronounced in English, *the good Sama-ritter*. He lauded *Sammy Ritter* to the very heavens, and poor Sammy, being present, could not for the life of him imagine what had gotten into the preacher, and became so confused that he rushed from the church, unable to identify himself.—D. H. B.

STAY ON THE GRIDDLE.

Some years ago, one of our clergymen preached on the text, "Ephraim is a cake not turned." He said that a cake not turned is a cake baked only on one side, half-baked, neither soft nor hard, neither bread nor dough, but a something between the two, not fit for use, disagreeable, and destined to be cast away. This, he said, was the character of some of the Jewish people in the prophet's time, and is the character of many modern professors of Christianity. The world seemed to be made up of three classes: Full-hearted, earnest and thorough Christians; those who make no pretensions whatever to Christian faith and devotion; and a third class, between these two, composed of such as cannot shake off all religious affections, accede to the requirements of Christianity in general, exhibit many points of true excellence, but still hold back in some matters which are needful to make them exemplary or satisfactory believers.

One of his parishioners came to him afterwards, expressing some anxiety and perplexity as to what she ought to do, as she was pretty well convinced that she belonged to the middle class, and did not wish to continue in that particular fellowship. She seemed to be conscious of a sort of half-and-half state of mind and character, which she wished to know how to cure. She even expressed serious doubts whether it was worth her while to continue her attentions to the church and religious duties, feeling as if it were not right to remain in such a feeble state of devotedness, and still not be able to make the necessary advances on what she had been. She said she knew she was only half-baked, and what should she do?

The clergyman said to her: "Well, madam, *I advise you to stay on the griddle.*" It was enough. The lady tells the story to her friends with much zest, as having been to her a word of great comprehensiveness, value and encouragement. She says she has been following the advice, and believes that it has helped her to be a better woman.—J. A. S.

About thirty-five years ago Rev. J. Scherer was pastor of St. John's Church in South-Western Virginia. At that time hymn books were scarce; perhaps there were not half a dozen in the congregation. The man who "raised the tune" had none. Father S. parceled out the hymn by twos, as was the custom. After reading the last lines he quickly laid down his hymn book, opened his Bible, and as soon as the singing ceased, read his text, "This is a faithful saying," &c. The "Clerk" supposing it was a continuation of the hymn, *commenced singing the text!* The preacher put a stop to it by hammering upon the pulpit, saying, "These are the words from which I wish to address you."—J. A. B.

Once on a time he was called on to baptize an infant in a private house. Having asked the name of the child, "Sam," said the father. The preacher proceeded. "Samuel, I baptize you." "Not *Samuel*" said the father, "*Sam.*" Father Scherer attempted to explain, saying that Sam was only a contraction of Samuel, which was the proper name, and again continued, "Samuel, I baptize you." "Not Samuel, *I say, Sam,*" exclaimed the father, and his demand had to be complied with.—J. A. B.

He was requested, on one occasion, to attempt a reconciliation between two of his parishioners who had gotten into a difficulty about the location of a road. Father S. heard each party give his version of the matter in a very excited manner, and after a few moments pause, simply remarked, "Well, all I have to say to you, brethren, is, that whilst you are quarreling about your roads here, take care that the road to heaven is not shut up to you," and extending his hand gave them good bye. That remark accomplished more than an hours' harangue.—J. A. B.

THE ECCENTRIC STUDENT WITH AN IRON CONSTITUTION.

If the normal condition of a good student be, as some say, "a sound mind in a sound body," then Mr. K. must have been a good student, especially in so far as the body is concerned. He was a German, a full-grown German in soul and body. His frame was square, solid, and plump. He had a broad Teutonic chest, a full, round Lutheran face, and a strong pair of leathern lungs. His voice was strong, coarse and guttural, just made for the German language. Mr. K's mind partook to some extent of the qualities of his rough and athletic body. He was rather dull and slow in his intellectual movements; it always took him some time to get even a plain idea fairly fixed in his mind, but when he got it there it generally stuck. We were students together at Gettysburg forty years ago, and I had a good opportunity of studying this queer specimen of the Genus Homo, for it was my misfortune to be his room-mate for a whole winter. Like most of his countrymen, he was genial and kind-hearted when he was in a good humor, but passionate and unreasonable when angry. He was quick as powder. Poor K. wanted to be pious, but it was hard work for him; he could not govern himself; often for the most trivial thing he would become excited to such a degree that he would foam with pure rage. But he was what may be called a hard student. He had not enjoyed the advantages of an early classical education, and as he had to keep up with the class in Greek Exegesis, it worked him hard. He had an inquisitive mind, and was not destitute of intellectual pride, hence he would not leave a Greek word until he knew all about it. I have known him to pour over his Greek Testament and Lexicon all night, and never close an eye. More than once have I gone to bed, at a proper hour, and in the morning, when I awoke, there stood (for he most studied in that position) the man with the iron constitution. If ever a man "trimmed the midnight lamp," it was he. Then he would continue his studies all day too; not a moment would he waste. He took no relaxation, his whole student-life was study, study, study. In his deportment he was stern and serious; life with him seemed to be one continued stream of moroseness, except when broken in upon by anger. Such was the violence of his temper that those students who had offended him, had to keep out of his way until his anger had subsided. Woe be to the wight who would play a trick on him! Mr. K. at last left the seminary, and received a license from the West Pennsylvania Synod. He was sent out into the mountains of Pennsylvania to hunt up the scattered Lutherans. As a missionary he accomplished some good, but as a settled pastor he never succeeded. He was once invited to preach to a German congregation, on the Alleghany mountains, as a candidate. The roads were very rough and rocky, especially the one that led to the church: it was almost impassable. And when within sight of the church, his horse stumbled over a large stump, and threw him sprawling into a mud hole! Here was a fix, and some cause for his wrath to take fire. When he came to church he was covered with mud, and immediately let loose upon the members for not mending their ways. "Why," says he, "I venture to say the heathen have better roads to their temples, and you have no better roads—you are no christians—you are not fit to have the gospel preached to you." The poor, innocent people looked on with amazement, and soon came to the conclusion that such an angry pastor would not suit them. So poor K. had to continue his mission work. Mr. K. was very much opposed to noisy and extravagant meetings. We students used to have preaching at school-houses and private houses. On one occasion, the Allbrights, who are a very noisy set of christians, got one of their revivals started at one of our preaching places. The meeting was one, as they call it, of "great power;" the noise and confusion were very great. I had heard of it, and expected a scene when I would have to preach there in my turn. I prevailed on Mr. K. to go with me. Long before we came to the house we heard the loud singing and shouting. The Allbright preachers had got there before us, and had commenced the meeting. When we entered the private house in which the meeting was held, the scene that we witnessed was beyond description; some were singing with the "holy swing," &c., rocking to and fro, clapping their hands and stamping their feet—others were shouting at the top of their voices—others stretched out on the floor—it was an awful scene. So we remained in the kitchen for some time. At last Mr. K. said, "Let us go in and preach." "Oh no," I replied, "we can't do anything here." "Yes we can." So in we went. Mr. K. took the hymn book, and commanded order with his rough, harsh voice. "I want you to be still; this is not the way to worship God; bodily exercise will not save your souls," and gave them a terrible overhauling. All became silent as the grave; he preached them a good, faithful gospel sermon on Faith in Christ, which no doubt did the people ten times more good in the end than their noisy and turbulent meetings. Poor K. has long since gone to his reward, and it is hoped has been cleaned and purified in the blood of the Lamb.—A. W.

SINGULAR CIRCUMSTANCE.

A Synod was held at ...., on which occasion there was an applicant for ordination. Some time previous he was called upon to baptize a sick child. He went, and the child died in the arms of its mother during the ceremony. A charge was brought against his application to the effect that he had baptized a dead child. He thought this charge too futile to merit even a refutation. The consequence was that he was denied ordination. His brother and another man, two ordained ministers, took him to a large oak tree near the church, and ordained him, and they three formed a new Synod. In a few weeks afterwards the lightning struck the oak tree and shivered it to splinters, down to the very roots.—D. H. B.

REV. JESSE HOOVER, OUR FIRST LUTHERAN MISSIONARY TO THE FAR WEST.

This enterprising pioneer of our church was born in Dover, York county, Pa., in 1809. He was, like myself, instructed in the principles of religion and confirmed by the Rev. Dr. J. G. Schmucker, in 1828. He came to Gettysburg, I think, in the fall of 1829. He was an apt scholar and a diligent student, and, of course, made rapid progress. He had enjoyed the advantages of a good common-school education. He was a short, thick-set man, somewhat under the average size of men. He was full of life and animation, and was a genial and pleasant companion, and was, of course, a general favorite among the students. He was a member of our "Famous Brotherhood," and remained a prominent member of it until it broke up, on the completion of the seminary building, when the students were all required to take rooms there.

In his piety he was exemplary and consistent. He had a great flow of spirits, and was a man of great energy and perseverance. What he undertook to do, he did with all his might. As an illustration, I think it was in 1830, when the mechanical labor scheme that had been started at Andover reached Gettysburg, and, encouraged by Prof. Schmucker, we also determined to set up a theological carpenter shop. Prof. Schmucker gave us fifty dollars, and requested all the theological students to collect funds for the purpose of purchasing tools; so each one had his little book. I went to York, and, by the aid of Dr. J. G. Schmucker, C. A. Morris and Philip Smyser, I raised some sixty dollars. I congratulated myself with the certainty that I would, of course, be able to return more money than any other one. But I was sadly disappointed—Brother Hoover was fifteen dollars ahead of me! He had collected, by little driblets, seventy-five dollars in and about Dover.

I left Gettysburg in the fall of 1832; in 1833 Brother Hoover left Gettysburg. He took charge of a private school in Hagerstown that had been taught by Rev. S. K. Hoshour, the latter having taken charge of the Lutheran Church in that place.

As students, the subject of missions was often discussed among us. Brother Hoover had made up his mind to become a missionary in the West; so, in 1834, I think, he started for the far West, and located in Fort Wayne, Indiana, where he commenced his work. I had a number of letters from him whilst laboring under great difficulties. How long he labored there I have forgotten, but not long; for he soon fell a martyr to the then inhospitable climate. He died, as almost every third man did in those early days, of the fever common in the swamps of Indiana. He was the first of the noble band of Lutheran missionaries who penetrated into the miasmatic regions of the far West. I think Rev. W. G. Keil, J. Henry Hoffman and M. Ruth, and perhaps Rev. Mr. Greenwald, had settled in Ohio before 1834; but none of our men had gone so far West as Fort Wayne. I do not know where Brother Hoover received his license—perhaps from the Synod of Maryland, before he started for the West.

Soon after 1834. Rev. A. A. Trimper, Jacob Sherer and Count Lehmanowsky went to the far West, and formed the Synod of the West. This Synod included Indiana, Illinois, Michigan, Kentucky, and all the "regions round about." It would require some considerable counting now to tell how many Synods—English, German and Scandinavian—have grown out of the Synod of the West. There are now on that field perhaps not less than twenty Synods, and nearly half the Lutherans in the United States. What a wonderful change in forty-three years! Who would have thought, in 1834, when a solitary young man located in the swampy and miasmatic regions of Indiana, and commenced gathering a few poor Germans into a Lutheran congregation in Fort Wayne, that in so short a time the Lutherans should be counted by hundreds of thousands?

Brother Hoover once wrote to me thus: "I am laboring here to build up a church, but it is hard work. I have a few good, substantial members; but many who call themselves Lutherans are a disgrace to our church, and I do not know what the result of my labors will be. We have secured a house (such as it is) in which we can now worship. I sometimes think of giving up the work and returning to the East; but, as I came out here to raise the standard of Lutheranism, by the help of God I'll do it." And he did it, but at the expense of his life. He fell at his post, with his harness on. When the General Synod met at Fort Wayne, in 1864, I was there, and I went out to the cemetery and found a neat tombstone erected by the congregation over his remains: "To the Memory of Rev. Jesse Hoover, Pastor of the Lutheran Congregation of Fort Wayne." Although it was nearly thirty years after his death, I could not help but shed tears over the remembrance of a dear friend and beloved fellow-student. And when I stood at his lonely grave, and memory called up to my mental view the image of my departed brother, I could not but admire the courage and moral heroism that had led him on to make the sacrifices that he had to make. While standing at his grave the thoughts of James Montgomery occurred to my mind: "Servant of God, well done."—R. W.

OVERSETTING A SERMON.

A minister of ours once attended the religious service of one of the smaller of the German sects. There were two preachers present, and one of them said in the beginning, "Brother Schmitz will breach in *Sharman*, and denn I will *overset* it in English." He meant *translate*, literally rendering the German word *uebersetz*, but the English *overset* conveys quite a different idea.

"HE FELL TO EXHORTIN."

An elder of one of our country churches once described the effect of his minister losing his manuscript, by the wind blowing it off from the pulpit, one day in summer, when the window was open. He said, "Look, die wint plowed it off and none of dem stupid councilmen had sense enough to bick it up and hant it to him. Vell, you see, his sarment was gone, and vot could he do? He *straitway fell to exhortin.*

IN DANGER OF BACKSLIDING.

A minister of our church once told me that in his vicinity, two female members of another denomination, whose houses joined each other, were, one day, engaged in a most violent altercation across the garden fence. The most opprobious epithets were freely interchanged, and, in general, language more forcible than chaste or polite was mutually used. The poor, henpecked husband of one of them, who, from painful experience, knew that it was at his peril to interfere resolutely in his wife's quarrels, or to oppose her will in any way, stood by in patient submission for a while, and finally ventured to remonstrate gently, and laying his hand upon her shoulder, in expostulating and humble tones, said, " You'd better take *keer*, Betsy—don't scold so much—don't swear so hard, or else may be *you might lose your religion!*" The indignant wife exclaimed with a terrific adjunct, "I feel jist now as ef I hadn't one bit!"

A SLIGHT DISAPPOINTMENT AND REBUKE.

A wealthy and respectable old gentleman had several young and interesting daughters, who lived in the country, a few miles distant from one of our theological seminaries. Two students from a certain city, who had more self-conceit than brains, proposed visiting these country lasses, for the purpose of showing off their city manners and displaying their irresistible charms. They openly boasted that they would overwhelm the simple minded and plain bred daughters of the Lutheran elder. The old gentleman happened to hear of their intended visit, and of their design. The students rode up to the house, where they were very politely received by the father, who invited them into the parlor, and engaged in a long conversation about the seminary, the professors and church affairs generally. He then begged to be excused and left the room. "Now," said they, " he will bring in the ladies." He soon returned, and instead of introducing the daughters, he brought in an armful of magazines and papers, and said, ' Gentlemen! you must excuse me, I must attend to some farm business, but amuse yourselves with these papers until I return; stay and dine with us." The newspapers had no interest for them, and thus they were compelled to pass several wearisome hours. Then dinner was announced, at which they were introduced to the family, but there was no opportunity of direct conversation with the ladies. After dinner, they returned to the parlor, hoping that surely the ladies would now appear, but they did not come. Such was their disappointment, that they soon rushed out, ordered their horses, and rapidly returned to the seminary.

It is said that whenever a paper is handed to either of those men, he blushes blue.

DISINTERESTEDNESS.

On the farm on which Rev. W. Carpenter (one of our old time preachers in the South), lived, he raised more than was required for his own use. The surplus he disposed of, but he always had a fixed price for his corn. In his day, he thought twenty-five cents a fair equivalent for a bushel. He would, however, never sell to speculators. On one occasion, corn rose to one dollar a bushel, but he still continued to sell in small quantities to his neighbors, for twenty-five cents. Some speculators having heard of this, brought their teams and proposed to take all he had at that price. His reply was, "No, you cannot have it at any price." *Stoever, Sprague's Annals*, 87.

He was a man of great uniformity of character, faithful to whatever trust was committed to him, unwearied in his industry and unostentatious in his benevolence. He disdained petty intrigue and scorned a mean action. His habits of life were plain and simple, his affections warm, earnest and manly. There are many incidents, illustrative of his peculiar traits of character, given by those who were brought within the range of his influence. He was, even in his early days, interested in the study of Meteorology, and it was his practice every night, before retiring, to walk out and observe the clouds. One night he discovered that the door of his corn-crib was open, and, on approaching the spot, found a thief filling his bag. When the poor fellow ascertained that he was detected, he immediately commenced emptying the sack, but Father Carpenter directed him to fill it, and also helped him to put it on his horse. "Now," said the good man, "go, and steal no more!" As the offender happened to be a neighbor, whom he did not wish to expose, he concealed his name, even from his own family, and to this day it is unknown.

WOODEN BIBLE.

At a late sale in Frederick, the effects of a book binder were sold. Among the articles offered, was his sign, consisting of a large box, made and painted in imitation of a Bible. "That," said a papist present, "I will buy for the Bible Society." "Oh! no," replied a Lutheran, "I intend to buy it for a priest, for as he forbids his people to read the open bible, this being shut, will suit him exactly." The papist wilted.—*Lutheran Intelligencer*, vol. III, 70.

APOSTOLIC SIMPLICITY TRIED IN OUR DEGENERATE TIMES.

A brother in the West once told his people, that raising salaries by subscription was altogether wrong, and contrary to the Apostolic usages. He said that he blamed the ministers for it, to some extent at least. He further said that if ministers would trust the people, the simplicity of Apostolic times could be restored. He then proposed that he would preach for them a year, and at the end they should pay him just what each one thought their preacher's services had been worth. The congregation was dismissed, and no more said of salary for the year. Upon the last Sunday in the year, he reminded the people of his proposition, and confidence in them, and said, "Now let each one come forward and place upon the altar table whatever he thinks I ought to have for my services to him, and I will be content with the aggregate." He gave out a hymn and sat down in the pulpit. One old lady walked up, and no one else. The congregation was dismissed, and the "Apostolic" preacher came down from the pulpit and found twelve and one-half cents upon the table.—D. H. B.

A MINISTER ANXIOUS ABOUT HIS WIFE'S HEALTH.

Rev. N. N. married for his second wife, a most amiable and estimable lady, but very corpulent, weighing considerably over two hundred pounds. He came to the Synod some years ago, and on his way overtook Rev. M. M. going to Synod also. M. asked N. in regard to his health, and that of his family. N. answered as follows, "I am very well, but my wife, I am sorry to say, is not so well. She is pining away and losing flesh rapidly." "What seems to be the matter?" asked M. "Well," said N., "the thing is this. I have been a member of this Synod for a score of years, and have never been its president. My wife asked me why it was so, and as I could not give her a satisfactory reason, she imagines that it must be incompetency. From that time on her health has been declining. Now Brother M., you have me proposed and elected president of Synod, and I think my wife's health will be restored."—D. H. B.

A LEARNED DISPUTANT.

Rev. G. preached in a community of Dunkards. These people annoyed him greatly by opposing his doctrines, and advocating their own, especially in regard to baptism. One day, one of their preachers sent the old man a challenge for a public debate upon the subject. G. accepted the challenge, and appointed a day for disputation. (It was all in German, but I will give you a full translation in the vernacular.) The two champions met to measure theological swords. G. commenced—"Now, my friend, I propose that we investigate this subject, exigetically, hermeneutically, philosophically and historically. What system of exegesis would you prefer?" "Exegesis!" said his antagonist, "I do not know what that is." "Well then," said G., "let us try it hermeneutically. Whose hermeneutics shall we use?" "I do not know what hermeneutics is," said the Dunkard. "Then let us try it philosophically. What system of philosophy would you prefer? Is it the inductive system or the a priori system?" "I do not understand you," said the poor, bewildered man. G. turned to the audience and said, "You see, dear hearers, that this man knows nothing at all!" and, taking up his hat, walked out of the assembly. He was never troubled afterwards.

PENNSYLVANIA DUTCH.

Rev. H. J. G. preached to some country congregations. In one of his churches there were several Pennsylvania families who dogged him continually to preach them a German sermon. He finally consented, and preached them a sermon of an hour's length in the broadest Pennsylvania *dutch*, mixing things up terribly with distorted English and hideous provincialisms. His audience looked at him in perfect amazement. At the conclusion, one old fellow remarked to another, "'s war gut, aver 's war net schriftmäsig."—D. H. B.

POWER OF ELOQUENCE.

A reverend brother was preaching one Sunday morning in his usual vehement style, when a large black cat came in at the front door, took one look over the assembled congregation, and hastily ran up the side steps on the gallery. Finding the gallery crowded, she took the front of the gallery, and ran, very much frightened, to the pulpit end near the speaker. There she halted to reconnoitre. Just at that moment the preacher uttered an emphatic sentence in a stentorian voice, and brought his fist with force upon the pulpit board. The cat wheeled and ran, following the front of the gallery until she came directly opposite the speaker, just above the aisle below. At this moment he uttered another thundering sentence, and the cat dropped down dead upon the lower floor. A hearer told Brother B. that the power of eloquence killed the cat.—*Ibid.*

A NEW SUIT UNSUITABLY USED.

When ...., now professor at ...., was pastor at .... , he was very poor, and, of necessity, shabbily clad. Esquire L. had a store in the place, and one day called the preacher into his store and presented him with an entire suit of clothing, good and fine. The next Sunday he appeared in his new suit and preached. It was a good fit, and very becoming. On Monday morning Esquire L. had occasion to visit the minister on some business. He was not at the house, but his wife said he was at the stable, and proposed to call him. The Esquire was in a hurry and said he would go to the stable to see him. He went to the stable and found him in his new suit of clothes busily engaged *in currying his horse.*—D. H. B.

DR. H. E. MUHLENBERG.

He had lost a favorite mare, and upon the occasion of her death he remarks, "The old cunning beast had a presentiment of the severe winter which was at hand, and of the scarcity of provisions, and left me when I had expended all my best food upon her. In her way, and by a service of ten years' duration, she had been a very faithful friend to me." At the close of these remarks he has the following epitaph upon her: "*Fida et sagax equa, bene fureta, ne esuriret, aliquando debet esse.*"

I conclude with the remark that his good nature was sometimes imposed upon. The two following cases were communicated to me by an aged clergyman of our Church. On one occasion, a strolling beggar had succeeded in obtaining some money in the way of alms from him, and, after spending it for drink at a neighboring tavern, returned to the parsonage, and there, in front of the door, cried out in a loud voice, whilst he was whirling his hat round his head, "Hurrah, Dr. Muhlenberg gave me money to become intoxicated." At another time, a person of the same description came into his study, and, when refused alms, pretended to fall down upon the floor in a fit. The Doctor, hereupon, suspecting the state of the case, immediately said to a friend, my informant, "I will try what virtue there is in iron," and, began to heat the poker in the stove. For a short time the man remained perfectly motionless, but when, after an interval, he heard the Doctor going to the stove and saying to his friend, "I will apply this heated iron to the tip of his ear," he sprung up from the floor in indescribable haste, flew out of the door, and nothing more was seen of him.

TOO SHORT BY A FOOT.

During the time that Dr. H. was pastor at F., Dr. B., then preaching at M., Va., paid him a friendly visit. The prevailing fashion of coats was the long-tailed, and very long-waisted style. Dr. H. towers up to six feet two, whilst Dr. B. reaches five feet eight. The time was Saturday evening, and Dr. H. invited his guest to preach for him next morning. The arrangements were all completed, and Dr. H. went over to visit his Sunday school, leaving Dr. B. in the parlor reading over his sermon. The hour for preaching was at hand, and Dr. H. hastily entered the room, stating that the hour for service had arrived. Dr. B. said he was ready. But Dr. H. observing that he had on a checked linen coat, told him to change for a cloth coat. Dr. B. had no such article with him. Dr. H. ran to his wardrobe, and, hastily snatching up a cloth coat of his own, said, "here put this on and come after me. The bell has ceased ringing, and the people will be impatient," and left for the church. The audience were all waiting, and Dr. B. appeared, with his sleeves turned up about six inches, being just so much too long for him, and the very long-waisted coat, with the exceedingly long-tail, about two inches from the floor. It was with difficulty the audience could pay proper respect to the sanctuary and services. After service Dr. H. said, "Well, you made yourself ridiculous to-day." "Next time let me preach in my own coat," was the only reply.—D. H. B.

SINGULAR VISITATION OF PROVIDENCE.

Rev. L. G., when pastor of congregations in ...., held a protracted meeting. In this meeting he was disturbed every evening by a wicked young man who lived in the vicinity, and attended a saw-mill, after talking both publicly and privately with this young man, to no effect, prayed one evening that if there was any one in the assembly whose doom was fixed in the councils of heaven, and who might be in the way of others' salvation, the Lord would suddenly remove such a one out of the way. The next day he had occasion to visit the place where the young man was employed. He went to the saw-mill, and as he approached the young man said, "Mr. G., you tried to pray me to hell last night, but you see I am not there yet." Before Mr. G. could make any reply, the young man's foot slipped, and he fell with his neck just before the circular saw, in full motion. In an instant his head was severed from his body and rolled upon the floor of the saw-mill.—D. H. B.

PERSECUTION.

Occasionally, a minister has been subjected to severe trials by even professed christians. The following is taken from the Observer of 1842:

"*Eine feste Burg ist unser Gott.*"—Our esteemed and excellent friend and brother, Shindel, of Sunbury, has been tried—awfully tried in the "fiery furnace," and has come forth unscathed and triumphant. He is one of our most faithful and devoted men, and has been laboring with great success in the Lutheran ministry for upwards of thirty years. During the last few years his zealous labors have been attended by some of the most extensive and powerful revivals that have taken place in our churches. In the midst of these distinguished sanctions of divine grace, it pleased the Lord, no doubt for wise and good purposes, to permit one of the severest trials to befall him. Had the devil and his instruments succeeded in their malignant schemes, the fair character of this man of God would have been blasted, and his future usefulness destroyed. He never could have recovered from such a master-stroke of diabolical malevolence. But the Lord watched over him, and vouchsafed to him a mighty and glorious deliverance from the machinations of his enemies. Bless the Lord for his great mercy. We congratulate Brother Shindel; and while his faith and confidence in God's providence cannot but be greatly strengthened, we pray that his wily but discomfited foes may be deeply humbled and brought to speedy and thorough repentance. He can truly exclaim with the much persecuted, but at last triumphant Luther: "Eine feste Burg ist unser Gott"—a stronghold is our God. O praise ye the Lord, for he is good, and his mercy endureth forever.

A CONSPIRACY CRUSHED.
From the Harrisburg Democratic Union.

The Dauphin county court is at present in session in our borough. Among the business despatched on Monday, was a case of exceedingly delicate nature, involving the standing of an eminent Lutheran pastor—the Rev. Peter Shindel, of Sunbury. This most estimable man has had charge, also, of a congregation at Gratztown, in this county, for a period of nearly thirty years, during all which time he has maintained a reputation as fair and unblemished as has fallen to the lot of any man. Several months since, however, some two or three miscreants in the neighborhood became dissatisfied with the "revival measures" introduced by Mr. Shindel into the Gratztown congregation, and, to gratify their vindictiveness, commenced a series of persecutions against him of the most fiendlike malignity. Among other means resorted to by the wretches, was an attempt to fix upon Mr. Shindel the commission of a criminal offence, which was dated back some *twelve or fourteen years*, but which they professed to have kept in profound silence until now! We are gratified to state, however, for the information of Mr. Shindel's extensive circle of friends, that the Grand Jury on Monday last, by a *unanimous vote*, ignored the bill containing the allegations against him, and directed *the prosecutors to pay the costs!* We are gratified at this result, as the whole affair was plainly a conspiracy of the most atrocious kind, to blast the reputation of a man universally beloved. Perhaps no man in the same section of country has such a host of true and beloved admirers as Mr. Shindel, and certainly none deserves them better. As a christian and philanthropist, Mr. Shindel may serve as an examplar to the world, and we are rejoiced that this attempt to assail him in that which is dearer than life—his good name—has met such a signal rebuke at the hands of the constituted authorities.

Since the above was written, we learn that the prosecutors have made a public recantation of all their charges against Mr. Shindel, which makes his triumph still more conclusive.

HIND PART FOREMOST.

There was once a fashion of making shirts closed on the bosom and open on the back of the neck, to be fastened by a button behind. The wife of Rev. F. S., made her husband a set of shirts in the new style. On the following Sunday she handed him one, and he put it on and proceeded to church to hold service. His wife was not with him. After preaching he came home, and complained that his shirt was a bad fit, and rather uncomfortable. His wife looked up, and to her surprise and mortification, found that he had put on his shirt with the bosom on his back, and the collar, being fastened to the shirt, and pointed, stuck out behind his head in a very laughable manner.—D. H. B.

THE DISCOMFITTED GATE KEEPER.

Rev. J. I. M., whilst a student at college, was often invited by the neighboring ministers to preach. Upon one occasion, after filling an appointment, he started on horseback, for the college, and the minister told him that he need not pay toll at the next gate, if he stated the fact that he had preached for him the day previous. The student started, and soon arriving at the gate, the toll-gatherer came out and demanded toll. He stated that he had preached for B. yesterday. The man demanded his credentials, saying, at the same time, that about half of the people that passed the road were preachers, if their word was to be taken. He then came forth, and, taking the rein of the bridle, detained M. in the road. The man had no hat on, and a hot July sun was beating upon his bare head. M. drew from his pocket a copy of "Pilgrim's Progress," and commenced reading. He read one page, and was proceeding with the second, when the man hissed through his clenched teeth—" Whether you are a minister of the gospel or not, I don't know. One thing I do know, that you are a blasted fool!" And with that he gave M's horse a kick in the ribs, and sent him on without toll.

MARRYING MINORS.

A few years ago the law in Maryland imposed a heavy fine upon ministers who united minors in matrimony without their parents' consent. The law is somewhat modified at present, and the court which issues the license assumes the responsibility to some extent. Some poor ministers have been severely fined, by being deceived by the false representations of the parties, but in most cases, I believe, the governor has remitted the penalty.

I was once caught in a similar scrape, but I escaped by the exercise of a little audacity. One night a tall, stalwart countryman, accompanied by a genteel young woman, came to be married without any previous announcement. He was fortified with a regular license, and everything else seemed right. I did not ask him his age, for his appearance indicated at least twenty-five. There was no question either as regarded the lady. They were married, and the fellow gave me a dollar as a fee.

In a few days, an ill-dressed, rough, unshaved countryman came and asked me whether I had married such and such a man. I was green enough at that time promptly to answer, *yes*, not suspecting his design. I should have declined answering and thrown the proof upon him, but I was a young man, and not yet up to the ways of the world. He said the young man was his son, and a minor, and that he had determined to prosecute me. I felt myself in an ugly position, for it was plain he had the advantage of me. He stated that he would demand heavy damages, for his son's services were worth some hundreds of dollars a year, and he was resolved to get that out of me for two years at least. I at first mildly reasoned the matter with him, but he would listen to no argument or expostulation. I then changed my course and put on a very severe air. I told him I would employ the first lawyers in the city, for they were my personal acquaintances; that I could afford to pay men of that standing and he could not; that I would compel him and his son to leave their work for weeks together, in attendance upon court; that I would appeal the case to Annapolis, if it went against me in the lower court; that I knew the Governor would remit the fine which the

State had imposed; that the damages, if any at all, would not be enough to pay his expenses; that I would do many more things damaging to his character, and his slender purse. I observed that the old chap was shrinking all the way through, and by the time I was done, he had completely wilted. After catching his breath with an effort, he meekly said, "Well, what fee did my son give you for marrying him?" "Sir," said I, in an imperious tone, "that's none of your business; I allow no man to enquire impertinently into my private affairs!" He began to apologize in humble strains, and said he had a particular reason for asking that question. I then relaxed a little myself, and said, "Well, Sir, he gave me a dollar." "Now, parson" he rejoined, "if you give me that dollar, I'll say no more about the whole matter, *for he stole that money from me.*" Glad to get rid of him on these terms, I gave him the dollar, which I could not keep after he said that, true or false. As he was going out, I called to him, "Hold on, here, I'll give you fifty cents in addition, to buy your old woman a new night cap, for judging from your appearance, I dare say she needs it." Taking it, he bolted.

JUDGED.

Some years ago the Albright Sect was anxious to form a congregation in a section of Pennsylvania, inhabited by none but Lutherans and Reformed, who had a church and regular services of their own. These sectarians used the unscrupulous means peculiar to these people, of going from house to house, and moving earth and heaven, to make one proselyte. About that time a number of thunder-storms visited that region, and several barns owned by Lutherans were struck by lightning. This was taken advantage of by the unprincipled proselyter, who declared it to be a manifestation of the wrath of God against the Lutherans, and a reason for leaving the Lutheran Church and joining his sect. He succeeded in frightening a few weak-minded people into his party, where he promised them security against divine thunderbolts. It was then proposed to build a frame meeting-house of their own, directly opposite the Lutheran parsonage. This was done, and a steeple was raised to some height. Scarcely was the edifice completed, when a flash of lightning split it from top to bottom. The effect can be imagined. The meeting-house has been called, *Die Blitz Kirche* (The Lightning Church) ever since. But whether the preacher thought of "Out of thine mouth will I judge thee" (Luke 19: 22), is not known.

BOLD AND NOBLE DARING OF A LUTHERAN MINISTER IN THE MIDST OF GREAT DANGER.

I was well acquainted with the Rev. H., a young man of fine talents and attainments. He had studied theology, I think, at Göttingen, and came to this country as a "candidate," i. e., as a young licensed preacher who had never had a charge in Germany. He was received into one of our Synods, and was sent into the mountain-regions of Pennsylvania, where he was elected pastor of a Lutheran congregation. He was active and efficient as a pastor, and was much respected by the community. He had a wife and two children at the time the scene I am about to relate occurred. He lived in T.—a considerable stream flowed through this town; one night there fell an extraordinary rain, some said it was a water-spout, and in the morning the waters rose to a fearful and unprecedented height—greater part of the town was overflowed—houses were swept away, and many persons were drowned—it was a terrible scene. Whilst a large number of citizens were standing upon the banks, watching the progress of events, a building was seen coming down the stream, and a voice of a woman was heard shrieking even above the roaring of the angry waters; this woman, with her babe in her arms, had got on the upper side of the house that was floating down the stream, and was calling for help! Her case excited great consternation and sympathy, but there was no one bold and daring enough to go to her assistance. No rope or boat could reach her, and a short distance below there was a high mill-dam where she would be sure to meet her end. If rescued, at all, it must be there. It was a fearful moment—just then the Rev. Mr. H. came to the spot on horseback, he rode a noble animal, and had great confidence in his strength and docility. He soon comprehended the state of affairs, his generous impulses prompted him at once to attempt the rescue of the unfortunate woman. "I will rescue that woman or perish in the attempt." All remonstrated and said it was madness to make an attempt; but he plunged into the foaming stream, and bravely did his noble horse deport himself; he reached the side of the house, and told the woman to cast herself and her child into the water, and he caught them and placed them on his noble animal! The excitement on the shore was intense; no one spoke a word until the woman seemed to be safe on the horse; then there went up a shout from the multitude that seemed to drown the roaring of the waters! There were now hopes that they would be saved, but alas! those hopes were soon blasted; the load was too great for the noble animal, and the current too strong; bravely did the horse struggle, but all in vain: he sank, and with him his precious freight! They all perished, and that was the last of Brother H.—R. W.

A SLIGHT MISTAKE IN INTERPRETATION.

During my studies, preparatory to the ministry, I spent some months with a private instructor in Shenandoah county, Va. There lived in that region an aged, patriarchal Menonite preacher, who was a living example of every christian virtue. He was a leading minister among that singular people, and their most popular and useful preacher. I used to go to hear him when our own pastor was absent, if he had an appointment in the neighborhood. He was a good old man, and an artist would have chosen him as a model for "Paul the aged." He occasionally preached English, but he had never looked into Murray's Grammar or any other book that would have taught him the proprieties of our language. He had never studied music, and as he officiated as chorister as well as preacher, he usually sung a common metre tune to a long metre hymn, and would stumble all through without ever being sensible of any disharmony. In all his English harangues, he would introduce the parable of Nathan (2. Sam. XII), and, when Nathan speaks of the *ewe* lamb, the good old man would pronounce it *e-we*, and really thought it was the vulgar diminutive, which I believe is of Scotch origin, though common among many other common people. He would lean down, and lifting his hand three or four inches from the ground, he would say, "It was a little *e-we* bit of a lamb, joost so big!"

A COMPLIMENT.

One day a simple-minded parishioner, who had never seen a library, stepped into my study, and, after a cursory glance at my collection of books, which was not very large, but still respectable for a poor man, stared all around and thought he owed me a compliment, and would now pay it. He gravely turned to me, and in perfect sincerity, observed, "Well, I guess it will take you about a month to read all them books through."

When I was a young man, and just fresh from the seminary, I was staying a day or two with a worthy old farmer, and I thought it would gratify him by saying, "That his growing *wheat* looked very promising." He cooly replied, "Wheat! wheat—that's not wheat; it's rye—is that all you learned at the seminary?" I took the rebuke, only quietly muttering, "That we were not taught farming at that school," and inwardly resolving, "Old Gent, I'll pay you for that before I leave you." Some hours after I took my Greek Testament from my pocket and went to him, saying, "Mr. S., here is a passage in 1. Cor. which is not clear to me, I wish you would translate it for me." "What do I know about Greek; we do not learn them things on a farm." "Neither do we at the seminary learn to know the difference between growing crops!" He at once perceived what I was about, laughed heartily, and said he had been fairly caught.

THE SHABBY TREATMENT OF MINISTERS BY THE PENURIOUS AND MISERLY.

In the early part of my ministry I was rather more guileless and simple-hearted than now. Would to God the wicked world would have permitted me to remain in that state of happy innocence! But, no! I was compelled to arm myself at all points, and to deal with men as though they were not all honest. Thus, I was simple enough to make no contract with my first charge. Three large congregations solemnly promised to give me a living. At the end of the year I came out minus about one hundred dollars. And I certainly labored hard and energetically, if not wisely. After that I took the precaution to bind up the charge to give me a specific amount; sometimes I got it, and sometimes I did not. After I had been in the gospel harness twenty-eight years, I sat down and looked over my accounts (for I have them all recorded); I found that I had lost just about one hundred dollars a year; this made twenty-eight hundred dollars that the congregation had chiseled me out of! But this was not all, as the following incident will show: I once engaged a load of hay from an elder for ten dollars; the season was very wet, and much hay was spoiled, and as nobody would purchase wet and spoiled hay, and as the prudent elder did not want to put it on his own mow, he brought it to his pastor, and in his absence put it on his mow. It was utterly useless, and we had to pay a man for throwing it out in the manure-yard. When I came to settle for it, having stated my case fairly, and showing clearly that it was utterly worthless, the old, rich miser seemed to have been touched with a streak of generosity, and said in a kind of compassionate and charitable tone, "Well, as it is you, I will not charge you the full price of ten dollars; I will only charge you nine dollars and fifty cents." I paid it, and, thinks I to myself, that man has a soul that would not fill the inside of a flea! This elder was rich, I was poor. Another time I had a grist of a few bushels of wheat at the mill; I requested the miller to send it to my house: a rich farmer, a member of the church, was at the mill, and came home with an empty wagon right past my house. The miller requested him to take a small grist for the pastor; he did so. Out of politeness I asked him what he charged. "Oh," says he, "about a dollar." I paid him the dollar, and came to the conclusion that my preaching could not do any man much good who had so little a soul. On another occasion I bought two small pigs from a member of the church; he promised either to bring them in himself, or send them. So one day, another member going past his house with an empty wagon, and going right past my house, was requested to bring them. He did so, and charged fifty cents for the job. What made this case worse was, that a few days before, at his own request, I had visited his sick father and administered the Holy Sacrament to him, and thus spent half a day in his service. One of my deacons, who was a merchant, once treated me in the following shabby manner: I owed him a bill of seventy dollars; when I left the charge he had on his subscription list seventy-five dollars. I made a settlement with him, and he agreed to collect the amount of his bill from the back-standing subscriptions. Some two years afterwards I had to pay him the seventy dollars with interest. He never accounted to me for a dollar of the subscription! My successor, in the same charge, had to sell his only horse at the end of his second year to pay a bill he owed the same man.

One of the hardest cases was that of Rev. G. B., one of the most pious and simple-hearted men I ever knew; he was about sixty years of age, and had no family; and as he had entered the ministry at an advanced age, and as he was more concerned about the next than the present world, he had laid up nothing for a rainy day. It happened that he took sick, and was not able to preach for some three months; so his church council had a meeting, in which it was resolved that if their pastor did not very soon recover, they would take him to the poor-house! A good, pious, Lutheran samaritan, of another congregation, having heard of the unchristian determination of that wicked church council, sent word to those religious Goths, that if they could not support their old pastor, rather than disgrace themselves and the Lutheran church they should bring him to his house, and he would take care of him. But the poor old pastor died soon after, and went to that place "Where the wicked cease from troubling, and the weary are at rest."

In Virginia a Lutheran congregation elected a man for a deacon who had been a gambler, but had professed to be reformed. So one day he was out collecting money for the pastor, and succeeded in collecting over one hundred dollars, but, on his way home in the evening, he fell in with some of his old cronies, and he gambled away the pastor's money! What was to be done; the man was poor, and had no credit. The church council met, and, out of compassion, agreed to stand half the loss. The pastor had to lose the rest.

Rev. Mr. T. told me that one of his members once paid off his subscription by bringing him rotten wood that could not be used.

But let these instances of fraud and penuriousness suffice. These are, of course, exceptions, and we hope many exceptions to the general rule. There are many noble and generous members in our churches who know how to treat their pastors. We have looked at the dark side, now for a short view of the bright side.

There was Mr. L., one of my elders, who used to give his pastor fifty dollars a year, and always paid it at once, as he said, so it would do some good. He also used to send his pastor twenty bushels of apples, and as many potatoes, and as much wood as he needed, for nothing. There was Mr. A., who also paid fifty dollars, and made the pastor a present of about fifty more. There was Mr. F., who made his pastor a present of a horse, besides giving a large subscription. There was Mr. N., a well-to-do farmer, said to his pastor, "I don't want you to purchase any feed for your horse, I have made up my mind to supply you with that." There was the wealthy Mrs. C., who (as her pastor informed me) made it a rule every time her pastor visited her to slip a fifty dollar note into his hand on parting. There was old Mr. S., a man of great wealth, but with a rough outside, built a house at an expense of four thousand dollars, and told the pastor to move in. This same man also built a church at his own expense, and deeded it to the Lutheran congregation. Thus we might name hundreds of green spots, as offsets to the miserly tricks of the few penurious members in our churches.— R. W.

REV. MR. STORK, SR.

This pious old gentleman was once visited by a neighboring minister, who found him sick in bed, and much depressed on account of the languishing state of the church.

He asked his visitor, "What news?—not political, nor literary, nor any neighborhood gossip; but can you tell me something good about the church, for I am sick at heart on account of Zion, and have been in bed a week!"

The visitor began to relate several encouraging events, which so animated the old gentleman that he exclaimed to his son (afterwards a D. D.), "Gottlieb, Gottlieb! bring me my clothes and shoes. I am well now and will get up. Brother H's good news has cured me."—C. S.

I was present once at a Synodical supper. The good lady of the house had a table spread with all that was good and nice. She insisted upon our eating long after we had all done our very best in that line, and, although enormous quantities of her abundant provision had been consumed, and the proportions of many a dainty had been spoiled, she still besought us to continue, concluding with the remark, "La! me! you have all been so moderate, and so much is still left, that one can't see what you have eat." Dr. B. Kurtz, who was one of the guests, observed in an under tone, "I guess she would not fancy now *seeing* what we have eat!"

EARLY COLLEGE STRUGGLES.

When one starts for college, and has no money, and does not know where it is to come from, it makes one feel queer. It is now more than forty years since I started on such an expedition, by the advice of my good old pastor. I was a young man, had made a profession of religion, and the good old pastor thought I was the right kind of young man to be educated for the ministry. I had only a few dollars, not enough to pay the stage fare (for there were no railroads in those days), so I determined to take it afoot; my friend, C. A. M., of York, who had been my Sabbath school teacher, went with me to the end of the town, and, although he was not rich then, yet he slipped a handful of silver into my hand, with the remark that I might need it. (God has since blessed that man with abundant riches, and with his riches his benevolence has kept pace). Well, I traveled on all day, and near night I came in sight of the town of Gettysburg. I was glad my journey was at an end, for, after walking over thirty miles, my feet were sore, and my limbs ached with pain. I stopped at a hotel. Next morning I called to see the Professor, who assigned me my place. He took me into his study, where he sat upon a curiously constructed chair with a writing desk all around it. He examined me very closely, and I suppose came to the conclusion that I would do. While there, another student was ushered into the room, and he looked like a very learned man; he was dressed in black, like a preacher; had on a white neck-cloth, wore green glasses, and had a thin, pale face. I was more afraid of him than of the Professor. But we are often deceived by appearances. I afterwards found that this very learned-looking man had a very low grade of intellect, and no learning at all! Well, I set in, after having passed muster. There were only a few of us; I think sixteen, all told, with a few town boys. The old gymnasium was then our college, taught by D. J., one of the best teachers I ever knew. I spent some three years in the gymnasium, and entered the seminary when the college classes were started. I should have entered the college; it was one of the greatest errors of my life, and I would advise no young man to commit the same blunder. It is true I have tried hard to make up the great loss I sustained in not passing through a regular college course, but, an active pastor as I have been, cannot find the time to study those branches thoroughly which are studied in a college course. I might just as well have taken a full course. Although my struggles to raise the necessary funds were great, I might have succeeded in remaining another year or so. Sometimes my funds were very low, and I had no idea how my purse was to be replenished, yet it always was replenished. I was often driven to the greatest straits; this would drive me nearer to God in prayer. God always opened a way to have my wants supplied. My friend, C. A. M., and his excellent wife, who, like Mary, frequently broke the alabaster box of ointment, never forgot me. I also tried to earn money by my own efforts. I acted as agent of the Bible Society, and of the American Tract Society—and labored with my own hands—and by God's blessing I always had enough to pay my way. No young man who puts his trust in God need despair of entering the ministry. After spending five years at G., I left with just funds enough to carry me to the charge that had elected me pastor! I had but two dollars when I commenced my studies, and when I was done I had two dollars and fifty cents left, after having spent about seven hundred dollars. The students of the present extravagant and expensive age may perhaps wonder how I could get along with so small a sum, when they can now scarcely live two years for seven hundred dollars. I will explain the matter in a few words. I paid only two dollars a week board while in a boarding house, and the greater part of the time, like many others, I lived in what was called the "Brotherhood," where our boarding cost only one dollar per week, and for one session only ninety-four cents! One young man, who made no mean figure in our church, boarded himself a whole session for thirty cents a week. He ate nothing but corn bread and molasses, and he told me if he had not indulged in the sumptuous luxury of half a pound of butter, he could have lived on eighteen and three-quarter cents a week! In those days corn was selling at forty cents per bushel, and molasses at twelve and a half cents per quart. Now it is well known in all the slave States that a peck of corn is considered a sufficient quantity for a laboring slave a week, and surely a student ought not eat more than a laboring man! In our Brotherhood we, however, carried the matter, "riotous living," so far as to eat meat once a day, and butter on our bread twice a week, and sometimes cabbage and potatoes! And once, and only once, we ventured upon the extravagant luxury of a mess of sweet potatoes! We drank nothing but cold water, and I have no doubt we left the institution with stronger nerves than those who indulged in coffee and tea. And this is the history of our going to college forty years ago.—W.

A DANCE BROKEN UP BY A STUDENT OF THE BROTHERHOOD.

It is now well nigh unto forty years since a very amusing scene occurred at G. Near the Brotherhood lived a man who was on friendly terms with the students. We often visited his family, and, even occasionally, held prayer-meetings in his house. All at once, however, the bad spirit seemed to get into the man of the house, and he would have no fellowship with us—even went so far as to speak disrespectfully of us, so that I, as the head of the establishment, was obliged to remonstrate with him, and admonish him, which it seems he did not take in good part. So to annoy and insult us he had a ball appointed at his house. It was known all over town that on such a night there was to be a ball at Mr. H's., and many of the wildest young men in town were invited, and as many girls as they could induce to go. This dance gave us a good deal of trouble. There was Mr. B., one of Mr. Finney's converts, who took the matter very hard, and, as he was strong in faith and prayer, he prayed against it, but it went on. And finally the time came—the young men and the young women in their white dresses came—the house was full—the fiddler began to draw his bow—and presently the dance commenced, and they seemed to have a regular break-down! Brother B. felt bad about it, and came to me and insisted upon it, that I, as the "Haus Vater," should put a stop to it, but I could not see it. "Well," says he, "if you don't do something, I will." "Well, how will you get at it." "Why, I'll go in and turn the whole thing into a prayer-meeting." I remonstrated, but found he was determined to do, what I considered, a fool hardy thing. And knowing that there were wild, desperate and half-drunken young men there, I was afraid they might abuse Brother B. I told him to go, and I would back him! I called on Brother V., a man of gigantic stature and a brawny arm, that could swing a club like old Hercules, and upon Brother H., a small, thick set, compact, little chap, but he had a lion's soul, and told them to stand by me; with these two men I would have invaded the gates of the lower regions. Well, Brother B. went in and commenced a powerful exhortation—the fiddler slunk out as fast as he could—the attack was so sudden and so unexpected, that the attacked party had no time to think. Very soon Brother B. had the whole party on their knees, and were engaged in prayer—the girls weeping; as soon as he was done praying, I called him out, for I knew if the party had time to recover their senses, there would be a fray. The dance was broken up, and we were no more annoyed in that quarter. This scene, of course, made a ten days' talk in G. Prof. J. got to hear it, and rather held me responsible for it. I explained the whole matter to him, and he seemed to be satisfied with it, only remarking that he hoped Brother B. would act more prudently in the future.—R. W.

SLIGHT MISTAKE IN QUOTING SCRIPTURE.

A very excellent layman of our church once forgot the precise language of a certain scripture passage, in expressing his admiration of one of our recently deceased ministers, who, during many years, was the honored head of a Lutheran institution. He was walking with a friend in the vicinity of the college, and after a general eulogy on the virtues of the deceased, wound up by saying, "Yes, we may write upon its walls *Obadiah, Obadiah! the glory has departed from thee!*" He meant *Ichabod!*—c. s.

RATHER INAPPROPRIATE.

Sometimes lay leaders of prayer-meetings select hymns and passages of scripture that do not suit the time nor the occasion. Sometimes ludicrous as well as unprofitable selections are made.

At a prayer-meeting of theological students, who were all bachelors, the leader chose the 877th hymn of our collection, evidently having just cast his eye upon the first line, "United prayers ascend to thee!" But the heading certainly escaped his notice, which is, "*After the Baptism of an Infant.*" He read the whole hymn, which consists of a prayer for the father, mother, and especially for the "*babe*" just baptized. Some of those present attempted to sing a part of it, but it soon struck them all as so inappropriate, and the whole affair was so utterly ridiculous, that some of them rushed out of the room to give full vent to their uncontrollable laughter.—c. s.

GERMAN EDITOR.

When I was pastor in Central Pennsylvania, writes a friend, I preached a number of sermons on temperance. One of my parishioners was editor of a German newspaper in the village, and handled me severely in his columns. Among other things he said, "There is a heaven-wide difference between the present preachers and the Apostle Paul. Ministers now abuse taverns, but Paul on the contrary thanked God and took courage when he saw "Three Taverns," as you can see in Acts 28: 15."

A SHORT GRACE.

This is related of several of our ministers who were on the way to Synod in the olden time, on horseback. They arrived at a country tavern tired and hungry, and were compelled to wait a long time for dinner. One of them was asked to say grace, which he thus commenced and ended, "Thank God for a good appetite; S. hand that sauer-kraut and speck this way!"

SEVERE REBUKE.

One of our ministers, in his early clerical life, was a most edifying and plain gospel preacher, but he took to metaphysical preaching and lost his influence in the pulpit. One of our staid, sober-sided older brethren went to hear him, and next morning he said to him, "Well, Bro. G., I went last night to your service, expecting to have my bread buttered on both sides, as on former occasions, but, alas! you gave me nothing but a dry, hard crust to gnaw!"

CHOICE OF A WIFE.

Perhaps among all classes of men, gospel ministers often make the greatest blunders in choosing a suitable help-mate. I remember the case of the second marriage of Rev. .... In making his second choice he visited a serving-girl, perhaps pious, but totally uneducated. Brethren remonstrated with him, but all in vain. Said he, "I intend to gratify my own fancy." She had a very pretty face and a nice, neat little person. When called to one of the churches in .... , the ladies of the church politely called on her. She was unable to converse even on the plainest and every-day topics. Thus did the dear sainted brother block up his own way to extended usefulness there. But the good Lord of the vineyard soon took her home, thus removing (perhaps) an obstacle out of the way of usefulness. I think I know a number of similar cases. How wisely ought we "men of God" to act in all our movements, looking to the great end of our holy ministry?—A. R.

A DARK REBUKE.

I occasionally preached for the colored people in a school-house of their own. On one of these occasions a number of white men were gathered outside, and were talking and laughing so loud as to annoy me. I requested one of the colored *Breddern* to go out, and beg the disturbers to be quiet. He was an old and generally respected man. He went, and standing on the threshold exclaimed: "See, jeah! you *white niggers* out yer must be quiet;" and they subsided.

AFRAID OF RESULTS.

I was once sent for to see a dying man in the country. After having instructed him and prayed with him, I asked whether he felt reconciled to God and was not afraid to die? He was silent for a while, and then replied: "I am not afraid to die, but I do not like these after-claps; it's the after-claps I am afraid of."

TAKING IT COOLLY.

Once, as I was preaching in a school-house, in the mountains of Pennsylvania, I noticed an old lady rising near the centre of the room, and making her way towards the table, behind which I was standing, she deliberately took one of the candles and proceeded to light her pipe. Perceiving that I hesitated somewhat, she coolly remarked in words heard over all the meeting: "Hope it won't make you cough!" and puffed away to her infinite satisfaction. It was some time before I recovered my composure.

A STRAY SHEEP.

While preaching one summer afternoon, the door being open, a sheep deliberately walked up the aisle and gravely looked me in the face. This caused a general titter, but as the irreverent beast walked to the opposite door, the sexton cautiously slipped behind the unsuspecting creature, and administering a severe kick, sent it head foremost out of the house. Many of the people laughed outright. A wag suggested to me afterwards that if I were the Shepherd I ought to protect my sheep from such rough treatment.

A DOGMATICAL ELDER.

I had a worthy Elder who hated dogs most intensely. It so happened one Sunday morning that a dog followed his mistress to the house of God. But, unfortunately for the dog, the pews had doors to them, and Carlo could not find the friend with whom he came. In order to spy out the object of his search, he came on the pulpit while I was preaching and surveyed very deliberately the entire audience. I at once comprehended the situation, and dreaded the result, for I knew, if the dog descended from the opposite side of the pulpit, near which the dog-hating Elder sat, a dog-fight would ensue. Sure enough, down went the dog, and up jumped the Elder and seized the dog, and the dog, with a hideous yell, snapped the Elder in the hand, and the Elder not wishing to retain his hold threw the dog half the length of the church down the aisle, then ran and caught the dog again, this time by the back of the neck, and bore him in triumph, yelling with all his might (the dog I mean) to the stairway, and threw him down in such a manner that the dog regarded it as a notice to quit the premises. During the latter part of the performance I stood in the pulpit a silent spectator of the contest, which ended in the discomfiture of the dog and the Elder resuming his seat amid much confusion in the congregation.

RETRIBUTIVE PROVIDENCE.

During the first year of my ministry I assisted Brother S. at a protracted meeting. The meeting became very interesting, and there were many asking: "What must I do to be saved?" We were tormented by a man of the iron-side Baptist persuasion, who, with Bible in hand, sought out the enquirers during the intervals between services, and tried to persuade them to be dipped in the river, close by, asserting that nothing more was necessary to salvation. He would mutter and laugh during the time I was preaching, and in many ways showed his opposition to the good work. Being called on to pray at the close of the meeting, on a Monday evening, after having been very much annoyed by this man, I became very much excited, and thinking of David's prayers, recorded in the Psalms, I earnestly besought God to convert the opposing sinner; or, if he, in his infinite wisdom, saw he would not repent, he should remove the stumbling block and carry on the good work. Tuesday afternoon, as he was crossing the river on horseback, in company with a neighbor, they stopped to let their horses drink. When, struck with palsy, and being about to fall off, he was caught by his friend, held on the horse until they reached the shore, when he was taken from his horse and instantly died on the river bank. On Wednesday afternoon he was buried. The effect on the community was tremendous. Besides his entire family, many were added to the church. But the preacher was believed and said to have prayed the Baptist to death!

NOT EXACTLY.

A worthy Episcopal clergyman said to me the other day, that at a recent mission meeting of the bishops and others at New

York, *seven* German ministers who, he thought, were Lutherans, had applied for the ordination of one of them as a bishop. They stated that they were weary of the present system of independency in the German churches, and wanted an authorized head who would direct and control them. I replied that a good many German ministers and people would be better off by having a *despotic* ecclesiastical ruler, but I did not think that the Episcopal authority, as exercised in this country, was strong enough to control some of the Germans outside of our Synod. "But," said I, "I do not believe that these applicants for a master were Lutherans, or members of any Lutheran Synod," and just so it turns out. They belong to that mongrel body of ecclesiastical odds and ends, "The United Evangelical Church," located somewhere in the West, I believe. The two men who made personal application for Episcopal power were Messrs. Eisenhauer and Weissgerber, both significant names. Whether they got a German bishop is not known, but they were courteously received by the bishops, who, I dare say, will be in no hurry in granting them their request. I wonder whether these men think that they will carry their congregations over into the Episcopal church when they get a bishop? That was once tried some years ago in our own Synod by a recusant, and to his infinite disgust not one of his congregation followed him. This was an English church, and much less will a German congregation adopt the forms and submit to the government of the Episcopal church.

Not one of the above *seven* applicants for admission into the Episcopal ministry has continued in that church. There were no churches to give them, and they could not form any for themselves. Some of them are now in our ministry, and others are "to let" to the highest bidder.

A MINISTER IN A SCRAPE.

As an impartial chronicler I dare not pass by any fact that relates to our profession. We are sometimes accused of concealing each other's sins; but the charge is false. I wish I could consistently ignore the following *stunning* fact, but, as an unso-*fist*-icated reporter, I must let the world know it. About the time of Hallow-eve, the mischievous boys in this city ring violently at doorbells and then run away. A certain old lady about here was grievously annoyed by these *bell*-igerent attacks and determined to watch for the offender. She stationed herself just inside the door, and soon the bell rung out sonorously. The lady hastily opened the door, caught the offender by the collar, boxed his ears right and left most soundly. He was a diminutive person, and it being dark she could not recognize him. At every whack he protested: "Madam, why madam!" "Don't *madam* me, you young rascal!" she exclaimed, and another blow made his ears smart painfully. He begged, implored. "Don't beg for mercy, you graceless scamp!" was the only reply, accompanied by another thundering thump upon his auditory apparatus. Finally, becoming exhausted by her combative demonstrations, she dragged the little man into the hall that she might recognize the offender by the gaslight, and "tell his mother," as she said, when whom should she discover in the person of her victim but her own minister, who had called to pay a friendly visit!

A QUEER SUBJECT.

A few weeks ago a young man whom I did not know, expressed his desire to study for the ministry. I, of course, enquired into his moral and mental character, and I will give you the substance of the dialogue: "Who is your pastor?" "I have none." "Of what church are you a member?" "Of none." "Where do you go to church?" "Nowhere." "Are you a professor of religion?" "No." "Do you read the Scriptures?" "No!" "Do you pray?" "No!" "Have you any sense of personal guilt, and do you feel the need of a Redeemer?" "Not particularly." "What is your motive in seeking the ministry?" "O, I think it is a respectable sort of life." "And you expect to make money, do you?" "Yes, enough to live upon."

This was about the substance of a long talk, and what do you think of that?—did you ever encounter a case like that?—did anybody?

The man was not insane, nor drunk, and yet such were his answers. How did I *treat* him you ask? Well, how do you *think?* I was not severe but I showed up his folly and stupidity in a way that will do him good all his days. You may conceive what a sensible man would say to such an infatuated youth, and just intensify it ten-fold, and you will have the character of my preaching to him. I do not think he will come again until his heart is changed. He went away thanking me for my candor and fidelity.

He said he never saw the subject set forth in that light before, and he concluded "to seek some other respectable profession."

HOW A YOUNG MINISTER FAILED BEING ELECTED.

One of our ministers, at present pastor of one of our most prominent city churches, was a candidate for a church when a young man, but was not elected. His sermons pleased everybody, his character was irreproachable, his talents of the first grade, and his manners mild and gentlemanly. All the members had made up their minds to vote for him, but to their surprise, on election day, an old and influential elder rose and objected. The people were surprised and demanded the reasons. The old man replied, "Well, brethren, I will tell you. Several years ago, when this candidate was a student in the seminary, one Sunday morning I was passing his boarding-house and I heard some one splitting wood in the cellar; I looked into the cellar window, and there I saw this young man hard at work, and I will not vote for any man as our minister who, when a student, *would split wood on Sunday!*" And he was defeated!

DRESSING FOR ORDINATION.

One of our young men about to be ordained, and desirous of being more than usually neat in his toilet, asked his land-lady for some hair oil. She directed him to go to her chamber, and he would find a bottle on her toilet table. He went, and, it being twilight, he unfortunately got hold of a bottle of Winslow's syrup and bathed his head liberally with that saccharine mixture. In attempting to comb his hair, he found great difficulty, and what was he to do, as the church bells were already ringing! He applied soap, and that made it worse. He rushed away in a phrenzy, and when the administrating minister, who had laid his hands upon his head in the act of ordination, was about to withdraw them, the candidate's hair stuck to his fingers, and it was raised several inches, leading the celebrant to believe that the candidate's wig was coming off. Young men, do not mistake Winslow's syrup for Macassar hair oil!

SHORT MOTTO.

One of our German ministers was asked by the bell-founder, what motto he should put on a bell which he was making for the minister's church steeple. The latter instantly replied, *Voco vocatos.* This is equal to Melanchthon's short grace at table, *Benedictus benedicat.*

DAIRYMEN.

At a western Synod when several candidates were licensed, the minister who read the instructions to them pronounced several words in a way that was not classic. He told them "they were now *licensures* and were expected to keep a *dairy*" (diary). For some years they were called by their brethren, the *Dairymen!*

THE RULING PASSION.

A pastor told me that he was once called in a great hurry to see a dying parishioner. He went and found the man, as he thought, near his end. He thought he would not have much time to talk to him before his expected decease, and after a few words, knelt and fervently prayed for the dying brother. He had hardly pronounced his amen, and had not yet risen from his knees, when the man who was thought to be dying and his mind fixed on eternal things, said, "Domine, have you set out your cabbage plants yet!"

SHARP REBUKE.

The late Dr. P. Sahm was engaged in a protracted meeting in an unevangelized section of the country. The ministers were often disturbed by turbulent scamps. One evening the Doctor preached on "The Terrors of the Law," and depicted the awful condition of the finally impenitent. In the midst of his earnest discourse, a young man exclaimed, "Doctor, where is hell?" The large assembly were amazed at the boldness of the man, and some of them thought that the Doctor would be so confused as to be unable to reply. But he looked at the audacious disturber, then, in a loud voice, he replied, "Young man, hell is at the end of the road on which you are traveling!" It is needless to say that the intruder subsided and the preacher continued without further interruption.

LOCKED-OUT AT A FUNERAL.

While preaching in Wayne county, one of my members, a young lady who lived with her parents near an old Lutheran church, died, and I attended the funeral. It was expected that I would preach in the church, but when the procession, I being in front, got to the church, we found the doors locked against the dead and the living, and we had to go into the woods, and there hold our services. I never before had a proper idea of the wickedness of these poor, old, unconverted people. There was the deacon with the key in his pocket, and others like him standing around, sneering at the preacher and the congregation.

I stood up beside a big tree, and announced as my text: "We must all stand before the judgment seat of Christ." I just felt like preaching from such a text; but I was not angry, my heart was tender, but I felt like preaching, and God gave me great power to preach in the woods that day. Among other things I showed how that deacon would feel in that terrible day, with the key in his hand, when Christ would ask him, why he locked the door against the dead, whose spirit he had received into heaven? I also said, I would not be surprised if that deacon would hang himself inside of a year, and stand before an insulted God. Though I am no prophet, yet this did actually come to pass; he hanged himself during that year. How dreadful the thought! Another one of the same party fell from a tree and broke his back the same year.—S. R.

A SINGULAR PROVIDENCE.

At the end of my second year in Wooster charge, I felt it my duty to leave and go where I thought I might be more useful. I presented my resignation to the council of the East Union congregation, and after proper consideration they agreed to accept it and let me go. There was a neighborhood of very wicked people some three miles from this church, who frequently came to hear me preach, and being hit pretty severely every time they came, they would go away complaining, and often swearing at me. When they heard that I was about to leave, and that the council had agreed to it, they went to the council and urged them to recall that action, saying they feared they would all go to perdition if I left. Through them the council were induced to call a meeting of the whole church, and take a vote on the subject. The result was a general vote of Lutherans, other Christians and all sinners, that I should remain another year. I did so, and that year we had a gracious revival, in which sixty-five were converted, and among these converts were many of those sinners in that neighborhood just referred to.—S. R.

ANOTHER PROVIDENCE WORTHY OF RECORD.

In the fall of 1841 the Synod met in Bucyrus. A number of us were on our way to Synod on horseback; as we came near the town of Galion, late in the evening, the subject of remaining over night was introduced among the preachers. There were but few members of our church in the town, and we feared they could not keep us all with our horses. As I had preached here some years previously, I was determining in my own mind how many such and such families might entertain. I had made out a place for all in our company, excepting myself; just as we came up to a tavern, where a sign was elevated upon a long pole, one of the brethren remarked: "Brother Solomon, you had better stop here." They all laughed, and to carry out the joke I turned about and went in. I found a very excellent lady and nice little children, but the husband and father was intoxicated. I remained over night, was very well treated, and in the morning had a long talk with the man, when he was sober, and prayed with the family. I felt that I was in the right place, and that good would result.

On our return from Synod we found the sign and pole lying flat on the ground. The man had reformed and cut down the sign. Soon afterwards he united with the church. One of his sons is now a minister of the Lutheran church. So much was accomplished by jokingly turning into the old tavern that night. Brethren, never shun a sinner's house. Don't despise a drunkard, but reform him if you can.—S. R.

LOCKED-OUT AGAIN—A GAY TIME.

While preaching at Bolivar, I went out into the country to preach in an old Lutheran and German Reformed church four miles from town. As I walked up towards the old castle, two stories high, the church council met me with red faces and sour looks, a great crowd following them, and forming a circle around me. It resembled somewhat a shooting-match fight. The council informed me that the church was locked, and I could not preach in it. I asked them why? They answered, "Because you are one of them *Schwermers*." I then asked them whether they had bees at home? They said they had. I asked if they ever swarmed? They answered, "Yes." By this time the crowd became funny. I asked them then what became of bees if they don't swarm any more? They said they died. I replied, "That will be the case with you old Lutherans, if you don't swarm soon." This made a gay time for a little while. The council were mad, and the crowd laughed immoderately. I then told them there was more room outside than inside, that the air was much purer and more healthy, and I would preach under the trees. The people then gathered and sat on the fence, on logs, and on the grass, and I preached from the text Rom. x. 2: "For I bear them record that they have a zeal of God, but not according to knowledge." I went at it in earnest to give those old Jews a good dressing. They needed it. So passed that precious time, and we, somehow, all went home edified.—S. R.

WONDERFUL CONVERSIONS.

A worthy minister of our church, now deceased, was led to serious reflection by visiting the "infernal regions," a representation of hell, in a Cincinnati theatre. Horrible flames and flashes of fire are seen, with numerous skeletons rising and gnashing their teeth as though in awful agony. He rushed from the room, nearly frantic, with the thought fixed in his mind, "If this be a mere representation, what must be the reality." This impressed his mind so deeply that he betook himself to prayer, which resulted in his conversion.

Another, yet living, when a student at Gettysburg, and unconverted, visited a theatre in Philadelphia. In the progress of the play a lady appeared on the stage, and dropping upon her knees, made a prayer. He said the appearance of the lady, her manner, her tone of voice and her prayer were all those of his mother. He was startled, and suddenly rushed from the theatre, went to his room, fell upon his knees and gave himself to God and to the ministry.

Two of our ministers in their youth and wickedness agreed to hold a burlesque Sunday school. This they would attend on Sunday morning for sport, and then engage in all sorts of wickedness in the afternoon and evening. In a few months one of them became either tired or ashamed of this conduct and proposed to the other to stop. To his utter amazement his friend told him that it was no more fun with him, but serious earnest. The next Sunday A. offered an extemporaneous prayer that produced such an effect upon the mind of G. that they spent the afternoon in prayer, and both gave themselves to God and dedicated themselves to the ministry.

HOW PEOPLE DO TALK.

Last Sunday I happened to fall in with a group of persons, some of whom had just come out of a large German lecture-room, (I cannot call it a *church*, it formerly was, but alas!) I could not help hearing their conversation, and I was interested in it. One of the persons was a Jewess, who has some reputation here as a vocalist, who had evidently been employed to assist the choir, on that day, at least, with her splendid voice. She was asked: "What do they preach in that church?" "Well," said the pretty Jewess, "he preached to-day that Christ was a good man, who gave laws a little better than Moses, but evidently he didn't make much more of Christ than of Moses—but," she continued, "he said that Luther committed many errors, and that sounded queer to me, for they call themselves Lutherans!" There it is, you see, but fortunately for us, all well-informed people here know that the rationalistic concern alluded to is not Lutheran; neither do the lecturer, nor his hearers, belong to any Lutheran Synod, nor would they be received into any with their present unscriptural and un-Lutheran opinions.

CHURCH ATTACHMENT.

One Sunday morning after service, my sexton came to me and said there was a youg man at the church door who desired to see me. I went, and a young stranger of foreign appearance addressed me in the most imperfect English. From his accent I discovered he was a Frenchman, and I soon put him at ease on the score of language. He was overjoyed, and in a pure Parisian style expressed his extreme gratification at my ability to converse with him. Upon inquiry, I learned that he was a French Lutheran from Paris, and although his unassuming manner and unaffected politeness were calculated to beget confidence, yet I put a few questions to him about certain Lutheran ministers and the locality of some Lutheran churches in Paris, which at once removed any suspicions I might have entertained, which are so natural to us Americans who have sometimes been deceived by the pretensions of foreigners. Upon asking him how he found out my church, rather than some others in the city, he said he had been in the city but a few days, and the first thing he did was to learn from the directory the location of the Lutheran churches, and mine happened to be the nearest to his boarding-house. He understood little or nothing of my sermon, but he wanted to worship in a Lutheran church. I found him a pious, intelligent and well-educated young man, who, on that occasion and in subsequent interviews, gave me much interesting information respecting Lutheranism in Paris. He is still here pursuing business, and is a regular communicant in the church.

This affair is not important in itself, but it shows the excellency of strong church attachment, and is a good example for young men in a strange place to find out the churches of their fathers, to make themselves known to the ministers and to associate with their own people, and is a rebuke to those who, when they leave home, too often forget their church obligation, or join the communion of others.

ANOTHER.

A member of our church who resided in a section of country where there were no Lutherans, worshipped with Methodists and Presbyterians. He was a very active Christian, and of course was very desirable as a member. One party promised him the position of class-leader if he would join them; the other had the office of elder to offer him; but he would not leave the church of his fathers. In telling me this fact, he added: "I thought of what Martin Luther might say to me in heaven the first time he would meet me, "Bro. W., I'm ashamed of you for leaving your brethren down there in the world!" and what could I say in excuse? No, I'll not leave my mother-church, even though I be the only Lutheran in this neighborhood."

ANOTHER.

In the early days of my ministry I was present and heard a conversation between two aged fathers of the church, who have now rested in their graves forty years. Said one: "Brother, if an enemy stood here with a drawn sword, and said to me: 'Deny thy faith, or I will strike off thy head;' I would say: 'Strike, in God's name.'" "So would I," replied the other. "I wouldn't turn a hair's breadth from my faith to save my life." And I have no more doubt than I have of my existence, that both would have suffered martyrdom if they had been put to the test.—*Lintner, Hist. Disc. p.* 21. *Note.*

WRITTEN SERMONS.

Some years ago I heard a young gentleman preach, who was fresh from the Seminary of Gettysburg. I will not say that he had completed his studies, for that I hope he will never do until he completes his earthly existence. I was pleased with the logical arrangement of his discourse, and the studied propriety of his language, the simple elegance of his illustrations, and the rich, suggestive thought which the sermon displayed. There was, besides, a glow of piety and a modest energy of elocution which were very impressive. I said to him afterward: "I presume, my young friend, you have just preached a *written* sermon." I shall never forget his reply. "Yes, sir," said he, "and at my time of life I should be ashamed to preach any other." I shook him warmly by the hand and congratulated him upon his success. He then remarked, that he felt a holy ambition to preach well, and was perfectly satisfied that no young man *could* preach well who did not fully write out his sermons. I coincided in his opinion, and so will all who are competent to form a reasonable opinion upon this subject. We both agreed that mere fluency of utterance and energy of action did not constitute good preaching.

BAD MANNERS.

I shall never forget a circumstance that is said to have occurred in the house of a minister, which effectually cured an awkward country parson of the impolite habit, so common, of tilting the chair against the wall and planting the feet upon the cross-stick below. It is an indecent and slovenly posture. One day this man was not quite so near the wall as he thought, and tilting back, down he went, smashing a pan of milk that the good wife of the house had set near the stove to thicken, nearly annihilating one cat that was lying there, and so frightening another as to cause her to rush out of the room through a broken pane of glass that had been mended with a sheet of paper. The squealing cat, the broken jar, with its milky contents all bespattered over the clothes and face of the "fallen hero," his convulsive struggles in rising and the noise of his scrambling, beside his indescribable appearance, all presented a very ludicrous scene, and yet he bore it all with much patience. At length he gravely began to scrape the milky material from his coat, and being somewhat of a wit, dryly remarked, "That he was *scraping* a very intimate acquaintance, and studying the nature of the milky *whey*, but he would rather have this half-elaborated *schmeer kaes* on his bread than on his back," and wound up by asking, "Whether our cat was going into the circus business and practicing jumping through a hoop covered with paper?" and concluded that he never saw such a house, for it had no room that would hold a cat or a chair that would hold a man.

AN HONEST CONFESSION.

Some years ago two of our northern ministers were seated on a bench in the capitol grounds at Washington. They had been lifelong friends, and had always belonged to the same Synod. It was on the fast-day appointed by President Harrison, in 1841. They were both sad and disposed to a mutual exhibition of their "inner life." After freely exchanging views and feelings very fraternally, the elder of the two, since deceased, with some emotion said: "Brother P., I now tell you, candidly, that for some years of my ministry I was under the malign influence of rationalistic notions imbibed from my theological preceptor, and I preached only *at the heads* of my people, and endeavored to make them upright and religious by the precepts of morality, but it was not till I preached *to their hearts* and told the tale of Calvary, and unfolded the doctrine of justification by faith in the atoning blood of Christ, that souls were converted, and I began to make full proof of my ministry."—H. N. P.

A MINISTERIAL SELF-DENIAL.

A ministerial self-denial was lately reported, of which, I think, you newspaper men did not make enough. The church of one of our Western German ministers was in peril of being sold by the sheriff. The minister was sorely distressed; his people were too poor to pay the debt; they could not borrow the money; and the minister, rather than be deprived of his house of worship, absolutely sold his own small residence to raise the money, with very little prospect of ever having it returned. That I call missionary pluck; and if it had happened in some other churches I know, there would have been newspaper plaudits loud as thunder.

THEOLOGY AND METAPHYSICS.

Bro. H., of C., was once invited to address the theological class of W. college. There were present, among others, R. and S. R.

H.'s theme was "The claims of a thorough training in mental philosophy upon the ministry." He gave entire satisfaction to all except R., who, on the following evening, preached in the college church, and took occasion to denounce H.'s position and spoke of the utter futility of all metaphysics. S. R. was in the pulpit with him and very much chagrined at the course pursued. R. concluded and called upon S. R. to close with prayer. He arose and began his prayer something like this: "O Lord, we thank thee for the Bible and its holy influences. We thank thee for the intimate union between theology and metaphysics as mutual aids to each other and our advantages therefrom, but O, Lord, have mercy upon those ministers who have neither theology nor metaphysics," etc.

A WEDDING DANCE BROKEN UP.

A student of Gettysburg of many years ago, relates the following:

Music and dancing were going on briskly over there, while some of us were studying and others sleeping. Suddenly there was a change in the noise over at the *shebang*. Instead of the sound of the fiddle and foot-pats, there was singing, praying and weeping. One voice was heard above all the rest—and it was terrible. All the students, together with Black Jim, were roused up and rushed to the door and windows of the "Brotherhood" to see and hear what was wrong. The students were all in quarters but Brother B. Perhaps he may be down town—out late. But no, it is his awful voice over yonder, and he must be there. Yes, behold, he is there praying, and the whole company down weeping. What a talk among the students of the "Brotherhood." Yes, it is B.! What a voice! What a venture! What boldness! What will be the result! All sorts of opinions were expressed among the young prophets. Presently there was a turning out from the *shebang*, and a hurrying home—some weeping and others in very earnest conversation. The dance is completely broken up. One large fat man, who at first fell on his knees with others, rose up before the prayer was ended, and hurrying down the street, reported to the serenading party, who were coming up to greet the wedding folks with all kinds of music, such as horns, cow-bells, etc. This party being greatly disappointed, became exceedingly mad, and came up to the "Brotherhood" making a terrible noise, running their horns into the windows and blowing at an awful rate, determined to have revenge upon us. Brother B. kept very quiet, and it was well he did. Brother J. B. D., a very smooth speaker, acted as Aaron for us. He stepped out and made a speech to the crowd, and succeeded in getting up such a division among them that they could do nothing, and were compelled to leave the ground. Thus ended this dreadful matter, and we all retired to rest.

AN APPRECIATIVE DOG, AN UNCOMPROMISING DEACON, AND A SPRIGHTLY IRISHMAN.

In this same old log meeting-house I also, at one time, got into a rather funny predicament. Here not only the Christians and ugly rowdies, and noisy babies, but even the dogs came to the meeting. One time I noticed, after going into the pulpit, a large, respectable looking dog lying in front of the altar railing, panting and looking up at me. As he was quiet, I concluded he might remain, perhaps he would behave as well as some of the other folks in that neighborhood. So I gave out my text and commenced preaching. The text was Isa. xxviii: 20. "The bed is shorter than that a man can stretch himself on it, and the covering narrower than that he can wrap himself in it."

I went on to show that the bed represented the foundation upon which sinners rested their hopes of salvation, and why it was too short, what was meant by the covering and why it was too narrow.

Well, the dog was among my best hearers; for while some slept and others misbehaved, he watched me closely, and occasionally, when I became loud and violent in my gestures, he responded with a slight bark. One of my deacons, becoming annoyed with this, determined to put the dog out. He came forward and abruptly ordered the dog out, but the only answer was a look and a growl. I asked the deacon to let him alone and not interrupt the service, but his wrath was kindled by the dog growling at him, and he savagely grabbed the poor creature by the tail and ran, dragging him backwards toward the door, the dog scratching for dear life and trying to hold on to the floor with his claws, but the deacon had the advantage, and the dog had to go out. Poor dog! I wished the uncompromising old deacon no harm, but, like many others in the house, I did wish the dog would bite him just a little.

This took place just as I had ended my first division—*the short bed*. You may suppose this little episode caused a rather amusing break in the sermon just here. I stood there looking on, and seeing how the congregation enjoyed it, all the time wondering how I could collect my thoughts and get the attention of the people back again to the sermon. I had noticed a little Irishman in the congregation who was very attentive to the sermon and who paid very little attention to the fuss with the dog, but looked serious all the time. I concluded he was a better man than I, for I was so full of laugh that I could scarcely commence again.

By way of introducing the matter again, I looked up and remarked, that during this funny little episode with the dog, I had almost forgotten where I left off in the sermon. Upon this, the little Irishman sang out—"If ye plase, sir, ye lift off jist where the bed was too short." This startled the congregation again worse than ever, and I was in the same fix with them, but I finally got command of myself again and went on with the second division, but made it very short and closed up the meeting.—S. R.

INVITATION TO A BALL.

In the spring of 1840 I organized the English Lutheran church of Wooster with twenty members. We worshipped in an old frame building which had been the first court-house. Our church was among the small things of earth, but we had a noble, devoted little band. At that time Wooster was a great place for drinking, dancing, etc. I preached earnestly and faithfully against all such folly and wickedness. This made the devil's children mad, and they sought a way to hurt my feelings. On the occasion of a big ball, they sent me a ticket as they did to some rowdies. My impulse was to go, and do my duty as a good minister of Jesus Christ, but my council objected and advised me not to go, for fear I might be handled roughly if I commenced to preach, sing or pray there. So, instead of going, I sat down and wrote as polite a letter as I could, in which I gave them eleven reasons why I could not attend their ball, as a Christian and a minister of Christ, and concluded by extending to them an invitation to come to my very humble little church the next Sunday and hear me preach. I sent this letter to the judge of the court, who was one of the party, and requested him to read it to all in the ballroom, which I was informed he did.

The next Sunday they came in a company to my church, and it was crowded full of the gay and feathery girls and their gallants.

It was a fashionable congregation for once. It had been intimated to me that they would come, and I prepared to preach on the text, "God forbid that I should glory, save in the cross of our Lord Jesus Christ." I prayed for an humble tender heart, that I might not say a hard or unbecoming word that day. The Lord answered my prayer and I preached with great liberty and power, and had the satisfaction to see some tears in the eyes of the dancers. Only one *black-leg* tried to laugh and excite vanity. The young lady who had accompanied him and sat by his side, showed him by her looks that his conduct was not satisfactory to her and he desisted. On the way out of church she told him that he must learn how to behave, if he wished to accompany her hereafter. In a year from that time nearly all of that crowd were converted and received into the different churches. So all went right.—S. R.

WARNED OUT OF THE TOWNSHIP.

Smithville was a part of my charge when at Wooster, and finding it cheaper to live in the little town of Smithville than in Wooster, I moved there. There was great excitement about this time concerning old and new measures. When my enemies found that I had moved to Smithville, they laid a plan to either get me away or disgrace me. According to a law in that region, it was the privilege of persons, when any one moved to the township, to warn him out, if there was any danger that he would become a township charge. They had to go before a justice and swear that they believed such danger existed. Then the constable was sent with a written notice to the person commanding him to leave. Well, one poor, miserable, old sinner, who hated me very bitterly, went and took the oath that there was danger of R. becoming a township charge, and lo! one day the constable comes along and notifies me to leave the township. O! The old sinner that made this oath was a *German* (ought to be) *Reformed*, and if no one had given any more to support ministers than he did, they would all have become township charges.

But I didn't go, and this old sinner and others like him, were very much disappointed. They were ignorant of the law, and thought I would have to go, but all that the law intended was that a person so warned could not afterwards become a charge to the township, though he might remain in it and become ever so poor.

Thirty-two years have passed since then, and the act stands on the record against me to this to-day. I stayed there until it suited me to leave, and I have since returned and lived there again, and had charge of my old church. But when I came back the old sinner was dead and had gone to his reward. I hope he repented before he died.—S. R.

EXORCISM.

In a manuscript left among the papers of Thomas Winfield, a deserter from the British army in the war of 1812, and who lived and died in the mountain, near Wolfsville, in Maryland, I read the following:

In the neighborhood of Beard's church, in Washington county, there lived a young man by the name of Sullivan. He did nothing, had no visible means of support, and yet seemed always to have money. He was a stranger and refused to tell whence he came. He lived thus for a number of years, when suddenly he became very melancholy. Finally, he went to Rev. Mr. Hase, then pastor at Middletown, and told him that he (Sullivan) had sold himself to the devil for one dollar. This dollar he had spent as often as fifty times a day, and still had it. But his time was nearly expired and the devil would come to claim him at a certain time. Hase went for Schroeder, then stationed some where in Pennsylvania, and a professed exorcist, and appointed a meeting at Beard's church, to which meeting Sullivan was summoned. Services were held, prayers recited, and exorcism performed, and Sullivan was received as a member of the Lutheran church. He remained faithful to his vows of confirmation, went to work, and is now highly spoken of by old people in the neighborhood of Beard's church.—D. H. B.

JOHN GEORGE BUTLER.

John George Butler was one of the early pioneers of our church in Western Maryland. He removed to Cumberland in 1805, and died in 1816, aged sixty-three. The following picture of frontier ministerial life is taken from a letter written by him in 1811, and published in the *Evangelishes Magazin*. It will give some idea of the extent and success of his labors and the fervor of his spirit:

"It will be six years next October since I came to live here. I serve at present eight congregations. Of these, one is forty-seven and the other sixty miles from my home. I receive from all these churches about one hundred and fifty dollars. I was requested, in August, 1807, to hold divine service some miles from my place of residence. With the consent of my principal congregation, I set out upon my journey. I was absent six weeks, traveling and preaching. And blessed be the Lord who assisted me and crowned my labors with his blessing to old and young. I instructed a number of young persons in the Catechism, and the nearer the close of the course of instruction approached so much the nearer did God come to us with his blessing, so that very often our hearts were melted and one flood of tears followed another. The Lord moved my heart and tongue, and gave me grace to speak so as never before. On, Friday previous to communion, whilst I preached in the forenoon with great freedom, from the words, 'Blessed are they who do hunger and thirst after righteousness, for they shall be filled,' God approached as in a special manner, and several of my hearers were powerfully affected; and towards the close of this afternoon's instruction, the King of Glory came to us and wrought a powerful awakening. In short, the following three days were blessed days, during which, in the hearts of the aged and the young, the Lord kindled a fire that burns still to the praise of his name. In October, 1809, I was called to a place sixty miles from this, to instruct children, on Tuesday previous to the celebration of the Lord's supper. God came especially near to us. I thought I could perceive that some of the children would like to speak to me alone, if fear did not prevent them. Hence, I exhorted them that, if they desired to disclose to me any thing resting upon their hearts and consciences, they should not fear at all, or be ashamed to do so, but should be free and openhearted towards me. This evening I went home with six of the catechumens. After supper one of them came to me and said, 'Sir, I wish to speak to you alone.' I went, and found the young person awakened and deeply wounded in heart. So soon as the rest saw this, a divine arrow seemed to penetrate the hearts of them all. I found one of them to be in the deepest anguish on account of his sins. I pointed him directly to Jesus, the friend of sinners. He desired me to pray for him. I called together the other catechumens and prayed, but in a very few moments I could not hear my own voice by reason of their weeping and crying for grace and mercy. I arose and permitted them and our blessed God to treat with each other alone. They prayed in one strain for a whole hour, and one of the children prayed two hours, when all its strength was exhausted. In short, God did here begin a work, such as I cannot and shall not attempt to describe. * * * * * * * On the last Sabbath in October, 1808, I held a general meeting of all the catechumens from all my congregations. At this meeting the Lord kindled a holy fire, which he has also carried to other neighborhoods, and which continues to burn. Again, on the last Sabbath of August, 1810, I held in town a general meeting of the catechumens. The meeting continued three days. We saw here wonderful displays of the grace of God."—*Sprague's Annals*, 74.

In visiting a neighborhood remote from his own residence, he usually remained from four to eight weeks, holding a protracted meeting, preaching and catechizing the youth daily, visiting the people from house to house and praying with them. * * * * These visits were almost always followed by extensive awakening. Before leaving such a neighborhood, it was his custom to preach a farewell sermon at a school house, or some other convenient place. * * * At the close of the service, he would call upon all to unite with him in a farewell hymn; while the first verse was being sung, the fathers would come forward, one after the other, and give him the parting hand. They would pass out of the house, generally weeping as they went. The mothers did the same, while the next verse was being sung. Then those whom he had confirmed; then all the rest. Then in front of the house all arranged themselves in a circle—he taking his place in the centre—and thus they sang the remaining verses. After that, in imitation of Paul with the Ephesian elders, he kneeled with them all upon the ground, and spreading his hands to heaven, he prayed. Then followed the doxology and benediction. And now, in an instant, he was upon his horse and away he went, perhaps to return no more. The impression made by such a scene was overpowering.—*Focht: Sprague's Annals*, 75.

The effect of his reproofs was sometimes wonderful—almost incredible. After he had preached on a certain occasion, in a small mill, he heard a young man, who was present, say that he would not forgive some person who had offended him. Mr. Butler went instantly to him, took him by the hand and told him, with tears, that if he could not forgive the person who had injured him, neither could he hope to be forgiven by God, and that if he continued to indulge that spirit, his soul must inevitably be lost. The young man was at once overwhelmed with a conviction of his guilt and fell prostrate in the open road, and cried aloud for mercy. Mr. B. knelt by his side and prayed for him. The young man then exclaimed, in the bitterness of his soul, "I will forgive—I will cheerfully forgive—but what shall I do? Will my Lord forgive me, a poor, helpless sinner?" "O, yes!" said Mr. B., "if you truly hate and forsake all your sins and believe in Jesus with all your heart, God will freely forgive you for Christ's sake." That young man found peace in believing, and, after he had reached old age, he was accustomed to say, that no one had done so much for him, or was so dear to him, as the man who had reproved him for an unforgiving spirit.—*Ibid*, 76.

On a certain occasion Mr. Butler was attending a prayer-meeting at the house of a widow, and, while he was speaking with great energy and unction, and with visible effect upon the minds of many present, the eldest son of the family, unable to restrain his rage, was just about to lay hands on him and thrust him out of the house. At that moment the mother rushed between her son and Mr. Butler, and, falling upon her knees, cried out, "Oh, do not put the preacher out until he has told me what I must do to be saved."

JOHN CHRISTOPHER HARTWIG.

He was one of the most eccentric of men; and in nothing did his eccentricity discover itself more strikingly than in his great aversion to the female sex. He seems to have had just as little interest in women as was consistent with the belief that they are rational and immortal beings. Mr. Davidson, a highly respectable man, who lived on the tract of land, which he, Mr. Hartwig, with other corporators, had, with the consent of the Colonial Government, purchased from the Indians, gave me an amusing account of a visit which he received from him, while that part of the country had only begun to be inhabited. He said he was then a young man, and he and his wife occupied a log hut, in which there was only one bed-room and one bed. Their only sleeping accommodations they very cheerfully gave up to their clerical guest and stretched themselves out on the floor before the kitchen fire. In the course of the night Mrs. D. awoke and found that the weather had become much colder, and it instantly occurred to her that the occupant of her bed might not have sufficient clothing over him to render him comfortable. Her concern for his comfort led her to get up and go silently into his room and spread upon his bed a part of her own very simple wardrobe. But such a thing was not to be done by a woman, and yet escape the observation of such a woman-hater. No sooner had the offence been committed, than her guest arose, dressed himself, made his way out of the house to the stable, saddled his horse and rode off. It was not an uncommon thing for him, if he saw that he was about to meet a woman in the street, to cross over in order to avoid her. It is said, that on one occasion, when he was disturbed in preaching by the presence of a dog, he exclaimed, with a good deal of earnestness, "That they had better keep their dogs and children at home, and it would not be much matter if they kept their women there too."

All tradition concurs in representing him as very slovenly in his habits (often preaching in his blanket coat and not always with the cleanest linen), eccentric in his manners, curt, and, at times, irritable in his intercourse with others, and an exceedingly undesirable inmate of the social and domestic circle. So much was this the case that those who occasionally entertained him did not hesitate to prescribe limits to his visits and to tell him plainly, "You may stay here so many days and then you must go."—*Pohlman: Sprague's Annals*, 32.

PRESENTIMENT OF DEATH.

Rev. Mr. Hartwig lived to green old age, yet his faculties remained unimpaired. He was venerable in years, and, like a shock of corn, fully ripe for the sickle. * * * * His departure took place in 1796, on the day he completed the eightieth year of his age. The manner of his death was singular, and furnishes a remarkable instance of the power of imagination over the mind. Forty years before his death, the impression of a dream on his birth-day, that he would just live forty years longer, had become so strong that he felt persuaded the dream would be fulfilled and his life would be protracted to the close of his eightieth year. As the period fixed upon in his mind approached, all doubt respecting the certainty of the time was dispelled. On the day preceding the completion of his eightieth year, he came to the residence of Hon. J. R. Livingston, his intimate friend, * * * and announced that he had come to die at his house. He appeared to be in full possession of health, entered freely into religious conversation with the family, and in the evening conducted the devotional exercises of the house. The next morning he left his bed in apparent health, breakfasted and engaged in conversation with the family until the approach of the hour his imagination had fixed upon as the moment of his departure. This was eleven o'clock in the morning. A few minutes before the time, he requested permission to retire to rest. Mr. Livingston, unobserved, followed him to the room and noticed that he was undressing. Just as the clock struck the hour, he was in the act of removing the stock from his neck; at that moment he fell back on his bed and expired.—*Evangelical Review*, VII, 171.

THE EFFECT WHICH THE READING OF LUTHER ON THE GALATIANS PRODUCED IN HANOVER COUNTY, VA., AMONG ENGLISH SETTLERS IN 1742.

We now carry our indulgent readers to Virginia, where we will meet with an interesting circumstance, which, though having occurred more than a century ago, will, no doubt, be as new and fresh to many in our church as it was to the writer when he first met with it in one of the volumes of the Library of the University of North Carolina, at Chapel Hill.

We will find it faithfully and graphically described in Howison's History of Virginia, Vol. II, p. 174, et sqq., which we will copy.

"In the county of Hanover, about the same time (1742), lived Samuel Morris, a planter possessed of wealth and influence. It is remarkable that his mind was directed to religion, not by the accustomed agency of preaching, but by reading the works of men who had made the Scriptures their practical study.

"An old copy of Luther on the Epistle to the Galatians fell into his hands. He read, pondered and felt. This short Epistle furnished to the great reformer all the weapons he needed to cut Popery to the heart. Justification by faith alone, and a holy life to prove *that* faith, are its prominent doctrines. Morris believed, and hastened to impart to others the means of his own happiness.

"His friends were assembled, and he began to read to them the much prized volume they had heard again and again with interest and pleasure. Gradually their numbers swelled; other books were introduced; the thoughts of old John Bunyan became familiar, and, in 1743, a copy of Whitefield's sermons fell into their possession.

"Mr. Morris caused to be erected a 'reading house' for the accommodation of the hearers, and this was filled to overflowing on every Sabbath. He never attempted to preach, or to exhort, or to introduce prayer or any regular worship; he did nothing but read; yet the word of God, explained by consecrated minds, kindled in the hearers a flame of which they had known nothing heretofore. The interest thus excited became so general that the friends of the church felt alarm. Morris and his principal adherents were summoned before the Court of Magistrates to answer for the crime of absenting themselves from the regular services. They were asked to what denomination they belonged. Here was a difficulty, they were anything but churchmen; they were not Quakers; they were not Baptists; they knew nothing of Presbyterians. Suddenly a bright thought flashed upon them. Knowing that Luther was a great reformer, and remembering their obligations to him, they declared that they were Lutherans. The Magistrates were puzzled; they could find no laws against such a sect, and the men were accordingly dismissed without punishment. But, persecution was not thus easily satisfied; finding that their meetings were continued, informers again brought them before the court; fines were inflicted and greater rigor threatened. Mr. Morris himself paid more than twenty fines under the systematic opposition to which he was exposed."

Still their march was onward. In 1743 a member of one of the Augusta congregations crossed the Blue Ridge to barter his grain for iron and salt. Meeting with some of Morris's hearers, he conversed with them, and was astonished to find that their views of religion coincided with his own. He advised them to send to the valley and invite a minister whom he had left there, to come and preach to them. This was the Rev. Wm. Robinson, an Evangelist, ordained by the Presbytery of New Brunswick, and a man to whom the Presbyterians of Virginia owe a heavy debt of love. Embarrassments, caused by youthful indiscretion, had driven him from England, but, soon after coming to America, he professed himself a christian, and devoting his life to the ministry, he carried into his sacred duties the ardor which had distinguished him in the pursuit of vicious pleasures. He obeyed the call of Mr. Morris, and, coming to H——, preached his first sermon on the 6th of July. The people attended in crowds, and recognizing from his lips the same doctrines which they had long heard from the books read by Mr. Morris, they received him with open arms. Deep seriousness prevailed at their meetings, and gradually an interest was awakened, such as men feel when they begin to compare sin with holiness, and time with eternity. The lives of many were changed; regular congregations were formed; proper modes of worship were introduced; the people took the name of Presbyterians and formed a connection with the Presbytery of New Brunswick, whose ministers were then a part of the Synod of New York.—B.

Rev. C. is a wit, and sometimes carries his fun too far. But I want to tell you of a trial of it, having a practical end in view. Going from B. to C., to meet an appointment, on foot, and becoming wearied, he descried ahead on the railroad a company of Irish track-hands with a hand-car. A happy idea led him to think of riding with them. Approaching, he sat down, and entered into conversation. As they gathered up their tools, one of them asked what business he was engaged in. He promptly replied, "I'm a *fortune-teller*." He was asked his price to tell the fortunes of the six. "Let me ride to C. with you, and I'll do it," he answered. They agreed, and were placed in a row, laughing at the prospect of fun, while he drew forth a book; then read the words: "*Except ye be converted, ye shall all likewise perish.*" They agreed that "the praist" was too much for even Irishmen, and with many bursts of laughter paid the fee demanded, and the parson got the ride.

Rev. Mr. W., who ministered to a Lutheran congregation in a mountain village, although a very good man, spent much of his time about the stores and shops in familiar gossip with the people who congregated there.

One Monday morning he was lounging in a saddler's shop, when the proprietor of the establishment called his attention to a woman on the street who was selling blackberries. "You had better go and buy them," he said; "they are doubtless very fine, and, besides, may be set down as *Lutheran* blackberries." This appeal to the brother's denominational feelings prompted him to go and make the purchase. He pronounced them very good; but he asked, "Why do you think they are *Lutheran* berries? The woman does not know anything about Luther, nor does she belong to our church."

"Oh," replied the saddler, "you see, they are brought here on Monday morning, and, as they were probably picked on *Sunday*, I judged them to be Lutheran berries."

"There now," said an eminent Lutheran divine, when he heard this; "see what a propensity the world has to charge our Saviour and the Lutherans with breaking the Sabbath."

A prominent man having been disciplined for irregular conduct, went with his whole family to the Lutheran church. When Dr. C., the pastor, asked one of the bright-eyed daughters, "Why are you a Lutheran?" she quickly replied: "Because Mr. D. was going to put pap out of the meeting."

Years ago when I lived in ...., I was called upon to preach the funeral sermon of an old lady, in a school-house. It was in the summer, in the afternoon, and, as she was much beloved in the community, the house was filled, and many were standing around the windows and door. I had been exceedingly annoyed during the introductory exercises, by a young man standing at one of the windows, when, in the midst of the singing of the hymn, just before the sermon, I stopped and said, without weighing my words, "*If that young man, with the red head and yellow coat, standing at the window, don't stop his talking, I'll be apt to point him out to the congregation.*"

The fellow stretched open his eyes, ran out his tongue, and I never saw him again.—S. R.

It is said that some ministers are fond of showing off their Latin and Greek, by sometimes finding fault with our good, old translation of the Bible. I have always thought the effect was bad upon a plain congregation, besides the contempt which sensible people feel for such ridiculous displays. If men will exhibit themselves in this way, let them do it in the style of a certain minister, who was once preaching upon the parable of the Ten

Virgins. He told his hearers that the word *lamps* was an incorrect translation, and said, "The original *Hebrew* word is *lampadas*, and should have been translated *torches!*" This is just about as wise and edifying as many other pulpit criticisms we sometimes hear.—s. r.

It is not always safe to preach other men's sermons, if you care anything about being detected. I could tell some very interesting facts concerning this matter, and so could some other men I know. Sometimes a man is compelled to acknowledge his delinquency, as the following fact will illustrate, and which was told me by the very minister concerned. He narrated it as a good joke, and such it really is:

"Upon descending from the pulpit one day, he was warmly complimented by one of his church officers upon a particular passage, part of which he repeated. The minister candidly observed, 'Well, brother, I will not take any credit for that passage, for it is an extract from Chalmers.' 'Ah, indeed'—rejoined the other, 'Then I wish the whole sermon had been from Chalmers!'"

There was once a trial between Luther and some of his friends who could say the shortest grace at table. The award was given to Melanchthon, who proposed, "*Benedictus benedicat,*" (may the blessed one, bless,) which is short and sweet.

Some of our men are occasionally given to innocent mirth. One of them writes me the following: "I was traveling to a clerical meeting with Brother Peter, as I will here call him. As we were descending a hill, he said to me, 'Brother, do you think there can be such a thing as *living faith*, and yet the man a liar, drunkard, and blasphemer.' I at once replied, no! 'Be not so sure,' he rejoined, 'for I have the demonstration before me. Do you see that man ploughing in the field before us?—well, that man is guilty of all these sins, his name is *Faith*, and you will admit he is *living Faith*.' I gave it up and said, 'Brother Peter, if I had broken every law in the decalogue, I could yet say, I never fell from grace! and I have the demonstration before me. My mare's name is *Grace*, and I never fell from *her!*'" "True, true, he exclaimed, we are now even, and we'll quit joking while descending this abrupt hill." "A few months afterward, whilst riding over a road as level as a floor, my mare stumbled and pitched me over her head, and I fell from Grace."

SOME BLUNDERS.

About sixteen years ago a timid young minister occupied my pulpit. His sermon proceeded very acceptably until the peroration was reached, when the speaker warmed up and his words flowed more rapidly. Then came the solemn reminder: "The christian must be like a city set on a candlestick." I sat behind him in an open pulpit. What passed after that expression to the end of the sermon, I can hardly tell. Yet, strange to say, there were probably only two other persons in the house who noticed the blunder.

Twenty-five years in the past I was a student of Theology at G. One Wednesday evening we assembled at our weekly devotional lecture in the chapel of the church in town. A preacher from the State of New York had happened along, and was impressed into service. In tone and manner he proved himself not a little stilty and pompous, at least to students who are trained into the art of criticism. The speaker seemed to have laid himself out for a special effort to impress the prospective preachers. He grew fervent, then poetic. Snatches of hymns were called into use, when a quotation from Cowper, on this wise:

> "There is a fountain filled with blood,
>   Drawn from Immanuel's veins;
> And sinners plunged beneath that flood,
>   Lose all their guilty souls."

It is now more than a dozen years since, when many of our ministers were assembled in Synod, in a pleasant borough on the Susquehanna. It was at the time when there was much excitement and wise speculation concerning the reported use of Greek fire as a destructive agent in the harbor of Charleston. There was introduced into the Synod a subject that called forth considerable animated discussion. One brother, who was particularly watchful against all temptation, began to fear that possibly harm might come to the tempers of some of the speakers. He, for some time, refrained from uttering a word, but, by and by, when he could justify his silence no longer, he hurriedly rose and called out, in substance, "Brethren, let me implore you speedily to dispose of this question, as it would be very disastrous to have fire hurled into the midst of us." He had scarcely closed his first sentence when a voice called out, "What sort of fire?" Instantly a cry came from another part of the house, in a sharp falsetto, "Greek fire!" In a twinkling we witnessed about as much of a bustle in that chamber as if the veritable article had been magically introduced.

PASTORAL EXPERIENCE.

Every minister of long standing will be able to give many and varied experiences, some peculiar, so much so that they cannot very well be produced on paper without losing much of their point and pith. The one which I now propose to give is of this character.

Whilst pastor of .... in Pennsylvania, I was called on in turn to preach to a vacant congregation, situated in one of the many little valleys lying between short ranges of mountains, some miles distant from any railroad, or from any of the large towns in the State. Such being the location of the church, I found the people comparatively free from many of the follies, as well as many of the vices, so prevalent in the more populous and fashionable portions of the country.

On Sunday morning, at ten o'clock, I reached the house of worship, which was one of those old time log houses, two stories high, nearly square, with a high gallery on three sides, and, I was going to say, a higher pulpit, of the old time wineglass pattern, perched on a pillar some eight feet high, and, when seated on the little bench inside, I could not see over the top so as to have a view of the congregation below; I could see only those in the gallery.

The time came for opening service, which I did in the usual way, and nothing to attract my attention particularly, until the singing of the first hymn commenced.

There were neither organ nor choir in the church, but there was a leader in singing, not so soon to be forgotten, at least by any stranger happening into that church.

Well, I gave out the hymn and took my seat in the pulpit, and waited for the singing, whereupon the said leader, after clearing his throat several times, and after sundry soundings on the tuning fork, *pitched* the tune, and away went the singing in real congregational style. At the end of the first stanza my ears were startled by hearing an *organ interlude*, and yet I knew there was no organ there; how or what could it be? To satisfy myself I peeped out from behind my tall pulpit, and what should I see and hear but our leader standing with his back against one of the gallery posts, his head thrown back, his eyes closed, and his mouth wide open trying to *imitate* an organ!!

Some years ago, when the question of disposing of the emancipated slaves was agitating the country, I had a regular hearer in my church who was not a member. One Sunday I preached on the conversion of the Eunuch, and happened to remark that he was a colored man, and yet that the Spirit and Philip thought he had a soul to save as well as white men.

My hearer absented himself from church from that day, and sometime after I heard that he was grievously offended at me for preaching *politics!*

I happened to meet him one day in the street, and plainly rebuked him for neglecting church, and challenged him for proof that I had preached what he called *politics!*

He replied, "You said that fellow you were preaching about was a *nigger*, and *you know our party can't stand the nigger!*" I burst out into an uncontrollable fit of laughter, not unmingled with pity for his stupidity, and left him after observing, "Sir, the time is not far off when you as well as the other party will court the *nigger* vote!" which really happened sooner than I expected.

All the following anecdotes refer to that very remarkable and godly man, Rev. F. D. Wyneken, of the Missouri Synod, who died a year or two ago in San Francisco, whither he had gone on a visit to his son-in-law, Rev. Mr. Buehler.

These anecdotes are taken from an admirable biographical sketch of Wyneken, by Prof. Lindeman, in the Almanac of the Missouri Synod for 1877.

The firmness of Wyneken's faith at that time, and the determination with which he confessed it, appeared in his exemplary conduct at an examination of candidates that he attended shortly before his departure to America.

The unbelieving, Consistorial Court Officer, M., to whom Wyneken's decided christian character was well known, had selected the doctrine of miracles with the intention of sounding the stability of his faith and perplexing his mind. He opened the examination somewhat as follows: "Evidently miracles do not occur now. The only question therefore is, whether miracles really did occur in former times." Thereupon he put the question to Wyneken: "What do you say to this?"

Without hesitation he replied, "God is a God whose miraculous works are of daily occurrence, and I am surprised that you, sir of the Consistorial Court, deny this."

Astonished at such an answer, M. proceeded: "But you certainly know what Spinoza has written on this subject?"

With cheerful good humor, but decided firmness, Wyneken replied: "Well, but what have you and I to do with the philosophical speculations of this Atheistic Jew? The Scriptures, the Scriptures, my dear sir, are our rule!!"

This high spiritual dignitary had never before met with such courage, for all other candidates, who had appeared before him, were much more inclined to tremble than to contradict him. He hurriedly rose from his chair and appealed to a mass of seeming proof, by which he expected to justify his position.

When Wyneken found opportunity to speak again, he also was carried away with excitement, and, likewise springing to his feet, refuted in terms of eloquence all that the examiner had adduced.

So the examination was changed into a discussion, to the immense astonishment of the gentlemen at the green-table and the hearers assembled in the ante-room. The most remarkable of all, however, was this, that the modesty, the affable manner, and the good humor of the candidate, that characterized his entire heroic defence, so won the heart of the examiner, that he openly commended him and gave him a certificate of the highest order.

PASTORAL FIDELITY.

One of his catechumens was almost deaf, and had also a very weak mind and memory. W. was, at first, at a loss how to treat her, but he soon found the right way. He had her to visit him during the entire winter, several times a week at his house, and shouted the catechism in her ears, a little at a time, until she had, at last, grasped so much of it, that he could, with a good conscience, confirm her.

GETS A PAIR OF PANTS.

For occasions of public worship, Wyneken strove to keep on hand a respectable black suit of clothes, which, however, usually exhibited numerous signs of increasing age and of a life in the forest. In his travels he wore whatever he could call his own, regardless of its color or style. During rainy and muddy weather his dress was likely to be something like this: a felt hat, old and full of holes, secured to his head with a red handkerchief tied over it; his body wrapped in a large cape overcoat, of green cloth or felt, and his legs were encased in *yellow* trowsers.

The yellow trowsers were given to him in the neighboring village of Decatur. He had entered the store of a Catholic, who was a drunkard. The man was occupied with measuring a piece of yellow cloth, so called "English leather," for a customer. Wyneken, whose pantaloons were very much worn, was looking on, perhaps with an expression indicating the thought, that such a pair of trowsers would be good for him also. "Do you wish a piece of this?" was the unexpected question of the merchant. Wyneken replied: "No, I have no money." "Well, how if I give you a pair?" "I would not accept a gift from you!" "Indeed, and why not?" "Because my lips would then be closed, so that I could not rebuke your drunkenness!" "Indeed? Ha, ha! Is that it? Well, here is the cloth; take it, and rebuke me to your heart's content!"

Wyneken accepted the gift as a favor of God, to whom he had already commended himself in his poverty. He took the cloth home with him, and had a pair of pantaloons made of it. But when his deacons saw this new piece of wearing material, it surprised them, and they asked each other, "Where in all the world did our pastor get those yellow trowsers?" ("In aller Welt, wo hat den unser Pastor de gaele Boexen her?") They soon discovered the truth, but were not willing to let that Catholic drunkard enjoy the opportunity of boasting that he had given anything to *their* pastor. They collected a wagon load of corn, and one of them drove up before the merchant's house and unloaded it there. It was now his turn to be surprised. "What are you doing here?" was his question. "I have bought no corn of you!" The man replied, "This is your pay for our pastor's pantaloons! You, sir, shall not say that you are obliged to provide for our pastor!"

A man came to him in Fort Wayne, desiring permission to attend the communion. W. looked at him sharply for a few seconds and said bluntly, "You cannot come to the communion." "Why not?" inquired the man. "Because you are a drunkard," was the short and decided reply. "What? I a drunkard!" exclaimed the man with indignation. "How do you know that? Who told you that? I'll make it hot for the shameless liar! I wish to know, sir, who told you that!" "Well, I was told so by a man who knows it perfectly well, and whom you will not contradict." "Why, who is that?" "Come here, I'll show him to you!" replied W., rising, seizing the man by the hand, and leading him before the looking-glass. With deep earnestness he then exclaimed, "Now, just look in there! That man, with the bloated face, with the red nose, the dripping eyes, and trembling hands; he told me! Look that man, now, right square in the face, and say, No! if you can!" He then added with deep emotion, "My dear friend, just think; you are a creature of God; he has created you in his own image; you have been redeemed by the precious blood of the Son of God; and yet you, whom God has so honored and valued—you throw yourself like a sow into the mire, and wallow there."

The man turned pale, and with trembling confessed his sins, asking in terror if there was yet help for him—if he might yet hope for forgiveness. "Yes," replied W., "sit down; there is help even for you." He now preached to him the grace of God in Christ, and showed him how to become a partaker of it.

As the man finally arose and started for his home, W. called after him, "I almost forgot; you may come to the communion!"

Another case was that of a man whom Wyneken had, on account of his indecent behavior, called a "dirty hog." This provoked the man, and he openly threatened to castigate the pastor for it. A few days later they met on the street. "Well," said Wyneken, "I am glad to see you; it is your intention to give me a pounding; this would be a good opportunity!" "Yes," said the man with some hesitation, "I will. You have called me a dirty hog." "Certainly, I have done so," responded Wyneken, "and I must abide by what I have said; for you are what I have called you!" "What? No one dare say that of me!" replied the man, whose anger was now fully aroused. In the mean time some twenty or more spectators had gathered about, anxious to see how the altercation between the two men would end. Wyneken promptly met the boldness with which he attempted to justify himself, saying: "We shall see," and turning to the assembled crowd, called for a decision. "Friends," said he, "you have all known this man a long time. What do you say? All of you who think that he is a dirty hog please say yes!" "Yes!—yes!—yes!" was the unanimous decision. The man was thoroughly ashamed of himself, and quietly left the place. But Wyneken quickly followed him, and spoke to him so cheeringly and encouragingly, that he soon had the pleasure of knowing him and speaking of him as a better man.

Wyneken had great presence of mind and an astonishing amount of ready humor at his constant command, so that he always knew what to speak, and very seldom failed to silence the lips of scorners. This trait in his character is illustrated by numerous incidents in his rich and varied experience.

On one occasion he had in his travels taken refuge in one of the hotels of the country. While quietly seated at the table, enjoying his frugal meal, a foppish young fellow entered the room, and as soon as he saw the preacher, sneeringly accosted him with the assertion: "Well, you surely must be a priest." "Yes," was the prompt response, "and, fortunately for you, this is the only circumstance that prevents me from kicking you out of the house!"

A similar anecdote may be related in this connection, though the circumstance occurred at a much later date. Wyneken had been absent from Fort Wayne for some time, when he returned to the city and called at the drug store of Mr. Meyers. At this place he met an old acquaintance who accosted him with much familiarity: "Hallo, Mr. Wyneken, how do you do? Are you still the old pietist that you have been?" "Yes," replied Wyneken, "and are you still the old miser that you formerly have been?" The old man had nothing more to say.

On one occasion he had denied the Holy Supper to a man who was guilty of adultery. The sin, however, had not yet become public: indeed, the circumstances were of such a nature, that if he had been disposed to deny it, Wyneken might have had some difficulty in furnishing satisfactory evidence of his guilt. On this state of affairs the proud and hitherto much respected Mr. P. had based his mode of attack. At a congregational meeting he made the demand, that Wyneken should mention the reason why he had refused the Holy Supper to him. Wyneken replied, that he, Mr. P., knew the reason well enough, and that it could therefore not be necessary to make mention of it. But the adulterer insisted upon it, and several of his friends very warmly supported him in making the demand. Wyneken asked him whether he remembered what had been said to him at the time when he announced his name. Mr. P. replied that he did! Wyneken further desired him to state whether he could deny the truth of the things then stated to him? Mr. P. refused to answer this question; but continued to insist on a statement of the reason why he could not receive the Lord's Supper! Wyneken still maintained that he had told him; if, however, Mr. P. desired that the congregation should know it, he himself might relate the affair. Thereupon Mr. P. suddenly declared, "You have accused me of being an adulterer!" "Very true," Wyneken replied, "so I told you *between thee and me alone;* you yourself have now made the matter public, and you must accept the consequences. I am now obliged to relate to the congregation the reasons why I accused you." Wyneken then told the story; unexpectedly witnesses were found who knew what had transpired; Mr. P. was exposed, but continued proud and impenitent; full of wrath he left the meeting to return no more.

Toward the fallen who confessed their sin Wyneken was very ready to show mercy and sympathy. Nothing was more disagreeable to him than hard and uncharitable reports and judgments concerning persons who had sinned in infirmity or ignorance. At such times he could severely rebuke the "just," and likewise administer correction to the "wise," who could patronizingly say of some new member who was about to be received: "His only defect is, that he is in need of a right knowledge of the truth."

His benevolence in giving can best be portrayed by a few examples. While residing in Indiana, the people in the neighboring settlements often urged him to take something, either money or provisions, home with him. But he seldom reached home with his supplies. He would either give all to some needy person whom he met on the way, or to poor people who were residing along the road.

At one time, while he was yet staying with Mr. Rudisill, he came riding home in his *stocking feet;* his boots had been given on the way to a poor man whom he had met, and who asked him for help. The man's shoes were worn out, and Wyneken gave him the boots.

At another time his father-in-law had given him money to buy a pair of boots, as his own were somewhat leaky. He started for the shop to make the purchase, but returned with neither boots nor money. On the way he had met poor people who needed the money more than he.

Of a very sympathizing and liberal man it is sometimes said, "He will, if necessary, give the shirt he is wearing." Wyneken, on one occasion, literally did this. He entered a house in which several men were occupied in laying out the body of a man who had recently died. He observed that the men were looking for something that they could not find, because it was not there—a clean shirt. As soon as Wyneken discovered this, he said, "Wait a moment; I know where to find one." He went out into the wood-shed, and returning gave them his own shirt. His vest, however, was buttoned up to his chin.

To his clothing Wyneken paid little attention while acting as missionary. Even his best suit was usually threadbare and somewhat patched. The rents in his black pantaloons were not unfrequently hastily sewed up with white thread. It became somewhat unpleasant to the congregation to see their pastor wearing such poor garments. Especially the yellow pantaloons, that have already been mentioned, were very disagreeable. He, however, was pleased with them, because they were "indestructible," and he wore them in the city as well as in the country.

Every one knew that Wyneken never kept money in his house, and that he had none with which to purchase better clothing.

The deacon, Ernst Vosz, accordingly, at one time, collected forty dollars for him (at that time a very considerable amount), brought the money to him with great joy, and very urgently requested him to procure a respectable suit of clothes. Vosz was still present when a poor woman came to Wyneken, complaining bitterly. She related that her husband had long been prostrated by sickness, that the rent had not been paid for months, that her landlord would wait no longer, that she had neither money or food, that she and her children were suffering with hunger, that, altogether, she was in extreme want. Vosz listened to this recital a while, and then, regarding his presence as superfluous, took his departure.

The congregation now hoped soon to see their pastor appear in a new outfit; however, he wore the old suit a long time. Some began to think strange of this, and, one day, Vosz asked him in regard to the new suit, whether it would not be finished soon? "New suit?" responded Wyneken, "What new suit? Where should I get money to buy new clothes?" "But," said Vosz, very unpleasantly surprised, "did I not bring you forty dollars for this purpose? And now you have no money?" "Yes," said Wyneken very cheerfully, "you see, that is perfectly natural. Did you not at that time see the poor woman who, with bitter tears, told me her want? I gave the money to her, because she needed it more than I. Why, you see, my clothes are good enough yet." Vosz began to remonstrate, but Wyneken interrupted him, saying, "Well, do not make so much ado about it; our faithful God can restore the money twofold, and give me a pair of pantaloons besides, when I need them!" "Yes, such is your way of speaking," replied Vosz somewhat despondingly. "What?" said Wyneken, "do you doubt this? You are a fine christian! Do you know what the first article says? I believe that God richly and daily provides me with all the necessaries and enjoyments of life." Vosz was silent, but the expression of his face seemed to say, "God had provided for you; you have given it away; now you may do the best you can!"

Together the two men went to the city. They had not gone far, when Postmaster R. cried out, "Wyneken, here is a letter for you!" "From what place?" said Wyneken with surprise and pleasure; for in those days letters were less common than they are now. "From Germany," was the reply. Wyneken took the letter, and knew, as soon as he had seen the address, that it had come from his relatives. He opened it, and the first thing he drew from the envelope was a draft for eighty dollars, sent to him by his brethren, "to keep him from starving in the forest." He showed the draft to Vosz, saying, "Do you see? you unbelieving Thomas!"

They passed on and came to a store, the proprietor of which, who was standing in the door, kept ready-made clothing. When he saw Wyneken he said, "Parson, will you please come in?" Wyneken, still accompanied by Vosz, complied with his request. "See here," said the merchant, "I have a pair of pantaloons that were made for a man who lives in the country; he is a man of your size; it would be a great favor to me if you would try them on before I send them away, so that I could know that they fit him!"

Wyneken, feeling slightly out of humor at such a request, at first refused to comply. When the merchant, however, urged him to do so, he went to the apartment provided for such purposes, put on the garment and came out, showing them to the merchant. "Well," said the latter, "how do you like these pantaloons? They are very fine wear, the very thing for a preacher!" "Yes," said Wyneken, "such things are not for me! Ever since I have been a preacher, I have never had such pantaloons; *now* I could not make use of them at all." "Well, Parson," said the merchant, "the pantaloons are yours; you must keep them; they were made for you and—are paid!"

Wyneken was reluctant to accept the gift; he went back again to put on his old comfortable yellow garment; but it—was gone, and he was obliged to return home in the new pantaloons.

"Well, Vosz, what have you to say now?" said Wyneken, extending his hand to the person addressed. The tears were in his eyes, as he pressed his pious pastor's hand and went away.

Wyneken often emptied his wife's pantry and flour-barrel. Usually he was confined to the latter, for there was nothing else at hand that he could give away. On this account his good wife was not unfrequently embarrassed, and sometimes complained. On such occasions he would say: "*Only be of good cheer. Our faithful God is exceedingly rich, and will provide for you, so that you will again have something to cook and bake. Be full of courage. It is more blessed to give than to receive.*"

At one time his wife had a fine cloth coat made for him. But because his old gray duster felt more comfortable, he continued the wearing of it, leaving the new coat for a long time hanging in the wardrobe unused. When he was preparing to go to the next Synod, his wife desired to pack the new coat into his traveling bag. She opened the wardrobe, but could see nothing of it. She looked for it everywhere, but could not find it. At last she asked her husband what he had done with the new coat. "Yes," said he, "you see, *a poor fellow at one time came here, a dilapidated German candidate, for whom the coat was an admirable fit, and he went away with it in great glee.*"

It is self-evident that wretched impostors frequently abused Wyneken's hospitality. In Baltimore a poor man came to him, who claimed to have been rich in Germany. He complained of his too great difficulty in learning the English language, in consequence of which he desired to return to Germany, and accordingly requested of Wyneken a small contribution for his traveling expenses. Wyneken gave him the *last half dollar he had*, and afterwards had the pleasure of very frequently seeing this tired wanderer in America on the streets of the city. After such experiences he was in the habit of saying, "*It is a good thing that I did not cheat him,*" and at the next opportunity he gave again what he had.

At another time as he was in the same drug store, and just upon the point of leaving, a man who had for some time been attending his preaching, stepped up to him, and said with an earnest air: "Tell me now honestly, pastor, do you really believe what you preach? I don't believe it!" "Only stand by that!" replied W. at once, "and when the devil collars you and drags you into hell, only keep on crying out: I don't believe it. I don't believe it yet!" With this he sprang upon his horse and rode away. The wit also left; but after a few days returned to the shop, inquiring for W. and saying: "That man's words have troubled me; I must have a talk with him." The meeting took place, and the man became a believer.

Occasionally some one would remain after the sermon to complain of some of his views and expressions. In a sermon on the eleventh Sunday after Trinity, upon "The two church-goers," he said, that among the poor sinners who enter the church, there are always some Pharisees to be found. The latter he then suitably considered and pictured their character in his peculiar style. After the sermon two old members of the congregation came to him and expressed their doubts as to whether there were really any such Pharisees among them. But W. soon convinced them that they need not look at a very great distance for the Pharisee, but could find him very near home. They left, and did not soon again undertake to criticise his sermons.

While acting as President of Synod, he visited a distracted congregation in the far West. At the conclusion of a noisy and ineffectual meeting which had lasted to midnight, he was standing in the dark vestibule of the church, while the pastor of the congregation put out the lights. While here, he overheard some of the most violent of the opposition, principally young men, disputing violently about him on the other side of the street, and threatening to thrash him. Without any hesitation, W. stepped suddenly in front of them, and said in Platt-Deutsch; "Young men, I want to say something to you. I am not afraid of the devil, and do you think that I will be afraid of you? You are a miserable set of fellows, &c." He gave them a severe overhauling, and then quickly left them. The men looked at one another in bewilderment; they had conceived a sudden respect for the Platt-Deutsch President, and gave proof of it in the next meeting, by peacefully submitting. One of them became later a live member of the congregation.

www.ingramcontent.com/pod-product-compliance
Lightning Source LLC
Chambersburg PA
CBHW021224300426
44111CB00007B/412